A History of Ancient Philosophy

SUNY Series in Philosophy

Robert Cummings Neville, Editor

Giovanni Reale

A History of Ancient Philosophy

II. Plato and Aristotle

EDITED AND TRANSLATED FROM THE FIFTH ITALIAN EDITION BY

John R. Catan

State University of New York Press

Published by
State University of New York Press, Albany

For information, address State University of New York
Press, State University Plaza, Albany, N.Y. 12246

Library of Congress Cataloging-in-Publication Data

Reale, Giovanni.
        A history of ancient philosophy.

        Translation of: Storia della filosofia antica.
        Includes bibliographies and indexes.
        Contents: 1. From the origins to Socrates / edited
and translated from the fourth Italian edition [by]
John R. Catan--2. Plato and Aristotle / edited and
translated from the fifth Italian edition [by] John R.
Catan--3. The systems of the Hellenistic Age / edited
and translated from the third Italian edition [by] John
R. Catan.
        1. Philosophy, Ancient--History. I. Catan, John R.
II. Title.
B171.R4213   1990   180   84-16310
ISBN 0-7914-0516-8 (v. 2)
ISBN 0-7914-0517-6 (pbk. : v. 2)

10 9 8 7 6 5 4 3 2 1

To My Friend and Colleague
The Reverend Doctor Denis J. M. Bradley

CONTENTS

Third Section

THE ETHICAL-RELIGIOUS-ASCETIC COMPONENT OF PLATONIC THOUGHT AND ITS NEXUSES WITH THE PROTOLOGIC OF THE UNWRITTEN DOCTRINES

Fourth Section

THE POLITICAL COMPONENT OF PLATONISM AND ITS NEXUSES WITH THE PROTOLOGIC OF THE *UNWRITTEN DOCTRINES*

Fifth Section
CONCLUSIONS CONCERNING PLATONIC THOUGHT

Second Part

ARISTOTLE AND THE SYSTEMATIZATION OF PHILOSOPHICAL KNOWLEDGE

First Section
THE RELATIONSHIP BETWEEN ARISTOTLE AND PLATO THE CONTINUATION OF THE "SECOND VOYAGE"

Fifth Section
CONCLUSIONS ABOUT ARISTOTELIAN PHILOSOPHY

PREFACE

This second volume of my *History of Ancient Philosophy* contains the treatment of Plato and Aristotle, and hence the most remarkable heights achieved by Greek thought.

We have been concerned with these two authors many times in wide-ranging research, but on Plato only in the last few years have we arrived at a satisfactory summary overview, especially in our work *Toward a New Interpretation of Plato. A Rereading of the Metaphysics of the Great Dialogues in the Light of the Unwritten Doctrines* (a preliminary edition in 1984; a revision and amplification as well as a third and fourth edition in 1986; and in $1987^5;1989^6;1990^7$ were published).

We came to this overall understanding through a series of works done in the past, especially following the publication of the volume by H. Krämer, *Platone e i fondamenti metafisica*, written at our request that we translated and that was published by Vita e Pensiero, in 1982 ($1987^2;1989^3$) [an American edition was published by State University of New York Press in 1990]. To complete this work, we have also translated all the principal testimonies concerning the Platonic *Unwritten Doctrines* handed down through the indirect tradition (some for the first time in Italian) and consequently had to reinterpret the entire problematic and with a series of detailed and analytic works systematically re-evaluated the tradition. We might also mention that Krämer has returned afterwards to these issues in the volume entitled *La nuova immagine di Platone* (Naples: Bibliopolis, 1986).

In addition, in 1985 Thomas Szlezák published the volume *Platon und die Schriftlichkeit der Philosophie* (De Gruyter, Berlin) which overturned the traditional model for reading Plato and, although proceeding from a different starting point, reached hermeneutic conclusions perfectly convergent with the basic conclusions of the School of Tübingen, that is, with the works of H. Krämer and K. Gaiser.

The 1980s, therefore, signal a progressive spreading and domination of the new model for reading Plato. It would seem that the time is ripe for acquiring and understanding at the synthetic level this model of interpretation, for reasons that we will explain, and that, generally, the reader can find in our volume, *Toward a New Interpretation of Plato* [to be published by Rutledge & Kegan Paul], all the specific and detailed clarifications.

The fulcrum of the metaphysical discovery of the supersensible (which Plato presented as a result of the *second voyage*) is for us, as in the preceding editions, the position from which Plato can be understood; but, with the new interpretative paradigm that we advance, this discovery is further clarified in ways that we will carefully explain.

This discovery of the supersensible is, in our view, not only the fundamental phase of ancient thought—which as we will see, will be characterized in certain ways when it is accepted, and then will be obscured and finally will be reacquired in its full significance—but, more generally, it constitutes a milestone in the flow of Western philosophy, for reasons that we will go into in detail in the course of our treatment. For this reason we allowed, in the exposition of Platonic ontology, a series of issues and problems to be taken up that normally are not encountered in a summary work such as ours. We have presented, in fact, a Plato, so to say, in three dimensions, because it seems to us that the three fundamental interpretations proposed in the course of the centuries reveal three functioning facets of our philosopher, three essential components of his thought: the theoretic, the mystical-religious, and the political. Each of these components takes on a singular and particularly Platonic meaning from the *second voyage*. But we have shown that only in the light of the *Unwritten Doctrine* handed down through the indirect tradition, do these three components (especially the *second voyage* itself) acquire their full meaning and so only in this way do we achieve a unitary conception of Plato's thought, which we have sought out.

The interpretation of Aristotle we propose depends, in large measure, on that of Plato. In our judgment Aristotle, read without preconceptions, is, in the essential nucleus of his thought, not the antithesis, but the truthfulness of Plato. The image of the antithesis, as pictured by Raphael in his painting "The School of Athens" (depicted on the dust-cover of the Italian edition) depicts Plato with his forearm upraised and his index finger pointing to the heavens (that is, metaphysical transcendence) and Aristotle is shown with his arm extended and his hand with palms down to the earth (that is, toward the phenomena of the empirical world). This is, in reality, the graphic representation of the interpretation that Humanism and the Renaissance had made of the two philosophers; that is, the picturing of the conflict between the spiritualism of the *humanae letterae* (of which Plato had been designated the emblem) and the naturalism of science (of which Aristotle had been made the symbol). We will see instead that Aristotle was unique among thinkers closest to Plato in being the one who developed, at least in part, his *second voyage* and even carrying it beyond in terms of certain of its aspects. Naturally, the new interpretation of Plato implies further developments and clarifications of the relations between Aristotelian and Platonic thought. This cannot be accomplished in a work such as this, in so far as it would embrace the understanding of the polemics of Aristotle against Plato and the precise rooting of the Aristotelian doctrines in the *Unwritten Doctrine* of Plato. On the other hand, the systematic-unitary interpretation of Aristotle that we have previously supported converges in an exemplary manner with the new systematic-unitary interpretation of Plato, and so we have deemed any further modifications and additions to be useless.

The systematic-unitary reading of the esoteric works of Aristotle (the extant ones), after being contested beginning in 1922, is by now accepted not only as allowable, but as the only possible reading, for reasons that we have previously stated. We will reread Aristotle, therefore, in a unitary and systematic way and go on to the analyses of some particular doctrinal positions that are usually reserved to treatments in monographs, because only in this way can the two distinctive traits of his thought emerge, that is, the way in which he tries to overcome and confirm the Socratic-Platonic positions and the way in which he formally creates the system of philosophical knowledge.

We mention, finally, the following volumes in which can be found the fully matured theses on Aristotle maintained in this volume: namely, *Il concetto di filosofia prima e l'unità della Metafisica di Aristotele* (Milan: Vita e Pensiero, 1961 [1985[4]; American edition, trans. J. R. Catan, Albany: State University of New York Press, 1980]) and my translation and commentary of the metaphysics of Aristotle entitled, *La metafisica di Aristotele* (2 vols. Naples: Loffredo, 1968, 1978[2]).

We mention finally to the interested reader two works on the thought of the Stagirite that we have published and that can complement this work of synthesis. From the collection "I Filosofi" of the house of Laterza, we published an *Introduzione a Aristotele* (Bari, 1974; 1989[5]; translated into Spanish by V. Bazterrica [Barcelona: Editorial Herder, 1985]) takes up (although within a smaller format) parts of this *History*, so it offers a series of integrations on the development of Aristotle, on the exoteric writings, on the destiny of Aristotle, as well as an ample bibliography. For the collection, "Filosofi antichi" and the house of Lofreddo we published the first Italian version (with Greek text on facing pages, introductory monograph, critical commentary, complete annotated bibliography, and a full glossary of Greek terms) of the *Trattato sul cosmo per Alessandro* (Naples, 1974), which (although simply as a working hypothesis but later accurately confirmed even to details) we attributed to Aristotle as a work written in the exoteric style for the lectures that he gave to Alexander, when he was called to the court of Philip of Macedon as teacher of the young prince Alexander.

We refer the reader who desires further reasons for the interpretation of Aristotle that we here propose to all the aforementioned works, just as for the explanations of the interpretation which we propose for Plato we suggest to the reader the volume entitled, *Toward a New Interpretation of Plato*.

We wish to thank in a special way, Dr. S. Raiteri, who, by means of appropriate devices and availing himself of the competence in graphics design of G. Facetti, achieved in a nearly perfect way the design that we had for a long time cherished (and that the preceding editions had partially realized).

Giovanni Reale

PREFACE TO THE AMERICAN EDITION

This second volume of my *History of Ancient Philosophy* is published last; that is, after the third, the first, and the fourth volumes for a fundamental reason.

The volume treats of Plato and Aristotle, indeed in these last years I have concentrated on Plato and thoroughly rethought my interpretation, and consequently I started anew the whole exposition of Platonic thought contained in this volume.

Because I initiated my scholarly activity in ancient philosophy beginning from Aristotle, first with the volume *Il concetto di filosofia prima e l'unità della metafisica di Aristotele* (translated into English by John Catan previously) and then with a translation and systematic commentary on the *Metaphysics* of Aristotle (2 Vols. Loffredo, Naples, 1968), I firmly believed (and still do so) that I would be an Aristotelian, or generally follow along the Aristotelian positions.

Instead, I had begun to study Aristotle, but ended up with Plato. I had begun, that is, with the disciple in order to come to the master.

And notwithstanding I have always continued to study Plato and had translated and commented upon many of his dialogues, only in the last ten years or so I have achieved a comprehensive understanding of his thought with which I am satisfied.

Remember that my volume Per una nuova interpretazione di Platone, issued provisorily in 1984, and three editions of which followed in 1986, one in 1987, and one in 1989 and another two published in 1990) is what permitted me to achieve these new perspectives which, on the whole, are presented also in this second volume of my *History of Ancient Philosophy*.

John Catan had already translated my new monograph on Plato, but the publication was delayed again for some time, because we wanted to include all the innovations that were in it and hence its definitive structure. I think that I will complete this work toward the end of 1991, and then the English translation can be published in the following year.

About my interpretation of Aristotle the American reader already has a clear idea flowing from the translation of my *Concetto di filosofia prima*. The lack of support for the historical-genetic interpretation of Jaeger and his followers who had been among the first ones to support him, by now the greater part of scholars acknowledge it and it has returned to a reading that tries to restore to that great philosopher unity, or, at least, "his" unity.

About my interpretation of Plato, it has matured as a result of a systematic interaction with the Platonic school of Tübingen (its two leaders, H. Krämer and K. Gaiser [d. 1989] composed, at my invitation, two books that summarize the best of their thought), that resulted in a repositioning of Platonic research on a new epistemological plane, and when the English translation of Krämer's book by Catan is published, the American reader can easily comprehend (Krämer's "Italian Plato" was translated by John Catan and will be published in 1990 by State University Press of New York with the title *Plato and the Foundation of Metaphysics*}. Here we mention only two issues.

Leibniz wrote that "if anyone can reduce Plato to a system, such a one will render a great service to human kind." Goethe, referring to the well known "irony" that pervades the Platonic dialogues repeated an analogous sentiment.

Well then, from the pages of this second volume of my *History of Ancient Philosophy* the reader can draw his own indications for what way to follow to achieve the objective that Leibniz and Goethe so greatly hoped for.

But it has been the study for over ten years of Aristotle that has assisted me in understanding Plato, how and why the reader who attentively reads these pages can understand.

I wish this American edition the greatest success and that the long labor given to it by John Catan will be rewarded.

Giovanni Reale

TRANSLATOR'S NOTE

I would like to thank all those who have been of assistance to me in the writing and production of this volume. Especially Professor Giovanni Reale and his gracious wife. I had the assistance of a copy editor for which I am grateful to State University of New York Press and Mr. William Eastman and my production editor Ms. Ruth East. Of course all errors are mine.

I had completed the translation of this volume many years ago, but, as Reale points out, the Plato section was completely revised and rewritten with I think outstanding results. Perhaps with the scholarly reputation and erudition of Reale, the theses of the School of Tübingen will get a fair hearing among American scholars especially in the form presented by Reale.

I dedicated this volume to my long-time friend and now professor at Georgetown University Father Denis Bradley as a public acknowledgement of his support and esteem through what were many trying years.

J. R. Catan

Adams Basin, New York

Plato and Aristotle

If any were worthy of the encomium
teacher of human-kind, then it is
precisely Plato and Aristotle.
Hegel, *Lectures on the History
of Philosophy*

First Part

PLATO AND THE DISCOVERY OF THE SUPERSENSIBLE CAUSE
THE SECOND VOYAGE

τὸν δεύτερον πλοῦν ἐπὶ τὴν τῆς αἰτίας
ζήτησιν ᾗ πεπραγμάτευμαι βούλει σοι,
ἔφη, ἐπίδειξιν ποιήσωμαι, ὦ Κέβης;

"do you wish me, O Cebes, said he, to
give you an account of the way in which I
have conducted my second voyage in
quest of this cause."

Plato, *Phaedo* 99C-D

THE GREAT RIFT BETWEEN THE WRITTEN CULTURE AND THE ORAL CULTURE AND THE DIFFERENT WAYS OF COMMUNICATING THE PHILOSOPHICAL DOCTRINE OF PLATO

λέγεται δ ὅτι Σωκράτης, ὄναρ εἶδε κύκνου νεοττὸν ἐν τοῖς γόνασιν ἔχειν, ὅν καὶ παραχρῆμα πτεροφυήσαντα ἀναπτῆσαι ἡδὺ κλάγξαντα· καὶ μεθ ἡμέραν Πλάτωνα αὐτῷ συστῆναι, τὸν δὲ τοῦτον εἰπειν εἶναι τὸν ὄρνιν.

It is stated that Socrates in a dream saw a cygnet on his knees, which all at once put forth plumage, and flew away after uttering a loud sweet note. And the next day Plato was introduced as a pupil, and thereupon he recognized in him the swan of his dream.

Diogenes Laertius 3.5

I. The Mediation Attempted by Plato between the Written and the Oral and the Structural Relationship between the Written and the Unwritten

1. Why it is necessary to surpass the traditional criterion and acquire a new one to understand the thought of Plato

That Plato[1] constitutes the most remarkable height of ancient thought is by now a well-supported conviction. But, if we remain within the sphere of ancient thought, the fact that Platonic philosophy directly constitutes the most important support of the Greek way of thinking is confirmed in a most surprising way. Aristotle himself, as we will show, depends in a structural manner on Plato, and after the Hellenistic Age, as we will see in the fourth volume. For about six centuries everything that was most important that came from the Greeks depended on the reinterpretation and development of the thought of Plato, directly or indirectly. Let us keep in mind also the influence that in late antiquity Plato exercised on the Fathers of the Church, who drew from him the most important metaphysical categories by which they elaborated and expressed rationally the great spiritual doctrine contained in the faith of Christians. In sum, the philosophy of Plato has been the most "influential," to use a modern term, and the most stimulating for well over a millennium.

What is the basic reason for all of this? The response to such a question is simple, because, in a certain sense, Plato himself has already given it, as we will see. He taught us to look at reality *with new eyes* (with eyes ruled by spirit and soul)[2] both to interpret it in a *new dimension* and by a *new method*. It is a method that accepts all the positions achieved step by step by previous thought, grounding them and unifying them by carrying them to a new level of inquiry achieved with what he himself has called the *second voyage* (δεύτερος πλοῦς),[3] which is a truly emblematic metaphor to which we have many times had recourse in the first volume, and which we are now going to explain.

But, before facing this issue, it is necessary to solve a series of complex preliminary questions of a methodological and epistemological nature, which were in the forefront of the awareness for our philosopher more than for all the other ancient thinkers.

The first of these questions to be answered is what had been the criterion with which traditionally (starting from the beginning of the eighteenth century) Plato was read and interpreted, why this criterion has worn thin, and how, at this time, a new and alternative one has to a great extent imposed itself.

The traditional criterion can be summarized in a very simple argument.

(*a*) Writing is, in general, the fullest and most important expression of the thought of an author; and in particular this is true in the case of Plato, who was endowed with extraordinary capacities both as a thinker and as a writer.

(*b*) Furthermore, we have been handed down intact all the written works of Plato that the ancients cited as his and that are considered authentic (a happy accident unique among authors of the Classical Age).

(*c*) Therefore, it is possible to draw forth with confidence all his thought from all his extant writings.

This argument, which for such a long time has convinced an enormous number of scholars, is today without foundation. It is in error in its major premise and correct only in its second premise, which has been by now completely confirmed; but, by destroying the major premise, the conclusion is also completely vitiated and so the whole reasoning process. Actually, two remarkable facts, emerge today into the forefront, belying the first premise. (*a*) In the self-testimony of the *Phaedrus* Plato says expressly that the philosopher *does not put into writing* the things "which are of greater value" (τὰ τιμιώτερα),[4] which are simply those things that make a man a philosopher; and this is largely confirmed in the *Seventh Letter*. (*b*) There exists an indirect tradition that attests to the existence of the *Unwritten Doctrine* of Plato, and refers to its principal contents.

Hence, both Plato with the explicit statements made in his writings, and his followers with the testimonies that have come down to us on the existence and the principal contents of the *Unwritten Doctrines* prove, in an irrefutable manner, the fact that the writings have not been for Plato the full expression or the most important communication of his thought. Consequently, even if we possess all the writings of Plato, we are not able to draw forth *from all these writings all his thought*, and therefore *the reading and the interpretation of the dialogues are to be reassessed through a new vision*.

Let us examine, in the first place, these two important facts, emerging into the full light from the most recent researches, which force upon us the necessity of introducing a new and more adequate criterion to read and understand Plato.[5]

2. The judgment of Plato on writing in the *Phaedrus*

The model that has been the point of reference for the majority of modern scholars on Plato has been formed in part in the course of seventeen centuries, but it was F. D. Schleiermacher at the beginning of the eighteenth century who consolidated and compelled its use.[6] The basic hermeneutic thesis of this model is centered on the conviction of the *autonomy of the Platonic writings* and hence on the presumption of the monopoly alleged in favor of them at the entire expense (or generally outstanding enough) of the indirect tradition, an understanding that goes back to immediate followers who had frequently heard Plato and had lived with him for some time in the Academy. On the contrary, this conviction has been impugned by Plato himself in the *Phaedrus* and in the *Seventh Letter*, where he explains, in a very careful way, that writings are understandable within limitations, *because they are not in the appropriate form for communicating to the reader some essential things, both from the point of view of method and from the point of view of content.*

The fact that the model about which we are speaking convinced many scholars for a long time, notwithstanding the self testimony of Plato, which implies the opposite conclusion, ought not to surprise us. The modern age is the most typical expression of a culture wholly based *on writing*, considered as the preeminent *medium* of every form of knowledge. Only in the last decades has there arisen and become widely diffused a different type of culture, based on various types of audio-visual communication of the *mass-media*, which arouses great problems about the function and nature of communication itself. Hence, today we live in a period of time in which there is a verifiable rift between the two cultures; and, this fact makes us capable of understanding the kind of situation (even if there are many dissimilarities) in which Plato was situated and his judgment about writing, which can be grasped correctly only by comparing it to this background. In effect, Plato lived at the moment in which the aspect of *orality*, which constituted a supporting arm of ancient culture, was losing its strength to the *written* word. Consequently, Plato experienced the rift between the two cultures in a very exacerbated fashion and in a certain sense even an extreme fashion: on the one hand, there was his teacher Socrates who personified in a paradigmatic and total way the model of culture based on *orality*; on the other hand, he vigorously accepted the attitudes of the upholders of the culture based upon *writing*, and he himself possessed the endowments of the writer, which placed him among the greatest in antiquity as well as for all time. We are, hence, able to understand much better than would be possible in the past the sense in which there can be a rift between two different cultures, and hence to understand why so great a writer could be convinced of the *limited character of the communicative function of writing*; and therefore we are finally in a position to interpret his *self-testimony* contained in the *Phaedrus* in a correct manner, whereas in the past there was the attempt to reduce its hermeneutic force and to change what it signified in various ways.

Actually, even in the past some understood that the self-testimony of the *Phaedrus* should be taken very seriously; but they were isolated instances, while the community of scholars followed a different view. Perhaps the finest and best example was given by no less a person than F. Nietzsche. Simply by taking a position against the thesis of Schleiermacher, who upheld the position that the writings are precisely the means to bring to knowledge those who do not possess it and hence the writings constitute the means that bring us as close as possible to the oral teaching, Nietzsche wrote:

"The whole hypothesis [of Schleiermacher] is in contradiction with the explanation which is found in the *Phaedrus*, and is maintained by means of a false interpretation. In fact Plato says that writing has its meaning only for those who already know, as a means of bringing it back to mind. Therefore the most perfect writing ought to imitate the technique of oral teaching: literally with the goal of bringing to mind the way in which those who know become aware. Writing ought to be (a treasury for bringing to mind) for the one who writes and for the philosopher and his companions. Instead for Schleiermacher writing must be the means, which is *the best of a poor lot, to bring those who do not know to knowledge.* The whole of the writings therefore has its own general function of teaching and education. But according to Plato writing in general *does not have the function of teaching and educating, but only the function of bringing to mind for those who are already educated and possess knowledge.* The explanation of the passage of the *Phaedrus* presupposes the existence of the Academy, and the writings are the means of bringing to mind for those who are members of the Academy.[7]

Nietzsche was completely correct, and the most recent research has shown this in detail; in fact, the passage of the *Phaedrus* even states that the philosopher is truly such if and only if *he does not entrust* "the things of greater value" *to writing but only to oral discourse.* Here is the well-articulated reasoning of Plato, which is spelled out as follows.[8]

(*a*) Writing *does not increase the wisdom of men*, but it increases the appearance of wisdom (that is, opinion); in addition *it weakens the memory*, but only offers a means to bring to mind things that are already known.

(*b*) Writing is dispirited and does not have the capacity to speak in a responsive way; in addition, *it is incapable of being of assistance and defending itself against critics*, but always awaits the active intervention of the author.

(*c*) The living and spirited conversation between those who have had knowledge impressed on their souls is much better and much more powerful than a written presentation. Written discourse is like an *image*; that is, a copy of actual spoken discourse.

(*d*) Writing involves a great deal of *play*, whereas oral discourse involves a notable *seriousness*; and so the play in certain writings can be quite attractive, but the promise of oral dialectic is much more beautiful concerning the same issues treated in written discourse and the results achieved are much more credible.

(*e*) Writing, to be conducted according to the rules of art, implies a *knowledge of the truth* dialectically grounded and, at the same time, *a knowledge of the soul of those to whom it is addressed*, hence the consequent structure of the discourse (which may be simple or complex, according to the capacities of soul of those who are to receive it); still the writer ought to be able to give an account in writing that cannot be of great *certainty and clarity*, precisely because in it there is a good deal of playfulness; the writing cannot teach or make anyone learn in an adequate manner, but can be used only as an aid to bring to mind things that are already known to the reader. In fact, only in oral dialectic can we find clarity, completeness, and seriousness.

(*f*) A writer and philosopher is one who composes works, being aware of their truth, and one who, therefore, *is capable of assisting and defending them* when necessary. Hence he is in a position to demonstrate in what sense the things written are of *small value* (τὰ φαῦλα) with respect to those things of *greater value* (τὰ τιμιώτερα) that he possesses but has no intention of entrusting to writing; rather he is going to reserve these for oral discussion.

Here are two of the most important passages in the *Phaedrus*, which explain completely the meaning of the hypomnematic function that Plato gave to writing and the limited character in form and content that *he attributed to it*:

> *Socrates*: He who thinks, then, that he has left behind him any art in writing, and he who receives it in the belief that anything in writing will be clear and certain, would be an utterly simple person, and in truth ignorant of the prophecy of Ammon, if he thinks written words are of any use except *to remind him* (ὑπομνῆσαι) *who knows the matter about which they are written.*
>
> *Phaedrus*: Very true.[9]
>
> *Socrates*: We have amused ourselves with talk about words long enough. Go and tell Lysias that you and I came down to the fountain and sacred place of the nymphs, and heard words which they told us to repeat to Lysias and anyone else who composed speeches, and to Homer or any other who has composed poetry with or without musical accompaniment, and third to Solon and whoever has written political compositions which he calls laws:If he has composed his writing with knowledge of the truth, and is able to support (βοηθεῖν) them by discussion of that by which he has written, and has the power to show by his own speech that the written words are of little worth (φαῦλα), such a man ought not to derive his title from such writings, but from the serious pursuit which underlies them.
>
> *Phaedrus*: What titles do you grant them then?
>
> *Socrates*: I think, Phaedrus, that the epithet "wise" is too great and befits God alone; but the name *"philosopher,"* that is, *"lover of wisdom,"* or something of the sort would be more fitting and modest for such a man.
>
> *Phaedrus*: And quite appropriate.
>
> *Socrates*: On the other hand, *he who has nothing more valuable* (τιμιώτερα) *than the things he has composed or written,* turning his words up and down at his leisure, adding this phrase and taking that away, will you not properly address him as poet or writer of speeches or of laws?
>
> *Phaedrus*: Certainly.[10]

3. The self-testimony contained in the *Seventh Letter*

The precise nature of the "things of greater value" (τὰ τιμιώτερα) that the philosopher does not trust to writing can be drawn from a series of convergent indications in the *Phaedrus*. They are those things that alone are able to support (βοηθεῖν)[11] the writings in the ultimate sense and on which the *certainty*, the *clarity*, and the *completeness* of the reasoning depend. In the ultimate analysis, they coincide, in the highest sense, with the supreme and primary Principles.

But although Plato says this in hints of various kinds in the *Phaedrus*, he instead in the most explicit manner affirms it in the *excursus* contained in the *Seventh Letter*.[12] The direct testimonies contained in the *excursus* are truly irreproachable and are presented in a well-contrived manner, which is spelled out in the following points.

(*a*) First, Plato explains the nature of the test, to which he subjected those who are attracted to philosophy, to determine whether they had the proper attitude to practice it.

(*b*) Immediately afterward, Plato explains the very bad results of the test carried out in the meeting with the tyrant Dionysius (II) of Syracuse who insisted that Plato return to his court in order for him to learn his philosophy. Consequently, Dionysius after having heard only one oral lesson of Plato thought that he could put into writing even those things considered "the greatest things"; that is, about those things that Plato had firmly denied the appropriateness and utility of writing, *because they require a series of discussions made with persistence and with a strict communion between teacher and pupil*; and it is through this continued application and communion of research and life-style that leads to the truth, that like a spark is ignited in the soul and then nourishes itself. To write on these things, *which are the greatest*, would not prove useful because those few who could profit from it are capable of finding the truth for themselves, in the communion of research and life-style, with just a little instruction given to them; on the contrary, it would be damaging for the ordinary run of men who are not capable of dealing with these things and they would end in deriding and contemning them or oppositely end in being puffed up with the presumption of learning and understanding what in fact they do not understand.

(*c*) To better understand these reasons, Plato recalls some basic epistemological arguments, thus demonstrating how complex the path that leads to the truth is, and how, consequently, the many would become lost on this way in a variety of ways. Only those few who possess the right disposition can pursue this path in all its manifestations and achieve the knowledge of "that which has the nature of the good." But, for the men who have this disposition of kinship to the things they seek after, writing is unnecessary; whereas, for the others who do *not* have the "proper disposition," it is totally futile to write on things that are above their capacity, because not even Lynceus himself could make such men see.

(*d*) In conclusion, anyone who pretends to write about these highest things; that is, about the "primary and supreme Principles of reality," as

Dionysius tried to do (and others like him), did not do so for good reasons but for evil purposes.

Here are some of the most important passages from the excursus of the *Seventh Letter*, which truly propose a model in all its detail for the reading of Plato:

> But this much I can certainly declare concerning all these writers, or prospective writers, who claim to know the subjects which I seriously study, whether as hearers of mine or of other teachers, or from their own discoveries; it is impossible, in my judgment at least, that these men should understand anything about this subject. *There does not exist, nor will there ever exist, any treatise of mine dealing therewith* (οὔκουν ἐμὸν γε περὶ αὐτῶν εστιν σύγγραμμα οὐδὲ μήποτε γένηται).
>
> For it does not at all admit of oral expression like other studies, but, as a result of continued application to the subject itself and communion therewith, it is brought to birth in the soul on a sudden, as light that is kindled by a leaping spark, and thereafter it nourishes itself.
>
> Notwithstanding, of thus much I am certain, that the best statement of these doctrine in writing or in speech would be my own statement; and further, that if they should be badly stated in writing, it is I who would be the person most deeply pained. And if I had thought that these subjects ought to be fully stated in writing or in speech to the public, what nobler action could I have performed in my life than that of writing what is of great benefit to mankind and bringing forth to the light for all men the nature of reality? *But were I to undertake this task it would not, as I think, prove a good thing for men, save for some few who are able to discover the truth themselves with but little instruction; for as to the rest, some it would most unseasonably fill with a mistaken contempt, and others with an overweening and empty aspiration, as though they had learnt some sublime mysteries.*[13]
>
> And this is the reason why every serious man in dealing with really serious subjects carefully avoids writing, lest thereby he may possibly cast them as a prey to the envy and stupidity of the public. In one word, then, our conclusion must be that whenever one sees a man's written compositions—whether they be the laws of a legislator or anything else in any other form,—*these are not his most serious work* (σπουδαιότατα), if so be that the writer himself is serious: rather those works abide in the fairest region he possesses. If, however, these really are his serious efforts, and put into writing, it is not "the gods" but mortal men who "Then of a truth themselves have utterly ruined his senses."[14]

Therefore, concerning whatever "the whole" (τὸ ὅλον), that is, the all, "the most important," (τὰ μέγιστα), "the true and the false of the whole of existence," (τὸ ψεῦδος ἁμα καὶ ἀληθὲς τῆς ὅλης οὐσίας), "the most serious things," (τὰ σπουδαιότατα), that is, "the supreme Principles of reality," (τὰ περὶ φύσεως ἄκρα καὶ πρῶτα)[15] involves, Plato does not wish to write, nor would he ever write about such things. For the many, in his judgment, writing on these issues would be *damaging*, for the reasons previously explained;

instead, for the few who are capable of grasping such exalted issues it would be useless, in addition to the reasons already given, also for the fact that *the supreme truths are able to be summarized in a few propositions* (ἐν βραχυτάτοις), and so, anyone who correctly grasps them fixes them firmly in his soul and will not forget them. And, then, the hypomnematic function (that is, the bringing to mind), which for Plato is the real function of writing, in this case will prove to be totally useless: "Since there is no fear lest anyone should forget the truth if once he grasps it with his soul, seeing that it occupies the *smallest possible space* (ἐν βραχυτάτοις)."[16]

4. The essential attributes of the *Unwritten Doctrine* of Plato were preserved through the indirect tradition

Everyone should certainly appreciate the truly remarkable importance that the indirect tradition has to assume, insofar as it carries a knowledge of the essential characteristics of those doctrines that Plato reserved to oral expression within the Academy.

Aristotle himself has told us that these teachings that Plato communicated only in oral discussions were called the *Unwritten Doctrines* (ἄγραφα δόγματα).[17] And Simplicius, citing Alexander of Aphrodisias, writes:

> Alexander says: "According to Plato, the Principles of the whole of things and the Ideas themselves are the One and the indeterminate Dyad, that he called great-and-small, as Aristotle also reports in his work *On the Good*. But one might also have got this from Speusippus and from Xenocrates and the others who attended Plato's lecture *On the Good. For all of them wrote down and preserved his opinion and say that he made use of these same Principles.*" (trans. Findlay, p. 414)[18]

And again Simplicius also mentions that "Heracleides" "Hestiaeus," and other friends of Plato[19] were present at these discourses and wrote down Plato's "*Unwritten Doctrines.*" Furthermore, Plato, although he rejected putting these orally expressed doctrines into writing, was willing to bring them publicly outside the Academy at least in a lecture or in a cycle of lectures. The results that occurred were exactly what he maintained his writings on such arguments would eventually provoke; that is, they aroused incomprehension and hence disapproval and outrage, as this important testimony tells us.

> Aristotle was wont to relate that most of those who heard Plato's discourse (ἀκρόασις) *On the Good* had the following experience. Each came thinking he would be told something about one of the recognized human goods, such as Wealth, Health, or Strength, or, in sum, some marvelous Happiness. But when it appeared that Plato was to talk on Mathematics and Numbers and Geometry and Astronomy, leading up to the statement that the Good was Unity (ὅτι ἀγαθόν ἐστιν ἕν), they were overwhelmed by the paradox of the whole matter. Some then pooh-poohed the whole thing and others were outraged by it. (trans. Findlay, p. 413)[20]

Hence there is incontrovertible certainty about the existence of the *Unwritten Doctrine* of Plato. But how is it possible to justify and preserve the writings of his pupils on these doctrines since Plato has pronounced a categorical verdict against all such writing for the past and the future on these topics? The response to this question is not as difficult as it might appear at first glance. In fact, Plato did not say that his *Unwritten Doctrines* were not of themselves capable of being written (on the contrary, he clearly says that he could write them down in the best manner possible), but he says that it would be *useless*, and even *damaging* to expose them to a public neither equipped or capable of understanding them. And, especially, he rejected all those writings on his oral doctrine produced by those who, like the tyrant Dionysius II, are not suitable, lacking adequate preparation and knowledge.[21] For, among those who do not understand these doctrines it is not appropriate to include his better pupils whose writings and testimonies have came down to us on this matter. And it is Plato himself who gave us a very clear and unconditioned positive judgment about these followers, by saying that they understood quite well the doctrines in question; and he counterposed them to such types as Dionysius II, as can be gathered from his unambiguous statement: "For if he [Dionysius II] deems them worthless he will be in conflict with many witnesses who maintain the opposite, men who should be vastly more competent judges of such matters than Dionysius" (trans. R. G. Bury).[22] Then it is clear that the followers who have written about the *Unwritten Doctrines* of the Teacher have not tried to do what Plato had maintained was objectively and structurally impossible, but simply had done what he maintained was *ineffectual, useless,* and for some *dangerous* with respect to the incomprehension of the many. In sum, the prohibitions of Plato on writing about certain doctrines were not of a purely theoretical character, but were rooted in a conviction that was chiefly ethical, educative, and pedagogical, and assimilated from the example of Socrates. Hence it is based on the conviction of the supremacy of the *oral expression* over the *written expression* of certain important philosophical doctrines. But the followers of Plato were, by now, so far removed from Socrates that they did not feel fundamentally restricted by these convictions, and hence maintained that they could not put into writing anything philosophical, without restriction or limitation. So much more now that the written culture had become the clear victor and those who were immediate followers of Socrates did not experience the effects of the rift between the two cultures, that, instead, Plato had experienced. And, in every instance, most of the better followers of Plato did not put into writing the *Unwritten Doctrines* to spread them among a inadequately prepared public, as all those who Plato censured would have done, but probably to circulate them only within the community of the Academicians.

But there is more.

The followers of Plato, by transgressing the great prohibition on writing about his *Unwritten Doctrine*s in the sense that we have explained, *handed down to us those keys that permit us to open the doors, that for so many generations would remain closed forever and for everyone*, and hence they did us, their posterity and history a great service. Therefore, the indirect tradition must be considered as fundamental evidence along and together with the *Dialogues*, as we will see.[23]

5. How the term *esoteric* is understood when referred to the *Unwritten Doctrine* of Plato

Long ago scholars introduced the term *esoteric* to designate these *Unwritten Doctrines*, by distinguishing, hence, an *esoteric* Plato from an *exoteric* Plato. By the *exoteric* is understood that thought that Plato destined for his writings and also aimed at those *outside* the School (*exoteric* derives from ἔξω, which means *outside*). By *esoteric* is understood, instead, that thought that Plato reserved solely to the circle of followers *within*; that is, *inside* the School (*esoteric* is derived from ἔσω, that means *inside*). But in the past *esoteric* was understood in a rather vague manner and indicated generically a doctrine destined to remain hidden under a cloak of mystery, almost like a kind of metaphilosophy for the initiated.[24] Against this way of understanding Plato's *esoterica*, Hegel seems to have done justice to everything, in this passage that is excellent in our judgment:

> A...difficulty arising from the obvious distinction between *esoteric* and *exoteric* philosophy. Tennemann states: "Plato used by right, what was appropriate in any thinker, to communicate only that part of his discoveries that he thought appropriate, and to communicate them only to those who he believed were capable of accepting them. Even Aristotle had an *esoteric* and an *exoteric* philosophy, with this difference though, that for him the distinction concerned only the form, while in Plato it involved the content of the discourse." Prattle! It would be almost like saying that the philosopher was in possession of his thoughts like some external thing: instead the philosophic idea is anything but that, it is the philosophic idea that possesses the man. When philosophers speak of philosophical arguments, they necessarily express themselves according to their ideas and they do not hold them closed up in their pockets. Even if some philosophers were to express their ideas in an extrinsic manner, nevertheless the idea is contained in their discourse, whereas very little of the external thing they are considering is contained. To express an external object not much is required, but to communicate an idea a capacity must be present, and this always remains something *esoteric*, so that there has never been anything purely *exoteric* about what philosophers say.[25]

Now, the Plato of the *Unwritten Doctrines* is an *esoteric* Plato, but in a wholly different sense. Gaiser explains:

> By calling...this theory of the principles of Plato [expressed in the *Unwritten Doctrines*] *"esoteric,"* means that Plato wanted to speak of these things only in the restricted circle of his followers, that, after a long and intense mathematico-dialectic preparation were capable of appropriating them in an adequate manner. It must not be understood, on the contrary, to mean an arbitrary secrecy, that can be found in the conventions of religious worship, or in sectarian laws or in elite groups.[26]

In sum: *'esoteric'* must be understood in the sense of *'intra-Academic'*; that is, as qualifying the *doctrine professed within the Academy*, and reserved to the followers of the Academy itself.

Hence, the peculiar meaning of the Platonic *esoterica* is the same as what characterizes the choice of oral dialectic to express the doctrine of the primary Principles. The way of access to the *esoterica* is identical with that difficult educative apprenticeship about which the *Laws* and the *Republic* expressly speak.[27] The *Republic* even speaks (as we will see) of an apprenticeship that lasts until fifty years of age. On the other hand, the supreme Principles that express the ultimate meaning of things are truly accessible to man only by means of a very long apprenticeship; that is, by traversing the "long way of being," without hope of finding a comfortable shortcut.

Understood in this precise sense, the term *esoteric* applied to the *Unwritten Doctrines* of Plato entirely escapes the criticism of Hegel. Quite the reverse, for Plato what Hegel said is confirmed; that is to say, that when philosophers speak of philosophical arguments, they necessarily express themselves according to their ideas and they do not hold them shut up in their minds. Even if some philosophers were to express their ideas in an extrinsic manner, *nevertheless the idea is contained in their discourse,* whereas very little of the external thing they are considering is contained." In fact, Plato, as we will see, in his *exoteric* writings directed to a vast audience outside of the Academy, simply by expressing himself on a particular question in a way that was to some extent extrinsic, *has manifested his conception by allusions and with continual reminders.* In sum, *the purely exoteric* is never present *in Plato.* Therefore, if there were no indirect tradition, we could not comprehend and reconstruct the *esoterica* present in the *Dialogues*, because they are variously interwoven with the *exoteric works* and thus somewhat veiled in very complex allusions and in various reminders.

6.   Significance, characteristics, and purpose of the Platonic writings

On the basis of what we have said earlier, it is evident that the necessity of reviewing the Platonic writings according to a new vision is imposed. The ancient problem "what is the nature of the Platonic writings" now can be seen to have a different solution at least in outline that is more complex, more articulated, and even more pregnant with possibilities.[28] First, we must remember that the form of the dialogue in which almost all of the writings of Plato have been constructed has its origins in the form of Socratic philosophizing. For Socrates to philosophize meant to examine, to prove, to bring to health and purify the soul. This can be accomplished only through living dialogue (that is, in oral discussion), that places directly soul with soul and permits the use of the maieutic-ironic method. But between the total rejection of writing on the part of Socrates and the consequent choice of oral dialectic as the single valid (on the one hand) expression and the rigid systematic treatment of the Naturalists or the rhetorical writings of the Sophists (on the other), Plato held that it was possible to go between the horns; that is, to produce a mediation that would (although only partially, and within limits that we have explained) be valid. Actually, he could well have written in prose (a σύγγραμμα),[29] by rejecting the rigidity of dogmatic exposition and discourse as practiced by the Sophists and the rhetoricians, and try to reproduce the Socratic spirit, without sacrificing it entirely.

So it is a matter of trying to reproduce in writing *Socratic* discourse, by imitating his special qualities; that is, by reproducing his artless questioning, with all that it evoked through his penetrating sallies, with its unexpected pain of recognition acting as midwife to bring forth the truth, without ever revealing it in any systematic or dogmatic sense, but attracting the soul to seek it out, with the dramatic breaks, that structurally open further areas of questioning: in sum, by making use of all those precisely Socratic dynamics. Thus was the *Socratic dialogue* born, that became a literary genre, adopted by the followers of Socrates and then even by later philosophers, of which Plato can be said to be the inventor and of which he was, generally, the greatest representative when compared to other practitioners. Indeed, he is the single true representative, since in him alone is recognizable the authentic nature of Socratic philosophizing, that in the other writers decayed into mannered or artificial prose. Therefore the judgment given by Plato himself in the *Phaedrus* is to be applied even to the dialogue as conceived and examined earlier. This means that, for Plato, the supreme philosophic truth; that is, *the things of greater value*, cannot be trusted to *writing* in any of its forms, not even to the dialogue, but *only to oral dialectic*. Therefore the dialogues achieve *some goals*, but not all the goals (certainly not the ultimate one) at which Plato aimed as a philosopher.

To put the issue succinctly:

(*a*) In the first dialogues, that are the closest to the spirit of Socrates, Plato has *protreptic*, moral, and educative goals in view, analogous to those that Socrates himself proposed with his moral philosophy. The purification of the soul from false opinions, the maieutic preparation for the truth and the educative discussion are certainly constants to be found in all the Platonic writings, but that in the youthful dialogues are certainly given primacy of place and are their principal objectives. Subsequently although they are muted, they still are present as constants.

(*b*) The Platonic dialogues *never* reflect *actually occurring discussions*, but they represent *ideal models of discussions*; that is, models of philosophical communication crowned by success, or by a lack of success. This idealization of the discussion allows a more accurate rendering of the primacy of the method, that has clearly taken on a regulative function, probably with many clear nexuses with the discussions that developed in the Academy. In particular, the dialogues present orchestrated magisterial dialectical discussions, in which the *elenchic* method; that is, the method of inquiry about the truth through the *rejection of inconsistent adversaries*, is perfectly exemplified.

(*c*) In the exposition of the doctrines contained in the "self-testimonies" in the *Phaedrus* and in the *Seventh Letter* we have already seen that Plato assigns to writing a precise *hypomnematic function*. The writer, therefore, must fix and place at the disposition of the author and the others conceptual material *achieved in some other way*; that is to say, in preceding discussions and hence *in antecedent oral discussions*. This "recalling to mind" function emerges into the foreground, from the moment in which the Platonic dialogues acquire a considerable doctrinal fullness, and hence especially in the span of those dialogues from the *Republic* (and partially also from the dialogues immediately preceding) to the *Laws*. Keep in mind that as we have already shown, the writings are useful for "recalling to mind" a series of doctrines, but, for reasons that we have explained earlier, not the ultimate doctrines concerning the supreme Principles of reality. Nevertheless these supreme doctrines are destined to remain unwritten, because they have no need of memory aids (insofar as they can be summarized in a few "short propositions" that when understood can no longer be forgotten), the writings make clear references to them *through various references and allusions*. It is a matter, therefore, of allusions that may well be called *hypomnematic allusions*, valid for those who know the doctrines achieved by means of other means of communication, but nothing more.[30]

(*d*) Plato verbally denies the capacity of effectively communicating doctrines to written discourse, reserving this capacity to oral discourse. Nevertheless the hypomnematic function would evidently not be possible, if the communicative function of written discourse were in fact totally absent. Notwithstanding the affirmations that excluded it that we read in the *Phaedrus*, it is clear, therefore, that Platonic writings are also an instrument for *philosophical communication*. Even if their author expressly denies it in his words, nevertheless, *as a matter of fact*, at least in the measure in which he has written and in the manner in which he has written, he ends with assuming it and indeed in demonstrating it.

(*e*) In addition, "the didactic procedure of Plato the writer gives way to a cognitive process that achieves the goal not yet in the writings, but in the activity of oral teaching of the Academy."[31] Therefore, "we can comprehend the Platonic dialogues in their totality only if we give an account that refers them in particular and in general to a justification of vast proportions that is not explicated in the written works, but that is presupposed in every one of its parts."[32] The circle in which Plato seems to enclose the reader with his writings, within its circumference, in reality refers many times to the *unwritten*, because the *unwritten* constitutes a wider circle, that includes the sphere of the writings and limits it.

(*f*) A confirmation of this viewpoint comes from a recent contribution of Szlezák, who, beginning from the examination of the dialogues and staying within that sphere (and hence without entering into the issue of the *Unwritten Doctrines* transmitted by the indirect tradition), demonstrates that the *assistance* of the oral doctrines that is brought to the writings and of which the *Phaedrus* speaks constitutes *the structural member of all the Platonic writings*, beginning right from the youthful ones. Plato "conceived philosophical writing right from the beginning as non-autarchic writings; that is, as writings that from the point of view of their content are to be transcended, if one wishes to understand them fully. The work of the philosopher must have the justification of his arguments beyond itself."[33] The detailed demonstrations furnished by Szlezák are particularly interesting because they show how this *assistance* is realized at different levels, as well as in a very extensive manner. At some levels, this assistance is enumerated in successive parts of the same work; on another level, they imply doctrines that are present in other dialogues; but the assistance that leads to the ultimate foundation is not found in the dialogues, and it is exactly that which Plato does not wish to put into writing and that the indirect tradition has handed down to us.

7. The *assistance* that the indirect tradition brings to the Platonic writings

That the indirect tradition can bring a series of *assistances* or *supports* to the Platonic dialogues has begun to be understood beginning from the early part of our century, but limited to the late dialogues. Instead the most advanced research of the last few years has shown in an ever increasing manner how even many obscure passages of the dialogues of the middle period are perfectly understandable only with the *assistance* of the *Unwritten Doctrines*. Therefore, it should be concluded that beginning from the foundation of the Academy, Plato already had the framework of the *Unwritten Doctrines* and a clear conception of the relations between the *written* and *oral* doctrines. Consequently, all the most significant dialogues of Plato, always considered as necessary points of reference for reconstructing his thought, are undergirded by the general theoretical framework of the *Unwritten Doctrines*.

Consequently, the *assistance* that the indirect tradition brings to the Platonic dialogues consists in this: by considering the *Unwritten Doctrines* as always being in the background, the central parts of many of the dialogues, that in the past were without clear explanations or explained only in a partial or forced manner, become clear and perfectly intelligible, and on a clearly objective and historical basis; that is, in the measure in which those who heard Plato *face to face* were able to furnish us with the key.

In conclusion, within the sphere of the new interpretative model *the loss of the autonomy of the dialogues* must validate the indirect tradition, but it does not mean a loss in their value, on the contrary, it means *an increase in it, since they are illuminated in shadowy areas*, and hence, they are very clear, very rich with positions and tensions and move us toward more wide-ranging areas of interest. In addition, that *increment* revealed by the indirect tradition is reduced to a very short set of statements. The doctrine on the *ultimate foundations* given to us by the indirect tradition is, in fact, always very brief: it is like the final part of the ascent to the summit, that is the shortest stretch, but at the same time the most compelling. The Platonic writings journey all over the mountain, but they do not achieve its summit; the indirect tradition, instead, puts us in the condition of *even* achieving the summit.[34]

II. THE IMPORTANT PROBLEMS THAT HAVE BESET THE INTERPRETATION OF PLATO AND THEIR MOST PLAUSIBLE SOLUTION IN THE LIGHT OF THE NEW RESEARCH

1. The problem of the unity of Platonic thought

Applying this new model of interpretation of Plato, we can resolve a whole series of problems that up to the present have not been solved. The biggest of the problems that have been tackled by the interpreters of Plato from the ancient period to the present is the reconstruction of the *unity* of Platonic thought and the achievement of a *synthetic and organic vision* that would bring order into that complex conceptual material that the dialogues offer, in which multiple perspectives intersect of various kinds, aporetic and problematic positions, references to different dimensions, irony often masking uncertainty as well as provocative surprises. Leibniz, who lived in an epoch in which the many centuries of Neoplatonic interpretations (that was directly and chiefly on the basis of an allegorical reading of the dialogues) was by now on the way to a radical disintegration writes: "*If anyone can reduce Plato to a system, such a one would render a great service to mankind.*"[1]

This then is the great enigma that needs to be resolved, in order to penetrate Platonic thought and understand it thoroughly.

Consequently, the indirect tradition, in the measure in which it reveals what would for Plato be the supreme foundations of reality and the nexuses that connect the whole of reality to the supreme Principles, in great part fills up this lacuna that the dialogues present and hence helps us solve the enigma. Actually from what we can draw from the testimonies that are extant, there is no doubt that Plato wanted to present a system, in order to embrace reality in its entirety and in its essential parts. And, although these testimonies are incomplete and very summary, they permit us, nevertheless, to reconstruct the essential traits and the structural nexuses of this system. But, because this discovery at a stroke makes a whole series of interpretations about Plato's work obsolete (and in particular those with skeptical, problematic, existentialistic, and antimetaphysical tendencies), it is necessary to explain in what sense the term system is being used when it refers to the thought of Plato. It is not being understood in the Hegelian or neo-idealistic sense, but in the sense that, right from the start, the Presocratics, Greek philosophy has shown as a defining characteristic and as a necessary connotation of philosophical thought. To explain means to unify, in function of concepts operating as grounds, that imply structural connections between them and over which there is a central or supreme concept that embraces them all. Hence a system is an organized connection of concepts, in function of a central concept (or of some central concepts). And, naturally, understood in this way, the system does not involve any rigid, dogmatic, closed ordering, but rather it is an open-ended project of chief supporting axes of researches and of connected supporting axes and their implications.[2]

Krämer seems to be correct in his explanation of this issue: "It can therefore be said to be a nondogmatic but heuristic project and it is in its detail even on the programmatic level an outline, and hence an open system; not, however, surely, of an antisystemic kind, full of fragments of theories, without any precise connections. Instead it certainly ought to be thought of in terms of its tendency to be holistic and in general as a coherent and consistent project."[3] Gaiser, in his turn, writes analogously:

> With the qualification "systematic" is meant that with this theory is understood and accomplished a *complete composition, a universal synthesis, a speculatively synoptic statement of the individual knowledge* acquired in all the possible spheres of reality. This adjective therefore does not mean that there can be drawn from it a rigidly closed complex of propositions, in a deductive manner, established once and for always. Until the present in the individual sciences what is of value for the whole of ontology is a type of living dynamic system, that insofar as it is "open," attempts to represent reality only in a hypothetical and dialectical way. The Platonic system therefore, if understood correctly, did not exclude, in fact involved a constant further development: even if the fundamental conceptions, like a crystallizing nucleus, remained for a long time unchanged, it was always possible to integrate new individual knowledges in the complex system.[4]

Therefore, the indirect tradition, by revealing the essential characteristics of the *Unwritten Doctrines*, and hence offering us that *plus* that the dialogues lack, bring us to a knowledge of the chief supporting axes (that highest concept or those highest concepts) that organize and unify in a remarkable way the various concepts presented in the dialogues.

But we will see this fully further on.

2. The problem of irony and its function in Platonic dialogues

What Leibniz said with respect to the problem of the reconstruction of the Platonic system is correctly stated also by Goethe, with similar words, about the problem of irony: "Certainly, he who wants to explain what men like Plato stated seriously, through comedy, or in a jocular manner, and what they stated through conviction or simply so to speak, would render an extraordinary service and would make an infinitely great contribution to our culture."[5]

Actually, Plato together with the Socratic dialogues also must necessarily take up irony. He introduces it in his writings as an essential constituent, with all the difficulties and with all the problems it involves. In Socrates irony consists of an easy play carried on under the mask of ignorance in all its various

shades and colors with the purpose of unmasking the unacknowledged ignorance of his blustering questioners. As is well known, in the various guises
of the simulation Socrates even goes as far as to pretend to accept the ideas
and methods of his adversary as if they were his own, he exasperates them to
more easily make weak positions emerge and defeats them, by making use of
the same logic that belongs to their methods.[6] Consequently, in Plato both
aspects of irony are to be found: the first, which is somewhat emphasized in
the early dialogues, reduces little by little its sharpness and importance, in the
measure in which the dialogues are enriched in doctrinal content and in the
measure in which the constructive aspect, in them, overcomes the aporetic
aspect. The second aspect, instead, tends to be widened and to become ever
more complex until it achieves the maximum place even in the very important
dialogues, such as in the *Parmenides*. And it is this aspect of Platonic irony that
makes certain dialogues difficult to interpret, because the philosopher does
not expressly acknowledge the ironic fiction as such and changes masks
without ever allowing them to fall off entirely. Platonic irony has a profound
methodological value, that has its roots in Socratic *maieutic* [midwifery]: the
reader of the dialogues becomes himself involved in the conventions and in
the play of the fictions for the purpose of obtaining his total involvement, that
has for its purpose to provide the condition for the arousal of the spark of
truth within.

Hence, Platonic irony does not have any relationship, as Jaspers has
correctly pointed out in his reconstruction of Platonic thought, with a *nihilistic
vision*, that follows the path of sheer negation and involves ridicule that batters
and humiliates. On the contrary, Platonic irony *implies the possession of
something positive*, which is not expressed directly, to avoid a misunderstanding
in one who is in no condition to understand the truth. Jaspers write:

> Philosophical irony is instead the expression of the certainty of an original
> content. Perplexed when faced with the univocity of the rational need and
> by the multiplicity of meanings that the phenomena possess, *it desires to
> grasp the truth, not by speaking it but by arousing it*. It wishes to give a sign
> of a hidden truth, whereas nihilistic irony is empty. In the vortex of the
> phenomena it would lead to an authentic unveiling in the ineffable presence
> of its truth, whereas vacuous irony falls through the vortex into nothingness.
> Philosophical irony is reserved in the presence of every direct truth. It
> prohibits any wholly immediate misunderstanding.

With irony–Jaspers says again–"it seems that Plato wanted to say: those
who do not understand ought not misunderstand."[7]

Consequently, by accepting the new interpretative paradigm not a few
dialogues cease to be enigmatic, and what Plato meant seriously and with
conviction can be understood now. The precise indications drawn from the
indirect tradition spread a lot of light, as we will see, on many dialogues,

especially on the enigmatic parts of some dialogues (that sometimes objectively reach the limits of indecipherability), and offer the key to understanding the ironic play and make masks fall away; hence, they allow us to factually identify the Platonic philosophical doctrine. In any case, the *panironic interpretation* of the Platonic dialogues, in which irony sweeps everything away, even itself, in the light of the reevaluation of the indirect tradition is no longer tenable, whereas ironic play reveals, eventually, its philosophical seriousness and its constructive purposes.

3. The critical problem of the evolution of Platonic thought

With respect to the crucial problem of the evolution of Platonic thought Theodore Gomperz writes at the end of the eighteenth century:

> Let us accept for a moment the luxury of a sweet dream. Let us suppose that one of Plato's intimate friends, for example, his nephew Speusippus...had done that which no longer can be done, using fifteen minutes of his leisure and, so become famous in the history of philosophy beyond his wildest dreams; that he would make a list of the writings of his uncle on a tablet, in chronological order and, that a copy of such a list had come down to us. We would possess, in that case, the best assistance for the scholar interested in the intellectual development of Plato.[8]

Gomperz noticed that this would not supply for the absence of a diary, of a rich supply of letters, of reports of his conversations; furthermore, the directive point of view concerning the chronological development and that concerning the continuity of doctrinal content would always strive with each other for supremacy; nevertheless, a catalogue of that kind would be helpful for the resolution of the biggest problems, since the thought of Plato was in a continuous process of development.

Consequently, today this conviction, on the basis of what we have stated above about the relations between the written and the oral in Plato, is in part overcome, and in any case reorganized in a structural manner. But, to understand this problem well and the solutions that are quite often offered today, it is necessary that we explain some essential features of this issue.

The concept of the "evolution" of the thought of Plato was introduced by Hermann in 1839,[9] in a work that marks an important shift in Platonic studies, by articulating in new way the interpretative model proposed by Schleiermacher. The thesis found exceptional agreement, and the conception of the *evolution of Platonic thought* became an accepted rule of interpretation; also it received some important confirmations on the basis of the application of the method of stylistic analysis, statistical linguistics, and with the aid of the sophisticated methods of modern philology.

It began from the *Laws*, which we know for certain to have been the final written work of Plato; and, with an accurate determination of the stylistic characteristics of this work, it attempted to establish what other writings correspond to these characteristics, and it concluded consequently (giving value to collateral criteria of various kinds) that the writings of the last period are, in order, probably as follows: *Theaetetus, Parmenides, Sophist, Statesman, Philebus, Timaeus, Critias, Laws.* It further established that the *Republic* belongs to the central phase of Platonic literary production, which is preceded by the *Symposium* and the *Phaedo* and followed by the *Phaedrus*. It can likewise be ascertained that a group of dialogues represent the period of maturity and the passage from the youthful phase to the more original: the *Gorgias* probably belongs to the period immediately prior to the first voyage to Italy and the *Meno* to that immediately following it. The *Cratylus* probably goes back to this period of maturity. The *Protagoras* is perhaps the crown of the early activity. The other dialogues, especially the short ones, are certainly youthful productions, as, moreover, is confirmed by the specifically Socratic thematic discussed therein. Although some of these may have been reworked in the mature period of Plato's literary activity.

Here are the conclusions that can be drawn from the theoretical and doctrinal point of view and that illustrate the schema we have upheld in the past too.

At first, Plato worked from a chiefly ethical (ethical-political) problematic, by proceeding exactly from the position at which Socrates had arrived. Next, and simply by analyzing in all dimensions the ethical-political problematic, he grasped the necessity of reevaluating the requirements of the philosophy of *physis*. He understood that the final justification of ethics cannot come from ethics itself, but only from a knowledge of being and the cosmos of which man is a part. But the recovery of the onto-cosmology of the Physicist occurred in a very original manner, and, indeed, through an authentic revolution of thought; that is, with the discovery of the supersensible (of superphysical being). The discovery of supersensible being and its categories started a process of revision of a series of ancient problems and also allowed to arise likewise a series of new problems that Plato posed and investigated little by little, in the dialogues of his maturity and old age, in a tireless manner. The achievement of the concept of the supersensible gave a new sense to the Socratic *psyché* and the Socratic care of the soul; it gave another meaning to man and his destiny, another meaning to Divinity, to the cosmos, and truth. In the other areas of interest achieved through the discovery of the supersensible Plato presented an antithesis between Heraclitus and Parmenides, he grounded the teleological intuition of Anaxagoras, he dissolved many of the aporias of Eleaticism, and gave a new meaning to Pythagoreanism. In the period of maturity, the Eleatic positions were quite pressing, not only inspiring entire dialogues like the *Parmenides*, but even leading, as we have already stated, to a substitution for Socrates as the central protagonist: in the *Sophist* and in the *Statesman*, in fact, the true protagonist will be the *Eleatic Stranger*. In the phase of old age, finally, the Pythagorean positions emerge into the foreground (however from the *Gorgias* onward they were always present and operative in various ways), to the point that, in the great final cosmo-ontological synthesis of the *Timaeus*, as protagonist Plato chose the Pythagorean *Timaeus*. According to the majority of scholars, finally (as well as those scholars who were among the first to reevaluate them), the *Unwritten Doctrines* would conclude the evolutionary sweep of the works of Plato.

This literary journey that we have sketched briefly naturally has a series of variants (some quite well known) among various interpreters. In particular it must be noted that many scholars believed that they could retrace in the dialogues after the *Republic* expressions of a crisis, of overcoming, of "self-criticism," of "self-correction" of various kinds of the original Platonic thought, especially with respect to the central doctrine; that is, the theory of Ideas. And it should be noted that the problem of the relations between evolution and system have been variously resolved, mostly with the tendency to give preeminence to evolution as a hermeneutic principle to the detriment of system; that is, to the unity of Platonic thought.[10]

Now, if the new interpretative paradigm is accepted, the genetic reconstruction of Platonic thought, as a whole with all the claims that accompany it, receives a drastic rearrangement, because the very presuppositions on which it is based fall under its attack. It would be appropriate to remember in summary fashion the focal points of this question.

(*a*) In the first place it should be noted that the studies of the Platonic dialogues using the genetic principle achieve results that depend on the consideration of Plato as a writer, but not at the same time bringing to bear the fact that he is a *thinker*. Indeed, Plato the writer is a long way from being systematically and wholly identifiable with Plato the thinker, as can be seen from what we have stated earlier, and as will emerge in detail in the remarks that follow.

(*b*) The genetic interpretation applies, without any demonstration forthcoming, the principle according to which Plato would have in mind *only* that grasp of his doctrine and theoretical awareness that he expresses in the dialogues written a little at a time.

(*c*) The different purposes and the different objectives that inspired the various dialogues impose, for structural reasons, different levels of doctrinal treatment; that is, *more or less in the quantity or quality of the doctrines* involved, that produce a notable gap in the play of the inferences on which the genetic method is based. Certain dialogues, for example, present a minor doctrinal content, simply by the fact that they propose to achieve more limited ends in comparison to others, and what is more they are adapted depending on what figures are involved in the dialogue.

(d) In the *Phaedrus*, moreover, Plato clearly states, as we pointed out earlier, that the moment of *verbal expression* of doctrines *comes first* and that only in a second moment do the doctrines achieved through oral discussion (or at least *some* of them) become fixed, with a hypomnematic function, in writing. In this respect, moreover, it is easy to notice a mobility within the limits between the written and the unwritten. With the passage of time, in fact, Plato is pushed to put always more into writing and to come to a halt only in front of those "things of greater value"; that is, before those doctrines that, for the reasons explained earlier, must remain "unwritten" for always.

(e) In addition, he has made a *series of references* to these *Unwritten Doctrines*, which in many dialogues, for an unbaised reader are unequivocal.

(f) The conclusions are, therefore, evident. Plato, when he composed the dialogues, moved in a conceptual area of interest *much wider* than his piecemeal writings of them. The correct evaluation of the indirect tradition permits us to reconstruct, with fair success, this area of interest of his thought. Once the essential nucleus of his *Unwritten Doctrines* is ascertained, it is seen to arise from a period very much prior to what was considered to be the case in the past. It is evident then that the question of the evolution of Platonic thought is imposed in a radically new way, and precisely on the basis of the relations between the written and the oral teaching; that is to say, on the basis of the relations between the two extant traditions, taking into account likewise all the circumstances spoken about above.

(g) It will be necessary, in any case, to distinguish different levels of the evolutionary arc: that of *Plato the thinker;* that of *Plato the writer in general;* that of the *structure of the relations between the written and oral expression,* that in a certain measure is slowly narrowed.

4. Myth and logos in Plato

Another problem of enormous proportions, proximate to that just examined, is produced by the fact the Plato reevaluated myth alongside the notion of logos; and, beginning from the *Gorgias* until the late dialogues, he attributes a singular importance to them.

What is the explanation for the fact? How does philosophy ever get involved in myth, from which in various way it has tried so hard to extricate itself? Is it, perhaps, an involution, a partial abdication of philosophy's own prerogatives, a renunciation of consistency, or, in any case, a symptom of a lack of confidence in itself? In short, what does myth mean in the Platonic writings? There have been various responses to this question. The extreme solutions have come from Hegel and the School of Heidigger.

Hegel wrote in this regard:

> Myth is a form of exposition that, insofar as it is very ancient, appeals always to sensible images that it adopts for presentation, not for thought; *but this*

attests to the impotency of thought, that does not yet know how to rule from its own resources, and hence is not yet fully liberated. Myth is part of the pedagogy of the human race, since it excites and attracts to concern us with content; but just as in it thought is contaminated by sensible forms, thought cannot express that which it wishes to express. *When the concept reaches maturity, it has no need of myth.*[11]

Therefore, Platonic myth belongs to an exterior and representational form; philosophical conceptions are always divorced from myth, it is mixed with myth only because it is in part still immature. Thus myth in Plato has a negative (philosophical) value.

The School of Heidigger has come to diametrically opposed conclusions, they point to myth as the most authentic expression of Platonic metaphysics. The logos, that is deployed in the theory of Ideas, is revealed as capable of stating *being*, but incapable of explaining *life*. Myth comes to its assistance in explaining life and, in a certain sense, overcomes logos and makes it mythology. Mythology would then be the most authentic meaning of Platonism.[12]

Between these two extremes, naturally, there exists a range of various intermediate solutions.[13]

In our judgment, the problem is solvable only if the precise reasons that brought Plato to repropose the myth are uncovered. And these reasons are to be found in the reevaluation of some basic theses of Orphism and of its mystical tendency, and, in general, in the predominant power of the religious component, beginning from the *Gorgias*. Myth, in sum, in Plato arises not only as an expression of the *imagination*, but rather as an expression of what we may call faith (Plato used the term *hope*, ἐλπίς in the *Phaedo*).[14]

Platonic philosophical discourse on certain eschatological themes, actually, from the *Gorgias* onward, in the greater part of the dialogues, becomes a form of rational faith: myth seeks a clarification of the logos and the logos *complements myth*. The power of faith which is explicated in the myth, Plato entrusts sometimes with the task of carrying and elevating the human intelligence into the ambit and sphere of a superior vision, *to pure dialectical reason*, alone, in which pure reason fails to ascend but can nevertheless take possession in a mediate form; at other times, instead, Plato entrusts to the power of myth the task, when reason has achieved its extreme limits, of intuitively overcoming these limits and thus to crown and complete this effort of reason, by elevating the intelligence to a vision or at least to a transcendent tension.

Here is how Plato expressly responds to the rationalistic negation of the value of myth in the preceding sense, in addressing Callicles and the champions of Sophistic hyperrationality:

> Now perhaps all this [the myth of the beyond the grave] seems to you like an old wife's tale and you despise it, and there would be nothing strange in despising it if our searches [with reason alone] could discover anywhere a

better and truer account, but as it is you see that you three, who are the wisest Greeks of the day, you and Polus and Gorgias, cannot demonstrate that we should live any other life than this, that is plainly of benefit also in the other world. (trans. W. D. Woodhead, Bollingen, p. 306)[15]

Moreover special attention ought to be paid to the following: the myth which Plato methodically used is essentially different from prephilosophical myth that is not yet aware of logos. Here is a myth that not only, as we have stated, is an expression of *faith* more than of *imaginistic wonder,* but likewise it is *a myth that does not subordinate the logos to itself, but tries to stimulate logos and fecundate it in the sense that we have explained, and therefore it is a myth that, in a certain sense, enriches logos.* In conclusion it is a myth that while being created, comes from the logos despoiled of its merely fantastic elements to maintain only its allusive and intuitive powers. But here is the clearest exemplification of what we have affirmed, in a passage of the *Phaedo,* that follows immediately after the telling of the most famous eschatological myth in which Plato attempted to recreate the destiny of the human soul in the hereafter:

> *Now it would not be fitting for a man of sense to maintain that all this is just as I have described it,* but that this or something like it is true concerning our soul and their abodes, since the soul is shown to be immortal, *I think he may properly and worthily venture to believe*; for the venture is well worth while; and he ought to *repeat such things* [these beliefs] to himself as if they were magic charms, *which is the reason why I have been lengthening out the story so long.*[16]

But the problem is still more complex, insofar as myth in Plato also presents other meanings, in addition to this just discussed, which is chiefly connected to the eschatological perspective. A second and remarkable meaning is, in fact, that of a *likely story* that concerns all those things that undergo generation. The *logos* in its purity can be applied only to unchanging being; whereas to changing being the *logos* could not be applied, but true opinion, indeed, a *likely story* can. Actually, Plato explains that between knowledge and the things known is a *structural affinity.* Argument and discourse that look to stable and certain being are simply those that are stable and immutable and grasp the pure truth; instead, reasoning and discourse that look to realities that are generated are probable and based upon belief.

And here is the position to which we must give adequate attention: *simply insofar as the changing cosmos is an image of pure being, which is the "original model," and it is also knowable; and simply because of the fact that it is an "image" it has a different cognitive status than the model.*[17]

The conclusions of Plato are, therefore, the following: With respect to the physical universe (that is not pure being, but its image), it is not possible to give true reasons in the absolute sense, but it is possible to give only some *probable or likely reasons.* Human nature, in this sphere, must, therefore, be content with myth in the sense of a likely story, because it is impossible to give anything else, because of the nature itself of the object of inquiry:

> Wherefore, Socrates, if in our treatment of a great host of matters regarding the Gods and the generation of the Universe we prove unable to give accounts that are always in all respects self-consistent and perfectly exact, be not thou surprised; rather we should be content if we can *furnish accounts that are inferior to none in likelihood,* remembering that both I who speak and you who judge are but human creatures, so that it becomes us to accept the *likely account* (τόν εἰκότα μῦθον) of these matters and forbear to search beyond it.[18]

Consequently, the whole of the cosmology and physics are myth in this sense.

But there are still further meanings to *myth* in Plato. Sometimes our philosopher presents it even as *an exorcism of a typically magical kind.* And it has been correctly pointed out that with this "he intends to characterize the particularly persuasive power of poetic-mythic discourse, that is capable of reaching not only the rational, but the emotive levels of the soul as well."[19]

And even, in certain cases, Plato intends through myth every kind of narrative exposition on philosophic subjects, that are not done in a purely dialectical form (and hence all his dialogues, or a large part of them).[20]

The reader should understand clearly that the importance of myth for Plato is quite exceptional. If we wanted to summarize with a minimum common denominator the things just explained, we would say that for our philosopher *to speak through myth* (μυθολογεῖν) is to express oneself through images, that at various levels remains valid, *insofar as we think, besides through concepts, also through images.*

The Platonic myth in its most elevated form and power is a thinking-through-images and not only in the physico-cosmological dimension, but also in the eschatological and even the metaphysical, as we will see. The μυθολογεῖν becomes, in this way, one of the emblematic signatures of the human spirit, that Plato, as a matter of fact, has given an ample place of importance.

5. The multiphased and polyvalent character of Platonic philosophy

In the exposition and understanding of Plato's philosophy the interpreters have generally followed two opposed positions. Some have espoused it in a systematic manner inspired by the schemas validated by Aristotle onward, or, even, according to the Hegelian schema (as for example Zeller, who presents his treatment of Platonism according to the dialectical triadic schema of Idea-Nature-Spirit). Others, on the contrary, after the discovery of the criteria that permit us to fix a succession although purely approximate of the more important dialogues, and with the conviction that Platonic thought went through a profound evolution, about which we have spoken, preferred to explain a dialogue through other dialogues. But the first method undoubtedly ends in being a Procrustean bed, insofar as it proceeds to amputate too many parts of Plato's thought to make it systematic. The second ends, instead, in essentially being dispersive, and at the end evades rather than solves the problem of reading Plato; in fact, to clarify, the reading of a philosopher must be done in accordance with some fundamental keys, some essential concepts, and in sum, some constants or structural notions around which the whole body turns.

Let us try to find a third path that goes between the other two, by attempting to recover the system of Plato in the sense explained earlier. Plato has slowly revealed different aspects in the course of centuries, perhaps it is simply this *diversity of faces* that can disclose his thought.

(*a*) It is to begin by starting from the philosophers of the Academy, reading Plato *in a metaphysical and epistemological key*, locating the fulcrum of Platonism in the theory of Ideas and the supreme Principles. (*b*) Next, with Neoplatonism, it is to put credence in finding the most authentic Platonic doctrine *in the religious thematic*, in the anxiety about the divine and generally in the mystical dimension, massively present in the greater number of the dialogues. (*c*) These two interpretations, in various ways, have been pursued right up to modern times, then, in our century, there arose a third way, original and suggestive, that points to the *political thematic*, or better the ethico-politico-educative thematic, as the essence of Platonism; a thematic almost wholly obscured in the past, or at least obscured in its correct valence.

We believe that the true Plato is not recoverable *in any of these three perspectives taken individually as uniquely valid, but rather he is recoverable in all three directions together and in their dynamic interrelationship.* The three proposed readings, in fact, illuminate, as we have said, the three actual faces of the polyvalent and multiphased Platonic thought, three dimensions or three components or three lines of force, that constantly emerge, variously accentuated or angled, from individual writings as well as all of them together.

It is certain that the theory of Ideas with all its metaphysical, logical, and epistemological implications, especially in the dialogues of the mature period and old age, is at the center of Platonic thought. But it is likewise true that Plato did not have an abstract metaphysics: the metaphysics of the Ideas has a profoundly religious sense, and the cognitive process itself is presented as a conversion (*metanoia*), and the Eros that elevates to the supreme Idea is presented as power of ascending that leads to mystical contemplation. And it is true, finally, that Plato did not place in contemplation the stage in which the philosopher must conclude his journey, since he prescribes that the philosopher must return, after having seen the truth, to save others and to pledge himself politically to construct a just State, in that dimension only is it possible to live a life of justice: and in the political task, in the *Seventh Letter*, as we will see, he has expressly pointed out the fundamental passion of his life.

According to these three dimension, therefore, we will present and interpret the thought of Plato. Nevertheless, the key position; that is, the supporting axes about which these three dimensions will be articulated, remain the protologic revealed in the *Unwritten Doctrines*. The protologic is reserved to the domain of oral expression and is referred to by the indirect tradition, thus in a certain sense, it constitutes a fourth dimension. Nevertheless, in another sense, it gathers up on a different plane and, hence, is not on the same level as the other three. It constitutes, rather, the final attribute (as we will see) of metaphysics, but, at the same time, also the summit of the ethico-religious dimension and the political dimension. Therefore, the protologic is *the general unifying summit*; that is, what makes the whole complex of Plato's thought a system, giving it unity of structure. Hence, we will speak in a wide sense of the protologic of the unwritten both as second feature and summit of metaphysics, and as summit of the other two components and hence the background of all the themes, by regarding, in this way, the unity that gives the highest meaning of Platonic thought.

Second Section

THE METAPHYSICAL-DIALECTICAL COMPONENT
OF PLATONIC THOUGHT

Θῶμεν οὖν δύο εἴδη τῶν ὄντων, τὸ μὲν
ὁρατόν, τὸ δὲ ἀιδές.

shall we assume...two kinds of beings,
one visible, the other invisible?

Plato, *Phaedo*,79A

I. The Second Voyage as a Journey from the Physical Inquiries of the Presocratics to the Metaphysical Level

1. The meeting with the Physicists and the verification of the inconsistency of their teachings

One of the most famous and most imposing passages that Plato has left in his writings, is without doubt the central part of the *Phaedo*.[1] Long ago scholars recognized it, even considering it the first description in European literature "of a spiritual history traced throughout its various phases, just as the first...clear affirmation of the teleological or ideal vision";[2] but it could also be said more accurately, that it is *the first rational perspective and demonstration of the existence of a supersensible and transcendent reality.* In our judgment, it could even be said that this passage is, for reasons that are better explained further on, *the "magna charta" of western metaphysics.*

Let us examine the grounding concepts in its key passages.

The most important metaphysical problems and the possibility of their solution is connected to the great questions concerning *generation, corruption,* and the *being* of things, and in particular they are connected with the specification of the "cause" that is their foundation. The basic questions, therefore, are the following: *Why are things generated? Why do they corrupt? Why do they exist?* Consequently, Plato says (through Socrates) that beginning from his youth he was concerned with these basic problems, searching for knowledge about the "inquiry into nature"; that is, that type of inquiry pursued by the early philosophers, examining many times from the beginning other solutions that these philosophers had furnished to this questions. On the basis of the method of this kind of inquiry, the replies to these problems are to be characterized as purely physical. For example, life is generated because of a process sustained by hot and cold; though, in addition, it is produced from blood (as Empedocles maintained for example), or from air (as for example, Anaximines and Diogenes of Apollonia maintained), or fire (as Heraclitus maintained), or from the brain understood as a physical organ (as Alcmeon thought). And the replies that the Physicists gave to the various problems concerning corruption and in general regarding the various phenomena of the heaven and the earth are all analogous.

But the repeated attempts to solve the problems and the various types of replies furnished for these problems, according to Plato, have a disappointing result: what was formerly known clearly comes to be obscured, simply as a result of these inquiries. The philosophers of Nature let stand, in a very wide-ranging way, the inconsistencies generated by the different foundations having a naturalistic character (on which common opinion is also based) and their contradictions; and this enlargement manifests the incapacity of such convictions to explain things adequately. Each view contradicts the others, but the same method (natural things as elements) was used by all naturalistic philosophers, so the conclusion is inevitable that the method is at fault and must be abandoned.

2. The meeting with Anaxagoras and the verification of the inadequacy of the Anaxagorean theory of cosmic mind as it was proposed by him

Before getting involved in the new kind of inquiry that brought him to the solution of the problems aroused, Plato examines the conception of Mind presented by Anaxagoras, that was to provide a quite important contribution for the solution of these problems, but that failed entirely for reasons that we will soon see. Actually, Anaxagoras was correct in stating that Mind was the cause of all, but he did not succeed in giving to this affirmation an adequate foundation and a necessary consistency, because the method of inquiry of the Naturalists, that he followed, did not permit it.

Here are the very important reasons adduced by Plato for this failure.

To affirm that Mind orders and is the cause of all things, means to affirm that it disposes all things in the best manner possible. This implies that *Mind* and the *Good* are structurally connected, and that it is impossible to speak of one without the other. Therefore, Mind posited as cause implies *by that fact* putting the *best (the Good)* as condition of generation, corruption, and the being of things. In particular, Anaxagoras maintained the thesis of the ordering Mind and ought to have explained the criterion of the best in function of what it does; and on the basis of this criterion he must explain the conditions; that is, its way of acting, of being acted upon, and the being of the earth, of the sun, of the moon, and the stars, their motions and the relations of their movements, and, in sum, the various phenomena. In short, he must explain how the various phenomena are structured in function of the *best*, and hence with an accurate knowledge of the *best* and of the *worst*. But Anaxagoras does not do this. He introduces Mind, but he does not attribute any role to it as just indicated; but he continued to assign the role of cause to the *physical elements* (air, aither, water, etc.) instead of to the best. But, if these physical elements are necessary to produce the structures of the phenomena of the universe, *they are not the "true causes"* and should not be confused with them.

In conclusion; Anaxagoras committed the same error that would be committed by all those who maintained that Socrates did everything that he did by use of the mind, but then wish to explain the "cause" for his going to and remaining in prison, by referring to his organs of locomotion, to his bones, sinews, etc., and not to the *true cause*; that is, his *choice of "justice" and the "best" made with Mind.* It is evident that, if Socrates did not have physical organs, he would not be able to do what he wished to do; nevertheless he acts *by means of* these organs but *not because of* these organs. The "true cause;"

that is, the "cause of being" (τὸ αἴτιον τῷ ὄντι), *is the "Mind" that operates in function of the best.*

Therefore, Mind and physical elements are not sufficient to "bind" and to "bring together" things: hence, it is necessary to achieve another dimension that brings us to the awareness of the "true cause" (τὸ αἴτιον τῷ ὄντι); that is, precisely to that which Mind refers. It is this *dimension of the intelligible* that can be achieved solely with a different kind of method from that followed by the Physicists, and that Plato now points out with the important metaphor of the "second voyage," which represents the most magnificent symbol of what it is to philosophize. Here is the superb text:

> "Whoever talks in that way [those who place Mind among the physical elements and not with the best] is unable to make a distinction and to see that in reality *a cause is one thing, and the thing without that the cause could never be a cause is quite another thing.* And so it seems to me that most people, when they give the name of cause to the latter, are groping in the dark, as it were, and are giving it a name that does not belong to it. And so one man makes the earth stay below the heavens by putting a vortex about it, and another regards the earth as a flat trough supported on a foundation of air; but they do not look for *the power that causes things to be now placed as it is best for them to be placed* nor do they think it has any divine force, but they think they can find a new Atlas more powerful and more immortal and more all-embracing than this, and in truth they give no thought to the good, that must embrace and hold together all things. Now I would gladly be the pupil of anyone who would teach me the nature of such a cause; but since that was denied me and I was not able to discover it myself or to learn of it from anyone else, *do you wish me, Cebes,"* said he, *"to give you an account of the way in which I have conducted my second voyage* [δεύτερος πλοῦς] *in quest of the cause?"* "I wish it with all my heart," he replied. (trans. H. N. Fowler)[3]

3. The important metaphor of the Second Voyage as a symbol of the ascent to the supersensible

The *second voyage* is a metaphor taken from the sailor's vocabulary, and its most obvious meaning seems to be that furnished by Eustachius, who, referring to Pausanius, explains: "It is called the 'second voyage' when the journey is interrupted by the absence of wind, and the journey continues using the oars."[4] The "first voyage" made with the wind in the sails would correspond, hence, to that followed completely by the Naturalists and their method; the second voyage made with the oars, and hence the very tiring and difficult, *corresponds to a new type of method*, that lead to the conquest of the sphere of the supersensible. The wind in the sails of the Physicists were the *senses and sensations*, the oars of the second voyage are *reasonings and hypotheses*; and the new method is based on these. Here is the new method:

"Well, after this," said Socrates, "when I was worn out with my physical investigations, it occurred to me that I must guard against the same sort of risk that people run when they watch and study an eclipse of the sun; they really do sometimes injure their eyes, unless they study its reflection in water or some other medium. I conceived of something like this happening to myself, and I was afraid that by observing objects with my eyes and trying to comprehend them with each of my other senses I might blind my soul altogether. *So I decided that I must have recourse to theories, and use them in trying to discover the truth of things.* Perhaps my illustration is not quite apt, because I do not at all admit that an inquiry by means of theory employs 'images' anymore than one that confines itself to facts. But however that may be, I started off in this way, and in every case *I first lay down the theory that I judge to be the soundest, and then whatever seems to agree with it–with regard either to causes or to anything else–I assume to be true, and whatever does not I assume not to be true."* (trans. H. Tredennick, Bollingen, p. 79)[5]

The teaching of Plato in this way become clear: the method of the Naturalists based on the senses does not clarify, but obscures knowledge; the new kind of method, therefore, will be based on *logoi* (definitions), and by means of them it must attempt to grasp the truth of things. Here is the nature of this "truth of things":

"But I should like to express my meaning more clearly, because at present I don't think that you understand."

"No, indeed I don't," said Cebes, "not a bit."

"Well," said Socrates, "what I mean is this, and there is nothing new about it. I have always said it; in fact I have never stopped saying it, especially in the earlier part of this discussion. As I am going to try to explain to you the theory of causation that I have worked out myself, I propose to make a fresh start from those principles of mine that you know so well–that is, *I am assuming the existence of absolute beauty and goodness and magnitude and all the rest of them...*'"

"Then consider the next step, and see whether you share my opinion. *It seems to me that whatever else is beautiful apart from absolute beauty is beautiful because it partakes of that absolute beauty, and for no other reason. Do you accept this kind of causality?'*"

"Yes, I do."

"Well, now, that is as far as my mind goes; I cannot understand these other ingenious theories of causation. If someone tells me that the reason why a given object is beautiful is that it has a gorgeous color or shape or any other such attribute, I disregard all these other explanations–I find them confusing–and I cling simply and straightforwardly and no doubt foolishly to the explanation *that the one thing that makes that object beautiful is the presence in it or association with it, in whatever way the relation comes about, of absolute beauty. I do not go so far as to insist upon the precise details–only upon the fact that it is by beauty that beautiful things are beautiful.* This, I feel, is the safest answer for me or for anyone else to give, and I believe that while

I hold fast to this I cannot fall; it is safe for me or for anyone else to answer *that it is by beauty that beautiful things are beautiful. Don't you agree?"*
"Yes, I do."
"Then it is by largeness that large things are large and larger things larger, and by smallness that smaller things are smaller?"
"Yes."
"So you too, like myself, would refuse to accept the statement that one man is taller than another 'by a head,' and that the shorter man is shorter by the same. You would protest that the only view that you yourself can hold is that *whatever is taller than something else is so simply by tallness–that is, because of tallness–and that what is shorter is so simply by shortness; that is, because of shortness.* You would be afraid, I suppose, that if you said that one man is taller than another by a head, you would be faced by a logical objection–first that the taller should be taller and the shorter shorter by the same thing, and secondly that the taller person should be taller by a head, that is a short thing, and that it is unnatural that a man should be made tall by something short. Isn't that so?"
Cebes laughed and said, "Yes, it is."
"Then you would be afraid to say that ten is more than eight 'by two,' or that two is the cause of its excess over eight, instead of saying that it is more than eight by, or because of, *being a larger number,* and you would be afraid to say that a length of two feet is greater than one foot by a half, instead of saying that it is greater *by its larger size*–because there is the same danger here too?"
"Quite so."
"Suppose next that we add one to one. You would surely avoid saying that the cause of our getting two is the addition, or in the case of the divided unit, the division. *You would loudly proclaim that you know of no other way in which any given object can come into being except by participation in the reality peculiar to its appropriate universal, and that in the cases that I have mentioned you recognize no other cause for the coming into being of two than participation in duality, and that whatever is to become two must participate in this, and whatever is to become one must participate in unity.* You would dismiss these divisions and additions and other such niceties, leaving them for persons wiser than yourself to use in their explanations, while you, being nervous of your own shadow, as the saying is, and of your inexperience, would hold fast to the security of your hypothesis and make your answers accordingly?" (trans. H. Tredennick, Bollingen, p. 79)[6]

4. The two phases of the Second Voyage: the theory of Ideas and the doctrine of the Principles

The vision of the "second voyage," as we have seen, is the discovery of a new type of "cause" consisting in purely intelligible realities. What necessitates the postulation of the existence of these realities is the explanation of all things precisely in function of these realities, and the exclusion of that which is physical and sensible as able to be considered within the realm of a "true cause," and hence the reduction of the sensible to the status of a means and of an instrument through that the "true cause" is realized.

Consequently, it would explain beautiful things not with the physical elements (color, shape, and similars), but in function of the beautiful-in-itself and smallness-in-itself; it would explain that ten is more than eight not by two, but by plurality; and it would explain that the way in which two and one are obtained is not by means of the physical operations of "division" and "addition," but by means of the participation in Duality and Unity, as we have read in the long passage previously quoted.

In general, hence, the first stage of the second voyage consists in taking as a basis the most solid hypothesis, *which is the admission of intelligible realities as "true causes," and in the upholding, consequently, as true those things that agree with this hypothesis and as not true those things that are not in agreement with it* (and hence, in the rejection of all those physical realities that we erroneously adopt as "true causes").

At this point what we have called the first stage of the second voyage terminates, with positive allusions to the One in the new dimension; that is, with a repeated recall to that which we will see is the focal point of the *Unwritten Doctrines.*

But there is a much stronger recall of the protologic that Plato made in the discussion, which follows immediately on this one.

If someone were to attack the *hypothesis itself* on which the theory of Ideas rests, what must be done? Before confronting the objections, all the consequences that derive from the hypothesis must be examined prior to giving an answer; that is, to ascertain if they are in agreement or not. And to justify the hypothesis, it is necessary to look for *a still higher hypothesis,* and we must proceed in this way until we have reached *an adequate hypothesis*; *that is, that hypothesis that has no need of any further hypothesis.* Here is the text:

> If anyone should fasten upon the hypothesis itself, you would disregard him and refuse to answer until you could consider whether its consequences were mutually consistent or not. And when you had to substantiate the hypothesis itself, you would proceed in the same way, *assuming whatever more ultimate hypothesis* [ὑπόθεσις] *commended itself most to you, until you reached one that was satisfactory* [ἐπὶ τι ἱκανόν]. (trans. H. Tredennick, Bollingen, pp. 82-3)[7]

And beyond the Ideas, as we have seen many times repeated, the indirect tradition states that Plato precisely placed the *first and highest Principles.* But Plato himself, in our text in the passage immediately following that which was read, used the very term "Principle" (ἀρχή), although in the unique allusive manner permitted him by his choice of not putting in writing this doctrine; that is, giving to the discussion a very general but nevertheless a very suggestive value.

You would not mix the two things together by discussing both the *principle* [aÂrxhÈ] *and its consequences, like one of these; destructive critics–that is, if you wanted to discover any part of the truth.* They presumably have no concern or care whatever for such an object, because their cleverness enables them to muddle everything up without disturbing their own self-complacence, *but you, I imagine, if you are a philosopher, will follow the course that I describe.* (trans. H. Tredennick, Bollingen, p. 83)[8]

And if that is not enough, the entire argumentative procedure of the dialogue, that is precisely based on its postulation of the Ideas, concludes by pointing out in a impressive manner what follows:

"As a matter of fact," said Simmias, "I have no doubts myself either now, in view of what you have just been saying. All the same, the subject is so vast, and I have such a poor opinion of our weak human nature, that I can't help still feeling some misgivings."

"Quite right, Simmias," said Socrates, "and what is more, *even if you find our original hypotheses* [ὑποθέσεις] *convincing, they still need more accurate consideration. If you and your friends examine them closely enough* [ἱκανῶς], I believe that you will arrive at the truth of the matter, insofar as it is possible for the human mind to attain it, and if you are sure that you have done this, you will not need to inquire further." (trans. H. Tredennick, Bollingen, pp. 82-3).[9]

Evidently only the highest Principles can constitute what, once achieved, does not require a search for anything higher.

In the passages read, Plato points out exactly what is that level which by his ethico-pedagogic-moral choice he wants to maintain in the area of oral expression; it is the *"things of greater value,"* that the philosopher, simply because he is such, does not put into writing. In the next to last (# 8) passage just read, after having spoken of the "Principle" and how it is to be treated, he concludes with the explication of the term *philosopher*, saying in an emblematic way: "But you, I imagine, if you are a philosopher, will follow the course that I describe." The *philosopher* (as we have seen in the *Phaedrus*) is one who does not entrust to writing, *but only to oral expression*, the things of greater value; that is, the doctrine of the supreme and primary Principles to which he makes reference.

5. The three great focal points of Platonic philosophy: the theories of Ideas, of the Principles, and of the Demiurge

The central passage of the *Phaedo* that we have taken up and interpreted truly presents a project that embraces the entire outline of Platonic metaphysics; and in a particular way places in the foreground the three focal points of the metaphysics and hence of all Plato's thought.These three focal points are indeed (*a*) *the theory of Ideas*, (*b*) *the theory of the primary Principles* and (*c*) *the doctrine of the Demiurge*. The theory of Ideas is expressly based on a clearly metaempirical inference; the theory of the Principles is referred to with wide and constant allusions;the doctrine of the Demiurge is amply expressed by means of the problem of the Mind that orders and governs the cosmos, with indications of the way in which (unlike what Anaxagoras did) it is to be based; that is, *in connection with the Good, the primary and supreme Principle.*

But the comprehension of these three focal points, and hence of the global sense of Platonic thought, is difficult enough, and Plato has informed the readers of his work of this in the most explicit manner.

(*a*) Of the theory of Ideas, he has written that the many find it the most difficult to comprehend and that hence they maintain that there are none, or that, if there are any, they are beyond the grasp of human nature. The man capable of grasping them and communicating them to others must truly have an exceptional nature. Here are his precise words that he has Parmenides proclaim, as the protagonist of the dialogue by that name:

> "And yet, Socrates," Parmenides went on, "these difficulties and many more besides are inevitably involved in the forms, if these characters of things really exist and one is going to distinguish each form as a thing just by itself. The result is that the hearer is perplexed and inclined either to question their existence, or to contend that, if they do exist, they must certainly be unknowable by our human nature. Moreover, there seems to be some weight in these objections, and, as we were saying, it is extraordinarily difficult to convert the objector. *Only a man with exceptional gifts will be able to see that a form, or essence just by itself, does exist in each case, and it will require someone still more remarkable to discover it and to instruct another who has thoroughly examined all these difficulties."*
> "I am in agreement with you, Parmenides," said Socrates, "in fact you certainly speak my thought." (trans. F. M. Cornford, Bollingen, p. 100, some changes, emphasis added)[10]

(*b*) We already know what Plato thought about the theory of the Principles: only a few can grasp it, and these few grasp it chiefly in the dialectic involved in its oral expression. Writing, for these few who understand it, would be useless, and for the majority of men, it would be damaging, because of their incomprehension and the consequences that it involves. Therefore Plato writes: "On these things there exists *no writing* of mine and *there never will be.*" [11]

(*c*) Plato has stated his strongly held convictions about the Demiurge that are completely analogous to those expressed about the theory of Ideas: "But the Maker and Father of this universe is very difficult to find and impossible to speak about to everyone."[12]

It is impossible to speak of it to all, not for esoteric reasons that are used about the theory of the Principles and with which by now we are quite familiar, but for reasons connected the problem of the Demiurge is part of the issue related to the belief or non-belief in the existence of a God, over that always man has struggled. There is again (and there probably always will be) the "terrible" man on duty (the scientist) who denies a divine ordering Mind of the universe; and, therefore, it is necessary that those who believe in it are not limited to repeating the convictions of their predecessors who favored the existence of a divine Mind, but that they face the risk of opposition. Here is what Plato states in the *Philebus*:

> *Socrates*: Are we to say, Protarchus, that the sum of things or what we call this universe is controlled by a power that is irrational and blind, and by mere chance, or on the contrary to follow our predecessors in saying that it is governed by reason and a wondrous regulating intelligence?
>
> *Protarchus*: A very different matter, my dear good Socrates. What you are suggesting now seems to me sheer blasphemy. To maintain that reason orders it all does justice to the spectacle of the ordered universe, of the sun, the moon, the stars, and the revolution of the whole heaven, and for myself I should never express nor conceive any contrary view on the matter.
>
> *Socrates*: Then are you willing that we should assent to what earlier thinkers agree upon, that this is the truth? *And ought we not merely to think fit to record the opinions of other people without any risk to ourselves, but to participate in the risk and take our share of censure when some clever person asserts that the world is not as we describe it, but devoid of order?*
>
> *Protarchus*: I am certainly willing to do so. (trans. R. Hackforth 1105-6, emphasis added)[13]

In our exposition, therefore, we will follow this order: we will first take up the Ideas, then the Principles, and finally the Demiurge, all of which mutually presuppose each other. We ask the reader to be attentive to what we say on this matter, because on the understanding of these issues depends not only the comprehension of the whole of Platonic metaphysics, but also the other dimensions of his thought in their fundamental significance.[14]

II.THE PLATONIC THEORY OF IDEAS
AND SOME PROBLEMS CONNECTED TO IT

1. Some determinations of the term Idea and its meaning

To face the problem we must consider first the issue of the word Idea that is generally used to translate the Greek words ἰδέα and εἶδος. Unfortunately the translation (that in this case is a transliteration) is an unhappy one, because, in modern languages, Idea has taken on meanings that are extraneous to those of Plato. The exact translation of the term would be "form," for reasons that will be completely explained in the pages ahead. In fact, we moderns understand by the term Idea a *concept, a thought, a mental presentation*, something in sum that stays on the psychological and mental level. Plato,on the contrary, understood by the term Idea, in a certain sense, something that is the *specific object of thought*; that is to say, that about which thought is concerned purely, that without which thought would have nothing to think about: in sum, the Platonic Idea is not in any way a simple mental entity, since it is a being, indeed, *that being that is absolutely, the really real*, as we will see amply.

In addition, keep in mind the following comments. The terms ἰδέα and εἶδος are both derived from ἰδεῖν, which means "to see," and in the Greek language prior to Plato it was employed especially to refer to the *visible forms of things*; that is, the exterior form and shape that can be seen with the eye, hence the sensible "vision." Next, the terms ἰδέα and εἶδος became used by transference to refer to the *interior form*; that is, the *specific nature* of a thing, more technically, the *essence of a thing*. This second use, rare before Plato, became instead an established philosophical term for our philosopher.

Plato, therefore, speaks of the Idea and of the Eidos especially to point out this *interior form*, this *metaphysical structure* or *essence* of the things of nature precisely as *intelligible* (and he used as synonyms likewise the terms οὐσία; that is, substance or essence, and finally, φύσις, in the sense of an intelligible nature, the inner most reality of things).[1] Consequently, the problem that we are now trying to comprehend is precisely this: how does a term that originally was used to refer to the *objects of sight*, come to be used to express the *highest metaphysical form of being*. To understand at bottom the reasons that brought Plato to the invention of the theory of Ideas means to understand that synthetic nexus which for the Greek man structurally unites "to see"–"form"–"being." Let us try therefore to comprehend this synthetic nexus, that is so characteristically Hellenic.

It has been pointed out many times by scholars that the Greek spiritual civilization has been a civilization of "vision" and hence of the "form" that is the object of vision; and that in many respects it is opposed, for instance, to Jewish culture, in which the dominant notion, instead, has been "listening" and "hearing" (hear the "word" and the "voice" of God and God's prophets).

This remark is accurate and is of very great importance for the historical and philosophical comprehension of the Platonic theory of Ideas, since, in the philosophical ambit, this theory is, in a certain sense, the most important and highest expression of that general Greek uniqueness. Democritus had previously used the term ἰδέα to refer to the atom, understood in the sense of the indivisible geometric shape and conceived as invisible to the physical eye and graspable only with mind. The atom-idea of Democritus is, therefore, the "plenum" *quantitatively* differentiated and determined; it is visible, yes, but only to the mind and not to the senses, but is nevertheless of a physical nature. The "form" of the Atomists is, therefore, purely material, as we have stated; it is determined and differentiated only quantitatively. Hence, it can be said that before "the Platonic Idea, which is *qualitative, immaterial, and purposeful*, there was the Democratean Idea, which is quantitative, material, and governed by necessity."[2] But even Anaxagoras was pushed in this direction in an analogous way. His admission of seeds (the *homoiomeries*), infinite in number, is not demonstrated. This togetherness of the *homoiomeries*, in fact, is a "formed" world, in which, as has been correctly pointed out, "is crystallized and so to speak sublimated every form, insofar as the infinite differences of the real are not only justified in its innumerable variety, but even demonstrated infinitely more true than it would seem." [3] In a famous fragment Anaxagoras has expressly used the term ἰδέα, speaking of the "seeds" that have "forms (ἰδέας), colors and taste of every kind." [4] Even this "original qualitative" is graspable in its purity only with thought and not with the senses, but it does not bring us outside the physical realm. Once again, we remain, therefore, in the sphere of the material, as we have seen already in the case of the Atomists.

The fundamental leap of Plato becomes possible only through the second voyage: the forms or Platonic Ideas are *immaterial qualitative originals* and, hence, are *realities of a metaphysical and not a physical nature*. Friedländer writes correctly: "Plato possessed...the plastic eye of the Greeks, an eye akin to that by which Polykleitos perceived the *canon*...; and also to the eye by which Greek mathematicians looked at the pure geometric forms. Plato seems to have been aware of this gift, stronger in him than in any other thinker."[5] The proof of this awareness is in the fact that Plato was the creator of the expressions "the vision of the mind,""the vision of the soul," to indicate the capacity of intellectual thought and the grasp of the essence.[6]

The analogy is hence clear: the things that we grasp with the bodily eye, are *physical* forms; the things that we grasp with the "eye of the soul" are, instead, *non-physical forms*: the vision of the intellect grasps *intelligible forms*, that are precisely *pure essences*. The "Ideas" are thus these eternal essences of the Good, the True, the Beautiful, the Just, and similar things, that the intellect, when it is stretched to its maximum capacity, and moved in the pure realm of the intelligible, succeeds in "determining" and "grasping." And this analogy bring us to securely understand the problem that we have been treating. Actually for Plato there is a metaphysical connection between the vision of the eyes of the soul and to what we owe this vision. Intellectual vision implies as its reason for being *what the Intellect sees*; that is, the Ideas. *For this reason the Idea implies a radical concise nexus, as we have stated earlier; that is, precisely a unified structure between vision-the object of vision-form-being. Therefore, in the theory of Ideas, Plato truly expresses one of the spiritual characteristics of the Greeks.*

2. The metaphysical and ontological attributes of the Ideas

The Ideas represent the speculative stature of Platonic thought that has had the greatest success, that has stimulated the greater number of theoretical interpretations, and that has inspired some of the greatest thinkers on central positions of their own doctrines, with a whole series of consequences easily imaginable, that has not simplified, but has complicated their comprehension.

The basic characteristics of the Ideas—on the objective basis of the texts—can be summarized in the six following statements that are referred to repeatedly in many writings, and that constitute points of reference that are truly unavoidable:

(*a*) *intelligibility* (the Idea is the quintessential object of the mind or intellect and graspable only by it);

(*b*) *incorporeal* (the Idea belongs to a realm totally different from the sensible corporeal world;

(*c*) *being in the full sense* (the Ideas are the beings that are really real);

(*d*) *unchangeable* (the Ideas are devoid of any kind of change beside generation and corruption);

(*e*) *self-identical* (the Ideas are in and of themselves; that is, absolutely objective);

(*f*) *unities* (the Ideas are, each of them, a unity, unifying a multiplicity of things that participate them).

The concise examination of these six attributes,[7] besides helping us to grasp the metaphysical status of the Ideas, helps us to understand some of the basic reasons why, although offering an explanation of sensible realities at a very high level, the Ideas still require a further justification and hence an ultimate explanation.

On the basis of what was said in the previous section, it is clear that the first of the attributes that define the metaphysical stature of the Ideas is that of their "intelligibility," that is strictly connected to their "incorporeality," and with which this is in a large measure identified. Actually, the new method characteristic of the "second voyage," that Plato opposed to that of the Naturalists based chiefly on the senses and the sensibles, is reasoning based on the *realities that are grasped only through reason; that is, the intelligible realities of the Ideas.* Intelligibility, hence, expresses an essential characteristic of the Ideas opposed to the sensibles, which makes manifest that realm of realities *existing beyond the sensibles themselves.* They are precisely graspable only by the intelligence that is able to disengage itself from the senses. Let us read the most important passage of the *Phaedo* in this respect:

> *"Is it not in the course of reflection,* if at all, that the soul gets a clear view of facts?"
> "Yes."
> *"Surely the soul can best reflect when it is free of all distractions such as hearing or sight or pain or pleasure of any kind–that is, when it ignores the body and becomes as far as possible independent, avoiding all physical contacts and associations as much as it can, in its search for reality?"*
> "That is so."
> "Then here too–in despising the body and avoiding it, and endeavoring to become independent–the philosopher's soul is ahead of all the rest."
> "It seems so."
> "Here are some more questions, Simmias. Do we recognize such a thing as absolute *uprightness*?"
> "Indeed we do."
> "And absolute *beauty* and *goodness* too?"
> "Of course."
> *"Have you ever seen any of these things with your eyes?"*
> "Certainly not," said he.
> *"Well,* have you ever apprehended them with any other bodily sense? By 'them' I mean not only absolute tallness or health or strength, but the real nature of any given thing–what it actually is. Is it through the body that we get the truest perception of them? *Isn't it true that in any inquiry you are likely to attain more nearly to knowledge of your object in proportion to the care and accuracy with that you have prepared yourself to understand that object in itself?"*
> "Certainly."
> *"Don't you think that the person who is likely to succeed in this attempt most perfectly is the one who approaches each object, as far as possible, with the unaided intellect, without taking account of any sense of sight in his thinking, or dragging any other sense into his reckoning–the man who pursues the truth by applying his pure and unadulterated thought to the pure and unadulterated object, cutting himself off as much as possible from his eyes and ears and virtually all the rest of his body, as an impediment that by its presence prevents the soul from attaining to truth and clear thinking? Is not this the person, Simmias, who will reach the goal of reality, if anybody can?"*
> "What you say is absolutely true, Socrates," said Simmias. (trans. H. Tredennick, Bollingen, pp. 48-9)[8]

This is the remarkable *distinction of the metaphysical realm from the physical realm* made in the sharpest fashion for the first time in the history of Western thought. *The distinction of the two realms (or of the two "regions" or "spheres") of reality, that of the intelligible and that of the sensible, is truly the principal path of all Platonic thought*; hence it is no wonder that all the writings make reference to it implicitly and explicitly, as we will repeatedly verify further on.

But here we wish to insist again on this point to which we earlier made reference. The intelligible, precisely insofar as it is not graspable by the senses, that can only grasp the bodily, can be grasped only by the intelligence that transcends the physical and bodily realm and that is in its nature *"incorporeal"*: *"for immaterial things* [ἀσώματα], that are the noblest and greatest, can be exhibited by reason only, and it is for their sake that what we are saying is said."[9]

Just so, with Plato, the term incorporeal takes on the meaning and conceptual value that to this day we attribute to it. *And it is exactly the "second voyage" that made possible the discovery of this dimension of being.* But because this is a point little emphasized and not much recognized, it would be better to mark that the term incorporeal has been used also by other thinkers before Plato, but in a different perspective; that is, in the naturalistic realm of the "first voyage." We refer to Anaximenes, who said that "air" (that for him was the principle of all things) was *"close to incorporeal"* because it is "an unlimited and rich source that never becomes less."[10] Melissus, the Eleatic understood incorporeal being, in saying:"If, hence, being is, it cannot not be one. And, by being one, it must not have a body." And again: "By being one it must not have a body; in fact, if it were solid, it would have parts, and hence it would no longer be a unity."[11]

Consequently, in the Presocratics (on the contrary, in this case, we would say in the Preplatonists) the term *incorporeal* indicates "the not having of any determinate form" (evidently form in a physical sense); so true is this that the "incorporeal" is connected with the "unlimited," that precisely does not have limits, or confines, or determination, and therefore lacks any form.[12] Plato radically changed this meaning: the incorporeal, for him, becomes an *intelligible form* (that is, a *metasensible, metaphysical*) and hence a determined being that acts as determining cause, a delimited being that acts as cause of limitation; that is, a *true and real cause*, as is said in the *Phaedo*.

Another definitional characteristic of the metaphysical stature of the Ideas is that focused on *being*. The Ideas are repeatedly specified by Plato as *true being*, as that which is *being in the fullest sense*, and as that which is *really real.*[13]

This attribute has the closest relations with the two already analyzed and with those we will examine below, and *constitutes a nexus that brings them together in a tight relationship.* The "being" of the Ideas is that type of being that is purely *intelligible* and *incorporeal*, that *neither comes into being or perishes* in any way, and it is, hence, *in itself and for itself* in the widest sense:

> "does that *absolute reality* [αὐτη ἡ οὐσία] that we define in our discussions [being] [εἶναι] remain always constant and invariable, or not? Does ab-

solute equality or beauty or any other independent entity [τὸ ὄν] that really exists ever admit change of any kind? Or does each one of these uniform and *independent entities* remain always constant and invariable, never admitting any alteration in any respect or in any sense?"

"*They must be constant and invariable*, Socrates," said Cebes.

"Well, what about the concrete instances of beauty–such as men, horses, clothes, and so on–or of equality, or any other members of a class corresponding to an absolute entity? Are they constant, or are they, on the contrary, *scarcely even in the same relation in any sense* either to themselves or to one another?"

"With them, Socrates, it is just the opposite; they are never free from variation."

"And these concrete objects you can touch and see and perceive by your other senses, but those constant entities you cannot possibly apprehend except by thinking; they are invisible to our sight."

"That is perfectly true," said Cebes.

"*So you think that we should assume two classes of things* [δύο εἴδη τῶν ὄντων], *one visible and other invisible?*"

"Yes, we should."

"The invisible things invariable, and the visible never being the same?"

"Yes, we should assume that too." (trans. H. Tredennick, Bollingen, 61-2)[14]

And also here, as earlier, the precise affirmations about the *existence of the two realms of being* [δύο εἴδη τῶν ὄντων] are particularly interesting: that of physical being (visible being; that is, sensible), and that of the *superphysical* or *metaphysical* (that is, not visible being, not sensible being). But it is very interesting also that another passage of the *Phaedo* in which Plato presents the attribute of being as the "seal" that characterizes the Ideas and expresses their ontological absoluteness: "Our present argument applies no more to equality than it does to absolute beauty, goodness, uprightness, holiness, and, as I maintain, all those characteristics that we designate in our discussion by the term '*absolute*' [αὐτο ὃ ἔστι]" (trans. H. Tredennick, p. 58).[15]

Let us also read the famous passage of the *Phaedrus* that speaks of the realm of Ideas as a "hyperouranos" and that we will discuss further on,[16] it is perfectly convergent with those we have read to the present. Finally, let us recall that in the *Republic* the thematic of being becomes very central with considerable epistemological amplifications: only *true being* is *truly knowable*; the sensible world, that is a mixture of being and nonbeing, is only opinable, whereas about nonbeing there is only pure ignorance.[17] It should cause, therefore, no wonder that Plato calls the same inquiry made by the philosopher as a "yearning for being," as a study capable of showing "that being that is always and does not change through generation and corruption," just as the soul leads "by day that is night to a true day;" that is, as "an ascent to being"; and even that he qualifies the sciences that prepare the soul for dialectic (and hence for true philosophy) as "a winch that draws the soul from becoming to being" without mentioning, then, the other famous images and similes of the *Republic* about which we will have occasion to treat further on, like the simile of the divided line and the myth of the cave.[18] This character of *absolute being* belonging to Ideas is perfectly clarified with the same reasoning that we have given earlier. *To truly explain becoming, Ideas ought not become themselves, but must have their own being that becoming does not have as its own, but must borrow and receive.* (Becoming as such is not being but only has being, in fact, it always implies nonbeing; and therefore, insofar as it has being, it must have it through *participation* with another.) With this, the way is open for a recovery both of Heraclitus and Parmenides and for a mediation between Heracliteanism and Eleaticism. The world of becoming is the sensible world; the world of being and immobility is the intelligible world. In other words, the world of sensible things has those characteristics that Heraclitus, and especially the Heracliteans, attributed to the whole of reality, while the world of the Ideas has those characteristics that Parmenides and the Eleatics attributed to the whole of reality. Plato arranged the antithesis between the two schools with the distinction of the *two realms of reality*: not *all* reality is covered by the Heracliteans, but only sensible reality; and analogously not *all* reality is covered by the Eleatics, but only intelligible reality, the Ideas. The realm of *being* (naturally interpreted again in a correct fashion) of which Parmenides speaks is the "cause" (the "true cause"), the *becoming* of which Heracliteans speaks is instead that which is "caused."

We now come to the characteristics of "immutability" and "self-identity" of the Ideas, which is a further specific explication and determination of the character of "pure being." Plato strictly connected these two traits, and that is very important for understanding his thought. However, there arose profound criticisms against Plato by Aristotle and even today they are repeated (although in a different sounding fashion) because of these traits and in particular against the notion of *"self-identity."* Actually, the absolute objectivity of Ideas in the Platonic context has a very complex meaning and theoretically is quite cogent. In fact, Plato had matured and fixed his theory of Ideas *in opposition to two forms of relativism that were very closely connected to each other.*

(*a*) The first form of relativism is that of Heraclitean origin (to that Aristotle himself refers, but in a strongly reductionist fashion),[19] that proclaimed the *perennial flux and the radical mobility of all things*; and he ended up, both as a matter of fact and necessarily, dispersing every thing in an irreducible multiplicity of *related mobile states* and hence ended with making it elusive, unknowable, and unintelligible.

(*b*) The second form of relativism is Sophistic-Protagorean, that reduces every reality and every action to something that is *purely subjective* and made of the subject itself the *measure*; that is, the *criterion of the truth* of all things.[20]

Let us seek to explain these two characteristics of the "immobility" and "self-identity" of the Ideas on the basis of some appropriate texts.

(*a*) The individual beautiful things; that is, the experiential and particular sensible things, change and move but the Beautiful-itself does not and cannot change. A change of an Idea would mean that it was absurdly *separate from itself* and it had *become other than itself*: sensible things can, it is true, go from being beautiful to being ugly, but precisely insofar as they are experiential and sensible; instead, Beauty-itself, which is the cause (the "true cause") of the beautiful sensible, cannot at all become ugly. Actually, a change of the Idea itself of Beauty; that is, its becoming not-beautiful, would imply the total destruction also of every participating beautiful thing, and hence the disappearance also of every empirical beautiful thing, because the cause being compromised, *by that fact* also the effect is compromised. In other words, by speaking of the Idea as *immutable*, Plato has affirmed the concept that the *true cause that explains that which changes cannot itself change, otherwise it would not be the "true cause;" that is, it would not be the ultimate reason.* Remember, the Ideas have been expressly introduced, as we have seen, as that *hypothesis* that it is necessary to introduce to overcome those contradictions into which the explanation, of the sensible by the sensible, and, hence, the changeable by the changeable, would otherwise fall. Here is how the characteristics of *immobility* and *self-identity* emerge in the context of the polemic against Heracliteanism conducted by Plato in the *Cratylus*:

> *Socrates*: There is another point. I should not like us to be imposed upon by the appearance of such a multitude of names, all tending in the same direction. I myself do not deny that the givers of names did really give them under the idea that all things were in motion and flux, that was their sincere but, I think, mistaken opinion. And having fallen into a kind of whirlpool themselves, they are carried around, and want to drag us in after them. There is a matter, master Cratylus, about which I often dream, and should like to ask your opinion. *Tell me whether there is or is not any absolute beauty or good, or any other absolute existence.*
> *Cratylus*: Certainly, Socrates, I think so.
> *Socrates*: *Then let us seek the true beauty* [αὐτὸ], not asking whether a face is fair, or anything of that sort, for all such things appear to be in a flux, but *let us ask whether the true beauty is not always beautiful.*
> *Cratylus*: Certainly.
> *Socrates*: *And can we rightly speak of a beauty that is always passing away, and is first this and then that*? Must not the same thing be born and retire and vanish while the word is in our mouths?
> *Cratylus*: Undoubtedly.
> *Socrates*: *Then how can that be a real thing that is never in the same state? For obviously things that are the same cannot change while they remain the same, and if they are always the same and in the same state, and never depart from their original form, they can never change or be moved.*

Cratylus: Certainly they cannot.

Socrates: Nor yet can they be known by anyone, for at the moment that the observer approaches, then they become other and of another nature, *so that you cannot get any further in knowing their nature or state, for you cannot know that which has no state.*

Cratylus: True. (trans. Benjamin Jowett, Bollingen, pp. 473-4, with emphasis added)[21]

Even in the passages from the *Phaedo* that we had just read in the preceding section this concept is unambiguously stated.

(*b*) Here is how the characteristic of "self-identity" in the sense of the *certainty* and *stability* of the Ideas emerges from the argument against Sophistic-Protagorean relativism (that Plato associates also with its opposite form, Eleaticism, that holds that all things are always together in the same way, and hence they are not objectively differentiated, but are confusedly together):

Socrates: But would you say, Hermogenes, that the things differ as the names differ? And are they relative to individuals, as Protagoras tells us? For he says that man is the measure of all things, and that things are to me as they appear to me, and that they are to you as they appear to you. Do you agree with him, or would you say that things have a permanent essence of their own?

Hermogenes: There have been times, Socrates, when I have driven in my perplexity to take refuge with Protagoras, not that I agree with him at all.

Socrates: What! Have you ever been driven to admit that there was no such thing as a bad man?

Hermogenes: No, indeed, but I have often had reason to think that there are very bad men, and a good many of them.

Socrates: Well, and have you ever found any very good ones?

Hermogenes: Not many.

Socrates: Still you have found them?

Hermogenes: Yes.

Socrates: And would you hold that the very good were the very wise, and the very evil very foolish? Would that be your view?

Hermogenes: It would.

Socrates: But if Protagoras is right, and the truth is that things are as they appear to anyone, how can some of us be wise and some of us foolish?

Hermogenes: Impossible.

Socrates: *And if, on the other hand, wisdom and folly are really distinguishable you will allow, I think, that the assertion of Protagoras can hardly be correct. For if what appears to each man is true to him, one man cannot in reality be wiser than another.*

Hermogenes: He cannot.

Socrates: Nor will you be disposed to say with Euthydemus that all things equally belong to all men at the same moment and always, for neither on his view can there be some good and other bad if virtue and vice are always equally to be attributed to all.

Hermogenes: There cannot.
Socrates: *But if neither is right, and things are not relative to individuals, and all things do not equally belong to all at the same moment and always, they must be supposed to have their own proper and permanent essence; they are not in relation to us,or influenced by us, fluctuating according to our fancy, but they are independent, and maintain to their own essence the relation prescribed by nature.* (trans. Benjamin Jowett, Bollingen, pp. 424-25, with added emphasis)[22]

In conclusion, by pondering over these two forms of relativism Plato conceived and fixed two fundamental characteristics of the Ideas, precisely, *immutability* and *self-identity*; that is, their objective stability. Therefore, it is clear that he wanted to affirm that they have a reality that is not enmeshed in becoming and that is not relative to the subject, a reality that is not sometimes subject to change and is not manipulable at the caprice of the subject, but that structurally implies reliability and stability. If it were not so, all our knowledge and judgment (and in particular our moral judgment) would be deprived of any significance, and our speech would be devoid of meaning. In a word, *the immutability and self-identity of the Ideas implies their absolute character.*

3. The highest metaphysical character of the unity of the Ideas

A final characteristic of the Ideas about which it is worthwhile to give special attention because it has a truly exceptional importance (unfortunately, in the sphere of the studies inspired by the traditional paradigm it has in large measure been obscured, or generally, undervalued) is that of "unity." Each Idea is a "unit," and as such it explains sensible things that participate in them, constituting in this way a unified multiplicity. For this reason, true knowledge is in knowing how to unify multiplicity *in a concise vision, grouping together the sensorial multiplicity in the unity of the Idea on which they depend.*

Note how, for Plato, the nature itself of philosophy is manifested in knowing how to grasp and hold this unity together, as he tells us in the *Republic* in this important passage:

"Whom do you mean, then, by the true philosopher?"
"Those for whom the truth is the spectacle of which they are enamored," said I.
"Right again," said he, "but what sense do you mean it?"
"It would be by no means easy to explain it to another," I said, "but I think that you will grant me this."
"What?"
"That since the fair and honorable is the opposite of the base and ugly, they are *two*."
"Of course."
"And since they are *two*, each is *one*."
"That also."

"And in respect of the just and the unjust, the good and the bad, and all the Ideas or Forms, the same statement holds, that *in itself each is one*, but that by virtue of their participation with actions and bodies and with one another as they present themselves everywhere, each as a *multiplicity* of aspects."(trans. Paul Shorey, with slight changes and added emphasis, Bollingen, pp. 715)[23]

And here is what discriminates between ordinary man, who is limited to the sensible, and the philosopher: the former reaches multiplicity and even clings to it and rejects unity. Furthermore: "who cannot endure to hear anybody say that the beautiful is *One* and the just One, and so of other things" (trans. Paul Shorey, p. 719, with emphasis added)[24] and "lose themselves and wander amid the *multiplicities* of multifarious things, are not philosophers (Shorey, p. 720).[25]

The philosopher, instead, is simply one who can *see the connection and can grasp the unity in the multiplicity*. Plato summarizes his thought in this astonishing maxim: "For he who can *view things in their connection* [συνοπτικὸς] is a dialectician; he who cannot, is not" (Shorey, p. 769).[26]

This definitional characteristic of the Ideas is important to such an extent that the Academics even based one of the arguments intended to demonstrate the existence of the Ideas on it, and they called it precisely "the proof derived from the one over many," that can be formulated in the following way: If there are many men and each of them is indeed a man, and hence if there is something that is predicated of each and all men without being identical in each of them, then it is necessary that there is something beyond each of them, separated from them and eternal, and that indeed is so insofar as this can be predicated of all men who differ in number in an identical way. And precisely this "one over many" is the Idea that transcends them and is eternal.[27]

But the implications of this basic character of the Ideas can be examined for the reasons stated only further on in connection with the protologic problematic.

4.   Platonic dualism is an expression of transcendence

After what we have said, it would be inevitable to speak of the "dualistic" conception of reality in Plato: experiential realities are sensible things, whereas the Ideas are intelligible things; physical realities are mixed with nonbeing, whereas the Ideas are being in the pure and total sense; sensible realities are corporeal, whereas the Ideas are incorporeals; sensible realities are corruptible, whereas the Ideas are stable and eternal realities; sensible things are relative, whereas the Ideas are absolute; sensible things are multiple, while the Ideas are unities. Actually, many scholars, repeating and developing in various ways the criticisms made by Aristotle (especially that contained in the passages we read), heavily contest this "dualism," by maintaining that the "separation" of the Ideas from sensible realities; that is, their "transcendence" compromised their role as "causes."

But this is in reality a purely theoretical prejudice to be rigorously avoided if you wish to understand Plato. First of all, it is revealed that the Ideas are as much "immanent" as they are "transcendent"; something that is frequently not mentioned or simply neglected. For Plato, the transcendence of the Ideas is simply the reason of being (that is, the foundation) of their immanence. The Ideas could not be the cause of sensible things (that is, the "true cause") if they were not *to transcend* the sensible things themselves; and indeed by ontologically transcending them, they can ground their immanent ontological structure. In sum, *the transcendence of the Ideas is precisely what allows them to function in the role of "true cause."* To confuse these two aspects, or generally, to reduce them to the same level means to totally forget the "second voyage" and its results.

It is, in any case, interesting to note that the first characteristic of the Ideas Plato revealed is that of their immanence. The first dialogues present, in fact, the aspect of the Ideas as that which remains identical in things, as that which makes each thing to be what it is and nothing else, that which fixes things in their nature and consequently makes them intelligible. Then Plato especially beginning from the *Phaedo*, where he made his "second voyage" and its results the subject of consideration, develops, besides the attribute of immanence, the attribute that, with proper theoretical precision, can be called, in a quite correct manner, "transcendence."[28] If the Ideas are opposed to experiential things as the intelligible to the sensible, being to becoming, incorporeal to corporeal, immobile to mobile, absolute to relative, unity to multiplicity, then it is clear that *they represent a different dimension of reality, a new and higher realm of being itself.* Plato is very explicit concerning the existence of two different realms of being, as we saw in some passages we quoted earlier and read, and he states it solemnly in the *Timaeus* in an admirable passage that we will now take into consideration and read:

> Is there such a thing as "five just in itself" or any other things that we are always describing in such terms, as things that "are just in themselves"? Or are the things we see or otherwise perceive by the bodily senses the only things that have such reality, and has nothing else, over and above these, any sort of being at all? Are we talking idly whenever we say that there is such a thing as an intelligible Form of anything? Is this nothing more than a word?
>
> Now it does not become either of us either to dismiss the present question without trial or verdict, simply asseverating that it is so, nor yet to insert a lengthy digression into a discourse that is already long. If we could see our way to draw a distinction of great importance in few words, that would best suit the occasion.
>
> My own verdict, then, is this.

If intelligence and true belief are *two different kinds*, then these things–
Forms that we cannot perceive but only think of–certainly exist in themselves; but if, as some hold, true belief in no way differs from intelligence, then
all the things we perceive through the bodily senses must be taken as the
most certain reality. *Now we must affirm that they are two different things,
for they are distinct in origin and unlike in nature.*The one is produced in us
by instruction, the other by persuasion; the one can always give a true
account of itself, the other can give none; the one cannot be shaken by
persuasion, whereas the other can be won over; and true belief, we must
allow, is shared by all mankind, intelligence only by the gods and a small
number of men. (trans. F. M. Cornford, 188-9)
*This being so, we must agree that there is, first, the unchanging Form,
ungenerated and indestructible, that neither receives anything else into itself
from elsewhere nor itself enters into anything else anywhere, invisible and
otherwise imperceptible; that, in fact, that thinking has for its object.*
*Second is that which bears the same name and is like that Form; is sensible;
is brought into existence; is perpetually in motion, coming to be in a certain
place and again vanishing out of it; and it is to be apprehended by belief
involving perception.* (trans. F. M. Cornford, p. 192 emphasis added)[29]

Anyone who has followed us attentively up to this point, will agree that
all the elements are now in place that are needed to draw the conclusions about
the authentic meaning of the theory of Ideas, which is the first and very
remarkable achievement of the "second voyage." Plato with the Ideas, as we
have pointed out many times, discovered the *realm of the intelligible as the
incorporeal and metaempirical dimension of being.* And this world of the
incorporeal intelligible, transcends, it is true, the sensible, not in the absurd
sense of "separation," but in the sense of being a metaempirical cause (that is,
"a true cause"); and hence, it is the true reason of being of the sensible. In
conclusion, *the dualism of Plato is nothing other than the dualism of anyone who
admits the existence of a supersensible cause as a reason of being of the sensible
itself and maintains that the sensible, by reason of its self-contradictory nature,
cannot be in its totality its own reason for being.* Therefore, the metaphysical
"dualism" of Plato has absolutely nothing to do with that ridiculous dualism
that is the hypostatization of the sensible and then is conceived as the opposite
of the sensible itself.

Finally, it needs to be pointed out that Plato presents, besides the
aforementioned, another form of dualism, that concerns the supreme Principles that are precisely two; but of this we can speak only further on, by reason
of the complexity of the problems that it implies, which can then be adequately
treated in a detailed manner to assist our understanding this other form of
dualism.[30]

We must yet recall an important point, in turning to "dualism" understood as an expression of transcendence, concerned in a particular way with
the famous great myth of the Hyperouranos, about which there are many

ambiguities. Actually the "myth" is not an abstract logos and is correctly understood for what it is; that is, as a metaphorical expression and symbol, as something speaking through images. But let us read the passage of the *Phaedrus* that has become very famous, in which Plato speaks about the Hyperouranos:

> Of that *place beyond the heavens* (Hyperouranos) none of our earthly poets has yet sung, and none shall sing worthily. But this is the manner of it, for assuredly we must be bold to speak what is true, above all when our discourse is upon truth. *It is there that true being* [οὐσία ὄντως οὖσα] *dwells, without color or shape, that cannot be touched; reason alone, the soul's pilot, can behold it, and all true knowledge is knowledge thereof.* Now even as the mind of a god is nourished by reason and knowledge, so also is it with every soul that has a care to receive her proper food; wherefore when at least she has beheld being she is well content, and contemplating truth she is nourished and prospers, until the heaven's revolution bring her back full circle. And while she is borne round she discerns Justice, its very self, and likewise temperance, and knowledge, not the knowledge that is neighbor to becoming and varies with the various objects to that we commonly ascribe being [= phenomenal being], but the veritable knowledge of being that veritably is. And when she has contemplated likewise and feasted upon all else that has true being, she descends again within the heavens and comes back home. (trans. Hackforth, p. 494 slight changes and emphasis added)[31]

"The Hyperouranos" means the "place beyond heaven," and hence is an image that, if correctly understood in what it expresses, indicates a place that is not quite a place in the physical sense, but a *metaphysical* place, the realm of the supersensible. The "heaven" is the "visible," (and hence sensible); the "beyond-the-heaven" is the "beyond-the-visible,"(that is, precisely the supersensible, the metaphysical). But note again how in the myth of the Hyperouranos, clearly to avoid misunderstanding, the Ideas that occupy that "realm" are immediately described as having these characteristics, that have nothing to do with what can be seen: they are *without shape, without color, invisible,* etc. and are graspable by us only with that part that rules the soul; that is, only by the intelligence.

In conclusion, through the theory of Ideas, as we have seen many times, but that it is necessary to repeat, Plato wanted to say this: *the sensibles are explained only by the supersensible realm, the corruptible by the incorruptible entities, the mobile by the immobile, the relative by the Absolute, the multiple by the One.*

5.   The important problem about the relationship between the world of Ideas and the world of the senses

The problem of the relation between the One and the many, which arises when we try to understand the relationship between the different Ideas and to explain their derivation from a first principle, is taken up again, as we have many times before hinted, also within the realm of the explanation of the relations existing between the Ideas themselves and sensible things.

In this regard remember that the interpretation of the relations of the sphere of the Ideas and the sensible world was already misunderstood by some contemporaries and by some followers of Plato, which is so true that Plato in the *Parmenides* takes aim at and in part refutes some interpretations that recall those maintained even in the *Metaphysics* of Aristotle about which we have previously spoken and to that we will return in a more detailed fashion further on.

Actually, Plato in his writings presents different perspectives in this regard, affirming that between the sensible and the intelligible spheres is (*a*) a relation of *mimesis* (μίμησις) or imitation, (*b*) or of *metexsis* (μέθεξις) or participation, or (*c*) of *koinonia* (κοινωνία) or community, (*d*) or again of *parousia* (παρουσία) or presence.[32] And great discussions have been generated because these terms are not conceived within their correct limits and measure. But Plato in the *Phaedo* has explicitly stated that these terms must be understood as simple hypotheses on which he does not entirely insist and to which he does not intend to give the cogency of an ultimate answer; what he was concerned with was simply to establish that the Idea is the true cause of the sensible, that it is the principle of these things, their *ratio essendi* [reason for being], their metaphysical foundation and condition for being. He intended, in sum, to stop at the first level achieved in the first stage of the "second voyage." Actually, to achieve the ultimate response, it would be necessary to take into account the protologic of the *Unwritten Doctrines*, thus the perspective of the highest Principles.

Considering all of this, these Platonic terms about which we have been speaking, will be clear enough from what follows, naturally remaining on the level of the achievement of the first stage of the "second voyage," as well as allowing them to again open up into big problems on that level, as we will see.

(*a*) The sensible is an imitation or *mimesis* of the intelligible because it imitates it, although without ever becoming equal to it (in its continual becoming it draws near, growing toward the ideal model and then it corrupts and retreats).

(*b*) The sensible, in the measure in which it realizes its essence, *participates*, that is it shares in the intelligible (and in particular, through its *sharing* in the Idea, it is and is knowable).

(*c*) It can be said that the sensible has a *communion* with; that is, a contact with, the intelligible, since this is its cause and foundation: whatever the sensible has of being and knowability is derived from the intelligible, and, in the measure in which it has this being and this intelligibility, it has "communion" with the intelligible.

(*d*) Finally, it can also be said that the intelligible is *present* in the sensible in the measure in which the cause is in the effect, the principle is in that which is principled, the condition in that which is conditioned.

In this way the Platonic terminology becomes clear. It clarifies the famous term paradigm; that is, "model," with which Plato designates the role of the Ideas in relation to the sensibles that "imitate" them and of which they are almost the "copies." Plato expresses with the term paradigm what, with modern language, could be called the "normative ontology" of the Ideas; that is, *how things ought to be, the obligatory being of things*. The Idea of health is a "paradigm" because it expresses how things or actions *ought* to be done and be to promote health; the Idea of beauty is a "paradigm" because it expresses how things ought to be formally structured to be and become beautiful and so on.[33]

In this conception, therefore, the problem remained open, in addition to the protological problems of the relation of the One to the many, also that problem which the metaphysical map of the *Phaedo* presents as essential (from which even the "second voyage" began), but that it then left unresolved: the relations between things and Ideas cannot be conceived as immediate, and therefore a *mediator* is necessary; that is, a principle that produces the imitation, secures the participation, actualizes the presence and grounds the community between the Ideas and things. This is the considerable problem of the ordering *Intelligence* and its role. Evidently, as we will see better ahead, Plato possessed a complete solution for the problem at the time when he wrote the *Phaedo*, so true is it that he anticipated it in any number of dialogues immediately after the *Phaedo*, beginning from the *Republic*, but formulating it with the greatest amplitude, according to the schema that has become classic in the *Timaeus*. The mediation between the sensible and the intelligible is the work of a supreme Intelligence, that is associated with the classic figure of the "Demiurge," the figure of an Artisan or Craftsman who molds the *chora* (that is, undetermined space, a kind of substrate or informal receptacle), according to the "model" of the Ideas, making each thing similar to, and an imitation of, in the most perfect way possible, the "ideal paradigms or Ideas." But as we have pointed out many times and as further on we will seek to demonstrate in a satisfactory manner, unless a large infiltration of a protological character is acknowledged, the solution to this problem will not be achieved basically. Plato will take into account, chiefly in the *Philebus* the metaphysical categories of *limit, unlimited*, and their *mixture* and the *cause of their mixture* to explain the work accomplished by the Ideas on the undetermined *chora* (on the substrate of a material kind) and hence the things that arise from this "mixture," as a result of the cause operating on the mixture, which is precisely the demiurgic Intelligence. And this operation is, in the final analysis, the specific action exercised *by the One on the undetermined many as a result of Intelligence*; and the "mixture" that is brought forth is a "unity-in-multiplicity." Moreover in the *Timaeus* itself, at a certain point, Plato reveals to us expressly what follows: "divinity has knowledge and power sufficient to blend the *many into one* [τὰ πολλὰ εἰς ἕν] and to resolve the *one into many* [ἐξ ἑνὸς εἰς πολλά], but no man is now, or ever will be, equal to either task" (trans. F. M. Cornford, *Plato's Cosmology*, p. 278).[34] Whoever has followed us up to this point will have understood in a satisfactory manner that to solve the various problems that the theory of Ideas arouses and that are the topic under consideration, he needs to confront and decide at every step what to do about the great problem of the interpretation of the protologic; that is, the unwritten metaphysics of Plato. And we are now going to direct our attention to this issue.

III. THE UNWRITTEN DOCTRINES OF THE FIRST PRINCIPLES AND THE HIGHEST AND MOST IMPORTANT METAPHYSICAL CONCEPTS CONNECTED TO THEM

1. The first Principles are identical with the One and the Dyad of the great-and-small

The time has now arrived to come to terms with that highest *hypotheses* about which the metaphysical map traced by Plato in the Phaedo spoke and which the *Republic* (considering it as the summit of all the hypotheses) and placed it beyond the hypotheses themselves,[1] which coincide with those *things of greater value* about which the Phaedrus spoke; that is, the first and highest Principles reserved for oral dialectic. We have referred earlier to these Unwritten Doctrines many times; and here we want to trace in their essential parameters in detail, because by now as every reader is well aware, only in their light can the ontology of the Ideas (and consequently the total thought of Plato) acquire its complete meaning.

A good start for a preliminary understanding of the protological discourse (that to many interpreters of Plato continues to appear extremely unpalatable) can be achieved, in addition to what we have pointed out many times earlier, by a general remark concerning an essential characteristic of the mode of thought of the Greeks. A basic conviction, which animates all the philosophy preceding Plato, consists in the conviction that to explain means to unify. This conviction supports, in the first place, the discourse of all the Physicists, who proceed to explain the multiplicity of phenomena concerning the cosmos, precisely by reducing them to the unity of a principle or of some principles, unitarily conceived and in addition reaches its extreme expression in the doctrine of the Eleatics, who dissolve into unity the totality of being, leading to a radical monism. But this conviction also supports Socratic discourse, pivoted entirely on the question *what-is-it,* which implies in general the systematic reduction of the subject of the discussion to a unity. And in particular, in the ethical sphere (about which Socrates was chiefly concerned), what we are explaining is made quite evident: all the complex manifestations characterizing the moral and political life are reduced to the unity of the virtues that in its turn is reduced as is well known to a science (the many virtues are explained by their reduction to a single essence, consisting precisely in the unity of true knowledge).[2]

Then, the doctrine of the Ideas of Plato, in its entirety, has arisen exactly from an analogous conviction and from a noticeable accentuation of the importance of the function of the synoptic vision, which steers the methodical procedure of the *unification* of the multiplicity that it intends to explain. The plurality of sensible things is explained precisely by means of the concise reduction to the unity of the corresponding Idea. Except that *as we have already explained* the theory of Ideas has at its head a further plurality, although simply on the new metaphysical level of the intelligible. In fact, if the many sensible men are unified and explained by the corresponding Idea of Man, the many trees by the Idea of Tree, the many manifestations of beauty by the Idea of Beauty, and so on for all the experiential realities we have mentioned having the same name, then it is evident that sensible multiplicity is simplified and resolved into the unity of the intelligible Ideas; but the intelligible multiplicity in its turn is not reduced to unity simply of itself. In addition take into account that Plato admits the Ideas not only for those things that we call substantial realities (like man, animals, and vegetables), but also for all realities and all aspects of things able to be grouped concisely (Beauty, Great, Double, and so on), so that the pluralism of the world of Ideas (that is, the pluralism of intelligible realities) is truly quite obvious, as Aristotle already, in the passage quoted earlier, stressed in a very marked fashion.[3] It is evident, then, that the theory of Ideas could not be the final level of explanation. In fact, the sensible *multiple* is explained by an intelligible *multiple,* which demands a further explanation; consequently, it imposed the necessity of going beyond to a second level of metaphysical grounding. Consequently, in his dialogues and for those readers who limit themselves to the reading of the dialogues, Plato maintained that the first level of metaphysical grounds would be sufficient; since, the theory of Ideas once achieved, the various teachings that he entrusted to the writings are adequately justified. But with his followers within the Academy, to solve the problems that the theory of Ideas itself aroused, he made it an object of discussion, and in a very considerable way it belongs to the second level of grounding.

Also the final stage of the "second voyage" was achieved in this way to its conclusions precisely according to the plan traced in the metaphysical map of the Phaedo. The schema of reasoning that supports the bipolarity of the metaphysical foundation is the following. Just as the sphere of the sensible multiple depends on the sphere of the Ideas, so also, the sphere of the multiple within the Ideas depends on a further sphere of reality, from which the Ideas are derived, and this is the first and highest sphere in the absolute sense. This sphere is, therefore, that of the first Principles (which are the One and the indefinite Dyad, about which we will speak immediately below). Plato called them expressly, as we know, τὰ ἄκρα καὶ πρῶτα,[4] and it is just for this reason that we propose to call protologic (the discourse concerning the first Principles) the teaching that is concerned with them.

This doctrine contains the ultimate foundation, because it explains the nature of the Principles from which the Ideas arise (which in their turn explain the remaining things), and therefore gives the explanation of the totality of the things that exist. It is clear, therefore, in what sense the ontology of the Ideas and the protologic or the theory of Principles constitute two distinct levels of grounding, two succeeding levels of metaphysical inquiry; that is, two stages of the second voyage. Here are three central testimonies:

> Since the Forms [= Ideas] were the causes of all other things [on the first level], he thought their elements were the elements of all things. As matter or element of the Forms [Ideas] he posited the Great-and-small, and as formal cause the One [on the second level]. (trans. W. D. Ross, p. 701, with some changes and emphasis added)[5]

> Plato, then, declared himself thus on the points in question; it is evident from what has been said that he has used only two causes, that of the formal and the material cause. In fact the Ideas are formal causes of the other things [on first level], and the One is formal cause of the other Ideas [on second level]. And to the question what is the matter having the function of substrate, of which the Ideas are predicated in the sensible realm [first level], and of which the One in the sphere of the Ideas [second level] are predicated, he replied that it is the Dyad; that is, the Great-and-small. (trans. W. D. Ross, p. 702, with some changes and emphasis added)[6]

> But if certain incorporeals exist before the bodies, these are not already of necessity elements of existing things and primary principles. For see how the Ideas, which are incorporeal, exist before the bodies, according to Plato, and everything which becomes becomes because of its relation to them [on first level]; yet they are not principles of existing things since each Idea taken separately is said to be a unit, but two or three or four when taken in conjunction with one or more others, so that there is something which transcends their substance, namely number, by participation in which the terms one or two or three or a still higher number than these is predicated of them.

> There are, then, two principles of existing things, the First One, by participation in which all the numbered ones are conceived as ones, and also the Indefinite Dyad, by participation in which the definite Dyads are dyads [second level]. (trans. R. G. Bury, 3.337, 339 with slight additions and emphasis added)[7]

The quintessential metaphysical problem for the Greeks is as we stated earlier, the following: *why are there many?*, or *why and how are the many derived from the One?* [8] The novelty of Plato, on the protological level, is, indeed, in this attempt to give a radical and ultimate "justification" of multiplicity in general according to the Principles of the One and the indefinite Dyad and their bipolar structure. The *Dyad* or *indeterminate Duality* is therefore obviously not the number two, just as the One in the sense of the Principle is not the number one. Both of these Principles have a metaphysical status, and hence are meta-mathematicals. In particular we must note that the *Dyad* is the Principle and root of the multiplicity of beings. It is conceived as the Dyad of the great-and-small in the sense that it is infinite quantity and infinite smallness, insofar as it tends to be infinitely great and infinitely small. It is precisely by reason of this two-fold direction toward (infinitely great and infinitely small) that it is called the *infinite Dyad* or *indefinite Dyad,* and consequently, it is likewise specified as the Dyad of the great-and-small, of the more-and-less, of the greater-and-lesser, and as structural inequality. With a more specific and technical terminology even if not used expressly by Plato, we can, therefore, say that the Dyad is a kind of *intelligible matter,* at least at the highest levels (excluding; that is, the cosmological sphere, in which the Dyad becomes sensible matter, as we will see). It is an in-determinate and in-definite multiplicity that functions as substrate for the action of the One, producing the multiplicity of things in all their forms; and hence, besides being Principle of horizontal plurality, it is Principle also of the hierarchical gradation of the real. The problem from which we began is solved in this way: plurality, difference, and gradation of entities arise from the action of the One that determines the opposite Principle of the Dyad, which is an indeterminate multiplicity. The two Principles are therefore equally present at the origin. The One cannot effectively be productive without the Dyad, even if it is hierarchically superior to the Dyad. For accuracy's sake we must say that it would be imprecise as such to speak of two Principles, if the "two" is understood arithmetically. In fact, numbers are subsequent to the Principles and derived from them, they cannot be applied to them except in a metaphorical sense. Therefore, we will speak of two Principles but understanding the *two* in a proto-typical sense. It would be perhaps more exact to say, in this case, not that the Principles constitute a dualism, but rather a *polarity* or a *bipolarity,* insofar as the Principles require each other structurally or necessarily.

2. Being as the synthesis (mixture) of the two Principles

The action of the One on the Dyad is a kind of delimitation, a determination, and definition of the unlimited, of the indeterminate, and of the in-definite, or, as it appears that Plato has also said, about equality and inequality.[9] *The entities derived from the activity of the One on the Dyad are therefore a kind of synthesis that is displayed as unity-in-multiplicity, which is a definition and a determination of the indefinite and indeterminate. And this is the fulcrum of the Platonic protologic: being is produced by two originative principles and hence is a synthesis, a mixture of unity and multiplicity, of determination and indetermination, of limit and unlimited.* Plato concerning this theme will be pressed into even presenting a compressed version in his writings, in particular in the *Philebus.*

On the status of the One conceived as beyond being the documentation of the indirect tradition is scarce. One testimony says that the One is *melius ente* [*a better entity*],[10] but Plato is forced to give us the most remarkable example of this position presented in the greater part of his writings. Therefore

on the metaphysical status of the One (that coincides with the Good) understood as beyond being we will return further on, interpreting the Platonic
affirmations found in the Republic, where the Good is expressly defined as
beyond being (ἐπέκεινα τῆς οὐσίας).[11]

Instead on the status of the Dyad as nonbeing; that is, as below being it is
stated:

> "All this, in virtue of a negation of Being, can be said to be unstable,
> shapeless, boundless, and unreal. For such negativity there is neither Prin-
> ciple nor Essence, but it rushes about in a certain unjudgeable condition"
> (trans. J. N. Findlay 425.16).[12]

But we must insist on this point. This conception of the two supreme
Principles connected by a bipolar nexus and the consequent conception of
being (at all levels, from the lowest to the highest) as a *mixture* of a structure
always bipolar in character, reflects in a perfect way, in the metaphysical
dimension, the characteristic type of thought of the Greeks in all areas, in
particular in the teleological, philosophical, and moral areas.

If we examine the most complete expression of Greek theology, which is
contained in the Theogony of Hesiod, it will be noted that right from the
beginning the Gods and the cosmic forces are divided into two opposed realms,
at their head Chaos and Gaia, having respectively, as has been pointed out,
the characteristics of *formlessness* and of *form*, which, precisely with this
opposition make up the totality of reality. Also in the second phase of the
theogony; that is, with the advent of the reign of Zeus and hence of the
Olympian Gods, this basic conception is quite evident. The Titans defeated by
Zeus are thrown down into Tartarus, which is the *counter-world at the opposite
pole* from Olympus. But there is more. Each of the Gods is like a mixture of
forces having a polar opposite character. Apollo, for example, even has as his
typical symbol the sweet sounding lyre and the bow and cruel arrows; Artemis
is a virgin and at the same time is the protectress of childbirth, and so on. In
addition, every divinity has another divinity as its polar opposite, as for
example, Apollo has at his polar opposite Dionysius, Artemis has as her polar
opposite Aphrodite, and so on.[13]

Paula Philippson, therefore, has correctly affirmed that *the polar form* is
the basic structure of the Greek theogony and the Greek way of thinking in
general. Let us read the conclusions of her argument, which are fitted in a
perfect fashion to the thought that we have developed and that proves in an
eloquent way, in our opinion, the thesis that we have maintained:

> The polar form of thought sees, conceives, models and organizes the world,
> as a unity in pairs of contraries. They are the form in which the world is
> presented to the Greek spirit, in which this transforms and conceives in an
> arrangement and as arranging the multiplicity in the world. These pairs of
> contraries of polar opposites of thought are fundamentally different than

pairs of contraries in monistic thought or dualistic thought, in the sphere of what they exclude, or, if fighting each other, they are destroyed, or finally reconciled, they cease to exist as contraries....In the form of polar thought instead the pair of contraries are not only each indissoluble joined to the other, as the poles of the axes of a sphere, but they are so in their most intimate logical existence, precisely that is, as polar, they are conditioned by their opposition: losing the opposite pole, they perish in the same sense. This sense consists precisely in the fact that they, like contraries *in the same way as the axes that separates them and wholly joins them* are parts of a greater unity that is not definable exclusively on their basis: in other words to express it in geometrical terms, they are points of a sphere complete in itself. This polar form of thinking necessarily informs every objectivization of Greek thought. Because the Greek vision of the divine is also formed under its sign.[14]

The bipolar conception about which we have been speaking, constitutes indeed a fundamental framework for Greek thought, as Aristotle himself has recognized in a quite explicit way even with respect to philosophical thought:

> Again, in the list of contraries one of the two columns is privative, and all contraries are reducible to being and non-being, and to unity and plurality, as for instance rest belongs to unity and movement to plurality. And nearly all thinkers agree that being and substance are composed of contraries; at least all name contraries as their first principle–some name odd and even, some hot and cold, some limit and unlimited, some love and strife. And all the others as well are evidently reducible to unity and plurality (this reduction we must take for granted), and the principles stated by other thinkers fall entirely under these as their genera (trans. W. D. Ross, p. 735)[15]

Naturally, in addition to philosophical thought, we could call attention also to the moral thinking of the Greeks, especially as it was expressed by the Seven Sages and the gnomic poets, in whom this polarity and structural synthesis of opposite principles is evident. The widespread *use of a measure, nothing in excess, the best is the mean, a measure is the best thing*, presupposes in a clear and essential way a *limit* and an opposing *unlimited* (this latter is made of excess and defect); that is, connotes a synthetic polar vision. This thesis is the same that Aristotle fruitfully applied in his famous doctrine of the *ethical virtues*.

In conclusion, the Platonic theory of the Principles, simply with the characteristics that we have explained, represents indeed the highest, the most typical, and most profound philosophical doctrine of Greek thought in general, and of their imagination and sensibility, and therefore, it truly expresses the supreme signature of the spirituality of the Greeks.

3. The categoreal division of reality

The ideal Numbers are derived from the two supreme Principles just as the Ideas that have a numerical structure in the sense explained earlier, and, consequently, all things. This clearly emerges from the theories that we have explained so far. Nevertheless Plato does not limit himself to this deduction, and, as a confirmation; that is, as an argumentation of essential support, he also presented a general plan of categorial division of the whole of reality with the aim of demonstrating that all beings actually go back to the two Principles, insofar as they are derived from their mixture. It is an important theoretical and quite notable historical argument, because besides clarifying the basic lines of force of the "Unwritten Doctrines," it is also the basis of the successive teachings of the categories of Aristotle (that draws basic inspiration from it, even if it bends in a different direction).

This categorial division is attested to by good sources,[16] in a rather extensive fashion, and it also makes appearances openly enough in the dialogues themselves. Here is the schema synoptically:

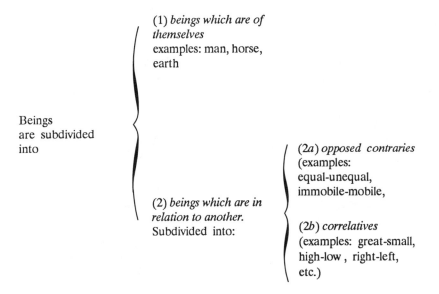

Beings are subdivided into

(1) *beings which are of themselves*
examples: man, horse, earth

(2) *beings which are in relation to another.*
Subdivided into:

(2a) *opposed contraries*
(examples: equal-unequal, immobile-mobile,

(2b) *correlatives*
(examples: great-small, high-low , right-left, etc.)

The distinction between (*2a*) contraries and (*2b*) correlatives may cause surprise, at first glance, since both are beings-in-relation-to-others. But the first is clearly distinguished from the second: in fact, the contraries cannot coexist together, and the disappearance of one of the contraries coincides with the appearance of the other (think for example of life and death, the mobile and the immobile); on the contrary the correlatives are characterized by the coexistence and codisappearance (there is no high without a low, there is no right without a left, and so on). In addition, the first does not admit a middle term (there is no middle state between life and death, between moving and not moving); the second, instead, admits a middle term (between the great and the small, there is a middle the equal, between the more or less there is the middle sufficient, between the sharp and the flat, there is the middle, the harmonious). It is hardly necessary to point out, as we have done previously for Numbers, that this categorial distinction, and hence these different categories, are not purely logical and abstract distinctions, but reflect the knowledge of the very structure of being. And the same obviously holds also for the relative opposites, both on a general level, and on the particular level. We find consequently opposed to these very general Ideas.

The process of this categorial distinction of the beings is based on a schema of relations, typical of the ideal world, that arises from species to genera; that is, toward the always more universal, according to the stages that follow.

(1) The *self-existent beings* (or substances) fall under the genus of Unity. In fact the self-existent beings or substances are perfectly differentiated, defined, and determined; and as we know everything is differentiated, defined, and determined precisely in the measure in which it is one (that is, through the appropriate action of the One).

(2a) The beings that are in the relation of the *opposition of contrariety;* that is, the contraries, enter into the genera of *equal* and *unequal* (diverse). The first of the members of this series are not subject to the *more and less,* where as the second are. For example, although that which is immobile cannot be more or less immobile, and analogously the suitable cannot be more or less suitable, that which is moved can be more or less moved, just as what is unsuitable can be more or less unsuitable. The *equal* is subsumed under the One, because the One represents equality itself in a fundamental fashion. The *unequal,* instead, insofar as it implies the more or less, implies excess and defect; and, hence, it is related to the Principle of indefinite Dyad.

(2b) The beings that are pairs of *relative* imply a reference to *excess and defect,* due to their mutual relations, that are structurally indefinite, insofar as each term can increase or decrease, and hence becomes *more or less.* For example, in the pair *great and small* the first term can be *more or less* what it is in a given moment and so also in a second moment. The same holds for the *high and low* and for other relatives. In fact, this type of relation is based on the indetermination of the two terms. These beings are placed under the genera of *excess and defect.* And the *excess and defect,* as we know, is subsumed under the Principle of the indefinite Dyad.

It is scarcely necessary, after what has just been clarified, to say that the reduction to the Principles as explained does not imply that some entities depend only on the first principle and others depend solely on the second, because everything that is subsequent to the Principles implies a mixture and synthesis of both. The reduction to the Principles instead implies that in some entities the action of the first Principle (that is, of the One) prevails, whereas in the other entities the action of the second (that is, of the indeterminate

Dyad) prevails. In any case, the unity remains the ontologically fundamental constituent even in the different kinds of prevalence of the opposite Principle.[17]

4. Ideal numbers and the numerical structure of reality

Another very grave obstacle to the understanding of the Platonic protologic, is constituted by the doctrine of the ideal Numbers and by the typical Platonic reduction of the Ideas to Numbers; that is, by the conception of the Ideas as ideal Numbers. We know that this connection between the Ideas and the ideal Numbers did not take place in coincidence with the discovery of the theory of Ideas, but successively.[18] Probably it took place together with the systematic and global formulation of the theory of Principles; that is, when Plato was capable of furnishing the protological foundation of his ontology of the Ideas.

A first clarification that is necessary to avoid a series of confusions and ambiguities. The ideal numbers with which we have been concerned are not mathematical, but metaphysical entities: they are; that is, for example, the Two as essence of duality, the Three as essence of threeness, and so on. The ideal Numbers are the essences of mathematical numbers and therefore *inoperable*; that is, not capable of supporting arithmetic operations. They have hence a metaphysical status, different from that of mathematical numbers, because they are not numbers but the essences of numbers. Consequently, it does not make any sense to add the essence of two to the essence of three, and to subtract the essence of two from the essence of three, and so on. The ideal Numbers are, therefore, the supreme ideal models. In addition, the ideal Numbers are presented as *first generated,* therefore (as has been pointed out by scholars), they represent in an original form, which is paradigmatic, that synthetic structure of unity-multiplicity that characterized all the different areas of reality and all entities in all areas. The essence of ideal Number is a determination and limitation specifically produced by the One on the Dyad that is indeterminate and unlimited multiplicity of great-and-small.

This explained we may now proceed to a series of key points for the understanding of this difficult doctrine.

(*a*) There is a strict connection between the Ideas and Numbers but not a total ontological identification.

(*b*) Each Idea is not reduced to a particular Number. Plato did not follow a view that was of a arithmological or arithmosophic character, thus not one conditioned by a kind of numeric mysticism. Actually, this doctrine belongs to the Pythagoreans and especially to the Neopythagoreans, whereas the way followed by Plato was of a strongly rationalistic character.

(*c*) This Platonic doctrine cannot be interpreted in terms of the modern concept of the whole number, expressing a determinate quantity, as well as being a purely conceptual abstraction. O. Töplitz has demonstrated that for the Greeks number is always conceived not only as a whole number; that is, as a kind of compact quantity, but as an articulated relation of quantity and of fractions of quantity, of logoi, of analogies. If this is so, the Greek logos is essentially united with the numerical sphere, and fundamentally it means therefore *relation*. Consequently, for the Greeks it is natural to translate *relations* by *numbers,* and to indicate relations with numbers, precisely because of this connection existing between number and relation.[19] On the basis of these explanations, here is the solution of the difficulties that we have been discussing. Each Idea is located in a precise position in the intelligible world, according to its greater or lesser universality and according to the form more or less complex of the relations that it has with other Ideas (that are above or below it). This web of relations, hence, can be reconstructed and determined by means of dialectic, and, for the reasons explained, can be expressed *numerically* (given that number expresses a relation). *Therefore, in the conception of number as relation (logos) is the key for the reading and the understanding of this truly very delicate position of the Unwritten Doctrines.*

(*d*) Ideal Numbers do not result in the multiplication of entities with abandon [traditionally called Plato's beard], without an adequate reason. Indeed Aristotle says expressly that Plato in the generation of the ideal Numbers *pushes up to the Decade.*[20] Therefore, he subordinated to the Decade and through it linked the deductive processes for all the other numbers. Probably he reduced whole numbers to the Decade, and understood all the other numbers as *logoi*, in the sense explained earlier.

Also this doctrine, just as the doctrine of the primary Principles, far from representing a deviation from Plato's thought, or a misunderstanding of his followers, represents a metaphysical summit, which reveals in a theoretical manner one of the most emblematic signatures of the Greek spirit.

Friedländer, to explain the theory of Ideas of the dialogues and the *visual* dimension that it implies, has written (as we have already quoted) that *Plato possessed...the plastic eye of the Greeks, an eye akin to that by which Polykleitos perceived the canon...and also to the eye by which Greek mathematicians looked at the pure geometrical forms.*[21] Here in our judgment, he uses it still more, for the reduction of the Ideas to Numbers, as the arts of the Greeks have shown in a perfect manner. In fact architecture and sculpture were based in Greece on a *canon* (corresponding to a nomos; that is, to the law that regulates music), that expressed (contrarily to those in force in the area of other civilizations) an essential *rule of perfection*, that the Hellenes indicated in a perfect proportion expressible in an exact fashion with numbers. Therefore, the *form (= Idea), which in various ways is realized in the plastic arts, for the Greeks was reducible to a numerical ratio and to number.* Indeed the perfection of figure and form retraced in sculpture in addition to being joined with the numerical relations of the parts among themselves and of the parts with the whole, *was also joined with the geometrical figure.*

Remember, for example, the famous representation that became classic and is designated with the expression *homo quadratus* (in Greek ἀνὴρ τετράγωνος), which included in a perfect way the man in a square and both in a circle, with a center in the umblicus. Even in the art of vase making there exists *canons* expressing *numerical ratios*, which rule the relations between the height and the width, and they go from the more simple to others more complex that reflect the ratio of the golden section, largely utilized also in the construction of buildings and statues. [22]

And here are the conclusions at which we wish to arrive. *The plastic eye of Greece had not seen the Form or Figure (Idea) as something ultimate; but it saw, beyond it, something further, that is to say number and numerical relation.* Think, now, of transferring all this onto the plane achieved by the *second voyage* of Plato; you will observe, in this way, the perfect correspondence on the metaphysical level of what the Greek artists had expressed with their creations. *The Ideas, which express the spiritual forms and the essences of things, are not the ultimate reason of things, but suppose something further, which consists, precisely, in Numbers and in numerical relations, and, hence, in the supreme Principles from which the Numbers themselves and the numerical relations themselves are derived.*

5.   Mathematical entities

We have explained that the *ideal Numbers* (just as the Ideas, which by having a numerical structure, are all specifiable as Number-Ideas) *are very different from numbers and mathematical objects in general*, which occupy a ontological position *intermediate* (μεταξύ); that is, a position *midway* between the ideal entities and sensible entities. Here is a very important testimony of Aristotle in this regard: "Further, besides sensibles things and Forms [= Ideas], he says there are objects of mathematics, *which occupy an intermediate position* (μεταξύ), differing from the sensible things in being eternal and unchangeable, from Forms in that they are many alike, while the Form itself is in each case unique" (trans. W. D. Ross, p. 701).[23]

This doctrine at first glance may cause surprise, but that in reality fits perfectly into the general outline of Platonic thought. These mathematical entities are *intermediates*, insofar as, on the one hand, they are *immobile* and *eternal* precisely as are the Ideas (and the ideal Numbers), and, on the other, they are *many of the same kind*. They have, hence, at the same time, a character fundamental to the Ideas and one typical of sensible things, and for this reason are, precisely, *intermediates*. Plato introduced them for the following reasons. (*a*) Numbers on which arithmetic operates, just as quantity on which geometry works are not sensibles, but intelligibles, as the sciences that inquire into them demonstrate. (*b*) On the other hand, numbers and quantity about which arithmetic and geometry are concerned cannot be ideal Numbers, nor ideal Quantity, because the arithmetical operations imply many equal numbers and the geometric operations and demonstrations imply numerous equal and multiple figures that are variations of the same essence (for example, many equal triangles and many shapes about which the demonstrations speak), whereas each of the ideal Numbers is unique, just as each ideal Figure is unique.

If this is kept in mind, the Platonic conclusions about the existence of *mathematical entities* having the character of *intermediates* between the intelligible world and the sensible world is easy to understand. The mathematical entities are like the intelligible entities, because they are immobile and eternal, while they are like sensible realities, because they are many of the same kind. The theoretical source of this doctrine is to be sought in the deeply rooted conviction of Plato of the perfect structural correspondence between knowledge and being (*for that which it is possible to know is the same as that which can be*),[24] at a determinate level of knowledge of a determinate type there must necessarily be situated a corresponding level of being.

Therefore, at the level of mathematical knowledge, which is superior to the level of sensible knowledge, but inferior to the level of dialectical knowledge, there must correspond a plane having the respective ontological connotations (in our case, of *many* similar *numbers* required operations, of *many* similar *figures*—many squares, many triangles, and so on—required by geometrical operations and demonstrations).

This *Unwritten Doctrine* is essential for understanding the Platonic epistemological system that is to be found in the dialogues (in particular in the *Republic*), so that it constitutes the fundamental bedrock of the system. It is with good reason that Gaiser, hence, affirms what follows: "…simply because mathematical realities in the strict sense stand in the middle of the structure of being and here manifestly unite in themselves the opposed properties of what is subordinate and what is superordinate, in the realm of the mathematical entities it is possible to see in the same way a *Model of the whole of reality*."[25] Naturally, it is a model in an *analogical* sense, insofar as mathematics and metaphysics remain quite distinct. In fact, "the structure of being itself is not in a special way of a mathematical type; and considered in their totality the mathematical laws do not have their foundation in the mathematical realm, but, in the ultimate sense, in the general principles of being."[26]

In sum, Plato did not mathematicize metaphysics, but, on the contrary, he has metaphysically grounded it; and, consequently, he has metaphysically utilized, *in an analogical key*, mathematics.

IV. THE METAPHYSICS OF THE IDEAS IN THE LIGHT OF THE PROTOLOGIC OF THE UNWRITTEN DOCTRINE AND THE ALLUSIONS THAT PLATO MAKES TO THE DOCTRINE OF THE PRINCIPLES

1. The interest paid by Plato in the *Republic* toward the Good and the remaining debt

In the passage of Hegel we read earlier,[1] we are informed (for good reasons) that the philosopher is not in possession of his thought as though it were an external thing, but, on the contrary, he is possessed by it, and *can express it*; therefore, anything can be expressed, generally by communicating the basic concepts contained therein. And this is true also in the case of Plato: in fact, even in his writings (besides in the area of oral expression), in spite of *maintaining silence about some things* (or at the least not expressing them *in explicit terms* [*expressis verbis*], he has made a series of references and allusions to them, even in a everincreasing way, *because no philosopher possesses the basic truth as a thing exterior to him, and no philosopher can put it aside and hide, because he is totally possessed by it.*

The fact remains, nevertheless, that today we can understand these unmistakable allusions and these continuous references only on the basis of some "aids" that come from the indirect tradition. Konrad Gaiser has produced a memorable image, that expresses accurately the meaning and structure of this way of speech and expression to be found in Plato's writings: "The reader...must force himself to grasp in these writings the truth not different from what forced him to understand the statements of the oracles. What Heraclitus said of the God at Delphi can be applied to the Platonic dialogues: 'He neither speaks nor conceals, but indicates'...(οὔτε λέγει, οὔτε κρύπτει, ἀλλὰ σημαίνει). There are texts, whose significance are revealed to the reader only through interpretation and a personal power of assimilation." [2] And naturally it is matter of a personal power of assimilation not only having been brought forward on a subjective basis, but also on an *objective* basis; that is, in the light of what the indirect tradition has handed down to us on the *Unwritten Doctrines*, which aid us in understanding what is "said" and "not said,'" but "alluded to" with a series of references, which in this way became illuminating.

Let us begin from a most important example, which is constituted by the *Republic*, the masterpiece that summarizes the achievements of all the previous Platonic writings and sets the foundation for all the subsequent ones.

The *Republic* in its central books contains a treatise *On the Good* that enters directly into heart of the thematic reserved for their treatment explicatively global in the cycle of lectures given by Plato within the Academy and hence orally expressed. The contact between the *written* and the *unwritten* expression in these books is hence highly significant, and the play of not affirming nor hiding, but speaking by means of a series of allusions, becomes clearly prototypical. In fact, Plato, after having explained that, to understand basically the nature of justice and virtue, one must have a *just measure*, and indeed a *perfect measure* (that is the supreme measure), and that hence it is necessary to go besides to what he stated in the first five books, where he explains that it is this "highest knowledge," for the achievement of which it is necessary to traverse the "long way," which implies a great labor and extraordinary struggle. This "highest knowledge," which is the achievement of the *highest precision and exactitude*, is the knowledge of the *Idea of the Good by which justice and virtue* (and in general every thing) derive their being, *usefulness, and beneficial character*. From it, hence, *every axiological value is derived*. Consequently, it is simply on the basis of the definition of this Idea; that is, through the *definition of the essence of the Good as in itself and for itself*, that the central books of the *Republic* ought to be focussed. Instead, Plato refers to another aspect and a different area. First, he says to the interlocutor that he has "heard" the doctrine of the Good already "not a few times" from him, in fact "many times"; and as it cannot really be said that any of the dialogues prior to the *Republic* speak of the Idea of the Good, the "many times" in which Plato has spoken refer obviously to "oral expression" (to have been heard in this way). Here is the most significant passage:

> "You remember," I said, "that when we had distinguished three parts of the soul, we discussed with reference to these parts the nature of each of justice, moderation, courage and wisdom."
> "If I did not remember that," he said, "I should not deserve to hear the rest."
> "And also what we said before that?"
> "What was that?"
> "We spoke as best we could at the time, and we said that to see these things most clearly there was a longer way round that would make them plain to anyone who traveled it, but that it was possible to deal with them on a level of proof compatible with what had been said up to then. You said that this was satisfactory; however, I thought that what was said then in that way was lacking in precision, but you might tell me if it satisfied you."
> "I thought you gave us *good measure* [μετρίως]" he said, "and so apparently, did the others."
> "*Any measure* [μέτρον], my friend," I said, "*that in these matters, falls short of reality to any degree, is not good measure* [μετρίως]. *Nothing that is incomplete is a measure* [μέτρον] *of anything, though sometimes people think it is already enough and that there is no need to search further.*"
> "They do this because they are lazy."
> "Laziness, however, is a quality that the guardian of a city and of laws can do without."

"Very likely."

"That sort of man should go round the longer way, my friend," I said, "and put as much effort into his studies as into physical training; *otherwise he will never reach the end of the most important and most appropriate study* [τοῦ μεγίστου τε καὶ μάλιστα προσήκοντος μαθήματος]."

"Are these virtues then," he said, "not the most important [μέγιστα] subject of study? Is there anything still more important than justice and the things we discussed?"

"There is," I said. "Also, we should not observe a mere outline of these things themselves, as we are doing now, *and neglect the most finished picture. Is it not ridiculous to strain every nerve to have a most exact and pure picture of other things of little value, and not to require the greatest accuracy for the greatest subjects?*"

"It certainly is," he said, "but do you think that anyone is going to let you off without asking you what this greatest study is, and what you say it is about?"

"No indeed," I said, "you too can ask me. *You have certainly heard it often enough*, but now either you are not thinking or you again intend to make trouble for me by your intervention. I rather think that the latter is the case, *for you have often heard it said that the Form of the Good* [ἡ τοῦ ἀγαθοῦ ἰδέα] *is the greatest object of study* [μέγιστον μάθημα], and that it is by their relation to it that just actions and the other things become useful and beneficial. *You probably knew that I was about to say this* and, besides, that *our knowledge of it is inadequate. If we do not know it, even the fullest possible knowledge of other things is no help to us, any more than if we acquire any possession without the good. Do you think there is any advantage to have acquired every kind of possession, if it is not good, or to have every kind of knowledge without that of the Good, thus knowing nothing beautiful or good?*"

"No, by Zeus, I do not." (trans. G. M. A. Grube, pp. 158-60 emphasis added)[3]

But evidently this reference to "having heard" is not sufficient, because the Good touches on the heart of the doctrines presented in the *Republic*, and, consequently, Plato must point out as much as necessary, at least in a certain respect, *to give a sense to his writing focussed on this statement*. And the way chosen by Plato is just right. The complete and exhaustive doctrine *On the Good* is like a big "price" or "debt" that is owed to another account; here, in the central books of the *Republic*, only *the interest* will be paid, but in a measure proportional to the debt, that will be paid off another time, in another place. Nevertheless, by playing with his great artistic talent, on the twofold meanings of the term τόκος, which means "interest" and "product," he associates it with ἔκγονος, that means "descendent," that is, "offspring" and hence "progeny" in an analogical sense, to say that *what he presents is indeed an interest-product of the Good*, and hence his "offspring," who reflects in a miniature fashion the father, like interest is proportioned to the principal (to use a modern financial term). Here are the exact words of Plato on the matter:

> "By Zeus, Socrates," said Glaucon, "do not stand off as if you had come to the end. We shall be satisfied if you discuss the Good in the same fashion as you did justice, moderation, and the other things."
>
> "That, my friend," I said, "would also quite satisfy me, but *I fear I shall not be able to do so, and that in my eagerness I shall disgrace myself and make myself ridiculous. But, my excellent friends, let us for the moment abandon the quest for the nature of the Good itself, for that I think is a larger question than what we started on, which was to ascertain my present opinion about it.* I am willing to tell you what appears to be the offspring [ἔκγονος] of the Good and most like it, if that is agreeable to you. If not, we must let the question drop."
>
> "Well," he said, "tell us. *The story of the parents remains a debt which you will pay us some other time.*"
>
> "*I wish,*" I said, "*that I could pay it in full now, and you could exact it in full and not, as now, only receive the interest* [τόκους]. *However, accept then this offspring and child* [τόκον τε καὶ ἔκγονον] *of the Good. Only be careful that I do not somehow deceive you unwillingly by giving a counterfeit account of this offspring.*"
>
> "We shall be as careful as we can. Only tell us!" (trans. G. M. A. Grube, p. 161)[4]

The "offspring" of the Good (the interest on the original principal) is represented by the Sun in a passage that, from many viewpoints, has become one of the best known or even most famous passages, because it presents a very remarkable and perceptive simile, which, imaginatively reveals all that Plato wanted to say about the Good insofar as it was possible to put into writing.[5]

The simile is crafted by Plato in the following way.

(*a*) The Craftsman of the senses (the Demiurge of the senses) has formed in the most valuable fashion the capacity of *seeing* and that corresponding to it, *of being seen*, in fact between sight and the visible he introduces a *third element* which joins them. Each of the other senses is directly joined to its object, whereas sight and the visible are joined by *a bond of greater value*; that is, by the light. So, the source of light is the Sun. But sight does not coincide with the Sun; and moreover, among the organs of the senses, it is the most similar to the Sun, and from the Sun derives its own capacities and its own power. In addition, as the Sun produces the capacity to see what is proper to sight, just so is it seen by it. Therefore, sight receives its capacity from the Sun, and through this it can also see the Sun.

(*b*) In addition, the Good can be understood through an analogy with the Sun, precisely because it has been presented as "offspring" of the Good. In fact, in the intelligible realm the Good is, in relation to the intelligible and to the intellect, in an analogy proportional to the role the Sun has in the sensible realm in relation to sight and the visible. When the eyes look at things in the obscure light of night, they see little or nothing; instead, when they look at things brightened by the Sun, they see them with clarity and sight takes on its proper role. And so it happens also with the soul, when fixed on that which is mixed with darkness; that is, that which is born and dies, then it is capable only of opinion and conjecture and seems almost not to have an intellect, whereas, when contemplating that which is illuminated by truth and being; that is, pure intelligibility, it takes on its proper stature and role.

Here is, therefore, how, by analogy with the Sun (the "offspring"), the Good (the "principle") develops its essential function and things are derived from it. The Idea of the Good gives to things known *truth* and to he who knows the *capacity of knowing the truth*; and, as such, the Idea of the Good is itself knowable. And as sight and the seen are not the Sun, but are akin to the Sun, so also the knowledge and the truth are not the Good, but they are akin to the Good. In addition, as the Sun is beyond vision and the visible, so *the Good is beyond knowledge and truth*. The Good is, hence, an extraordinary beauty, in fact *it is beyond the beauty of knowledge and truth*.

(c) But the comparison with the Sun involves further implications. As the Sun not only gives to things the capacity to be seen, it also causes generation, growth, and nutrition, although not being itself implicated in generation, analogously the Good not only causes the knowability of things, but *causes likewise, being and essence; that is, not being a "being" or an "essence," but beyond, and superior to being and to essence in dignity and power*. Here is the text, which has become very famous:

> "Say then," I said, 'that it is the Sun which I called the offspring of the Good, which the Good begot as analogous to itself. *What the Good itself is in the world of thought in relation to the intelligence and things known, the Sun is in the visible world, in relation to sight and things seen*."
> "How? Explain further."
> "You know," I said, 'that when one turns one's eye to those objects of which the color are no longer in the light of day but in the dimness of the night, the eyes are dimmed and seem nearly blind, as if clear vision was no longer in them."
> "Quite so."
> "Yet whenever one's eyes are turned upon objects brightened by sunshine, they see clearly, and clear vision appears in those very same eyes?"
> "Yes indeed."
> "So too understand the eye of the soul: whenever it is fixed upon that upon which truth and reality shine, it understands and knows and seems to have intelligence, but whenever it is fixed upon what is mixed with darkness that which is subject to birth and destruction it opines and is dimmed, changes opinions this way and that, and seems to have no intelligence."
> "That is so."

> *"Say that what gives truth to the objects of knowledge, and to the knowing mind the power to know, is the Form of Good. As it is the cause of knowledge and truth, think of it also as being the object of knowledge.* Both knowledge and truth are beautiful, but you will be right to think of the Good as other and more beautiful than they. As in the visible world light and sight are rightly considered Sun-like, but it wrong to think of them as the Sun, so here it is right to think of knowledge and truth as Good-like, but wrong to think of either as the Good, *for the Good must be honored even more than they."*
>
> "This is an extraordinary beauty you mention," he said, "if it provides knowledge and truth and is itself superior to them in beauty. You surely do not mean this to be pleasure!"
>
> "Hush!" said I, "rather examine the image of it in this way."
>
> "How?"
>
> "You will say, I think, that the Sun not only gives to the objects of sight the capacity to be seen, but also that it provides for their generation, increase, and nurture, thought it is not itself the process of generation."
>
> "How could it be?"
>
> *"And say that as for the objects of knowledge, not only is their being known due to the Good, but also their being, though the Good is not being but superior to and beyond being in dignity and power."*
>
> "Glaucon was quite amused and said: 'By Apollo! a miraculous superiority'!"(trans. G. M. A. Grube, pp. 161-3 emphasis added)[6]

And here is in what sense these passages read, of exceptional historical importance, contain *only* the "interest" of the original principal, the "offspring" and not the Father. Plato *refuses to reveal the essence of the Good*, that he says he has in mind; that is, that he knows. Moreover, he says only *that* the Good is the cause of being and truth (and hence of knowledge itself), and also of the value of every thing, but he does not tell us *why*. And finally, he says *that* the Good is *beyond being*, but is silent about *why* it is so. Therefore he reveals the that (the fact) and that means "to reveal the offspring" and "to pay the interest"; to reveal the why would mean to reveal the "father" and "to pay the principal" due *On the Good*; hence, to do this, it would be necessary to reveal *the essence of the Good itself.*[7]

But the "father" and the original principal are known to us only through the indirect tradition. *The essence of the Good is the One*, that delimits and determines in various areas the opposed Principle of multiplicity, indetermination, by producing in this way *being* (which is again one determination and delimitation of the indeterminate), the *knowability* of all things (that which is determined and limited is only and always knowable), the intellect itself (which in its nature and function is a unifier), and also the *value* of every thing (since value is order, harmonization, proportion, unity-in-multiplicity). The One is superior to being, because it is the cause (being is a "mixture," it derives from the One, and it determines its opposite Principle).

All these responses (knowledge of the *why*) is centered, hence, on the definition of the *Good* as *One*. And Plato, by achieving in this passage one of the great summits of his ability as a writer, tells us symbolically and through images (but confirming them also in various ways), simply with the use of that typical nonrevealing and nonsilencing but *alluding* discourse of the oracle. In fact, as it has come down to us,[8] the Pythagoreans symbolically called *Apollo*, the One, based on the alpha privative ($\bar{\alpha}$) and on *pollon* ($\pi o\lambda\lambda\acute{o}v$, which means many) and hence by understanding the term Apollo as a *"privation"-of-the-"many"*; that is, as the supreme "One." And Plato concludes his great passage, by saying precisely:

By **APOLLO**! a miraculous superiority!

an expression that means

By the **ONE** (A-pollon), *a miraculous superiority*!

And to be understood in what he wants to say with this truly significant allusion, Plato has embedded a series of references to the One at all the key places in his discourse.

And then it becomes not too difficult to understand that concluding moment of dialectic, which consists in the "definition" of the Idea of the Good with a definition that "prescinds" from all the other Ideas (by being based on that characteristic that is neither affirmed nor held silent, but *is spoken of by strong allusions* that enlivened the two passages on the Good that we have read): *the Good is the One, and the One is the supreme Measure of all things*, just as the indirect tradition and even the succeeding dialogues confirm for the most part.[9]

2. The *Parmenides* and its meaning

Another dialogue that is made much clearer by the new interpretation of Plato is the *Parmenides*, which is one of the most famous, and, at the same time, the most over-valued and under-valued among Plato's dialogues. In fact, numerous interpretations have been presented which go from those that see in it the remarkable summa of Platonic metaphysics and of dialectic to those that instead see in it a simple scholastic exercise, and even with an abundant "logical thicket"; and almost all have fallen in the excess of either too little or too much.[10]

The correct framework for a rereading of the *Parmenides* is, instead, the following. Plato in this dialogue pushes much further along in speaking of that which concerns the apex of metaphysics; that is, the Principles whose bipolar structure is revealed; nevertheless, *he does not at all uncover the dialectic in its entirety, and especially he does not reveal except very partially the essence of these Principles, and their foundational nexuses*. In particular, Plato is silent even throughout about the axiological foundational nexuses (he does not mention the Good at all). And this is completely consistent with his choice of the interlocutor (that is, the Eleatics) and with their interests, for whom the problematic of the Good is not an issue.

If we examine carefully the theoretical framework of the dialogue and if it is reduced to its essential lines, one can note that it follows accurately the great lines of the metaphysical map of the *Phaedo*: from the area of the sensible it must pass to that of the *intelligible*, achieving, first, the *doctrine of the Ideas* and then, *that of the Principles*.

In the first part, which has become very famous, we are given the interpretation and general framework of Zeno's dialectic. In brief, it explained how the famous arguments of Zeno could be understood as a proof in support of the positions of Parmenides. He affirmed that the All is One (that is, he affirmed the *unity* and *unicity of being*); and the adversaries from the affirmation "the One is" conclude to a whole series of absurd consequences contrary to the position in a systematic fashion, and hence destroying it. So, in his writing, Zeno gives tit for tat to the adversaries of Parmenides, by showing how the hypotheses of these adversaries, who maintain the opposite position that *"the many are"* (and hence that the *One is not*), would involve consequences still more absurd than those involved in the position of Parmenides. Consequently, the proof of the impossibility of the "pluralistic" thesis, opposed to that of the "monistic" one of Parmenides, is a dialectical confirmation of monism itself.[11]

In the second part, Socrates presents the theory of Ideas that is structurally multiple. The dialogue again defends plurality, *but positing it on another plane than the Pluralist adversaries of the Eleatics*. These latter, in fact, are moving on the plane of the sensible, whereas Plato, in our work, moves on the plane achieved with the "second voyage"; that is, on the plane of the intelligible. Now, as we already know, all the contradictions of sensible multiples are solved and overcome precisely with the doctrine of the Ideas. The participation of a thing in the Ideas explains, hence, all the contradictions encountered in the realm of the sensible multiple. It would be, therefore, a very serious matter if the contradictions revealed within the sphere of the sensible multiples were represented in the same form or in an analogous form on the new plane of the Ideas; that is, if the contradictions would be represented also in the realm of the intelligible plurality. It is thus to this problem that Plato calls our attention firmly.

This Socratic challenge provoked the intervention of Parmenides himself, who personally assumed the burden of refutation. Note that at this point *Eleatic dialectic is displaced, with a real switch to the plane achieved by the Platonic "second voyage."* Nevertheless at first the dialectic of Parmenides is limited to revealing aporias; that is, difficulties and contradictions included in the theory of Ideas itself (while in the third section it unfolds in all its power and value, pushing itself up to the level of the supreme Principles). Seven aporias are raised by Parmenides against the theory of Ideas, and some of them were evidently already much more widespread at the period of the composition of the dialogue (some of the principles return also in the *Metaphysics* of Aristotle and have become quite well known for that reason). It could already be said, in general, that these criticisms, and those that appear as the most damaging, in reality arise from a basic howler: they treat the Ideas, which are introduced by Plato as "cause," on the same level as the things of which they are the causes; that is, they demote the cause to the same ontological level as the effect, with all the consequences that this error implies, in particular with the total lack of understanding of the transcendence of the Ideas in the metaphysical sense. The response of Plato is contained in the third part; but already at the end of the second he gives the following important observations: (*a*) a privileged spirit is necessary to understand the theory of Ideas (that is, that which is very distant from the ordinary understanding of the many) and a still more privileged spirit is needed to be able to teach it and communicate to others; (*b*) the theory of the Ideas arouses aporias, therefore, if it is eliminated, thinking and dialectic is also eliminated; but with that philosophy would be finished.[12]

The third section of the dialogue (the longest and most complex)[13] opens as follows. This section has a kind of prologue that is methodological and programmatic, uncovering most of the intentions pursued by Plato. First of all, it says that the condition for not falling into those aporias that we have analyzed and hence to solve them, is an *exercise in dialectic* (that exercise of long duration and of great significance that Plato prescribed in the Academy). And it will certainly not be the old exercise of dialectic conducted on the physical plane of the Eleatics, but a new exercise conducted on the plane achieved by that which the *Phaedo* calls the "second voyage" and which we know well; that is, the dialectic on the level of the intelligible world. The dichotomous dialectic of Zeno is therefore taken up to a new plane and hence it produces an authentic shift already in part achieved with the theory of Ideas. The existence of an Idea must be hypothesized, and then see what follows from considering it in relation to itself and in relation to its contrary; hence the hypothesis that that Idea does not exist also must be posited and it must verify in an analogous fashion what follows that hypothesis considering it in relation to itself and in relation to its opposite. This must be done not only for the One and for the many, but likewise for the Ideas of similar and dissimilar, movement and rest, being and nonbeing and similar cases.

Parmenides, therefore, after having accepted the request, begins from the hypothesis on which is based his own philosophy (which Plato understands in a rigidly monistic sense); that is, from the hypothesis "if there is a One." From this hypothesis, hence, on the basis of the general outline proposed, they will analyze the dialectical consequences, concerning the *One itself* and the *Other from the One*, and then again the consequences derived from each of them, considered both in itself and reciprocally; hence, it will examine the opposed hypotheses, following the same logical distinctions. There would in this way be eight hypotheses, presented as antithetical horns of four antinomies.

Dialectic examination of each of these eight hypotheses involve positive and negative results that alternate; that is, concerning the One *nothing can be said and everything can be said*; also of the Other from the One, analogously, nothing can be said and everything can be said. To a cursory reader, it would seem that the most laborious effort must conclude with a laborious zero; that is, in a totally negative fashion. Actually, it is not at all like this. The hypotheses that suppose a contraposition and a radical divorce of the One from the Other and the Other from the One or those that reject the One or the Other than the One are absolutely without support. The two hypotheses that suppose a structural relation between the One and the Other than the One (the many) are supportable as well as give rise to aporias generally capable of being overcome. In particular, *Plato reveals at least some of his most significant cards, by speaking of the One that "participates" the Other, understood as infinite multiplicity, and by alluding to the function of the One as limit.*

The theoretical nucleus of the dialogue hence is the following: the monistic conception of the Eleatics does not offer support, because it falls into insuperable aporias; neither does a purely pluralistic position offer support (as for example that of the Atomists). But between monism and pluralism exists a concise middle way, which is that of admitting a *polar structure*, or better *bipolarity* of the real, *structured at the summit by two Principles*—the One and indefinite Plurality (Dyad)—such that one cannot be present without the other and vice versa; that is, the two Principles are indissolubly conjoined. In particular such a conception of the two highest Principles and their participation structure throws a wholly different light on the theory of Ideas. *The relation of Ideas and sensible things is reexamined in the light of the general bipolar structure of Unity and Plurality. And the plane on which the aporias are based of the second section is entirely overturned with this conception.*

Therefore, if the *Parmenides* is interpreted in this way—that has always been a kind of seed of discord for the interpretation of Plato, it is the writing more charged with exoterical elements, by reason of it contents and the people called in evidence—its fundamental doctrine becomes very significant and truly clear.

3.   The ontology of the highest genera in the *Sophist* and the metaphor of the parricide of Parmenides

The *Sophist* has become very well-known in the history of ontology more than for its basic thematic, regarding the nature and art of the "sophist" (which is radically differentiated from that of the philosopher), for being the "locus classicus" in which being and some of highest Ideas are discussed and for its overturning of the basic position of Eleaticism involving the "parricide of Parmenides," as we will see.

For these reasons the dialogue has been largely overvalued, insofar as it is believed that here Plato drew upon his supreme and ultimate metaphysical concepts. Actually, Plotinus was the first to lead the interpreters into this error, in the famous passage of the *Enneads* in which he presents the Ideas that are considered in the *Sophist* as an exhaustive list of the highest universals and hence as the table of the categories of the intelligible world.[14] Instead, as it emerges from the most careful of the modern studies, Plato speaks clearly of choosing only some of the Ideas that are considered the greatest. Therefore, Plato made a precise choice of those Ideas that were of interest to develop the specific theme of the "sophist," and hence the sweep of the totality of the Ideas is left outside of the treatment.

This clarified, let us see what is the nature of the dialectical nexuses that are involved with these most general genera (or Meta-Ideas) selected in the *Sophist* to develop its specific discussion.

Plato begins from the three following Ideas: "Being," "Rest," and "Motion." Among these the last two involve a negative relation, because they do not participate in each other. Instead the Idea of Being has positive relations with both of them, insofar as Rest "is" as well as Movement "is." But these three Ideas, simply by being three, must be each *different* than the others, and, at the same time, each *identical* with itself. Then, consequently, they involve other general Ideas, "Identity" and "Difference."

In this way, we have obtained the five most general Ideas. And here is the dialectical nexus that joins them, which Taylor puts in focus in a concise fashion in the following way:

> Motion is not rest, nor rest motion. But both *are* and are *identical* with themselves, and thus *"partake"* (μέτεχει) of Being and identity, and also, since each is different from the other, of *difference*. Thus we can say, e.g., that motion is—it is motion, but also *is not*—*it is not rest*. But in just the same way we can say that motion "partakes of" Being and so *is*. There is such a thing as motion; but motion is not identical with being, and in that sense we may say that it is *not*, i.e., it is not-being. The same line of thought shows that "not-being" may be asserted of all the five forms already enumerated, even of Being itself, since each of them is different from any of the others, and thus is *not* any of the others.[15] Here are, then, the results of the inquiry. We speak of "not-being" in two different senses: (*a*) one in which we understand it as the contradictory of Being (that is, as a negation of being); (*b*) the other, instead, we understand as "other" than being; that is, we understand it not as the contrary but as different than being. (*a*) In the first sense nonbeing cannot exist (because the negation of Being cannot

be); (*b*) instead, in the second sense, it can exist, because *it possesses its own specific nature (the nature of alteriety).*

It is in this way that we ought to understand what Plato himself called the "parricide" of Parmenides. In fact, Plato disguises himself in this dialogue as the Eleatic Stranger to transgress against the highest command of Parmenides according to which *not-being is not*. And, instead, the Platonic-Eleatic Stranger says in the text: *not-being is, if it is understood in the sense of "Difference."* Here is the great passage in which Plato presents us with the "parricide" of Parmenides:

> *Stranger*: Then I have another still more pressing request?
> *Theaetetus*: What is that?
> *Stranger*: That you will not think that I am turning into a sort of parricide.
> *Theaetetus*: In what way?
> *Stranger*: *We shall find it necessary in self-defense to put to the question that pronouncement of father Parmenides, and establish by main force that what is not, in some respect has being, and conversely that what is, in a way is not.*
> *Theaetetus*: It is plain that the course of the argument requires us to maintain that at all costs.
> *Stranger*: Plain enough for the blind to see, as they say. Unless these propositions are either refuted or accepted, anyone who talks of false statements or false judgment as being images or likenesses or copies or semblances, or of any of the arts concerned with such things, can hardly escape becoming a laughingstock by being forced to contradict himself.
> *Theaetetus*: Quite true
> *Stranger*: That is why *we must now dare to lay unfilial hands on the pronouncement, or else, if some scruple holds us back, drop the matter entirely.*
> *Theaetetus*: As for that, we must let no scruple hinder us! (trans. F. M. Cornford, p. 214-5 [Hamilton-Cairns ed., p. 985], emphasis added)[16]

Here is the passage that has become very famous in the history of ontology in which the "parricide" of Parmenides takes place on the ontological plane:

> *Stranger*: *So, it seems, when a part of the nature of the different and a part of the nature of a being are set in contrast to one another, the contrast is, if it be permissible to say so, as much a reality as Being itself; it does not mean what is contrary to 'a being,"* but only what is different from that being.
> *Theaetetus*: That is quite clear.
> *Stranger*: What name are we to give it, then?
> *Theaetetus*: *Obviously this is just that 'what-is-not' which we were seeking for the sake of the Sophist.*
> *Stranger*: Has it then, as you say, a Being inferior to none of the rest in reality? *May we now be bold to say that 'that which is not' unquestionably is a thing that has a nature of its own*–just as the tall was tall and the beautiful was beautiful, so too with the not-tall and the not-beautiful–*and in that sense 'that which is not' also, on the same principle, both was and is 'what is not,'*

a single form to be reckoned among the many realities? Or have we any
further doubts with regard to it, Theaetetus?
Theaetetus: None at all.
Stranger: You see, then, that *in our disobedience to Parmenides we have
trespassed far beyond the limits of his prohibition.*
Theaetetus: In what way?
Stranger: In pushing forward on our quest, we have shown him results in a
field that he forbade us even to explore.
Theaetetus: How?
Stranger: He says, remember, *'Never shall this be proved, that things that are
not, are, but keep back your thought from this way of inquiry.'*
Theaetetus: Yes, he does say that.
Stranger: *Whereas we have not merely shown that things that are not, are, but
we have brought to light the real character of "not-being."* We have shown
that the nature of the different has Being and is parceled out over the whole
field of a beings with reference to one another, and of every part of it that
is set in contrast to "that which is" *we have dared to say that precisely that
"is really" that which is not.*
Theaetetus: Yes, sir, and I think what we have said is perfectly true.
Stranger: Then let no one say that it is the contrary of the Being that we
mean by 'what is not,' when we make bold to say that 'what is not' exists. So
far as any contrary of the Being is concerned, we have long ago said good-bye
to the question whether there is such a thing or not and whether any account
can be given of it or none whatsoever. But with respect to the 'what-is-not'
that we have now asserted to exist, an opponent must either convince us
that our account is wrong by refuting it, or, so long as he proves unable to
do that, he must accept our statements that *the kinds blend with one another,
that Being and difference pervade them all, and pervade one another, that
difference [or different], by partaking of being, is by virtue of that participation, but on the other hand is not that Being of which it partakes, but is
different, since it is different from Being [or a being], quite clearly it must be
possible that it should be a thing that is not,* and again, being, having a part
in difference, will be different from all the rest of the kinds, and, because it
is different from them all, it is not any one of them nor yet all of the others
put together, but is only itself, *with the consequence, again indisputable, that
existence is not myriads upon myriads of things, and that all the other kinds
in the same way, whether taken severally or all together, in many respects are
and in many respects are not.*
Theaetetus: True. (trans. F. M. Cornford p. 291-2, 294-6 [Hamilton-Cairns
ed., pp. 1005-06] with some changes, emphasis added)[17]

The "parricide" of Parmenides does not happen only in the ontological
perspective; that is, on the basis of discussions of the concepts of *being* and
nonbeing, and in particular by reason of the admission of this latter, as normally
upheld. Plato, in fact, also brings to the fore the *henological* thematic of the
One and the *first Principles*, and likewise the perspective involving the necessity
for the admission of the *hierarchical structure of being*. Moreover, the imposing

dialectical exercise in the hands of the Eleatic Stranger in the *Parmenides*, as we have seen, brings to the fore the dialectical-polar structure of reality that Plato used to push Parmenides "to kill" himself, by bringing into focus this "polarity"; that is, which radically overturned Eleatic monism. But here is how, immediately after having spoken of the "parricide" of Parmenides, Plato subscribed to an assault on the "conclusions" of the father. This assault, note, is not part of the discussion about nonbeing, but rather arises from the discussion about Being itself and its structure, and in particular about *the lack of support for the conception of one-being in the Eleatic-monistic sense*:

> *Stranger*: It strikes me that Parmenides and everyone else who has set out *to determine how many real things there are and what they are like*, have discoursed to us in rather an offhand fashion. (trans. F. M. Cornford, p. 216 [Hamilton-Cairns ed., p. 986], emphasis added)[18]

Here are the aporias from which Parmenides does not escape, by identifying Being with the One and the Whole.

(*a*) So, "*Being*" and "*One*" are two names; but, to admit two names, since only the One is admitted and no other, is contradictory. But it will become even absurd to admit that a name *is*, because if it is different (insofar as it is a name) from the thing that it expresses, together with it, it will constitute *two* (*one thing* is the name and *a second thing* is that which the name indicates). Consequently, to be coherent absolute monism must also embrace in its unity the name.

(*b*) But the position of the Eleatics implies further complications, in the measure in which the *One* is made to coincide with the *Whole*. In fact, Parmenides, identified the Whole with a sphere and attributed to the Whole as a necessary consequence a center, extremities, and hence "parts." But what has parts can participate in the One, but cannot be the One itself; in fact, the one as such is indivisible, and hence is beyond parts. Parmenides in general could not identify *Being, One, and Whole*, because each of them *has its own distinct nature*: Being partakes of the One, and hence is not One; and the Whole is something more than One, insofar as it embraces Being and the One.[19]

This text *contains the "parricide" of Parmenides on the plane of henology in the new dimension achieved by Plato and reveals the following*. (*a*) The One in a primary sense is absolutely indivisible; that is, absolutely simple. (*b*) That which has parts can have unity, but only by partaking in the One. (*c*) Being partakes in the One, but does not coincide with the One (the One is beyond Being, and Being depends on the One). (*d*) The Whole does not coincide with the One or with Being, but is, in a certain sense, the area that includes them. (*e*) And because Being does not coincide with the Whole, because it implies unity outside itself, of which it partakes, Being is not of itself complete and it will include nonbeing (in the sense, well understood and clarified in our dialogue; that is, of difference: in particular, it is not One).

It is a question, as we will see, of some *protological points of primary importance*, even if Plato mixed them in various ways with the nuances of "play," which the work to that extent required of him.[20]

4.   The important metaphysical theses of the *Philebus*: the bipolar structure of reality, the four highest genera, and the supreme Measure as Absolute

The protological positions is considerably widened in the *Philebus*, as the ancients have already pointed out,[21] and as careful modern scholars have acknowledged.[22] There are three very significant passages on the protologic: in the first, Plato points out the bipolar structure of reality (One-Many) and, in connection with this issue, he focuses especially on the Ideas, explaining the numerical structure of the Ideas. In the second, he widens the area of this discussion, by extending it to all the areas of cosmology and anthropology, uncovering in this way the four highest genera of the really real. In the third, he states, by means of a series of allusions, many forced and to some degree even explicit, the essence of the Good as One and as supreme Measure.

Let us begin with the first position.[23]

After having expressed the importance of the questions on the relations of the One and the many, its correct connotations and its precise nature, and after having further emphasized that the identity of the One and the many established by reasoning is found constantly in every ███e, in all the things that have been spoken about, Plato explains that to bring to a head some of the difficulties that this involves, it is necessary to go on through that same path which has been followed in all the discoveries in the sphere of the arts. This knowledge of the relations between the One and the many, says Plato, coincides substantially with a "divine revelation," which the ancients have transmitted, according to that all things that are said *"to be"* are always constituted precisely by *"one"* and *"many"* and contain in themselves limitedness and unlimitedness. in other words, the bipolar stru█████e is the supporting axes of the whole of reality, and hence also of thought.

But in what does this revelation consist and more precisely this "gift of the Gods to mankind": *being itself as such contains the limit and the unlimited (the "peras" and the "apeiron"), which are therefore essential components of equal necessity.* This statement holds for *each and every being* and hence also for the *Ideas themselves*, as is clear in context and as the most careful scholars by now incontestably agree.

What are the subjects under discussion, it is necessary that they be reduced to the *unity of the Idea*; hence it is necessary to carefully examine this Idea, to see if it contains, in its turn, *two* or *more Ideas*, and then, further, if each of these Ideas is subdivided into other Ideas, up to the point of reaching the Ideas that are no longer further divisible. Up to the point in which it remains within the parameters of the Ideas, the *number* of the Ideas contained in a given general Idea is always *determinate*. But, when it reaches the Ideas that are no longer divisible it is no longer possible to continue in dialectical division, and then it passes into the *multiplicity of the empirical individuals*.

The division of the Ideas, therefore, again gives origin to the *limited quantity* of Ideas included in them. The peculiar task of dialectic is precisely that of establishing *what and how many these are*. And here precisely lies the most remarkable novelty of the *Philebus* put into the limelight beginning from Stenzel; that is, the joining together of the *diairetic structure of the Ideas with number. The doctrine of the Idea-Numbers emerges, as we have already pointed out, in the sense that we have explained earlier. It is possible to establish the structure of every general Idea, marking off again by divisions the particular Ideas in which it is spelled out, and hence to transpose this diairetic structure into a number (this means, in fact, to establish what and how many Ideas there are contained in a genera Idea).* Finally, after this procedure, it will be possible to go on to the indeterminate plurality of the individuals. This means that it is not possible *immediately* to go on from a general Idea (unity) to the plurality of empirical individuals, which are an indeterminate plurality, except *by means of the ontological and logical progression of the Idea in the various Ideas of which it is constituted and the determination of their number (that is, what and how many they are)*. Only the indivisible Ideas, once achieved, allow for the possibility of the passage to the corresponding innumerable empirical individuals. Hence, below the lowest Idea no longer further divisible is the *sensible apeiron*. Therefore, the Idea, in its turn, has a determinative function of unity with respect to the sensibles, as we will see better further on, but the following text is clear on the matter:

> *Socrates:*"When you have got your *one* (ἕν), you remember, what ever it may be, you must not immediately turn your eyes to the *unlimited* [ἐπ᾽ ἀπείρου φύσιν] but to a number [ἐπί τινα ἀριθμόν]; now the same applies when it is the unlimited that you are compelled to start with. You must not immediately turn your eyes to the *one*, but must discern this or that number embracing the *multitude*, whatever it may be; reaching the *one* must be the last step of all. (trans. R. Hackforth [Hamilton-Cairns ed., pp. 1094], emphasis added)[24]

Let us go on to the second point that we mentioned earlier.[25]

Plato takes these metaphysical arguments and draws some conclusions of the greatest importance. In fact the concepts of (*a*) *"unlimited"* and of (*b*) *"limit"* are taken with ontological-cosmological connotations. He affirms that what exists in the totality implies, precisely, these two factors in systematic fashion. But beside these two genera, he needs, to comprehend the ontological structure of physical reality, (*c*) to add the *"mixture"* of *limit* and *unlimited*, as a third genera, and (*d*) finally, and very important, the further *"cause of the mixture."*

These four highest genera are connected to the unwritten protologic in a very clear manner.

(*a*) *Apeiron* (or "indeterminate," "indefinite," "unlimited" consists in a "procedure always moving and not remaining firm" in two opposite directions, as is evident from Plato's examples of the hot and cold, which implies a *unceasing change* in the hotter and an *unceasing change* in the colder in the opposite direction. Nevertheless, the choice of "more and less" as the *distinctive character* of the nature of the unlimited is particularly revealing: Plato understands a ceaseless change in the "more" and a procedure of ceaseless change (in the opposite sense) in the "less"; that is, *in a process to infinity in the "two" opposed extremes, in a dyadic sense.* Therefore the reference to the principle of the Dyad of the great-and-small of the "Unwritten Doctrines" which expresses precisely an unlimited (the *indefinite* Dyad) in the twofold sense of a procedure toward an infinite greatness and toward an infinite smallness is evident. In any case, Plato who as we have said made allusions in great abundance, indicated explicitly *the greatest and the smallest* as the best kind of definitive examples, as evidently referring exactly to the *indefinite Dyad of the greater-and-smaller.*

(*b*) *Peras* (or "limit") implies all which that has a relation with the Ideas and in particular with their *numerical structure* and the capacity of determining the indeterminate *by means of numerical mediation.* Plato points out quantity, due measure, equality, numbers in relation to numbers, measure in relation to a measure. In particular he emphasizes that the *limit* is that which removes the relations of contrariety *by the introduction of number*, and in this way makes them well proportioned and harmonious. He also states that it is that which eliminates the excessive and creates measure and balance. Evidently, it is a matter of various ways in which the One in various areas and in various ways develops its function as a determining and ultimate Principle. And here Plato is even forced to say expressly that the *limit* "is One by nature" (ἐν φύσει).

(*c*) The *mixture* of limit and unlimited is consequently that which is measured and proportioned (the effect of the action of the *peras* on the *apeiron*), as for example in health, physical strength, music, the seasons, and in general all beautiful things as well as the positive states present in souls. And Plato explains, further, the mixture is "coming-into-being" (γένεσις εἰς οὐσίαν); that is taking on the One by the indeterminate plurality. Therefore, it is that *unity* which derives from the measure produced by the *peras* on the *apeiron*, and hence a *unity-in-multiplicity.*

(*d*) Whereas in the world of Ideas this "mixture" is eternal (it takes place over and over again), insofar as in the sphere of the intelligible world through the same bipolar structure of the Principles it does not require a further cause that would guarantee the structural mixture of *limit* and *unlimited*, in the sphere of change and in all that which implies "generation," *it is necessary to have recourse to a productive efficient cause of this "mixture,"* and this is Mind in all spheres. In particular, the *mixture* of the physical cosmos, in general and in particular of the things contained in it, implies a cosmic Mind; that is, the Demiurge (the universal Craftsman), just as the arts and the products of human activity imply the mind of man. But we will take up the complex of important problems in a specific way in the next chapter.

Let us now turn to the third point[26] that we pointed out earlier, which is contained in the conclusion of the dialogue. After having first stated (in the passages we have analyzed), by means of a massive series of allusions, that *the Good is the One*, in this definitively metaphysical passage Plato is even pushed to explain that at the summit of all values stands the *Measure*, and that all values whatsoever are derived from it. Pohlenz has pointed out this quite well previously: "By Measure Plato understood in reality the Absolute, and chose this name because the Absolute includes in itself not only the Good understood in the finalistic sense but also the Beautiful, and hence the principle of order and proportion, and it constitutes the first cause of their concrete existence and the norm of their exact mixture."[27] Consequently, we know from the indirect tradition that the supreme Measure is the nature itself of the One (in a metaphysical sense), as we have seen confirmed by the allusions in the *Republic*[28] and as in the *Philebus* Plato tells us again by means of further allusions almost to the point of openness, *by placing the Measure* [μέτρον] *at the summit of all values.*

And, in this way, what the Oracle at Delphi stated is confirmed in all senses "...neither speaks out nor conceals, but gives a sign" (Kirk-Raven, p. 211, n. 247).[29] But the explication of these hints (quite strong in the *Philebus*) is again possible today because of the "assistance" and aid rendered by the indirect tradition; and it is possible, if not entirely, at least in its essential characteristics in a truly remarkable manner.[30]

It is precisely this most significant way and most constructive manner of reading and understanding Plato, that in large measure has been imposed by the best research in our day.

V. THE DOCTRINE OF THE DEMIURGE AND COSMOLOGY

1. The position of the physical world in the sphere of the real according to Plato

This significant concept, which must be grasped to understand the doctrine of the Demiurge and the cosmology (one of the summits of Platonic thought), consists in the hierarchical structure of the real. It is one of the most outstanding supporting axes that guarantees the unity and the correct global understanding of Plato's thought. To the primary and supreme Principles of the One and the Dyad, according to Plato, there follow: (*a*) the sphere of the Ideas, (*b*) hence the intermediate sphere of the mathematical entities, (*c*) and finally, the sphere of the sensible world. Each of these spheres is articulated into further distinctions; that is, (*a*) the sphere of the Ideas has at its summit ideal Numbers and Figures after which there are very general Ideas (which some scholars have correctly called the Meta-Ideas) and then the more specific and particular Ideas; (*b*) the sphere of mathematical entities that include the geometrical entities, sphere and solid, objects of pure astronomy and objects of musicology, even souls; (*c*) the sphere of the physical world including all sensible realities.

It is scarcely necessary to remember that we speak of spheres by using a physical metaphor that, naturally is taken as an image to allude to a metaphysical structure; that is, to an ordered hierarchy. Here is an illustrative outline:

PRIMARY AND SUPREME PRINCIPLES:
ONE AND INDETERMINATE DYAD

Sphere of the Ideas	$\Big\{$	Ideal Numbers and Figures Very general Ideas or Meta-Ideas

---

Sphere of the mathematical entities	$\Bigg\{$	Objects of mathematics Objects of sphere of geometry Objects of stereometry Objects of pure astronomy

also the Soul of the world and souls in general

Sphere of the physical sensible world

The relation existing between the spheres is *unilateral nonsymmetrical* ontological dependence and not one that is *symmetrical* or *reciprocal*. The lower spheres cannot be (nor can they be conceived) without the higher spheres, but the higher spheres can be (and can be conceived) without the lower. It is this relation of priority and posteriority in terms of substance and nature to use an expression that Aristotle uses when he writes: "Some things then are prior and posterior in this sense, others in respect of *nature* and *substance*; that is, *those which can be without other things, while the other cannot be without them–a distinction that Plato used*" (trans. W. D. Ross, p. 764 emphasis added).[1]

The technical Platonic formula was the following: that which is dependent can be destroyed without destroying that on which it depends, with this destroyed, however that which depends on it, is also destroyed. This means that we basically found a kind of metaphysical dependence of the successive spheres of being one upon the other, which implies, so to speak, an enrichment at every succeeding stage of the Dyadic Principle, which is not deduced or systematically explained, but is simply presented as such. In this sense, the causation that the higher sphere involves is *necessary, but not sufficient*, because it explains only the metaphysically formal aspect of the successive spheres, but not its differences, which depend on the Dyadic Principle. This is a remark of enormous importance, because it categorically excludes the possibility of imprisoning this position of Plato in the parameters of pantheism and immanentism.[2]

Some further remarks will clarify better this complex Platonic metaphysical structure.

(*a*) We have already seen that the ideal Numbers are derived from two supreme principles (and hence all the Ideas, which, as we know, all have a numerical structure), through a process of limitation (equalization) on the part of the *One* working on the *indeterminate multiplicity* of the Dyad.

(*b*) The sphere of mathematical entities was explained by Plato as follows. (1) The mathematical numbers are deduced from the *monad* (unity of individual entities) and from the *plurality* of the many and few. (2) The geometrical and stereometrical figures were deduced from a particular kind of *point* that Plato called the *indivisible line* (a mathematical point having position), which acts as a formal principle, while he speaks of the "*short and long*" as a material principle of the line, "*wide and narrow*" for surfaces and "*high and low*" for solids. Evidently it is a question of determining the difference of the supreme Principle from the original Dyad of the great-and-small, which little by little contains an enrichment in (intelligible) materiality and multiplicity (although always on the level of intelligibility).

(*c*) By passing from successive ontological spheres we assist at the birth of the physical cosmos: and here the material principle also takes on a solidity such as to produce the *sphere of the sensible* and generate the world of becoming, (as we will see further on).

But–and this is the most important point to specify—even the sphere of the sensible is an intermediate, according to a different perspective. In fact, mathematical entities are intermediates *between two different kinds of being;* that is, between *an eternal being that does not change in any sense at all* (it is neither born, nor dies, nor increases, nor decreases, nor does it change) and *a being that is generated and becomes in all senses of the term.* As we have explained earlier, the mathematical entities are multiple as the sensibles; in addition, they are *intermediate* as well as being *intermediaries,* insofar as they make possible and explain the way the intelligible is articulated in the sensible sphere (as we will see better further on). On the contrary, the sensible world is intermediate, if we consider it in function of a perspective that also includes *not-being* between the steps in the hierarchical scale, as the following schema shows in outline:

---

(1) *Intelligible and eternal being:* Ideas, mathematical entities (being in the full sense)

---

(2) *The being that is born, dies, and changes* (being in a partial and incomplete sense)

---

(3) *Not-being*

It is precisely within this perspective that Plato in the *Republic* characterizes the physical world, which is changing, as intermediate between *pure being and pure not-being.*

Why did Plato speak in this way?

Parmenides did not have any doubts: that which is multiple and relative, changes and becomes, and hence is not; and is not in the strongest sense of the term; that is, it is nothing. Consequently, opinion or *doxa* grope into not-being and toward nothing which belongs to mortals, who by believing in the becoming of being, *are condemned to not-being.* But, as already with respect to the intelligible world (which has been identified simply with absolute being and hence interpreted with a category of Eleatic lineage) Plato has reformed the doctrine of Parmenides and has introduced not-being as the different or other to explain the ideal multiplicity, just as also with respect to the sensible world he is forced to reform (and no less radically) the doctrine of Parmenides and to concede to phenomena, to explain them, *their own reality and their own being.*

We have seen that the attempt of Parmenides to give an account of phenomena is broken up in his hands, because in the very position in which he attempts to give a place to phenomena in the riverbed of being, he does not preserve it, but rather destroys it entirely (Eleatic being, applied to phenomena, absolutizes them, immobilizes them, and resolves them into a total identity).[3] On the contrary, Plato (because of his second voyage) grasps that being of the sensible and phenomenal world exists, but is *structurally different* than true being (the really real), absolute being. It is clear, for Plato, that the being of the sensible world is a being in which there is division, conditioned by not-being; but is, for him, likewise clear that it is in no way absolute not-being; that is, a simple nothing, or generally something totally deprived of the imprint of metaphysical being. And it is likewise clear, for Plato, that, if true knowledge (the truth) is concerned solely with the really real (the intelligible world), the world of true being, opinion (*doxa*), the world of mortal opinion, concerns something which in some measure is (in the measure in which it reflects something of truth or being), and that it cannot be referred to not-being in the absolute sense, because there is no knowledge, but only ignorance of not-being.[4]

And here is, then, the Platonic response to the problem: the being of the sensible world is an intermediate (μεταξύ) between pure being (the really real) and pure not-being. Therefore, the sensible world, which is the world of becoming and change, is not being (not really real, not true or absolute being but note, it is real) but it has being and it has it *by partaking the world of Ideas* (that is, true being): it has being, so to speak, *changing being*.

Let us read a passage that expresses this conception, which is fundamental for the correct understanding of Plato. After having explained, on the basis of an analysis of the kinds of knowledge, sense cognition, that opinion cannot be referred to not-being or to being (because there is science of being, not opinion and of not-being there is ignorance) but to something intermediate, the philosopher writes:

> It would remain, then, as it seems, for us to discover *that which partakes of both, of to be and not to be*, and that could not be rightly designated either in its exclusive purity, so that, if it shall be discovered, we may justly pronounce it to be the opinable, thus assigning extremes to extremes and the intermediate to the intermediate. Is not that so?
> It is.
> This much premised, let him tell me, I will say, let him answer me, that good fellow who does not think there is a beautiful in itself or any idea of beauty in itself always remaining the same and unchanged, but who does believe in *many* beautiful things [= the many beautiful empirical phenomena] the lover of spectacles [merely phenomenal]. I mean, who cannot endure to hear anybody say that the beautiful is *One* and the just one, and so of other things [= the other Ideas]and this will be our question. My good fellow, is there any one of these *many* fair and honorable things [phenomena] that will not sometimes appear ugly and base? And of the just things [phenomena], that will not seem unjust? And of the pious things [phenomena], that will not seem impious?

No, it is inevitable, he said, that they would appear to be both beautiful in a way and ugly, and so with all the other things you asked about.

And again, do the many *double things* [phenomena] appear any less halves than the doubles?

None the less.

And likewise of the great and small things, the light and the heavy things - will they admit these predicates any more than their opposites?

No, he said, each of them will always hold of, partake of, both.

Then is each of these multiples [phenomena] rather than it is not that which one affirms it to be?

They are like those jesters who palter with us in a double sense at banquets, he replied, and resemble the children's riddle about the eunuch and his hitting of the bat-with what and as it sat on what they signify they struck it.[5] For these things too equivocate, and it is impossible to conceive firmly any one of them to be or not to be or both or neither.

Do you know what to do with them, then? said I. And can you find a better place to put them than that *midway between existence or essence and the not to be* [μεταξύ οὐσίας τε καὶ τοῦ μὴ εἶναι] For we shall surely not discover a darker region than not-being that they should still more not be, nor a brighter than being than they should still more be.

Most true, he said.

We would seem to have found, then, that the many conventions of the many about the fair and honorable and other things are tumbled about *in the mid-region between that which is not and that which is in the true and absolute sense.* (trans. Paul Shorey, Bollingen, p. 718-9)[6]

2. The Demiurge and his metaphysical role

If the meaning of the important passage that we have read is thoroughly grasped, we can also understand the physical cosmos by a simple *deduction* from the primary and supreme Principles and from the world of Ideas but Plato thought it was necessary to introduce the divine Mind as the originating metaphysical cause.[7] In fact, in his judgment, the being that changes implies the specific cause of the productive Mind and all that it involves. Here is how (in the marvelous theoretical prelude to the great cosmological discourse of the *Timaeus*)[8] Plato summarizes his thought in four axioms.

(*a*) *Being which is always* (intelligible being) is not subject to generation and becoming, because it remains always in the same condition; it is grasped by the intelligence through reasoning.

(*b*) *Becoming*, which continually is generated, and is never true being, because it is continually changing; it is the object of opinion; that is, it is grasped through sensorial perception, which is distinct from reason.

(c) All that which is subject to the process of generation requires a cause, because to be generated every thing has need of a cause that produces precisely its generation. This cause is a Demiurge, a Craftsman, that is to say an efficient cause.

(*d*) The Demiurge; that is, the Craftsman, always produces something, previously *looking to something as a point of reference*; that is, taking it as a *model*. So, the Craftsman could refer to two different kinds of models: (1) to that which exists always and in the same way (that is, to the type of being about which we spoke in the first axiom), (2) or to something that is subject to generation (that is the type of realities about which the second axiom is concerned). If the Craftsman takes as a model eternal being, that which is produced is beautiful; if, instead, he takes as a model something generated, that which is produced is not beautiful. Here is the text:

> We must, then, in my judgment, first make this distinction: [1] what *is* that which *is always* real and has no becoming, and [2] what *is* that which is always *becoming* and is never real? [1] That which is apprehensible by thought with a rational account is the thing that is *always unchangeably real*, [2] whereas that which is the object of belief together with unreasoning sensation is *the thing that becomes and passes away, but never has real being*. [3] Again, all that becomes *must needs become by the agency of some cause*, for without a cause nothing can come to be. [4] Now whenever the maker [δημιουργός] of anything *looks to that which is always unchanging* and uses a model of that description in fashioning the form and quality of his work *all that he thus accomplishes must be good*. If he looks to something that has come to be and uses a generated model, it will not be good. (trans. F. M. Cornford, *Plato's Cosmology*, p. 22, emphasis added)[9]

On the basis of these four axioms Plato, as we have already hinted, constructs the metaphysical and cosmo-ontological system of the entire treatment of the *Timaeus* and, at the same time, grounds the noetic structure and the justification of the methodology adopted. Because the object under discussion in the *Timaeus* is the heaven and the world; that is, the cosmos, it is necessary to establish, first of all, if it is a being that is always; that is, a being of that type about which the first axiom was concerned, or if it is a generated reality, one of the second type spoken about in the second axiom. Well, all the things that constitute this world are perceptible through the senses. But all that which is perceptible with the senses and is opinable, as is established in the second axiom, is in its nature generated and comes to be. On the basis of the third axiom, in addition, this world, insofar as it is generated, must be generated by a cause. But to find this cause of the universe in an adequate fashion is difficult; and when it is found it is difficult to make it understandable to all men (for the reasons we have explained earlier). Finally, on the basis of the fourth axiom it can be established what is the model to which the Demiurge looks as he constructs this world. In fact, this axiom has established that, *if this world is beautiful*, necessarily the Demiurge has looked *to an eternal model* in its construction; if, instead, it were not beautiful (but only in this case), the Demiurge would have used a generated model. But it is clearly demonstrable that the world is beautiful; and hence because of this, the Demiurge necessarily has looked to an eternal model. In fact, because the world is *the most beautiful* of generated realities, its Demiurge is consequently the *most good* of craftsmen; that is, as we will see, it is the Craftsman who has imitated and realized *the Good in the greatest possible degree.* Here is the text of Plato:

> So concerning the whole Heaven or World–let us call it by whatsoever name may be most acceptable to it–we must ask the question which, it is agreed, must be asked at the outset of inquiry concerning anything: Has it always been, without any source of becoming; or has it come to be, starting from some beginning? It has come to be; for it can be seen and touched and it has a body, and all such things are sensible; and, as we saw, sensible things, that are to be apprehended by belief together with sensation, are things that become and can be generated. But again, that which becomes, we say, must necessarily become by the agency of some cause. *The maker and father of this universe is a hard task to find, and having found him it would be impossible to declare him to all mankind.* Be that as it may, we must go back to this question about the world: After which of the two models did its builder frame it–after that which is always in the same unchanging state, or after that which has come to be? Now if this world is good and *its maker good* [ἀγαθός], *clearly he looked to the eternal;* on the contrary supposition (which cannot be spoken without blasphemy), to that which has come to be. Everyone, then, must see that he looked to the eternal; *for the world is the best of things that have become* [κάλλιστος τῶν γεγονότων], *and he is the best of causes* [ἄριστος τῶν αἰτίων]. (trans. F. M. Cornford, *Plato's Cosmology*, pp. 22-3, emphasis added)[10]

Hence, there exists a pure being graspable only by intelligence, and it is to this one that the Demiurge looks to as a model, to realize the sensible and changing world. Therefore, *the sensible cosmos is an image of a metasensible reality, carried out by the Demiurge.* "Having come to be, then, in this way, the world has been fashioned on the model of that which is comprehensible by rational discourse and understanding and is always in the same state. Again, these things being so, our world must necessarily be a *likeness* of something" (trans. F. M. Cornford, *Plato Cosmology*, p. 23, emphasis added).[11]

This conception of pure being as "*model*" and of becoming as "*image*" of that model and *the necessity of an efficient cause* (the Demiurge or Craftsman) to ground and justify this relation, constitutes a *fundamental supporting axis* of the written doctrine of Plato, which is given its most mature and complete expression in the *Timaeus.* And as we previously said the epistemological system of the entire cosmological treatment is supported by this metaphysical system: the original model, insofar as pure being, is the object of science, which achieves incontrovertible truths; the image of this model (and hence our physical cosmos, which is precisely an *image*) is the object of opinion, and this can be well founded, but not achieve epistemological certitude; hence it is "a myth" in the sense of a likely story, as we have explained earlier.

3. The material principle of the sensible world, its metaphysical role, and its connections with the Dyad

The important metaphysical distinction between the *intelligible*, immutable and eternal being of the Ideas understood as *"paradigms"* or *"models,"* and *sensible* being in continuous change, understood as its *image* or likeness, demands to be justified and grounded, a material Principle having the function of excipient and substrate of the image itself.

Actually, Plato said in the *Philebus*, with noteworthy clarity (as we have seen), that the whole of reality—in every area—is a "mixture, " which implies a synthetic bipolar connection of the two opposed principles (limit = unlimited); but he also explained that, although in the sphere of the intelligible the "mixture" is structural and *ab aeterno*, in the sphere of the sensible the "mixture" demands *a cause that accomplishes it* (a demiurgic Mind = Intelligence). Evidently, the necessity for the intervention of the demiurgic Mind depends on the fact that, although in the sphere of the intelligible the two opposed Principles that form the mixture are both of an intelligible nature, in the sphere of the sensible instead it is not so. In fact the material Principle takes on solidity to introduce the sensible, and consequently it is of a nature that, notwithstanding the tendency to be conjoined to its opposite Principle and the capability allowing itself to be dominated by it in large measure, only the intervention of a demiurgic Mind can produce the mediation. Moreover, for the *plus* that the sensible dimension involves, the material Principle that constitutes the sensible world can*not* be reduced *totally* to the structure of the ideal Principle, and for this reason it is the source of *being-in-becoming* (to a form of being *intermediate* between *pure being* and *not-being*).[12]

But there are two further important issues that must be dealt with to understand fully this complex doctrine of Plato.

(*a*) The material Principle participates (through the demiurgic Mind) in a very complex way in the intelligible, because this participation, which consists in the reception of the imprint of the images derived from the Ideas, happens in an ineffable and marvelous way (τρόπον τινὰ δυσφραστον καὶ θαυμαστόν);[13] that is, through a complex *mediation of a numerical and geometrical nature*, as (at least in part) we will see.

(*b*) Moreover, it is a good idea to consider what we have already pointed out; that is, that what the material Principle receives and with what it is mixed is not the Ideas themselves directly, but only the likenesses of those realities which are always, imitations of eternal beings, and hence likenesses or appearances of other realities:[14] *the images of the Ideas, obtained through the mediation of mathematical entities*.

But let us see, first of all, what are the essential properties of the sensible material Principle and what are its relations with the Dyad of the Unwritten Doctrines.

(*a*) Plato underlined in a very marked fashion that the kind of intelligible realities "which is always the same, ungenerated and imperishable, " and as such acts as model, for its ontological structure does not receive anything else into itself from elsewhere, nor itself enters ever into anything else anywhere. And conversely he notes that sensible realities are *copies* or *sensible images* of the intelligible model and are generated and in continuous movement, "*coming to be in a certain place* and then *vanishing out of it*." Consequently, it is necessary to admit another kind of reality: the spatiality or *chora* [χώρα], which furnish the *place* [τόπος] or the *seat* [ἕδρα] for all the realities that are born and perish, precisely because that which is born and perishes, is born in some place, in which and from which, then, it perishes. Let us read the Platonic text concerning this matter:

> [1] This being so, we must agree that there is, first, the unchanging Form, ungenerated and indestructible, which neither receives anything else into itself from elsewhere nor itself enters into anything else anywhere, invisible and otherwise imperceptible; that, in fact, which thinking has for its object. [2] Second is that which bears the same name and is like that Form; is sensible; is brought into existence; is perpetually in motion, coming to be in a certain place [τόπος] and again vanishing out of it; and is to be apprehended by belief involving perception. [3] Third is Space [χώρα], which is everlasting, not admitting destruction; providing a situation [ἕδρα] for all things that come into being, but itself apprehended without the senses by a sort of bastard reasoning, and hardly an object of belief. (trans. F. M. Cornford, *Plato's Cosmology*, p. 192, emphasis added)[15]

Then, Plato notes that referring to this reality, we tend to give it a superior importance extending its nature to all beings, and erroneously we attribute it an omni-comprehensive function. In fact, we maintain that one thing, to be, must be found precisely in some place, and that that which is not on earth or in some place in heavens is nothing.[16] Instead, the truth is this: the things that concern space are only *the realities that are generated*; that is, sensible realities, and hence *not intelligible realities in and of themselves*. Therefore, the things that concern space are only the *imitations* or *images* of the Ideas, not the Ideas themselves.

Therefore, the ontological *status* of the images carried on in the sensible (which coincides perfectly with that of the mixture of which the *Philebus* speaks) implies: (1) that of which it is the appearance or manifestation and to which it makes reference as a model, and (2) a substrate; that is, *a base on which it is supported*, which is precisely *spatiality* of which we are speaking and which is necessary as a *place for that which is born*. And therefore, as such the *chora* is eternally and not subject to corruption, insofar as it is a necessary condition for the existence of each thing that is generated (it is that which if taken away every form of generation would be eliminated also).[17]

(*b*) In addition to the conceptual connotation of spatiality [χώρα], Plato, to characterize the sensible material Principle, centers on the essential notion of *receptacle of all that which is generated* (ὑποδοχή, πανδεχές). The Receptacle is a reality that remains always identical with itself in its amorphous structure. In fact, it receives all things and is formable; that is, able to be formed variously, because it is an *amorphous reality* (lacking a formal structure of its own) and does not take on the form that it quickly assumes, in a definitive fashion; and, for this reason, it can continually and quickly take on other forms. It is comparable to an impressionable material, which is capable of quickly taking on different shapes, and appears precisely under those shapes. The things that enter and leave the receptacle are images of eternal realities (that is, imitations of the paradigms of the Ideas), and entering into it they form it and they impress a mark just as the gold and the material are marked and come to be formed by shapes they receive. Here is a truly very interesting text:

> Now the same thing must be said of that nature which receives all bodies. It must be called always the same; *for it never departs at all from its own character;* since it is always receiving all things, and never in any way whatsoever *takes on any character* that is like any of the things that enter it: by nature it is there as a matrix of everything, changed and diversified by the things that enter it, and on their account it appears to have different qualities at different times; *while the things that pass in and out are to be called copies of the eternal things,* impressions taken from them in a strange manner that is hard to express. (trans. F. M. Cornford, *Plato's Cosmology,* p. 182, emphasis added)[18]

Plato insists greatly on the lack of form in the structure of the Receptacle. That which receives the imprint, as the Receptacle receives it, is adequately prepared for this, *only if it is lacking every form,* because if it were to have any form, it could not accept and reproduce in an adequate way the form opposite to that which was present in it. In short, to accept all forms in an appropriate way, the Receptacle must not possess any.

(*c*) A further and very interesting conceptual connotation of the sensible material Principle is that of *source of generation;* that is, as a reality that is moved and shaken in a disordered and unregulated manner, draws forth rudimentary characters and traces of the elements (water, air, earth, and fire), and hence also the powers and dispositions connected with them, without order and balance. Therefore the material Principle is like a *bundle of powers, shaking disordered and chaotic movements.* Here are two very clear texts on the issue:

> God. . .took over all that is visible [sensible] and *not at rest,* but in discordant and unordered motion–and brought it from disorder into order. (trans. F. M. Cornford, *Plato's Cosmology,* p. 33)[19]
> Now the *nurse of Becoming* [τιθήνη γενέσεως], being made watery and fiery and receiving the characters of earth and air, and qualified by all the

other affections that go with these, had every sort of diverse appearance to the sight; but because *it was filled with powers that were neither alike nor evenly balanced,* there was no equipoise in any region of it; but it was *everywhere swayed unevenly and shaken by those things, and by its motion shook them in turn.* And they, being thus moved, were perpetually being separated and carried in different directions; just as when things are shaken and winnowed by means of winnowing-baskets and other instruments for cleaning corn, the dense and heavy things go one way, while the rare and light are carried to another place and settle there. In the same way at the same time the four kinds were shaken by the Recipient, which itself was in motion like an instrument for shaking, and it separated the most unlike kinds farthest apart from one another, and thrust the most alike closest together; whereby the different kinds came to have different regions, even before the ordered whole consisting of them came to be. *Before that, all these kinds without proportion or measure. Fire, water, earth, and air possessed indeed some vestiges* [ἴχνη] *of their own nature, but were altogether in such a condition as we should expect for anything when deity is absent from it* ...(trans. F. M. Cornford, *Plato's Cosmology*, p. 198)[20]

(*d*) Finally it must be noted that, as the primary meaning of material Principle (which in a certain sense involves somewhat generically the three meanings which we have explained) Plato names the concepts of necessity, [ἀνάγκη] and errant cause [πλανωμένη αἰτία]:

Now our foregoing discourse, save for a few matters, has set forth the works wrought by the craftsman of *Reason*; but we must now set beside them the things that come about of *Necessity*. For the generation of this universe was a *mixed result of the combination of Necessity and Reason.* Reason overruled Necessity by persuading her to guide the greatest part of the things that become towards what is best; in that way and on that principle *this universe was fashioned in the beginning by the victory of reasonable persuasion over Necessity.* If, then, we are really to tell how it came into being on this principle, we must bring in also the *Changeable Cause*—in what manner its nature is to cause motion. So we must return upon our steps thus, and taking, in its turn, a second principle concerned in the origin of these same things, start once more upon our present theme of our earlier discourses. (trans. F. M. Cornford, *Plato's Cosmology*, p. 160, slight change and emphasis added)[21]

By *Necessity* Plato understood here *the total lack of finalism* (sheer disteleology), which is something indeterminate and anomalous and hence casual, disorder in the global sense. And this is what is meant by the term *changeable cause* [errant cause] means; that is, *a cause that acts by chance and in an irregular way.*

And now we must explain what Plato expressly states in the *Timaeus,* and hence in writing, about the material Principle, we must ask ourselves what is the nexus that connects it to the *indefinite Dyad* about which the *Unwritten*

Doctrines speak and with which the indirect tradition connects it in a clear and explicit way.[22]

The expression *indefinite Dyad of the great-and-small* expresses in a concise way the nature of the material Principle. It consists in a tendency toward the indeterminate and the unlimited in the double direction of the great and the small in various ways.

This tendency *toward the great and the small;* that is, *toward the more and the less* in all the senses, *toward infinity,* evidently, applies to all that which in every area tends to the more or less, to excess and defect, to the unmeasured in opposite directions. Therefore, the *chora* of the *Timaeus* (and all that which the dialogues says involves the material Principle) *represents only a part of the Dyad,* or better an aspect, or, to speak in an even more precise way, the lowest level of it (the sensible level).

Therefore, the *chora* comes into the *Dyad,* but does not exhaust it at all. Evidently, the theory that we read in the *Timaeus* must occupy an important place also in the lectures of Plato, and perhaps with all four characteristics that we have pointed out; nevertheless it is limited only to what concerns sensible phenomena, and hence must be only as *a part of the vision of the whole.* In fact, the Dyad, as such, embraces a very extensive section, since it is involved *in the explanation of the whole of reality at all levels.*

In conclusion, we can certainly say that what Plato refers to concerning the material Principle in the *Timaeus* (and in general in various dialogues) is not exhaustive, and that, therefore, it is necessary to go up to the summit of the metaphysical abstraction achieved in the *Unwritten Doctrines,* in which the essential characteristics are preserved by the indirect tradition.

Evidently, the Principle antithetical to the One-Good is differentiated in the different levels of being, and in particular in the three great spheres: (*a*) the *ideal,* (*b*) the *intermediate,* (*c*) and the *sensible* spheres. In the sphere of the ideals the opposed Principle chiefly produces the differentiation and the graduation of the hierarchy; in the sphere of the intermediates it produces also the multiplicity of the same realities in a horizontal dimension and always at the intelligible level; instead, the *novum,* which is introduced in the sphere of the sensibles, is in being the origin of the very dimension of the sensible, with all its implications, with respect to the intelligible sphere.

Aristotle himself in the *Metaphysics* many times mentions the problem of the existence of an *intelligible matter* different than *sensible matter,* combining the problem of *intelligible matter* to the Platonic problem of the *Ideas* and the *mathematical entities.* Evidently, this essential position of the *Unwritten Doctrines* had exercised a rather remarkable influence on him, to the point that he felt obligated to bring it to our attention more than a few times.[23]

A final and very important point has still to be clarified. The indirect tradition states that Plato referred to the One as the cause of the Good and to the Dyad as the cause of *Evil.* However it does not say expressly that *all levels* of the Dyad were to be considered as such. Actually, it would be difficult to explain how on the intelligible level, where the Dyad acts as the principle of *plurality,* of *difference,* and *gradations,* it can be a cause of evil, and especially of what kind of evil. Or better, the only perspective according to which the Dyad can be considered as the cause of evil in the realm of the intelligible is the most general, in the measure in which the negative Ideas of the various pairs of contraries depend on it. Therefore, at the intelligible level, the Dyad is cause of negation (and in this sense of evil) only in the paradigmatic and abstract sense of the term. Instead, it is easy to understand in what sense the sensible Dyad must be considered cause of evil in the concrete sense. And what our philosopher says in the *Theaetetus* becomes clearer: that it is not possible that evil have a place near the Gods (that is, in the realm of the intelligible) but rather that it roams around in mortal nature, in this world.[24]

Thus, the Principle antithetical to the One-Good is the cause of evil chiefly (at least in a specific concrete way) at its lowest level. At the sensible level the Dyad is *not totally dominated* by the intelligible and the rational, and hence it allows openings to disorder and to a lack of measure very different from that which is verifiable on the level of the intelligible. There the Dyad causes, in the ultimate analysis, only *antithesis, difference, plurality,* and the *lowering of degrees,* whereas at the metaphysical level contrarily, in the sphere of the sensible the Dyad maintains an opening to the negative consequences of *becoming,* of *ontological malleability,* of *noetic insufficiency,* and *axiological problematicity,* in sum all the characteristics linked to the sensible sphere.

4.   The One as an emblematic key to the activity and works of the Demiurge

How exactly does the Demiurge work on this material Principle, forming it according to the world of the Ideas? Plato himself clearly responds by explaining that the Demiurge, insofar as he is good in the highest degree (that is, he is the best), works to achieve the best in the highest degree, by bringing order into disorder:

> He was good [ἀγαθός]; and in the good no jealousy in any matter can ever arise. So being without jealousy, he desired that all things should come as near as possible to being like himself... *Desiring, then, that all things should be good* [ἀγαθά] and, so far as might be, nothing imperfect, the God took over all that is visible—not at rest, but in discordant and unordered motion and *brought it from disorder* [ἐκ τῆς ἀταξίας] *into order* [εἰς τάξις], since he judged that order was in every way the better. Now it was not, nor can it ever be, permitted that the work of the *supremely good* (τῷ ἀρίστῳ) should be anything but that which is best (τὸ κάλλιστον). (trans. F. M. Cornford, *Plato's Cosmology,* p. 33 with emphasis added)[25]

In doing this, the Demiurge is grounded on the One (who, as we know, is, for Plato, the essence itself of the Good) and hence has worked to achieve *unity-in-multiplicity* in a variety of remarkable ways, by means of the *measure* and the *numerical and geometrical relations*.

Actually, Plato says, without the intervention of God everything (all the things that involve the material Principle) is without order or measure (ἀλόγως καὶ ἀμέτρως). And the ordering of the universe consists in producing *logoi*, numerical relations, measure, and hence in forming and modelling "according to forms and numbers" (εἴδεσι καὶ ἀρθμοῖς); and this produces the best and the most beautiful things (κάλλιστα καὶ ἄριστα). And now that which the Demiurge produces is a benefit infused in the material Principle by means of numerical relations (ἀναλογία) and with the proportioning of things in disorder according to numerical relations (συνηρμόσθαι ταῦτα ἀνὰ λόγον). In other words, the activity of the Demiurge-God consists in the bringing into those things that he finds to be lacking order (ἀτάκτως), measure, or symmetry (συμμετρία), and hence in bringing order and proportion to them, generally and particularly, in a way that leads them to be in an adequate relation with the measure (ὅπη δυνατὸν ἦν ἀνάλογα καὶ σύμμετρα εἶναι). And a few lines before these statements Plato tells us (in a passage to which we will return) that the science and the power of God are in the mixing up of *"the many into one"* (τὰ πολλὰ εἰς ἕν) and in the choice of the things *"from the many into the one"* (ἐξ ἑνὸς εἰς πολλά).[26]

Therefore, it is exactly by making reference to the *One (and to the various ways in which the One explicates and is realized in various areas)* that Plato has insistently characterized in general and in particular the activity and the works of the Demiurge, as we have said. Let us summarize in an outline this repeated insistence on the One as a key characterizing the activity and the work of the demiurgic Mind.

(*a*) The world is perfect, because it is realized as a *one* (ἕν). To be perfect it must be *one*, because the model in fact is one and the cosmos is the likeness of this model (*one* image of a *unique* model).[27]

(*b*) The *unity* of the cosmos, in addition, is guaranteed by the particular connection that the Demiurge has established between the four elements, which is a kind of connection which makes some things linked to a *one* in the highest degree (ὅτι μάλιστα ἕν). And indeed on this basis of numerical relation (ἀναλογία), which brings all things into *unity* (ἕν-πάντα), the Demiurge grounds *friendship* (φιλία); that is, the communion of all things among themselves.[28]

(c) In addition, the cosmos is constituted as a one-all; that is, as a *"one"*-*"whole"* (ἕν-ὅλον), because it is based on numerical calculation, which involves in a *one-whole* the *totality of things*, without allowing anything outside.[29]

(*d*) Also the spherical form of the cosmos realizes unity perfectly, since the sphere is a form that includes in itself all the forms (σχῆμα τὸ περι-ειληφὸς ἐν αὑτῷ πάντα ὁπόσα σχήματα) by realizing the maximum of likeness. And the same is repeated for rotational movement impressed on it, which is one form of movement in the same place and in the same way (and hence brings together stability and movement). And this holds also for autar-chic being, which makes the world one, insofar as it makes it have no need of anything outside itself.[30]

(*e*) Also time, created together with the cosmos, realizes a unity in its sliding, insofar as time imitates eternity that is a permanence *in unity* (ἐν ἑνί). And this imitation of the unity of eternity occurs *by means of number* (κατ' ἀριθμοῖς).[31]

(*f*) But in the creation (production) of the four sensible material elements, the Demiurge, by realizing the image of the ideal models, explicates a complex articulation of forms and numbers (εἴδεσι καὶ ἀριθμοῖς) that delimited the sensible material Principle, as we will see. And this is a perfect way of realizing the unity-in-the-multiplicity.[32]

(*g*) Finally, the soul itself, which the demiurgic Mind has created for the purposes of realizing a perfect model of the intelligible in the sensible, is one (*one* Idea, μία ἰδέα) and precisely *a unity* that consists of the *mixture of three realities* (ἐκ τριῶν ἕν) and a whole (ὅλον) structured according to the geometri-cal dimensions and numerical harmonies, which realize the Good; that is, Unity, Measure, Order, in a perfect way,[33] as we will explain better now.

5. The creationlike activities of the Platonic Demiurge against the Hellenic background

In this producing of *unity-in-multiplicity*, and hence in producing the "mixture" [34] of cosmological being and the structure that makes it possible, the *creative activity* of the Demiurge is explicated in the highest degree possible in the sphere of Greek thought. This notion is a form of semi-creatonism, if compared with that of the biblical notion. In fact, although the creative act of the biblical God is absolute or unconditioned, insofar as it does not presup-pose anything existent and is therefore a production *ex nihilo* (out of nothing), the creative activity of the Platonic demiurge is not unconditioned, insofar as it *presupposes*, in order for it to act, *the existence of two realities* having between them a bipolar metaphysical nexus: that of a being that is always identical, that functions as an *exemplar*, and that of a sensible *material Principle*, charac-terized by more-and-less, by unequal, by disorder and excess. *To bring this disordered reality into order is to bring it from not-being to being; that is, "to create" a generated being*, which is in the best possible way to realize sensibly ungenerated being (and this is the notion of creationism in the Hellenic sense). But to understand it thoroughly we must consider some concepts we have already acknowledged and summarize in a synoptic fashion the things we have stated and thus complete them.

(*a*) The mediation between the sphere of eternal being and sensible reality, and hence creation (passage from not-being toward being), implies, according to Plato, *a complex numerical and geometrical articulation; because only through this, in his judgment, is it possible to bring down the intelligible into the sensible.* But this very complex play of numerical and geometrical articulations would be incomprehensible, except it were considered the *metaphysical-numeric structure of the Platonic Ideas and the numerical nexuses* (ἀριθμοί, λόγοι), which locates in particular and in general each Idea with all the others; that is, the complex question of the Idea-Numbers, which the new hermeneutic paradigm has brought into the limelight and has perfectly clarified, as we have shown.

(*b*) This complex metaphysical-numeric system at a purely theoretical level implies an *intermediate mediating realm. The mathematical entities* with the numeric and geometrical system that they reproduce form exactly the *mediating structure* (and for this reason are said precisely to be intermediates) between the ideal Numbers, the Ideas or eternal Forms, on the one hand, and sensible things, on the other.

In effect, the mathematical entities are the necessary mediation between each Form or idea that is *"one"* alone (ἓν ἕκαστον μόνον) and the multiplication of the same in a plurality. And, precisely for this reason, the intermediate mathematical entities are immobile and eternal as the Forms; but they are many alike. Hence, the passage between the Ideas and the things corresponding to them, which is a passage that occurs between the *One* (ἕν) and the *Many* (πολλά), is explained with the introduction of *many eternal beings similar among them* (ἀΐδια καὶ ἀκίνητα—πόλλ' ἄττα ὅμοια), so that between the *ungenerated and incorruptible Form-one*—on the one hand—and the corresponding *many generated and corruptible similars*—on the other hand. The *many ungenerated and eternal similars* are posited as intermediates, which are precisely the "mathematical entities." [35] And this explains well, consequently, in general the unfolding of the bipolar structure of the real and in particular the complex fundamental nexuses existing between the transcendence of the world of Ideas with respect to the sensible world and its participation in the world of Ideas and the radical overcoming of the objections against the theory of Ideas and in particular the overcoming of the difficulties centered upon their transcendence.

Let us pause on three points that characterize in a most perfect manner the creative activity in the Hellenic sense of the Demiurge, which consists in the *bringing the One into the Many* by means of mathematical entities and the sphere of numbers: (*a*) by the creation of *time*, (*b*) the creation of the *elements*, and (*c*) the creation of the *soul*.

(*a*) Let us begin from the analysis of the creation of *time*. The exemplar to which the Demiurge refers in the creation of the cosmos is eternal (the eternal Living thing; that is, the global Idea of the cosmos that implies the essence of life). Now, the eternal is a perduring *in unity* (ἐν ἑνί). But how is it is possible to imitate this *perduring in unity*, which is the essential trait of eternity? Once again, the *mediation of number* makes possible the response. The image of eternity is the effect of the running together of time; that is, *the effect of the running together of the unity, according to numerical distinctions* realized in day and night, in month and year, and hence it is moved cyclically *according to number*. From this cyclical movement *numerically determined* arises the "it was" and the "it will be" of time. And for this "it was" and "it will be" cannot correctly be referred to eternal entities. For these hold only the "it is," because "it was" and "it will be" are nothing but the moving numbered *copy* of the eternal "it is," which remains in the one.[36] Here is the important text:

> Now the nature of that Living Being was eternal, and this character it was impossible to confer in full completeness on the generated thing. But he took thought to make, as it were, a moving likeness of eternity; and, at the same time that he ordered the Heaven, he made of eternity that abides in unity [ἐν ἑνί] an everlasting likeness moving according to number [κατ᾽ ἀριθμόν]—that to which we have given the name Time. (trans. F. M. Cornford, *Plato's Cosmology*, pp. 97-8)[37]

Hence for Plato time was generated together with the heaven, and "according to a model";[38] and thus, by reproducing this model, time and the heaven, made together, are and will be always (time will perish together with the heaven, if, by hypothesis, the heaven perish; and, naturally, also vice versa).

Therefore, Plato formulated a truly explosive, new, difficult and original thesis; that his own followers would not accept in a appropriate fashion, as they understood it in an allegorical-didactic key, or rejected it, as Aristotle did. The clear distinction between the eternal and the temporal, and the information that it is not correct to apply it to the eternal "was" and "shall be," solves at its root a whole series of difficulties, which in the history of Western thought have arisen at various levels and at various times.

(*b*) The production of the *four elements: water, air, earth, and fire* are most complex and articulated. As we have pointed out earlier, had originally only "some traces of itself" within the scope of the material Principle; that is, they were in a total state of *disorder*. God produces them (he "creates" them in the Hellenic sense) and he disposes them in a beautiful and good way by working on them *through forms and numbers*, hence by producing a "mixture" of the material Principle and that which of the Ideas of the four elements is realizable in the material Principle itself by means of numerical and geometrical forms. Here is an exemplary text, which we have already read in part:

Before that, all these kinds were *without proportion* [ἀλόγως] or measure [ἀμέτρως]. Fire, water, earth, and air possessed indeed some vestiges of their own nature, but were altogether in such a condition as we should expect for anything when deity is absent from it. Such being their nature at the time when *the ordering of the universe* was taken in hand, the god then *began by giving them a distinct configuration by means of shapes and numbers* [εἴδεσί τε καὶ ἀριθμοῖς]. That the god framed them *with the greatest possible perfection, which they had not before, must be taken, earlier all, as a principle we constantly assert.* (trans. F. M. Cornford, *Plato's Cosmology*, p. 198, emphasis added)[39]

In producing the four elements, the Demiurge starts from two forms of the most beautiful *triangles*: from a *right-angled isosceles triangle* and from that obtained by *dividing into two an equilateral triangle with a perpendicular* (or by dividing the same triangle into six triangles, tracing a perpendicular from each side to the opposite vertex). On the basis of the *isosceles triangle* only one of the four elements is produced by the Demiurge in the following way. Coordinating four isosceles triangles with right angles, joined about a center, *a square* is obtained, and combining six *squares* in a suitable manner he produces a *cube*; and this constitutes the atomistic structure that configures the element *earth*. By combining, instead six *triangles* of the second type, there are *equilateral triangles*, which suitably multiplied and combined in an exact fashion (which Plato indicates, but which here it is not possible to go into the details, because the discussion would carry us outside of our principal theme) give origin to (1) the *tetrahedron* (a regular pyramid on a equilateral base), which constitutes the structure of *fire*; (2) the *octohedron*, which constitutes the structure of the *air*; (3) the *icosahedron*, which constitutes the structure of *water*.

Evidently, these regular solids of a geometrical structure that constitute the four elements are not of themselves visible by reason of their smallness (being like atoms), although they become visible by rejoining together in great numbers.

In conclusion, the rationalization of sensible bodies and sensible corporeals in general depends exactly on their *geometrical and mathematical structure*. The physical-sensible corporeal reflects the structure of the intelligible corporeal (geometrical); that is, it is "the mixture of a combination of *necessity* and *intelligence*."[40] Points, lines, surfaces, three-dimensional structures on the plane of intermediate, and ideal entities are purely intelligible; instead, entities synthetically combined or "mixed" with the sensible material Principle they give rise to bodies that we see and touch, by means of a *capillary penetration* that channels the material sensible Principle, chaotic in itself, *down to the smallest particulars*, according to the atomistic structure on the basis of regular geometrical solids.

(*c*) The work of the creation of the *soul of the world* (and of souls in general) is a still more complex action. It is produced by means of a twofold mixture: one, so to say, in a *vertical* sense and one in a *horizontal* sense. With the mixture in a vertical sense, the Demiurge produces three intermediates in this way: (1) an intermediate Being between indivisible Being and divisible Being, (2) an intermediate Identity between indivisible Identity and divisible Identity, and (3) an intermediate Difference between indivisible Difference and divisible Difference. With the mixture we have called horizontal, instead, the Demiurge produces three intermediate realities (intermediate Being, intermediate Identity, intermediate Difference) in a way to form a *unity*, deriving from three realities (ἐκ τριῶν ἕν).[41]

Plato insists, moreover, on the *geometrico-dimensional structure* of the soul of the world (in an ideal sense of lines and surfaces, which form the global figure of the cosmos), which from the middle is extended to every part and wrapped up wholly about the world itself, in a circle, from outside. And, in addition to the *dimensional* structure of the soul, he insists on the *numerical* structure, showing that this numerical structure is identical with the *musical*, and because of this the movements that the soul imprints on the world are *harmonious* (the movements that in this way the soul imprints, reduce into harmonic order the chaotic movements of the material Principle).[42]

With the intelligence infused by the Demiurge, the Soul of the world has the function of realizing in concrete the great design of the Demiurge and through the Demiurge it participates the ideal world. The passage between the Ideas and the sensible corporeal world is based on its geometrical and mathematical dimensional structure, and hence it summarizes analogically the whole of reality, *constituting true union between the metaphysical world and the physical world.*[43]

Let us remember that the Demiurge also creates all the stars and the heavenly bodies as divine and eternal living beings, with spherical bodies made chiefly of fire, and all endowed with intelligent souls, strictly connected to the intelligence of the soul of the world. And, in addition, he creates the souls of men in a wholly analogous fashion. In the "mixture" out of which he creates these souls, he utilized what remains of the three elements with which he created the soul of the universe, by mixing them "almost in the same way," and in this way he makes men's souls immortal.[44]

Therefore, in all senses the creationism, the Demiurge is a *bringing order out of disorder in all parts with exactness according to numerical and geometrical perfectly proportioned relations.*[45]

6. The Demiurge (and not the Idea of the Good) is the God of Plato

The supreme God, for Plato, is the Demiurge (that is, the highest Mind), which, as the *Timaeus* states, it is "the best of intelligible beings" and "the best of causes." [46] The Idea of the Good, instead, is "the Divine" (τὸ θεῖον). In other words, the Platonic God is "he who is good" in the *personal* sense, whereas "the Idea of the Good" is the Good in the *impersonal* sense.[47]

To understand this, two essential points are to be noted:

(*a*) God for the Greeks has something beyond itself; from the hierarchical viewpoint, a rule or some supreme rules, to which it must refer or attend. And in this sense, the Platonic God, which is the supreme Mind, has beyond itself hierarchically a rule or some rules, to which it must attend and toward which it must direct its activities. Therefore, in this perspective, the Good is the supreme rule (and the world of Ideas in it complexity constitutes that totality of rules) by which God is inspired and to which God attend, for the purpose of bringing it into actuality in all areas; and for this He is absolutely the Good and the Best; that is, that being nearest to the Good, insofar as He is Mind that explicates and produces the Good in a global sense.

(*b*) Parmenides introduced to Greek thought the conception that Mind is possible only if it has being as its foundation and if it is expressed in and through being. Hence, also a supreme Mind, insofar as Mind, for the Greeks does not produce its own foundation, but presupposes it. And in this sense, also for Plato the supreme Mind implies as its foundation the Good (and in general the being of the Ideas and the primary and supreme Principles).

So, *God is the unconditioned Good*, because He acts in function of the Idea of the *Good*; that is, of the *One* and the *supreme Measure*, producing them perfectly in the measure possible. Therefore, God acts in the best way, by ordering and measuring the disorder, that derives from the material Principle antithetical to the Good, in the vision of the bipolar structure with which we are familiar; that is, unifying the multiple.

And God *wished*[48] that all things become as close as possible to Him, who realizes in the highest degree the One-Good, by fixing in them Good, Measure, and Order.

Hence, God, insofar as he achieves the supreme Measure is also the one who achieves *unity-in-multiplicity*; that is, *connects the One and the Many and the Many and the One in a perfect manner*. The *Timaeus* states it, as a matter of fact, continually; but it is pointed out expressly and conceptually many times, in a passage which we have made allusions, and that it is appropriate at this time to consider: "divinity has knowledge and *power* sufficient to blend *the many into one* [τὰ πολλὰ εἰς ἕν] and *to resolve the one into many* [ἐξ ἑνὸς εἰς πολλά], but no man is now, or ever will be, equal to either task" (trans. F. M. Cornford, *Plato's Cosmology*, p. 278).[49]

Naturally there is no man who, on his own account, taking himself as a measure of all things (as Protagoras said), knows or has the power to produce (even in a different way), what God does. Man, hence, if he wishes to act well, must do what God himself did after having created the Gods as models by imitating His power in the creation of things and achieving unity-in-multi-plicity, and in this way produce order and harmony. And this is indeed the way in which Plato also understood justice and virtue; that is, as manifestations of that *metaphysical nexus that unifies all things*. And it is an interpretation of *what binds all things together* (of *friendship* and *community, what makes the Whole one*) proposed at the highest level of Hellenic thought.[50]

VI. EPISTEMOLOGY AND DIALECTIC

1. Anamnesis, root and condition of knowledge in the *Meno*

We have spoken of the intelligible world, of its structure and the way in which it is reflected in the sensible. Now we must examine in what way man can gain access cognitively to the intelligible. And, in general, we must reply to the following questions: How does knowledge occur and what is it? How does the knowledge of the intelligible differ from knowledge of the sensible?

The problem of knowledge has been a concern of some of the preceding philosophers, but it cannot be said that any of them formulated the question in any specific or definitive way. Plato is the first to frame it clearly, even if, obviously, the solutions proposed in his writings, as always, are open to completion, and only in the *Unwritten Doctrines* achieve the highest summit.

The first response to the problem of knowledge is found in the *Meno*.[1] The Eristics (Sophists) had attempted to capriciously avoid the problem by maintaining that inquiry and knowledge are impossible: in fact, one cannot seek to know what is not known, because if one were to find it, it would not be recognized, since we lack the means to recognize it; and neither is it meaningful to seek what is already known, as it is already known: "Why, on what lines will you look, Socrates, for a thing of whose nature you know nothing at all? Pray, what sort of thing, amongst those that you know not, will you treat us to as the object of your search? Or even supposing, at the best, that you hit upon it, how will you know it is the thing you did not know?"[2]

It is to overcome this aporia that Plato found a new way: knowledge is *anamnesis*; that is, a form of "recollection," a reemergence from what has always existed within the interior of our soul.

Let us see the explanation of this Platonic doctrine, so frequently misunderstood. Many scholars say that it is only a myth and not at all of a dialectical and theoretical character and hence has little value. Actually, the issue is far from being that easily reduced and eliminated.

The *Meno* presents the doctrine in a twofold manner, one *mythically* and the other *dialectically*; and we need to examine them both in order not to risk betraying Plato's thought.

The first way, of mythico-religious nature, is referred to the Orphic-Pythagorean doctrine of priests, according to which, as we know, the soul is immortal and has been reborn many times: death is only the end of one life of the soul in the body; birth is only the beginning again of a new life, which is connected to a series of *preceding ones*. The soul, therefore, has seen and knows all reality in its totality: the realities here and the realities there (in the beyond). If this is so, Plato concludes, it is easy to understand how the soul can *come to know* and *comprehend*: it must simply be drawing *from itself* the truth that it essentially possesses, and that it has *always* possessed: and this "drawing from itself" is a "recollection." Here is the famous passage of the *Meno*:

> Seeing that the soul is immortal and has been born many times, and has beheld all things both in this world and in the nether realms, she has acquired knowledge of all and everything; so that it is no wonder that she should be able to recollect all that she knew before about virtue and other things. For as all nature is akin, *and the soul has learned all things, there is no reason why we should not, by remembering but one single thing–an act which men call learning–discover everything else,* if we have courage and faint not in the search. So we must not hearken to that captious argument: it would make us idle, and is pleasing only to the indolent ear, whereas the other makes us energetic and inquiring?[3]

Well, if Plato were limited to saying this, they would be perfectly correct who decry the merely mythological character of the doctrine, and hence there would be no support for a strictly theoretical understanding of "recollection": which as a matter of fact is based on myth–and as it is formulated recollection is indeed based on myth–therefore it could never have any other role than that of myth.

But, immediately nearby, in the *Meno*, the roles are exactly reversed: that which was a conclusion becomes speculatively interpreted and verified by a piece of factual experimentation, whereas that which at first was proposed as myth functions as a foundation and becomes instead a conclusion. In fact, after the mythological exposition, Plato makes a "maieutic experiment," which has an extraordinary demonstrative impact. Plato questions a slave boy who is absolutely ignorant of geometry, and the slave-boy begins to solve, only by means of Socratic maieutic questioning, a complex geometrical problem (in essence implying a knowledge of the Pythagorean theorem). Hence–as Plato then argues–since the slave boy did not learn geometry, and since he has not been given the solution, *he was capable of knowing how to reach the solution strictly by himself* (although with the assistance of the dialectical method). We must conclude then that he had drawn it from himself, from his soul; that is, he "recollected" it.[4] And here, as is clear, the basis of the argument, far from being a myth, *is a confirmation and proof of the fact, that the slave-boy, as every human being in general, can draw and recover from himself a truth that he did not know beforehand and that no one had taught him.*

Further, then, from the presence of truth in the soul, Plato infers the immortality or deathlessness of the soul: if the soul possesses some truths that were not previously grasped in its present life, which is hidden but that the soul can bring to awareness, this means that it has always possessed it from the beginning before its birth as a human being in which it now exists, again: the soul, then, is deathless, indeed, in a certain sense as permanent in being, as the truth is.

Here is the conclusion that the Platonic Socrates drew after showing up everybody, by means of the maieutic experiment, that the uncultured slave boy, guided only by appropriate questions, was able to solve a difficult geometrical problem and achieve the truth:

> *Socrates* - Without anyone having taught him [the slave boy], and only through questions put to him, he will understand, recovering the knowledge out of himself?
>
> *Meno* - Yes.
>
> *Socrates* - And is not this recovery of knowledge, in himself and by himself, recollection?
>
> *Meno* - Certainly.
>
> *Socrates* - And must he not have either once acquired or always had the knowledge he now has?
>
> *Meno* - Yes.
>
> *Socrates* - Now if he always had it, he was always in a state of knowing; and if he acquired it at some time, he could not have acquired it in this life. Or has someone taught him geometry? You see, he can do the same as this with all geometry and every branch of knowledge. Now, can anyone have taught him all this? You ought surely to know, especially if he was born and bred in your house.
>
> *Meno* - Well, I know that no one has ever taught him.
>
> *Socrates* - And has he these opinions, or has he not?
>
> *Meno* - He must have them, Socrates, evidently.
>
> *Socrates* - And if he did not acquire them in this present life, is it not obvious at once that he had them and learnt them during some other time?
>
> *Meno* - Apparently.
>
> *Socrates* - And this must have been time when he was not a human being?
>
> *Meno* - Yes.
>
> *Socrates* - So if in both of these periods - when he was and was not a human being - he has had true opinions in him which have only to be awakened by questioning to become knowledge, his soul must have had this cognizance throughout all time? For clearly he has always either been or not been a human being.
>
> *Meno* - Evidently.
>
> *Socrates* - And if the truth of all things that are is always in our soul, then the soul must be immortal; so that you should take heart and, whatever you do not happen to know at present—that is what you do not remember—you must endeavor to search out and recollect.[5]

Scholars have frequently repeated that the doctrine of *anamnesis* arose in Plato through the Orphic-Pythagorean influence; but after what we have explained, it is clear that we must give weight, for the origin of the doctrine, to the influence of the *Socratic maieutic method*. It is evident, in fact, that to produce the truth in the soul, *the truth must exist in the soul*. The doctrine of anamnesis is not only presented as a corollary of the doctrine of Orphic-Pythagorean reincarnation, but also as the *justification and confirmation* (that is, as an epistemologico-metaphysical foundation) *of the very possibility of the Socratic maieutic method.*

2.   Reconfirmation of the doctrine of anamnesis in the subsequent dialogues

A further proof of anamnesis is offered by Plato in the *Phaedo*,[6] chiefly in relation to mathematical knowledge (which had enormous importance in the determination of the discovery of the intelligible).[7] Plato argues essentially as follows. We notice the existence *of equal things, the greater and lesser, the square and the circular, and other similars*, with our senses. But, with a careful analysis, we discover that the data furnished by experience–all the data, without exception of any kind–is never completely adequate to *the corresponding notion that we undoubtedly possess.* No sensible thing is ever "perfectly" equal to another sensible thing, no sensible thing is ever "perfectly" and "absolutely" [in every respect] squared or circular, *rather we have these notions of "absolutely" and "perfectly" equal, square, and circular.* So it is necessary to conclude that there is a *inequality* between the data of experience and the notion and knowledge that we possess. Our knowledge involves *something more* than the data of experience.

But where can we have derived this *"more"*? If, as is obvious, it is not derived and cannot structurally come from the senses; that is, from outside, we can only conclude that *it comes from within us.*

Yet, it cannot be the product of the thinking subject: the thinking subject does not "create" this *extra*, he rather "finds" it or "discovers" it. It is instead imposed on the subject himself *absolutely.* Hence, the senses provide us with only imperfect knowledge. Our mind (our intelligence, our spirit) on the occasion of this data, dredges up and goes into itself and turns inward, finding there the corresponding perfected knowledge. And since it did not produce it, the only conclusion *remaining is that it found it within itself and recovered it from itself as an "original possession" "by bringing it to mind."*

In this way, mathematics reveals that our soul is in possession of *perfect knowledge*, which did not derive from sensible things, and which reflects, on the contrary, models or paradigms to which sensible things approximate, but without becoming identical with them, as we know from the exposition of Plato's ontological and metaphysical doctrine. The same argument is repeated by Plato with respect to various ethical and aesthetic notions (*good, beautiful, justice, health*, and similars). We find them within ourselves and make use of them in our judgments, and obviously, they were *not* derived solely from sensible experience, because they are more perfect than the data given in experience. Hence, they contain that *extra*, that cannot be justified except in the foregoing manner; that is, by coming to our awareness as an original and unalloyed *possession of our soul*, which is regained then in an explicit manner as a *recollection.*

Here is the passage of the *Phaedo* which contains the resolutive moment of the argument:

"Now then," he said, "do the equal pieces of wood and the equal things of which we were speaking just now affect us in this way: Do they seem to us to be equal as abstract equality is equal, or do they somehow fall short of being like abstract equality?"

"They fall very far short of it," said he.

"Do we agree, then, that when anyone on seeing a thing thinks, 'This thing that I see aims at being like some other thing that exists, but falls short and is unable to be like that thing, but is inferior to it,' he who thinks thus must of necessity have previous knowledge of the thing which he says the other resembles but falls short of?"

"We must."

"Well then, is this just what happened to us with regard to the equal things and equality in the abstract?"

"It certainly is."

"Then we must have had knowledge of equality before the time when we first saw equal things and thought, 'All these things are aiming to be like equality but fall short.'"

"That is true."

"And we agree, also, that we have not gained knowledge of it, and that it is impossible to gain this knowledge, except by sight or touch or some other of the senses? I consider that all the senses are alike."

"Yes, Socrates, they are all alike, for the purposes of our argument."

"Then it is through the senses that we must learn that all sensible objects strive after absolute equality and fall short of it. Is that our view?"

"Yes."

"Then before we began to see or hear or use the other senses we must somewhere have gained a knowledge of abstract or absolute equality, if we were to compare with it the equals which we perceive by the senses, and see that all such things yearn to be like abstract quality but fall short of it."

"That follows necessarily from what we have said before, Socrates."

"And we saw and heard and had the other senses as soon as we were born?"

"Certainly."

"But, we say, we must have acquired a knowledge of equality before we had these senses?"

"Yes."

"Then it appears that we must have acquired it before we were born."

"It does."

"Now if we had acquired that knowledge before we were born, and were born with it, we knew before we were born and at the moment of birth not only the equal and the greater and the less, but all such abstractions? For our present argument is no more concerned with the equal than with absolute beauty and the absolute good and the just and the holy, and in short, with all those things which we stamp with the seal of 'absolute' in our dialectic process of questions and answers; so that we must necessarily have acquired knowledge of all these before our birth." [8]

Recollection structurally supposes a mark impressed in the soul from the Idea, an original metaphysical "vision" of the ideal world that still, even if veiled, remains in the soul of each one of us.[9]

Plato has constantly maintained the theory of recollection and has expressly stated it in the *Phaedrus* (which is later than the *Republic*), as well as in the late dialogue, the *Timaeus*. In the *Phaedrus* he writes:

> For a human being must understand a general conception [κατ' εἶδος] formed by collecting into a unity [εἰς ἕν] by means of reason the many perceptions of the senses; and this a recollection [ἀνάμνησις] of those things which our soul once beheld, when it journeyed with God and, lifting its vision earlier the things which we now say exist, rose up into real being.[10]
>
> For, it has been said, every soul of man has by the law of nature beheld the realities, otherwise it would not have entered into a human being, but it is not easy for all souls to gain from earthly things a recollection [ἀναμιμνῄσκεσθαι] of those realities....[11]

And in the *Timaeus* the Demiurge, immediately after having created the souls destined to become human beings, and after having placed them within stars (in order that through them they would pass into bodies), shows them the original truths: those truths that, entering into bodies, are obliterated, but not entirely.

> And when He had compounded the whole [of what remained of the elements with which he had constructed the soul of the universe] He divided it into souls equal in number to the stars, and each several soul He assigned to one star, and setting them each as it were in a chariot *He showed them the nature of the Universe* [τὴν τοῦ παντὸς φύσιν ἔδειξεν] *and declared unto them the laws of destiny.* [12]

Just as we have exposed and interpreted, the Platonic doctrine of knowledge as a *recollection of the Ideas* becomes something less fantastic than some previously-mentioned interpretations would have lead us to believe. Some scholars have seen in the recollection of the Ideas *the first Western philosophical discovery of the a priori.* This expression is clearly not Platonic, but undoubtedly may be used as long as it is understood that it does not connote the Kantian *a priori* or the Neo-Kantian or generally any idealistic meaning,[13] because these involve a subjective *a priori* (although in a purely transcendental sense), but on the contrary it involves an objective *a priori*, which the Platonist Rosmini claimed against Kant. The Ideas are in fact absolutely objective realities, which, by means of recollection, are objects of the mind. And since the mind in recollection *grasps* and does not *produce* the Ideas, and grasps them *independently from experience*, even if within the context of experience (we must see the equal sensible things to "recall" the Equal-in-itself, and so on), we can properly speak of the discovery of the *a priori;* that is, of the first conception of the a priori in the history of Western philosophy.[14]

3. The kinds of knowledge delineated in the *Republic*

It is evident, nevertheless that more than knowledge, recollection explains the "root" or the "possibility" of knowledge, insofar as it explains essentially only this: knowledge is possible since we have in the soul *an original intuition of the truth.* The specific stages and ways of knowing have to be determined further, and Plato has specified them in the *Republic* and in the dialectical dialogues.

In the *Republic* Plato begins with the principle already known to us that knowledge is proportional to being, on condition that *only that which is really real is perfectly knowable, not-being is absolutely unknowable.*

But since we know that an *intermediate reality* exists between being and not-being; that is, the sensible which (we have seen earlier) is a mixture of being and not-being, then Plato concludes that this intermediate is a knowledge exactly intermediate between science and nescience, a knowledge that is not really knowledge and is called "opinion" *doxa.* Here is the passage of the *Republic* which expresses these concepts quite handily:

"Does he who knows know something or nothing: Do reply in his behalf."
"I will reply," he said, "that he knows something."
"Is it something that is or is not?"
"That is. How could that which is not be known?"
"We are sufficiently assured of this, then, even if we should examine it from every point of view, *that that which entirely 'is' is entirely knowable, and that which in no way 'is' is in every way unknowable?*"
"Most sufficiently."
"Good. If a thing, then, is so conditioned as both to be and not to be, would it not lie *between that which absolutely and unqualifiedly is and that which in no way is?*"
"Between."
"Then since knowledge pertains to that which is and ignorance of necessity to that which is not, *for that which lies between we must seek for something between nescience and science, if such a thing there be.*"
"By all means."
"Is there a thing which we call opinion?"
"Surely."
"Is it a different faculty from science or the same?"
"A different."
"Then opinion is set over one thing and science over another, each virtue of its own distinctive power or faculty."
"That is so".[15]

The forms of knowledge are therefore two: the lowest is *doxa* (δόξα), the highest is *episteme* (ἐπιστήμη) or science; the first concerns the *sensible*, the second the *supersensible*.

Opinion, nevertheless for Plato is often deceptive. It can also be *veracious* and *correct*, but *never can it guarantee its own correctness and it remains always fleeting, just like the sensible to which it refers*. To ground opinion and make it stable, it would be necessary, as Plato says in the *Meno*, to connect it to *causal reasoning*; that is, to stabilize it with the knowledge of the cause (of the Idea). But, then, it ceases to be simply an opinion and becomes true opinion or *knowledge* (*episteme*), and therefore it will move from the sensible to the supersensible.[16]

But Plato further specifies that both *doxa* and *episteme* each have two subdivisions: *doxa* is divided into *imagination* (εἰκασία) and *belief* (πίστις); knowledge is divided into *mediate knowledge* (διάνοια) and pure *intellection* (νόησις).

On the basis of this principle explained, each kind and form of knowledge is referred to a corresponding kind and form of reality or being. *Eikasia* and *pistis* correspond to two kinds of sensibles, respectively, the first refers to the shadows and images of sensible things, the second to the things and sensible objects themselves. *Dianoia* and *noesis* refer in their turn, to two kinds of intelligibles: *dianoia*is the knowledge of mathematico-geometrical reality, *noesis* is thepure dialectic of the Ideas.

Διάνοια (mediate knowledge, as some appropriately translate this term) can still be concerned with visible elements (for example, the figures that are drawn during a mathematical demonstration), but it is characterized especially by grasping mathematical entities that, as we know, are ontologically "intermediates." Νόησις grasps, by means of dialectic, the Ideas and the supreme and unconditioned Principle (that is, the Idea of the Good) with all their grounding and participating nexuses.[17]

Sphere of Knowledge		Sphere of Being	
δόξα (*doxa*) or opinion	εἰκασία (*eikasia*) or imagination	Sensible Images	Sensible World
	πίστις (*pistis*) or belief	Sensible Objects	

ἐπιστήμη (*episteme*) or science	διάνοια (*dianoia*) or mediate knowledge	mathematical objects (intermediate entities of the Unwritten Doctrine)	The Intelligible World
	νόησις (*noesis*) or intellection	Ideas and Idea of the Good	

We can outline visually the forms and kinds of knowledge and their respective forms and kinds of realities, according to what Plato[18] himself indicated, with the famous image of the line, as shown above.

4. Dialectic

Naturally, the ordinary man is confined to the first two kinds of 'knowledge;' that is, to opinion. Mathematicians reach *dianoetic* thinking. But only the philosopher rises to noesis, the highest science. The intellect and intellection, after learning, leave behind sensations and the sensible and every element linked to the sensible, it grasps the pure Ideas, in their positive and negative nexuses, with both a discursive and intuitive procedure, with all its implications and exclusive connections; and rising from Idea to Idea, it finally grasps the supreme Idea (which is the supreme and first Principle; that is, the Good = One) and hence to the unconditioned. And this procedure by which the intellect passes from sensibles to intelligibles and thence moves from Idea to Idea is "dialectic," so that the philosopher is the "dialectician." And it is understood, therefore, from the *Republic* onward, that Plato tried to deepen in all ways this concept of dialectic even in his written works in addition to his oral discussions (and so the dialogues after the *Republic* are called *dialectical* dialogues).

Now, there is an ascending dialectic, which frees the soul from the senses and from the sensible, and goes on to the Ideas and then, from Idea to Idea, to the supreme Idea with a *synoptic* method (which slowly embraces the multiplicity in a unity). On this aspect of dialectic, the *Republic* is based:

"Then," said I, "is not dialectics the only process of inquiry that advances in this manner, doing away with *hypotheses* [ὑποθέσεις] up to the first *principle* [ἐπ᾽ αὐτὴν τὴν ἀρχήν] itself to find confirmation there? And is it literally true that when the eye of the soul is sunk in the barbaric slough of the Orphic myth, dialectic gently draws it forth and leads it up, employing as helpers and co-operators in this conversion." (trans. Paul Shorey, LCL 203, 205)[19]

"And so you also call a *dialectician the man who can give a reasoned account of the reality of each thing*? To the man who can give no such account, either to himself or another, you will to that extent deny knowledge of his subject?"

"How could I say he had it?"

"How could I say he had it?"

"And the same applies to the Good. The man who cannot *by reason distinguish the Form of the Good from all others,* who does not, as in a battle survive all refutations, eager to argue according to reality and not according to opinion, and who does not come through all the tests without faltering in reasoned discourse–such a man you will say does not know the Good itself, nor any kind of good. If he gets hold of some image of it, it is by opinion, not knowledge; he is dreaming and asleep throughout his present life, and, before he wakes up here, he will arrive in Hades and go to sleep forever." (trans. G. M. A. Grube, p. 185, emphasis added)[20]

And there will be, then, a *descending* dialectic, which goes in the opposite direction, beginning from the highest Idea, or from the general Ideas and proceeding by division (a *diairetic* method). By distinguishing little by little particular Ideas contained in the generals on the basis of the articulations into which it is explicated, the soul reaches the Ideas that do not include in themselves further Ideas. Hence the soul arrives at a stable place that one given Idea occupies in the hierarchical structure of the ideal world and therefore it comes to comprehend the complex framework of the numerical relations that bind the parts and the whole.

But to comprehend what we have said; that is, to understand these two dialectical methods and their connections, it is necessary to make some further clarifications.

5. The protologic system of dialectic hinges on the one and the many

What we have stated so far does not yet touch the foundations and the protological system of dialectic; that is, those grounding and globally influential nexuses that are the framework of dialectic itself, in general and in particular.

Three points are worthy of special consideration. (*a*) In the first place, we need to consider the fact that the *synoptic* method and the *diairetic* method intersect in various ways and at different places, since one is understandable only in connection with the other, and vice versa. (*b*) In the second place, it is necessary to advert to the fact that the grounding nexuses consist in the relations of the One=many, and that the stages of the two dialectical methods are ones that bring us little by little *to embrace the multiplicity in a unity, to the point of coming to the highest form of unity.* The other carries to resolution diairetically the unity in the multiplicity and thus to understand how *the one is explicated in the many.* (*c*) In conclusion, dialectic in the global sense brings to perfect comprehension the "mirabile" [the wonderful] about which the *Philebus* states; that is, to understand that "the *many* are *one* and *one* is *many*," and, at its highest level, it is exactly that knowledge which the Demiurge (the divine Intelligence) possesses in a perfect manner, that is to say:

"Knowledge–to blend the *many* into *one* and dissolve them from *unity* into the *many*."[21]

Here are three basic passages which bring out the three points that we have pointed out:

> *Socrates*: For the most part I think our festal hymn has really been just a festive entertainment, but we did casually allude to a certain pair of procedures, and it would be very agreeable if we could seize their significance in a scientific fashion.
> *Phaedrus*: What procedures do you mean?
> *Socrates*: *The first is that in which we bring a dispersed plurality under a single form, seeing it all together–the purpose being to define so-and-so, and thus to make plain whatever may be chosen as the topic for exposition–*
> *Phaedrus*: And what is the second procedure you speak of, Socrates?
> *Socrates*: The reverse of the other, *whereby we are enabled to divide into forms, following the objective articulation; we are not to attempt to hack off parts* like a clumsy butcher–
> *Phaedrus*: That is perfectly true.
> *Socrates*: Believe me, Phaedrus, I am myself a lover of these *divisions* and *collections*, that I may gain the power to speak and to think, and whenever I deem another man able to discern an objective unity and plurality, I follow 'in his footsteps where he leads as a god.'(trans. R. Hackforth, Bollingen, pp. 511-2 with emphasis added)[22]

> *Stranger*: *Dividing according to kinds, not taking the same form for a different one or a different one for the same–is not that the business of the science of dialectic?*
> *Theaetetus*: Most certainly.
> *Stranger*: And the man who can do that discerns clearly [1a] *The Idea everywhere extended throughout many, where each remains a separated unity, and in addition* [1b] *many <Idea> as different from one another, embraced from without by one unique <Idea>*; [2a] *and again one single <Idea> connected in a unity through many wholes; and in addition* [2b] *many <Ideas> as entirely marked off apart.* That means knowing how to distinguish, kind by kind, in what ways the several kinds can or cannot combine. (trans. F. M. Cornford, Bollingen, pp. 999-1000 with minor additions, changes, and added emphasis)[23]

> We get this *identity of the one and the many* cropping up everywhere as the result of the sentences we utter; in every single sentence ever uttered, in the past and in the present, there it is. What we are dealing with is a problem that will assuredly never cease to exist; this is not its first appearance. Rather it is in my view, something incidental to sentences themselves, *never to pass, never to fade.* (trans. R. Hackforth, Bollingen, p. 1091)[24]

To this very complex specification of the nexuses One-many and many-One is reduced in its ultimate position the definition of the positive and negative relations among the Ideas, and the determinations of those Ideas that have some commonality, and those, instead, that do not share anything. The *Sophist* presents a specific example among a choice of *some* of the highest Ideas, and the *Parmenides* itself presents only a foreshortening, even if a quite important one, and a high point within a particular outlook.

A global outline of dialectic is not presented by Plato in his written works. The *Republic* has presented only a variety of hints as to how to ascend to the essence of the Good (that is, to the One), by proceeding from an Idea to another Idea and finally to those that are highest in the hierarchical arrangement, and by alluding (although in a somewhat marked manner) to how to arrive at the Idea of the Good (to the One), "by abstracting," that is, by separating it from all the others (and especially from the highest ones). The dialectical dialogues have presented *some* conspicuous diairetic sections and explained connections among some basic Ideas; but *only in the sphere of oral discussion does Plato present the complete framework of dialectic in its essential connections in the parts handed down to us by the indirect tradition.*

The passage from the One to the Many–remember–takes place on the basis of a bipolar relationship of the One with respect to the Dyad (the opposed Principle of indeterminate multiplicity), by means of determinate actions of the One on the Dyad. (*a*) The first stage, in an hierarchical sense, is indicated by the ideal Numbers (which are limited to the Decade), which represents Unity-in-multiplicity in the most elevated manner and in a prototypical and paradigmatic sense; (*b*) from ideal Numbers we pass to the most general Ideas (*c*) and then to particular Ideas, until we reach (*d*) those that are no longer divisible, and beneath these there are (*e*) the corresponding multiple sensibles.

All the Ideas are connected to Numbers in the sense that we have explained; that is, in the sense that Number (ἀριθμός) means a precise relation (λόγος); and hence the complex framework that each Idea implies with others and the nexuses that each Idea involves with those that are earlier and below it, is determinable in the Greek sense of "number" (in the sense that we can qualify as *arithmo-logos*).

The *bipolar structure* (One=Dyad, limit=unlimited) of all being belongs, consequently, *to the numerical-metaphysical structure of all reality.*

Plato in the *Philebus* presents us with one of the most remarkable passages on these dialectical nexuses, even offering it to us as a "gift of the Gods to human being":

Socrates: There is a gift of the Gods–so at least it seems evident to me–which they let fall from their abode, and it was through Prometheus, or one like him, that it reached mankind, together with a fire exceeding bright. The men of old, who were better than ourselves and dwelt nearer the Gods, passed on this gift in the form of a saying. All things, so it ran, that are ever said to be consist of a *one* and a *many*, and have in their nature a conjunction of *limit* and *unlimitedness*. This then being the ordering of things we ought, they said, whatever it be that we are dealing with, to assume a single form and search for it, for we shall find it there contained; then, if we have laid hold of that, we must go on from one form to look for two, if the case admits of there being two, otherwise for three or some other number of forms. And we must do the same again with each of the *'ones'* thus reached, until we come to see not merely that the *one* that we started with is a *one* and *unlimited* and *many*, but also just *how many* it is. But we are not to apply the character of unlimitedness to our plurality until we have discerned the total *number* of forms *the thing in question has intermediate between its one and its unlimited number*. It is only then, when we have done that, that we may let each *one* of all these intermediate forms pass away into the *unlimited* and cease bothering about them. There then, that is how the Gods, as I told you, have committed to us the task of inquiry, of learning, and of teaching one another, but your clever modern man, while making his *one*–or his *many*, as the case may be–more quickly or more slowly than is proper, when he has got his *one* proceeds to his *unlimited* number straightaway, allowing the *intermediates* to escape him, whereas it is the recognition of those intermediates that makes all the difference between a philosophical and a contentious discussion. (trans. R. Hackforth, Bollingen, pp. 1091-93, with slight changes, emphasis added)[25]

Only one point remains to be examined for us to conclude our analysis. That the One determines and limits the opposite Principle (the unlimited and indeterminate Dyad) is explained by the ideal Numbers and in the ideal numerical framework, that are the most perfect and ideally articulated *unity-in-multiplicity*, just as, analogously, the Ideas and the framework of the ideal world determine the sensible Dyad through the mediation of the "intermediate" mathematical entities that are between intelligible being and sensible being produced by the divine Intelligence (the Demiurge), in the way that we have seen.

Actually, the Idea can be *multiplied* in its "unity" and *descend into the sensible*, by means of the mathematical entities that are *eternal* like the Ideas, but, each, *multiplies* like the sensibles. And in this way they can determine the material Principle in an adaptive manner, in a way that reflects in the best way possible the intelligible world.

Consequently, the emblematic signature of Platonic dialectic becomes quite clear, and recalls the things stated that we can summarize in the following way: from the sensible dilectic brings to the intelligible (from the physical sphere to the metaphysical sphere), by gathering the multiplicity of the sensible at various levels into the unity of the intelligible; that is, into its corresponding Idea (this is the first stage of the second voyage); hence running through all the senses the multiplicity of the pyramidlike structure of the intelligibles, grasping in all senses the unity-in-multiplicity (and conversely, the unity acting in the multiplicity), that is to say the arithmo-logos structure of the intelligible in all its senses, right up to reaching the highest Ideas, and finally, to the ultimate abstraction of the unconditioned Unity.

Evidently, Plato took Pythagoreanism to its extreme metaphysical consequences. But, just as he recognizes in Parmenides a father with the metaphor of the "parricide of Parmenides," so in the dialectical dialogues, instead of the mask of an "Eleatic Stranger" he would put on the mask of a Pythagorean and likewise commit a "parricide of Pythagoras," insofar as he brought *number* from the purely quantitative to the metaphysical and axiological sphere, by the conversion from the purely mathematical still linked to the vision of the Physicists to an extraordinary new metaphysical perspective.[26]

VII. THE CONCEPTION OF ART AND RHETORIC

1. Art as far from being and truth

The Platonic problematic on art ought to be seen in close connection with the metaphysical and dialectical thematic, since only through this connection is it fully intelligible. Plato, in fact, in the determination of the nature, function, role, and value of art is concerned only about this: to establish just what its value is with respect to truth; that is, (1) whether and in what measure it approaches truth; (2) whether it improves a human being; (3) whether it has any value socially in terms of education.

And his reply, as is known, is wholly negative on all counts: (1) *art does not reveal* but obscures the truth, *because it does not know the truth*; (2) *it does not improve human beings* but to the contrary, corrupts them, *because it is practiced mendaciously*; (3) *it does not educate* but miseducates, *because it has its source in the irrational parts of the soul*, which are among the lower parts of man.

Let us try to thoroughly understand the reasons for this condemnation, which did not change throughout all the dialogues in any way. Right from the very beginning, in the first dialogues, Plato assumed a negative attitude toward poetry. He conceived it as obviously inferior to philosophy. The poet is never such through science and knowledge, but through irrational intuition. The poet, when he composes, is inspired, is "outside himself," is "possessed," and hence is unaware: he cannot give an account of what he has accomplished, nor can he teach how he does it to others. The poet is a poet through θείᾳ μοίρᾳ; that is, by divine fate, not by virtue of knowledge.[1] Here is a passage of the *Phaedrus*, which is most important in this respect:

> And a third kind of possession and madness comes from the Muses. This takes hold upon a gentle and pure soul, arouses it and inspires it to songs and other poetry, and thus by adorning countless deeds of the ancients educates later generations. But he who without the divine madness comes to the doors of the Muses, confident that he will be a good poet by art, meets with no success, and the poetry of the sane man vanishes into nothingness before that of the inspired madman.[2]

More precise and determined are the conceptions of art that Plato expresses in the tenth book of the *Republic*. Art, in all its expressions (that is, as poetry, including both the pictorial and plastic arts), is, from the metaphysical viewpoint, a *mimesis*; that is to say, an "imitation" of things and sensible occurrences. It is through poetry that the figurative arts in general describe man, things, deeds, and events of various kinds, trying to reproduce them in words, colors, and plastic mediums. Now, we know that sensible things are, from the metaphysical viewpoint, not really real, being but imitations of the really real. They are, therefore, "images" of the eternal "paradigms" of the Ideas and hence *are as distant from the truth as a copy is from the original.* Consequently, if art is an imitation of sensible things, then it follows that it is *a copy of a copy,* and hence quite distant from the truth even more so than sensible things are. It is therefore "three removed from the truth." Here are Plato's frank words in this regard:

> "To that is painting directed in every case, to the imitation of reality as it is or of appearance as it appears? Is it an imitation of a phantasm or of the truth?"
> "Of a phantasm," he said.
> "Then the mimetic art is far removed from truth, and this, it seems, is the reason why it can produce everything, because it touches or lays hold of only a small part of the object and that a phantom."[3]

Hence, the representational arts imitate the mere appearance and thus poets speak *without knowing and without awareness of that about which they speak,* and their speech is, from the metaphysical viewpoint, playful, lacking in seriousness:

> "Then the imitator will neither know nor opine rightly concerning the beauty or badness of his imitations."
> "It seems not."
> "Most charming, then, would be the state of mind of the poetical imitator in respect of true wisdom about his creations."
> "Not at all."
> "Yet still he will none the less imitate, though in every case he does not know in what way the thing is bad or good. But, as it seems, the thing he will imitate will be the thing that appears beautiful to the ignorant multitude."
> "Why, what else."
> "On this, then, as it seems, we are fairly agreed, that *the imitator knows nothing worth mentioning of the things he imitates,* but that imitation is a form of play, not to be taken seriously, and that those who attempt tragic poetry, whether in iambics or heroic verse, are all altogether imitators."
> "By all means."[4]

Consequently, Plato was convinced that art does not develop the best parts of the soul but *only those that are less worthy*:

> "...poetry, and in general the mimetic art, produces a product that is far removed from truth in the accomplishment of its task, and associates with the part in us that is remote from intelligence, and its companion and friend for no sound and true purpose."[5]

Art has therefore a corrupting influence and in large part has to be outlawed or even eliminated from the perfect State, unless it is subjected to laws concerned with truth and goodness.[6]

On this issue much has been written and said, some thought it best, because of its flinty and unyielding viewpoint, to ameliorate and soften it by referring to the fact that Plato placed on the highest level beauty and the Idea of Beauty to which he gave the privilege of being, alone among all intelligible realities "visible." And many times the passages from the *Symposium* and the *Phaedrus* are called to mind, which are true hymns to beauty. Actually, this attempt to bring together the problem of art with the problem of beauty is *historically* less correct, at least in the Platonic context. In fact, our philosopher groups *beauty* not only with *art* but rather with *eros* and the *erotic*, which, as we will see, *have an altogether different meaning and function*. It is hence quite useless to attempt, by using the accomplishments of modern aesthetics, to find in Plato what is not present there or to twist his statements into sense foreign to them.

The truth is that for Plato art does not have a truly *autonomous* sphere and value. It is of use solely if and in the measure in which it can or knows how to put itself at the service of truth.[7] Plato says about some verses that the fear of death inspired is paradigmatic; and these he proposes to strike out of the *Iliad* and the *Odyssey* in the project of his perfect State: "We will beg Homer and the other poets not to be angry if we cancel those and all similar passages, not that they are not poetic and pleasing to most hearers, but because the more poetic they are the less are they suited to the ears of boys and men who are destined to be free and to be more afraid of slavery than of death...."[8]

It is therefore evident that Plato did not at all deny to art its own power and magic, but he denied any validity to its power, when left to itself, standing alone, and when it was not put under the aegis of immutable laws of the truth-giving logos or reason.

In conclusion, Plato did not deny the power of art, but *rejected the idea that art by itself was of value*. Art either serves the truth or serves evil and *there is no middle ground*. Hence, if it wishes to "save itself" from the viewpoint of truth, art must subject itself to philosophy, which alone is capable of achieving truth, and the poet must be subjected to the rules and the dialectic of philosophy.

We moderns, who proclaim the absolute freedom of art and maintain irreproachable dogma of art for art's sake, can adduce against Plato's view many accomplishments of aesthetics and demonstrate the positive aspects of art for art's sake in various respects. Nevertheless, notwithstanding this, we cannot say that in the Platonic position there is no truth. Actually it is very difficult to deny that, cast loose from metaphysical and ethical truth, art risks frequently being reduced to empty posturing; or that in the end, it develops by attracting the worst parts of our being and it frequently contributes to a useless preoccupation with the appearances or the ephemeral, precisely as Plato has indicated, especially by reason of falling into excesses of an iconoclastic nature.

2. Rhetoric as the mystification of truth

In classical antiquity, rhetoric was extremely important, as can be seen in our treatment of the Sophists. It was not, as for us moderns, something that was done through literary affectation and that hence is on the margins of life, but it was a *civil and political power* of the very first rank. So much so that the Sophists, as the ethico-political teachers and educators of a new generation presented themselves as *rhetoricians* and as *teachers of rhetoric.*[9] Plato very early felt the need to examine rhetoric and establish what is its nature and value with respect to the truth. The results were very clear: rhetoric is to be condemned for reasons wholly analogous to that by which art had been condemned.

Rhetoric (the art of Athenian politicians and their teachers) is mere *flattery*, it is an *illusion*, it is *adulatory*, it is *totally opposed to the truth.*

As art it pretends to bring us to and to imitate all things *without having any true knowledge, but by imitating the mere appearance*, just so rhetoric pretends to persuade and *convince all about all without having knowledge about anything.* And as art creates mere phantasms, so rhetoric creates useless persuasion and illusory beliefs. The rhetorician is one who, although being ignorant (even boasting about his ignorance) has the ability in comparison with the many, to be *very persuasive* about what he really knows, because he plays upon their sentiments and passions and brings them not to the truth but only to the appearance of the truth.[10]

Rhetoric (like art) develops, hence, *the worst parts of the soul*, the parts that are susceptible to emotional manipulation, that which feels pleasure and the illusion of pleasure, the parts that are gullible and unstable.[11] Therefore the rhetorician is as far from the truth as an artist, and in fact even more so, because he intentionally produces phantasms of truth, the *appearance of the truth* and shows hence a roguishness that the artist does not possess, or has only partially.

And as *philosophy* is substituted for poetry, just so is "true politics" to be substituted for rhetoric, which we will see is identical with *philosophy*. Poetry and rhetoric stand with respect to philosophy as *appearances* stand in relation to *reality* and as *phantasms* of the truth stand with regard to the *truth*.

This somewhat exacting judgment on rhetoric, which we have stated is pronounced in the *Gorgias*, becomes somewhat softened in the *Phaedrus*, because there Plato admits that the arts of discourse; that is, rhetoric, viewed existentially, must come under the influence of truth and philosophy:

> "Well, do you think we have reproached the art of speaking too harshly? Perhaps she might say: 'Why do you talk such nonsense, you strange men? I do not compel anyone to learn to speak without knowing the truth, but if my advice is of any value, he learns that first and then acquires me. So what

I claim is this, that without my help the knowledge of the truth does not give the art of persuasion."

"And will she be right in saying this?"
"Yes, if the arguments that are coming against her testify that she is an art. For I seem, as it were, to hear some arguments approaching and protesting that she is lying and is not an art, but a craft devoid of art. *A real art of speaking,* says the Laconian, *which does not seize hold of truth, does not exist and never will.*"[12]

And to reach the truth, naturally, it is necessary to apprehend, first, the doctrine of the Ideas and *dialectic* (both in its ascending moment that goes from multiplicity to unity, and in its descending or diairetic moment that divides the Ideas according to their proper articulations).[13] Second, it is necessary to know the *soul*, because the art of persuasion is directed to the soul.[14] Only by knowing the *nature of things* and the *nature of the human soul* will it be possible to construct the true art of rhetoric; that is, a true art of persuasion through oral discussion.

It is evident after all we have pointed out that the "second voyage," with the discovery of the metaphysical sphere, has revolutionized the whole spiritual world of the Greeks, that prior to Plato had seen in the poet and the rhetorician its teachers about life and human excellence.

Third Section

THE ETHICAL-RELIGIOUS-ASCETIC COMPONENT OF PLATONIC THOUGHT AND ITS NEXUSES WITH THE PROTOLOGIC OF THE *UNWRITTEN DOCTRINES*

οὐ γάρ τοι θαυμάζοιμι᾽ ἂν εἰ Εὐριπίδης
ἀληθῆ ἐν τοῖσδε λέγει, λέγων· τίς δ᾽
ὃδεν. εἰ τὸ ζῆν μὲν ἐστι κατθανεῖν, τὸ
κατθανεῖν δὲ ζῆν; καὶ ἡμεῖς τῷ ὄντι
ἴσως τέθναμεν.

Well, life as you describe it is a strange affair. I should not be surprised you know,
if Euripides was right when he said,
"Who knows, if life be death, and death be
life?

Plato, *Gorgias* 492E

I. RELEVANCE OF THE MYSTICAL-RELIGIOUS-ASCETIC COMPONENT OF PLATONISM

Plato is not only a metaphysician and a dialectician: anyone who interprets him exclusively in this way has simply reduced him to a skeleton. Already the ancients had acknowledged that Plato's philosophy was impregnated through and through with a strongly religious sentiment, which is an inexhaustible source for persons thirsting for the divine. Some have even understood it almost as a mystical initiation: many Neoplatonists considered the dialogues as no more or no less than a response from an oracle, a divine revelation.[1] But although with a different vocabulary, the interest in Plato the mystic was renewed (omitting the medievals who did not directly know our philosopher's works) by the humanists of the circle of Ficino, and then by many modern interpreters and translators up to the present: this enthusiasm is not without foundation as we will see immediately.

The mystical dimension, latent in the early dialogues and in some almost totally absent, explodes, so to speak, for the first time, in the magnificent canvas of the *Gorgias* and it coincides with a moment of crisis in the life of Plato, which brought him to ponder the basic meaning of the 'Orphic way of life" and the 'Pythagorean life-style," it forced him not only to accept them, but to deepen them and then to show little by little, all their implications and consequences. [2] For the first time in the *Gorgias* Plato confronts all the basic problems related to the life of man, which he presented dramatically, as in none of his preceding writings, in all its stridency and tragic contradictions. Socrates the just man is killed and the unjust man seems instead to triumph. The virtuous and the just are at the mercy of the unjust and suffer injustice at their hands. The morally vice-ridden and the unjust seem instead to be happy and satisfied in their overbearing arrogance. The just politician succumbs to what is imposed without scruples. The good ought to triumph but instead the evil seem to be victorious. What is the truth here? Callicles, one of the protagonists of the dialogue, who gives voice to the most extreme position that could be found at the time (as we have seen stated by some of the teachers of the Sophists), does not shrink from stating with the most brazen shamelessness, that the truth rests with the strongest; that is, with those who do not care about anyone or anything, who know how to enjoy every pleasure, to satisfy all their passions, to satisfy all their desires and to seize the means to serve their needs. Justice is simply the invention of the weak; virtue is a joke; temperance absurd: anyone who abstains from pleasures, who moderates and tempers his appetites or passions is stupid, because the life that they live who adopt this style is actually death.[3] And it is simply in response to this extreme vision that Plato, going beyond Socrates, finds the truth in the teachings of the Orphic-Pythagoreans. Callicles and all his kind (pseudo-Sophists and

139

politicians of the time), of which Callicles is the model, say that the life of virtue, which controls the instincts and passions, is a life without meaning and hence death.[4] But what is life? And what is death? Could it not be that what we call *death* is instead *life*, and could it not be instead that *true life* begins with death?[5] It is clear then that for Plato the problem that Socrates consciously left unsolved, involves resolving the problem of the *eschatological destiny of the soul*. If the soul is immortal and if, with the death of the body, even the spirit of man is dissolved into nothingness, then the doctrine of Socrates would not be sufficient to refute that of Callicles. It is not enough to say that for Plato man is his *psyché*; as Socrates said; but it is necessary to establish if the *psyché* is or is not *immortal* (athanatos/deathless). Only the reply to this question is truly decisive in the argument with Callicles.[6] The doctrine of the immortality of the soul, consequently, emerges into the forefront and produces a new direction for ethics and politics.

To live for the body (as do the majority of human beings) means to live for what is destined to die; to live for the soul means, instead, to live for what is destined to be always, and hence it means to live by purifying the soul *through a progressive distancing from the body*.

If the just man, in this life, is victimized by the bullying of the unjust to the point of being frequently beaten with impunity, then he suffers bodily, and in the end he may lose his body; but, by losing his body, as we have pointed out already, he loses that which is mortal, while *he preserves his soul for eternity*.[7] This vision of life is not a simple revival or quantitative reelaboration, let us say, of an Orphic-Pythagorean position. It acquires a wholly new meaning after the "second voyage"; that is, after the discovery of the intelligible world. The existence of an *immortal soul*, which alone can give meaning to the vision of life that we have described, does not remain a mere hope or belief, or a simple trust or faith, but can be rationally demonstrated. In Orphism it was simply a mysterio-sophic doctrine; in those Presocratics who had accepted the Orphic vision it remained a presupposition in contrast with their physical principles; *in Plato it is grounded instead and is established completely on a metaphysical level; that is, in on the basis of the doctrine of the supersensible, of which it became almost a corollary*. The soul is the intelligible and immaterial aspect of man, and it is eternal as the intelligible and immaterial is eternal.

It is evident, hence, that *the proofs of immortality* of the soul are given great importance, because, with them, Plato proceeds beyond Socrates' doctrine and Orphism and ends by making a mediation between the rationalistic position of Socrates, on the one hand, and the mystical view of Orphism, on the other. We must now turn to the analyses of these proofs.

II. THE IMMORTALITY OF THE SOUL, ITS ULTRATERRESTRIAL DESTINY, AND ITS REINCARNATION

1. The proofs of the immortality of the soul

The *Phaedo* gives us three proofs for the immortality of the soul.[1] Putting aside the first, to which Plato himself gave scarcely any value and that brings into evidence categories of a physical nature and in particular of Heraclitean derivation, ending by bringing up recollection (analogously to what we saw already in the *Meno*).[2] We want to examine the other two proofs, of which at least one is among the most convincing of those proofs that the succeeding metaphysics has attempted to supply.

The human soul—says Plato—is capable (according to what we have seen earlier) *of knowing immutable and eternal entities*; but, to grasp these things, it must have, *as a necessary condition, a nature akin to them*: otherwise these entities will remain outside its capacity; and therefore, as these are immutable and eternal, so also the soul *must* be immutable and eternal. This is in essence the proof; but, since in our judgment it is a most fruitful proof, we want to analyze it closely. As we know, there are two spheres of reality: (*a*) the visible realities; that is, the perceptible and sensible ones, and (*b*) the invisible and intelligible realities. The first—we know—are those that do not stay in the same condition, the second are instead those that always remain the same. Let us ask ourselves now with that type of reality the two parts or components that constitute man, the *soul* and the *body*, are to be identified. There is no doubt that the body is akin to visible reality, the soul to *invisible* and *intelligible* reality; and, since the visible is immutable and the intelligible is immutable, the soul must be immutable. And in fact, when the soul relies on sensible perceptions, these lead it into error and confusion, because they are as changeable as the objects to which they refer. Instead, when the soul is elevated above the senses and grasps itself alone, then it no longer errs, but finds in the pure Ideas and in the intelligibles its appropriate object and discovers, indeed by knowing them, that it is akin to them, and remains immutable in knowing the immutable. (And a further confirmation of what was said is this: when the soul and body are together, the soul governs and leads; whereas the body obeys and is lead by the soul; but it is characteristic of the divine to command and of the mortal to be commanded; hence the soul—also from this viewpoint—is akin to the divine, whereas the body is akin to the mortal).[3] Given the importance of this proof, we wish to read it in the precise terms in which Plato formulated it:

> "Now," said he, 'shall we assume *two kinds of existences, one visible, the other invisible?*"

"Let us assume them," said Cebes.

"And that the invisible is always the same and the visible constantly changing?"

"Let us assume that also," said he.

"Well then," said Socrates, 'are we not made up of two parts, *body* and *soul*?

"Yes," he replied.

"Now to which class should we say the body is more similar and more closely akin?"

"To the visible," said he, 'that is clear to everyone."

"And the soul? Is it visible or invisible?"

"Invisible, to man, at least, Socrates."

"But we call things visible and invisible with reference to human vision do we not?"

"Yes, we do."

"Then what do we say about the soul? Can it be seen or not?"

"It cannot be seen."

"Then it is invisible?"

"Yes."

"Then the soul is more like the invisible than the body is, and the body more like the visible."

"Necessarily, Socrates."

"Now we have also been saying for a long time, have we not, that, when the soul makes use of the body for any inquiry, either through seeing or hearing or any of the other senses"for inquiry through the body means inquiry through the senses - then it is dragged by the body to things which never remain the same, and it wanders about is confused and dizzy like a drunken man because it lays hold upon such things?"

"Certainly."

"But when the soul inquires alone by itself, it departs into the realm of the pure, the everlasting, the immortal and the changeless, and being akin to these it dwells always with them whenever it is by itself and is not hindered, and it has rest from its wanderings and remains always the same and unchanging with the changeless, since it is in communion therewith. And this state of the soul is called wisdom. Is it not so?"

"Socrates, said he, what you say is perfectly right and true."

"And now again, in view of what we said before and of what has just been said, to which class do you think the soul has greater likeness and kinship?"

"I think, Socrates," said he, "that anyone, even the dullest, would agree, after this argument that the souls is infinitely more like that which is always the same than that which is not."

"And the body?"

"Is more like the other."

"Consider, then, the matter in another way. When the soul and the body are joined together, nature directs the one to serve and be ruled, and the other to rule and be master. Now this being the case, which seems to you like the divine, and which like the mortal? Or do you not think that the divine is by nature fitted to rule and lead, and the mortal to obey and serve?"

"Yes, I think so."

"Which, then, does the soul resemble?"

"Clearly, Socrates, the soul is like the divine and the body like the mortal."

"Then see, Cebes, if this is not the conclusion from all that we have said, that the soul is most like the divine and immortal and intellectual and uniform and indissoluble and ever unchanging, and the body, on the contrary, most like the human and mortal and multiform and unintellectual and dissoluble and everchanging. Can we say anything, my dear Cebes, to show that this is not so?"

"No, we cannot." [4]

The ultimate proof that is given in the *Phaedo* is derived from some structural characteristics of the Ideas. The contrary Ideas do not combine together, because insofar as they are contraries, they exclude one another. But the sensible things that participate in these Ideas cannot admit the contraries together. If this is so, then an Idea upon entering into a thing, necessarily excludes its opposite or else it would retreat from the thing (not only the Idea of great and of small cannot be combined but they clearly exclude each other when considered in themselves as well as excluding each other when they are present in things: if the one is present, then the other must leave the thing). And the same thing is true of not only the contraries themselves, but also of all those Ideas and things that, although not being their contraries, have in themselves the contraries as essential attributes: not only hot and cold exclude each other in the way just stated but also *fire* and *cold*, *snow* and *warm*. The fire never admits in itself the Idea of cold and snow never admits in itself the Idea of warm; the snow to overcome it must have the warm vanish and take its place, and for the fire to overcome it must have the cold vanish and take its place. Now we come to the soul and apply to it what we have established now. The soul has its essential attributes *life* and the *Idea of life*: it is, in fact, that which brings life to the body and maintains it (and this—it is well to consider— for the Greeks it is more obvious than for us, because even from the strictly linguistic viewpoint, *psyché* recalls the notion of life and also means, in many contexts, simply life). And, since death is the contrary of life, on the basis of the principle established, the soul, having as an essential character life, could not structurally accept in itself death, and therefore it will be immortal. Therefore, when death happens, the body is corrupted and the soul will then depart. In conclusion, the soul, that implies life essentially, cannot accept death indeed for reasons of a structural nature, because the Idea of life and the Idea of death totally exclude one another. The expression "a dead soul" is a pure absurdity, it is a contradiction in terms, like "warm snow," or "cold fire." Therefore soul = Idea of life = that which by its nature is and gives life = incorruptible = immortal (deathless, ἀθάνατός) = eternal.[5] A further proof for the immortality of the soul is to be found in the *Republic*. Evil is that which corrupts and destroys (whereas the good is that which preserves and benefits).

Every thing has its characteristic evil (just as it has its characteristic good), and it is and can be destroyed only by the evil that is proper to it and not by the evil of other things. Consequently, if we can find something that indeed has its evil that makes it bad, but that notwithstanding, is an evil that can neither destroy nor dissolve it, then we ought to conclude that such a reality is necessarily indestructible; since, if it cannot be destroyed by its characteristic evil, *a fortiori* [all the more so] would it not be destroyed by an evil proper to something else. Yet, such a thing is precisely true of the soul. It has its evil, which is *vice* (injustice, rashness, impiety and so on); but vice, no matter how great, does not destroy the soul, which continues to live, even if quite badly. This is quite the opposite of what occurs in the case of the body, which, when it has been touched by some evil (disease) is corrupted and dies. Therefore, if the soul cannot be destroyed by the evil of the body, since the evil of the body (due to the principle established) is alien to the soul and as such cannot touch it; and if it can never be destroyed by its characteristic evil, no matter how strong it is, then it is indestructible. Here is the conclusions of the Platonic argument:

> "You say well," I replied; "for when the natural vice and the evil proper to it cannot kill and destroy the soul, still less will the evil appointed for the destruction of another thing destroy the soul or anything else, except that for which it is appointed."
> "Still less indeed," he said, "in all probability."
> "Then since it is not destroyed by any evil whatever, either its own or alien, it is evident that it must necessarily exist always, and that if it always exists it is immortal."
> "Necessarily," he said."[6]

Finally, in the *Phaedrus* the immortality of the soul is derived from the concept of *psyché* understood as *principle of motion* (to say life means to say movement; hence the concept of soul as principle of movement is only a corollary derived from the concept of soul as principle of life): and the principle of movement as such can never perish. Here is the passage of the *Phaedrus* in which this demonstration is developed:

> Every soul is immortal. For that which is ever moving is immortal; but that which moves something else or is moved by something else, when it ceases to move, ceases to live. Only that which moves itself, since it does not leave itself, never ceases to move, and this is also the source and beginning of motion for all other things which have motion. But the beginning is un-generated. For everything that is generated must be generated from a beginning, but the beginning is not generated from anything; for if the beginning were generated from anything, it would not be generated from a beginning. And since it is ungenerated, it must be also indestructible; for if the beginning were destroyed, it could never be generated from anything nor anything else from it, since all things must be generated from a begin-

ning. Thus that which moves itself must be the beginning of motion. And this can be neither destroyed nor generated, otherwise all the heavens and all generation must fall in ruin and stop and never again have any source of motion or origin. But since that which is moved by itself has been seen to be immortal, one who says that this self-motion is the essence and the very idea of the soul will not be disgraced. For every body which derives motion from without is soulless, but that which has its motion within itself has a soul, since that is the nature of the soul; but if this is true,—that that which moves itself is nothing else than the soul,—then the soul would necessarily be ungenerated and immortal."[7]

In the dialogues prior to the *Timaeus* the souls seem to be without birth, in addition to being without end. Instead in the *Timaeus*, as we have already stated, the souls are generated by the Demiurge: they clearly have a birth, but, as a result of a divine decree they are not subject to death just as all the things directly produced by the Demiurge are not subject to death.[8] Beyond the technical formulation of the various proofs from which arises numerous discussions and perplexities of various kinds, a point is still secure, in order for anyone to believe in the possibility of metaphysics: *the existence and immortality of the soul only has sense if a supersensible, metaempirical being is admitted, which Plato called the world of Ideas, but which means in the ultimate analysis precisely this: that the soul is the intelligible, metaempirical, incorruptible aspect of man.* With Plato man has discovered the two aspects of his being. And this acquisition is irreversible, because even those who reject one of the two dimensions give to the physical dimension what they believe must be maintained, a meaning wholly different from that which it had when the other was unknown.

The soul, in which Socrates (overcoming the Homeric and Presocratic understanding and the irrational aspects of the Orphic vision) pointed out the "true man," by identifying it with self-awareness, intelligence, and morality, received with Plato its adequate ontological and metaphysical foundation and a precise place in the general understanding of reality.

2. The eschatological destiny of the soul

The immortality of the soul (which, as we have amply seen, is a position that Plato achieved by means of reasoning) involves *the further problem of its destiny after the destruction of the body.* But this problem is not amenable to being solved by the application of reason *alone*, and it is at this point that Plato decides to have recourse to myths.

It has been frequently noted, eschatological myths are different, in certain respects they involve mutual contradictions. Actually, the contradictions result from trying to interpret them according to rational principles (the logic of the logos) and not according to their own peculiar principles, which, as we have seen already, is that of soliciting belief by means of differing allusive representations, in a fundamental unique truth, which is metalogical but not antilogical, not susceptible of rational demonstration but in some way subject to the logos itself.

The basic truth which the myth intends to suggest and bring us to believe is a kind of "rational faith," as we discussed in the opening section. In outline, it is as follows. Man is on earth as on a journey and terrestrial life is a test. The true life is in the hereafter, in the Shades (the invisible). And in the Shades (the Underworld) the soul is "judged" on the sole basis of justice and injustice, of temperance and intemperance, of virtue and vice. The judges from beyond are not concerned with anything else: they do not take into account absolutely whether or not the soul is the soul of the Great King or one of his many low-born subjects: they take into account only the signs of justice and injustice contained in the soul itself. And the possible destiny that is earned by the soul is threefold: (*a*) if a soul has lived justly, it will receive a reward (it will go to a marvelous place called the Isle of the Blessed, or to a higher and indescribable place), (*b*) if a soul has lived unjustly to the point of being irredeemable, it will receive everlasting punishment (it will be thrown into Tartarus), and (*c*) if a soul was occasionally unjust; that is, it lived sometimes unjustly and sometimes justly holding itself back from profound injustice, then it will be punished for a limited time (when it has worked off its faults then it will receive the reward that it merited).

Because this issue is one of the most delicate points in Plato's thought, which many criticize (rationalists, idealists or postivists) and tend to undervalue or even eliminate, whereas, through the express declarations of our philosopher, he, on the contrary, sees it as an essential truth,[9] we will take the opportunity to explain it in a detailed way, on the basis of what is said in the *Gorgias* and in the *Phaedo*, which are two dialogues that differ greatly in their reasoning (the *Republic* and the *Phaedrus*, as we will see,[10] confirm this truth, but illustrate it from another perspective).

Above all we must speak of "judgment" that decides the destinies of the soul in the beyond. At the time of Cronos, Plato tells us, and even in the first period of the reign of Zeus, justice occurred *before* death and it risked being badly administered: the beauty of bodies, wealth, honors, the testimony of parents could in certain cases mask the brutish soul and confuse the judges, who judged them only in terms of their bodies and hence with the souls conditioned by them. And here is how the supreme decision of Zeus was made:

First of all then, said he, *men must be stopped from foreknowing their deaths*, for now they have knowledge beforehand. Prometheus has already been told to stop this foreknowledge. Next *they must be stripped naked of all these things before trial*, for they must be judged after death. And the judge must be naked too and dead, *scanning with his soul itself the souls of all immediately after death*, deprived of all his kinsmen and with all that fine attire of his left on earth, that his verdict may be just. Now I had realized all this before you, and *I have appointed my three sons as judges* two from Asia, Minos and Rhadamanthus, and one, Aeacus, from Europe. And when these are dead, they will hold court in the meadow, at the crossroads from which two paths lead, one to the isles of the blessed, the other to Tartarus. And Rhadamanthus will judge those who come from Asia, Aeacus those from Europe, and to Minos I will grant the privileges of court appeal, if the other two are in doubt so that their judgement about which path men take may be as just as possible. (trans. W. D. Woodhead, Bollingen, p. 304, with slight changes)[11]

Two affirmations strike us in a particular way in the passage. In the first place it is emphasized that the supreme judgment is made by a soul without a body on a soul equally without a body; that is, *in their purely spiritual aspect;* and in the soul, Plato immediately after explains, "when it lacks the body, its constitutive characteristics and affections which man has received for it by means of his mode of living in different circumstances is quite visible": it is a judgment then that is conducted entirely within the sphere of the soul. The other affirmation pointed out is that Zeus *establishes that his three sons* will do the judging. Can anyone avoid the surprising analogy with the evangelical maxim: "The Father judges no one, but entrusts judgment to the Son." [12] The judgment, as we have stated, rewards the just ones (especially the philosophers, who do not waste their time in the vain pursuits of life, but who care only for human excellence (virtue) with a happy life on the Isle of the Blessed and punishment for evil-doers in Hades.

Here is what Plato writes in regard to these punishments:

And it is proper for everyone who suffers a punishment rightly inflicted by another that he should either be improved and benefitted thereby or become a warning to the rest, in order that they may be afraid *when they see him suffering what he does and may become better men. Now, those who are benefitted through suffering punishment by gods and men are beings whose evil deeds are curable; nevertheless it is from pain and agony that they derived the benefit both here and in the other world, for it is impossible to be rid of evil otherwise.* But those who have been guilty of the most heinous crimes and whose misdeeds are past cure—of these warnings are made, and they are no longer capable themselves of receiving any benefit, because they are incurable—but others are benefitted who behold them suffering throughout eternity the greatest and most excruciating and terrifying tortures because of their misdeeds, literally suspended as examples there in the prison house in Hades, a spectacle and a warning to any evil doers who from time to time arrive. (trans. W. D. Woodhead, Bollingen, p. 305)[13]

This passage, in spite of a certain obscurity, contains one of the most powerful intuitions of our philosopher: the intuition about the remedial function of pain and suffering.

Here is the passage of the *Phaedo* that presents in a complete fashion the destinies of the soul in the afterlife:

> "Such is the nature of these things. Now when the dead have come to the place where each is led by his genius, first they are judged and sentenced, as they have lived well and piously, or not. And those who are found to have lived neither well nor ill, go to the Acheron and embarking upon vessels provided for them, arrive in them at the lake; there they dwell and are purified, and if they have done any wrong they are absolved by paying the penalty for their wrongdoings, and for their good deeds they receive rewards, each according to its merit. But those who appear to be incurable, on account of the greatness of their wrongdoings, because they have committed many great deeds of sacrilege, or wicked or abominable murders, or any other such crimes are cast by their fitting destiny into Tartarus, whence they never emerge. Those, however, who are curable, but are found to have committed great sins—who have, for example, in a moment of passion done some act of violence against their father or mother and have lived and repented the rest of their lives, or who have slain some other person under similar conditions—these must need be thrown into Tartarus, and when they have been there a year the wave cast them out, the homicides by way of Cocytus, those who have outraged their parents by way of Pyrithlegethon. And when they have been brought by the current to the Acherusian Lake, they shout and cry out, only to those to whom they have slain or outraged, thinking and beseeching them to be gracious and to let them come out into the lake; and if they prevail while they come out and cease from their ills, but if not, they are borne away again to Tartarus and hence back into the rivers, and this goes on until they prevail upon those whom they have wronged; for this is the penalty imposed upon them by the judges. But those who are found who have excelled in holy living and are free from these regents within the earth and are released as from prisons; they mount upward into the pure gold and dwell upon the earth. And of these, all who have duly purified themselves by philosophy live henceforth all together without bondage, and pass to still more beautiful abodes which it is not easy to describe, nor have we now time enough."[14]

We have already spoken about the truths contained in these myths. We have already noted the way that Plato demythologizes their fantastic elements, at the same time that he narrates them. Nevertheless let us turn and reread the passage in which our philosopher warns the reader from taking the myth literally and together reaffirms its capacity to go beyond through allusions, because such a passage contains the unique correct key reading of the whole Platonic mythology:

> "Now *it would not be fitting for a man of sin to maintain that all this is just as I have described it*, but that this or something like it is true concerning our souls and their abodes, since the soul is shown to be immortal, *I think he may properly and worthily venture to believe; for the ventures are*

worthwhile; and he ought to repeat such things to himself as if they were magic charms, which is the reason why I have been lengthening out this story for so long. This then is why a man should be of good cheer about his soul, who in his life has rejected the pleasures and ornaments of the body, thinking that they are alien to him and more likely to do him more harm than good, and has sought evil and after adorning his soul with no alien ornaments, but with its own proper adornment of self=restraint and justice and courage and truth, awaits his departure to the other world, ready to go when fate calls him. You, Simmias and Cebes and the rest," he said, "will go hereafter, each in his own time; but I am now already, as a tragedian would say, called by fate, and it is about time for me to go to the bathe where I think it is better to bath before drinking the poison, that the women may not have the trouble of bathing the corpse."[15]

3. Metempsychosis

This conception of the afterlife, of itself is clear enough and delineated. It intersects with the Orphic-Pythagorean doctrine of metempsychosis (reincarnation), without therefore being totally identical with it.

First, it is to be noted that the doctrine of reincarnation of souls in Plato assumes two forms and two different meanings.

The first form is that which is presented in the most detailed way in the *Phaedo*. Here it is said that the souls that have lived lives excessively attached to bodies, passions, loves, and their pleasures do not entirely separate themselves from them at death because they have become so attached to them. These souls hang around for a certain period, out of fear of Hades, staying around the grave like phantoms until, attracted by corporeal desires, they become linked to new bodies and not only of human beings but also of animals, on the basis of the quality of their moral life that they had formerly lived. Here is the famous passage of the *Phaedo* in which Plato expresses this belief:

> "But it will be interpreted, I suppose, with the corporeal which intercourse and communion with the body have made a part of its nature because the body has been its constant companion and object of its care? "
> "Certainly."
> "And, my friend, we must believe that the corporeal is burdensome and heavy and earthly and visible. And such a soul is weighed down by this and is dragged back to the visible world *through fear of the invisible and of the other world*, and so, as they say, it flits about the monuments and the tombs, where shadowy shapes of souls have been seen, figures of those souls which were not set free in purity but retain something of the visible; and this is why they are seen."
> "That is likely, Socrates."
> "It is likely, Cebes. And it is likely that those are not the souls of the good, but those of the base, which are compelled to flit about such places as a punishment *for their former evil mode of life*. And they flit about until through the desire of the corporeal which clings to them they are again

imprisoned in a body. They are likely to be imprisoned in natures which correspond to the practices of their formal life."

"What natures do you mean, Socrates?"

"I mean, for example, that those who have indulged in gluttony and violence and drunkenness, and have taken no pains to avoid them, how likely to pass into the bodies of asses and other beasts of that sort. Do you not think so?"

"Certainly that is very likely."

"Then those who have chosen injustice and tyranny and robbery pass into the bodies of wolves and hawks and kites. Where else can we imagine that they go?"

"Beyond a doubt," said Cebes, "they pass into such creatures."

"Then," said he, "it is clear where all the others go, each in accordance with its own habits?"

"Yes," said Cebes, "of course."

"Then," said he, "the happiest of those, and those who go to the best place, are those who have practiced, by nature and habit without philosophy or reason, the social and civil virtues which are called moderation and justice?"

"How are these happiest?"

"Don't you see? Is it not likely that they pass again into some such social and gentle species as that of bees or wasps or ants, or into the human race again, and that worthy men spring from them? "

"Yes."

"And no one who has not been a philosopher and who is not wholly pure when he departs is allowed to enter into the communion of the Gods, but only the lover of pure knowledge. It is for this reason, dear Simmias and Cebes, that those who truly love wisdom refrain from all bodily desires and resist them firmly do not give themselves up to them, not because they fear poverty or loss of property, as most men, in their love of money, do; nor is it because they fear the dishonor or disgrace of wickedness, like the lovers of honor and power, that they refrain from them."

"No, that would not be seemly for them, Socrates," said Cebes.

"Most assuredly not," said he. "And therefore those who care for their own souls, and do not live in service to the body, turn their backs upon all these men and do not walk in their ways, for they feel that they know not whither they are going. They themselves believe that philosophy, with its deliverance and purification, must not be resisted, and so they turn and follow it withersoever it leads."[16]

Does it speak here of a cycle of lives that occurs for the souls of evildoers after death, *before going to Hades*? Or is it a question only of a *different way* of representing the eschatological destiny (the punishment) of the souls of evildoers? It is difficult to find an answer. It is perhaps possible, in any case, that Plato remained faithful to his belief, since it is also pointed out in the late work, the *Timaeus*."The Demiurge, as we know,[17] constructs the souls destined to be put into bodies and to become human beings, and establishes for them this destiny:

"And he who should live well for his due span of time should journey back
to the habitation of his consort star and there live a happy and congenial
life; but failing of this, he should shift at his second birth into a woman; and
if in this condition he still did not cease from wickedness, and according to
the character of his deprivation, he should constantly be changed into some
beast of a nature resembling the formation of that character, and should
have no rest from the travail of these changes, until letting the evolution of
the Same and uniform within himself draw into its train all that turmoil of
fire and water and air and earth that have later grown about it, he should
control it's irrational turbulence by discourse of reason and return once
more to the form of his first and best condition." (trans. F. M. Cornford,
Plato's Cosmology, p. 144)[18]

But in the *Republic* Plato speaks of a second kind of reincarnation of souls,
quite different from this one. Souls are *limited in number,* so, if all were to have,
in the afterlife, an *eternal* reward or punishment, at a certain time none would
be left on earth. For this evident reason Plato maintained that the ultraterrestrial reward and the punishment for a life lived on earth must be of a limited
duration and fixed period. And since a earthly life endures maximally one
hundred years, Plato, clearly influenced by Pythagorean mysticism associated
with the number ten, maintained that the ultraterrestrial life must have a
duration of ten times one hundred years; that is, a thousand years (for the souls
that have committed very great and irredeemable crimes, the punishment
continues another thousand years). After this *cycle period* all the souls must
be reincarnated. In the famous myth of Er, with which the *Republic* closes, the
return of the souls to the earth are narrated in some wonderful pages.

Terminating their thousand year journey, the souls come up to a plain on
which is determined their future destiny. And here Plato works out a real
revolution within the context of Greek traditional beliefs, according to which
it would be the Gods and Necessity who decide the destiny of human beings.
The "paradigms of life instead,"[19] Plato states, are in the grip of Moira
Lachesis, daughter of Necessity, but they are not imposed but only proposed
to souls, and *the choice is entirely consigned to the liberty of the soul itself.* Man
is not free to choose whether to live or not to live, but he is free to choose *how*
to live morally; that is, to live according to virtue or according to vice:

"Now when they arrived they were straightway bidden to go before Lachesis,
and then a certain prophet first marshalled them in orderly intervals, and
there upon took from the lap of Lachesis lots and patterns of lives and went
up to a lofty platform and spoke, [this is the word of Lachesis, the maiden
daughter of necessity]. Souls that live for a day, now is the beginning of
another cycle of mortal generation where birth is the beacon of death. *No
divinity shall pass lots for you, but you shall choose your own deity.* Let him
to whom falls the first lot first select a life to which he shall cleave of necessity.
But virtue has no master over her, and each shall have more or less of her as

he honors her or does her despot. The blame is his who chooses: God is blameless."[20]

This said, the prophet of Lachesis throws lots to establish the order with which each soul must go to choose: the number that governs each soul is that which falls near it. Hence the prophet spreads out on the grass the paradigms of lives (paradigms of all possible human and even animal lives), in greater number than that of the souls present. The first on whom the lot falls has many more choices of paradigms of lives at his disposal than those who are last; but this does not irreparably cause difficulty in the matter of choices.

Here is the express words of the prophet Lachesis: "And at that time also the messenger from that other world reported that the prophets spoke thus: Even for him who comes forward last, if he make his choice wisely and lives strenuously, there is reserved an acceptable life, no evil one. Let not the foremost in the choice be heedless or the last be discouraged."[21] The choice made by each soul is then sealed by the other two Moira, Clotho and Atropos, and becomes, thus, irreversible. The souls drink, hence, the water of forgetfulness from the Ameles and then descend into bodies, in which they live their chosen lives.

We have stated that the choice depends on *liberty of soul,* but it would be more accurate to say, *on knowledge, or the science of the good and bad life; that is, on philosophy,* which for Plato becomes, hence, a healing power that preserves it here and in the beyond, for ever. The ethical intellectualism is here pushed to extreme consequences: "Yet if at each return to the life of this world *the man loved wisdom sanely,* then the lot of his choice did not fall out among the last, we may venture to affirm, from what was reported thence, that *not only will he be happy here but that the path of his journey thither and the return to this world will not be underground and rough but smooth and through the heavens.*"[22] The value that Plato gives to this myth is exactly that which he gives to the myths of the *Phaedo* and to the others: the value of an "incantation" to allay doubts and to help one's faith.[23] Moreover the words with which he ends resound unequivocally:

> "And so, Glaucon, the tale was saved as the saying is, and was not lost. *And it will save us if we believe it,* and we shall safely cross the river of Lethe, and keep our soul unspotted from the world. But if we are guided by me we shall believe that the soul is mortal and capable of enduring all extremes of good and evil, and so we shall hold ever to the upward way and pursue righteousness with wisdom always and ever, that we may be dear to ourselves and to the gods both during our sojourn here and when we receive our award, as the victors in the games go about to gather in theirs. And thus both here and in the journey of 1000 years, whereof I have told you, we shall fare well.[24]

Finally note that Plato has again proposed in the *Phaedrus* a vision of the hereafter still more complex.[25] The reasons are probably to found in the fact that none of the myths thus far examined explain *the cause of the descent of souls into bodies, the original birth of souls themselves, and the reasons for their kinship with the divine.* Originally the soul was near the Gods and lived among the Gods a divine life, and it fell into a body on earth *through a fault.* The soul is like a winged chariot drawn by two horses with a charioteer. Whereas the two horses of the Gods are equally good, the two horses of the souls of men are of a different breed: one is good and the other evil and the ride as a result is difficult (the charioteer symbolizes reason, the two horses are the irrational parts of the soul, about which we will speak further on). The souls go along behind the Gods, flying through the streets of heaven, and their goal is to come periodically together with the Gods, up to the summit of heaven, *to contemplate Being,* what is beyond the heavens, the Hyperouranos (the world of Ideas), or, as Plato says, "the Plain of Truth." But, unlike the Gods, our souls struggle in trying to contemplate Being, which is beyond the heaven, and to graze on the "Plain of Truth," especially because of the badly bred horse, which keeps trying to descend below. Just so it happens that some souls succeed in seeing Being, or at least a part of it, and for this reason continue to live with the Gods. Other souls do not succeed in getting to the "Plain of Truth": they are crowded, in a turmoil, not succeeding in rising the ascent that brings them to the summit of the heaven; they trample and tread upon one another, fall to brawling, in which their wings break off; and consequently these souls become heavy and fall to earth:

> "And this is a law of Destiny, that the soul which follows after God and obtains a view of any of the truth [the *Ideas*] *it is free from harm until the next period, and if it can always attain this, is always unharmed*; but when, through inability to follow it fails to see, and through some mischance is still with forgetfulness and evil and grows heavy, and when it has grown heavy, loses its wings and falls to the earth, then it is the law that this soul shall never pass into any beast at its first birth."[26]

Hence, as long as a soul succeeds in seeing Being and pastures on the "Plain of Truth" it does not fall into a body on earth, and, from cycle to cycle, it continues to live in the company of the Gods and of the daimons. (How long the cycle of going around the heaven lasts, Plato does not say, perhaps to suggest that it is a life *outside time*). Human life to which the soul, by falling, begins is the more morally perfect depending on the more it was able to see in the Hyperouranos and morally less perfect according to whether it saw less. At the death of the body, the soul is judged and for a millennium, as we know from the *Republic,* it will enjoy rewards or it will reap punishment, corresponding to the merits or demerits of its terrestrial life. And after the thousand years it will return again and be reincarnated.

But compared to the *Republic,* in the *Phaedrus* there is another novelty. After ten thousand years have passed, *all souls get back their wings and return to the vicinity of the Gods.* The souls that for three consecutive lives have lived according to philosophy are made an exception and enjoy a kind of privilege, in which their vings are refitted after only three thousand years. It is clear hence, that in the *Phaedrus*, the place in which the souls live with the Gods (and to which they return every ten thousand years) and the place in which they enjoy their reward every thousand years for each life that they live are wholly different.

Here is the passage of the *Phaedrus*, in which Plato expresses this complicated vision of things:

> For each soul returns to the place [= the place where they live with the Gods] whence it came in ten thousand years; for it does not regain its wings before that time has elapsed, except for the soul of him who has been a guileless philosopher or a philosophical lover; these, when for three successive periods of a thousand years they have chosen of such a life, after the third period of a thousand years become winged in the three thousandth year and go their way; but the rest, when they have finished their first life, receive judgment, and after the judgment some go to the place of correction under the earth and pay their penalty while the others, made live and raised up into a heavenly place by justice, live in a manner worthy of the life they led in human form. But in the thousandth year both come to draw lots and choose their second life, each choosing whatever it wishes. Then a human soul may pass into the life of a beast, and a soul which was once human, may pass again from a beast into a man. For the soul which has never seen the truth can never pass into human form."[27]

These complications are simplified in the *Timaeus*, because of the explication of the figure of the Demiurge, which, as we have seen,[28] directly creates souls, placing them in stars, it shows them original truth and entrusts to the "created Gods" the task of dressing them in mortal bodies. But the introduction of this fundamental theoretical personage, as well as the affirmation of the principle with which the Demiurge accomplishes all his work *by reason of the good*, must inevitably involve a change of the affirmation that the soul is found in a body *through a fault* and hence because of evil: it must bring us to interpret also this being in a body *in a positive way*. But Plato has not expressly developed this theme and has only simplified, as we read in the passage of the *Timaeus* reported earlier,[29] his eschatology, maintaining the cycle of reincarnations as expiation of a morally evil life and placing the return to the stars, to which the Demiurge originally had assigned the soul, as a reward for a good life.

From the *Gorgias* to the *Timaeus*, this fundamental principle is generally firm, although there are fluctuations in the way it is presented: what gives meaning to *this life* is the eschatological destiny of the soul; that is, *the other life* here has meaning only if it is related to a hereafter.

III. THE NEW MORAL ASCETIC

1. Anthropological dualism and the importance of the paradox connected
to it

We have explained, in the preceding section, how the relation between
the Ideas and things is not "dualistic" in the usual meaning of that term, since
the Ideas are the "true causes"; that is, the metaphysical foundation of things.[1]
Instead the Platonic conception of the relations between the soul and the body
is dualistic (in certain dialogues in a total and radical sense). In fact, in the
conception of the relations between *soul* and *body* there is introduced, beyond
the metaphysical-ontological dimension, the religious dimension of Orphism,
which transforms the structural distinction between the soul (= supersensible) and body (= sensible) into a *structural opposition*. For this reason the
body is understood not only as the receptacle of the soul, which gives the body
life and other capacities, and hence as an instrument at the service of the soul,
which is Socrates, understanding, but much more like a "tomb," a "prison" of
the soul; that is, as a place of expiation for the soul. We read in the *Gorgias*:
"Well, life as you describe it is a strange affair. I should not be surprised, you
know, if Euripides was right when he said, 'Who knows, if life be death, and
death be life?' And perhaps we are actually dead, for I once heard one of our
wise men say that we are now dead, and that our body is a tomb." (trans. W.
D. Woodhead, Bollingen, pp. 274-5)[2] Until we have a body we are dead,
because we are fundamentally our soul, and the soul, until it is in a body, is as
in a tomb, and hence mortified; our death (with the body) is life, because,
leaving the body, frees the soul from a prison. The body is the root of all evil
and the source of unhealthful desires, passions, hatreds, discords, ignorance,
and folly: all this mortifies the soul. This negative conception of the body is
attenuated somewhat in the final period of Plato, but it is never completely
erased.

This said, it is however necessary to point out immediately that Platonic
ethics is only in part conditioned by this exaggerated dualism; in fact, its basic
theorems and corollaries depend on the metaphysical distinction of the soul
(an entity akin to the intelligible) and the body (a sensible entity) rather more
than on the mystery-Orphic based opposition of soul (daimon) and body
(tomb and prison). From this last distinction the exaggerated and paradoxical
formulations of some principles are derived, which are, in any case, valid also
on the ontological level. The "second voyage" is in substance the true foundation of Platonic ethics.

To explain this, let us immediately analyze the two best-known paradoxes
of Platonic ethics, which have frequently been misunderstood, because they
are looked upon in terms of their external mystery-Orphic appearance more
than at their metaphysical substance: we allude to the two paradoxes of the

"flight from the body" and the "flight from the world." The first paradox is developed especially in the *Phaedo*. The soul ought to try to get as far away from the body as possible, and hence *the true lover of wisdom (philo-sopher) desires death and the true philosophy is the practice of death.* The meaning of this paradox is very clear. If the body is an obstacle for the soul with the weight of the senses and if the death is no more than the separation of the soul from the body, then death constitutes, in some way, the complete realization of that liberation that in this life the philosopher pursues through knowledge. In other words, death is an episode that ontologically involves only the body; it does not in any way harm the soul, but brings it great advantages, permitting it to live a pure life devoted to truth, a life wholly gathered into itself, without obstacles and veils, and entirely connected with the intelligible. This means that the *death of the body* discloses the *true life of the soul.* Therefore the meaning of the paradox does not change but by reversing the definition makes it even clearer: *the philosopher is one who desires true life* (= death of the body) *and philosophy is the practice of that life, of life in the purely spiritual sphere.* The flight from the body is the rediscovery of the spirit. Here is how Plato explains the sense of this paradox in the *Phaedo*, in this exemplary passage:

> "Then," said he, "all this must cause good lovers of wisdom to think and say one to the other something like this: 'there seems to be a shortcut which leads us and our argument to the conclusion in our search that so long as we have the body, and the soul is contaminated by such an evil, we shall never attain completely what we desire; that is, the truth. For the body keeps us constantly busy by reason of its need of sustenance; and moreover, if diseases come upon it they hinder our pursuit of the truth. And the body fills us with passion and desires and fears, and all sorts of fancies and foolishness, so that, as they say, it really and truly makes it impossible for us to think at all. The body and its desires are the only cause of wars and factions and battles; for all wars arise for the sake of gaining money, and we are compelled to gain money for the sake of the body. We are slaves to its service. And so, because of all these things, we have no leisure for philosophy. But the worst of all is that if we do get a bit of leisure inherent to philosophy, the body is constantly breaking in upon our studies and disturbing us with noise and confusion, so that it prevents our beholding the truth, and in fact we perceive that, if we are ever to be anything absolutely, we must be free from the body and must behold the actual reality with the eye of the soul alone. And then, as our argument shows, of when we are dead we are likely to posses the wisdom which we desire and claim to be enamored of, but not while we live. For, if pure knowledge is impossible while the body is with us, one of two things must follow, either it cannot be acquired at all or only when we are dead; for then the soul will be by itself apart from the body, but not before. And while we live, we shall I think, be nearest to knowledge when we avoid, so far as possible, intercourse and communion with the body, except what is absolutely necessary, and are not

filled with this nature, but keep ourselves pure from it until God himself sets us free. And in this way, freeing ourselves from the foolishness of the body and being pure, we shall, I think, be with the pure and shall know of ourselves all that is pure,—and that is, perhaps, the truth. For it cannot be that the impure attain the pure. Such words as these, I think, Simmias, all who are rightly lovers of knowledge must say to each other and such must be their thoughts."[3]

The meaning of the second paradox, "the flight from the world," is also made clear. Moreover it is Plato himself who unveils it in a specific way, explaining that the flight from the world means *to become virtuous and to try and become assimilated to God.* Here are his words:

"But it is impossible that evil shall be done away, Theodorus, for there must always be something opposed to good; and they cannot have their place among the Gods, but must inevitably hover about mortal nature and his earth. *Therefore we ought to try to escape from earth to the dwelling of the Gods quickly as we can; and to escape is to become like God, so far as this is possible; and to become like God is to become righteous and holy and wise.*"[4]

This passage can be further explained, if need be, with a reference to a parallel passage of the *Laws*:

"What conduct, then, is dear to God and in his steps? One kind of conduct, expressed in one ancient phrase, namely, that *'like is dear to like'* when it is moderate, whereas immoderate things are dear neither to one another nor to things moderate. *In our eyes God will be 'the measure of all things' in the highest degree*—a degree much higher than is any 'man' they talk of. *He, then, that is to become dear to such and one must needs become, so far as he possibly can, of a like character; and, according to the present argument, he amongst us that is temperate is dear to God,* since he is like him, while he that is not temperate is unlike and so as is also he who is unjust, and so likewise with the rest, by parity of reasoning."[5]

So, the two paradoxes have an identical meaning: to flee from the body means to flee from the evil of the body by means of virtue and knowledge; to flee from the world means to flee from the evil of the world, again by means of virtue and knowledge; to follow virtue and knowledge means to make oneself like God, who is the "measure" of all things.

2. The systematization and foundation of the new list of values

Socrates already, as we have seen produced a revolution in the sphere of values, which, probably, was the most radical produced in antiquity. He produced it on the basis of his fundamental discovery of the *psyché* as the essence of man. Real values are *only those of the soul*; that is, virtue and knowledge. Values of the body and exterior values are secondary and have been displaced and lost their traditional status.[6] Now, the new metaphysical status attributed by Plato to the soul gives a definitive foundation to the Socratic list of values.

And, if, in a first moment, Plato focussed almost all his attention on the values of the soul, as though they were unique values, little by little, attracted chiefly by his political interests, he mitigated the devaluation of the other values, so he could reach a deduction of a true and proper "list of values," the first systematic and complete list handed down from antiquity.

(*a*) The first and highest place was reserved for the Gods, and hence to the values which may be called *religious*.

(*b*) Immediately after the Gods came the soul, which, in man, is the highest and best part, with the values which belong to virtue and knowledge; that is, with spiritual values.

(*c*) The third place is given to the body with its values (the values vital to life, as we would say today).

(*d*) In fourth place the goods of fortune, wealth, and exterior goods in general.

As is evident also from a first reading of this list, the place that each of the values occupies corresponds exactly with the place that, in the general scheme of Platonic understanding of being, each of the beings to which they refer would occupy. Thus the sensible is entirely dependent on the supersensible, to the point that it alone exists in function of the supersensible, just as the values connected to the sensible are used only in function of the metasensible values. In particular keep in mind that the values in the third and fourth place are such only if subordinated to the higher values of the soul. In the case in which they presuppose or generally are opposed to the values of the soul, they become negatives, and hence they are disvalues.

Here is a passage of the *Laws* that is little known, but that ought to be better known for the light it sheds on this problem and because it is Plato's last word on the subject:

> "Of all of man's own belongings, the most divine is his soul, since it is most his own. A man's own belongings are invariably twofold: the stronger and better are the ruling elements, the weaker and worse those that serve; wherefore of one's own belongings one must honor those that rule above those that serve. Thus it is that in charging men to honor their own souls next after the gods who rule the secondary divinities, I am giving a right injunction. But there is hardly a man of us all who pays honor rightly, although he fancies he does so [there follows a list of actions that do not honor the soul, among which we choose two of the most suggestive examples]. Again, when a man honors beauty above goodness, this is nothing else than a literal and total dishonoring of the soul; for such a statement asserts that the body is more honorable than the soul,—but falsely, since nothing earth born is more honorable than the things of Heaven, and he

that surmises otherwise concerning the soul knows not that in it he possesses, and neglects, a thing most admirable. Again, when a man craves to
acquire wealth ignobly, or feels no qualm in so acquiring it, he does not then
by his gifts pay honor to his soul,—far from it in fact!—for what is honorable
therein and noble he is bartering away for a handful of gold; yet all the gold
on earth, or under it, does not equal the price of goodness."

"as for the third, everyone would conceive that this place *naturally* belongs
to the honor due to the body. But here again one has to investigate the
various forms of honor,—which of them are genuine, which spurious; and
this is the law giver's task. Now he as I suppose, declares that the honors are
these and of these kinds; —the honorable body is not the fair body or the
strong or the swift or the large, or yet the body that is sound in health,
—although this is what many believe; neither is it a body of the opposite
kind to any of these; rather those bodies which hold the mean position
between all these opposite extremes are by far the most temperate and
stable; for while the one extreme makes the soul puffed up and proud, the
other makes them lowly and spiritless."

The same holds good of the possession of goods and chattels, and they are
to be valued on a similar scale. In each case, when they are in excess, they
produce enmities and feuds both in States and privately, while if they are
deficient they produce, as a rule, serfdom."[7]

3. Platonic antihedonism

What of pleasure? Does a place exist in this "list of values," or is it to be
found in a grouping of another kind? Already Socrates, as we will see, rejected
pleasure as an autonomous value and the school of Aristippus, by erecting
pleasure to the status of supreme good, betrayed Socrates position, whereas
Antisthenes, qualified pleasure precisely as evil, pushing to extremes Socrates
thought in the direction of Cynicism.

The position of Plato, in this regard, went through an evolution that
moved from a radicalization, in the ascetic direction, of Socrates view, to a
recovery, clarified and deepened ontologically, of the Socratic position.

In the dialogues like the *Gorgias* and the *Phaedo* (and in part in the
Republic itself)—in which, in addition to the metaphysical distinction of
body-soul, the mystery-Orphic dualism plays a role, and in which the body is
seen also as the prisonhouse of the soul—it is clear that pleasure, which is
connected to the senses, cannot be but disvalued radically, and it is seen, in a
certain sense, as the antithesis of the good, in so far as it enslaves the soul to
the sensible and binds it to it. In sum, the dualistic scorn of the body belongs,
consequently, with the scorn of all pleasures and all enjoyment of the body.
Here is one of the most important texts in this regard:

> Now the soul of the true philosopher believes that it must not resist this
> deliverance [from the body], and therefore it stands aloof from pleasures
> and lusts and griefs and fears, so far as it can, considering that when anyone

has violent pleasures or fears or griefs or lusts he suffers from them not merely what one might think"for example, illness or loss of money spent for such lusts"but he suffers greatest and most extreme evil and does not take it into account."

"What is this evil, Socrates questioned" said Cebes.

"The evil is that the soul of every man, when it is greatly pleased or pained by anything, is compelled to believe that the object which caused the emotion is very distinct and very true; but it is not. These objects are mostly the visible ones, are they not?"

"Certainly."

"And when this occurs, is not the soul most completely put in bondage by the body?"

"How so?"

"Because each pleasure or pain nails it as with a nail to the body and rivets it on and makes it corporeal, so that it fancies that things are true which the body says are true. For because it has the same beliefs and pleasures as the body it is compelled to adopt also the same habits and mode of life, and can never depart impurities to the other world, must always go away contaminated with the body; and so it sinks quickly into another body again and grows into it, like seed that is sown. Therefore it has no part in the communion of the divine and the pure and the absolute."

"What you say, Socrates, is very true," said Cebes."[8]

A softening of this conception can be felt already in the *Republic*, where, on the basis of the distinction of the various functions or parts of the soul (on which we will return further on), pleasure is understood, although with some vacillations, as a prerogative of the soul more than of the body. And since there are three parts of the soul, the *thumos* (concupiscible), the *epithumos* (irascible), and the *logistikon* (rational), there are subsequently three kinds of pleasure: the pleasures linked to material things and to wealth (those of the concupiscible soul), the pleasures connected to honor and conquering (those of the irascible soul), and pleasures of knowledge (those of the rational soul). The pleasures of the third kind are far and away superior, first because of the great superiority of the rational faculty of the soul to which it refers, and second, because of the great superiority of the objects through which the pleasures of reason are procured in comparison to those through which the pleasures of the other parts of the soul are procured. But, only the pleasures of the third kind are "authentic," whereas the other two kinds of pleasures are "spurious." In fact, in general, pleasure is like the attempt to "stuff" or "fill" an emptiness; but neither the body nor the lower parts of the soul are such as to be able to attract and receive objects that would be capable of doing this, because their objects are not true being, whereas the higher part can be stuffed and filled with true being, in the highest grade pleasurable:

"Then is not that which is fulfilled of what more truly is, and which itself more truly is, more truly filled and satisfied than that which being itself less real is filled with more unreal things?"

"Of course."

"If, then, to be filled with what befits nature is pleasure, then that which is more really filled with real things would more really and truly cause us to enjoy a true pleasure, or that which partakes of the less truly existent would be less truly and truly filled and would partake of a less trustworthy and less true pleasure."

"Most inevitably," he said."[9]

Nevertheless, even "spurious" pleasures of the two lower parts of the soul, if they are condemnable when they overcome the higher, are instead acceptable if restrained by reason:

"Then," said I, "may we not confidently declare that in both the gain=loving and the contentious part of our nature all the desires that wait upon knowledge and reason, and, pursuing their pleasures in conjunction with them, take only those pleasures that reason approves, will, since they follow truth, enjoy the truest pleasures, so far as that is possible for them, and also the pleasures that are proper to them and their own, if for everything that which is best may be said to be most its 'own'?"

"But indeed," he said, "it is most truly its very own."

"Then when the entire soul accepts the guidance of the wisdom-loving part and is not filled with inner dissension, the result for each part is that it in all other respects keeps to its own task and is just, and likewise that each enjoys its proper pleasures and the best pleasures, and, so far as such a thing is possible, the truest."[10]

But in the Academy there arose rather quickly a lively debate about the nature of pleasure, which resulted in two opposite views. On the one hand, some Academics rejected the notion that pleasure could in any way be identified with the good; on the other, as we will see, Eudoxus reexamined pleasure and identified it with the good, bringing in evidence in favor of his position, the fact that both men and animals tend equally to pleasure and avoid pain.[11] Plato intervened in the dispute with his *Philebus,* attempting to bring the two views together. The ameliorating solution that he proposed, more than a modification of the philosophical presuppositions of his ethics, was rather an elimination of the excesses due to mystery-Sophist dualism of Orphic origin, and hence an attempt to make the ethical corollaries more cogent with his metaphysical premises.

A life of pure intelligence, which is undoubtedly a more divine life, does not suit man, who is a soul in a body, because it is more than a human life, it is the life of the eternal Gods. But neither is a life of pure pleasure suitable to man, which would be the life of an animal. Here the conclusion of the *Philebus* shows clearly that the ethics of the *Gorgias* and *Phaedo* are rearranged, but nothing at all is repudiated:

> But [we will] not [give] first [place to pleasure], even if all the cattle and horses and other beasts in the world, in their pursuit of enjoyment, so assert. Trusting in them, as augres trust in birds, the many [human beings] judge that pleasures are the greatest blessings in life and they imagine the lusts of beasts are better witnesses than are the aspirations and thoughts inspired by the philosophic muse."[12]

To man a "mixed" life of intelligence and pleasure is suitable. But, first, note that pleasures that Plato takes up into the "mixed life" are only the "pure pleasures," that is, the pleasures derived from spiritual activities and perceptions; in the second place, note that the domination lies entirely entrusted to intelligence and it alone:

> *Socrates*: Yes; but let us hear what follows. For I, perceiving the truths which I now have been detailing, and annoyed by the theory held not only by Philebus, but by many thousands of others, said that mind was a far better and more excellent thing for human life and pleasure.
> *Protarchus*: True.
> *Socrates*: But suspecting that there were many other things to be considered, I said that if anything should be found better than these two, I should support mind against pleasure in the struggle for the second place, and even the second place would be lost by pleasure.
> *Protarchus*: Yes, that is what you said.
> *Socrates*: And next it was most sufficiently proved that each of these two was insufficient.
> *Protarchus*: Very true.
> *Socrates*: In this argument, then, both mind and pleasure were set aside; neither of them is the absolute good, since they are devoid of self- sufficiency, adequacy, and perfection?
> *Protarchus*: Quite right.
> *Socrates*: And on the appearance of a third competitor better than either of these, *mind is now found to be ten thousand times more pain than pleasure to the victor.*"[13]

And also in the *Laws*, where Plato is concerned with pleasure a vocabulary is used that at first glance would even seem to anticipate Epicurus, things do not change. In the fifth book we, in fact, read what follows:

> "Thus, as regards the right character of institutions and the right character of individuals, we have now laid down practically all the rules that are of divine sanction. Those that are of human origin we have not stated as yet, but state them we must; for our converse is with men not gods. *Pleasures, pains and desires are by nature especially human; and from these, of necessity, every mortal creature is, so to say suspended and depended by the strongest cords of influence. Thus one should commend the noblest life,* not merely

because it is of superior fashion in respect of fair repute, but also because, if a man consents to taste it and not shun it in his youth, it is superior likewise in that all that man covet,—*an excess, namely, of joy and a deficiency of pain throughout the whole of life.* That this will clearly be the result, if the man tastes of it rightly, will at once be fully evident. But wherein does this 'rightness' consist? That is the question which we must now, under the instruction of our argument, consider; comparing the more pleasant life with the more painful, we must in this wise consider whether this mode is natural to us, and that other mode unnatural. We desire that pleasure should be ours, but pain we neither choose nor desire; the neutral state we do not desire in place of pleasure but we do desire it in exchange for pain; and we desire less pain with more pleasure, but we do not desire less pleasure with more pain; and when the two are evenly balanced, we are unable to state any clear preference. Now all these states—in their number, their quantity, intensity, equality, and in the opposites thereof—have, or have not, influence on desire, to govern its choice of each. So these things being thus ordered of necessity, we desire that mode of life in which the feelings are many, great, and intense, with those of pleasure predominating, but we do not desire the life in which the feelings of pain predominate; and contrariwise, we do not desire the life in which the feelings are few, small, and gentle, if the painful predominate, but if the pleasurable predominate, we do desire it. Further, we must regard the life in which there is an equal balance of pleasure and pain as we previously regarded the neutral state: we desire the balanced life insofar as it exceeds the painful life in point of what we like, but we do not desire it insofar as it exceeds the pleasant lives in point of the things we dislike. The lives of us men must all be regarded as naturally bound up in these feelings, and what kinds of lives we naturally desire is what we must distinguish; but if we assert that we desire anything else, we only say so through ignorance and inexperience of the lives as they really are."[14]

But immediately after having recognized this (which among others—note—is consciously motivated by the popular character of the *Laws*) Plato concludes that the life that affords the most pleasure *is only the virtuous life*, as in all the preceding dialogues:

"I would desire in the choice of lives not that pain should be in excess, but the life we have judged the more pleasant is that in which pain is exceeded by pleasure. We will assert then, that since the temperate life has its feelings smaller, fewer and lighter than the licentious life, and the wise life than the foolish, and the brave than the cowardly, and since the one life is superior to the other in pleasure, but inferior in pain, *the brave life is victorious over the cowardly and the wise over the foolish; consequently the one set of lives ranks as more pleasant than the other: the temperate, brave, wise, and healthy lives are more pleasant than the cowardly, foolish, licentious, and diseased.* To sum up, the life of bodily and spiritual virtue, as compared with that of vice, is not only more pleasant, *but also exceeds greatly in nobility, rectitude, virtue and good fame, so that it causes the man who lives it to live ever so much more happily than he who lives the opposite life.*"[15]

4. The purification of the soul, virtue, and knowledge

Socrates has placed in the "care of the soul" the supreme moral task of man. Plato states the Socratic commandment, but adding a mystic coloration, by explaining that the "care of the soul" means "the purification of the soul." This purification is realized when the soul, going beyond the senses, is possessed by the pure world of the intelligible and spiritual, and communing with it, as with that which is connatural and similar in kinship. Here *purification*, quite different than the initiation ceremony of the Orphics, *is identical with the process of rising to the supreme knowledge of the intelligible.* And it is actually on this value of purification recognized as *science* and *knowledge* (values that the ancient Pythagoreans in part already, as we will see, discovered) that we need to reflect upon to comprehend the novelty of Platonic "mysticism." It is not a ecstatic and alogical contemplation, but a cathartic effort of inquiry and progressive ascent to knowledge. And so it is easy to understand how, for Plato, the process of rational knowledge is at the same time a process of moral conversion: in the measure in which the process of knowledge is carried from the sensible to the supersensible, we are converted from one to the other world, we are carried from the false to true sphere of being. Hence the soul is cured, purified, converted and elevated *by knowing.* And this is virtue.

Here is an important passage of the *Phaedo*, in which *virtue, knowledge,* and *purification* are identified, and philosophy is made to coincide with the true initiation into the mysteries:

> "My dear Simmias, I suspect that this is not the right way to purchase virtue, by exchanging pleasures for pleasures, and pains for pains, and fear for fear, and greater for less, as if they were coins, but the only right point is, for which all those things must be exchanged and by means of and with which all these things ought to be bought and sold, is in fact *wisdom*; and courage and self-restraint and justice and, insured, true virtue exists ultimately with wisdom, whether pleasures and fears and other things of that sort are added or taken away. *And virtue which consists in the exchange of such things for each other without wisdom, is but a painted imitation of virtue and is really slavish and has nothing healthy or true in it*; but truth is in fact a *purification from all these things*, and self-restraint and justice and courage and *wisdom itself are a kind of purification.* And I fancy that those men who established the mysteries were not unenlightened, but in reality had a hidden meaning when they said long ago that whoever goes initiated and unsanctified to the other world would lie in the mire, but he who arrives there initiated and purified will dwell with the Gods. For as they say in the mysteries, 'the thyrsus-bearers are many, but the mystics few'; and these mystics are, I believe, those who have been true philosophers."[16]

And not only in the *Phaedo*, but the central books themselves of the *Republic*, state these doctrines: dialectic is the conversion to being, the initiation into the highest Good.

We will speak about the individual virtues in our exposition of the *Republic*. Here we point out again that in this fusion of mysticism and rationalism, Plato fully recovers Socratic intellectualism. We will, in fact, see that if he has placed in the soul alogical powers in order to explain more adequately human action, he nevertheless allows an indisputable supremacy to reason. And he even states, again in the last two dialogues, the Socratic paradox that *no one commits evil voluntarily*, acknowledging in this way the omnipotent power of knowledge.[17]

IV. THE MYSTICISM OF PHILIA
AND EROS

1. Friendship (love) and the "Primary Friend"

We have seen that Socrates had taken the inquiry into friendship into a philosophical framework. Plato took from Socrates the state of the question, but, in the solution, went beyond Socrates, once again on the basis of the results of the "Second Voyage."

Generally the Platonic treatments of love (*eros*) and friendship (*philÙa*) are considered together, but that is a mistake, because they are not identical, although having much in common. In Greek the term *philÙa* involves the rational element, or at least the absence of passion and that "divine mania" which is instead the peculiar characteristic of eros; and this is why Plato studied them separately, the former in the *Lysis* and the latter the *Symposium*, and, in part also in the *Phaedrus*.

Beyond the aporias generated in the *Lysis*, we can certainly determine the following points.[1] Friendship does not arise between similars nor between dissimilars; friendship does not arise between good and good nor between evil and good (or among good and evil). It is rather the intermediate (neither good nor bad) that is a friend of good. And the *intermediate* is friend of good because of evil, which is there in him (naturally it must be an evil that does not entirely condition the intermediate), and because of the desire of the good, which he lacks but that in some way belongs to him, due to the intermediate (the intermediate, note, can be defined, in addition as that which is *neither* good *nor* bad, even as that which is, instead, both good *and* bad).

But friendship for Plato does not develop in a purely horizontal way, so to speak, but it rises in a vertical sense; that is, transcendent. That which we seek in human friendship is again something further and every friendship has meaning only in function of a *"Primary Friend"* (πρῶτον φίλον). Here is the most important passage of the dialogue:

> Can we possibly help, then, being weary of going on in this manner, then is it not necessary that we advance at once to a beginning, which will not again refer us to friend upon friend, but arrive at that to which we are in the first instance friends, and for the sake of which we say we are friends to all the rest?
>
> It is necessary, he answered.
>
> This, then, is what I say we must consider, in order that all those other things, to which we said we were friendly, for the sake of that one thing, may not, like so many shadows of it, lead us into error, but that we may establish that thing as the first, to which we are really and truly friends. (trans. J. Wright, Bollingen, pp. 163, 164)[2]

And in the context of the dialogue it clearly emerges that this "Primary Friend" is nothing other than the primary and unconditioned Good. Friendship that binds human beings to human beings is authentic, for Plato, *only if it shows the way to rise to the Good.*

The conclusions that Plato draws in his analyses about love are analogous and we will consider them in detail.

2. "Platonic love"

We have already seen that the theme of beauty is not linked by Plato with that of art (which is imitation of mere appearances and does not reveal anything about intellectual beauty), since with the theme of eros and love, which is understood as a mediating power between the sensible and the supersensible, a power that gives wings and elevates, through various levels of beauty, to the metaempirical Beauty in itself. And since Beauty, for the Greeks, is identical with Good, or it is generally an aspect of Good, just so is Eros a power that elevates to the Good: *the Platonic erotic, far from being in contrast with Platonic mysticism and asceticism, is a fundamental aspect that is especially Hellenic in character.*

The analysis of Love is among the most beautiful that Plato has given.[3] Love is neither beauty nor good, but is a thirst for beauty and goodness. Love is hence not a divinity (God is always and uniquely Good) nor even a man. It is not mortal nor even immortal: it is one of those daimonic beings that are "intermediate" between man and God. Here is how these daimonic beings are described:

> They are the envoys and interpreters that fly between heaven and earth, flying upward with our worship and our prayers and descending with the heavenly answers and commandments, and since they are between the two estates they weld both sides together and merge them into one great whole. They form the medium of the prophetic arts, of the priestly rights of sacrifice, initiation, and incantation, of divination and of sorcery, for the divine will not mingle directly with the human, and it is only through the mediation of the spirit world that man can have any intercourse, whether waking or sleeping, with the Gods. And the man who is versed in such matters is said to have spiritual powers, as opposed to the mechanical powers of the man who is expert in the more mundane arts. There are many spirits, and many kinds of spirits, too, and Love is one of them. (trans. Michael Joyce, Bollingen, p. 555)[4]

And the *Daimon* Love has been produced from *Penia* (which means *Need*) and from *Poros* (which means *Plenty*) on the birthday of Aphrodite. And it is for this reason that Love has a *twofold nature*:

> Then again, as the son of *Plenty* and *Need*, it has been his fate to be always needy; nor is he delicate and lovely as most of us believe, but harsh and arid, barefoot and homeless, sleeping on the naked earth, in doorways, or in the

very streets beneath the stars of heaven, and always partaking of his poverty. But, secondly, he brings his father's resourcefulness to his designs upon the beautiful and the good, for he is gallant, impetuous, and energetic, a mighty hunter, and a master of device and artificeat once desirous and full of wisdom, a life long seeker after truth, and adept in sorcery, enchantment, and seduction. He is neither mortal nor immortal, for in the space of a day he will be now, when all goes well with him, alive and blooming, and now dying, to be born again by virtue of his father's nature, while what he gains will always ebb away as fast. So Love is never all together in or out of need, and stands, moreover, midway between ignorance and wisdom. (trans. Michael Joyce, Bollingen, pp. 555-6)[5]

Love is hence philo-sopher in the fullest sense of the term. *Sophia*; that is, wisdom is possessed only by God; ignorance is the condition of those totally alienated from wisdom; a philosopher is, instead, in the condition of one who is neither ignorant nor wise, who does not possess wisdom but aspires to it and is always in search of it, and when he finds it, it escapes him and so he must seek for it further as a lover does.

That which men commonly call love is only a small part of true love: love is a desire for *beauty*, for the *good*, for *wisdom*, for *happiness*, for *immortality*, for the *Absolute*. Love has many ways that bring to various levels of good (every form of love is a desire to possess the good permanently); but the *true lover* is one who knows how to pursue the beloved in all things until he reaches the supreme vision, until he achieves a vision of that which is absolutely beautiful.

The lowest grade in the scale of love is physical love, which is a desire to possess the beautiful body for the purposes of generation in beauty of another body, and already this physical love is a desire for the immortal and the eternal: "because generation, although in a mortal creature, is perennial and immortal."[6]

Then there are the different grades of lovers who are fruitful not in the body but in the soul, which carried the seed that is born and increased in the realm of the spirit. And among the lovers in the sphere of the spirit are found, by going little by little to the heights, lovers of souls, lovers of the arts, lovers of justice and laws, lovers of pure knowledge.

And finally, at the summit of the scale of love, there is the effulgence of the vision of the Idea of Beauty, of Beauty itself, of Absolute Beauty.

Let us read the marvelous pages in which Plato describes the steps of love, which bring us from the beautiful body to the pure Idea of Beauty: they are among the most elevated literature of all times:

Well now, my dear Socrates, I have no doubt that even you might be initiated into these, the more elementary mysteries of Love. But I don't know if you could apprehend the final revelation, for so far, you know, we are only at the bottom of the true scale of perfection.

Never mind, she went on, I will do all I can to help you understand, and you must strain every nerve to follow what I'm saying.

Well then, she began, the candidate for this initiation cannot, if his efforts are to be rewarded, begin too early to devote himself to the beauties of the body. First of all, if his preceptor instructs him as he should, he will fall in love with the beauty of one individual body, so that his passion shall give life to noble discourse. Next he must consider how nearly related the beauty of any one body is to the beauty of any other, what he will see that if he is to devote himself to loveliness of form it will be absurd to deny that the beauty of each and every body is the same. Having reached this point, he must set himself to be the lover of every lovely body, and bring his passion to the one into due proportion by deeming it of little or no importance.

Next he must grasp that the beauties of the body are as nothing to the beauties of the soul, so that wherever he meets with spiritual loveliness, even in the husk of an unlovely body, he will find it beautiful enough to fall in love with and to cherish–and beautiful enough to quicken in his heart a longing for such discourse as tends towards the building noble nature. And from this he will be led to contemplate the beauty of laws and institutions. And when he discovers how nearly every kind of beauty is akin to every other he will conclude that the beauty of the body is not, after all, of so great moment.

And next, his attention should be diverted from institutions to the sciences, so that he may know the beauty of every kind of knowledge. And thus, by scanning beauty's wide horizon, he will be saved from a slavish and illiberal devotion to the individual loveliness of a single boy, a single man, or a single institution. And, turning his eyes to the open sea of beauty, he will find in such contemplation the seed of the most fruitful discourse and the loftiest thought, and reap a golden harvest of philosophy, and so confirmed and strengthened, he will come upon one single form of knowledge, the knowledge of the beauty I am about to speak of. And here, she said, you must follow me as closely as you can.

Whoever has been initiated so far in the mysteries of Love and has viewed all these aspects of the beautiful in due succession, is at least drawing near the final revelation. And now, Socrates, there bursts upon him that wondrous vision which is the very soul of the beauty he has toiled so long for. It is an everlasting loveliness which neither comes nor goes, which neither flowers nor fades, for such beauty is the same on every hand, the same then as now, here as there, this way as that way, the same to every worshipper to every other.

Nor will his vision of the beautiful take the form of a face, or of hands, or of anything that is of the flesh. It will be neither words, nor something that exists in something else, such as a living creature, or the earth, or the heavens, or anything that is—but subsisting of itself by itself in an eternal oneness, while every lovely thing partakes of it in such sort that, however much the parts may wax and wane, it will be neither more or less, but still the same inviable hold.

And so, when his prescribed devotion to boyish beauties have carried our candidate so far that the universal beauty dawns upon his inward side, he is almost within reach of the final revelation. And this is the way, the only way, he must approach, or be led toward, sanctuary of Love. Starting from individual beauties, the quest for the universal beauty must bring him ever mounting the heavenly ladder, stepping from rung to rung—that is from one to two, and from two to every lovely body, from bodily beauty to the beauty of institutions, from institutions of learning and from learning in general to the special lore that pertains to nothing but the beautiful itself–until at least he comes to know what beauty is.

And if, my dear Socrates, Diotima, went on, man's life is ever worth the living, it is when he has attained his vision of the very soul of beauty. And once you have seen it, you will never be seduced again by the charm of gold, of…, of comely boys, or lads just ripening to manhood; you will care nothing for the beauties that used to take your breath away and kindle such longing in you, and many others like you, Socrates, to be always at the side of the beloved and feasting your eyes upon him, so that you would be content, if it were possible, to deny yourself the gross and necessities of meat and drink, so long as you were with him.

But if it were given to man to gaze on beauties very self-unsullied, unalloyed and freed from the mortal taint that haunts the frail loveliness of flesh and blood—if, I say, it were given to man to see the heavenly beauty face-to-face, would you call his, she asked me, an unenviable life, whose eyes has been open to the vision, and who had gazed upon it in true contemplation until it had become his own forever?

And remember, she said, that it is when he looks upon beauty visible presentment, and only then, that a man will be quickened with the true, and not the seeming virtue—for it is virtue's self that quickens him, not virtue's semblance. And when he has brought forth and reared this perfect virtue, he shall be called the friend of God, and if ever it is given man to put on immortality it shall be given to him. (trans. Michael Joyce, Bollingen, pp. 561-3)[7]

Plato in the *Phaedrus* sheds further light on the problem of the *synthetic* and *mediating* nature of love, by linking it with the doctrine of recollection. The soul, as we know, in its original life in the company of the Gods, has seen the Hyperouranos and the Ideas; then, by losing its wings and falling into the body, it has forgotten everything of this. But, by its own labor, by philosophizing, the soul "remembers" those things that it at one time saw. This recollection, in the specific case of Beauty, occurs in a totally particular way, because, along among all the other Ideas, Beauty has the privileged quality of being "extraordinarily clear and gentle."[8] This translucency of the ideal Beauty in the Beautiful sensible, inflames the soul, which is taken by the desire of flying with wings, to return there from whence it has descended. And this desire is precisely *Eros* which with the transcendent yearning for the supersensible rises again to gain again its ancient wings.

...But he who is newly initiated, who beheld many of those realities, when he sees the God-like face or form which is a good image of beauty, shudders at first, and something of the old awe comes over him, then, as he goes, he reveres the beautiful one as a God, and if he did not fear to be thought stark mad, he would offer sacrifice to his beloved as to an idol or a God. And as he looks upon him, a reaction from his shuddering comes over him, with sweat and unwanted heat; for as the affluent of beauty induce him through the eye, he is warmed; the effluence moisten the germ of the feathers, and as he grows warm, the parts from which the feathers grow, which were before hard and choked, and prevented the feathers from sprouting, become soft, and as the nourishment streams upon him, the quills of the feathers swell and begin to grow from the roots over all the form of the soul; for it was once all feathered."[9]

Love is nostalgia for the Absolute, transcending tension toward the metaempirical, a power which pushes us toward a return to our origins, *when we were near the Gods.*

V. PLATO A PROPHET?

Certain acritical Neoplatonic glorifications of Plato have undoubtedly brought a smile to modern readers. And the fact that, as we are told, Ficino placed an eternal flame before the statue of Plato in the Florentine Academy may equally cause amusement. And to contemporary man, having adopted an incredulous attitude, is perhaps almost irritated by the adulation (putting aside numerous examples that we could adduce and limiting ourselves to one of the most instructive ones) found in the dedication made by Acri (one of the most well-known translators of Plato in the modern era): "These books [the dialogues of Plato which he had translated] of the *pagan prophet of Christ* I put at the feet of the Vicar of Christ with a humble soul."[1]

Actually, that there are positions and affirmations in Platonism that can be understood as foreshadowings of Christianity is undeniable. Here is an example in a passage that overturns the moral sentiment of the Greeks and anticipates, almost, the Gospel precept, if anyone strike you on the cheek, turn the other cheek:

> But amid all these arguments...this alone stands steadfast, that we should be more on our guard against doing than suffering wrong, and that before all things a man should study not to seem but to be good, whether in private or in public life, and that if anyone proves evil in any way, he should be chastised, and next to being good the second best thing is to become good and to make amends by punishment, and that we should avoid every form of flattery, whether to ourselves or to others, whether to few or to many, and that rhetoric and every other activity should ever so be employed, to attain justice. If you will listen to me then, you will follow me where on your arrival you will win happiness both in life and after death, as our account reveals and you may let anyone despise you as a fool and do you outrage, if he wishes, yes and, you may cheerfully let him strike you with that humiliating blow, for you will suffer no harm thereby if you are really a good man and honorable, and pursue virtue. (trans. W. D. Woodhead, Bollingen, p. 306-7)[2]

But—putting aside various less eloquent exampleswe want to cite a single passage from the *Republic*, which is utterly baffling: "What they will say is this: that such being his disposition the just will have to endure the lash, the rack, chains, the branding-iron in his eyes, and finally after every extremity of suffering, he will be crucified...".[3]

And if, in regard to such a text, Acri writes: "here in an obscure way is foretold the God-Man," [4] anyone can judge whether or not what he said is without any probability. And the scientifically minded, as pure scientist, certainly does not have the means with which to pronounce either for or against such statements. But he who believes knows that the Spirit breathed wherever he wills. And why could he not have breathe on the Greek and pagan Plato?

VI. THE ETHICAL-RELIGIOUS COMPONENT OF PLATONIC THOUGHT AND ITS RELATIONSHIP WITH THE PROTOLOGIC OF THE UNWRITTEN DOCTRINES

The exposition that we have made about the positions and essential doctrines of the ethical-religious component of Platonic thought is based on the whole of his writings. We wanted to maintain this type of exposition, and to indicate only at the end their connections with the protologic, for the purpose of defending what we said earlier about the function of the protologic at the summit and, consequently, to delineate in a still clearer manner the theoretical coherence of Platonic thought and the centrality of the weight-bearing axes that unify the various components into which it is articulated (and hence that make it a "system" in the sense that we have clarified earlier). Indeed it is the same thematic considered in a global sense within the protological framework that Plato took up in large measure in his writings.

Here are some essential points which deserve to be emphasized in a particular way.

(*a*) First, the bipolar structure of all reality is understood as not being restricted or confined to the period of composition of the *Timaeus* and the synthetic bipolar structure of the soul, and in particular to its rational part. In fact, already from the *Republic* it emerges clearly that Plato conceived the soul, in its true nature (τῇ ἀλητεστάτῃ φύσει); that is, in its rational aspect, as a "mixture" like a composite of many elements (σύνθετόν τε ἐκ πολλῶν), and in particular as a composite in function of a beautiful synthesis (καλλίστῃ συνθέσει). Evidently, already from the period of the Republic Plato maintained only this rational aspect of the soul as immortal; actually, it is really qualified as being of a "divine nature."[1]

(*b*) In addition, an interpretation in a protological sense to the great myth of the "winged chariot," presented by Plato as a metaphysical image which was emblematic of the soul is newly applied.[2] Actually, if the charioteer of the "winged chariot" undoubtedly represents the rational aspect of the soul in its foundation, the pair of horses capable of going off in two different directions and that only the charioteer can control or subdue in a satisfactory manner, hardly represents the concupiscible and irascible aspects of the human soul. As a matter of fact, the pair of horses of the "winged chariot" have come to be interpreted generally in this way, as they would seem at first glance; but this does not explain some important elements, which are anomalous and which are capable of being understood only within the framework of the protologic.

First of all Plato also conceived the souls of the Gods as "winged chariots"; but it is clear that the souls of the Gods do not have need for an irascible and concupiscible aspect, which instead characterizes the human soul.[3] In addition,

177

if the concupiscible and the irascible constitute the mortal aspects of the soul, they cannot remain structurally joined to the rational soul in the Hyperouranos; that is, in the sphere of the intelligible world.

In modern times Robin has correctly called attention to these points, stating that in the two horses that go in opposite directions is an important image of the "dyad of the great and small"; that is, "an inequality and a dissimilarity, a multiplicity, a more or less." [4] Robin, in addition, explains:

> this duality is not in itself a danger, as far as inequality is submitted to order: it does not become a danger except in the souls in which this subordination is destroyed, and in mythical terms, at the moment when the charioteer is no longer able to subdue the horses; the fall of the soul is, hence, an effect of Necessity (understood in the sense of a dyadic Principle), because Necessity is a principle of disorder. Just as the two horses of the *Phaedrus* seem to represent exactly the essence of the Different and the necessary cause sometimes dominated by reason at others rebelling against it.[5]

Understood in this sense, the alogical aspect expressed by the two horses becomes quite coherent within the general metaphysical frame of reference, and it expresses in a surprising and truly effective way the presence and the function of the Dyad in the sphere of the soul, in its constitution and structure.[6]

(c) But even the concept of virtue (ἀρετή), becomes quite clear within the protological framework. Even beginning from the Gorgias Plato clearly emphasized the axiological-ontological structure of justice and virtue in general as the *order* and *harmony* (κόσμος, τάξις) of the soul and hence as the overcoming of *disorder, disorderliness*, and the *excessive*, with clear references to the protologic. Virtue, Plato explains, is an order brought into the soul analogous to that which is produced by the craftsmans (the demiurges) who in a way make the elements on which they work, giving them a shape, endowing each of them in the most appropriate way, up to the point of being ordered and complete. Let us read an important passage in this respect:

> *Socrates*: Then let us just quietly consider whether any of them had this quality. Well now, the *good* man who speaks for the *best* surely will not say what he says at random but with *some purpose in view*, just as all other *craftsmen* do not choose and apply materials to their work at random, but with the view that each of their productions should have a *certain form*. Look, for example, if you will, at painters, builders, shipwrights, and all other craftsmen—any of them you choose—and see how each one disposes each element *he contributes in a fixed order*, and compels one to fit and harmonize with the other until he has combined the whole into something well ordered and regulated. Other craftsmen in general and those we were speaking of just now, who have to do with the body, physical trainers and doctors, give order, I think, and discipline to the body. Do we admit the truth of this or not?
>
> *Callicles*: Let it be granted.

Socrates: Then harmony and order will make a building good, but disorder bad.

Callicles: I agree.

Socrates: Is it not the same too with the ship?

Callicles: Yes.

Socrates: And with our bodies also, we say?

Callicles: Certainly.

Socrates: And what about the soul? Will it be good if disordered, or rather if it achieves a certain order and discipline?

Callicles: Hereto our previous argument demands that we agree.

Socrates: Now what is the name of that bodily quality resulting from order and discipline?

Callicles: Health and strength, I suppose you mean.

Socrates: I do. And the effect of order and discipline in the soul? Try to discover and name it, as in the other case.

Callicles: Why do you not name it yourself, Socrates?

Socrates: Well, if you prefer that, I will do so, then do you, if you think I am right, agree; if not, refute me and do not let me escape. It seems to me that the word healthy is applied to all regularity in the body, and from this come health and general bodily excellence. Is it so or not?

Callicles: It is.

Socrates: And the words lawfulness and law are applied to all order and regularity of the soul, whence men become orderly and law-abiding, then this means justice and temperance. Yes or no?

Callicles: So be it. (trans. W. D. Woodhead, Bollingen, pp. 286-7)[7]

A little further on, our philosopher even drops an allusion to "geometrical equality," which sounds really symbolic, because of its relations with the protologic that we well know. This equality is the foundation of the "bond" and the "union," or universal "friendship"; and just as equality is cosmic law in general, so analogously, it is also the foundation of human excellence in particular. Here is a truly important text:

"This is then the position I take, and I affirm it to be true, and if it is true, then the man who wishes to be happy must, it seems, pursue and practice temperance, and each of us must flee from undiscipline with all the speed in his power and contrive, preferably to have no need of being disciplined, but if he or any of his friends, whether individual or city, has need of it, then he must suffer punishment and be disciplined, if he is to be happy. This I consider to be the mark to which a man should look throughout his life, and all his own endeavors and those of his city he should devote to the single purpose of so acting that justice and temperance shall dwell in him who is to be truly blessed. *He should not suffer his appetites to be undisciplined and endeavor to satisfy them* by leading the life of a brigand—a mischief without end. For such a man could be dear neither to any other man nor to God, since he is incapable of *fellowship*, and where there is no fellowship, *friendship* cannot be. Wise men, Callicles, say that the heavens and the earth, gods and men, *are bound together by fellowship and friendship, and order and temperance and justice,* and for this reason they call the sum of things the 'ordered' universe, my friend, not the world of this disorder or riot. But it seems to me that you pay no attention to these things in spite of your wisdom, but you are unaware that *geometric equality* [ἡ ἰσότης ἡ γεωμετρική] *is of great importance among gods and men alike, and you think we should practice overreaching others for you neglect geometry .*" (trans. W. D. Woodhead, Bollingen, pp. 289-90)[8]

And in the *Republic,* as we will see, this order (this *geometrical equality* hence proportional equality), will even be explained, with expressions completely unambiguous, as the realization of *unity-in-multiplicity;* that is, of the One-in-the-Many, completely interpretable and comprehensible only in the protological and henological sense.

The structure of life, hence, exactly corresponds in the ethical sphere, to the metaphysical structure of the whole of reality. The order in the disorder means at all levels (and hence also that of the ethical) bringing unity into multiplicity. As such, it implies the supreme knowledge of the Good (that is, of the One), and this is the "form" of which the *Gorgias* speaks, which must be brought within moral realities, to produce an adequate order.[9]

(*d*) The great ethical metaphor of the "flight from the world" also acquires a theoretical bite even more marked in the protological framework.[10] The "flight from the world" is the *flight from evil.* Consequently Plato connected evil with the Dyad, in the way in which we have explained. So that to flee the world and evil, by acquiring virtue (justice, holiness, wisdom) means to take away the preeminence of the opposite Principle (multiplicity and disorder) and to opt in favor of the Principle of the Good (that is, the One) in all its meanings. It means, in other words, *to stand on the base of this bipolar nexus focussed on the preeminence of the One-Good all of one's life,* and to develop, consequently, all human activities.

(*e*) And likewise the famous doctrine of the "assimilation to God" takes on within the protological framework more pertinent conceptual determinations. To assimilate to God means, in fact, to bring order into life, descending into realities, as Plato explains in the *Republic,* the order of those realities that are always the same and that are structured according to a numerical relation in the Hellenic sense (κατὰ λόγος). Actually it is the structure of the *logos-arithmos* which can bring order out of disorder, measure into the unmeasured; that is to say, unity-into-multiplicity.[11]

Consequently the Demiurge; that is, the supreme God, is He who brings order into disorder, by gathering the One and the many in the best possible way, as we explained earlier.

Hence, the supreme Measure of all things is the Good as One, and this is the Divine in the impersonal sense; that is, the supreme rule of which God himself (the Demiurge, the personal God) clings. But the personal God is He who has realized the Measure and the One in a perfect manner, and, in this sense, He is Measure *in a personal sense*. Man must imitate him as far as possible, trying, as He does, to bring to completion in the best way possible in private as well as in public life, and in general in all the forms of activity, precisely, *unity-in-multiplicity*.[12]

(*f*) Also the doctrine of Eros reveals strong connections with the protologic, although in different respects. First (to limit ourselves only to the essential nexuses) let us point out the parents from which Eros was born, and hence the composite and mediating nature of Eros itself, which is emblematic.[13] The mother of Eros, which is Need, the Goddess of Poverty, symbolizing the Dyad (one of its explications): it is, in fact, that power which is both lacking and, in its own way, at the same time, aspiring to be fulfilled (and hencewe may sayto be delimited and determined and therefore unified); and for this reason, on the day in which the birth of Aphrodite is celebrated, Need succeeds in capturing Resource and unites with him and is fructified by him. Instead, father Resource corresponds to the determined and delimiting Principle, and hence to a unifier (to one of its explications). And the *synthetic-dynamic* nature and mediating character of Eros, which eternally tends to further and higher acquisitions, *expresses the bipolar and dynamic relationship that characterizes the whole of reality* (and hence specifically man, in a special way); and therefore it expresses the increasing tendency in all the spheres of Multiplicity to be fructified in the direction of the Principle of the Good (and hence towards Unity), which is realized at each level by reproducing itself perennially, and in the way it achieves the stability and permanence of being.

Keep in mind that Plato, with his extraordinary ability of never saying in an explicit way the ultimate truths and nevertheless communicating them by means of strong allusions, in the *Symposium*, has Aristophanes say (and hence with a sensitivity demanded by the contrast between the *play* of comedy and the *seriousness* of the truth) that the essence of love is in the doing "*of two, one*," for the purpose of healing, and in this way, human nature in its shortcomings, and hence of "welding into a *unity*" men, in such a way, that from "two" that are (in various ways), they may become *one*. This is a truly superb vision, and from the artistic viewpoint even magnificent, of the striking conjunction of the Dyad and the One, conducted with the delicious play of comedy, placed in the mouth of the greatest of the Greek comedic writers. And with an Aristophenian coloring presented in a superior way, Plato presents mythically the original way that man existed as spheres; that is, as conjoined couples in a unity, *as a whole*, then cut into two halves by the Gods, to limit their excessive and dangerous power and vigor. Consequently, each "half" derived from the cutting into two, tries to return to the other "half" and to be reunited to it precisely to return to the original state of "wholeness." Therefore, what is manifested in various ways in the love of human beings is the *desire of Duality* (of the Dyad) for *Wholeness* (that is, for *Unity*). Consequently love is a desire to achieve the One in all areas even the highest and most elevated ones.[14]

(g) Finally, in connection with the protologic we also achieve an adequate explanation of the Platonic position that the Beautiful is the only Idea that has the privilege of being "visible." Actually, because the Beautiful, just as the Good, is *a way of explicating the One, through order and measure, it follows that in the Beautiful we see the One in its proportional and numeric relationships and in its numerical explications*, not only within the intelligible sphere, but also in the sensible sphere of the "visible."

As such, the Beautiful attracts and from sensible harmony it raises to intelligible harmony at all levels.

Hence, the One itself, by means of the Beautiful, charms *by making itself "seen"* in the relations of proportion, order, and harmony. And in this way the wings of the soul are renewed, carrying it to the highest levels in other words, to the heights from which it has fallen.[15]

Fourth Section

THE POLITICAL COMPONENT OF PLATONISM AND ITS NEXUSES
WITH THE PROTOLOGIC OF THE *UNWRITTEN DOCTRINES*

οἶμαι μετ᾽ ὀλίγων ᾽ Ἀθηναίων ἵνα μὴ
εἴπω μόνος, ἐπιχειρεῖν τῇ ὡς ἀληθῶς
πολιτικῇ τέχνῃ καὶ πράττειν τὰ
πολιτικά μόνος τῶν νῦν.

I think that I am one of the very few
Athenians, not to say the only one,
engaged in the true political art, and that
of the men of today I alone practice
statesmanship.

Plato, *Gorgias* 521 D

I. THE IMPORTANCE AND SIGNIFICANCE
OF THE POLITICAL COMPONENT
OF PLATONISM

1.   The affirmations of the *Seventh Letter*

The political direction of Platonism has been understood, in all its relevance and range, only in our century. First, the authenticity was vindicated of the *Seventh Letter*[1] in which Plato expressly stated, within the context of an autobiographical section, that *politics was the dominant love of his life.* Wilamowitz-Möllendorff in his by now classical biography of Plato,[2] used the content of the *Seventh Letter*, which verified as a matter of fact that, within the scope of his whole life, Plato nourished this passion for politics. Finally, Jaeger who grasped the importance of this love, tried to show (and he did so although falling into some excesses) that political problems constituted not only the central focus of Plato *the man*, but *the very substance of his philosophy.*[3] And to these three scholars others can be brought forward in evidence.[4]

Socrates never participated actively in the political life: he not only did not feel compelled to be concerned with it, but he considered it as something which was inconsistent with his life-style. Plato, on the contrary, whether because of noble birth, or through family tradition, or because of a deeply felt personal sense of mission, felt from his earliest years drawn to political life. Here is the statement of it from the *Seventh Letter*: "In the days of my youth my experience was the same as that of many others. *I thought that as soon as I should become my own master I would immediately enter into public life.*"[5]

But from the experience of the political life to which he was drawn, Plato quickly experienced the profound corruption it worked on men in government as well as the decay of the laws themselves and the customs (unwritten laws) both in and outside of Athens. Here are the conclusions he drew from the experience:

> When, therefore, I considered all this and the type of men who were administering the affairs of the City-State, with their laws too and their customs, the more I considered them and the more I advanced in years myself, the more difficult appeared to me the task of managing affairs of City-State rightly. Where it was impossible to take actions without friends and trusty companions; and these it was not easy to find ready to have, since our City-State was no longer managed according to the principles and institutions of our forefathers; while to acquire other new friends with any facility was a thing impossible. Moreover, both the written laws and customs were being corrupted, and that with surprising rapidity, consequently, although at first I was filled with an ardent desire to engage in public affairs, when I considered all this and saw how things were shifting about anyhow in all directions, I finally became dizzy; and although I continued to consider

186 / *Plato and the Discovery of the Supersensible*

by what means some betterment could be brought about not only in these matters but also in the government as a whole, yet as regards political action I kept constantly waiting for an opportune moment; until, finally, looking at all the City-States that now exist, I perceive that one and all they are badly governed; for the City-State of their laws as such has to be almost incurable without some marvelous overhauling and good luck to boot. *So in my praise of the rightful philosophy I was compelled to declare that by it one is enabled to discern all forms of justice of political and individual. Wherefore the classes of mankind (I said) will have no succession from evil until either the class of those who are right and true philosophers attains political supremacy, or else the class of those who hold power in the City-State becomes, by some dispensation of Heaven, really philosophic.*[6]

This is the mature conviction that Plato, as he immediately says in the next lines of this passage, came to during the years when he first voyaged to Italy, which is about the time of the composition of the *Gorgias*, when Plato was approximately forty years of age. This dialogue, which involves an explosion of mysticism, is also marked by an eruption of political passion containing *the proclamation of a new notion of the political art.*[7] The political art and the conception of the City-State have to be reorganized by the positions of Socraticism. Although the old politics and the old City-State had their most potent instrument in art of rhetoric (in the classical sense of the term that is well known), the new, the true politics and the new City-State must instead have its instrument in philosophy, *because philosophy represents the single secure path to the values of justice and the good, which are the true basis of every authentic politics and hence of the true City-State.* And so Plato does not hesitate to put on the lips of Socrates (with whom he identifies himself) this challenge: "I think that I am one of the very few Athenians, not to say the only one, engaged in the true political art, and that of the men of today I alone practice statesmanship" (trans. W. D. Woodhead, Bollingen, p. 302).[8]

2. Differences between the Platonic conception and the modern conception of politics

It is clear, hence, from what we have said that the total output of Plato the philosopher must be seen, altogether, as political work in the sense just witnessed. On the other hand, the titles themselves of his works that follow the *Gorgias* confirms this view: the central masterpiece of Platonic thought is the *Republic*, in the middle of the dialectical dialogues we find the *Statesman*, the final voluminous and wide-ranging work of Plato's old age is the *Laws*. Moreover, keep in mind the repeated attempts on the part of Plato with respect to Dionysius I, and Dionysius II, rulers of Syracuse, to realize the political ideals he had originated;[9] to contemplate the Truth and to direct the Academy was not sufficient: he was profoundly convinced that the True and the Good as contemplated ought to flower in all realities and better them, and thus be politically effective, not ineffectual ideals (but we will speak of this further on).

But before examining our reconstruction of the notion of the City-State thought up by Plato, we must first provide a clarification about the radical difference that runs through the *Platonic* conception of politics and the *modern* conception of the same, to avoid a whole series of ambiguities.

Plato is profoundly convinced that every kind of politics, if it is to be an authentic one, *must aim at the betterment of man*; but since man is fundamentally his *soul*, while his body is simply its transient and apparent covering, it is clear that true benefits for man will be spiritual benefits.[10]

These are then the lines of demarcation that divide the true and false politics: true politics must have as its aim the care of the soul (be concerned with the best in man), whereas false politics aims at the body, at the satisfaction of bodily desires and those things that are related to the unauthentic aspects of man. And since there is no other way of caring for the soul except by the practice of philosophy from which the identification of philosophy and politics is derived, as well as the identification (today so paradoxical, but in the Platonic context so obvious) of the philosopher and the statesman.[11]

On the other hand, it was not only the presuppositions of the Platonic system that arrived at these conclusions: the Greeks were always convinced (at least up to the time of Plato and Aristotle) that the City-State and the laws of the City-State were the paradigm of every form of life, as we already know; the individual was essentially a citizen, and the value and virtues of man were the values and virtues of citizenship: the City-State was not a relative sphere of interest but rather the unconditioned center and limits of a human life. Hence, if we add this understanding to the elements distinguished earlier, it is easy to understand how the Platonic conclusions were even inevitable.

Our conception of politics is instead at the antipodes to Plato's. The City-State has for a long time rejected being the font of *all* norms which regulate the life of the individual, because for a long time the individual and the citizen has ceased to be identified. The City-State, in addition, for a long time has not tried to take over those spheres of the interior life of the citizen that were chiefly of interest to Plato, permitting the free decisions of the individual's conscience within this sphere. Today, then, economic and aspirations of the commonwealth radically condition the practice and theory of politics, and it is frequently limited to being a system for the aggrandizement of material goods and benefits, in which Plato saw the source of all evil.[12] We are, in conclusion, the sons of Machiavelli and in certain respects we have even gone beyond what Machiavelli conceived: ours is a *realpolitik* that indicates the most radical overturning of the *political idealism* that was Plato's hallmark.

These observations, which we have introduced within the structure of the analysis, and without making any value judgments, while intending to contribute to historical comprehension of the Platonic conception, tries to raise a doubt. Certainly, Plato was conditioned in a twofold sense: by the suppositions of his own system and by a particular historical-social-cultural vision of the City-State both of them unrepeatable conditions. Nevertheless, beyond these conditions, he had pointed out a truth, which today more than ever before sounds a warning: a politics that disavows, in the regulation of the lives of men living in community, the spiritual dimension and structures itself exclusively in terms of the material necessities of human beings cannot rule for long: the exigencies of the spirit, denied or compromised, inexorably reimpose themselves and demand satisfaction.

But let us now proceed to a more detailed clarification of these concepts.

II. THE *REPUBLIC* OR THE CONSTRUCTION
OF THE IDEAL CITY-STATE

1. Perspectives for reading the *Republic*

The clarifications that we have just made ought to give us the sense of the correct perspective within which to read the *Republic*; that is, the masterpiece that is, in many ways, the *summa* of Platonism. To ask oneself, as some have done, whether or not it is a political or ethical work is to raise a spurious problem, which arises, as we have hinted, from a way of conceiving politics and ethics in a modern understanding but which does not belong to Plato, and in general to any classical Greek political thought. These badly stated questions have held back for a long time the recovery and appreciation of the political component of Platonism.

To illustrate and clarify specifically what we have stated generically in the previous paragraph, let us read some of the affirmations of one of the greatest of the modern exponents of Plato's thought, which clarify well enough the terms of the problem we have taken up:

> It has sometimes been asked whether the *Republic* is to be regarded as a contribution to ethics or to politics. Is its subject righteousness, or is it the ideal City-State? The answer is that from the point of view of Socrates and Plato there is no distinction, except one of convenience, between morals and politics. The laws of right are the same for classes and cities as for individual men. *But one must add that these laws are primarily laws of personal morality; politics is founded on ethics, not ethics on politics.* The primary question raised in the *Republic* and finally answered at its close is a *strictly ethical one*. (p. 265, Meridian Books edition)[1]
>
> The *Republic*, which opens with an old man's remarks about approaching death and apprehension of what may come after death, and ends with a myth of judgment, has all through for its central theme a question more intimate than that of the best form of government or the most eugenic system of propagation; its question is, How does man attain or forfeit eternal salvation? For good or bad, it is intensely other-worldly. Man has a soul which can attain everlasting beatitude, and this beatitude it is the greatest business of life to attain. The social institutions or the education which fit him to attain it are the right institutions or education; all others are wrong. The philosopher is the man who has found the way which leads to this beatitude. (p. 265-6 Meridian Books edition)[2]

Now note that such judgments (which, more or less varied, have been made authoritatively up to the middle of our century) contradict themselves. At the beginning, the passage reported acknowledged that for Socrates and Plato there is no distinction between ethics and politics, that simply in itself would be enough to overturn Taylor's conclusions or, at the least, admit that the *Republic* is a work of *politics* insofar as it is *ethical*. But here is what the same scholar is constrained to affirm: "At the same time, no man lives to himself, and the man who is advancing to beatitude himself is *inevitably animated by the spirit of a missionary to the community at large.* Hence the philosopher cannot be true to himself *without being a philosopher-king; he cannot win salvation without bringing it down to his society.* That is how the *Republic* views the relation between ethics and statesmanship" (p. 266 Meridian Books edition).[3] This means that the *Republic, simply by being an ethical work, must by that very fact be a political work,* because, for Plato, man can be morally explicated only if he is explicated *politically,* insofar as man is not yet conceived by him (as we have previously pointed out) as an individual distinct from a citizen, that is from a member of the political society. (Moreover Jaeger himself, who proposed the reinterpretation of Plato entirely within a political perspective, has shown handily that Platonic politics is nothing other than this, and that the Platonic City-State is nothing other than image written large of man: to form the true City-State, for Plato, means to form the true man.)[4]

A second set of problems is likewise damaging to the aim of understanding the *Republic* and the spirit that animates it. We allude to the problems aroused by those interpretations that we may call politicized, which have, it is true, acknowledged the political nature of the work, but have understood it by using the categories of modern political theory as their exegetical principles, in critical comparisons and value judgments.[5] These interpretations commit the same errors that we mentioned earlier, insofar as they maintain that the City-State and politics can have only the acceptations used in the modern period, and in addition they misunderstand in a very damaging manner the nature of Platonic discourse, reducing it to a very restricted sphere, as we will immediately see.

For example, some speak of Platonic communism and socialism, especially with respect to the necessity of having in common all possessions (including families and children) proclaimed by Plato for the classes who were to become the Guardians of the City-State, although those Platonic doctrines that touch upon communism only accidentally; they have, as we will see, a theoretical basis and spiritual motivation that has nothing in common with the modern political theories of Engels and Marx. In the other direction, there have not been lacking, especially in Germany and Italy attempts to find in the *Republic* characteristics of Nazism and Fascism.

Within this climate, the famous work of Karl Popper (which has been widely published especially within English-speaking countries), in which the conception of the City-State of Plato not only is said to be conservative and reactionary, but heavily totalitarian, and Plato is identified as the great enemy (the triad of Popper's great enemies of the open society is made up of, in addition to, Plato, of Hegel, and Marx) of the *open society;* that is, of those who on the basis of free choice and free decisions of individuals, the open society of the future, capable, with reason, strides into the unknown and uncertain future and constructes little by little their own security and freedom. Plato would be, instead, a promoter of a closed society, encased in a rigid structure, and in which the institutions (here including casts) are sacred cows and taboo. The Platonic City-State, in conclusion, would be the *very negation of freedom and liberty.* In short, Plato would be the enemy of a democratic society and of democracy.[6]

Out of Popper's work a whole new literature has arisen, and not a few scholars have rejected the totalitarian interpretation of Plato, by emphasizing terms and positions in a liberal and democratic spirit that are present or operative in the writings of our philosopher.[7]

It is clear, hence, that trying to read the *Republic* with categories derived from modern political ideologies, one may come up with everything and the contrary of everything one wishes to, whether it be totalitarianism (of the right or left) or its negation (anarchy): it is certain that, in this way of proceeding, one betrays the most authentic meaning of the Platonic political discourse, which is not in any way an ideology, but is above all a philosophy, metaphysics, and finally an eschatology of the City-State.

Hence the correct perspective for reading the *Republic*, the terrain cleared of the ambiguities just mentioned, is that which we have indicated earlier: *Plato wishes to know and form the perfect City-State to know and to form the perfect man.*

Man is his soul, Socrates said,[8] and Plato wrote this affirmation not only in the mystical dialogues, but even in the *Republic* indeed taking it to its extreme consequences therein. The City-State, as we will see, is the enlargement of the soul, and between soul and City-State we will see set up this reciprocal relationship: if it is true that the City-State is a projection of the soul written large, it is likewise true that, ultimately, the soul is the authentic seat of the true City-State and true politics and that the soul and the true City-State are to be interior cities, which is not outside but within man.[9]

2. The perfect City-State and the type of man corresponding to it

The problem from which Plato started the reconstruction of the ideal City-State springs from the necessity of replying in a decisive manner to the destructive criticism that the Sophists (especially in its degenerate current of political sophism, of which Thrasymachus is the emblematic figure in the *Republic*) made against justice, and concerning which we have already spoken in its appropriate place.[10] No one of the traditional arguments was ready to respond to these criticisms, because none touched the basis of the questions raised. And here is, then, the necessity of being able to put the question in a radical way and to answer it in a likewise radical way: *what is* justice (what is the essence or nature of justice?) What is its *value*, what value does it have for man? Does justice have an interior validity or only a merely external utility, is it mere conventionality or an expression of the power of the ruling group?

Consequently, since justice is rooted in the individual just as in the City-State, in the former as microcosm and in the latter as macrocosm, it will be necessary to examine it there where it is written large, to better understand it even there where it is written in small letters. Here is the passage in which Plato expresses this concept and that constitutes one of the principal keys to the reading of the whole of the *Republic*:

> The inquiry we are undertaking is no easy one, but calls for keen vision, as it seems to me. So, since we are not clever person, I think we should employ the method of search that we should use if we, with not very keen vision, were bidden to read small letters from a distance, and then someone had observed that these same letters exist elsewhere larger and on a larger surface. We should have accounted it a godsend, I fancy, to be allowed to read those letters first, and then examine the smaller, if they are the same.
> Quite so, said Adeimantus; but what analogy to this do you detect in the inquiry about justice?
> I will tell you, I said: There is a justice of one man, we say, and, I suppose, also of an entire city?
> Assuredly, said he.
> Is not the city larger than the man?
> It is larger, he said.
> Then perhaps, it would be more justice in the larger object and more easy to apprehend. If it pleases you, then, let us first look for its quality in City-State, and then only examine it also in the individual, looking for the likeness of the greater in the form of the less.
> I think that is a good suggestion, he said.
> If, then, said I, our arguments should observe the origin of City-State, we should see also the origin of justice and injustice in it?
> It may be, said he. And if this is done, we may expect to find more easily what we are seeking?
> Much more.
> Shall we try it, then, and go through with it? I fancy it is no slight task. Reflect, then.
> We have reflected, said Adeimantus; proceed and don't refuse. (trans. Paul Shorey, Bollingen, Pg. 614-5)[11]

Why and how did the City-State arise?

Because each of us is not autonomous; that is, because we are not self-sufficient.[12] The source of the City-State is hence our need. And our needs are manifold, so that each of us has necessity not only one or of a few, but of many other men who provide for these needs. Thus the different professions develop, which only different men can adequately exercise. Each man, in fact, is not born totally similar to others, since he has natural differences, and hence, does different work.[13]

But in the City-State, besides the classes of professions mentioned related to peace and that aim at the satisfaction of the essential needs of life, it is necessary to have a class of guardians and warriors. In fact, with the increase in needs, the City-State must annex new territories or, even, simply to defend itself from those who attack or, for analogous reasons, take possession of territories that belong to it.[14] Now, the guardians of the City-State, on the basis of the principle expressed earlier, must be endowed, above all, with an appropriate disposition: the guardians must be like a well-bred dog, endowed with both a gentleness and a ferocity; the guardians must be physically agile and strong, quick to anger and yet courageous and a lover of wisdom in the soul.[15] In addition, if for the first group of citizens no special education was necessary, due to the fact that the usual professions can easily be learnt, for the guardian class of the City-State a very precise education is indispensable. Culture (poetry and music) and gymnastics will be the most appropriate instruments for educating the body and the soul of the guardians. This is, of course, the ancient Hellenic ideal of paideia, which Plato, therefore, changed in his accustomed manner.[16] Poetry that feeds the soul of youths in the perfect City-State must be purified of all that which is morally objectionable and from all that is false, especially in those types that are about the Gods.[17] Analogously, with respect to music, sentimental or schmaltzy melodies that tenderize the soul ought to be eliminated and only those capacities on which warlike courage can be built are to be preserved as well as independent action in works connected with peace; and so only those rhythms in calisthenics that are appropriate and simple ought to be chosen.[18] Also gymnastics ought to be appropriate and simple, avoiding any kind of excess.[19] It will proceed to the education of the soul, since the good soul with its excellence can make the body good, but not vice versa.[20] The ultimate aim of "gymnastics" must be, not only and not just the strengthening of the body, as much as the strengthening of that element of our soul from which courage is derived.[21] Musical education, hence, forms and strengthens the rational part of the soul; gymnastic education, through the body, forms and strengthens the irascible part of the soul; both together produce perfect peace and harmony in the soul.

The distinction of the classes is still not completed. In fact, among the guardians, it will be necessary to distinguish those who *obey* from those who *command*. The latter, the rulers of the City-State, must be those who love the City-State above everything else and for their whole lives must pursue its advantage and good with the greatest zeal (as we will see, the true philosophers make up this third class).[22]

These three social classes, quite famous and much discussed, do not have anything to do with the notion of a *caste*, because they are each open and not closed, although not wholly and completely. In fact, if it is true that at the basis of the distinction into classes there is a different *human disposition*, it is likewise true that from parents of a given disposition, even if rarely, offspring are born who have a different nature, and so they will be made to go into the classes that correspond to their disposition, whether it be higher or lower and vice versa.[23]

To the first class, that of the workers, artisans, and merchants, the possession of goods and wealth is conceded (not much, but not a small amount either). Instead, to the defenders of the City-State no goods or wealth will be allotted; they are to have common residences and dining facilities and their expenses are the obligation of all the other citizens as compensation for their duties. This limitation is made necessary for the higher good of the City-State and its well-being: in the perfect City-State, in fact, no one class can be particularly well-off or happier, since in the measurement of happiness of the City-State it is in its interest that every class share in happiness only to the extent consistent with their natural endowment.[24]

The guardians, in addition, must be vigilant that in the City-State so constructed no changes are introduced, which will lead it to ruin. They must be watchful that in the first class there is no excessive accumulation of wealth (which produces laziness, a taste for luxury and a love of novelty) but neither should there be poverty (which produces the opposed vices, in addition to the desire for change), so that the City-State does not become too great or too small, so that the dispositions and natures of individuals correspond to the functions that they exercise, so that it proceeds to the appropriate education of the better youths, so that there is no change in the laws that govern education and the arrangement of the State is not changed.[25]

Now that the ideal City-State has been outlined, it is possible to see what is the nature and value of justice. And, to specify justice exactly, it is necessary to determine the four fundamental virtues (the well-known chief virtues; that is, besides *justice, wisdom, fortitude, temperance* as well). The perfect City-State must be in possession of all of them by necessity.

The City-State that we have described possesses *wisdom* (σοφία) because it has *good counsel* (εὐβουλία), and good counsel is a *knowledge* (ἐπιστήμη) different from the special knowledges and arts, because it has as its object the correct way of doing things by the City-State internally and externally with other City-States, and it is possessed only by the perfect guardians; that is, the governors. The City-State is wise only through the class of those who are governors.[26]

Fortitude or *courage* (ἀνδρεία) is the capacity of preserving with constancy the right opinion in dangerous affairs and those that are not, without allowing the victory to be carried by pleasures or pains or fears or passions. Courage is the particular virtue of those who are warriors and the City-State is strong through the class of those who are its courageous warriors.[27]

Temperance (σωφροσύνη) is a type of order, rule, or discipline (ἐγκράτεια) with regard to pleasures and desires. It is the capacity of submitting the lower part to the higher part. This virtue is found, it is true, particularly in the third class of citizens, but it is not exclusive to it, and in fact it extends to all the classes that make up the City-State, by bringing into complete harmony the lower classes with higher ones. The temperate City-State, hence, is that in which the weakest are in balance with the strongest, the higher with the lower in complete harmony.[28]

And we finally come to the consideration of *justice* (δικαιοσύνη). It is the very principle on which the ideal City-State is erected; that is, on the principle according to which *each ought to do only those things that by nature and hence by law he is called to do.* When each citizen and each class attends to its proper role in the best way, then the life of the City-State develops in a perfect manner and it is, hence, the just City-State.[29]

If, as we saw at the beginning, the City-State is only the individual man and his soul written large, there must correspond to the three social classes belonging to the City-State three forms or capacities in the soul: "Is it not, then, said I, impossible for us to avoid admitting this much, that the same forms and qualities are to be found in each one of us that are in the City-State?"[30]

Here is the proof upon which Plato based the threefold distinction of the powers of the soul. We notice three different activities in us: (*a*) we know and think, (*b*) we get excited and angered, (*c*) we pursue the pleasures of sex and food. Now we could not pursue these three activities with one and the same capacity, because "the same thing will never do or suffer opposites in the same respect in relation to the same thing and at the same time."[31]

Actually, the three activities about which we have spoken are involved thus: they act and they suffer contrary things in relation to the same things. In comparison to the same objects we remark that there is in us a tendency that pushes us to them and that is a *desire*, and another that instead draws us from them and that can dominate the desire and that is *reason*. But there is also a third tendency, which is that through which *we get angry* and which is neither reason nor desire. It is different than reason because it is passionate, but it is also different than desire because it opposed to desire (for example, when we get angry for yielding to desire as to a force that exerted violence on us). Hence, just as there are three classes in the City-State, so also there are three powers of the soul: the *rational* (λογιστικόν), the *irascible* (θυμοειδές), and the *appetitive* (ἐπιθυμητικόν); the irascible, by its nature, is related to reason although not being a part of reason, but it can be persuaded by it as well as the lowest part of the soul, if it is ruined by an evil education.

This correspondence between the classes of the City-State and the powers of the soul will involve a correspondance between the virtues of the City-State and that of the citizens. Here is the exemplary passage in which Plato expressed, in the analogy with the virtues of the City-State, the chief virtues of man:

> Just too, then, Glaucon, I presume we shall say a man is in the same way in which a city was just.

That too is quite inevitable.

But we surely cannot have forgotten this, that the City-State was just by reason of each of the three classes found in it fulfilling its own function.

I don't think we have forgotten, he said.

We must remember, then, that each of us also in whom the several parts within him perform each their own task–he will be a just man and one who minds his own affairs.

We must indeed remember, he said.

That is it not belong to the rational part to rule, being wise and exercising forethought in behalf of the entire soul, and to the principle of *high spirit* [irascible] to be subject to this and its ally?

Assuredly.

Then it is not, as we said, the blending of music and gymnastics that will render them concordant, intensifying and fostering the one with fair words and teaching and relaxing and soothing and making gentle the other by harmony and rhythm?

Quite so, said he.

And these too thus reared and having learned and been educated to do their own work in the true sense of the phrase, will preside over the appetitive part which is the mass of the soul in each of us and the most insatiate by nature of wealth. They will keep watch upon it, lest, by being filled and infected with the so=called pleasures associated with the body and so waxing big and strong, it may not keep to its own work but may undertake to enslave and rule over the classes which it is not fitting that it should, and so overturn the entire life of all.

By all means, he said.

Would not these two, then, best keep guard against enemies from without also on behalf of the entire soul and body, the one taking counsel, the other giving battle, attending upon the ruler, by its courage executing the rulers designs?

That is so.

Brave, too, then, I take it, we call each individual by virtue of this part in him, when, namely, his high spirit preserves in the midst of pains and pleasures the rule handed by the reason as to what is or is not to be feared.

Right, he said.

But wise by that small part that ruled in him and handed down these commands, by its possession in turn with it the knowledge of what is beneficial for each rather than for the whole, the community composed of the three.

By all means.

And again, was he not sober by reason of the friendship and concord of the same parts, when, namely, the ruling principle and his two subjects are at one in the belief that the reason was to rule and do not raise faction against it?

The virtue of temperance certainly, said he, is nothing else than this, whether in a City-State or in an individual." (trans., Paul Shorey, Bollingen, pp. 684-5)[32]

It is clear, then, that justice is that disposition of the powers of the soul which allows that each accomplishes the function proper to it (τὰ ἑαυτοῦ πράττειν) and, consequently, in accordance with which nature dominates or is allowed to dominate. Justice is something concerned not only with exterior but also interior activity; that is, the life of the soul itself. And from this also develops the problem of the value of justice. It is *according to nature*, and it is, as is virtue in general, the health, beauty, and well-being of the soul, whereas injustice and vice are the brutalization and perversion of the soul. And as the happy City-State is only the one that accomplishes its functions according to justice and the other virtues, so the happy soul, is only that which acts according to justice and the other virtues, means according to that which is its true nature (κατὰ φύσιν).[33]

3. The system of community of life of the warriors and the education of women in the ideal City-State

Before considering the forms of the degenerate City-State Plato examines two groups of questions. The first consists in a series of consequences that arise from having stated the principle that the guardians of the City-State *must have all things in common*, and hence, in addition to habitation and food, women, children, the raising and education of their offspring.[34]

A first consequence that Plato draws is to entrust to the wives of the guardians the same habitations that he entrusted to the men and hence to educate the women in the same gymnastic-musical paideia as is mentioned earlier. The reforms that Plato proposed are truly revolutionary for his time, since the Greeks roughly speaking limited their women within the domestic household chores, entrusting to them the care of the house and the raising of children, and kept them away from cultural activities, the use of the gymnasia, and the activities connected to war making or politics.

Here is the reasoning at the foundation of the Platonic work that conceptually overturned the role of the Greek women:

> Then there is no pursuit of the administrators of the City-State that belongs to a woman *because she is a woman* or to a man *because he is a man*. But the natural capacities are distributed alike among both creatures, and women naturally share in all pursuits and men in all—yet for all the woman is weaker than the man.
> Assuredly.
> Shall we, then, assign them all to men and nothing to women?
> How could we?
> We shall rather, I take it, say that one woman has the nature of a physician and another not, and one is by nature musical and another unmusical?
> Surely.
> Can we, then, deny that one woman is naturally athletic and warlike and another warlike and adverse to gymnastics?

I think not.

And again, one a lover, another a hater, of wisdom? And one high-spirited, and the other lacking spirit?

That also is true.

Then it is likewise true that one woman has the qualities of a guardian and another not. Were not these the natural qualities of the men also whom we selected for guardians?

They were.

The woman and the men, then, have the same nature and respect to the guardianship of the City-State, save insofar as the woman is weaker, the other stronger. Apparently."[35]

If this is so, then the identical disposition that is in both men and women will be educated in an identical way: women, as men, are to exercise in the nude in the palestra, girded with virtue rather than garments, and without having to be concerned with any other work, taking part in the guardianship of the City-State and also in war (it will be necessary to entrust to them less heavy tasks, because of their weakness as compared to men).[36]

A second consequence that derives directly from the preceding one, is the elimination of the institution of the family for the guardian classes since women (just as men) must be occupied with no other duty than that of guarding the City-State (the family is instead maintained just as property by the lower classes). The wives of guardians, hence, are held in common and the children are also held in common.[37]

Marriages are to be regulated by the City-State and declared sacred and they will be done in a way so that the better men will be joined with the better women, so that the offspring produced are the best possible. In addition, the City-State will use all the encouragement possible to make the best mingle with the best as many times as possible. And the children of the best couples must be educated, while the children of the worst couples are not, without, however, it being bruited about. And they will pretend to decide the matching by drawing lots, although the lots will be manipulated to ensure the desired results.[38]

Children will be immediately taken from their mothers; mothers and fathers will not know their children. In addition only men between thirty and fifty-five years of age and women between twenty and forty will have the right to beget children. If a child is conceived through an unregulated coupling of a man and a woman beyond these years mentioned, it will not be allowed to come to term, or, if it is born it will be exposed and not brought up.[39]

All infants are born between the seventh and the tenth months counting from the day on which a man and a woman have celebrated their marriage must be called their sons and daughters. On the other hand, these last will call fathers and mothers, all those men and women who have contracted marriage between the tenth and the eighth months prior to their births. Consequently, they will reckon as their brothers and sisters all those born in the period in which their fathers and mothers were procreating.[40]

These are the laws of the Platonic City-State that, as is obvious, have aroused the most vehement reaction and are considered by many to be absurd. But before going on to an evaluation of them it is necessary to understand the intention that animates them. Plato wanted to break the guardians attachment to *their individual families*, by offering them a larger family. In fact, not only the possession of material goods divides men, but also the possession of that peculiar good which is the family from which arises in various ways human individualism. Therefore, if the family were to be common, the guardians would not have anything to say "it is mine," or better they could say of everything "it is mine," because absolutely everything would be held in common, with the exception of the body.

Here is a passage that is most important in this regard and on which it is indispensable to think deeply, if one wishes to understand the particular meaning given to Platonic communitarianism:

> Do we know of any greater evil for a City-State than the thing that distracts it and makes it many instead of one, or a greater good than that which binds it together and makes it one?
> We do not.
> Is not, then, the community of pleasure and pain the tie that binds, when, so far as may be, all the citizens rejoice and grieve alike at the same births and deaths?
> By all means, he said.
> But the individualization of these feelings is a dissolvant, when some grieve exceedingly and others rejoice to the same happenings to the city and its inhabitants?
> Of course.
> And the chief cause of this is when the citizens do not utter in unison such words as [mine] and [not mine], and similarly with regard to the word [others]?
> Precisely so.
> That city, then, is best ordered in which the greatest number use the expression, [mine] and [not mine] are the same things in the same way.
> Much the best.
> And the city whose state is most like that of an individual man? For example, if the finger of one of us is wounded, the entire community of bodily connections stretching to the soul for "integration" with the dominant part is made aware, and all of it feels the pain as a whole, though it is a part that suffers, then that is how we come to say that man has a pain in his finger. And for any other member of the man the same statement holds, alike for a part that labors in pain or is eased by pleasure.
> The same, he said, and, to return to your question, the best governed state must nearly resemble such an organism.

> That is the kind of state, then, I presume, that, when any one of the citizens
> suffers for a good or evil, we'll be most likely to speak of the part that suffers
> as its own and will share the pleasure or the pain as a whole.[41]

It is clear, on the basis of these statements, that Platonic communism does
not have anything to do with modern collectivism, for both historical and
theoretical reasons. Modern collectivism, from the historical viewpoint,
presuppose the industrial revolution, capitalism, the proletariat of the large
cities, and is chiefly applicable in the economic sphere; from the theoretical
viewpoint, then, it springs from a materialistic conception of man. Platonic
communism, instead, arises from other presuppositions, precisely the need to
have the guardian class totally available for their role as guardians and for the
defense of the City-State and to place completely them outside the laboring
classes, which alone, produces and administrates the commonwealth. In addition the theoretical defense of this kind of communism is clearly spiritual and
even ascetic in character.

The guardians of the Platonic City-State, says Taylor quite well, "are much
more in the position of a medieval military monastic order than in that of a
collectivist bureaucracy."[42] And analogously Jaeger noted:

> The Church later solved this same problem by directing priests, its own
> ruling class, to remain unmarried and childless throughout their lives. Plato,
> who was not married himself, did not adopt that solution–both because he
> did not, like the Church, believe that marriage was morally worse than
> celibacy, and because the ruling minority in his state was physically and
> spiritually the cream of the crop, so that its offspring were necessary to
> produce a new elite. The prohibition of private property (including the
> possession of a wife), blended with the principle of racial selection, leads to
> the doctrine that the guards must have wives and children in common.[43]

In any case, to turn to the basic question, it remains true that, no matter
how noble the end that Plato pursued (to unify a City-State into a large family,
by cutting out at the root everything that supports human individualism), the
means that he used were not only inadequate, but deceptive. In all these
doctrines, the basic error is one consists in the consideration of the group as
more important than the individual, the collectivity as more than the person.
Plato, as all Greeks before him (and even after him, until the rise of Hellenistic
currents), did not have a clear concept of man *as an individual* and as a
irreplaceable singular, and hence he could not understand how to be a singular
and irreplaceable individual was the supreme human value.[44]

4. The Philosopher and the ideal City-State

In the outline of the ideal City-State that we have reconstructed so far
there is still lacking the most significant part; namely, the specific characteristic of the supreme "governors" or "rulers" of the City-State and their

particular *paideia* or *education*. It is surely the conception of the nature of the rulers that reveals, besides the theoretical foundation, the conditions for the realization of the Platonic City-State. The position is already known to us and can be therefore summarized as follows: the necessary and sufficient condition for the realization of the ideal City-State is that the rulers become philosophers or philosophers become rulers. Not only, therefore, is it the philosopher who brings to realization theoretically the perfect City-State, but it is likewise the philosopher who alone can bring it to completion practically, and then it can enter into history. Here is the famous passage in which the position is affirmed:

> Listen.
> I am all attention, he said.
> Unless, said I, *either philosophers become kings in our City-States or those whom we call our kings and rulers take to the pursuit of philosophy seriously and adequately, and there is a conjunction of these two things, political power and philosophic intelligence,* while the motley hoard of the natures who at present pursue either apart from the other are compulsorily excluded, there can be no cessation of troubles, dear Glaucon, for our City-States, nor, I fancy, for the human race either. (Bollingen, pp. 712-13)[45]

The affirmation is stated and extended, with respect to its possibility, beyond the present, to the past and to the future:

> For this cause and for seeing this, we then despite our fears declared under compulsion of the truth that neither city nor polity nor man either will ever be perfected until *some chance compels this uncorrupted remnant of philosophers,* who now bear the stigma of uselessness, *to take charge of the City-State whether they wish it or not, and constrains the citizens to obey them, or else until by some divine inspiration a genuine passion for true philosophy takes possession either of the sons of the men now in power and sovereignty or of themselves.* To affirm that either or both of these things cannot possibly come to pass is, I say, quite unreasonable. Only in that case could we be justly ridiculed as uttering things as futile as daydreams are. Is that now so?
> It is.
> If, then, the best philosophical natures have ever been constrained to take charge of the City-State *in infinite time passed,* or now or in some barbaric region far beyond our camp, or shall he raft to be, we are prepared to maintain our contention that the constitution we have described has been, is, or will be realized when this philosophic Muse *has taken control of the City-State.* It is not a thing impossible to happen, nor are we speaking of impossibilities. That it is difficult we too admit.
> I also think so, he said.[46]

The meaning of this affirmation (which Plato introduces with some circumspection, so that its apparent paradoxical nature does not prejudice its truth value, but at the same time he is definite about it) is easy enough to understand, if we keep in mind the notion of philosophy explained earlier and, in particular, the results of the "Second Voyage." The philosopher as constructor and ruler of the City-State means that the *Divine and the Absolute are the supreme measure and are the foundation of the City-State.* The philosopher, after having achieved the divine, contemplates it and imitates it, brings himself into conformity with it, and consequently, placed at the head of the City-State, he forms and conforms the City-State itself with the same measure.

Here is a fundamental passage of the *Republic*, in which Plato explains this conception in a clear way:

> For surely, Adeimantus, the man whose mind is truly fixed on eternal realities has no leisure to turn his eyes downward upon the petty affairs of men, and so engaging in strife with them to be filled with envy and hate, but he fixes his gaze upon the things of the eternal and unchanging order, and seeing that they neither wrong or are wronged by one another, but all abide in harmony as reason bids, he will endeavor to imitate them and, as far as may be, fashion himself in their likeness and assimilate himself to them. Or do you think it possible not to imitate things to which anyone attaches himself with admiration?
>
> Impossible, he said.
>
> *If the lover of wisdom associated with divine order will himself become orderly and divine in the measure permitted to man.* But calumny is plentiful everywhere.
>
> Yes, truly.
>
> If, then, I said, some compulsion is laid upon him to practice stamping on the plastic matter of human nature in public and private the patterns that he visions there [= the divine], *and not merely to mold and fashion himself,* do you think he will prove a poor craftsman of sobriety and justice and all forms of ordinary civic virtue?
>
> By no means, he said.
>
> But if the multitude become aware that what we are saying of the philosopher is true, will they still be harsh with philosophers, and will they distrust our statement that *no city could ever be blessed unless its lineaments were traced by artists who use the heavenly model?*
>
> They will not be harsh, he said, if they perceive that. But tell me, what is the manner of that sketch you have in mind?
>
> They will take the city and the characters of men, as they might a tablet, and first wipe it clean—no easy task. But at any rate you know that, this would be their first point of difference from ordinary reformers, that they would refuse to take in hand either individual or City-State or to legislate before they either received a clean slate or themselves made it clean.
>
> And they would be right, he said.
>
> And thereafter, do you think that they would sketch the figure of a constitution?
>
> Surely.

And then, I take it, in the course of the work they would glance frequently in either direction, *at justice, beauty, sobriety and the like as they are in the nature of things, and alternately at that which they were trying to reproduce in mankind, mingling and blending from various pursuits that hue of the flesh, so to speak, deriving their judgment from that likeness of humanity that Homer too called when it appeared in men the image and likeness of God.*
Right, he said.
And they would erase one touch or stroke and paint in another until in the measure of the possible they had made the characters of men *pleasing and dear to God as may be.* (Bollingen, pp. 735-6)[47]

The Platonic discussion achieved the maximum desirable clarity in proclaiming the supreme Idea of the Good, the Good in itself as supreme "model" or "paradigm" that the philosopher must use to regulate his own life and the life of the City-State.[48] And with this the Platonic City-State achieves its full definition: it wants to be the entrance of the Good into the community of men, though through a few men (in point of fact, philosophers) who themselves have risen to the contemplation of the Good itself. And since, as we have seen, the Idea of the Good is the Divine of the highest type, the Platonic City-State is consequently the attempt to organize the life of men who associate with one another according to the most elevated theological foundation. The Divine becomes thus, in addition to being the foundation of being and the cosmos and the private life of the individual, also the foundation of the life of men in the political sphere, the true hinge of the polis.[49]

Jaeger, in this regard writes: "Plato's chief work...is a *Tractatus Theologico-politicus*. Despite the close connection between religion and the state, the Greeks never had a priesthood supported by dogma. But in Plato's *Republic* Hellas produced a bold ideal worthy to be matched with the priestly theocracy of the Orient: *a ruling class of trained philosophers, their claim to rule founded on the ability of the human mind to seek out and find the good which is God"* (*Paideia*, 2:298-9).[50] This is, in reality, the true foundation of the Platonic ideal *City-State.*

5. The education of philosophers in the ideal City-State and "highest knowledge"

In the kind of City-State that Plato favored, the greatest importance devolved on the selection of youngsters endowed with an authentic philosophical inclination (that is, of youngsters in whom the rational part of the soul predominated over the other two) and their education.

For those destined to become philosopher-rulers the gymnastic-musical education, which was established for all the guardians in general, was only an introductory step. In fact this kind of education produces an individual whose life is well-ordered and harmonious, but it does not yield a knowledge of the cause on which this order and harmony depends. To put it briefly, we can say that the gymnastic-musical paideia produces the effects of the Good, but not the *knowledge of the Good*. Instead, this is the goal of a philosophical educa-tion: to reach the "highest knowledge" (μέγιστον μάθημα); that is, to possess the knowledge of the "Good in itself."[51]

To reach the "highest knowledge" there are no short cuts, but only the "long way,"[52] the way that goes from the sensible to the supersensible, from the corruptible to the incorruptible, from becoming to being, which is nothing more than the route of the "second voyage."

The long way of being passes through mathematics, plane and solid geometry, astronomy, and the science of harmony: all these sciences, in fact, force the soul to use intelligence and they carry it into contact with a part of privileged being (the mathematical-geometric entities and laws). But the most arduous and difficult part of the journey is dialectic, through which the soul completely puts aside the sensible to achieve the pure being of the Ideas and, proceeding through the Ideas, reaches the vision of the Good, to the "highest knowledge."[53]

In brief we can say that the method and content of the paideia of the guardians and rulers of the City-State is exactly the method and content of Platonic philosophy, which we have revealed already. Some Platonic positions have nevertheless still to be discussed.

The first mathematical lessons must be presented as though they were games and not serious study, because only in this way will they reveal the nature of the youngster:

> Now, all this study of reckoning and geometry and all the preliminary studies that are indispensable preparations for dialectics must be presented to them while still young, not in the form of compulsory instruction.
> Why so?
> Because, said I, a free soul ought not to pursue any studies slavishly; for while bodily labors performed under constraint do not harm the body, *nothing that is learned under compulsion stays with the mind.*
> True, he said.
> Do not, then, my friend, keep children to their studies by compulsion but *by play. That will also better enable you to discern the natural capacities of each.*"[54]

At twenty, those who had been singled out in these studies, in their work and in their capacity to confront dangers of various kinds will be educated to understand the relationships arising between the studies taken in the preced-ing cycle and to grasp the higher bonds of affinity existing between these studies and the *nature of being* (τοῦ ὄντος φύσις).[55] During this second cycle, which lasts from their twenties to their thirty-first year, is important to determine which of them is endowed with a dialectical nature: "And it is also, said I, the chief test of the dialectical nature and its opposite. For he who can view things in their connection is a dialectician; he who cannot is not."[56]

The nature of dialectic therefore is *the capacity to see things together* (σύνοψις), meaning that capacity which Plato himself defines as the tendency of the soul "towards the whole (ὅλον) and the all (πᾶν)."[57]

At the thirtieth year, those who have revealed a dialectical nature must be put to the test: "To see that of them is able to disregard the eyes and the other senses and go on to being itself in company with truth."[58]

In dialectic, those who pass the test, will be educated for five more years.[59]

From thirty-five to fifty they must be retested in terms of experiential realities by taking command of soldiers and various other commands.

At fifty years of age their training or paideia ends:

> Fifteen years, said I, and at the age of fifty those who have survived the test and have proved themselves altogether the best in every task and every form of knowledge must be brought at last to the goal. We shall require them to turn upwards the vision of their souls and *fix their gaze on that which sheds light on all, and when they have thus beheld the good itself they shall use it as a pattern for the right ordering of the City-State and the citizens and themselves throughout the remainder of their lives*, each in his turn, devoting the greater part of their time to the study of philosophy, but when the turn comes for each, toiling in the service of the City-State and holding office for the city's sake, *regarding the task not as a fine thing but a necessity*; so, when each generation has educated others like themselves to take their place as guardians of the City-State, they shall depart to the islands of the blessed and there dwell" [60]

And just as for the classes of the warriors Plato does not make any distinction between men and women, holding that beginning from birth they must receive the same education and exercise the same functions in the City-State, so consistently he points out the same principle is operative for the rulers:

> A most beautiful finish, Socrates, you have put upon your rulers, as if you were a statuary.
> *And on the woman too*, Glaucon, said I; *for you must not suppose that my words apply to the men more than to all women who arise among them endowed with the requisite qualities.*
> That is right, he said, if they are to share equally in all things with the men as we laid it down.[61]

This is undoubtedly the most revolutionary and daring reevaluation of the role of women that occurred in antiquity.

A final point to emphasize.

The philosopher, having reached the contemplation of the Good and the highest Being, would undoubtedly desire to live the remainder of her life in *contemplation*. But that would not be taking into account a precise debt contracted by her in relation to the City-State: she has arrived at these heights that only a very few achieve and has perfected her nature thanks to the *paideia* and to the concern of the City-State, therefore it is only fair that she be concerned with others, to share with them those advantages accruing from her achievement of the vision of the Good. The City-State cannot allow one of its classes to have the privilege of extraordinary happiness, but it must ensure that all classes are reciprocally enriched with those advantages according to their respective capacities.[62]

The highest "political power," within the Platonic framework, becomes therefore the highest and necessary "service" of those who, contemplating the Good, descend into reality through practical politics and dispense the advantages of their knowledge to others.

6. The corrupt City-State and the type of man corresponding to it

The construction of the perfect City-State and the analysis of the human type corresponding to it attempts to show, as we have seen, that there is a structural correspondence between human excellence and happiness, and that the latter is precisely the necessary and natural effect of the former. But Plato is not content with a direct proof, and in the eighth and ninth books of the *Republic*, he gives us a kind of *counterproof*, going on to the analysis of the kinds of degenerate constitutions and of human types corresponding to them, to show that in the measure in which they turn away from virtue, they likewise turn away from happiness.

Also all this part of the Platonic analysis arises from the principle of the perfect correspondence between the soul and the character of the individual and the institutions of the City-State: the rulers and constitutions, he says, "do not spring from the proverbial oak or rock," but rather, "from the moral character of the citizens of the City-State." [63]

The corrupt forms of government are, in order, the following: (*a*) *timocracy*, which is a form of government that depends on the recognition of honor (which in Greek is expressed by τίμος, hence the name timocracy) as the highest value; (*b*) *oligarchy*, which is a form of government founded on wealth understood as the highest value (and hence managed by those few who acquire wealth); (*c*) *democracy*, which Plato understood in the pejorative sense of demagoguery; (*d*) *tyranny*, which for our philosopher is the real scourge of mankind.

The ideal City-State described by Plato is an "aristocracy" in the strong and rich sense of the term, meaning a City-State that is righteous and correct directed by those who are the best by nature and upbringing, based on *human excellence* as the highest value, and hence characterized by the esteem for the rational part of the soul of the citizens.

"Timocracy" (which Plato identified usually with the governance of Sparta) destroys this necessary balance of the perfect City-State, because it substitutes virtue to honor, so to speak, by wanting the effect without the cause. In this form of City-State the wellspring of public life is the *drive for honor*, and hence ambition, whereas in the private life the path is found in the *drive for money*, cleverly still hidden and masked. In the soul of the citizens of this City-State there is present an imbalance between the various powers, between the rational and the two nonrational parts of the soul, as long as the intermediate part (the *"irascible"* or *"epithumos"*) does not end in overwhelming the others.[64]

"Oligarchy" is for Plato, as we have already pointed out, essentially a "plutarchy." It signals a further degradation of values, because for the rule of virtue, the rule of wealth is substituted, which is purely an exterior good. Only the wealthy manage public affairs; virtue and the good are eclipsed and poverty and the poor are despised. The conflict between *rich* and *poor* is inevitable, and it becomes a conflict without any possibility of mediation (because of the absence of any values seen as beyond wealth and poverty, thus the human excellence of both the rich and the poor is obscured). And so by spending time making money, the man of this City-State further upsets the balance of his soul, and ends in allowing the lower part, the concupiscible to dominate.[65]

The "democracy" that Plato describes is the stage that precedes and prepares for tyranny. As we have previously stated, the modern word should not be allowed to draw us into being deceived by the name, since what our philosopher has in mind is *demagoguery* and the *demagogic aspect of democracy*. The insatiable desire for wealth and money brings about little by little an oligarchy, in which nothing is important except accumulating wealth. Youngsters, grow up without any moral education, begin to spend without measure (the sense of "saving" for them is without meaning, because they are the inheritors of such great wealth) and they give themselves over to every kind of pleasure without discrimination (because they no longer possess any sense of limits, which could only be derived from a higher set of values). In this way the wealthy holders of power are weakened, both morally and physically, to the point where the subjects of poverty acquire an awareness of it and, at the first opportune moment, take the opportunity and impose a government of the people, proclaiming the equality of all citizens (the equal footing to both the equal and the unequal says Plato) and distribute the judiciary by a system of lotteries. The City-State is stuffed with "freedoms": but it is a liberty that, not being attached to values, degenerates into license. Every one lives as he pleases and, if he so wishes, can also not participate in public affairs. Justice is mild and tolerant; sentences are passed but frequently are not executed. Any one who wants a career in public office need not have the right disposition, education, and competence, but it is sufficient that "he say that he is a friend of the people."[66]

In this City-State in which liberty is license, the individuals that make it up have corresponding traits. For youngsters, desires and pleasures rule, which "in the end, I suppose,...seize the citadel of the young man's soul, finding it empty and unoccupied by studies and honorable pursuits and true discourses, which are the best watchmen and guardians in the minds of men who are dear to the gods."[67]

Such "bastard reasoning" bars entrance to and destroys any possibility of access to the arguments of the older who wish "to bring help and assistance."

And so respect proclaimed with these "reasonings" is described as stupidity, temperance now called unmanly is banished with insults, moderation and rules about spending are now a sign of miserliness. And analogously the opposite negative qualities are exalted: arrogance is now called good education, anarchy is said to be liberty, the spending of public moneys is now called liberality and impudence is now courage. And so the life of this young man is without order and without law, entirely dedicated to pleasures.[68]

Tyranny directly arises from democracy (understood in the sense just stated), because of insatiable freedom. The excess of freedom (which is license) falls into the opposite excess, which is slavery.

Here are some quite exemplary texts in which Plato describes the movement from democracy to tyranny (the casual tone and the subtle ironic interplay makes it even more effective):

> And now, said I, the fairest polity and the fairest man remain for us to describe, the tyranny and the tyrant.
> Certainly, he said.
> Come then, tell me, dear friend, how tyranny arises. That it is an outgrowth of democracy is fairly plain.
> Yes, plain.
> Is it, then, in a sense, in the same way in which democracy arises out of oligarchy that tyranny arises from democracy?
> How is that?
> The good that they propose to themselves and that was the cause of the establishment of oligarchies–it was wealth, was it not?
> Yes.
> Well then, the insatiate lust for wealth and the neglect of everything else for the sake of money making was the cause of its undoing.
> True, he said.
> And is it not the avidity of democracy for that which is its definition and criterion of good the thing which dissolves it too?
> What do you say its criterion to be?
> Liberty, I replied; for you may hear it said that this is best managed in the democratic city, and for this reason that is the only city in which men of free spirit were cleared to live.

Why, yes, he replied, you hear that saying everywhere.

Then, as I was about to observe, is it not the excess and greed of this and the neglect of all other things that revolutionizes this constitution too and prepares the way for the necessity of a dictatorship?

How he said?

Why when a democratic city athirst for liberty gets bad cup bearers for its leaders and is intoxicated by drinking too deep of that unmixed wine, and then, if its so-called governors are not extremely mild and gentle with it and do not dispense the liberty unstintedly, it chastises them and accuses them of being acursed oligarch.

Yes, that is what they do, he replied.

But those who obey the rulers, I said, it reviles as willing slaves in men of naught, but it commends and honors in public and private rulers who resemble subjects and subjects who are like rulers. Is it not inevitable that in such a City-State the spirit of liberty, should go to all lengths?

Of course.

And this anarchical temper, said I, my friend, must penetrate into private homes and finally enter into the very animals.

Just what do we mean by that? he said.

Why, I said, the father truly tries to resemble the child but is afraid of his sons, and the son likens himself to the father and feels no awe or fear of his parents, so that he may be forsooth a free man. And the resident alien feels himself equal to the citizen and the citizen to him, and the foreigner likewise.

Yes, these things do happen, he said.

They do, said I, and such other trifles as these.

The teachers in such cases fears and fawns upon the pupils, and the pupils pay no heed to the teacher or to their overseers either. And in general the young ape their elders and vie with them in speech and action, while the old, accommodating themselves to the young are full of pleasantry and graciousness, imitating the young for fear that they may be thought disagreeable and authoritative.

By all means, he said.

And the climax of popular liberty my friend, I said, is attained in such a city when the purchased slaves, male and female, are no less free than the owners who paid for them. And I almost forgot to mention the spirit of freedom and equal rights in the relation of men to women and women to men. Shall we not, then, said he, in Aeschylean phrase, say [whatever rises to our lips]?

Certainly, I said, so I will. Without experience of it no one would believe how much freer the very beasts subject to men are in such a city than elsewhere. The dog literally verified the adage and [like their mistresses become.] And likewise the horses and asses are one to hold on their way with the utmost freedom and dignity, bumping into everyone who meets them and who does not step aside. And so all things everywhere are just bursting with this spirit of liberty.

It is my own dream you are telling me, he said; for it often happens to me when I go to the country.

And do you note that the sum total of all these items when footed up is that they render the souls of the citizen so sensitive that they chafe as the slightest suggestion of servitude and will not endure it? For you are aware that they finally pay no heed to the laws written or unwritten, so that forsooth they may have no master anywhere over them.

I know it very well, said he.

Thus, my friend, said I, is the fine and vigorous root from which tyranny grows, in my opinion.

Vigorous indeed, he said; but what next?

The same malady, I said, that arising in oligarchy, destroyed it, this more widely diffused and more violent as a result of this license, enslaves democracy and in truth, any excess is want to bring about a corresponding reaction to the opposite in the seasons, in plants, in animal bodies, and most especially in political societies.

Probably, he said.

And so the probable outcome of too much freedom is only too much slavery in the individual and the City-State.

Yes, that is probable.

Probably, that, tyranny develops out of no other constitution than democracies–from the height of liberty, I take it, the fiercest extreme of servitude."[69]

The disease that corrupts democracy is located in the category of laziness that enjoys consuming. The most malevolent of these men drags the others, and, taking advantage of freedom, they act in a domineering way through words and action and they do not tolerate any one who speaks in any other way. With various strategies they try to take away from the wealthy their riches, doing in a way what people do who look out for their own benefit by taking for themselves the richest part. And when among them a man stands out and rises to become the leader acknowledged by the populace (a demagogue), he will very quickly become a tyrant; that is, by accusing his adversaries unjustly and banishing them from the City-State or even killing them. At this point there seems to be no other choice for him: either to be killed himself as a victim of the vengeance of his adversaries or to transform himself into a tyrant, and thus become a "predator." At first he will go among them in a gracious and smiling manner; but soon he will be forced to come out from behind the mask. Wars are stirred up continually, because he must arouse their desire for a strong leader. Hence "he will purge" the City-State, by eliminating all those elements in it that are disturbing it: and it will be the best who are eliminated. The tyrant will end by associating with useless men, and, in the end, he will finish his life with those who hate him even though they may have brought him into power: "A very parricide, said I, you make the tyrant out to be, and cruel nurse of old age, and, as it seems, this is at last tyranny opened and avowed, and, as the saying goes, the demos trying to escape the smoke of submission to the free would have plunged into the fire of enslavement to slaves, and in exchange for that excessive and unseasonable liberty as clothed itself in the garb of the most cruel and bitter servile servitude."[70]

In the rule of the tyrant, there is tyranny both at the top of the power structure but also among the citizenry. And the traits of the tyrannic citizen are the following: unrestrained freedom, which is really license and anarchy, to which he abandons himself, allowing full expression to those savage and illegal desires and passions, and to those terrible impulses that are present in each one of us, but that education and reason have tamed and that flourish only in our dreams.[71]

Preyed upon by these desires, he shakes from himself every residue of temperance, stops at nothing and wants to dominate not only human beings but even the Gods, and he touches bottom when he wholly buries himself in liquor, sex, and finally succumbs to psychic depression: "Then a man becomes tyrannical in the full sense of the word, my friend, I said, when either by nature or by habits or by both he has become even as the drunken, the erotic, the maniacal."[72]

It is clear that such men are incapable of being in relationship with other men, they are capable only of ordering or obeying and becoming alienated from persons with whom they come in contact especially if they do not get from them what it is they wish: "Throughout their lives, then, they never know what it is to be the friends of anybody. They are always masters or slaves, but the tyrannical nature never tastes freedom or true friendship."[73]

Just as tyranny is the City-State of absolute servitude–and this is not only the servitude of the subjects to the tyrant, but it is total enslavement (both in the tyrant and the subjects) of reason by the most base instincts–exterior enslavement is nothing if it is not the consequence and the manifestation of interior enslavement.

7. The City-State, terrestrial and ultraterrestrial happiness

We have stated earlier that Plato constructed the ideal City-State with the aim of seeing reproduced on a large scale the soul of human beings, his virtues and his vices, and hence his happiness and unhappiness. Already with Socrates happiness had been interiorized in the *psyché* and it was made to coincide with *areté*. And the Platonic *Republic*, from a certain viewpoint, is a proof written large of this thesis, explained in all of its details.

The ideal City-State and the ruling man or aristocrat to which it corresponds is characterized by the uncontested power of rationality, with which virtue essentially coincides (the virtue is fundamentally rationality) and also freedom (freedom is freedom of reason from arational instincts and impulses, and it reveals itself in the control it has over these): and not only does reason dominate in the ruling class of the City-State, but it also dominates the classes of the guardian-warriors, in the measure in which it controls their irascible nature from which their courage is derived, and the lower class, in the measure in which the concupiscible soul is controlled and produces temperance in them. The healthful City-State is happy.

In the City-State and in the corresponding timocratic man, rationality loses out to the irascible part of the soul. The first disruption of the balance is produced based on supremacy of ambition and the seeking of honor over virtue. In the City-State and in the corresponding oligarchic man rationality is overcome, further, by the concupiscible soul and then the desire for achievement and superfluous pleasures rises. In the City-State and in the corresponding tyrannical man, finally, the balance of the soul is completely disrupted, and the most unrestrained and bestial desires emerge and become dominant. With the progressive regression from rationality, sickness, spiritual bankruptcy and hence unhappiness reign in the City-State and in the soul, they achieve their extreme limit in the City-State and corresponding tyrannical man.

The highest happiness for the man who lives according to the politics of the perfect City-State; that is, one who lives the philosophical life, emerges also from the further considerations concerning pleasure, to which we have already referred. Happiness cannot consist in anything but the highest form of pleasure, which is that of the rational part of the soul. This pleasure is also that which is most true (and even the only one), because the object that obtains it is the most true object, it is the *being* and the *eternal* contemplated by the soul.

The philosophical life in the ideal City-State is the victory of the divine element over the bestial element in man; it is construction of the divine man.[74]

And as a seal for this position, Plato, in the final book of the *Republic*, adduces a final argument, which he intends as a definitive counterproof, an ultimate verification: the time that runs between birth and death is short and the rewards of virtue in this live are only relative; the true reward of virtue is in the afterlife.[75] So that the political life of the ideal City-State guarantees happiness in the here and now just as in the hereafter, in life and after death; that is, for always. The magnificent eschatological myth of Er that closes the *Republic* returns thus to the final sense of Platonic politics: *true politics* is that which saves man not only in the temporal order but for eternity.[76]

8. The City-State in the interior of man

Does the Platonic *Republic* present us with a myth and an utopia or an ideal and moral reality? It is very easy to respond to this question: in the Platonic construction there is undoubtedly utopian and mythical aspect, but they are, if not marginal, at the very least unessential. The Platonic *Republic* fundamentally expresses a *realizable ideal* (even if historically speaking the ideal City-State does not exist) *within the heart and soul of man*. If the true City-State does not exist *outside us*, we can nevertheless construct it within ourselves, following within ourselves true politics. Here is a page in which Plato expresses this concept quite clearly:

> And the wise man will bend all his endeavors to this end throughout his life; he will, to begin with, prize the studies that will give this quality to his soul and disprize the others.
>
> Clearly, he said.
>
> And then, I said, he not only will not abandon the habit and nurture of his body to the brutish and irrational pleasure and live with his face set in that direction, but he will not even make health his chief aim, or give the first place to the ways of becoming strong or healthy or beautiful unless these things are likely to bring with them soberness of spirit, but he will always be found attuning the harmonies of his body for the sake of the calm chord in his soul.
>
> By all means, he replied, if he is to be a true musician.
>
> And would he not deal likewise with the ordering and harmonizing of his possessions? He will not let himself be dazzled by the felicitations of the multitude and pile up the mass of his wealth without measure, involving himself in measureless ills.
>
> No, I think not, he said.
>
> He will, rather, I said, *keep his eyes fixed on the constitution in his soul* and, taking care at watching lest he disturb anything there either by excess or deficiency of wealth, will so steer his course and add to or detract from it as well on this principle, so far as may be.
>
> Precisely so, he said.
>
> And in the matter of honors and office too this will be his guiding principle: he will gladly take part in and enjoy those which he thinks will make him a better man, but in public and private life he will shun those that may overthrow the established habit of his soul.
>
> Then, if that is his chief concern, he said, he will not willingly take part in politics.
>
> Yes, by the dog, said I, *in his own city he certainly will, if not perhaps in the city of his birth*, except in some providential conjuncture.
>
> I understand, he said; *you mean the city whose establishment we have described, the city whose home is in the ideal; for I think that it can be found nowhere on earth.*
>
> Well, said I, perhaps there is a pattern of it laid up in Heaven for him who wishes to contemplate it and so beholding to constitute himself its citizen. *But it makes no difference whether it exists now or if it will come into being. The politics of this city only will be his and of none other.*
>
> That seems probable, he said."[77]

Only in recent times has the meaning of this passage been understood, which is in many respects decisive and it has been so understood best of all by Jaeger, who writes:

> Ancient and modern interpreters who expect to find in The *Republic* a handbook of political science, dealing with the various existing forms of

constitution, have tried again and again to find the Platonic state somewhere on this earth, and identified it with some real form of state which seemed to resemble it in its political structure. But the essence of Plato's state is not its external structure (if it has any) but its metaphysical nucleus, the idea of absolute reality and value round which it is built. It is not possible to realize Plato's *Republic* by imitating its external organization, but only by fulfilling the law of absolute good which is the soul of it. Therefore he who succeeds in realizing that divine order in his individual soul has made a greater contribution to the realization of Plato's state than he who constructs an entire city which externally resembles Plato's political scheme but is deprived of its divine essence, the Idea of the Good, the source of its perfection and happiness.[78]

It goes without saying, that inevitably in the historical State the citizen who lives the political life of the ideal City-State becomes estranged, and the more he becomes so, the more does he become conformed to the political ideal. What arises here for the first time is the idea of the citizen of two City-States, of the terrestrial City-State and of the divine City-State, hence, a political dualism. Jaeger maintains that such an idea is "the product of the inner dissolution of the Greek unity of man and polis,"[79] and it is nothing other than "to explain the real situation of the philosophical man in the polis of his [of Plato] time, as manifested in the representative life and death of Socrates."[80] In reality this is true only in part. First it should be noted that the otherworldly vision that Plato took from Orphism plays a role no less important than the life and death of Socrates in carrying him to his conclusions. But especially keep in mind that Plato does not seem to be at all aware of the character of the affirmation about which we are concerned, so that it is true that he does not pursue this issue and does not draw from this powerful intuition the consequences that it imposes, but he rather goes back on it. Since in the succeeding political works of Plato (the *Statesman* and the *Laws*) the Greek unity of the individual and the City-State is still ruling: the definitive break in this unity would occur only in Hellenistic thought.

III. THE MAN OF THE STATE, WRITTEN LAWS, AND CONSTITUTIONS

1. The problem of the *Statesman*

What else can be said by our philosopher, with respect to politics, after the magnificent construction of the ideal City-State? The reply is simple, if we keep our focus on the purpose of the Academy. The School that Plato founded aimed to educate, essentially, political men, men formed in a new way for a new City-State. The historical realization of the ideal designated in the *Republic* was impossible, and Plato himself, explicitly stated that it was realizable only within the spiritual dimension (in our souls). On the other hand, as we have pointed out, the time was not yet ripe to go further into the intuition of the *two Cities* (the heavenly and the earthly) and man as a *citizen of two Cities*. It was necessary that the philosopher provide, in addition to the model of the ideal State, a more realistic point of reference, something *historically capable of being realized*, and hence Plato reproposes the political problematic from another perspective. Indeed to respond to these exigencies, Plato matured the design of the "second State"; that is, of the State that comes *after the ideal one*: a state that explains, in a different way than the first, not only about *how man ought to be*, but *how he actually is*; a State, in short, easier to produce in actuality.

The *Statesman* signals the first phase in this work of mediation between the ideal politics and historical reality, which culminates in the *Laws*. In discussing the definition of the citizen and the art of statesmanship, Plato, in the *Statesman*, by considering men and the State just as they actually are, asks whether or not the citizen is beyond the law or, vice versa, whether the laws are sovereign. It is clear that in the case of the ideal State of the *Republic* this dilemma does not exist, because in that State the statesman (the philosopher) and the law are not found to be in conflict necessarily, insofar as the law is nothing other than the way in which the statesman realizes within the State the good which he contemplates in the Absolute. But in the historical State things do not proceed in this manner: the statesman who *can actually realize* this ideal do not exist; and out of this understanding the problem just stated is produced.

Plato, note, in the *Statesman* does not renounces his ideal State, and he emphasizes that the better form of government would be that of a man who would govern "with virtue and knowledge"[1] beyond the law, which is always abstract and impersonal and hence frequently inadequate. But, at the same time, he recognizes that men endowed with this virtue and knowledge are not only exceptional, but, as a matter of fact, nonexistent; hence, in the historical State, the supremacy must be given to the law, and it is necessary to elaborate an inviolable written constitution:

Stranger: So then we have the tyrant and the king, then oligarchy and aristocracy, then democracy, all of which arise when men turn down the idea of the one true and scientific ruler. Men doubt whether any man will ever be found fit to bear such perfect rule. They despair of finding any one man willing and able to rule with moral and intellectual insight and to render every man his due with strict fairness. They feel sure that a man with such absolute power will be bound to employ it to the hurt and injury of his personal enemies and to put them out of the way. *But it remains true that if the ideal ruler we have described were to appear on earth he would be acclaimed, and he would spend his days guiding in strictest justice and perfect happiness that one and only true State worthy of the name.*

Young Socrates: That is so of course.

Stranger: *We must take things as they are, however, and kings do not arise in cities in the natural course of things in the way the royal bee is born in a bee-hive—one individual obviously outstanding in body and mind and capable of taking charge of things at once. And therefore it seems men gather together and work out written codes, chasing as fast as they can the fading vision of the true constitution.*[2]

2. The forms of possible constitutions

The realistic recognition of the principle that we have discussed brought about a reevaluation of the different forms of constitution, which in the *Republic* were presented as the pathologies of the ideal State. In the *Statesman* it is shown, instead, that they are necessary and that they have their validity, indeed, because the perfect form of government does not exist, which as we have seen, requires impossibly the existence of an extraordinary man.

The historical constitutions are "imitations" of the ideal ones.[3] If it is only one man who governs and imitates the political ideal, then there is *monarchy*. If instead it is a multitude of the wealthy who govern and imitate the ideal, then we have an *aristocracy*. If instead the whole people govern and try to imitate the political ideal, then we have *democracy*. These three forms of government are just in the measure in which he (they) who govern respect the laws and customs. If, instead, the law is not respected, then the three corresponding corrupt forms of government come into being: monarchy degenerates into *tyranny*, aristocracy into *oligarchy*, and finally democracy degenerates into *corrupt democracy* (we may call it *demagoguery*).

Among these historical constitutions which are better, or not as bad (since they are in any case mere imitations), and which are worse? Which is the most supportable and which the least supportable? Here is the reply of Plato:

Stranger: Before, when we were in search of the right government, this division was of no use, as we showed at the time; but now that we have set that apart and have decided that the others are the only available forms of government, the principle of lawfulness and lawlessness bisect each of them.

Young Socrates: So it seems, from what has been said.

Stranger: Monarchy, then, when bound with good written rules, which we call laws, *is the best of all six*, but without law it is hard and most oppressive to live with.

Young Socrates: I fancy it is.

Stranger: But just as few is intermediate between one and a multitude, so the government of the few must be considered *intermediate, both in good and in evil*. But the government of the multitude is *weak* in all respects and able to do nothing great, either good or bad, when compared with the other forms of government, because in this the powers of government are distributed in small shares among many men; *therefore of all these governments when they are lawful, this is the worst, and when they are all lawless it is the best; and if they are all without restraint, life is most desirable in a democracy, but if they are orderly, that is the worst to live in*; but life in the first kind of City-State is by far the first and best, with the exception of the seventh, for that must be set apart from all the others, as God is set apart from man.[4]

3. The "just mean" and the art of politics

In the *Republic* the science of politics is identical with the knowledge of the supreme Good and the Ideas and hence with philosophy. In the *Statesman* it is defined more specifically and more realistically, in agreement with the general tendency of the dialogues.

There are two ways of proceeding in the *measurement*, by means of two different criteria. There is the measurement based on the reciprocal relation of great-small, long-short, excess-defect, which is of a mathematical nature. There is also the measurement "according to the essence which is necessary for generation,"[5] that is based on the "just mean" or on the "just measure"(τὸ μέτριον);[6] that is to say on the Ideas or essences of things and this is a measurement that could be called axiological, because it refers to the ideal values (qualities) and not to mere quantities.

The introduction of this second kind of measurement is, as is obvious, *a clear overcoming of Pythagoreanism, which is completely analogous to that produced in relation to Eleaticism by the introduction of "nonbeing" as equivalent to "difference,"* as Plato has taken some pains to expressly point out:

> *Stranger*: Then just as in the case of the Sophist we forced the conclusion that not-being exists, since that was the point at which we had lost our hold of the argument, so now we must force this second conclusion, that the greater and the less are to be measured in relation, not only to one another, but also to the establishment of the standard of the mean, must we not? For if this is not admitted, neither the statesmen nor any other man who has knowledge of practical affairs can be said without any doubt to exist.
>
> *Young Socrates*: Then we must by all means do now the same that we did then.
>
> *Stranger*: This, Socrates, is a still greater task that was; and yet we remember how long that took us; but it is perfectly fair to make about them some such assumption as this.

Young Socrates: As what?

Stranger: That sometime we shall need this principle of being for the demonstration of absolute precise truth. That our belief that the demonstration is for our present purpose good and sufficient is, in my opinion, magnificently supported by this argument–that we must believe that all the arts alike exist and that the greater and the less are measured in relation not only to one another but also to the establishment of the standard of the mean. For if this exists, they exist also, and if they exist, it exists also, but neither can ever exist if the other does not.

Young Socrates: That is quite right. But what comes next?

Stranger: We should evidently devise the science of measurement into two parts in accordance with what has been said. One part comprises all the arts which measure number, length, depth, breadth, and thickness in relation to their opposites; the other comprises those which measure them in relation to the moderate, the fitting, the opportune, the needful, and all the other standards that are situated in the mean between the extremes.[7]

By applying this fundamental distinction (which is applicable in general to all the arts) in a specific way to the art of governing, we will say that it has as its object the just mean, the obligatory, the appropriate, the fitting in the most important area of the life of the City-State.[8]

The activity of politics is properly distinguished in this way from a series of activities that are connected to it, but that turn out to be subsidiary and subordinate to it. Just as rhetoric is distinguished from politics, because, whereas the former is persuasive, the latter instead is an activity that decides *whether or not it is appropriate* to persuade (or to resort to force) and thus is not only different but superior as well. By analogous reasoning we can extend this to the art of warfare, which is concerned with prosecuting and winning the war, but it is not concerned with deciding whether or not it is correct to go to war or to maintain the peace, because this decision belongs to the political art. Even the activity of the judiciary is different than the art of governing and is subordinated to it, because the former is limited to applying the law, whereas the governments establish law.[9]

But the just measure or the just mean that the art of governing pursues is found chiefly in its fundamental task, which is that of constructing the unity of the State by bringing together heterogenous elements and especially those opposed to one another to give them a single power and a single identity. In fact men can be distinguished according to two fundamental tendencies and two opposed virtues: one is the mild or timid and the other is the audacious, courageous, and strong. The statesman must be able to harmonize these opposing temperaments, as if components of a piece of cloth or of a covering used by those who are ill and obstinate. This covering in being weaved will fix the divine part of man (the soul) with a divine "knot" and the animal part (the body) with a human "knot." The divine knot is the knowledge of the highest values, which tempers the audacious soul and makes sensible the cautious soul, both being united in relation to the good and the beautiful by a unified opinion. The human knot consists instead in producing through the appropriate marriage the opposed natures conjoined, just as the opposed temperaments are tempered also from the biological viewpoint.[10]

Here is the conclusion of the dialogue:

> This, then, is the end, let us declare, of the web of the City-States's activities, the direct interweaving of the characters of retrained and courageous men, when the kingly science has drawn them together by friendship and community of sentiment into a common life, and have perfected the most glorious and best textures, closed with it all the inhabitants of the City-State, both slaves and freemen, holds them together by this fabric, and omitting nothing which ought to belong to a happy City-State, rules and watches over them.[11]

IV. THE "SECOND STATE" OF THE LAWS

1. The purpose of the *"Laws"* and their relationship with the *"Republic"*

The *Laws* are the final work of Plato and also his political testament. They not only trace a general plan for a State, but go into the particulars, by developing a model of legislation of a City-State almost complete. The reason why Plato submitted to the exhaustive labor that the drafting of this work undoubtedly entailed, given the heavy element of juridical knowledge it involved, is better understood in the light of modern historiographic reconstruction, which we have already in part explained. Taylor writes, for example,

> ...in the fourth century the Academy was constantly being asked, as a recognized society of experts in jurisprudence, to do the same sort of work. Plato himself is said to have been requested to legislate for Megalopolis, and, though he declined, work of the same kind was done by his associates for many foundations. Hence it was eminently desirable that men contemplating the probability of being called on to "legislate," should be provided with an example of the way in which the work should be gone about, and the *Laws* is meant to furnish just such an example.[1]

Considered from this perspective, the *Laws* are undoubtedly a work of great importance and, for not a few, of great value, but properly for their practical significance they are not the *summa* of all of the political positions of Plato, but only the *summa* of what in these positions Plato judged was immediately realizable.

Thus the conception of the philosopher-king and the authentic State from one such man is still expressly stated as the ideal, even if at the same time he recognizes, as earlier in the *Statesman*, the necessity of retreating to a more realistic conception positing the laws as sovereign:

> Yet if ever there should arise in man competent by nature and by a birthright of divine grace to assume such an office, he would have no need of rulers over him; *for no law or ordinance is mightier than knowledge, nor is it right for reason to be subject or enthralled to anything, but to be lord of all things, if it is really true to its name and free in its inner nature*. But at present such a nature exists nowhere in all, except in small degree; *wherefore we must choose what is second best*, namely ordinance and law, which see and discern the general principle, but are unable to see every instance in detail.[2]

And the superiority of the community life is expressly stated again and hence implicitly emphasized even the theoretical presupposition that platonic "communism" implies:

> That State and polity come first, and those laws are best, where they're observed as carefully as possible throughout the whole State the old saying

that "friends have all things really in common." As to this condition,– whether it anywhere exists now, or ever will exist,–in which there is community of wives, children, and all chattels, and all that is called "private" is everywhere and by every means rooted out of our life, and so far as possible it is contrived that even things naturally "private" have become in a way "communized",—eyes, for instance, and ears and hands seem to see, hear, and act in common,–and that all men are, so far as possible, unanimous in the praise and blame they bestow, rejoicing and grieving at the same things, and that they honor with all their hearts those laws which render the State as unified as possible,—no one will ever lay down another definition that is truer or better than these conditions in point of super-excellence. In such a State, be it gods of sons of gods that dwell in it,–they dwell pleasantly, living such a life as this wherefore one should not look elsewhere for a model constitution, but hold fast to this one, and with all one's power seek a constitution that is as like to it as possible. That constitution which we are now engaged upon, if it came into being, would be very near to immortality, and would come second in point of merit. The third we shall investigate hereafter, if God so wills; for the present, however, what is this second best polity, and how would it come to be of such a character?[3]

2. Some fundamental concepts of the "*Laws*"

The State of the "*Laws*" is, hence, almost a copy of the original model and for this "comes as second"[4] after the original "which is first."[5] For this reason, an exposition of the "*Laws*" can gain its correct emphasis only by descending to particulars, a thing that can be done only in the course of a treatment of monograph length. In this perspective we must try to emphasize two important points.

The constitution which Plato proposes in the "*Laws*" as more adequate is a "mixed constitution," which unites the advantages of monarchy with those of democracy and eliminates their mutual defects:

> *Athens*: Listen. There are two mother-forms of constitution, so to call them, from which one may truly say all the rest are derived. Of these the one is properly termed monarchy, the other democracy, the extreme case of the former being the Persian Polity, and of the latter the Athenian; the rest are practically all, as I said, modifications of these two. Now it is essential for a polity to partake of both these two forms, if it to have freedom and friendliness combine with wisdom. And that is what our argument intends to enjoin, when it declares that a state which does not partake of these can never rightly be constituted.
> *Clinaeus*: It could not.
> *Athens*: Since the one embraced monarchy and the other freedom, unmixed and in excess, *neither of them has either in due measure*....[6]

In fact, in Persia little by little the people were pushed into complete slavery (and hence it was a form of absolute tyranny); in Greece the people were forced to accept total liberty (and hence democracy became demagoguery). Absolute liberty (anarchy) is of less value than a tempered and regulated liberty.[7] Liberty tempered by authority is hence the "just measure" and it is the goal which the mixed constitution embraces.

Plato also took up the issue of equality. He held that even in this case, it is necessary to find the "just measure," and the just measure is not found in an abstract egalitarianism, but in a *proportional equality*:

> For slaves will never be friends with masters, nor bad men with good, even when they occupy equal positions—for when equality is given to unequal things, the resultant will be unequal, *unless due measure is applied*; and it is because of these two conditions that political organizations are filled with feuds. There is an old and true saying that "equality produces amity," which is right well and fitly spoken; what the equality is which is capable of doing this is a very troublesome question, since it is very far from being clear. For there are two kinds of equality which, though identical in name, are often almost opposites in their practical results. The one of these any State or lawgiver is competent to apply in the assignment of honors,namely, equality determined by measure, weight and number,—by simply employing the lot to give even results in the distribution; but the truest and best form of equality is not an easy thing for everyone to discern. It is the judgement of Zeus, and men it never assists save in small measure, but insofar as it does assist either States or individuals, it produces all things good; where it dispenses more to the greater and less to the smaller, giving due measure to each according to nature; and with regard to honors also, by granting the greater to those that are greater in goodness, and the less to those of the opposite character in respect of goodness and education, *it assigns in proportion what is fitting to each*. Indeed, it is precisely this which constitutes for us "political justice," which is the object we must strive for, Clinias; this equality is what we must aim at, now that we are settling the State that is being planted. And whoever founds a State elsewhere at any time must make this same object the aim of his legislation,—not the advantage of a few tyrants, or of one, or of some form of democracy, but justice always; and this consists in what we have just stated, namely, the natural equality given on each occasion to things unequal.[8]

In general, the "just measure" dominated the *Laws* from start to finish, and, thus, Plato pointed out its foundation, once again in the theological, by affirming that for human beings, "the measure of all things is God."[9]

V. THE POLITICAL COMPONENT OF PLATONIC THOUGHT AND ITS RELATIONSHIP WITH THE PROTOLOGIC OF THE UNWRITTEN DOCTRINES

After the full exposition we have given to the thematics that constitute the political component of Platonic thought, on the basis of what we have explained in the preceding part, the concluding problem becomes all the more necessary: what relations do the political doctrines, which Plato entrusted in large measure to his writings and on which he focussed even his masterpiece, have to the *"Unwritten Doctrines"*; that is, to the doctrine of the first and highest principles?

Now, after the explanations that we have given on the precise connections between the metaphysical foundations of the *Republic* and the protologic, the solution to the difficulty is not hard to find.

We know that the Good is the "cause of all the things that are right and beautiful";[1] and we know that, therefore, the true statesman, having seen and contemplated the Good in itself, must preserve it as a "model" to give "order to the State," and likewise to regulate his life as a private citizen.[2] We know, in addition, that the *the Good is the One*, and that it is the *measure of all things*. The One-Good is the cause of all things right and good, because it brings unity, order, and stability, and hence a just measure to all things. In fact, all things are good, simply because they are "definite" and "ordered," and as such imply stability, that *unity-in-multiplicity*.[3] Hence, the authentic, ordered and harmonious statesman, brings unity-in-multiplicity to all levels.

Consequently, the *good* City-State will be that in which *unity* predominates at all levels, whereas the City-State that is not good will be one in which *multiplicity* predominates; that is, the Principle that is antithetical to the One.

Here is a very significant text, in which Plato not only hinges his reasoning on his Principles of *One/Many*, but especially joins the *Many* with the *Two* (with an evident allusion to the Dyad):

> "When happy innocence," said I, "to suppose that you can properly use the name city of any other than the one we are constructing."
> "Why, what should we say?" he said.
> "A greater predication," said I, "must be applied to the others. For they are each one of them many cities, not a city, as it goes in the game. There are two at the least at emnity with one another, the city of the rich and the city of the poor, and in each of these there are many. If you deal with them as one you will altogether miss the mark. But if you treat them as a multiplicity by offering to the one faction the property, the power, the very persons of the other, you will continue always to have few enemies and many allies. And so long as your city is governed soberly in the order just laid down, it will be the greatest of cities. I do not mean greatest in repute, but in reality, even though it have only a thousand defenders. For a city of this size that is

really one you will not easily discover either among Greeks or barbarians–
but of those that seem so you will find many and many times the size of this.
Or do you think otherwise?"
"No, indeed I don't," said he.[4]

Plato expresses, then, this concept, in a certain sense quite emphatically, and with some expressions of extraordinary effectiveness, by stating explicitly that the "greatest good" for a City-State is that which links together and makes it "one," whereas the "greatest evil" is that which divides its unity, and hence makes it become "many instead of one." Here is a passage that constitutes not only an allusion, but almost an explicit framework for his esoteric concepts:

> "Is not the logical first step towards such an agreement to ask ourselves what we could name as *the greatest good* (τὸ μέγιστον ἀγαθόν) for the constitution of a state and the proper aim of a lawgiver in his legislation, and what would be *the greatest evil* (μέγιστον κακόν), and then to consider whether the proposals we have just set forth fit into *the footprints of the good* (τὸ τοῦ ἀγαθοῦ ἴχνος) and do not suit those of the evil?"
> By all means," he said.
> "Do we know of any greater evil for a state than the thing that divides it and makes it *many* (πολλάς)instead of *one* (ἀντί μιᾶς), or a greater *Good* (ἀγαθόν) *than that which binds it together and makes it one* (ἂν συνδῆ καὶ ποιῇ μίαν)?"
> "We do not."[5]

This passage introduces the complex thematic of the community of men, women, and children and the various benefits that have been explained with arguments of different kinds, but that on the henological level of the *"Unwritten Doctrines"* become even clearer. In fact, the community of men, women, and children and benefits is conceived and presented by Plato as one of the highest forms of *unification*; that is, of the *realization of unity among human beings*: nothing, in the perfect State, must be divided into "mine," "yours," and "his," and hence slide into "multiplicity" (into the disorder of egoism), which is derived in various senses; all ought, instead to be joined into "ours," which brings *unity into multiplicity in the global sense*.

It is perfectly understandable, consequently, that the just man par excellence, *who only does that which is within his ken* (that is, what fulfills justice in its essence, which consists in the τὰ ἑαυτοῦ πράττειν), according to the henological perspective of the protologic that we already know, the just man we are told by Plato (and directly *through writing!*) is the one who binds and harmonizes his different faculties and everything connected to them, by way of *becoming one out of many*. Thus the metaphysical essence of the just person and of justice consists in the *making unity out of multiplicity*; and "wisdom" is the science of this unification. Here is a truly programmatic text:

"But the truth of the matter was, as it seems, that justice is indeed something of this kind, yet not in regard to the doing of ones own business externally, but with regard to that which is within and in the true sense concerns oneself and the things of oneself—it means that a man must not suffer the principles in his soul to do each the work of some other and interfere and meddle with one another, but that *he should dispose well* what in the true sense of the word is probably his own, and *having first attained to self-mastery* and beautiful *order* within himself, and *having harmonized these three principles*, the notes or intervals of three terms quite literally the lowest, the highest, and the mean, and all others there may be between them, and having linked and bound all three together and made of himself a unit, *one man out of many* (ἔνα γενόμενον ἐκ πολλῶν), self-controlled and in unison, he should then and then only turn to practice if he find aught to do either in the getting of wealth or the tendance of the body or it may be in political action or private business, *in all such doings believing the just and honorable action to be that which preserves and helps to produce this condition of soul, and wisdom the science that presides over such conduct; and believing and naming the unjust act to be whatever tends to overthrow this spiritual condition, and brutish ignorance to be the opinion that in turn presides over this.*"

"What you say is entirely true, Socrates."

"Well," said I, "if we should affirm that we had found the just men and state what justice really is in them, I think we should not be much mistaken."

"No, indeed we should not," he said.

"Shall we affirm it, then?"

"Let us so affirm."[6]

Hence, not only the civil community realizes the *Good* by the actuality of *Unity*, but even each individual human being can actualize in himself the Good by realizing himself in a unified way, *by unifying* his potentialities and activities. In fact, a single person cannot realize *many* arts and hence control *many* activities, but only *one* (one, only one).

Virtue itself, in its essence, is said to be *only one*, whereas vices are said to be *infinite* in their variety (just as the Dyad is infinite). And in all their range the political constitutions proceed, from the highest to the lowest, with a progression determined by "multiplicity," which belongs to inequality, disorder, and excess, which little by little overcomes their unity.[7]

No less evident are the connections that the political problematic, even in the way it is proposed in the *Statesman* and in the *Laws*, has with the *Unwritten Doctrines*.

In the *Statesman*, as we have seen, the concepts of the "just mean" and the "just measure," which are precisely *unities in multiplicity* are developed. Consequently, the final foundation of these concepts involves a precise demonstration of *absolute exactness*; that is, of the supreme Measure, which is the One; and hence it refer to oral dialectic in a quite obvious way.

Aristotle himself, in a dialogue entitled *Statesman*, and hence inspired by the Platonic *Statesman* of the same name, states quite clearly that: *"the good is the most perfect Measure."*[8] And the most perfect Measure is precisely the One.

This capacity to produce unity-in-multiplicity, permits the statesman to realize the "mixture"; that is, that great "interwoven web" which constitutes the political fabric of the State, by mixing the extremes, and securing them with bonds, in relation to the Good and the Beautiful; that is, in relation to the just measure, in function of the most perfect Measure. And with this message (political reality as a mixture of the opposites in function of the Measure) the dialogue concludes in the passage just reported.

In the *Laws*, and in all the parts that we have read earlier, these same concepts emerge concerning the "mixed constitution" and the "mean between the extremes," which has a necessary structural connection with the protologic. The just mean and order (as we already know) are a unity-in-multiplicity, and hence a way of *being one* derived from the originating Unity.

And the just measure, which strongly inspired all the *Laws*, found an emblematic expression in that affirmation which is well known, according to which "God is the measure of all things."[9]

Let us keep in mind in conclusion that God is the measure of all things, because indeed He possesses the knowledge and the power to bring the One into the Many and to bring together the Many out of the One, as Plato not only says in the *Timaeus*, but also comes back to it again in the *Laws*, where he points out that the divine governor of the world forms *"many things from one and one from many."*[10]

And this is truly a golden sign, meaning a decisive mark of the thought of Plato.

CONCLUSIONS CONCERNING PLATONIC THOUGHT

Θεὸς μὲν τὰ πολλὰ εἰς ἓν
συγκεραννύναι καὶ πάλιν ἐξ ἑνὸς εἰς
πολλὰ διαλύειν ἱκανῶς ἐπιστάμενος
ἅμα καὶ δυνατός, ἀνθρώπων δὲ οὐδεὶς
οὐδέτερα τούτων ἱκανὸς οὔτε ἔστι νῦν
οὔτε εἰς αὖθίς ποτε ἔσται.

God has knowledge and power sufficient
to blend the many into one and to
resolve the one into many, but no man is
now, or ever will be, equal to the task.

Plato, *Timaeus*, 68D

ὁ δὴ θεὸς ἡμῖν πάντων χρημάτων
μέτρον ἂν εἴη μάλιστα, καὶ πολὺ
μᾶλλον ἤ πού τις, ὥς φασιν, ἄνθρωπος.

In our eyes God will be "the measure of
all things" in the highest degree—a degree much higher than is any "man" they
talk of.

Plato, *Laws* IV, 716C

I. THE MYTH OF THE CAVE AS A SYMBOL OF PLATONIC THOUGHT IN ALL ITS FUNDAMENTAL VALENCES

At the center of the *Republic* is a very famous Platonic myth, the "Allegory of the Cave."[1] The myth has slowly been seen as symbolizing Platonic metaphysics, epistemology, dialectic, and even ethics and the mystical ascent; actually, it symbolizes all this and even Platonic political theory, and today we are capable of recognizing even the strong allusions of a protological character present in a very poetic manner. It is the myth that expresses the whole Plato; and with it, hence it is fitting that we conclude the exposition and the interpretation of his thought.

Let us imagine some individuals who live in a subterranean cave, a cave in which the opening is toward the light in the whole of its breadth, with a steep ascent; and let us imagine that the inhabitants of this cave are bound hand and foot and neck in such a way that they cannot turn their heads around, and hence can fix their gaze only on the back wall of the cave. Let us imagine then, a fire behind the prisoners in front of which is a walkway and behind the walkway are men who carry on their shoulders images, statues made out of wood, stone, and other materials, which look like all the kinds of things that exist. Let us imagine, finally, that the cave has an echo and that men who pass beyond the wall speak to each other their voices bouncing around and producing an echoing effect.

Consequently, if this were so, these prisoners could not see anything except the shadows of the statuettes that project on to the back wall of the cave and they would hear the echoes of voices: but they would believe, not having experienced anything else, that these shadows were the only true reality and would believe in them, even that these echoed voices were truly the voices produced by these self-same shadows. Now let us suppose that one of these prisoners arises and frees himself from his bonds. Then, he would with great difficulty habituate himself to the new vision that appeared to him; and being habituated, he would see the statuettes moved above him on the wall and understand that these are more true than those he had first experienced and that now appear as shadows. And then let us suppose that someone takes our prisoner outside the cave and the ramp. He would be first blinded by the light; then having become habituated to it he would begin to see the things themselves, first in their shadowy appearance and then in their reflections in puddles and pools of water. Finally he would see them directly, as well as the sun, and understand that only these are the true realities and that the sun is the true cause of all that which he had seen. Let us record the whole text, because it is truly fundamental:

"Next," said I, "compare our nature and respect of education and its lack to such an experience as this. Picture men dwelling in a sort of subterranean cavern with a long entrance open to the light on its entire width. Conceive them as having their legs and necks fettered from childhood, so that they remain in the same spot, able to look forward only, and prevented by the fetters from turning their heads. Picture further the light from a fire burning higher up and at a distance behind them, and between the fire and the prisoners and above them a road along which a low wall has been built, as the exhibitors of puppet shows have partitions before the men themselves, above which they show the puppets."

"All that I see," he said.

"See also, then, men carrying past the wall implements of all kinds that rise above the wall, and human images and shapes of animals as well, wrought in stone and wood and every material, some of these bearers speaking and others silent."

"A strange image you speak of," he said, "and strange prisoners."

"Like to us," I said; "for, to begin with, tell me do you think that these men would have seen anything of themselves or one another except the shadows cast from the fire on the wall of the cave that fronted them?"

"How could they," he said, "if they were compelled to hold their heads unmoved through life?"

"And again, would not the same be true of the objects carried past them?"

"Surely." "If then they were able to talk to one another, do you not think that they would suppose that in naming the things that they saw they were naming the passing objects?"

"Necessarily."

"And if their prison had an echo from the wall opposite them, when one of the passersby uttered a sound, do you think that they would suppose anything else than the passing shadow to be the speaker?"

"By Zeus, I do not," said he.

"Then in every way such prisoners would deem reality to be nothing else from the shadows of the artificial objects."

"Quite inevitably," he said.

"Consider, then, what would be the manner of the release and healing from these bonds in this folly if in the course of nature something of this sort should happen to them: when one was freed from his fetters and compelled to stand up suddenly and turn his head around and walk and to lift up his eyes to the light, and in doing all this felt pain and, because of the dazzle and glitter of the light, was unable to discern the objects whose shadows he formerly saw, what do you suppose would be his answer if someone told him that what he had seen before was all a cheat and an illusion, but that now, being nearer to reality and turned toward more real things, he saw more truly? And if also one should point out to him each of the passing objects and constrain him by questions to say what it is, do you think that he would be at a loss and that he would regard what he formerly saw as more real than the things now pointed out to him?"

"Far more real," he said.

"And if he were compelled to look at the light itself, would not that pain his eyes, and would he not turn away and flee to those things which he is able to discern and regard them as in very deed more clear and exact than the objects pointed out?"

"It is so," he said.

"And if," said I, "someone should drag him thence by force up the ascent which is rough and steep, and not let him go before he had drawn him out into the light of the sun, do you not think that he would find it painful to be so haled along, and would chase at it, and when he came out into the light, that his eyes would be filled with its beams so that he would not be able to see even one of the things that we call real?"

"Why, no, not immediately," he said.

"Then there would be need of habituation, I take it, to enable him to see the things higher up. And at first he would most easily discern the shadows and, after that, the likenesses or reflections in water of men and other things, and later, the things themselves, and from these he would go on to contemplate the appearances in the heavens and the heaven itself, more easily by night, looking at the light of the stars then the moon, then by day, the sun and the sun's light."

"Of course."

"And so, finally, I suppose, he would be able to look upon the sun itself and see its true nature, not by reflections in water or phantasms of it in alien setting, but in and by itself in its own place."

"Necessarily," he said.

"And at this point he would infer and conclude that this it is that provides the seasons and the courses of the year and resides over all things in the visible region, and is in some sort the cause of all these things that they had seen."

"Obviously," he said, "that would be the next step."

"Well then, if he recalled to mind his first habituation and what passed for wisdom there, and his fellow bondsmen, do you not think that he would count himself happy in the change and pity them?"

"He would indeed."

"And if there had been honors and commendations among them which they bestowed on one another and prizes for the man who was quickest to make out the shadows as they passed and best able to remember their customary precedences, sequences, and coexistences, and so most successful in guessing at what was to come, do you think he would be very keen about such rewards, and that he would envy and emulate those who were honored by these prisoners and lauded among them, or that he would feel with Homer and greatly prefer while living on earth to be serf of another, a landless man, and endure anything rather than opine with them and live that life?"

"Yes," he said, "I think that he would choose to endure anything rather than such a life."

"And consider this also," said I, "if such a one should go down again and take his old place would he not get his eyes full of darkness, thus suddenly coming out of the sunlight?"

"He would indeed."

"Now if he should be required to contend with these perpetual prisoners in [evaluating] these shadows while his vision was still dim and before his eyes were accustomed to the dark—and this time required habituation would not be very short—would he not provoke laughter, and would it not be said of him that he had returned from his journey aloft with his eyes ruined and that it was not worthwhile even to attempt the ascent? And if it were possible to lay hands on him and to kill the man who tried to release them, and lead them up, would they not kill him?"

"They certainly would," he said.[2]

What does the Myth of the Cave symbolize exactly?

(*a*) Primarily *it symbolizes the various ontological grades of being*, that is, the levels of sensible being and supersensible being, with their subdivisions: the shadows of the cave are the appearances of sensible things, whereas the statues and the artifacts represent all sensible things; the wall represents the division that divides sensible things from supersensible things. The things beyond the wall, symbolize the true things and the stars represent realities in their true being; that is, the Ideas; the sun, then, symbolizes the Idea of the Good.

What do the shadows and reflections in water of the true things, which the prisoner sees beyond the wall represent? It is apparent that the direct shadows and images reflected in the water, outside the cave and beyond the wall, are indeed the *shadows and images* of the true *realities produced by the light of the sun*, and, hence, are completely different than the shadows that the prisoner sees at the base of the cave's interior wall, which are, on the contrary, those produced by the statues and the artificial objects seen in the light of the fire. In other words, they are truly "in the middle" between the Ideas and the things that reproduce them and hence they express quite well the "intermediate entities," which are precisely *ontologically intermediate*, as we quite well know.

The stars and the heavenly bodies, which, evidently, are still beyond individual real things, what do they symbolize? The response is already quite clear, and, with Krämer, it is possible to say that it would not be incorrect "if it is recognized, here, the Meta-Ideas of identity and diversity, of equality and inequality, of the equal and unequal."[3] Therefore, the real things symbolize the individual, specific Ideas, the stars and the heavenly bodies the Meta-Ideas and the ideal Numbers, whereas the sun symbolizes the Idea of the One-Good.

(*b*) In the second place, the myth symbolizes the *degrees of knowledge* in their different levels and in their various grades. The vision of the shadows in the cave symbolizes the εἰκασία or imagination, whereas the statues and the artifacts symbolize πίστις or opinion.

The *transition* from the sight of the statues to the sight of the corresponding true objects, which occurs, first by means of reflections and images and then of mathematical entities, symbolizes διάνοια, which is mediate or intermediate knowledge structurally linked to the mathematical sciences. The most elevated sight begins with the perception of real entities and, through the sight of the stars and celestial bodies and the moon at night, comes to the sight of the sun and the clear light of day, symbolizes the great path of dialectic in its essential stages; that is, in its progress and in its reaching from Idea to further Ideas until it achieves the highest Idea, and through further progress to the Idea of the good itself, to the Principle of the Whole.

(c) In the third place, the Myth of the Cave symbolizes the *ascetic, mystical, and theological aspect* of Platonism: the life in the cave represents life governed by the senses and the sensible, whereas life in the light of day symbolizes life lived by means of intelligence and mind. The liberation from the chains and the "conversion," that is, the turning around from the sight from the shadows to the light, represents the "turning around" from the sensible to the intelligible. Finally, the highest sight of the sun and daylight represents the sight of the Good and hence the knowledge and the fruition of the One and of the highest Measure of all things and thus of the unconditioned Divine, with the consequent decision inspired by it in all the activities such a life involves.

Note, especially, Plato indicates the liberation from the seeing of shadows to seeing by daylight as a "turning around" that the prisoners in the cave perform (περιάγειν τὸν αὐχένα), to raise their sight toward the light (πρὸς τὸ φῶς ἀναβλέπειν).[4] And this image indicative of *turning the head from the opposed parts is taken and developed a little after and specified as a "conversion"* (περιαγωγή) of the soul from becoming to being, as the necessary condition to achieve and see being in its greatest splendor; that is, the Good that is the Principle of the Whole.[5]

This metaphor of "conversion" is taken up and developed by Christians in a religious sense, as Jaeger has already pointed out, by stating that those "who approach the problem, not from the point of view of the religious *phenomena* of conversion, but of the origins of the Christian *conception* of conversion, we must acknowledge that Plato was its originator. The word was transferred to Christian experience in the circles of early Christian Platonism."[6] But the religious and ascetic connections (naturally in an Hellenic sense) is already largely present in Plato, and the "conversion" in the global sense of "turning around" of the soul from illusion to truth, with all that follows that, in Plato is already strongly present, as is demonstrated in this myth of the Cave in an extraordinary manner.

(d) The Myth of the Cave also expresses *a precisely Platonic political conception*. Plato speaks, in fact, likewise of a *"return" into the cave by those who have been liberated from their chains, a return that has as its goal breaking the chains that hold those who were the former companions in slavery.*

This "return" is undoubtedly the return of the philosopher-statesman, who, if he were to follow his desires, would remain in contemplation of the

Good, but instead, overcoming his desire, descends to try to save the others (the true statesman, according to Plato, does not love power and command, but uses his power and command as a service to the City-State, to actualize the Good).

But, are those to whom he goes capable of understanding his mission? He, by passing from the light to the shadows, does not see very well, until he becomes habituated to the shadows again; going back to his old ways does he not risk not being able to persuade them and being taken for a fool and arousing in them a profound aversion? And could it not end in their taking his life? The allusion is certainly to Socrates, but the judgment undoubtedly goes far beyond the case of Socrates.

Plato means to say this: it would be a dangerous thing to change the illusions that envelop human beings; they do not tolerate the truths that overturn their comfortable way of life based upon appearances and the more fleeting side of being, and they fear those truths that appeal to the whole of being and eternity and he who brings to them a message of ontologically revolutionary truth can be put to death, as if he were a charming swindler! Just as it happened to Socrates "the one true statesman" of Greece, as Plato calls him, and so it was and will be or could be for anyone who presents "statesmanship" in that total dimension.

II. SOME SUMMITS OF THE THOUGHT
OF PLATO REMAIN REFERENCE POINTS
IN THE HISTORY OF WESTERN THOUGHT

(*a*) One of the high points of Platonic thought—which has endured within the history of Western philosophy perhaps the most significant and most stimulating reference point, not only in the ancient period, but also in the modern age—is the theory of Ideas. Let us give some perspicuous examples.

Aristotle, although he made the theory the object of a far-reaching criticism of a theoretical character, still drew from it the basic inspiration for his conception of "form" that structures matter. With Middle Platonism the Ideas become the thoughts of the Divine Intellect, and in this sense the Fathers of the Church understood them also. And both of these interpretations involved important issues for the Scholastics. For the modern age we will refer to two examples, which are the most significant ones: Kant will interpret the Ideas as the supreme categories of Reason, and, although denying to them any cognitive value, he will attribute to them a "regulative" role that is structurally of great importance; Hegel, then, will judge the theory of Ideas as the "true speculative greatness" of Plato and even as an authentic "landmark" in the history of philosophy, and finally in "universal history."

It could be stated, on solid grounds, that a history of the interpretation and the theoretical reinterpretation of the theory of the Ideas would cover a wide area of the history of Western philosophy, in many of its essential points. Actually, the principal weight-bearing axis of the thought of Plato as presented in his dialogues (that is, in the sphere of the "written") is the metaphysics of the Ideas, and on this issue the reader's attention is focussed, in all ages, to interpret Plato.

(*b*) From the strictly theoretical viewpoint, and for reasons that we have discussed earlier, the most perspicuous high point of Platonic thought is the theory of the Principles (on which the theory of the Ideas depends), which Plato has entrusted chiefly to the "oral" dimension, but to which, with references and allusions that are clear enough, he has made precise references even in his writings. Such a doctrine brings us (as indeed by the allusions stated expressly even in the *Republic*) to the "principle of the Whole" (τοῦ παντὸς ἀρχή),[1] and hence to the global metaphysical explanation of reality in all its aspects.

Within the perspective of the modern interpretation of Plato the theory of the Principles has been recovered and understood in its importance only in recent years, for reasons that we have already gone into; but, from the historical perspective, at least within the sphere of ancient thought, it has developed truly auspicious influences.

Already in 1912 Werner Jaeger recognized that Platonic philosophy, to which Aristotle referred in his Metaphysics, is not that of the dialogues, but rather that of the *"Unwritten Doctrines."*[2] And in effect, in very large measure, both through his polemic as well as the theoretical reinterpretations, Aristotle owed a great deal to the *"Unwritten Doctrines."*

The Neoplatonists, then, will start their theoretical interpretation from this point and their systematic developments of the philosophy of Plato. The One-Good, which is the foundation of the thought of all Neoplatonists (about which we will speak at length in the fourth volume), is the "Principle of the Whole" of Plato, with this difference: in Plato the highest Principle has a *bipolar structure* (the One acts on the Dyad, which is hierarchically subordinated to it, but coessential and coeternal with it); whereas in the Neoplatonists the Principle *does not have a bipolar but a single and unconditioned structure*, in the sense that everything is derived from it, including the Dyad itself, with all that follows from it.

(*c*) An acquisition of Plato, which is strictly connected with the preceding and stands on its base, is the conception of the hierarchical structure of reality. The conclusions of the Phaedo, always maintained by Plato as valid, are those on which we have insisted many times during the course of this volume: "we posit...two kinds of being: one visible and other invisible" (θῶμεν...δύο εἴδη τῶν ὄντων, τὸ μὲν ὁρατόν, τὸ δὲ ἀιδές).[3]

On the basic meaning of this "dualism," which is linked to transcendence, we will turn immediately; here we only want instead to call attention not to the basic distinction between the *physical* and the *superphysical*, but rather on the *complex articulation of this distinction* (which we have explained earlier), which begins from the first and supreme Principles, on which the sphere of the hierarchical structure of the Ideas follows, and then further the sphere of the mathematical entities hierarchically structured, and finally, the sphere of sensible realities. Each of these spheres is articulated, according to an hierarchical structure (with the emergence and the particular importance of the sphere of the Ideas, which is articulated in the ideal Numbers, the more general Ideas or the Meta-Ideas, specific Ideas), with a structural dependence of the lower level on the higher (and not vice versa) and in various ways with a dependence mediated of all reality at all levels on the primary Principle.

This conception of the hierarchical structure of the real has had an important and truly remarkable influence. The immediate successors of Plato cannot be understood except on this basis. Aristotle himself, as we have seen in this volume, introduces such a conception in his theorizing and even as one of the important hinges on the basis of which he erects his metaphysics. The Neoplatonists, then, as we will see in the fourth volume, will bring it in a systematic way to its extreme consequences, with its fullest development to be found in Proclus.

(*d*)We have many times over used the terms *Divine* and *God* in presenting the thought of Plato and here we want to pause for a moment and summarize what we have stated and determine what the meaning of Platonic theology is. Some have stated that Plato is the founder of Western theology.[4] The statement is correct, if it is understood in its proper sense. The "Second Voyage," that is, *the discovery of the supersensible, must be attributed to Plato to acknowledge for the first time the possibility of seeing the divine in the perspective of the supersensible.* This connection of the two notions will then be made in every succeeding conception of the divine. Actually, even today we hold fundamentally an equivalent belief in the divine and the supersensible, on the one hand, and deny the divine and reject the supersensible, on the other. Within this perspective, Plato is undoubtedly the creator of Western theology, in the measure in which he has discovered the (immaterial) category according to which alone the divine can be and ought to be conceived (the succeeding positions of the Stoics and the Epicureans, which maintain material divinities, as we will see, present a confusion of aporias, made more strident by the fact that they go back to Presocratic categories, which inevitably after Plato and Aristotle could not possibly be supported in their original sense).

Nevertheless it is immediately necessary to add that Plato, in having achieved the new level of the supersensible and by having impressed upon it the theological problematic, takes up again the perspective (which we are already familiar with and which will remain a constant for the whole of Greek philosophy) according to which the divine is structurally multiple.

First, in the theology of Plato, we ought to distinguish the impersonal "Divine" from a personal "God." The Ideal world is divine, on all its levels, and, especially, the Idea of the Good is divine (the One), but it is not a person-God [a subject but only a predicate]. Hence, at the summit of the hierarchy of the intelligible there is a divine Entity (impersonal) and not a (personal) God, just as the Ideas are divine entities (impersonal) and not (personal) Gods.

The traits of a person, that of God, are instead those of the Demiurge, who *knows and wills*; but he is inferior to the world of the Ideas in its complexity, since he did not create it, but epistemologically and normatively he is dependent on it (although he is positioned at the top, immediately after the Idea of the Good). The Demiurge does not even create the material Principle, which preexists him, as we have seen.

The Gods created by the Demiurge are, then, the stars and the world (conceived as intelligent and animated), and perhaps some divinities about which ancient polytheism is concerned and that Plato seems to support (or at least that he does not reject in any clear and categorical way). The soul of the world is divine, the souls of stars are also divine as well as human souls, among which can be placed even the protecting *daimons* and the mediating daimons, of which a typical example is Eros.

Nevertheless, it gives some sense to the concept of creationism (although simply in the sense of Hellenic *semicreationism*). All these other Gods depend structurally on the first, and hence, although somewhat distant, as required, Plato has stepped into a pathway that leads toward a form of monotheism, at least in an Hellenic way.

The famous words that the Demiurge ("creator" God in the Hellenic sense) directs to the *created Gods* are illustrative in a certain sense, almost emblematically, in the sense that we have indicated:

> Gods, of Gods where of I am the maker and of work the father, those which are mine own handiwork are indiscernible, save with my consent. Now, although whatsoever bond has been fastened may be unloosed, and only an evil will could consent to dissolve what has been well fitted together and is in a good state; therefore, although you, have come into being, are not immortal nor indiscernible all together, nevertheless you shall not be dissolved nor taste of death, finding *my will* a bond yet stronger and more sovereign than those where with you were bound together when you came to be.
>
> *Now, therefore, take heed to this that I declare to you.* There are yet left mortal creatures of three kinds that have not been brought into being–be not born, the heaven will be imperfect; for it will not contain all the kinds of living being, as it must if it is to be perfect and complete. But if I myself gave him birth and life, they would be equal to Gods. In order, then, that mortal things may exist and this All may be truly all, turn according to your own nature to the making of living creatures, *imitating my power in generating you.* In so far as it is fitting that something in them should share the name of the immortals, being called divine and ruling over those among them who at anytime are willing to follow after righteousness and after you–that part, having sown it as seed and made it a beginning, I will hand over to you. For the rest, do you, with a mortal to immortal, make living beings; bring them to birth, feed them, and cause them to grow; and when they fail, receive them back again. (trans. F. M. Cornford, *Plato's Cosmology*, p. 140)[5]

Beyond the Platonic God, as we have stated earlier, is the Divine in the highest sense (the One-Good and the Principle and, in a certain measure, the Ideas considered in their totality, even if, hierarchically, the Demiurge is the greater of all the entities[6] and ontologically and metaphysically subordinated only to the first and highest Principles). Aristotle, as we will see, inverted this hierarchy, putting at the summit a God having a personal intelligence, and hence, in this sense, he goes beyond Plato, although in a partial and problematic manner; but the fifty-five intelligences that "move" the celestial spheres that he introduces (about which we have previously spoken) are Gods that are inferior to Him and coeternal with Him, whereas Plato on this point seems to be pushed further, in holding that all the Gods are created by the Demiurge.

(*e*) As we have already written, Plato achieved the most advanced notion of "creationism" by any Greek philosopher.[7] Let us remember that in addressing this problem there has been verified (and still is verified) strong reactions and warnings on the part of many interpreters, which is conditioned by an aversion of various kinds to the thematic of divine "creation." Such an dislike has generated not a few confusions, or generally it has managed to place in parentheses this problematic and relegated it to the periphery of the interpretation of Plato.

Again, some maintain that *it is not possible to speak of a "creation" in any sense, with reference to Greek authors, unless the way of thinking of the Greeks is simply put aside.*

Instead, Plato speaks of a *demiurgic activity* in the sense of a *bringing from nonbeing to being* (ἐκ τοῦ μὴ ὄντος εἰς τὸ ὄν);[8] and he clearly says that the Demiurge produces the universe, living things, vegetables, minerals, and even not only the things that are generated, but also "those things that are derived from the things that are generated";[9] that is, the elements (water, air, earth, and fire).

But how are we here to understand this aspect of Plato's philosophy? *Being is a "mixture,"* and consequently the creation of the Demiurge *is a creation of the mixture*; that is, the production of order out of disorder, because being is precisely this ordering of that which is disordered (a *uni*fication of an unlimited *multiplicity*).

But on this point Plato springs far ahead, in a truly astonishing manner. Although, as we have already stated, he goes a very long way beyond in this respect all Greek thinkers both prior and posterior to him, *he still remains on the conceptual terrain of Greek thought.*

Actually, he is limited not only to saying that the Demiurge combines in the mixture preestablished elements, but he even clearly states that he makes them. In other words, the Demiurge forms both the material elements from which he derives things, and the formal elements that permit the realization of the ideal world in the sensible world, and in this way he actualizes the Good (the One) in the highest way possible, in particular by means of numbers and mathematical and geometrical structures, as we have already shown.

(*f*)Plato, as we have seen, has identified the philosopher with "dialectician" and has defined the dialectician as one who has the capacity to look at reality in a *synoptic vision*; that is, *one who has the capacity to see the "whole,"* which means to gather together a plurality into a unity, *the many into a one.*

The concept of dialectic has had one of the most outstanding developments in Western thought, and it has been pushed far beyond the areas that concerned

Plato, especially in the person of Hegel (and with thinkers of various perspectives dependent on Hegel), who had the advantage of the presuppositions and the precedents belonging to Plato.

Actually, dialectic has its origins in the sphere of Eleatic thought, especially with Zeno, but in the ambit of ancient thought *achieved its summit with Plato.* Aristotle himself, as we will see, reduced it to the sphere of his logic. But it takes on a new life with the Neoplatonists, with interesting and remarkable developments, but not with the essentially grandiloquent and paradigmatic directness that it had in Plato.

As we have seen, beyond the different interpretations that we can give of Platonic dialectic, its precise outlines emerge as grounded in his first and highest Principles and on the consequent bipolar structure of the real; that is, on that cognitive procedure that is capable of bringing together the many (πολλὰ) into a unity (ἕν) and, at the same time, break up the unity into many, by means of diairetic steps, as we have seen and documented.

The dialectic with the synoptic procedure and with the diairetic becomes truly, for Plato, *the highest signature of thought and the foundation of every capacity and power to produce, and, in this sense, also the essential characteristic of the Divine Intellect and of his works.*[10]

(g)Precisely in this sense, the "assimilation to God" (ὁμοίωσις θεῷ)[11] that is "making oneself like God in the way that it is possible for man"(εἰς ὅσον δυνατὸν ἀνθρώπῳ ὁμοιοῦσθαι θεῷ),[12] about which Plato speaks (and to which many make reference in every period, in various perspectives) ought to be understood. Therefore to imitate God for Plato means *to achieve the knowledge and the capacity of realizing unity-in-the-multiplicity, which God possesses in its fullness.* And this achievement in knowledge, in power, and in practical activity, is the most significant factor in the whole of Platonic philosophy, in all its aspects: metaphysical, epistemological, ethical-religious, and political. In short, the imitation of God is the crowning knowledge, which joins man to God who is the Measure of all things and brings actuality in all things.

(h) The greatness of the conception of man for Plato consists in the famous perspective of the nature of *man in two dimensions,* material and spiritual. But in this regard, the aporias in which he is trapped are remarkable in the measure in which he proposes in an exaggerated dualistic way body and soul (as he did not counterpose, instead, Idea to thing: soul is the prisoner of the body, whereas the Idea, far from being a prisoner of the things of which it is the Idea, is the cause, reason, and foundation of that very thing). Plato sees in the body something evil and a kind of shadowy counterpart of man, a conception that involves an excessive rigidity, which almost becomes obdurate at some points.

Further, to the discovery, simply proclaimed on the intuitive level in the *Phaedo* that life is sacred and can no longer for any reason be suppressed, since it is not our possession but that of the Gods, Plato, at least in the *Republic* in the way we have seen; that is, proclaims the necessity of killing the malformed, the chronically and terminally ill. This admission is much more disconcerting because Plato does not stop saying that man is his soul and that the evil of the body does not touch the soul. But the absolute character of human life is adequately grounded only if it is directly connected to the Unconditioned and is joined to him: this was not achieved by any Greek thinker, for the reasons that we have already explained.

(*i*) A further remarkable advance of Plato is the extraordinary value he gave to Beauty: the beautiful, in his view, is related to Truth in an unusual way, because it is a "clear image" of the intelligible (of beauty itself, and hence of the Good; that is, the Principle of all things).

But to understand Plato fully on this point, it is necessary to keep in mind that for him (as well as for the Neoplatonists) art does not give access to the fruition of the beautiful, but Eros (Eros in the Hellenic sense) and hence the erotic with its ascending scale (it is Platonic "love," to use a well-known phrase). Hence, not art but the erotic ("Platonic love") implies a cognitive experience, ground on this dimension of the human spirit, which from the Beautiful brings us to the Unconditioned.

However, there is a further fundamental point to grasp, if the reader wishes to grasp what Plato intended in the treatment of this theme. The beautiful is the only transcendent Idea that is accessible through the senses, but only through that which is for him the most elevated sense; that is, through vision but not even through hearing, which reveals the beautiful for example through music (with all the consequences which follow). On this point Plato uses an expression taken directly from Hellenic culture, in the ambit of which the "visible" has a clear and hierarchical structural predominance over "hearing," which instead, has dominance within other cultures, as we have pointed out.

This enables us to grasp the *extraordinary relevance that form and figure would have for the Greeks* (and hence the *idea* and the *eidos*, which precisely means form and figure, and which in Plato has an extraordinary metaphysical role that is well known). In particular, for our philosopher, the Good is the One and the highest Measure; and the Beautiful (just as the Good) *is explicated by means of number and measure*; that is, *as a unity-in-multiplicity*; and it is this we "see" in the sensibly beautiful: the explication of the unity in the multiplicity according to order and harmony, which manifests itself at various levels and in various ways. In short, the Beautiful (first the sensible and then the intelligible) is shown with respect to the Good, because it is shown with respect to the One and its various and multiple explications at the highest levels.

(j) All the things we have spoken about are the most important results of what Plato called his "Second Voyage." We have already spent a sufficient amount of time on this notion. Plato with a strongly metaphorical tinge called the "Second Voyage" the "conversion" of the soul, the "liberation from bonds," as we have seen.

We can then in conclusion state that the Platonic "Second Voyage" is an acquisition that signals in a certain sense, as we have pointed out from the beginning, *the most important stage in the history of metaphysics.* In fact, all Western philosophy will be conditioned, in a decisive way, by this conception, both insofar as and in the measure in which it accepts it (and this is obvious), and, also, insofar as or in the measure in which it does not accept it; in fact, in this last case it must polemically justify the nonacceptance of this conception and from this polemic it will remain dialectically conditioned.

After the Platonic "Second Voyage" (and *only* after it) we can speak of the *corporeal* and the *incorporeal*, the *sensible* and the *supersensible*, the *empirical* and the *metaempirical*, the *physical* and the *metaphysical*. And in the light of these categories (and only in the light of these categories) the prior Physicists can be materialists, both nature and the physical cosmos no longer are the totality of the things that *are*, but only the totality of the things that appear. Philosophy has reached into the *intelligible world*, the sphere of the realities that *are not sensible, but only intelligible.* Against all the predecessors and against many contemporaries, Plato did not tire, for the whole of his life, to point out that his fundamental discovery was indeed revolutionary: there are very many things about which your philosophy limited to the physical world does not know! In our judgment this is the "possession for all time" that Plato has transmitted to posterity.

The West, for the first time, to the question "why being exists and not nothing?" With Plato, can now respond in function of the "Second Voyage": because being is good; and in general, all things that exist are so because they are positive, because it is good that they be just as they are, in the sense that we have explained. *The positive, order, and the Good are the basis of being.*

Second Part

ARISTOTLE AND THE SYSTEMATIZATION OF PHILOSOPHICAL KNOWLEDGE

ὑπολαμβάνομεν δὴ πρῶτον μὲν ἐπίστασθαι πάντα τὸν σοφὸν ὡς ἐνδέχεται.

We maintain, in the first place, that the wise man knows all things, insofar as that is possible.

Aristotle, *Metaphysics* A 2.982a8–9

THE RELATIONSHIP BETWEEN ARISTOTLE AND PLATO
THE CONTINUATION OF THE "SECOND VOYAGE"

εἴ γε ἀΐδιον μηθέν ἐστιν, οὐδὲ γένεσιν εἶναι δυνατόν.

If nothing were eternal, even becoming would not be possible.

Aristotle, *Metaphysics* B 4.999b5

Ἀριστοτέλης...γνησιώτατος τῶν Πλάτωνος μαθητῶν.

Aristotle was the most faithful disciple of Plato.

Diogenes Laertius 5.1

I. A CRITICAL PREMISE: THE HISTORICAL-GENETIC METHOD AND THE MODERN INTERPRETATION OF ARISTOTELIAN THOUGHT

It is now appropriate, in our judgment, to speak about Aristotle:[1] before taking up the fate of the Platonic Academy and its first scholars since, to anticipate the discussion in the third volume, not only did the Platonic inheritance not increase in the first Academy, it was also gravely compromised and undermined almost to the point of disappearing, with consequences, as we will see, that were very momentous. Aristotle, on the contrary, first as a faithful Academician, then as a dissident, and finally as the founder of his own school in competition with the Academy (viz., the Academy directed by Speusippus and by Xenocrates), attempted a systematic verification of Platonic argument, achieving results, in many cases, an authentic "confirmation" of the Platonic positions. Diogenes Laertius wrote that "Aristotle was the most faithful disciple of Plato."[2] And that judgment still stands in our view, contrary to what many modern scholars believe. A faithful disciple of a great master is certainly not one who repeats his teacher, limiting himself to preserving the doctrine intact, but rather one who moves from the aporias of the master and tries to overcome them in the spirit of his teacher, and thus goes beyond his teacher. This is precisely what Aristotle accomplished with respect to Plato.

But, before we can deal with this point in detail, it is necessary as a preliminary to posit and solve a critical and methodological difficulty. In 1923 Werner Jaeger, in a work that seemed to radically overturn the understanding that over the centuries had been handed down by Aristotelian scholars,[3] maintained the following thesis.

The systematic-unitary method with which Aristotle had always been read was erroneous because it was ahistorical; viz., it did not take into account the historical development and genesis of his thought, which is not a monolithic and compact mass that is simply to be believed. The true picture is that Aristotle began from an initial position of Platonism and continued on with a penetrating criticism of Platonism and the Platonic notion of the transcendent Ideas, to reach a metaphysical position hinging on his interest in the immanent *form* and *entelechy*. Finally, Aristotle achieved a position, if not of repudiation, at least of disinterest in metaphysics in favor of the empirical sciences and verified and organized empirical data.

In sum, from the Jaegerian viewpoint, the spiritual history of Aristotle would be the history of Aristotle's turning away from Platonism and from metaphysics and, from thence, a conversion to empiricism and naturalism. But, as the thesis is formulated it does not yet reveal all its implications. In fact, according to Jaeger, the expression of the Platonic aspect of Aristotle's thought would be found not only in his exoteric works, which (as we have seen in the biographical note) were composed and published when Aristotle was still an official member of the Academy, *but likewise whole sections of the esoteric works*.

These esoteric works, which we know are constituted of the *logoi* derived from the teaching activity of Aristotle; that is, the material that served as his lecture and course materials, and they would have been composed in successive stages, beginning from the period spent by the philosopher at Assos. They would have their origin from some original nucleus, which would have been added to little by little, always becoming something new in the process, in which the Stagirite again proposed the problems from new starting points. Therefore, the works of Aristotle that we read today would have arisen from successive strata and not only would they not have any literary unity, but more important they would not even have any speculative homogeneity; viz., a unity of a doctrinal and philosophical character. The treatises would present themselves, in fact, as a series of prospective problems and solutions arising from various moments within the evolution of Aristotelian thought, not only distant from each other in time but also far removed in their theoretical inspiration and hence they would present contrasts and in some cases clear contradictions within themselves.

Using this regulating idea Jaeger reconstructed some of the exoteric works on the basis of some fragments, then went on to the esoteric works dismembering them by isolating the various strata and coming in this way to limn in a picture of an Aristotle who moved from Platonic idealism and became at the end an empiricist. The ability, the talent, and the sheer erudition of Jaeger guaranteed his book a great success, such that anyone would have hesitated not to accept his conclusions as almost definitive. But the historic-genetic method of Jaeger had scarcely begun to be applied by other scholars, when it began to reach results different than those to which he had come and even brought some scholars to the complete overturning and different specification of the presumed evolutionary arc of the Stagirite's development. In the course of a half a century, by applying Jaeger's genetic method, it was possible to demonstrate every position and its contrary, and thus all the conclusions drawn about the different strata and evolution of the works of the school were reduced to zero.[4] Therefore it comes as no surprise that the number of scholars in the ranks of the followers of the Jaegerian method became thinned, and they are by now confined to peripheral positions. In fact, the genetic method's failure was inevitable for the following reasons.

(*a*) School logoi were not conceived and written as books to be published, and they constitute the substance of Aristotle's teaching activity; therefore not only did they never leave the hand of their author, but they remained always, so to speak, capable of further development.

(*b*) Consequently, it is absurd to think that chronological strata can be distinguished in any determinate way; the successive rearrangements, which certainly would have been integrated by their author, would not have left clearly recognizable traces because of the very plasticity of the material.

(*c*) The historic-genetic method, to be *historical* must be constructed on the basis of *data* that is incontrovertible, on *data*; that is, which are certain and verifiable; instead both characteristics are completely lacking with respect to the works that are the result of the teaching activity of Aristotle.

(*d*) The historic-genetic method does not solve in any way the difficulties that the reader of the *Corpus Aristotelicum* encounters, but rather it multiplies them.

(*e*) Thus, in conclusion, the genetic method has arrived at almost none of the objectives that it had proposed with respect to the interpretation of the works of the school. It has promoted a great renewal of scholarship concerned with the Stagirite. It demonstrated the literary informality of this kind of written work. And it has enormously refined the techniques of research and exegesis of the text. But it has not reconstructed the "history of the intellectual evolution" of the philosopher, which was its aim.

(*f*) A balanced judgment, instead, requires us to recognize that the method inaugurated by Jaeger has given its best results in the treatment of the basic problems that arise from the exoteric works of Aristotle, of which we have recovered many fragments, sometimes sizable. But the fragments of these works do not prove Jaeger's thesis; they prove instead that in the period during his stay in the Academy some of Aristotle's results were maturing, which would then become very prominent in the esoteric works.[5]

In our *History of Ancient Philosophy*, we are not be concerned with the fragments discovered of the exoteric works (that would be properly done in an analytic monograph);[6] we will however say that in them Aristotle already revealed *in essentials* his own intellectual character. He is revealed in them as a disciple who reinterprets but does not repeat his teacher, and thus goes beyond him, while staying true to his spirit.

Instead, in what concerns the esoteric works on which our exposition is based, we will assume, as a datum already acquired, after the bankrupt attempt to understand them in a genetic way, the thesis that they have a unitary meaning within their development (both in the case that some parts of them arise from the period at Assos or even during his stay in the Academy, as well as those which were made and refined in successive periods). They manifest then a basic unity and a *speculative homogeneity* that only those who read them pretending at all costs to perceive a chimerical evolutionary parabola are able to deny. Moreover, as has been recently stated, no philosopher could be understood, except by assuming that he is in every moment responsible for his work, when he has not expressly denied some part of it.[7] The way in which the followers of the historic-genetic method interpret Aristotle presupposes precisely the rejection of this principle: a rejection that at least implies upon reflection, the rejection of the statement that Aristotle was an authentic philosopher.[8]

II. THE BASIC POINTS OF CONTACT BETWEEN PLATO AND ARISTOTLE: THE TRUTHFULNESS OF THE "SECOND VOYAGE"

Aristotle cannot be understood except by beginning with establishing what specific positions he took in comparison with Plato. And, in effect, almost all historians of philosophy, even prior to the work of Jaeger, began the exposition of the thought of Aristotle with the theme: "the criticism by Aristotle of the theory of the Ideas."

Nevertheless to begin an exposition of Aristotle from this position, if it may be correct from a particular viewpoint, from another viewpoint can produce a series of errors into which many scholars have fallen. Actually to maintain the right balance, it is necessary to articulate this question in the right way, in reference both to the historical perspective and the philosophical one; but this, for many reasons, is difficult.

First, it is necessary to realize that the numerous and continuous criticism that Aristotle made against Plato are not solely concerned with the theory of Ideas, but at what we have seen to be the stages of the "Second Voyage"; that is, they are aimed, at the same time, against both the doctrine of the Principles, and the theory of Ideas. In fact, in a certain measure, the discussions on the protological positions connected with the theory of the Principles and the things based on it are more frequently the subject matter in dispute. Jaeger, in his first work on Aristotle,[1] had even affirmed that the criticism the Stagirite had mounted against Plato did not refer to the doctrine in the dialogues, but to the doctrines connected to the lectures that Plato held in the Academy (and hence, to the *Unwritten Doctrines*). The German scholar did not push his position any further and went off in another direction, to which we have referred earlier; but, today, this position has been entirely confirmed. Consequently, the position that Aristotle took concerning the doctrine of the Principles and about the theory of Ideas, even considered in many implications and in its complex consequences, would seem to be, at least at first glance, a polemical position, wholly negative, globally and categorically, whereas, in reality this is not the case at all, as we will see.

In addition, it is necessary to comprehend and adequately note that the weighty criticism levelled by the Stagirite against the theory of Ideas, if isolated from the context of Aristotelian metaphysics and from the new theoretical paradigm that we have proposed and hence interpreted outside of the complex historical nexuses from which they arose, inevitably falls into an error of perspective (as has happened to many scholars) insofar as it leads to the belief that Aristotle, by rejecting the doctrine of the Principles and the theory of

Ideas, likewise rejected (as a consequence) the Platonic "Second Voyage" almost entirely.

The truth of the matter is, objectively speaking, quite different. Aristotle had heavily criticized, it is true, the doctrine of the Principles and the doctrine of the Ideas and in addition went on to deny the existence of the One-Good and all the transcendent Ideas or Forms. Nevertheless–and this is the principal and indispensable point to grasp correctly–he did not in any way intend to deny that some *supersensible realities* existed. He, in fact, wanted instead to demonstrate that the *supersensible did not have the nature that Plato conceived it to have* (or at least, only in part and with a different understanding).

Since as we have pointed out, this is an absolutely fundamental point, we must clarify it further in an appropriate way. Plato pointed out in the transcendent One-Good the Principle of the whole of reality. On the contrary, Aristotle denied the existence of the transcendent One-Good; *nevertheless, he did reiterate that there existed a transcendent reality in a firm, unequivocal manner.* However, he attributed a general function to this reality conceived at the supreme vertex as supreme Mind, precisely as a thinking on thinking, as the immobile Movent of all things, affirming explicitly that "on such a Principle depend the heaven and nature,"[2] and hence all realities.

In the supersensible Ideas, moreover, Plato had pointed out the "cause" of sensible things. Insofar as they are the *causes* of things, the Ideas have immanent relations with things and at the same time, through their metaphysical status, they are *other* than the things that are sensible; that is, they are metasensibles, transcendent. The Ideas thus can be both immanent and transcendent although Plato did not succeed, in his writings, and did not wish to basically explain them, except, at least in a certain measure, in the dialectical dialogues, and particularly in the *Timaeus*,[3] whose narrative was understood by Aristotle from a partial perspective and according to his new categories. In any case, Plato was not interested in sensible phenomena as such either, specifically or particularly.[4] He was concerned more with inquiring into the structure of the ideal world as such and not with its relationship with the sensible world. And certainly the followers of Plato in the Academy imposed their arguments according to the perspective and the transcendent aspect of the Principles and of the Ideas, by trying to deduce the relations that mutually bound them and by trying to establish that all beings could be deduced from the first principles; and thus they end by obscuring these phenomena and the physical world, which the Principles and the Ideas had to explain. Consequently the energetic reaction of Aristotle is quite understandable. If the Principles and Ideas are *supersensible* and *transcendent*, then they do not serve the goal for which they were introduced: qua transcendent they cannot be either the *cause of the existent* or the *cause of the knowledge* of sensible things, because the *causa essendi et cognoscendi* [*cause of being and the cause of knowledge*] of things must be *in* the things themselves and not *exterior* to them. All the numerous Aristotelian criticisms (which the reader can see in our commentary on the *Metaphysics*)[5] theoretically are reduced to this fundamental nucleus, which can be summarized in the following way: in the place of the transcendent Principle of the One-Good, he will need to introduce the Good understood as *final cause* of the whole of reality (as "that towards which everything else tends");[6] in the place of the transcendent Ideas he needs to introduce the Forms or immanent essences as act, understanding them as the intelligible structure of the whole of reality and of the sensible world in particular.

Let us put aside the problem of whether Plato wholly merited this criticism and whether Aristotle completely grasped Plato's meaning; what is of interest to us is instead a still more important point. Does the interpretation of the Good *within the conception of final cause* and making the Ideas immanent, understood as *intelligible forms*, as the act of sensible things, *perhaps mean the repudiation, on the part of the Stagirite, of his conviction that the supersensible exists?*

This is the error that many have fallen into by believing that the immanent forms as acts would uniquely succeed the Platonic Ideas, whereas in Aristotle the successors to the theory of the Ideas are *two quite distinct doctrines*: (*a*) the one is that which has already been discussed; that is, *the conception of the immanent intelligible structure of the sensible world* (form as act); (*b*) the other, on the contrary, is a *new and higher conception of the supersensible, centered not on the transcendent Intelligible, but on the transcendent Mind.*

Anticipating what we will discuss at length, we can say that Aristotle achieved a new conception of the supersensible precisely following from his criticism of the theory of the Principles and the transcendent Ideas; in fact, by reinterpreting the Platonic metaphysics through a process of nutritive assimilation, he absorbed *in large part that doctrine within his own perspective.*

Here is an important summary of the issues. After having demonstrated, in his new perspective, the truth that Plato had achieved with his "Second Voyage" (that is, *that the sensible would not exist, if the supersensible did not also exist*), Aristotle went on to locate the supersensible in the following realities:

(*a*) God or the first immobile Movent;

(*b*) A certain number of other realities analogous to the first Movent, but hierarchically related to it in a lower astronomical position;

(*c*) The intellective soul or mind that is in man.

The first Movent is a mind, a self-thinking thought; the other Movents are also minds in every way equal to the first; the intellective human soul is a mind or intellect "which comes from the outside."[7]

Therefore, as we stated previously, *Aristotle substituted a conception of the supersensible understood chiefly as Mind as act (Intelligence as act) for the Platonic conception of the supersensible understood chiefly as the intelligible.*

In this sense, it can be said that, for Aristotle, within limits, it is even possible to find something more than in Plato (at least within a certain metaphysical paradigm); that is to say, a tendency toward greater coherence and consistency (and within the areas of interest opened up by the "Second Voyage") that is not present in Plato. The supersensible in a global sense is the world of Intelligence (the highest Good is itself the highest Intelligence). The great world of Ideas becomes *the intelligible content of the sensible.* The material principle, chiefly, conceived as disordered and irrational necessity becomes, in a very marked way (but with a framework already traced by Plato)[8] *potentiality* and *connection* to the intelligible form. Thus the phenomena acquire more concreteness and are "preserved": *therefore they are preserved in the form; and the whole universe (as we will see) is presented as a magnificent ladder that rises upward from forms anchored in matter step by step, with each level hierarchically superior to the other levels, in a perfect way, up to the purest immaterial form; that is, the Intelligence.*[9]

In addition (and this is also not usually noted, because it is not well understood) it could even be said that in Aristotle, from the theoretical viewpoint, there is, in a theoretical sense, a more robust and metaphysically fruitful Platonism than in the other Academics of whom there are extant testimonies, as we will see in the third volume. Eudoxus, to overcome Plato's notion of the transcendent, proposed the hypothesis of the "mixture" among the Ideas and things, against which Aristotle himself vehemently reacted. Speusippus eliminated the Ideas, by maintaining only mathematical entities. Xenocrates tried to go back to that which had been lost, but with meager success (by taking a typical position of the follower).

Therefore, Aristotle, with his doctrine of separate Mind, in a certain sense *showed himself to be theoretically more Platonic than some of the other Academics, because, by rejecting the existence of a first Principle understood as impersonal One-Good, he reaffirmed it as the supreme Mind, achieving speculative vertices with regard to those of the other Academics, who were definitively below his achievements.*

In addition, with his theory of immanent forms Aristotle was also more Platonic than the other Platonists, because, although he denies the transcendence of the Ideas, *he held the Platonic conclusion of the metaphysical priority of the form*, making the form as act the intelligible content of the sensible in large part; and, furthermore, *he maintained the fundamental eidetic conception* gravely compromised by some exponents of the Academy (in particular by Speusippus), as we will have an opportunity to discuss fully subsequently.

Within this framework, the statement by Diogenes Laertius that Aristotle was the most authentic; that is, the most legitimate (γνησιώτατος),[10] of the followers of Plato, seems truly emblematic and, according to this understanding, we will present our interpretation of the philosophy of the Stagirite.

III. THE BASIC DIFFERENCES BETWEEN ARISTOTLE AND PLATO

It is clear, then, in what sense we can say that Aristotle understood and completed the Platonic "Second Voyage." The discovery of the supersensible is not only maintained, but is vigorously developed. The points of opposition between Aristotle and Plato are in another direction.

First of all, the mystical and religious spirit is missing in Aristotle through which Plato's poetic genius took wing in specific flights and sorties. In Aristotle, the connection to the eschatological dimension and its tension is missing but all this estrangement, in great part, of the mystical and religious from the sphere of the properly metaphysical and philosophical is conceived in Aristotle as something that is added to the properly philosophical.

In this regard, however, it is necessary to make a clarification. The mystical-religious spirit and the eschatological beliefs about the destiny of the soul are still present, and even with a quite striking power, in the early Aristotle, that is to say in the exoteric works, whereas they are almost entirely neglected in the esoteric works. Here for example is an explicit testimony of Proclus in this regard:

"Aristotle in emulation of him treats physically of the soul in the de Anima, saying nothing either about its descent or about its fortunes; but in his dialogue [that is, in the exoterica] he dealt separately with those questions."[1] Here is some more from the same author:

> The divine Aristotle, also, states the reason why the soul on coming hither from yonder forgets the sights it saw there, but on going from here remembers yonder its experiences here. We must accept the argument; for he himself says that on their journey from health to disease some people forget even the letters they had learned, but that no one ever has this experience when passing from disease to health; and that life without the body, being natural to souls is like health, and life in the body and being unnatural is like disease. For there they live according to nature, but here contrary to nature; so that it naturally results that souls that pass from yonder forget the things there, while souls that pass yonder from this world continue to remember the things in it.[2]

In the *Protrepticus*, then, Aristotle, by going completely beyond Plato, assimilated the body not only to the notion of being the tomb of the soul but even of being a horrifying punishment for the soul: "And that is true which Aristotle says, that we are punished much as those who once upon a time, when they had fallen into the hands of Etruscan pirates, were killed with studied cruelty; their bodies, the living with the dead, were bound exactly as possible one against another: so our minds, bound together with our bodies, are like the living joined with the dead."[3]

Consequently, it is precisely the mystical, religious, eschatological component that is dropped during the evolution of Aristotle's thought; but, we have seen, it is a Platonic component that has its source in the Orphic religion and has its source more in a faith than in a metaphysics and dialectic. Aristotle undoubtedly intended by dropping this component from his esoteric works to continue his thinking by making the purely theoretical argument more rigorous, thus to distinguish what is based only on logos from what is based on religious belief.

A second basic difference between Plato and Aristotle is this: Plato was interested in the mathematical sciences but not in the empirical sciences (with the exception of medicine). Plato does not have any interest in empirical phenomena as such. Aristotle, on the contrary, has a very keen interest in almost all the empirical sciences (and somewhat less for mathematics) and for the phenomena as such; that is, for the concrete things of experience, and hence he is diligent likewise in collecting and classifying specimens, even where their consideration is in function of philosophical categories. But, as is well known, this component, which is absent in Plato and is present in Aristotle, must not be exaggerated and become a source of error. It proves only that Aristotle had, *in addition* to purely speculative interests, interests *also* in empirical sciences that his teacher did not share, and hence it is true that the teacher and the pupil were different but from the *anthropological* standpoint and not necessarily from the *speculative* standpoint. The scholars of Humanism and the Enlightenment (and then many modern scholars) fall into this difficulty. The painting of Raphael representing the School of Athens offers a splendid tableau capturing this interpretation, by placing Plato with his fingers pointing toward heaven; that is, toward the transcendent, and Aristotle instead with his hand toward the ground; that is, the empirical and immanent sphere of the phenomena. Actually we will see that the truth is exactly the opposite; Aristotle, notwithstanding all the love that he had for the phenomena, never tired of repeating that, from the speculative standpoint, they are "preserved" only by the metaphenomena, only by putting them in relation to an immaterial, immobile, and transcendent cause.[4]

We can briefly summarize the differences that we have spoken of up to this point: Plato, in addition to being a philosopher, is *also* a mystic (and a poet); Aristotle, on the contrary, in addition to being a philosopher is *also* a scientist. However this *plus* has an ambivalent meaning that markedly differentiates the two men, differentiating them precisely in their extraphilosophical human interests, so to speak, *although not in the speculative core of their thought.*

Finally, a further difference can be uncovered. The Socratic irony and maieutic, joined to exceptional poetic power, was the source in Plato for a form of argument that was always open to a way of philosophizing as an inquiry without rest. The opposite scientific attitude of Aristotle was necessarily accomplished in a organic systematization of various results, by means of a distinction of themes and problems according to their nature and also by means of a separation of methods with which the different kinds of problems were confronted and resolved. Thus to the Platonic mobile spiral that tended to involve and link together all the problems he let follow a stabilized systematization that once and for all will fix in outline the problematic of philosophical knowledge (and it will be precisely an outline that will mark the path on which all the successive problematics of philosophical knowledge will trod: metaphysics, physics, psychology, ethics, politics, aesthetics, and logic).

But, also in this respect, their differences are no less radical from what at first glance they may seem to be. In fact, Plato was forced by the weight of his discoveries to fix, if not dogmas, at least solid positions, and sacrifice the flexibility of his poetry to the insistent rigor of the *logos*, and hence to mitigate somewhat its aporetic tensions. Aristotle himself, on the one hand, when he is read adequately, not only did not eliminate the aporias, but institutionalized them, so to speak, and proclaimed the awareness of the structure of the aporias as a necessary condition for opening the impasse to the truth. The aporias are like knots and their solution is like untying a knot, but as we know a knot cannot be untied unless it is recognized and its structure analyzed as such. Here also, therefore, the differences between Plato and Aristotle have been exaggerated because of an optical illusion: the very different *way* in which the two philosophers express their thought is not always taken into account (the one values the movement of the dialogue leading to the logos through the power of poetry, the other values an impersonal and dry argument dense with complex notions) frequently it cannot but appear (or be made to appear) that these thinkers are more different than they are, or, simply different when they are not.

In conclusion, then, the relationship between Plato and Aristotle is not antithetical; instead, to use a Hegelian vocabulary completely suited to the situation, as was already said, it is a relationships such that it brings the pupil to *surpass* his teacher, which brings him to the truth of his basic achievement. In addition to the truth in Aristotle antithetical to Plato, there is also one *complementary* to Plato, which leads to that systematization of philosophical knowledge, about which we have already given hints and from which emerged the outline of philosophical knowledge on which Western philosophical thought will be supported for centuries.

METAPHYSICS AND THE THEORETICAL SCIENCES

αἰ μὲν οὖν θεωρητικαὶ τῶν ἄλλων
ἐπιστημῶν αἱρετώτεραι, αὕτη δὲ τῶν
θεωρητικῶν.

The theoretical sciences are greatly to be
preferred to the other sciences, and, this
(metaphysics) is greatly to be preferred
to the other theoretical sciences.

Aristotle, *Metaphysics* E 1.1026a22

I. METAPHYSICS

1. The concept and characteristics of metaphysics

Aristotle has divided the sciences into three great branches: (*a*) *theoretical sciences*, viz., the sciences that seek knowledge for its own sake; (*b*) *practical sciences*, viz., sciences that seek knowledge to achieve moral perfection; and (*c*) the *poietic or productive sciences*, viz., the sciences that seek knowledge in view of making something with the goal of producing a determined object. The highest sciences in dignity and value are the first branch, in which *metaphysics, physics* (which also includes *psychology*), and *mathematics* are found.[1]

We will now begin our exposition from the theoretical sciences and indeed from the highest of them, since it is from it and in function of it that all the other sciences acquire their adequate and correct perspective.

Just what is metaphysics?

Let us begin with a clarification of the term itself. It is well known that *metaphysics* is not a term used by Aristotle (perhaps it was coined by some Peripatetics, if not it was certainly in use on the occasion of the edition of the works of Aristotle made by Andronicus of Rhodes in the first century BCE).[2] Aristotle used the expression *first philosophy* for the most part or even theology in opposition to *second philosophy* or *physics*, but the term metaphysics is certainly more pregnant with meaning, or better it was felt as more pregnant and thus became canonic throughout subsequent centuries. Aristotelian metaphysics is, in fact, as we will immediately see, the science concerned with realities that are beyond the physical, about realities that are transphysical or superphysical, and as such, are opposed to the physical. Metaphysics was denominated as such definitively and consistently, on an Aristotelian basis, and so is every attempt of human thought to surpass the empirical world to achieve metaempirical realities.

We must specify in a detailed manner the precise values that Aristotle attributed to that science which he named *first philosophy* and posterity *metaphysics,* after having given this general clarification. The definitions that Aristotle gave to his metaphysics are four in number: (*a*) metaphysics inquires into the *first and supreme causes and principles*,[3] (*b*) metaphysics inquires into *being qua being*,[4] (*c*) metaphysics inquires into *substance*,[5] (*d*) metaphysics inquires into *God and supersensible substance*.[6] Who followed us to this point will have no difficulty in gasping the meaning, whether historical or speculative, of the four definitions of metaphysics; but they do give complete form and expression to those lines of force according to which all the preceding speculations from Thales to Plato developed, lines of force that Aristotle unites now in a powerful synthesis. (*a*) In the first place, all the monistic philosophers of nature were inquiring into nothing other than the *arché*; viz., the primary principles or causes. The primary causes and principles were also sought by the pluralistic Physicists and the "true causes" were sought by Plato himself through his theory of Ideas. Therefore, the Aristotelian determination of metaphysics as "aitiology" or "etiology" (the inquiry into the primary causes and principles) is completely in line with all of preceding thought. (*b*) In the second place, Parmenides and his school inquired into *being, pure being,* and Plato, by developing the Eleatic position, construed everything as an elaborated "*ontology*" (of the Ideas, without taking into account that the same doctrine of *physis* is a doctrine of being or an "ontology," because physis is true reality, viz., true being); therefore, the determination of metaphysics as "theory of being" was inevitable. (*c*) Also the third determination of metaphysics (which we will name *ousiology*) is easy to understand. Once Eleatic monism is put aside as antiquated and it is then seen that many beings exist, viz., different forms and different kinds of being, it was necessary *that the fundamental kind of being* be established that is *ousía* or substance; viz., it was necessary to determine what things are to be considered as "being" in the strongest and truest sense of the word (*ousía* or substance indicates precisely the truest being). (*d*) Finally, the determination of metaphysics as "theology" is well explained, we have seen that all the Naturalists denominate their principles as God (or as the Divine); the same thing, at a higher level, made Plato identify the Divine with the Ideas, and the same thing would also be done by Aristotle.

But not only "note" are the four Aristotelian definitions of metaphysics in harmony with the speculative tradition that preceded the Stagirite, but they are also completely in harmony among themselves; the first necessarily carries us to the next one and then on to all the others in turn, ending in a complete unity.[7]

Let us consider this unity in detail. One who inquires into the causes and principles *must necessarily encounter God.* God is, in fact, the primary cause and principle par excellence. Therefore, the aitiological inquiry opens structurally into theology. But also beginning from the other definitions we come to identical conclusions, for example, to ask what being is means to ask whether any beings besides sensible beings exist or if supersensible and divine being also exist (theological being). Again, the question, What is substance? implies the question, What kinds of substances exist? as well as, do only sensibles *or supersensibles and the divine also exist*? hence, the theological problem.

On this basis it is easy to understand that Aristotle undoubtedly used the term *theology* to indicate what is called today metaphysics, insofar as to the theological dimension necessarily brings us the other three dimensions. The inquiry into God is not only an *aspect* of the metaphysical inquiry, it is *the essential and defining aspect.* The Stagirite, moreover, says, with total clarity, that if it were not supersensible substance there would not be any metaphysics:

"If substances other than the sensible were not to exist, then physics would be the primary science."[8]

This statement is easy to understand for these reasons: if there were no supersensible, the causes and principles would be only sensible ones; viz., those of the physics. If there were no supersensible being, all beings would be reduced to natural beings, viz., physical beings; if there were no supersensible substances, only natural substances would exist, viz., physical ones. In sum, if there were no supersensible realities, there would be nothing but nature and natural causes and the highest science would be nothing other than that of nature and natural causes, viz., physical ones. The new science, therefore, arose fundamentally from the Platonic "Second Voyage." It wishes to reach substance or superphysical being, and both in fact and in principle merits to be called *meta-physics*.[9]

We have said earlier that the theoretical sciences are superior to the practical sciences as well as to the productive sciences, and again metaphysics is superior to the other two theoretical sciences. Metaphysics is the absolutely primary science, the highest and the most sublime.[10] But of what use is it, someone might ask. To ask this question means to put oneself in a position antithetical to that of Aristotle, viz., it is an unintelligible question within an Aristotelian context. Metaphysics is the highest science, he says, precisely because it is not bound to any material necessities. Metaphysics is not a science ruled by a practical or experiential goal. The sciences that have such goals are subservient to those goals and do not have value in and of themselves, but only in the measure in which they lead to those effects. Instead, metaphysics is a science that *is valued in and for itself*, because it has in itself its own goal, and in this sense it is the "liberal" science par excellence.[11]

But, it might be objected, how did it arise, and what is its reason for being? Metaphysics, Aristotle replies, was born from the wonder and the amazement that man feels in the presence of the wonderful; it arises, therefore, from a pure love of knowledge, it arises from the need to grasp the *ultimate why* rooted in the very nature of man. In fact, metaphysics prescinds from any practical advantage whatsoever that such knowledge can achieve, and man desires it only for itself. Metaphysics is, therefore, a science attempting to satisfy *nothing other than the human need for knowledge*. This is the most solid and authentic defense and justification of metaphysics and with it of philosophy in general, at least of philosophy classically understood, which, as was seen in detail already in the course of the preceding volume, is a purely speculative enterprise; viz., contemplation.

All the reasons are now clear–as we have already said–to understand why Aristotle named metaphysical science *divine*. God alone can possess this kind of knowledge, which he has as his only goal. God possesses it entirely, completely, and continuously; we, instead, possess it partially, incompletely, and only on occasion. But within these limits, man has a point of contact with God.

The man who is metaphysical is, therefore, closest to divinity, and in this possession, Aristotle has placed the greatest happiness of man. God is happiest by knowing and contemplating himself. Man is happiest by knowing and contemplating the supreme principles of things, and, hence, God *in primis et ante omnia* [*first and foremost among things*]. In this knowledge man completes his nature and his essence, which consists in reason and intelligence. As we will see in the ethics, in this way he also achieves his most authentic happiness. With this in mind, Aristotle has written: "All the other sciences are more necessary for men, but to this one none is superior."[12]

This is an affirmation that can also be correctly reversed in another way. The other sciences would be more necessary to achieve particular practical and pragmatic goals, but metaphysics is still the most necessary because in it and through it man fulfills his nature as a rational being, which is his highest *areté*, and thus he satisfies the most profound, original, and unavoidable demand that arises from his nature, the unalloyed need to know.

2. The four causes

Let us proceed now to the explanation of the content, after having analyzed and clarified the definitions, of metaphysics from the formal viewpoint. We have said that metaphysics is, in the first place, presented by Aristotle as an inquiry into the *primary causes and principles*. We must, therefore, establish the nature and number of these "causes." Aristotle stated that the causes must necessarily be finite in number, and that, with regard to the world of becoming, they are the following four (already glimpsed–although confusedly–he said, by his predecessors): (*a*) *formal cause*, (*b*) *material cause*, (*c*) *efficient/moving cause*, (*d*) *final cause*.[13]

The first two are simply the *form* or *essence* and the *matter* that structure all things, and about which we must speak in greater detail further on. (Remember that *cause* and *principle*, for Aristotle, mean that which *grounds*, that which *conditions*, that which *structures*).[14] Now let us keep in mind that through matter and form the being of things is considered from a static viewpoint, which is necessary to explain them. If instead we consider things dynamically, viz., in terms of their development, in their becoming, in their production and their corruption, then this analysis is not sufficient although necessary. It is evident, in fact, that if we consider a given man statically or formally, he is reduced simply to his matter (flesh and bones) and to his form (soul). But if we consider him dynamically and ask the question, How did he come into being? or Who generated him? or Why does he develop and grow? then it is necessary to have recourse to further reasons or causes: the *efficient or moving cause*, viz., the father who was the generator, and the *final cause*, viz., the *telos* or the goal to which the becoming of the man tends. Let us examine, in brief, each of these four causes.

(*a*) The *formal cause* is, as we have said, the form or essence (εἶδος, τὸ τί ἦν εἶναι) of things: the soul for animals, those given formal relations for different geometrical figures (the circumference, for example, is the position of points equidistant from the center), a determinate structure for different objects of art, and so on.

(*b*) The *material cause* (ὕλη) is "that from which" (τὸ ἐξ οὗ, *id ex quo* [*that out of which*]) a thing is made: for example, the matter of animals is flesh and bones; the matter of a bronze sphere is bronze, of a cup of gold is gold, of a wooden statue is wood, of a brick house is the bricks and the cement, and so on.

(*c*) The *efficient or moving cause* is that by which the change and movement of the thing originates: the father is a movent cause of the son, the will is a movent cause of the various actions of a man; a blow that impels this ball is the efficient cause of the movement of this ball, and so on.

(*d*) The *final cause* is the goal or the end of the thing or action; it is that in view of which or in function of which (τὸ οὗ ἕνεκα, *id cuius gratia* [*that on account of which*]) each thing is or becomes; and this, says Aristotle, is the good (ἀγαθόν) of each thing. The being and the becoming of things, therefore, in general demands these four causes. These are the proximate causes; but, beyond these, there are further causes given by the movements of the heavens and the highest cause, the primary immobile Movent, of which we will speak in what follows.[15]

3.   Being and its meanings and the meaning of the formula "being qua being"

We have seen that metaphysics besides being defined as a doctrine of the causes by Aristotle is also defined as a doctrine of "being" or also, of "being qua being." Let us see, therefore what is being (ὄν, εἶναι) and being qua being (ὄν ᾗ ὄν), in the context of the Aristotelian theoretical science.

What, therefore, is being? Parmenides and the Eleatics believed that being can be only *absolutely identical* being; viz. (in Aristotelian terms), it can be understood only in a *single meaning, univocally.* Now, *univocity*, in the case of being, implies also *unicity*; and, in fact, throughout Zeno, Melissus, and the School of Megara, Eleaticism is crystallized in the doctrine of the One-Being, with the total absorption of all reality into this One-Being, and goes on to the immobilization of the All. Now Aristotle completely specified the root of the error of the Eleatics and, in his disagreement with them, formulated his great principle of the *original multiplicity of the meanings of being*, which is the basis of his metaphysics. Being does not have a univocal meaning, but is rather said homonymously or equivocally (ὄν is not said μοναχῶς, but πολλαχῶς).[16]

Neither Plato nor the Platonists knew how to achieve this essential and advantageous position, according to Aristotle, notwithstanding their criticism of Parmenides. Plato and the Platonists attempted a *deduction of multiplicity* it is true; but, in doing this, they were still victimized by the Eleatic presupposition, especially, insofar as they understood their Being as a *transcendent genera, as a substantialized universal,* existing in itself and through itself beyond things. For this reason the true recovery of multiplicity and becoming necessarily evaded them and that is why the Platonists could not truly overcome Parmenides.[17] Here is how, in detail, Aristotle characterized being.

(*a*) As we said, being cannot be understood univocally in the manner of the Eleatics, or as a transcendent genera or as a substantialized universal in the manner of the Platonists.

(*b*) Being expresses originally a "multiplicity" of meanings. Not for this, therefore, is it purely "homonymous," viz., an "equivocal" by chance. Between univocity and equivocity by chance is a *middle way,* and being is precisely within this middle way. Here is the famous passage in which Aristotle enunciates this doctrine:

> There are many senses in which a thing may be said to 'be,' but they are related to one central focus, one definite kind of thing, and are not homonymous. Everything which is healthy is related to health, one thing in the sense that it preserves health, another in the sense that it produces it, another in the sense that it is a symptom of health, another because it is capable of it. And that which is medical is relative is the medical art, one thing in the sense that it possesses it, another in the sense that it is naturally adapted to it, another in the sense that it is a function of medical art. And we shall find other words used similarly to these. So, too, there are many senses in which a thing is said to be, but all refer to one focal-point.[18]

Let us put aside for the present the question of the more detailed specification of this principle and proceed with the general characterization of the concept of being.

(*c*) Being because of what has been established cannot be characterized as a "genera" much less a "species." It is, therefore, a *transgeneric* concept in addition to being *transspecific,* which means it is wider in extension than a genera as well as a species. The medievals will say that it is an *analogical concept* but Aristotle did not use this term in his discussion of being. It can certainly be used, but only by keeping in mind that the analogous character of Aristotelian being is different than the medieval notion of the analogy of being and that Aristotle's notion is defined by very precise characteristics, which we will immediately explain.

(*d*) If the unity of being is not a unity of species nor genera then what kind of unity does it possess? Being expresses different meanings, but all of them have *a precise relationship with a single principle or a single reality,* as is well illustrated in the example of "health" and "medical," in the passage quoted earlier. Therefore, the various things which are said to be "beings," express it is true different meanings of being but at the same time *they all imply a reference to a single thing.*

(*e*) What is this single thing to which reference is made in equivocal predication? It is οὐσία, substance. Aristotle says it quite clearly at the conclusion of the previously mentioned passage quoted earlier which we read only in part:

> So, too, there are many senses in which a thing is said to be, *but all refer to one focal-point*; some things are said to be because they are substances, others because they are affections of *substance*, others because they are a process *towards substance*, or destructions or privations or qualities of substance, or productive or generative *of substance*, or of things which are relative to substance, or negations of some of these things or of *substance itself.*[19]

In conclusion, the unifying focal-point of the meanings of being is οὐσία, substance. The unity derives to the various meanings of being by the fact that *being is said in relation to substance.*

From all this it is clear that Aristotelian first philosophy must distinguish and make precise the nature of the various meanings of being. But it cannot at all be reduced to a mere phenomenology or a phenomenological description of the various meanings of being *because the various meanings that being can take on always imply a basic reference to substance.* Take away substance and that would take away all the meanings of being. Consequently, it is clear that Aristotelian first philosophy must be fundamentally focussed on substance, which is the principle in relation to which all the other meanings of being exist. And in this sense we can say that Aristotelian first philosophy is fundamentally an *ousiology*.

The clarifications offered must put the reader in a position to interpret the famous formula "being qua being" (ὄν ᾗ ὄν). This formula cannot mean an abstract, uniform, and univocal *ens generalissimum* [*most general being*], as many believe. We saw, in fact, that *being* is not only not a species nor a genus, but that it expresses a transgeneric and transspecific concept. Therefore, the formula "being qua being" can express only *the multiplicity itself of the meanings of being and the relations that formally bind them and makes them precisely what each one is.* Then "being qua being" will mean substance and all that which in any way is referred to substance.[20] Consequently, it is beyond discussion that, for Aristotle, the formula "being qua being" loses any significance outside the context of the argument about the *multiplicity of the meanings of being*; anyone who attributes the meaning of being in its most general sense or in the sense of pure being, within or beyond the *multiple determinations of being*, is the victim of an archaic mode of reasoning derived from the Eleatics and completely betrays the meaning of the Aristotelian methodological reformation.[21]

4. The Aristotelian list of the meanings of being and its structure

We must now specify the nature and number of these meanings having grasped the notion of being and the principle of the original and structural multiplicity of its meanings, since Aristotle outlines a precise "list" of them. Here is the enumeration and the elucidation of the meanings of being.[22]

(*a*) Being is said, on the one hand, to be an *accident*, viz., as accidental or contingent being (ὄν κατὰ συμβεβηκός). For example, when we say that "the man is musical," or "the just is musical," we indicate accidental being; in fact, being musical does not express the nature of man, but only *that which happens to the being of a man*, a pure *happening*, a mere *accident* or nonessential occurrence.

(*b*) Opposed to accidental being is *being per se* (ὄν καθ' αὐτό). It indicates not that which is being through another, as accidental being, but that which is being *essentially or necessarily* [being *per se*]. As for example, of *ens per se* Aristotle indicates, for the most part *substance* only; but, sometimes, also *all the categories*; in addition to the essence or substance, quality, quantity, relation, action, passion, where, and when. In effect (different from what can be found in medieval speculation) in Aristotle the categories other than substance are more solid than those that are purely accidental (by which the purely fortuitous is meant), insofar as, although purely subordinate to substance, they are, as we will immediately see, a foundation of a second level of the other meanings of being.

(*c*) Third in the list of the meanings is *being as true* to which its contrary is the meaning of nonbeing as false. This meaning of being is the one that we will call the meaning found in "logical" discourse; in fact, being as true points out the being of true judgment, whereas nonbeing as false indicates the being of the false judgment. This is in some respects a purely mental being, viz., a being that has its being only through mind and in the mind that knows and reasons.

(*d*) The final entry in the list is being as *potency and act*. We may say, for example, that someone is seeing both when he sees potentially; that is, when he *can* see (viz., someone who has the capacity to see but who has his eyelids closed momentarily) and when he *actually* sees; or we may say that someone is knowledgeable, although he is not making use of his knowledge (for example, someone who knows arithmetic, but who is not actually using it) as much as he who is actually using it. Analogously, we may say also that a statue is actually sculpted, as well as saying that it is potentially within the block of marble on which the sculptor is working; and in the same sense we may say that the seedling is wheat, in the sense that it is potentially wheat, whereas we may say that the mature stalk is actually wheat. Aristotle states that being according to potency and act *extends to all the meanings of being that were distinguished so far*. There can be accidental being in potency or act; there can be a true judgment and a false judgment in potency or act; and there can be potency or act *according to each of the different categories*. (But we will speak about this issue more fully further on.)

The list of the meanings of being consists, therefore, of four meanings. But it would be more exact to say of four groups of meanings. We have seen this already, in fact, implicitly but we will immediately make it explicit further on, that being is not understood in an univocal manner nor within the ambit of each of the four meanings.

Both to reduce to a schema the things said and to conclude, we will state that the meanings of being are the following four arranged by proceeding from the most important to that of least importance:

(*a*) being according to the different categories;
(*b*) being as act and potency;
(*c*) being as true and false;
(*d*) being as accidental or contingent.
The meanings of nonbeing are, instead, only three:
(*a*) nonbeing according to the different categories;
(*b*) nonbeing as potency (= nonbeing-in-act);
(*c*) nonbeing as false.

Accidental being does not have a corresponding nonbeing, as the other three meanings of being have, because of itself it is already, for Aristotle, "something close to not-being;"[23] viz., almost not-being.

5. Clarifications of the meanings of being

We have noted earlier that the four meanings of being are in reality four groups of meanings. In fact, each of these groups further signifies similars, but not identicals; that is to say, not univocally but analogically.

(*a*) In the first place, the *different categories* do not go back to identical or univocal meanings of being; being according to each "of the categories," in other words, constitutes a different meaning from that of any of the others. Consequently, the expression "being according to the categories" designates as many diverse meanings of being, as there are such.[24]

Aristotle says expressly that being belongs to the different categories not in the same way nor in the same degree: "Being is predicated of all the categories, but not in the same way, since it is said of substance in a primary way and of the other categories in a derivative way."[25] And again:

> For it must be either homonymously that we say that these are, or by making qualifications and abstractions (in the way in which that which is not known

may be said to be known),-the truth being that we use the word *neither homonymously nor in the same sense, but just as we apply the word 'medical' when there is a reference to one and the same thing, not meaning one and the same thing, nor yet speaking homonymously*; for a patient and an operation and an instrument are called medical neither homonymously nor in virtue of one thing, but with reference to one thing.[26]

This last reality referred to is obviously substance. As can be seen, that which holds in general for the different meanings of being, holds, then, in particular for the categories; the remaining categories are being in relation to the first category and in virtue of it.

But, consequently, it may be asked, besides the unity that is proper to all the meanings of being, What specific connection unites the different "categories" in a single group, what is precisely the basis for grouping together the "categories"? The reply is as follows. The categories go back to the primary and basic meanings of being; they are, therefore, the original distinctions on which the distinctions of the further meanings are supported necessarily. The categories represent, therefore, the meanings in which being was divided originally;[27] they are the highest divisions of being, or, as Aristotle also states, the highest "genera" of being.[28] In that sense it is easy to grasp how Aristotle indicates in the categories the group of the meanings of being "per se," precisely because it is a question of the primary meanings.

How did Aristotle arrive at the number of the categories and their listing? This is a very complex problem that has not been resolved up to now and is probably insoluble. Logical and linguistic research would be able to make a contribution, but a phenomenological and ontological analysis especially would be conclusive.[29] Here is the list of the categories:

(1) Substance or essence (οὐσία, τί ἐστι, τὸ τί ἦν εἶναι);
(2) Quality (ποιόν);
(3) Quantity (ποσόν);
(4) Relation (πρός τι);
(5) Action or to act (ποιεῖν);
(6) Passion or to suffer (πάσχειν);
(7) Where or place (ποῦ);
(8) When or time (ποτέ);
(9) To have (ἔχειν);
(10) To lie (κεῖσθαι).

(b) Also *being according to act and potency* does not have one meaning. First of all, it is clear that with the expression "being according to act and potency" is indicated two very different and in a certain sense contrary modes of being. Aristotle, in fact, even calls the being of potency not-being, in the sense that, with respect to being-in-act, being in potency is not-being-in-act.

The expression, therefore, ought not deceive us, since Aristotle maintains that he achieved an essential concept for the purposes of the explanation of reality and being, precisely through the discovery of *potential* being, as resulted from his argument with the Megarics. The experience tells us, in fact, that in addition to *actual* being, there is *potential* being; therefore it is that mode of being which is not actual but is the capacity to be actual. Anyone who denies that there is some other way of being besides actual being enmeshes reality in an actualized immobility excluding any kind of becoming or movement. It is clear, therefore, why Aristotle gave such a great importance to the distinction between being-in-potency and being-in-act.[30]

But—and this is the point to which we have been trying to arrive—potential being and actual being, also taken individually, do not have a single meaning, but, once again, *they have a multiplicity of meanings*. In fact, act and potency extend to all the categories and likewise assume different meanings, insofar as there are different categories. This means that there is one form of actual being and potential being according to *substance*; a different form of actual being and of potential being according to *quality*; another and different form of act and potency according to *quantity*; and so on.

Apart from the numerous questions to which these affirmations would give rise, but of which this is not place to speak, a point remains to be clarified. Being as potency and being as act (which are joined in one grouping since they are comprehended and measured only in function of each other) do not exist outside or over and above the categories, *but they are modes of being that rely on the very being itself of the categories, they are included in all the list of the categories and are different according to which category they are referred*.

(*c*) Also the third meaning of being, being as *true* and as *false* is understood in different ways, it is included in the being of the categories. But since metaphysics is not concerned with it, but logic, there is no need to explain it here.

(*d*) Finally there remains *accidental* being. We state that the question of accidents (and consequently of accidental being) is complex enough, insofar as the term *accident*, in Aristotle, is among the most fluctuating notions. Nonetheless, when the Stagirite speaks of accidental being (ὄν κατὰ συμβεβηκός), he understands it as fortuitous or contingent being, viz., being that depends on another being, to which, therefore, it is not bound by any necessary connection. It is, therefore, a kind of being that is *not always nor for the most part but only sometimes, fortuitous, and contingent*.[31]

Frequently categorial being and accidental being are confused, but this is an obvious error. It must not obscure the fact that Aristotle himself (but especially later thought) sometimes calls the same categories *accidents*. We will see, in effect, that among the categories, only the first is an autonomous being, and the others suppose this first one and are structurally inserted into it. In such a sense, all that which is not substance cannot be per se in the strict sense and therefore is an accident. But when Aristotle speaks of "accidental being," he is not aiming to simply refer to another or to being in another. Accidental being is that which can not be, that which is not always nor for the most part. Consequently, it is obvious that the categories, viz., that categorial being as such, cannot be precisely said to be contingent being, or it cannot be said that it can either be or not be, or that it is always or for the most part. Being (at least sensible being) is inconceivable without the categories, which means that, as such, they are necessary. An example will serve to clarify this notion and bring us to a conclusion. It is not precisely necessary that a man be pale or angry; that a man have *these* qualities is accidental, it is fortuitous, it is contingent, in the sense that they could indifferently be or not be; but *it is necessary that man have some qualities* (it does not matter what they are). The example can be duplicated for every category. The fact that a thing has a given measure can be contingent but it is not contingent and not accidental that it have measure (a sensible thing without any quantity is inconceivable). That something is found in a particular place can be accidental, but it is not purely accidental that he is in a place. And so the examples can be multiplied. In conclusion, truly and properly accidental and accidental being can be grounded (as moreover also the other meanings of being) only on the categories, and they are distinguished totally, insofar as the category is necessary, whereas the accident is the affection or the occurrence that is merely fortuitous, that is located according to every category. So accidental being is *the contingent affection or the contingent event that takes place according to (necessary) different categories.*

Let us recapitulate the results of the discussion of this section. It has been shown that the four meanings of being are, in reality, four groups of meanings, all referring to the first; that is, to the categories. Being as potency and act is located according to the different categories and only according to them; it does not exist outside of them or over and above them. Being as true, which consists in the mental operation of joining and separating are based on the categories, which are, precisely, that which is united or is separated. Finally, accidental being is based also on categorial being and is only an accidental affection or an occurrence according to the different categories. Therefore, all the meanings of being presuppose the being of the categories; but–and this is a point that has emerged many times and that now must be deepened–*the various categories, in their turn, do not all stand on the same level; between substance and the other categories is a radical difference, a difference in a way that is like that between the categories in general and the other meanings of being.* All the meanings of being presuppose the being of the categories; in its turn the being of the categories depends entirely on the being of the first category, viz., οὐσία or substance. If, therefore, all the meanings of being presuppose the being of the categories, and if, the being of the categories in their turn presuppose the being of the first of the categories and are wholly grounded on it, it is evident that the radical question about the meaning of being will be focussed on *ousía* or substance. Therefore it is easy to understand the precise statements of Aristotle: "And indeed the question which, both now and of old, has always been raised, and always been the subject of aporia, viz.,what being is, is just the question, what is substance?...And so we also must consider chiefly and primarily and almost exclusively what that is which is in this sense."[32]

We must therefore conclude that the ultimate meaning of being is unveiled through the meaning of substance. What, consequently, is οὐσία or substance?

6. The problem of substance in general

We must point out immediately that substance is the most delicate, the most complex, and in a certain sense, also the most enigmatic problem–all who wish to understand Aristotelian metaphysics must reject summary solutions to which the systematizing textbooks have habituated them.[33]

Nevertheless we must make clear that the general question about substance involves two strictly connected and essential problems, one of which develops in two directions. These problems we will clarify in a preliminary way. The predecessors of Aristotle had given to the problem of substance wholly antithetical solutions: some had seen in *sensible matter* the only substance, Plato instead had pointed it out in *supersensible entities*, and the common conviction seemed to point it out in *concrete things*.

Aristotle began the problem *ex novo* [*anew*] by structuring it in a correct manner. After having reduced the metaphysical problem to its central nucleus, viz., to the question of *ousía*, he says, with full awareness that the starting point will be in the determination of what substances there are, *whether there are only the sensibles* (as the Naturalists claim) *or are there also supersensibles* (as the Platonists insist). Note, this is the problem of problems and the *quaestio ultima* (*the most profound problem*), the question par excellence of the Aristotelian metaphysics just as of every metaphysics in general. It is a question, in the last analysis, of deciding on the validity or at least on the results of the "Second Voyage" of Plato.[34]

But, to resolve this specific problem, Aristotle must first solve the ousiological problem, *What is the nature of substance in general*? Is it *matter*? Is it *form*? Is it the *composite*? This general problem must be solved before any other in order to be methodologically correct. It would be, in fact, more precise to say if there exists *only* the sensible or *also* the supersensible, if it were to be first established what is, in general,οὐσία. If, for example, *ousía* were only the matter or the concrete composite of matter and form, it would be clear that the question of supersensible substance would be *by that very fact* [*eo ipso*] eliminated; whereas if *ousía* were found to be also other or even chiefly other than matter, then the question of the supersensible would present itself in all its fullness.

What basis is there for Aristotle to treat of substance in general? Obviously on the basis of substances that no one would contest, *the sensible substances*. Aristotle expressly writes: "It is agreed that there are some substances among sensible things, so that we must look *first among these*. For it is in an advantage to advance to that which is more intelligible. For learning proceeds for all in this way–through that which is less intelligible by nature [= the sensible things] to that which is more intelligible by nature [= the intelligible things]."[35]

In conclusion, of the two problems of Aristotelian ousiology, the first, What is the nature of substance in general? is prior to the second, What substances are there? (the theological problem). In addition, the first problem (the preliminary one) can only be solved based on sensible substance, which is the only one that we know, before ascertaining whether supersensible substance exists or does not exist.[36]

7. The problem of *ousía* in general: form, matter, the composite, and the definition of the concept of substance

And now we must finally ask, What is the nature of *ousía* in general? Aristotle, as we have already noted, found in his predecessors contrasting replies: for the Naturalists substance was matter or the material substrate, for the Platonists, form and the universal; according to popular opinion instead it seemed that it was the individual substance and the concrete thing. Who is right? The Stagirite replies everyone and no one. The answer to the problem cannot be simple, but must be necessarily complex.

The reader will probably already be oriented toward the Aristotelian answer to the problem posed by what we have said previously. The Stagirite says that *ousía* can be understood in different respects, as (*a*) *form*, (*b*) *matter*, and (*c*) the *synolon* or composite of matter and form. With that Aristotle acknowledges each of his predecessors as correct in part and indicates the error in their onesidedness. Let us briefly explain the three meanings.

(*a*) Substance is in a sense the form (εἶδος, μορφή). *Form*, according to Aristotle is not obviously the external form or exterior shape of things (or it is only so in a subordinate manner), but it is the intimate nature of things, the *what-is* or the intimate essence (τὸ τί ἦν εἶναι) of them. The form or essence of man, for example, is his soul, viz., that which makes him a living rational being; the form or essence of an animal is the sentient soul and that of plants the vegetative soul. Again, the essence of the circle is that which makes what is that given shape with these given qualities; and the same can be repeated for different things. When we define things, we refer to their form or essence in general and the things are knowable only in terms of their essence.[37]

(*b*) However, if the rational soul does not inform a body, we do not have a man; if the sentient soul does not inform a certain matter, we do not have an animal; and, again, if the vegetative soul does not inform other matter, we do not have a plant. The same can be said according to all the objects produced by the activity of an art, if the essence or form of the table is not carried out in the wood, then we do not have that instantiation, and the same is to be repeated for all other things similar to this. In this sense also the matter is fundamentally within the constitution of things, and therefore it can be said—at least within certain limits—that it is the substance of things. It is clear, yet, that these limits are well defined; in fact, if there were no form, the matter would be indeterminate and would not suffice to constitute things.

(*c*) On the basis of what has been said already the third meaning is also quite clear; that of the *synolon* (σύνολον). The *synolon* is the concrete union of matter and form. All concrete things are nothing other than the *synolon* of matter and form. Therefore, all sensible things are whatever can be considered in their form, in their matter, in their composition; and substance (*ousía*) is in different respects (in the senses seen) both the form and the matter and the *synolon*.[38]

We have said that Aristotle attributed substance to form, to the *synolon*, and to matter *in different respects*. Consequently, the Stagirite developed the problem of *substance in general* in a second direction, he also tried to determine what are these "respects" on the basis of which something can rightly be said to be substance. This second direction in the texts is not always explicitly distinct from the first and frequently it is interwoven in various ways with the other view. However it is essential to distinguish them to grasp Aristotelian thought in all its complexity.

The Stagirite seems to establish the definition of substance as numbering four, or better as five, if we take into account a characteristic that is on a somewhat different level than the others.

(*a*) In the first place, he names as substance only *that which does not inhere in another and is not predicated of another* but which is a subject of inherence and of predication of all the other modes of being.

(*b*) In the second place, substance can be only an entity that can *subsist through itself or separately from the rest* (a χωριστόν), having an autonomous form of being.

(*c*) In the third place, he names as substance only that which is a *determined something* (τόδε τι); a general attribute or something that is universal or abstract cannot hence be a substance.

(d) In the fourth place, *substance* must be something *intrinsically unitary* (ἕν) and not a mere aggregate of parts or something multiple and disorganized.

(e) Finally, note the characteristic of *act* and *actuality* (ἐνέργεια, ἐντελέχεια); only that which is act or actual is substance. And this characteristic, which we have stated stands somewhat outside this order, is very important.

Now let us reexamine and compare these definitional attributes of the substantiality to *matter, form,* and the *synolon*; that is to say, those that we stated—in different respects—signify *ousía*. In what measure do matter, form, and the composite fulfill these requirements?

Matter undoubtedly possess (a) the first of these characteristics: it does not inhere in another nor is it predicated of another; in some way all the rest inhere in it and are predicated of it; form itself inheres and in a certain sense it refers to the matter. The matter, however, does not possess some of the other entitative characteristics. (b) It does not have being precisely through itself because where there is only matter there is no possession of form. (c) It is not a *determinate something* (*tode ti*) because such can be only something that is or has a form. (d) It is in no way something *unitary*, because unity is derived from form. (e) Finally, it is not *act*, but it exists only in potency. We will say, then, that matter is substance solely in the *weakest and most improper sense of the term*. Keep in mind at this point that Aristotle at times denies that matter is substance and at others affirms it; it has only the first characteristic of being and not the others.

Instead the *form* and the *composite* even if not in identical manner have all the characteristics of substance (οὐσία).

The form (a) does not have its being in another and is not predicated of another; it is true"note"that the form inheres in matter and that it refers in a certain sense to matter, but, in a wholly exceptional sense (it inheres in matter as that which informs the matter and has more being–as we will see immediately–than the matter); hierarchically it is the matter that depends on the form and not vice versa. (b) The form can be separated from the matter in two senses; (1) it is the form that gives being to the matter and not vice versa and hence the form is, in general, at least conceptually always separable; (2) there are substances that are entirely form and that do not have any matter, and in these cases, the form is absolutely separated. (c) The form is a determined something (τόδε τι), as Aristotle repeatedly states; the form is a determined something and also *determining* because it is that which accounts for the thing being what it is and not something else. (d) The form is unity eminently, since it is the Principle that accounts for the unity of the matter that it informs. (e) Finally, the form is act eminently, it is the Principle that accounts for act, to the point that Aristotle frequently uses *form and act as synonyms*.

And what of the *synolon*? The composite of matter and form also possesses the previously mentioned characteristics, because the composite is precisely the union of matter and form. The *synolon* that is the concrete individual thing (*a*) is the substrate of inherence and predication of all the accidental determinations; (*b*) it subsists of itself and independently in the full sense of the term; (*c*) it is a "this," a determinate something (τόδε τι) in the concrete sense; (*d*) and it is a unity, insofar as it has all its material parts unified by the form; (*e*) it is in act because its material parts are actualized by form.

The matter—as has been seen—is somewhat less substance than *form* and the *synolon*. The question then lies between the form and the *synolon*, Is there a further differentiation with respect to their entitative character (viz., in what respect do they fulfill the conditions of beingness)? The question is somewhat complex. In certain passages Aristotle seems to consider the *synolon* or the concrete individual as substance in the fullest sense; in other passages, instead, he seems to consider the form to be such. But there is no contradiction in this, as instead at first glance there might seem to be. In effect it depends on the context in which the statement is located whether Aristotle responds in the first way or in the second way. *From the empirical and verifiable point of view* it is clear that the *synolon* or the concrete individual seems to be substance in an eminent fashion. Not so, instead, *from the strictly metaphysical or speculative viewpoint*. In fact, the form is the Principle, the cause, and the reason for being; that is to say the foundation, and with respect to it the *synolon* is instead that which is based on the Principle, that which is caused, and that which is grounded. Consequently, in this sense, the form is substance eminently and with the best conformity with the characteristics of *ousía*. In sum, *quoad nos* [*for us*], in the clearest sense and that closest to our experience, *ousía* is the concrete individual; but *in itself and in its own nature* and furthest from our experience the form is instead *ousía* eminently.

On the other hand, this result is fully confirmed if we think that the *synolon* does not exhaust the notion of substance as such. If the *synolon* were the only substance as such, there would be nothing but the *synolon* as substance; and, in this way, God and in general the immaterial and supersensible would not be substance! The form can be said instead to be substance eminently; God and the intelligent movents of the celestial spheres are pure immaterial forms, whereas sensible things are forms that inform matter. The form is essential to the individuals and to other entities, although in very different ways.[39]

To conclude, we will say that the meaning of being is fully determined in this way. Being in its strongest meaning is substance; and substance in an improper sense is matter, in a secondary (more proper) sense it is the *synolon*, and in a third sense (and eminently) it is form. Being is hence matter, being in a higher sense is the *synolon*, and being is, in the highest sense, form. In this way the notion is grasped since Aristotle has named the form even as "the primary cause of being,"[40] precisely insofar as it informed matter and grounds the *synolon*.

8. The Aristotelian "form" is not a universal

Viewed from the standpoint we have proposed, the Aristotelian doctrine of substance (οὐσία) appears less aporetic than many modern scholars have claimed following the lead especially of Zeller.[41] The distinctions of the multiple meanings of *ousía* were not proposed simply because of merely linguistic considerations and to satisfy linguistic requirements, but it was made as a result of a metaphysical analysis and to satisfy the requirements of a comprehension of reality in its multiple aspects. And just as Zeller did not understand the three meanings of *ousía* and in particular the two principal meanings (that of the *synolon* and form), he could only—for structural reasonsmake an argument in terms of *aut-aut* [*either-or*], so at all the costs he must remain in the area of one of the meanings, but he should have made an argument instead in terms of *et-et* [*both-and*] as we have seen. Aristotelian metaphysics cannot begin, as succeeding ones do, by a *reductio ad unum* [*a reduction to one (meaning) of being*] at all costs; it is rather developed by distinguishing the various aspects of reality, and when it has distinguished them it does not proceed to a further unification, but declares them irreducible, and precisely as such considers them expressions of the multidimensional structure of reality.

So also another difficulty raised by Zeller is easily solved. It is difficult"he says"to conceive as immutable the forms of things that change, as Aristotle had conceived them. Actually Aristotle expended a good deal of energy on this point on the immutability of the *eidos*. Consequently, how can Aristotle affirm that the *eidos* is immutable, without falling into the position of the "transcendence of the form" for which he insistently reproached the Platonists? Simply because the immutability of the Aristotelian *eidos* is nothing other than the immutability of the metaphysical cause, or of the condition, or of the Principle in relation to that which is caused, conditioned, and empirically based on the Principle.[42]

We wish to conclude finally in our considerations of substance by pausing over a frequently obscured point about which the Zellerian control over the phrasing of the question is the one to which most scholars are indebted and that must inevitably impede its comprehension. We are speaking of the relationship between form and the universal. Aristotle shows that, whereas the matter, form, and *synolon* have a title to be considered *ousía*, it would seem, the universal that the Platonists elevate to the rank of substance in the highest sense does not have absolutely any title to be considered substance, because it does not have any of the characteristics that we saw earlier to be proper to beingness.[43]

But, one might say, is not the Aristotelian *eidos* a universal? The response is unequivocally negative. Most of the time Aristotle qualifies his *eidos* as a τόδε τι, an expression that indicates a determined something that is opposed to the abstract universal; and, moreover, we have seen, as all the characteristics of *ousía* belong to the *eidos*. The Aristotelian *eidos* is a metaphysical Principle, an ontological condition; in modern terms we would say an ontological structure. Let us quote as confirmation just one passage—the most important one—which is positioned at the end of the book concerned with substance (οὐσία). After having stated that substance is "a Principle and a cause," Aristotle shows that there must be an inquiry into such a Principle and such a cause. The thing or the fact about which the cause or Principle is sought must be known beforehand, and the inquiry requires this: Why is this thing or this fact thus or such? This means, Why is (or does the matter constitute) the matter of this determinate object? Here is Aristotle's detailed answer to the question: "This matter is a house, why? Because there is present in it the essence of house. And we can inquire thus, why this given thing is a man? Or why this body has these characteristics? Therefore in the inquiry into the why, we seek the cause of the matter; that is to say, *the form for which the matter is a determinate thing, and this is precisely the substance.*"[44] But here is the most eloquent example with which Aristotle seals his inquiry:

> As regards that which is compounded out of something so that the whole is one–not like a heap, however, but like a syllable,–the syllable is not its elements, **ba** is not the same as **b** and **a**, nor is flesh fire and earth; for when they are dissolved the wholes, i.e., the flesh and the syllable, no longer exist, but the elements of the syllable exist, and so do fire and earth. The syllable, then, is something–not only its elements (the vowel and the consonant) but also something else; and the flesh is not only fire and earth or the hot and the cold, but also something else. Since, then, that something must be either an element or composed of elements, if it is an element the same argument will again apply; for flesh will consists of this and fire and earth and something still further, so that the process will go on to infinity; while if it is a compound, clearly it will be a compound not of one but of many (or else it will itself be that one, so that again in this case we can use the same argument as in the case of flesh or of the syllable. But it would seem that this is something, and not an element, and that it is the cause which makes this thing flesh and that a syllable. And similarly in all other cases. *And this is the substance of each thing; for this is the primary cause of its being.*[45]

As we can see, the *ousía-eidos* of Aristotle as the immanent metaphysical structure of the thing cannot be confused in any way with the abstract universal at all. The universal is instead the *genus* (γένος) that does not have a separate metaphysical reality. The soul of man as *eidos* is a Principle that informs a body and makes it into a man, and it has its own metaphysical reality; instead animal, understood as the *genus* of animal, is only a common abstract term that has no reality *in itself* and does not exist except in the *man* or in another *form* of animal.

Yet it is appropriate to point out that the Aristotelian *eidos* has two aspects: one of these is *metaphysical* as we have seen, the other is the aspect that we may call *logical*. The Stagirite does not analyze and emphasize the two aspects and their relative differences, but he moves in various instances from one to the other without giving any sign of difficulty. We note also that for linguistic reasons we emphasize the differences because once again we are forced to translate *eidos* in two different ways: sometimes with the term *form* and at other times with the term *species*. In what concerns the metaphysical aspect of *eidos*, that is to say the form, Aristotle correctly states that it is not a universal. But what of the *eidos* in the logical sense of the species? Evidently the *species is precisely eidos insofar as it is conceived by the human mind*. And therefore it could be said that as the metaphysical structure or the metaphysical Principle, the *eidos* is not a universal; instead as it is conceived and constructed by the human mind, it becomes a universal. But let us repeat when Aristotle is concerned with emphasizing the first point he does not focus on the second aspect. (So much is this so in his eyes that the *eidos also considered as species* is the specific "difference" that gives determinateness to the genera, precisely "differentiating them" and hence redeeming them within their abstract universality,[46] as we will see when we take up Aristotle's logic.)

These difficulties must not dissuade us from looking into what was first stated about the metaphysical status and reality of the *eidos*. The *eidos* is not only not a universal, but *possesses more being than the matter and more being than the composite*, insofar as it is a principle that by structuring the matter accounts for the *synolon* itself as a being.[47]

9. Act and potency

The doctrine presented must again be integrated with some clarifications regarding potency and act as referred to substance.[48] Matter is *potency*–that is, potentiality, in the sense that it is a *capacity* to assume or to receive the form; the bronze has a potency for being a statue, because it is a positive capacity both to receive and to take on the form of the statue; the wood is the potency for various objects that can be made with the wood, because it is the positive capacity to take on the forms of the various objects—whereas the form is aligned with act or the actualization of the capacities. The composite or *synolon* of matter and form will be, if it is considered as such, chiefly act; if it is considered in its form, it will be undoubtedly act or entelechy; and if it is considered in its materiality, it will be instead a composite of act and potency. All the things that have matter have always hence, as such, to a greater or lesser degree potentialities.[49] Instead if, as we will see, there are immaterial beings; that is, of pure form, they will be pure acts, devoid of potentiality.[50]

Act, as we have already emphasized, is also called by Aristotle an *entelechy*. Sometimes it seems that between the two terms there is a certain difference of meaning, but, for the most part and especially in the *Metaphysics*, the two terms are synonymous. Therefore, act and entelechy bespeak something fulfilled, actualized perfection, or the actualized. The soul, hence, insofar as it is essence or form of the body, is the act and entelechy of the body; and in general all forms of sensible substances are act and entelechy. God, we will see, will be pure entelechy (and just as the other movent Intelligences of the celestial spheres).

Act, Aristotle again says, has absolute "priority" and superiority over potency; potency in fact cannot be known, as such, except by relating it to the act of which it is the potency. In addition act (which is form) is a condition, rule, and goal of potentialities. Finally act is superior to potency, because it is the mode of being of the eternal substances.[51]

The doctrine of potency and act is, from the viewpoint of metaphysics, of the greatest importance. With it Aristotle was able to solve the Eleatic aporias about becoming and movement; becoming and movement enter into the river of being, because they involve a passage from nonbeing to absolute being, since it moves from *being in potency* to *being in act*; that is, from being to being.[52] In addition with it he has solved completely the problem of the unity of matter and form; the former being potency, the latter act or the actualization of matter.[53] Finally, the Stagirite has used them at least in part, for demonstrating the existence of God and understanding his nature.[54] But also in the ambit of all the other sciences the concepts of potency and act have in Aristotle an unrivaled role to play.

Now we are ready to move on to the last of the metaphysical issues: that of supersensible substance, which is the decisive one.

10. Demonstration of the existence of the immobile Movent

Are there supersensible substances, or are there only sensible substances? Aristotle replied to the question (which, as we know, was the question aroused by the Platonic "Second Voyage") and not only, as we have emphasized, has he reconfirmed its results, but he even went further and reached a position that, both in the clarity of its method of formulation and in its conclusion, goes beyond Plato.

We say immediately that, for the Stagirite, three kinds of substances exist hierarchically ordered. Two are of a sensible nature: (*a*) the first is constituted of the sensible substances that come into being and perish, (*b*) the second is constituted by the sensible substances that are incorruptible. These "sensible" substances although "incorruptible," are the heavens, the planets and the stars, which, according to Aristotle, are incorruptible, because they are structured by incorruptible matter (the ether, or fifth essence), capable only of change or local motion and hence not capable of alteration, or augmentation, or diminution and much less of generation and corruption. Instead corruptible sensible substance is the support of all kinds of changes, precisely because the matter of which it is constituted includes the possibility of all the contraries; because the things of this world (the sublunaries), besides being able to move themselves, are subject to addition and diminution, to alteration, and to generation and corruption. Beyond these, there are then, (c) the immobile, eternal substances transcending the sensible substances, they are God or the immobile Movents and the other movent substances of the various spheres of which the heaven consists, as we will see.

The first of these two kinds of substances are constituted by matter and form; by the four elements (earth, water, air, and fire) of these sensible corruptibles, by pure ether, as we already said, of these incorruptibles. The supersensible substance is instead an absolutely pure form devoid of matter. Physics and astronomy is concerned with the first two kinds of substances; the third kind of substance constitutes the special subject matter of metaphysics as we know.

We must, therefore, examine in brief, the procedure by which Aristotle demonstrates the existence of supersensible substance and its nature, whether it is unique or whether there are many, and the relations between such a substance and the world. The existence of the supersensible is demonstrated in the following way.

Substances are the primary realities, in the sense that all the other ways of being, as we have fully seen, depend on substance. If, hence, all the substances were corruptible, there would not exist anything at all that was incorruptible. But—Aristotle says—time and movement are certainly incorruptible. Time is not generated or corrupted; in fact, prior to generation of time, there would have to be a "before," and after the destruction of time there would have to be a "after." Now, "before" and "after" are precisely time. In other words, for the reasons presented, there is always a time before or after something is placed as a beginning or ending of time; therefore, time is eternal. The same reasoning holds also for movement, because, according to Aristotle, time is simply a determination [numbering] of motion; hence, there is no time without movement, and hence, the eternity of the former postulates the eternity of the latter.

But under what condition can an eternal movement (or time) exist? The Stagirite replies (on the basis of the Principles that he established by studying the conditions of motion in the *Physics*); only if a primary Principle exists that is the cause of its eternality.

How must this Principle be to be the cause of the eternality of the celestial motions? In the first place, Aristotle says, the Principle must be eternal, if movement is eternal, the cause of movement must be eternal. Or, in other words, to explain an eternal motion, the cause of such a motion can only be eternal. If it were not so, the eternality of motion would not be accounted for.

In the second place, the Principle must be *immobile*, because only the immobile is the absolute or unconditioned cause of the mobile. In the *Physics*, Aristotle has demonstrated this point with rigor. All that which is in motion, is moved by another. A rock, for example, is moved by a stick, the stick in its turn is moved by the hand, and the hand by the man. In sum, to explain every motion at the beginning there is need of a Principle that is in motion through itself and not moved by another, at least with respect to that which it moves. It would be absurd, in fact, to conceive of moving from movent to movent *ad infinitum* because a process to infinity is always inconceivable, in these cases. Now, if this is so, not only must these be the Principles or relatively mobile movents, which are placed at the beginning of each individual motion, but–and *a fortiori*–there must be an absolute primary Principle, absolutely immobile that is at the head of the motion of the whole universe.

In the third place, the Principle must be devoid of all potentialities; that is, pure act. If, in fact, it were to have potentialities, it would be also not moved in act; but that is absurd, because in such a case, it would not be a eternal movement of the heavens; that is, a movement always in act.

In conclusion, because there is eternal movement, it is necessary that there be an eternal Principle that accounts for it, and it is necessary that such a Principle is (*a*) eternal, if that which it causes is eternal; (*b*) immobile, if the absolutely primary cause of the mobile is the immobile; (*c*) pure act, if the movement that it causes is always an act.[55] Immobile Movent is the supersensible substance for which we have been seeking.

But, how can the Primary Movent remain *absolutely immobile*? Is there, in the ambit of things that we know, something that moves, without being moved itself?

Aristotle responds by adducing the example of a thing that is the object of desire and intelligence. The object of desire is that which is beautiful and good; or the beautiful and the good attract the will of man without moving themselves in any way; just so the intelligible moves the intelligence without being moved itself. And this type of causality is also the kind exercised by the primary Movent, viz., the primary substance; the primary Movent "moves" as an object of love and draws the beloved (ὡς ἐρώμενον κινεῖ)[56] and, as such, remains absolutely immobile.

As is evident, the causality of the primary Movent is not a causality of the efficient kind, of the kind exercised by a hand that moves a body, or that of a sculptor who carves the marble, or of the father who generates a child. God, instead, attracts; and He attracts as an object of love, viz., as a goal; the causality of the immobile Movent is hence properly final causality. The interpreters have had long discussions on this question, with different results.

There are, for example, some who claim—by digging in various ways into the texts of Aristotle and by explaining the presuppositions of certain assertions—to have found in Aristotle, more than implicitly, the concept of creation, and hence a true and proper efficient causality of the immobile Movent.[57] But, in reality, the Aristotelian texts and their contexts do not authorize such an interpretation; moreover the knowledge of creation was not achieved by Greek speculation and it was instead achieved only by succeeding medieval speculation. It seems correct instead to say with Ross, "God is an efficient cause because of its being a final cause, but in no other way."[58]

The worldeven if it is totally influenced by God, by the attraction that He exercises as highest goal, hence by the yearning for perfection—does not have a beginning. There is no moment in which there was chaos (or the noncosmos), precisely because, if it were so, it would be contradictory to the conclusion of the priority of act over potency; first; that is, would be chaos, which is potency, then there would be the world, which is act. But this is most absurd, insofar as God is eternal, being eternal God has always attracted as an object of love the universe, which, hence, has always had to be what it is.[59]

11. Nature of the immobile Movent

This Principle, on which "depends the heaven and nature," is Life; and what kind of life? That which is most excellent and perfect, a life that for us is possible only for a brief period, a life of pure knowing, a life of contemplative activity. Here is the astonishing passage in which Aristotle–extremely rare for him–is touched, and in which his language becomes almost poetic and lyrical:

> On such a Principle, then, depend the heavens and the world of nature. And its life is such as the best which we enjoy, and enjoy for but a short time. For it is ever in this state (which we cannot be), since its actuality is also pleasure. (And therefore waking, perception, and thinking are most pleasant, and hopes and memories are so because of their reference to these)–If then God is always in that good state in which we sometimes are, this compels our wonder; and if in a better state this compels it yet more. And God is in a better state. And life also belongs to God; for the actuality of thought is life, and God is that actuality; and God's essential actuality is life most good and eternal. We say therefore that God is a living being, eternal, most good, so that life and duration continuous and eternal being belong to God; for this is God.[60]

But what does God know? God knows the most excellent thing. But this most excellent thing is God himself. God, therefore, knows himself, it is the contemplative activity with himself as its object, it is a self-knowing knowing (νόησις νοήσεως). Here is the precise statements of the philosopher:

> And knowing in itself deals with that which is best in itself, and that which is known in the fullest sense with that which his best in the fullest sense. And

knowing knows itself because it shares the nature of the object of knowing; for it becomes an object of knowledge in coming into contact with and knowing its objects, so that knowing and the object of knowing are the same. For that which is capable of receiving the object of knowing i.e., the *ousiá*, is knowing. And it is active when it possess its object. Therefore the latter rather than the former is the divine element which knowing seems to contain, and the act of contemplation is what is most pleasant and best.[61]

And again: "If therefore the divine Mind is that which is most excellent and it knows itself, and its knowing is a knowing of knowing." [62] God is therefore eternal, immobile, pure act devoid of potentialities and of matter, a spiritual life, and a self-thinking thought. Being such, obviously "he cannot have any magnitude," but must be "without parts and indivisible." And he must likewise be "impassible and unalterable."[63]

12. Unity and multiplicity in the Divine

Yet, Aristotle believed that God alone is sufficient to explain the eternal movement of all the spheres he conceived as constituting the heavens. God directly accounts for the primary mobile—the heaven of the fixed stars—but between this sphere and the earth are many other concentric spheres, below and enveloping one another. What accounts for eternal motion of these lower spheres?

The response would be twofold: either their eternal motion is to be accounted for by a motion derived from the first heaven, which is transmitted mechanically one to the other; or their eternal motion is to be accounted for by other supersensible movents, immobile and eternal, that account for eternal motion in a manner like the primary Movent.

The second solution is that embraced by Aristotle. In effect, the first could not be squared with the conception of the diversity of the various eternal motions of the different spheres. The eternal motion of the different spheres was, in fact, according to the opinion of the astronomers, different and nonuniform, with the goal of producing, by combining in various ways, the motion of the planets (which is not a perfectly circular motion). Therefore it could not be grasped (it would be incomprehensible) that from the motion of the first heaven could be derived different motions or the others could be derived from a uniform attraction of a single Movent. Here is why Aristotle introduces the multiplicity of movents, which he understood as capable of moving as God moves; that is to say, as *final causes* (as final causes relative to the individual ensouled celestial spheres).

On the basis, then, of the calculations of an astronomer of his time, Callippus, and by working with some corrections that he found necessary, Aristotle established the number of the spheres as fifty-five, admitting, still, a possible diminution to forty-seven. And if such is the number of the spheres, likewise that must be the number of the eternal and immobile Movents that account for their eternal rotational movement. God or the primary Movent accounts for the eternal rotational movement of the first sphere, the outermost sphere, the other fifty-five supersensible substances account for the eternal rotational motion of the other fifty-five spheres.[64]

Is this view of Aristotle's a form of polytheism?

For Aristotle, just as for Plato, and in general for the Greeks, the Divine designated a wide area, in which, under various titles, as the readers of this *History of Ancient Philosophy* already well know, many and different realities enter. The Divine for the Naturalists included structurally many entities. The same holds for Plato; for example, the Ideas of the Good and the Beautiful are divine and, in general, all the Ideas; the Demiurge is divine; souls are divine; the stars are divine and the world is divine. Analogously, for Aristotle, the supersensible immobile Movents of the heavens are divine; the stars are divine; the astral beings and the spheres and the aither (or quintessence) that constitutes them are divine; and the intellective soul of human beings is divine. In sum, all that which is eternal and incorruptible is divine. The Greek (and in this work we have fully shown also this point) does not have a sense of the antithesis of the unity and multiplicity of the divine; and hence it is a purely contingent fact that the question has been explicitly stated in those terms.

Given all of this, and the *mental set* [*forma mentis*] of the Greeks, the existence of fifty-five supersensible substances besides the primary one; that is, besides the immobile Movent, must seem a thing less strange than it does to us. Consequently, based on this understanding we must say that there is undeniably an attempt at unification on the part of Aristotle. First of all he has explicitly called with the term *God* in the strongest sense only the primary Movent. In the same place where he espoused the doctrine of the plurality of the movents, Aristotle points out the unicity of the primary Movent–God in the true and proper sense–and from this unicity deduces also the unicity of the world. And the theological book of the *Metaphysics*, as is known, closed with the solemn affirmation that things do not claim to be badly governed by a multiplicity of Principles, the notion of which was sealed, almost to give greater solemnity, from an important verse of Homer: "Government by the many is not good, one alone should be in charge."[65]

It is clear, consequently, that Aristotle can have conceived the other immobile substances which move the individual celestial spheres only as hierarchically inferior to the primary immobile Movent. And in effect, their hierarchy results from the data about the order of the spheres that move the heavens. Therefore the movents of the fifty-five spheres are inferior to the primary Movent and further they are hierarchically organized each with respect to the other.[66] This explains well how they can be individual substances different from one another; they are purely immaterial forms, one inferior to the other. However they are each in their way inferior Gods.

In Aristotle there is therefore a kind of monotheism derivable from the orientation of his reasoning rather than one present literally in the text. It is a necessary conclusion, because Aristotle tried to separate clearly the primary Movent from the others, by positing it on a totally different level; in order to be able to legitimately call it one and from this unicity to deduce the unicity of the world. But this necessity is fragile because the fifty-five movent substances are equally eternal immaterial substances that *do not depend on the primary Movent for their being*. The Aristotelian God *is not the creator* of the fifty-five movent intelligences; and from this arises the difficulties that we have been discussing.

The Stagirite, then, has left completely unexplained the precise relationship existing between God and these substances and, also, between these substances and the spheres that they move. The Middle Ages will transform these substances into the famous movers or "angelic intelligences," but it could work this transformation precisely in virtue of the concept of creation.

13. God and the world

God (and speaking of God we allude to the primary Movent), as we will see, knows and contemplates Himself. Does He also know the world and the men who are in the world? Aristotle has not supplied a clear solution to this question either; and he seems at least in a certain measure to be inclined toward the negative.

What the world is and what are the universal Principles of the world is a knowledge that the Aristotelian God certainly possess. On the other hand, if God is Himself a highest Principle, it is clear; also that He must know Himself as such, He will know; that is, Himself, as the object of love and attraction of the whole universe.

It is certain, yet, *that the individuals as such*, viz., in their limitations, deficiencies, and poverty, are not known to God, since this knowledge of the imperfect, in the eyes of Aristotle would represent a *diminution* for God. Here is the most eloquent texts:

> Further, whether its substance is the faculty of knowing or the act of knowing, what does it know? Either itself or something else; and if something else, either the same always or something different. Does it matter, then, or not, whether it knows the good or any chance thing? Are there not some things about which it is incredible that it should know? Evidently, then, it knows that which is most divine and precious, and it does not change; for change would be change for the worse, and this would be already a movement.[67]

And immediately afterward, by demonstrating that the Divine intelligence is in its very nature act, the Stagirite adds:

> First...if it is not the act of knowing but a capacity, it would be reasonable to suppose that the continuity of its thinking is wearisome to it. Secondly, there would evidently be something else more precious than knowing, viz., that which is known. For both knowing and the act of knowing will belong even to one who has the worst of knowledges. There if this ought to be avoided (and it ought, for there are even some things which it is better not to see than to see), the act of knowing cannot be the best of things. Therefore it must be itself that knowing knows (since it is the most excellent of things), and its knowing is a knowing of knowing.[68]

From these passages it would seem, therefore, to be concluded that the concrete individual, according to Aristotle, is unworthy, precisely in his individuality, of being the object of the divine knowledge.

Another limitation of the Aristotelian God–which has the same foundation as the preceding one; since *He does not create* the world, man, individual souls–consists in the fact that He is the object of love, but He does not love (or, better, He loves only himself). Individuals, as such, are not precisely the object of the divine love; God does not incline toward *individual human beings*. Each of them, as each individual thing, inclines in various ways toward God, but God, since He cannot know them as individuals, cannot love any individual human beings.[69]

This state of affairs occurred because the notion of creation had not been achieved, but Greek speculation never did attain such a notion, not even the Neoplatonists.[70]

II. PHYSICS

1. The characterization of Aristotelian physics

The second theoretical science for Aristotle is *physics* or "second philosophy," which has as its object the inquiry into *sensible realities*, intrinsically characterized by movement, just as metaphysics has as its object the supersensible realities, intrinsically characterized by the absolute absence of motion.[1]

The distinction between a metaphysical problematic and a physical problematic is imposed structurally as a result of the acquisitions of the Platonic Second Voyage; if there are two levels of reality or, to express it in more Aristotelian terms, if there exists two different genera of substances structurally distinct, the genus of the supersensible and the genus of the sensible, then the sciences having these two different realities as the object of their inquiry likewise will necessarily be different. The distinction between metaphysics and physics will involve the definitive overcoming of the limitation of the philosophy of the Presocratics and it will also involve a radical change in the ancient meaning of *physis*, which will now signify sensible being, rather than signifying the totality of being, and *nature* will be said chiefly of *sensible nature*[2] (but a sensible thing in which the form is the dominant principle).[3]

The modern reader can be deceived by the word *physics*; for us, in fact, physics is identified with the science of nature understood as Galileo did, viz., quantitatively. Aristotle, instead, is in the opposite direction, his is not a quantitative science of nature, but a *qualitative* one; compared to modern physics, the physics of Aristotle is more than a *science*, it is an *ontology or metaphysics of the sensible*. We find, in sum, in it a *viewpoint of nature that is totally philosophical*; and this outlook, moreover, will endure up to the Galilean revolution.

It will, therefore, come as no surprise to find abundant physical considerations (in the sense defined) of a metaphysical nature in the books of the Metaphysics, and vice versa, in the books of the Physics abundant considerations of a metaphysical character, since the spheres of the two sciences are structurally interdependent. The supersensible is a cause or reason of the sensible, and the supersensible completes both the metaphysical inquiry, and (even if in a different sense) the inquiry of the physics itself. In addition, the methodology applied in the two sciences is identical. Moreover, the exposition that follows–which for reasons of space is limited only to some of the basic issues–will adequately demonstrate this point.

2. Change and movement

We have said that the essential characteristic of nature is movement, and to the analysis of movement and its causes Aristotle dedicated, consequently, a great deal of the *Physics*.[4]

What is movement? We already know what movement is although it becomes a philosophical problem only after it was denied by the Eleatics, to whom it appears as an illusion; that is, about which no consistent *logos* can be given. We also know already about movement from the Pluralists, for whom it was partially recovered and partially justified. However, no one, not even Plato, up to this point in time, knew how to establish its essence and its metaphysical status.

The Eleatics had rejected becoming and movement because on the basis of their basic position, they could only be supported by giving being to *not-being* (becoming in general involves a passage from either being to *not-being* or from *not-being* to being, in either case the admission of *not-being* is required, so for example, birth and death would be passages from not-being alive to being alive and from being alive to not-being alive), but of course, *not-being simply is not*. The solution of the aporia is achieved by Aristotle in the most brilliant manner.

First, movement is a datum that is experientially undeniable, hence it cannot be placed in doubt. But how can it be justified? We know (from metaphysics) that being *has many meanings* and that a group of these meanings goes back to the pair *being as potency* and *being as act*. With respect to being-in-act, being-in-potency can be said to be not-being, precisely not-being-in-act; but it is clear that this is a relative not-being, since *potency is being*, because it is a positive capacity to become actual. Consequently, coming to the point that is of interest to us, *movement or change in general is precisely the passage from potential being to actual being* (movement is the actualization of that which is potential insofar as it is potential, says Aristotle).[5] Therefore, movement does not precisely suppose the Parmenidean not-being, because it develops within being and it is the passage from being (potential) to being (actual); and with this account movement was rescued definitively from the grip of not-being, which was the reason that the Eleatics believed they had to reject it, and it is thus fundamentally accounted for by Aristotle's metaphysical doctrine of act and potency.

But Aristotle supplied further analyses about movement that are of capital importance, by establishing the nature of all the possible forms of movement and their metaphysical structure.

Let us go back to the original distinction of the various meanings of being. We have seen that potency and act involve the various categories and not only the first of them. Consequently, also movement, which is a passage from potency to act, will *concern the various categories* (all the categories or at least the principal ones).⁶ For this reason it is possible to figure out the various forms of change. Some of the categories actually do not involve change. This is true for example for the category of relation, because it is sufficient if one of the two terms of the relation is changed since the other will be also, so even though remaining unchanged the relation will be changed (and hence if we admit movement according to relation, then we will have to admit the absurdity of a movement without movement; that is, for the second term). The categories of *action and passion* are already themselves movements and it is not possible to have movement of a movement. Finally, also the *when* or *time*, as we have already seen, is a specification of movement. There remain, therefore, the categories (*a*) of *substance*, (*b*) of *quality*, (*c*) of *quantity*, (*d*) of *place*, and it is precisely according to these categories that change takes place. Change according to substance is *generation and corruption*. Change according to quality is *alteration*. Change according to quantity is *augmentation and diminution*. Movement according to place is *local motion*. *Change* is a generic term that may be used for all of these forms and for any one of the four forms. *Movement* is instead a term that designates the last three and particularly the final one.⁷

In all its forms becoming supposes a substrate (which is a potential being), which passes from one opposite to the other opposite; in the first category, form passes from one contradictory to the other contradictory, and in the other three forms from one contrary to the other contrary. Generation is the taking on of form by matter, corruption is the loss of the form. Alteration is a change of quality, whereas augmentation and diminution are a passage from small to large and vice versa. Local motion is a passage from one place to another. Only the composite (the *synolon*) of matter and form can change because only matter implies potentiality; the hylomorphic structure of sensible reality necessarily implies matter, therefore potentiality is the root of every change and movement.⁸

These considerations are related to the problem of the four causes already known to us. Matter and form are the intrinsic causes of becoming. The external causes are instead the movent, agent, or efficient cause. No change within nature takes place without this cause, because there cannot be any passage from potency to act without that which is *a movent already in act*. Finally we must take up the final cause, which is the goal and the reason for becoming. The final cause indicates essentially the positive sense of every becoming that in Aristotle's eyes is fundamentally a progress toward the form and a realization of the form. Far from being a movement toward nothing, becoming appears to Aristotle as the path to the fullness of being; that is, the way that things move toward their full actuation, to be fully that which they are, to fulfill their essence or form (and in that sense it is easy to understand why the Aristotelian *physis* is, in the ultimate analysis, this form).⁹

In this regard it is to be noted that Aristotelian theology is incomplete, not simply through the limitations that he expressly makes in some famous passages of the *Physics*,[10] but by reason of the basic unresolved metaphysical aporia; that is, that the world exists not through a plan of the Divine, but by an almost mechanical and necessary attraction of all things for perfection, which is intuited and affirmed by the Stagirite but is not rigorously justified. The late Plato, with the doctrine of the Demiurge of the *Timaeus*, had seen more deeply into the basic reason for universal finality; and, indeed, either we admit a Being who plans the world and who made it to be in function of the good and the best, or universal finality cannot be supported.

3.   Place and the void

Connected to the concept of movement is the concepts of *place, void,* and *time*.[11] Objects are not in not-being, which does not exist, but are in a *where*, viz., a *place*, which, therefore, is something that is. Place exists and it is, therefore, undoubtedly a reality, if we advert to the fact that there is a reciprocal replacement of bodies (in the container where once there was water, when it leaves, air enters, and, in general, a different body always occupies the same place that was occupied by a body that moves out, by substituting for it): "So that clearly the place or space into which and out which they passed was something different from both."[12]

In addition, experience shows that a "natural place" exists to which each of the elements tends, when they are not impeded; fire and air tend toward the *heights*, earth and water toward the *depths*. High and low are not something relative to us, but something objective and are natural determinations: "It is not every chance direction which is up, but where fire and what is light are carried."[13]

What is the nature of *place*? A first characterization Aristotle achieves by distinguishing between the place common to many things and the place proper to each object: "Place, on the other hand, is common and in which all bodies are, on the other hand, it is that particularly in which a bodies is immediately...and if place is that which immediately contains each body, it will be, then, *a kind of limit*."[14] Furthermore, Aristotle states that: "place is what contains that of which it is the place and which is not part of the thing it contains."[15] By uniting the two characterizations he defines place as: "the limit of the containing body, insofar as it is in contact with the contained body."[16]

Finally Aristotle states again that *place* is not to be confused with the *container,* the first is immobile whereas the second is mobile; it is possible to state in a certain sense that place is the immobile container whereas the container is a mobile place:

> Just as the vessel is a transportable place, so also place is a vessel which cannot be transported. So when what is within a thing which is moved, is

moved and changes, as a boat on a river, what contains plays the part of a vessel rather than that of place. Place, on the other hand, is rather what is motionless; therefore, it is the whole river that is place, because as a whole it is motionless. Therefore *place is the first immobile limit of what contains a thing.*[17]

This very famous definition the medievals would keep secure in the famous formula: *terminus continentis immobilis primus* [*the first immobile limit of that which contains*].

And from this definition of place it follows that a *place outside of the universe* is inconceivable or a place in which the universe exists as in a container:

But prescinding from the whole universe, there is nothing outside of the whole universe, and for this reason all things are in the heaven; for the heaven, we may say, is the whole universe! The heaven, instead, is not a place, but, we may say, the extremity of the heaven, and it is [an immobile limit] contiguous with mobile body; and for this reason the earth is in water, and this is the air, and the air in the aither, and the aither in the heaven; *but the heaven is not in anything else.*[18]

And just as the movement of the heaven as a totality is possible only in the sense of a rotational motion, so there is no place for it to move in the sense of local motion. In a place is–note–all that which is moved (and what is moved tends to go toward its natural place); that which is immobile is not in a place, God and the other movent intelligences do not structurally need a place.

From the definition of place Aristotle has given, the impossibility of a void also follows. The void was intended as a "place in which there is nothing" or "a place in which there is no body."[19] But it is obvious that a *place in which there is nothing* due to the definition given of place as a *terminus continentis* [as a container] is a contradiction in terms. And so the notion of place destroys the chief presupposition on which the Abderite had constructed the doctrine of the atoms and the mechanistic conception of the universe.

4. Time

Aristotle had dedicated a profound analysis to the concept of *time* that even anticipated some concepts that Saint Augustine was to develop and make famous.[20] Here is the focal point of the Aristotelian doctrine of time:

That it [time] does not exist or that its existence is obscure and barely recognizable, can be suspected from the following considerations. One part of it has been and is not, while the other is going to be and is not yet. Yet time is made up of these, both in its infinity and any you may wish to take. It would seem impossible that it is composed of non-existents, possesses any being. Further, if a divisible thing is to exist, it is necessary that, when it exists, all or some of its parts must exist. But of time some parts have been, while others are going to be, and no part of it is, though it is divisible into parts. For the "now" is not a part of time; in fact a part has a limit, and the whole must be composed of its parts, while time does not seem to be made up of "nows".[21]

What then is the nature of time? Aristotle asks the question to solve the difficulty in function of two points of reference; *movement* and the *soul*. If both are prescinded, the nature of time is impossible to state.

First, time is not movement nor change but it essentially implies movement and change: "The existence of time...is not...possible without change; when, in fact, nothing changes within our mind or we do not notice it, it does not seem that time has elapsed at all."[22] Since time strictly implies movement, it can be maintained as an affection or a *property of movement*. What is this property? Movement that is always movement through continuous place is itself consequently continuous, and time also must be continuous since the quantity of time that passes is always proportioned to the movement. A *before* and *after* is distinguished in the continuous that consequently has a correspondence in movement and hence in time: "When we have marked a movement according to the distinction of 'before' and 'after,' we also recognize time, and then we say that time has elapsed *when we have perceived before and after in motion*."[23]

Here is the well known definition of time: "Time is the numbering of a motion with respect to 'before' and 'after'."[24]

Consequently, the perception of the *before* and the *after* and hence of the numbering of a motion *necessarily presupposes soul*: "When we think of the extremes as different from the middle and the *soul prompts us that the 'nows' are two*, one *before* and one *after*, it is then that we say that time exists between these two 'nows,' since time would be what is specified by the 'now' and this is like its foundation."[25]

But if the soul is the rational principle that calculates and hence the condition of the distinction of that which numbers and that which is numbered, then the soul is the *necessary condition* of time itself; and it is well to grasp the aporia that Aristotle comes to grip with in this passage of unmeasurable historical importance:

> Whether...time would exist if soul did not exist could be a difficulty. In fact, if the existence of the one who enumerates is not admitted, it is also impossible for the numerable to exist, because obviously, there would be no number. Number, in fact, is either what has been or can be numbered. *But it is true that in the nature of things only the soul or the mind which in the soul has the capacity to enumerate, so the existence of time without that of the soul is impossible.*[26]

This conception is strongly anticipatory of the Augustinian perspective and of the spiritual conception of time that only recently has been given the attention it deserves.

Aristotle was quite specific that to number motion it is necessary to have a unit of measure, just as it is necessary to have a unit of measure to measure anything. This must be sought in the uniform and perfect motion; and since the only uniform and perfect motion is circular; consequently that unit of measure is the rotational movement of the spheres and of celestial bodies.[27] God and the movent intelligences, just as they are outside of place insofar as they are immobile are also outside of time.

5. The infinite

Finally we have to say something about the concept of the *infinite*.[28] Aristotle denies that an *actual infinite exists*. When we speak of the infinite he understand chiefly an *infinite body*; and the arguments that he adduces against the existence of an actual infinite are precisely against the existence of an infinite body. The infinite exists *only as potency or in potency*. The potential infinite is, for example, a number, since it is always possible to add to some number a further number without coming to an extreme limit beyond which it would not be possible to proceed. Space is also the potential infinite, since it is infinitely divisible insofar as the result of the division is always a magnitude that is further divisible. Finally, time is also the potential infinite whose moments (units) cannot exist together actually, but time does go on endlessly.

Aristotle does not in any way foresee the idea that *the infinite could be immaterial*, precisely because he locates the infinite within the category of quantity, which only holds for the sensible. This also explains why he ends up supporting definitively the Pythagorean notion (and in general almost all the Greeks support it) according to which the finite is perfect and the infinite is imperfect. Aristotle says in an exemplary passage:

> The infinite is...if we take it as a quantity, that to which it is always possible to add something else. On the other hand, what has nothing outside it is complete and whole. For thus we define the whole, that from which nothing is lacking, as for example, a whole man or box. What is true of each particular is true of the whole properly speaking, the whole is that of which nothing is outside; but that from which something is lacking and outside, however small that may be, is not "whole." Instead, the "whole" and "complete" are either identical in every respect or something quite similar in nature. But nothing is complete which has no end and the end is a limit.[29]

This makes quite understandable the reason why Aristotle necessarily must deny that God is infinite. More than ever, after this theorizing about the infinite as potentiality and imperfection, the ancient intuition of the Milesians, of Melissus, and of Anaxagoras, which conceived the Absolute as infinite, must be obliterated; it must be judged idiosyncratic with respect to the thought of all the Greeks and to be recovered it must await the discovery of a further metaphysical areas of interest.

6.   The "fifth essence" and the division of the sublunar world and the heavens

Aristotle distinguished sensible realities into two clearly differentiated spheres: on the one hand the so-called sublunary world and on the other, the superlunary world or the celestial, and as we have hinted at before, the metaphysical. Here we must further clarify the reasons for the divisions.

The sublunary world is characterized by all the forms of change among which predominate generation and corruption. Instead the heavens are characterized by only local motion, and precisely by circular movement. In the celestial spheres and in the astrals there can be no place, no generation, no corruption, no alteration, no augmentation, no diminution (in all ages men have always seen the heavens just as we see them; therefore, it is the same experience that says that they were never born and just as they were never born so also are they indestructible). The difference between the superlunary world and that of the sublunary that is equally sensible is nothing other than the difference in the matter out of which they are constituted:

> Nor does eternal movement, if there such, exist potentially; and, if there is an eternal movent, it is not potentially in motion (except in respect of "whence" and "wither"; there is nothing to prevent its having matter for this). Therefore the sun and the stars and the whole heaven are ever active, and there is no fear that they may sometime stand still, as the natural philosophers fear they may. Nor do they tire in this activity; for movement does not imply for them, as it does for perishable things, the potentiality for opposites, so that the continuity of the movement should be laborious; for it is that kind of substance which is matter and potentiality, not actuality, that causes this.[30]

This matter, which is in potency to contraries, is determined by the four elements (earth, water, air, and fire) that Aristotle against the Eleaticizing Empedocles, considers transformable one into the other precisely to give a reason at bottom for what Empedocles could not explain of generation and corruption. Instead, the other matter that possesses only the potency of passing from one place to another and that hence is susceptible of receiving only local motion, is called *aither*, simply because it runs always (ἀεὶ θεῖν).[31] It was also called "fifth essence" because it was added to the four essences of the other elements (earth, water, air, and fire).[32] And while the movement characteristic of the four elements is rectilinear (the heavy elements are moved from high to low, the lighter ones from low to high), that of the aither is instead circular (*aither* is not therefore either heavy or light). Aither is ungenerated, incorruptible, not subject to increase and to alteration, not to any other affections that imply these changes, and it is for this reason that the heavens that are constituted of aither are incorruptible.

This doctrine of Aristotle will be accepted by medieval thought, and only at the beginning of the modern age will the distinction between the sublunary world and the superlunary world fall together with the presupposition on which it was supported.

We have said at the beginning that Aristotelian physics (and also a great part of the cosmology) is really a metaphysics of the sensible and hence it is no surprise to the reader that the *Physics* is full of metaphysical considerations and even culminates with the demonstration of the existence of a primary immobile Movent. Fundamentally convinced that "if there are no eternal entities there would not exist any becoming,"[33] the Stagirite has crowned his physical inquiries by demonstrating in detail the existence of this principle. Once again the result of the Platonic Second Voyage is shown to be absolutely determinative.

III. PSYCHOLOGY

1. The Aristotelian concept of the soul

The Aristotelian physics does not inquire only into nature in general and its principles, the physical universe and its structure, but likewise the beings that are in the universe, those that are inanimate, those that are animate without reason, and these that are animated beings with reason (human beings). To the animated beings the Stagirite dedicated a very close attention, by composing an enormous quantity of treatises, among which stand out for profundity, originality, and speculative value the famous treatise *On the Soul*,[1] which now we must analyze (the greater part of the other treatises contain doctrines that are of more interest to the history of science, than to the history of philosophy).[2]

The animate beings are differentiated from inanimate beings *because they possess a principle that gives them their life* and *this principle is soul*. What is the nature of the soul?

Aristotle, to respond to the question, refers to his hylomorphic metaphysical conception of natural things. All things in general are a *synolon* of *matter* and *form* and the matter is potency whereas the form is *entelechy* or *act*. This holds naturally also for living beings. Now, the Stagirite observes that living bodies *have* life but *are not* life; and therefore they are like the material substrate and potentiality of which the soul is form and act. Aristotle writes: "It is necessary, hence, that soul is substance as form of a natural body potentially having life. But substance as form is *entelechy* [= act]. Soul hence is *entelechy* of a body as characterized above."[3] Hence, soul is the first *entelechy* (ἐντελέχεια ἡ πρώτη) of a natural body potentially having life.[4] "If we must give a definition which is correct for each kind of soul, it would be necessary to say that it is the first entelechy of a natural body having organs."[5]

It is clear, first, already from this simple definition that the Aristotelian *psyché* is presented with new characteristics both with respect to that of the Presocratic *psyché*, because this was identified more with a physical principle, or generally reduced to an aspect of it; and with respect to the Platonic *psyché* conceived dualistically as opposed to the body and incapable of an harmonic reconciliation with it, since the body was seen as prison and a place of expiation of the soul. (After the *Phaedo* Plato will understand the soul as a principle of motion, by tempering but not overcoming the whole of his original position.) Aristotle takes an intermediate position, by unifying the first two points of view and attempting a mediating synthesis, as moreover he tried to make in the solution of all speculative problems. The Presocratics are correct in seeing the soul as something intrinsically united to the body, but Plato is also correct in seeing in it an ideal nature; it is not therefore simply a reality existing in itself irreconcilable with the body, but it is a form, an act, or an *entelechy* of the body. It is the intelligible principle that structuring the body makes it to be that which it must always be. And with this is preserved the *unity of the living being*.

But the substantial Platonic discovery of transcendence, just as it is preserved in the metaphysics with the doctrine of the immobile Movent, is not lost even in the psychology, since Aristotle did not consider the soul as *absolutely immanent*. The intuitive thought, the speculation that reaches to the knowledge of the immaterial and eternal, which carries man, if only for brief moments, almost to touch divinity, *evidently is but the prerogative of something in us that is congenital, or akin to that which is known, as Plato had demonstrated in the Phaedo*. And so Aristotle, at the price of leaving an aporia unresolved, does not hesitate to affirm the necessity that a part of the soul is "separable." Here are the most significant passages in this regard:

> There is no doubt that the soul is not separable from the body, or at least certain of its parts are not, if it is by nature divisible; in fact, the entelechy of some part of it are the *entelechy* of the corresponding parts of the body. But nothing prevents that there be some parts which are separable, because they are not the *entelechies* of any body at all.[6]

> With respect to the mind or the theoretical capacity, nothing in a certain respect is clear; it would seem that *it is a different kind of soul and it alone can be separated from the body as the eternal is from the corruptible*. On the contrary, the other parts of the soul it is clear...are not separables.[7]

Again in the *Metaphysics* he clearly says: "But we must examine whether any form also survives [corruption] afterwards. For there is nothing to prevent that the soul may be of this sort–not the whole soul but only mind; for doubtless it is impossible that all soul should survive but only the intellective part."[8] As can be seen the results of the Second Voyage are to be found here further and fully confirmed.

2. The tripartition of the soul

But to basically understand the meaning of these affirmations we must first examine the general doctrine of the soul and the meaning of the famous threefold distinction of the "parts" or "functions" of the soul. Plato had already beginning from the *Republic* spoken of the three parts or functions of the *psyché*, distinguishing a *concupiscible* [*thumos*] soul, an *irascible* [*epithumos*] soul, and an *intellective* [*logistikon*] soul; but such a tripartition, based fundamentally on the analysis of the ethical behavior of man and introduced to explain it, has very little in common with the Aristotelian tripartition, which arises instead from a general analysis of living things and their essential functions and hence on the terrain of biology rather than psychology. Since the phenomena of life–as Aristotle reasons–supposes determinate and constant operations clearly differentiated (to the point that some of them can exist in some beings without the others), then also the soul, which is the principle of life, must have the capacities or functions or parts that are in charge of these operations and ruled them. And since the basic phenomena and the functions of life are (*a*) of a vegetative character, as birth, nutrition, and growth; (*b*) of a movent sensorial nature, as sensation and movement; (*c*) of an intellectual character, as knowledge, deliberation, and choice; consequently, that is why, for the reasons clarified earlier, Aristotle introduces the distinctions of (*a*) a vegetative soul and (*b*) a sentient soul, and (*c*) an intellectual or rational soul. The Stagirite writes: "The powers of the soul about which we have spoken are found...some beings have all of them, some beings have only some of them, and still others have only one of them." [9]

Consequently the plants possess only the vegetative soul, the animals the vegetative and the sentient, human beings the vegetative, the sentient, and the intellective soul. To possess the rational soul man must possess the other two and just as to possess the sentient soul animals must have the vegetative; yet it is possible to have the vegetative soul without the succeeding ones:

> It is now evident that a single definition can be given of soul only in the same sense as one can be given of figure. For, as in that case there is no figure apart from triangle and those that follow in order, so here there is no soul apart from the forms of soul just enumerated. It is true that a common definition can be given for figure which will fit all figures without expressing the peculiar nature of any figure. So here in the case of soul and its specific forms. Hence it is absurd in this and similar cases to look for a common definition which will not express the peculiar nature of anything that is and will not apply to the appropriate indivisible species, while at the same time omitting to look for an account which will. The cases of figure and soul are exactly parallel; for the particulars subsumed under the common name in both cases–figures and living beings–constitute a series, each successive terms of which potentially contains its predecessor, e.g., the square the triangle, the sensory power the self-nutritive. Hence we must ask in the case of each order of living things, What is its soul, i.e., What is the soul of plan, man, beast? Why the terms are related in this serial way must form the subject of examination. For the power of perception is never found apart from the power of self-nutrition, while–in plants–the latter is found isolated from the former. Again, no sense is found apart from that of touch, while touch is found by itself; many animals have neither sight, hearing, nor smell. Again, among living things that possess sense some have the power of locomotion, some not. Lastly, certain living beings–a small minority–possess calculation and thought, for (among mortal beings) those which possess calculation have all the other powers earlier-mentioned, while the converse does not hold–indeed some live by imagination alone, while others have not even imagination. *Reflective thought presents a different problem.*[10]

Among the three souls, therefore, there is a distinction more than a separation: "...the division which the soul admits—writes Ross—is not that of qualitatively different parts, but in each part it has the qualities of the whole. The soul, in fact, although Aristotle does not say it, is a *homoemeria,* as a whole and not as an organ. And though he frequently uses the traditional expression 'parts of the soul,' the word that he prefers is faculty.' "[11]

Exact observations, we will see, clarify some things, but accentuate the aporetic character of certain others; in particular it make problematic the relation between the intellective soul and the others. Moreover, in the passage read, Aristotle himself is emphasizing that for the theoretical intellect the argument is different.

Let us consider the three functions of the soul individually.

3.   The vegetative soul

The vegetative soul is the most elementary principle of life, and since the most elementary phenomena of life are, as we have already pointed out, generation, nutrition, and growth, just so the vegetative soul is the principle that governs generation, nutrition, and growth. And just as clearly, the explanation of the vital processes, which the Naturalists give, is surpassed. The cause of growth is not fire or heat or in general matter; fire and heat are moreover cocauses and not the true causes. In any process of nutrition and growth a rule is present that apportions magnitude and increase, which fire of itself cannot produce and which therefore would be unexplained without something other than fire; that is, without the soul. So also the phenomena of nutrition consequently cease to be explained as the mechanical play of relations between similar elements and similar elements (as some have maintained) or among certain contrary elements; nutrition is the assimilation of the dissimilar and becomes possible always from the soul by means of heat: "The process of nutrition involves three factors, what is fed, that wherewith it is fed, and what does the feeding; of these what feeds is the first soul, what is fed is the body which has that soul in it, and that with which it is fed is the food."[12]

Finally, the vegetative soul governs reproduction, which is the goal of every form of life ending in time. In fact, every form of life even the most elementary is made for eternity and not for death. Aristotle writes:

> The acts in which it manifests itself are reproduction and the use of food, because for any living thing that has reached its normal development and which is unmutilated, and whose mode of generation is not spontaneous, the most natural act is the production of another like itself, an animal producing an animal, a plant a plant, in order that, as far as its nature allows, it may partake in the eternal and divine. That is the goal towards which all things strive, that for the sake of which they do whatsoever their nature renders possible....Since then no living thing is able to partake in what is eternal and divine by uninterrupted continuance for nothing perishable can for ever remain one and the same, it tries to achieve that end in the only way

possible to it, and success is possible in varying degrees; so it remains not indeed as the self-same individual but continues its existence in something like itself–not numerically but specifically one.[13]

Also the most insignificant vegetable, therefore, by reproducing itself tries to be eternal, and the vegetative soul is the principle that at the lowest level makes possible this perpetuation in perpetuity.

4. The sentient soul

Animals, besides the functions examined in the preceding section, possess *sensations, appetites,* and *movement*; therefore it will necessarily admit a further principle that has control over these functions and this is the *sentient soul.*

Let us begin with the first function of the sensitive soul; that is, *sensation,* which in a certain sense among the three just distinguished is that most important and certainly the most characteristic. Some of the predecessors of Aristotle had explained sensation as an affection, or passion, or alteration in which the similar submits to the similar (see, for example, Empedocles and Democritus), others as an action in which the similar submits to the dissimilar. Aristotle took the hint from these attempts, but went beyond them. The key to the interpretation of sensation is found once again *in the metaphysical doctrine of potency and act.* We have a sentient faculty that is not in act, but in potency; that is, a capacity of receiving sensations. They are like the combustible that does not burn except through contact with what is burning. So the sentient faculty from the simple capacity of sensing becomes sensing in act through contact with the sensible object as long as there is nothing intervening:

> Everything that is acted upon or moved is acted upon by an agent which is actually at work. Hence it is that in one sense, as has already been stated, what acts and what is acted upon are like, in another unlike; for the unlike is affected, and when it has been affected it is like.[14]

> As we have said, what has the power of sensation is potentially like what the perceived object is actually; that is, while the beginning of the process of its being acted upon the two interacting factors are dissimilar, at the end the one acted upon is assimilated to the other and is identical in quality with it.[15]

The interpretation proposed by Ross is correct therefore: "Sensation is not an alteration of the type of a simple substitution of one state with its contrary, but of the type of a fulfillment of a potency, of progression of something towards itself and towards actuality."[16]

But–it will be asked–what does it mean to say that sensation is *being made similar* to the sensible? It is evidently not a process of assimilation of the type that takes place in nutrition; in the assimilation of nutrition, in fact, the matter is also assimilated, instead in sensation only the form is assimilated. Aristotle expressly writes:

> Generally, about all perception, we can say that *a sense is what has the power of receiving into itself the sensible forms of things without the matter*, in the way in which a piece of wax takes on the impress of a signet-ring without the iron or gold; in a similar way the sense is affected by what is colored or flavored or sounding not insofar as each is what it is, but insofar as it is of such and such a sort and according to its form.[17]

The Stagirite passes then to the analysis of the five senses and the sensibles that are proper to cach of these senses. When a sense grasps the *proper sensible*, then the related sensation is infallible. In addition to the proper sensibles there are also the common sensibles that, as for example *motion, rest, shape,* and *magnitude*, are not perceived by any of the five senses in particular, but can be perceived by all of them:

> Further, there cannot be a special sense-organ for the common sensibles either; that is, the objects which we perceive incidentally through this or that special sense, for example, movement, rest, figure, magnitude, number, unity; for all these we perceive by movement, for example, magnitude by movement, and therefore also figure (for figure is a species of magnitude), what is at rest by the absence of movement: number is perceived by the negation of continuity, and by the special sensibles; for each sense perceives one class of sensible objects. So that it is clearly impossible that there should be a special sense for any one of the common sensibles.[18]

By considering these clarifications, we can speak of a "common sense" (and Aristotle in effect speaks of it) that is like a nonspecific sense or, better yet, it is a sense that acts in a nonspecific manner. In the first place, precisely in the passage read, sensation is seen grasping in a nonspecific way the common sensibles. In addition, we can undoubtedly speak of a common sense with respect to the sensing of sensing or the perception of that which is sensed, or also when we distinguish or compare the sensibles.

On the basis of these distinctions Aristotle established that the senses are infallible when they grasp the objects that are proper to them, but they are only so in this case. Here is a quite famous passage in which this doctrine is formulated:

> Perception of the special objects of sense is never in error or admits the least possible amount of falsehood. Next comes perception that what is incidental to the objects of perception is incidental to them: in this case certainly we may be deceived; for while the perception that there is white before us cannot be false, the perception that what is white is this or that may be false. Third comes the perception of the common attributes...for example, of movement and magnitude; it is in respect of these that the greatest amount of sense-illusion is possible.[19]

Imagination is derived from sensation that is a production of images and *memory* that is the preservation of images (and from the accumulation of mnemonic facts derive further *experiences*).

The other two functions of the sentient soul we have mentioned at the beginning of the section are *appetite and movement*. Appetite consequently arises from sensation:

> Plants have none but the first, the nutritive, while another order of living things has this plus the sensory. If any other order of living things has the sensory, it must also have the appetitive; for appetite is the genus of which desire, passion, and wish are the species; now all animals have one sense at least, viz., touch, and whatever has a sense has the capacity for pleasure and pain and therefore has pleasant and painful objects present to it, and wherever these are present, there is desire, for desire is appetition of what is pleasant.[20]

Movement of living beings, finally, is derived from desire: " The movent is single, the appetitive faculty" [21] and precisely desire is "a species of appetite." [22] Desire is put in motion by the object desired that the animal grasps by means of sensations and of which generally he has a sensible representation. Appetite and movement depend therefore strictly on sensation.

5. The rational soul

As sensibility is not reducible to simple vegetative life or to the principle of nutrition but contains a *plus* that cannot be explained except by the introduction of a further principle beyond the sentient soul, so thought and the operations connected to it like rational choice are irreducible to sentient life and to sensibility, but it contains a *plus* that is not explained except by the introduction of a further principle, the *rational soul*. Concerning this principle we must now speak.

The intellective act is analogous to the perceptual act insofar as it is a reception or assimilation of the intelligible sensed forms, just as sensation was an assimilation of the sensible form but it differs profoundly from the perceptive act because it is not mixed with the body or the corporeal. And here is how Aristotle characterized the mind or intellect in one of the most sublime pages that ever issued from his pen, in which the ancient intuition of Anaxagoras takes definitive form thanks to the categories achieved through the Second Voyage, and consequently they become acquired as an irredeemable possession:

> Turning now to the part of the soul with which the soul knows and (whether this is separable from the others in definition only, or spatially as well) we have to inquire what differentiates this part, and how thinking can take place. If thinking is like perceiving, it must be either a process in which the soul is acted upon by what is capable of being thought, or a process different

from but analogous to that. The thinking part of the soul must therefore be, while impassible, capable of receiving the form of an object; that is, must be potentially identical in character with its object without being the object. Thought must be related to what is thinkable, as sense is to what is sensible. Therefore, since everything is a possible object of thought, mind in order, as Anaxagoras says, to dominate; that is, to know, must be pure from all admixture; for the co-presence of what is alien to its nature is a hindrance and a block: it follows that it can have no nature of its own, other than that of having a certain capacity. Thus that in the soul which is called thought (by thought I mean that whereby the soul thinks and judges) is, before it thinks, not actually any real thing. For this reason it cannot reasonably be regarded as blended with the body; if so, it would acquire some quality, e.g., warmth or cold, or even have an organ like the sensitive faculty: as it is, it has none. It was a good idea to call the soul 'the place of forms,' though this description holds only of the thinking soul, and even this is the forms only potentially, not actually. Observation of the sense-organs and their employment reveals a distinction between the impassibility of the sensitive faculty and that of the faculty of thought. After strong stimulation of a sense we are less able to exercise it than before, as e.g. in the case of a loud sound we cannot hear easily immediately after, or in the case of a bright color or a powerful odor we cannot see or smell, but in the case of thought thinking about an object that is highly thinkable renders it more and not less able afterwards to think of objects that are less thinkable: the reason is that while the faculty of sensation is dependent upon the body, thought is separable from it. When thought has become each thing in the way in which a man who actually knows is said to do so (this happens when he is now able to exercise the power on his own initiative), its condition is still one of potentiality, but in a different sense from the potentiality which preceded the acquisition of knowledge by learning or discovery; and thought is then able to think itself.[23]

Also intellectual knowledge just as sense knowledge is explained by Aristotle in function of the metaphysical categories of *potency* and *act*. The intellective part of the soul is of itself a *capacity*, a *potency* of knowing the intelligible forms. At the same time, the forms are contained in potency in the sensations and in the images of the imagination. It is necessary therefore that something brings into act this twofold potentiality in such a way that thought is actualized by grasping the form; and the form contained in the image becomes an intelligible in the act of being grasped and possessed.

In this way the distinctions arise that became the source of innumerable problems and arguments both in antiquity and in the medieval period about *the-mind-that-makes-all-things* (the *intellect as act*) and *the-mind-that-be-comes-all-things* (the *intellect as potential*) or, to use a terminology that will become canonic (but that is not found in Aristotle except potentially), between the *possible intellect* and the *active intellect*. Let us read a passage that contains this distinction because it will be for centuries a constant point of reference:

Since in every class of things, as in nature as a whole, we find two factors involved, a matter which is potentially all the particulars included in the class, a cause which is productive in the sense that it makes them all (the latter standing to the former, as e.g. an art to its material), these distinct elements must likewise be found *within the soul.* And in fact thought, as we have described it, is what it is by virtue of becoming all things, while there is another which is what it is by virtue of making all things: this is a sort of positive state like light; for in a sense light makes potentially colors into actual colors. Thought in this sense of it is separable, impassible, unmixed, since it is in its essential nature activity (for always the active is superior to the passive factor, the originating force to the matter)....Because *separate, it is alone that which it is, and this alone is immortal and eternal.*[24]

Two affirmations contained in the passage must be emphasized. In the first place is the analogy with light; as colors would not be visible and they could not be seen, except for the presence of light, so also the intelligible forms contained in the sensible images would remain in a potential state and the potential intellect could not in its turn grasp them in act, unless there were an *intelligible light,* which permits the intellect to "see" the intelligible and to see them *in act.* It is an analogy and it is the same analogy with which Plato presented the highest Idea of the Good; but, to explain the highest of the human powers, Aristotle could not present it except as an analogy, precisely because such a power is irreducible to something further and represents an impassible limiting point.

The other affirmation is that this "active intellect" is "in the soul." Hence the interpretations among the ancients fail that maintain that the "agent intellect" is God (or generally a divine and separate Mind) that as we saw in the appropriate place, had characteristics that were necessarily irreconcilable with those of the "agent intellect." And it is true that Aristotle affirms that "the intellect *comes from the outside* and that only it is divine,"[25] whereas the lower powers of the soul are already in potency in the masculine source and thus are passed into the new organism that is formed in the maternal source. But it is likewise true that through coming "from the outside," it stays in the soul (ἐν τῇ ψυχῇ)[26] for all the life of man. The affirmation that the intellect comes *from the outside* means that it is irreducible to the body by its intrinsic nature and that therefore it transcends the sensible. It means that in us is a metaempirical, superphysical, and spiritual aspect. This aspect is the divine in us.

But if the "agent intellect" is not God, he does yet reflect the characteristics of the divine, chiefly his absolute impassibility:

But thought seems to be an independent substance implanted within us and to be incapable of being destroyed. If it could be destroyed at all, it would be under the blunting influence of old age. What really happens is, however, exactly parallel to what happens in the case of the sense organs; if the old man could recover the proper kind of eye, he would see just as well as the young man. The incapacity of old age is due to an affection not of the soul but of its vehicle, as occurs in drunkenness or disease. Thus it is that thinking and reflecting decline through the decay of some other inward part and *are themselves impassible* (ἀπαθές). Thinking, loving, and hating are affections not of thought, but of that which has thought, so far as it has it. That is why, when this vehicle decays, memory and love cease; they were activities not of thought, but of the composite which has perished; thought is, no doubt, something more divine and impassible.[27]

And just as, in the *Metaphysics*, Aristotle achieved the concept of God with the characteristics we saw and could not solve the numerous aporias that that achievement aroused, so also in producing the concept of the spiritual that is in us (the-mind-that-makes-all-things) he could not solve the numerous aporias that followed upon it.

Is this mind an individual? How can it come "from the outside"? What relationship does it have to our moral behavior? Is it completely subject to some eschatological destiny? In what sense does it survive the death of the body?

Some of these questions are not even raised by Aristotle and would be commonly destined to not have an answer within the confines of Aristotle's doctrine; for to be taken up and adequately answered they would demand the presence of some notion of creation philosophically elaborated, which as we know is alien not only to Aristotle but to all the Greeks.

Aristotle dedicated his attention to the eschatological problems in the works of his early period. Instead in the esoteric works he allowed the mystical-religious component to wither (which in the writings of the early period he had borrowed much from Plato) and together with them also those problems. It is a question of problems that reason alone cannot solve but to which a full response would be provided only by the stimulation of a religious faith.

IV. MATHEMATICS

Aristotle did not concern himself in any special way with the mathematical sciences since he had less interest in them than Plato, who made mathematics a quasi-obligatory entrance requirement to the metaphysics of the Ideas and who on the portal of the Academy had inscribed: "do not enter herein without geometry." However the Stagirite also in this area made his own singular and relevant specific contribution, in determining for the first time correctly the *ontological status of the objects of the mathematical sciences*. This contribution hence is worthy to be recorded in a precise manner.

Plato and many of the Platonists understood numbers and mathematical objects in general as *ideal entities separate from the sensibles*. Other Platonists had tried to mitigate this uncompromising notion by making the mathematical objects immanent in sensible things maintaining yet firmly the conviction that they should be treated as intelligible realities distinct from the sensibles. Aristotle rejected both of these conceptions, judging one view as more absurd than the other and hence absolutely unacceptable.[1]

What is the nature then of number and mathematical-geometrical entities if they are not intelligible entities endowed with their own existence? Here is the Aristotelian solution to the question. The mathematical objects are not real entities much less something unreal. They exist potentially in sensible things and our reason *separates them* by means of subtraction (abstraction). They are, therefore, *mental entities* that exist in act only in our mind in virtue of our capacity of "abstraction" (viz., existing as separates only in and through the mind) and in potency exist in the things as their properties.[2]

We can explain this better. The sensible things have a multitude of properties and determinations. We can consider all these properties but we likewise focus on some of them while prescinding from the others.

Thus we can, for example, consider sensible things only insofar as they have the characteristic of *being in motion*, prescinding from all the rest; but not for this reason, obviously, is it necessary that the moving thing exists as something in reality and separate from the rest. It is enough that our power of "abstraction" and the capacity of our mind consider that characteristic of sensible things to prescind from all the rest.

Analogously, following this same procedure we can prescind from motion, and we can regard sensible things *only insofar as they are three-dimensional bodies*. Again, we can proceed in the process of "abstraction," considering things only *according to two dimensions*, viz., *as surfaces*, prescinding from all the rest. Further we can consider things as *only having length* and then as *indivisible unities* having therefore place but no extension; that is, *only as points*. Finally we can consider things also as *pure unities*, viz., as indivisible entities and without a place or extension, viz., *as numerical unities*.

It is clear, consequently that mathematical objects and arithmetical objects have their foundation in the *characteristics to be found in sensible things*, which therefore exist as affections of those things. But, like geometricals and mathematicals, they are considered as existing *only by way of "abstraction [subtraction]."* Here is a very important text in this regard:

> Thus since it is true to say without qualification that not only things which are *separable* but also things which are *inseparable* exist–for instance, that *moving things* exist–it is true also to say, without qualification, that the objects of mathematics exist, and with the character ascribed to them by mathematicians. And it is true to say of the other sciences too, without qualification, that they deal with such and such a subject–not with what is accidental to it (e.g., not with the white, if the white thing is healthy, and the science has the healthy as its subject), but with that which is the subject of each science–with the healthy if it treats things qua healthy, with man if man qua man. *So too is it with geometry*; if its subjects happen to be sensible, though it does not treat them qua sensible, *the mathematical sciences will not for that reason be sciences of sensibles–nor, on the other hand, of other things separated from sensibles*. Many properties attach to things in virtue of their own nature as possessed of some such property; e.g., there are attributes peculiar to the animals *qua female* or *qua male*, yet there is no female nor male separate from animals. And so also *there are attributes which belong to things merely as lengths or as planes*....The same account may be given of harmonics and optics; for neither considers its objects qua light-ray or qua voice, but *qua lines and numbers*; but the latter are attributes proper to the former. And mechanics too proceeds in the same way.[3]

It is exactly this interpretation of the mathematical objects as "abstractions" of the mind that permitted Aristotle to resist the tendency to reify mathematical objects, which is what the late Plato risked falling into and which helped Aristotle develop instead the eidetic aspect of the Platonic metaphysics, as we saw. It is this same interpretation that permitted him to completely grasp the basic error of pan-mathematicism into which some Academics fell as we will see and thus dissolving for the most part the very achievements of the Second Voyage.[4]

Third Section

THE PRACTICAL SCIENCES: ETHICS AND POLITICS

ἡ τοῦ θεοῦ ἐνέργεια, μακαριότητι
διαφέρουσα, θεωρητικὴ ἂν εἴη· καὶ τῶν
ἀνθρωπίνων δὴ ἡ ταύτῃ συγγενεστάτη
εὐδαιμονικωτάτη ἐφ' ὅσον δὴ διατείνει
ἡ θεωρία, καὶ ἡ εὐδαιμονία.

The activity of God, which is the most excellent blessedness, is contemplative activity; therefore also among the human
activities that which is most capable of
rendering him happy...as far as, therefore, he achieves theoretical thought, so
also he achieves happiness.

Aristotle, *Nicomachean Ethics*,
K 8.1178b21

I. ETHICS

1. The relations between ethics and politics

After the theoretical sciences, in the Aristotelian systematization of knowledge, the practical sciences come as a second group, as we have seen. They are arranged hierarchically lower than the first, insofar as in them knowledge has no other purpose than itself, but is subordinated and hence in certain sense, subject to practical activity. These practical sciences concern, in fact, the conduct of human beings, as well as the goals towards which this conduct hopes to progress, both considered as individuals, and considered as being part of a society, chiefly political society. In fact, Aristotle calls *politics* in general[1] (but also "the philosophy of the affairs of man")[2] the complex science of the moral activity of men both as individuals and as citizens; then he divides *politics* (or "philosophy of the affairs of man"), respectively, into *ethics* and *politics*, properly speaking, (a theory of the State).

In this subordination of ethics to politics is clearly incised in a specific way the Platonic doctrine we have amply illustrated earlier, which moreover, as we know, gave paradigmatic form to that typically Hellenic conception that only succeeded in seeing man as a citizen and posited the City-State completely earlier the family and individual human beings. The individual was for the City-State and the City-State was not for the individual. Aristotle expressly states it: "If, in fact, the good for the individual and the city-state is identical, it seems more important and more complete to choose and defend the good of the city-state; it is certainly desirable also with regard to only one person, but it is more seemly and more divine with regard to a people and the city-state."[3]

Therefore, an *architectonic* function belongs to politics, viz., that of command; and to it belongs also the determination of "what sciences are necessary in the City-State, and what each must grasp and up to what point."[4] It is quite true, yet, as some scholars have pointed out, by proceeding little by little in his *Ethics*, the relationship between the individual and the City-State threatens to reverse itself "and at the end of the work he speaks as if the State had a simple ancillary function with respect to the moral life of the individual, furnishing elements of compulsion to render the desires of man subject to his reason."[5] However this fact, which simply is very important, is not carried by Aristotle to the level of a conscious criticism, much less does he ever come to treat those consequences that would have broken the general outline of the "philosophy of the affairs of man." The historical-cultural conditioning had a heavier weight than the speculative conclusions and the polis remained for the Stagirite fundamentally the sphere of interest enclosing the values of human beings.

2. The highest good for man: happiness

In the various actions man tends always to a determined ends that are considered as goods. Just so the *Nichomachean Ethics* begins: "Every art and every inquiry and similarly every action and every undertaking seems to aim at some good; therefore with reason the good has been defined as: *that at which all things aim.*"[6]

Consequently there are goals and goods that we desire in view of further goals and goods and that therefore are relative goals and goods; but since it is inconceivable that a process go on to infinity from goal to goal and goods to goods (such a process would even destroy the very concept of goods and goals that are necessarily implied in the term), we must acknowledge that all goals and goods to which man tends are in function of some ultimate goal and highest good. The Stagirite states: "If then there is an end of our actions that we choose for its own sake, while the others we choose only in view of that end, and we do not desire everything for the sake of something else (which would obviously lead to a process to infinity, so that our tendency would be empty and vain), in such a case it is clear that this must be the good and *the highest good.*" [7]

What is this highest good? Aristotle does not have any doubts, all men, without distinction, hold that such a good is *eudaimonia*; viz., happiness: "As far as its name, the greater part is in agreement: we call it *happiness both the multitude and persons of refinement* those who suppose that to be happy consists in living well and in being successful." [8] Therefore happiness is the goal to which all human beings consciously tend. But what is the nature of happiness?

We see this essential and collateral point. Most human beings hold that happiness consists *in pleasure and the enjoyment thereof.* But a life dedicated to pleasure is a life made "like a slave's" and an "existence worthy of beasts."[9]

In more evolved persons and more cultivated places the highest good and happiness in *honor.* Honor is sought chiefly by those who are dedicated actively to the political life. Except that this cannot be the ultimate goal for which we ought to search because as Aristotle notes *it is something external and dependent on others*: "In fact it seems to depend more on he who confers the honor than on he who is honored; we instead hold that the good is something individual and inalienable."[10]

In addition, men seek honor not for itself but rather as a confirmation and public acknowledgement of their worth and of their value, which therefore is something more important than honor.

If the type of life dedicated to pleasure and that dedicated to seeking honors is inadequate for the reason discussed, they still have their *apparent plausibility*, but the same cannot be said for the type of life spent in the amassing of wealth, which in the judgment of our philosopher does not even have apparent plausibility: "A life...dedicated to commerce is something contrary to nature, and it is evident that wealth is not the good which we are seeking; in fact it is only good in view of being useful and a means to something else."[11]

Pleasures and honors are sought for themselves, not however, wealth; the life spent to amass wealth is, therefore, the most absurd and the most unauthentic since it is spent in seeking things that are more valued as *means* not as *goals*.

But the *supreme good* of man cannot even be that which Plato and the Platonists had pointed out as such, viz., the *Idea of the Good*, the transcendent *Good-in-itself*: "If, in fact, the good were a unity or something predicable in common and existed separately by itself [as it is precisely the Idea of the Good], it is evident that it will not be attainable or realizable by man; but for what we are searching is instead our own good."[12]

Therefore it cannot be conceived as a *transcendent Good* since it is an *immanent Good*, nor as a good already once and for all achieved, since it is a realizable and actualizable good of and for man. (The good, for Aristotle, is not a single and univocal reality, but just as we have seen with regard to the notion of *being*, it is something polyvalent, different in different categories and different also in different realities entering again into each category and always linked by an analogical [homonymous] relationship).

But what is the nature of the supreme Good *realizable by man*?

The response of Aristotle is in perfect harmony with the sharply Hellenic conception of *areté*, which is by now well known, and we cammpt prescinds from it, in order to understand Aristotle.

The good of man is that which consists in the work that is peculiar to him; that is, in that work which he and only he can accomplish, just as in general, the good of each thing consists in the *function* that is peculiar to that thing. The *function* of the eye is to see, the *function* of the ear is to hear, and so on. *What is the function of man?* (*a*)It cannot be the simple fact of living given that living is proper to all vegetative beings. (*b*) It cannot be to sense given that to sense is common to all animals. (*c*) It remains, therefore, that *the function peculiar to man is reason and the activity of the soul in accordance with reason.* The real good of man, therefore, consists in this *function or activity* of reason and, more precisely, in the complete explication and actualization of this activity. This is, therefore, the "virtue" of man and here he will seek his happiness. But let us read an entire section of the *Nichomachean Ethics* that develops these concepts since it is one of the most illuminating pages reflecting the Aristotelian mental attitude as well as that of the whole of the moral thought of the Greeks:

> If to say that happiness is the highest good seems to be something already agreed to, however we still need something more precise to be said about

its nature. We could quickly arrive at it, if we were the examine the function (ἔργον) of man. As in fact for the flutist, the maker of statues or artisan of any kind, and in general anybody who has some function or activity it seems that the good resides in their function, just so it would also be for man, if there exists some function proper to him. Perhaps therefore to the carpenter or the shoemaker are there proper activities and functions, while there is no function proper to man but he is born without a function? Or rather must we not assume that, just as the eye, the hand, the foot and each of the various members of the body manifestly has a certain function of its own, so a human being also has a certain function of its own, so a human being also has a certain function over and above all the functions of his particular members? What then precisely can this function be? The mere act of living appears to be shared even by plants, whereas we are looking for the function peculiar to man; we must therefore set aside the vital activity of nutrition and growth. Next in the scale will come some form of sentient life; but this too appears to be shared by horses, oxen, and animals generally. There remains therefore what may be called the practical life of the rational part of man. This part has two divisions, one rational as obedient to principle, the other as possessing principle and exercising intelligence. Rational life again has two meanings; let us assume that we are here concerned with the active exercise of the rational faculty, since this seems to be the proper sense of the term. If then the function of man is the active exercise of the soul's faculties in conformity with rational principle, or at all events not in dissociation from rational principle, and if we acknowledge the function of an individual and of a good individual of the same class, for instance, a harpist and a good harpist, and so generally with all classes to be generically the same, the qualification of the latter's superiority in excellence being added to the function in his case (I mean that if the function of a harpist is to play the harp, that of a good harpist is to play the harp well); if this is so, and if we declare that the function of man is a certain form of life, and define that form of life as the exercise of the soul's faculties and activities in association with rational principle, and say that the function of a good man is to perform these activities well and rightly, and if a function is well performed when it is performed in accordance with its own proper excellence–from these premises it follows that *the Good of man is the active exercise of his soul's faculties in conformity with excellence or virtue,* or if there be several human excellences or virtues, in conformity with the best and most perfect among them. Moreover this activity must occupy a complete lifetime; for one swallow does not make spring, nor does one fine day; and similarly one day or a brief period of happiness does not make a man supremely blessed and happy.[13]

This beautiful section that we have read shows in an exemplary manner what we have pointed out earlier the *substantial adherence of Aristotle to the Platonic-Socratic doctrine that endowed the essence of man in the soul and precisely in the rational part of the soul, in the spirit.* We are our reason and our spirit. The good man Aristotle expressly says:"...for he does it on account of the rational part of himself, and *this appears to be present in each of us.*"[14] And again:"It is therefore clear that *a man is or is chiefly the dominant part of himself and that a good man values this part of himself most.*"[15] And finally:"And if it [the rational soul and in particular the most elevated part of him; that is, the intellect] is the better and dominant part, *it would seem that each of us consists precisely in it.*"[16]

Because this is the same foundation we saw of the Socratic-Platonic ethics, we must not be surprised if Aristotle, having accepted the foundation, ends with Socrates and Plato more often than is ordinarily conceded. The authentic values also for the Stagirite (as we have implicitly emphasized) could not be those exterior goods (like wealth), which only touch man tangentially, nor those of the body (like pleasures), which do not concern the true self of man, *but only those of the soul* since the soul is the true man. The Stagirite explicitly says: "Having therefore divided goods into three kinds; those *exterior*, those of the *soul*, and those of the *body, those relative to the soul we say which are the principal and most complete goods.*"[17]

In conclusion, it can be said that the true goods of man are the spiritual goods that consist in virtue of his soul, and in nothing other than these is happiness. When we speak of human excellence we do not intend at all to speak of the virtue of the body–states in an unequivocal way Aristotle–*but it is that of the soul; and we say that happiness consists in an activity proper to the soul.*

The Socratic "care of the soul" remains hence also for Aristotle the way, the only way that leads to happiness. Unlike Socrates and especially Plato, however, Aristotle held that being sufficiently endowed with the possession of exterior goods and the blessings of fortune was indispensable; in fact, although their presence does not guarantee happiness, in their absence they can, however, spoil and compromise it (at least in part). And to this partial reevaluation of external goods is associated also a certain reevaluation of pleasure, which for Aristotle crowns the virtuous life and is the necessary consequence of which virtue is the antecedent, as we will see.

But these affirmations are stated more from good sense (and from a good sense determined by the Greeks) than from Aristotelian realism, the nature of which we well know. In fact, he does not hesitate to make affirmation like these:

> Nevertheless it is manifest that happiness also requires external goods in addition, as we said; for it is impossible, or at least not easy, to play a noble part unless furnished with the necessary equipment. For many noble actions require instruments for their performance, in the shape of friends or wealth or political power; also there are certain external advantages, the lack of which sullies supreme happiness, such as good birth, satisfactory children, and personal beauty; a man of very ugly appearance or low birth, or childless and alone in the world, is not our idea of a happy man, and still less so is one who has children and friends that are worthless, or who has had good ones

but lost them by death. As we said therefore happiness does seem to require the addition of external prosperity.[18]

Moreover, Aristotle is convinced that bad luck compromises happiness, not ordinary bad luck but the great misfortune, viz., that from which there is no recovery in a short time. Therefore, he says no one can be truly happy "if they were to have the end of Priam."[19] But, if this is so, not even Socrates could be said to be happy, not even Socrates who lived the whole of his life seeking and attaining virtue. Evidently, the experience of life and especially of the *happy* death of Socrates, who in complete tranquillity of spirit drank the hemlock, conscious of having attained fully his destiny, is not considered by Aristotle, and this view contrasts with the assertions we have read. Moreover, that which Aristotle himself will say about the contemplative life radically reoriented these concessions to common sense.[20]

3. The deduction of the "virtues" from the "parts of the soul"

Happiness consists, therefore, in an activity of the soul according to excellence [virtue]. It is clear, then, that some further analysis of the concept of excellence (*areté*) depends on an *analysis of the concept of the soul*. Now, we have seen that the soul is distinguished, according to Aristotle, into three parts: two nonrational; that is, the vegetative soul and the sentient soul; and one rational, the intellective soul. And as each of these parts has its own singular activity, so it has its own singular excellence or virtue. However *human excellence is only that into which the activity of reason enters*. In fact, the vegetative soul is common in all living things: "The excellence of this faculty hence appears to be common to all living beings and not specifically the human."[21]

Instead, the argument about the sentient and concupiscible soul is different, although itself not rational, it does participate in a certain way in reason:

> Nevertheless it cannot be doubt that in the soul also there is an element beside that of principle, which opposes and runs counter to principle....But this second element also seems, as we said, to participate in rational principle; at least in the self-restrained man it obeys the behest of principle, and no doubt in the temperate and brave man it is still more amenable, for all parts of his nature are in harmony with principle. Thus we see that the irrational part, as well as the soul as a whole, is double. One division of it, the vegetative, does not share in rational principle at all; the other, the seat of the appetites and of desire in general, does in a sense participate in principle, as being obedient and amenable to it.[22]

It is clear then, that there is a virtue in this part of the soul, which is *specifically human* and which consists in the domination, so to speak, of these tendencies and these impulses that are of themselves immoderate; and this the Stagirite calls "ethical virtue."

Finally, if there is also in us a purely rational soul, then it must likewise have its own peculiar virute and this will be the "dianoetic virtues," viz., rational virtues.

4. The ethical virtues

Let us begin the examination of the ethical virtues, which are just as numerous as the impulses and the sentiments they must moderate. The ethical virtues derive *from attitudes* in us. We, by nature, are potentially capable of forming them and by means of their exercise precisely to change this capacity in us to actuality. By carrying out just acts over time, we become just, viz., we acquire the virtue of justice, which then remains in us, stabilized, as a *settled disposition* or *hexis*, which successively makes it easy for us to accomplish further acts of justice. By carrying out over time acts of courage, we become courageous, viz., we acquire the hexis of courage, which then we can easily bring to completion acts of courage. And so on in succession. In sum, for Aristotle, ethical virtue is grasped in the same way in which the various arts are grasped, which are pure *hexai*: "For example, men become builders by building houses, harpists by playing on the harp. Similarly we become just by doing just act, temperate by doing temperate acts, brave by doing brave acts."[23]

This argument although somewhat helpful for the sake of clarity does not reach to the heart of the problem; it tells us; that is, how we acquire and then possess these virtues, but it does not tell us again in what the nature of virtue consists. What is the nature common to all the ethical virtues? The Stagirite responds in detail, there is never a virtue when there is *excess* or *defect*, viz., when there is too much or too little; virtue implies instead the *correct proportion that is the mean between excess and defect.* Here are the precise words of our philosopher:

> Now of everything that is continuous and divisible, it is possible to take the larger part, or the smaller part, or an equal part, and these parts may be larger, smaller, and equal either with respect to the thing itself or relatively to us; the equal part being a mean between excess and deficiency. By the mean of the thing I denote a point equally distant from either extreme, which is one and the same for everybody; by the mean relative to us, that amount which is neither too much nor too little, and this is not one and the same for everybody. For example, let 6 be many and 2 few; then one takes the mean with respect to the thing if one takes 6; since 6 - 2 = 10 - 6, and this is the mean according to arithmetical proportion. But we cannot arrive by this method at the mean relative to us. Suppose that 10 lb. of food is a large ration for anybody and 2 lb. a small one: it does not follow that a trainer will prescribe 6 lb., for perhaps even this will be a large ration, or a small one, for the particular athlete who is to receive it; it is a small ration for a Milo [who was an exceptional athlete], but a large one for a man just beginning to go in for athletics. And similarly with the amount of running or wrestling exercise to be taken. In the same way then an expert in any art

324 / Aristotle: The Unification of Wisdom

avoids excess and deficiency, and seeks and adopts the mean–*the mean; that is, not of the thing but relative to us.*[24]

But–it will be asked–the "excess," "defect" and "correct proportion" of which you speak with respect to ethical virtue, what precisely is its object? They are concerned exactly with *sentiments, passions,* and *actions*–Aristotle replies:

> For example, one can be frightened or bold, feel desire or anger or pity, and experience pleasure and pain in general, either too much or too little, and in both cases wrongly; whereas to feel these feelings at the right time, on the right occasion, towards the right people, for the right purpose and in the right manner, is to feel the best amount of them, which is the mean amount–and the best amount is of course the mark of virtue. And similarly there can be excess, deficiency, and the due mean in actions. Now feelings and actions are the objects with which virtue is concerned; and in feelings and actions excess and deficiency are errors, while the mean amount is praised, and constitutes success; and to be praised and to be successful are both marks of virtue. Virtue, therefore, is a mean state in the sense that it is able to hit the mean.[25]

In conclusion, ethical virtue is precisely mediated by two vices, one of which is reached through defect and the other through excess. It is obvious, for anyone who understood this doctrine of Aristotle, that the *mediation* is not only not *mediocrity* but it is its antithesis; the "correct proportion," in fact, is clearly beyond the extremes representing so to speak their overcoming, and hence as Aristotle puts it nicely it is a "culmination," viz., the most elevated point of view of value, insofar as it marks the affirmation of reason over the nonrational: "Hence according to its essence and according to the reason which establishes its nature, virtue is a mean, but *with respect to the good and to perfection, at its highest point.*"[26]

Here is almost a synthesis of all of Greek wisdom that has found typical expression in the poets and in the Seven Sages who had pointed out many times the *middle way,* the *nothing too much,* the *correct measure*–the highest rule of moral action-rule that is like an exemplary code of the Hellenic sensibility. And here, too, is the acquisition of the Pythagorean lessons that point out perfection in the limit (the πέρας), chiefly a precise exploitation of the notion of "correct measure," which had such importance especially in the late period of Plato's writings.

This doctrine of ethical virtue as the "just measure" between extremes is illustrated by a full analysis of the principal ethical virtues (or better, of that which the Greeks then considered as such). Naturally they are not deduced in accordance with any detailed outline but rather empirically and almost in unconnected lists. The virtue of *courage* is the "just measure" between the excess of impulsiveness and faintheartedness; courage is therefore the just measure imposed on the sentiment of fear that if deprived of rational control, can degenerate by defect into faintheartedness or by excess into impulsiveness. *Temperance* is the "just measure" between the excesses of intemperance or dissoluteness and insensibility; temperance is therefore the attitude that reason takes on when faced with determinate pleasures. *Liberality* is the "just measure" between avarice and prodigality; it is therefore the just attitude that reason takes on when faced with the action of spending money. And so on in succession.

In the *Eudemian Ethics*, Aristotle furnishes us the following list of virtues and vices:

gentleness is the mean between irascibility and lack of feeling;
courage is the mean between foolhardiness and cowardice;
modesty is the mean between shamelessness and shyness;
temperance is the mean between intemperance and insensibility;
indignation is the mean between envy and the opposed excess which has no name;
justice is the mean between gain and loss;
liberality is the mean between lavishness and meanness;
sincerity is the mean between boastfulness and self-depreciation;
friendliness is the mean between adulation and hostility;
dignity is the mean between servility and stubbornness;
greatness of spirit is the mean between vanity and meanness of spirit;
magnificence is the mean between extravagance and pettiness.[27]

In all these manifestations, ethical virtue *is the just measure that reason imposes on sentiment or on actions or on attitudes that, without the control of reason, would tend towards one or another excess.*

Among the ethical virtues, the Stagirite does not hesitate to add that justice is the most important one (and to the analysis of it he dedicates an entire book).[28] In a primary sense, justice is the respect for the laws of the state. And since the laws of the state (of the Greek City-State) cover the whole area of the moral life, justice, in this sense, in some way comprehends all the virtues. Aristotle writes:

"This is why justice often seems to be the most important of the virtues and more sublime than the evening or the morning star; and we have the proverb–*in justice is all virtue found together.*"[29] But the most proper meaning of justice (which is that most attentively analyzed by Aristotle) consists in the *just measure with which goods, advantages, and earnings* (and their contraries) are distributed. In this sense justice is "the mean" but not as the other virtues are, "because justice is related to a mean, while injustice is related to the extremes."[30]

In general, the many and fine analyses of the various aspects of individual ethical virtues made by Aristotle remain, mostly, on a purely phenomenological level; yet it can be said that frequently the moral convictions of a society to which Aristotle belonged influenced the philosopher in a decisive way, as for example in the case of the description of magnanimity, which must be a kind of embellishment of the virtues but which, instead, is a weighty mortgage that the taste of the time placed on the Aristotelian doctrine.[31]

5. The "dianoetic" virtues

Beyond the ethical virtues, according to Aristotle are other virtues that as we have already pointed out, *are the virtues of the most elevated part of the soul, that is, the rational soul,* and that hence are said to be the dianoetic virtues; viz., virtues of reason. And since there are two parts or functions of the rational soul, the one that knows contingent and variable things and the other that knows necessary and immutable things, then there will be logically both a perfection or virtue of the first function, and a perfection or virtue of the second function of the rational soul.[32] These two parts of the rational soul are in substance the practical reason and the theoretical reason and the respective virtues are the perfected forms with which practical truth and theoretical truth are grasped. The typical virtue of the practical reason is "prudence" (φρόνησις), and the typical virtue of the theoretical reason is "wisdom" (σοφία).

Prudence consists in knowing correctly how to direct the life of man; viz., in knowing how to deliberate about that which is good or evil for man. ("It–says Aristotle–is a practical disposition, accompanied by truthful reason about that which is good and evil for man.")[33] It should be noted, for the purposes of an exact understanding of the Aristotelian doctrine, that *prudence* or wisdom assists us in deliberating correctly about the true aims of man *in the sense that it points out the suitable means to the achievement of true goals.* It helps us; that is, to specify and follow out these things that lead to those ends; therefore *it does not point out or determine the ends themselves.* The true ends and the true aims are grasped by ethical virtue that directs the will in a correct way. Aristotle states precisely: "For *virtue makes us aim at the right mark,* and *practical wisdom makes us take the right means*" (trans. W. D. Ross, p. 1034 McKeon ed.).[34] It is clear hence that the ethical virtues and dianoetic virtue of prudence are linked by their twofold mandate, in fact, Aristotle says: (*a*) It is not possible to be virtuous without prudence, or (*b*) to be wise without ethical virtue."[35]

(*a*) In reality, if ethical virtue as we saw "is a habit of choice consistent with the mean in ourselves, determined *by reason* and as the *wise man* would define it,"[36] it is clear that it cannot be had without this reason, or better without this *right reason,* and this right reason is only that of the *wise man;* viz., that precisely which is *in conformity with prudence.* Moreover it is evident, on the basis of this, that if only prudence can point out the means to achieve the good, if then, hypothetically, we can achieve the good without prudence, but we will achieve it only by a kind of natural inclination, viz., in an unreflective way; however, this would not be authentic virtue. Prudence is thus the necessary condition (although not sufficient) of each and every ethical virtue and constitutes also the element that in a certain way unifies them all.[37]

(b) On the other hand, it is also true that it cannot be prudence without ethical virtue; in fact, prudence is not simply cleverness, a capacity in general of finding and following the means to achieve some goal, but it is so *only when it specifies a capacity of finding the just means that carries us to the highest goal of man, to the moral good.* Prudence may be said to be only cleverness that is in the service of moral actions.[38]

This twofold bond, which, at the present, scholars have pointed out, ends by falling into a vicious circle. Zeller wrote previously: "virtue basically is the maintaining of the just measure, and this can be determined only by prudence; if things are this way, the task of prudence does not consist only in seeking of the means in order to achieve ethical goals; without it is not possible even to determine exactly those goals and on the other hand cleverness is worthy of the name of prudence only when it is dedicated to realizing ethical goals." [39] It is an aporia that derives from other aporias that are more difficult and of which we will speak at the end.

Wisdom (σοφία), as we stated, is the other and most elevated dianoetic virtue. It is constituted both by the intuitive grasp of principles through the mind and by discursive knowledge of the consequences that derive from these principles. Wisdom is a higher virtue than prudence, because whereas prudence is concerned with human beings and hence of what is changeable in man, *wisdom regards those things that are higher than man.* Man is the best of living beings, however Aristotle states that: "There exist other things much more divine than man in their nature, as, to mention the most visible things, the stars of which the universe is composed. From which it can be clearly said that wisdom is both the demonstrated conclusions and the immediate knowledge of the most excellent things of nature."[40] In other words, wisdom coincides with the theoretical sciences and indeed coincides in special way with the highest of them, viz., with metaphysics.

6. Complete happiness

Since, as we have seen at the beginning, happiness is an activity in conformity with excellence, it is by now clear in what that happiness will consist. In the first place, it will consist in the activity of the mind in conformity with virtue; the mind, in fact, is that which is most elevated in man and the activity of mind is the perfect activity, it is self-sufficient, it is the activity that has in itself its own end insofar as it tends to knowledge through itself. In the activity of the contemplative mind man achieves the vertex of his possibilities and there is then present that which is the highest that is in him. Aristotle writes:

> If...the activity of the mind is felt to excel in serious worth, consisting as it does in contemplation, and to aim at no end beyond itself, and therefore augmenting its activity; and if accordingly the attributes of this activity are found to be self-sufficiency, leisureliness, such freedom from fatigue is possible for man, and all the other attributes of blessedness; it follows that it is the activity of the mind that constitutes complete human happiness—provided it be granted a complete span of life, for nothing that belongs to happiness can be incomplete. Such a life as this however will be higher than the human level; not in virtue of his humanity will man achieve it, but in virtue of something within him that is divine; and by as much as this something is superior to his composite nature, by so much is its activity superior to the exercise of the other forms of virtue. If then the mind is something divine in comparison with man, so is the life of the mind divine in comparison with human life. Nor ought we to obey those who enjoin that a man should have man's thoughts and a mortal the thoughts of mortality, but we ought so far as possible to achieve immortality, and do all that man may to live in accordance with the highest thing in him; for though this be small in bulk, in power and value it far surpasses all the rest.[41]

In second place will go the life in conformity with the ethical virtues. In fact, they involve the composite structure of man, and as such, they alone can yield human happiness.

On the contrary, the happiness of the contemplative life carries us beyond the merely human, it achieves so to speak a contact with divinity, for which life can only be the contemplative life. Aristotle writes:

> It follows that the activity of God, which is transcendent in blessedness, is the activity of contemplation; and therefore among human activities that which is most akin to the divine activity of contemplation will be the greatest source of happiness. A further proof is that the lower animals cannot partake of happiness, because they are completely devoid of the contemplative activity. The whole of the life of the Gods is blessed, and that of man is so insofar as it contains some likeness to the divine activity; but none of the other animals possess happiness, because they are entirely incapable of contemplation. Happiness therefore is co-extensive in its range with contemplation; the more a class of beings possesses the power of contemplation, the more it enjoys happiness, not as an accidental concomitant of contemplation but as inherent in it, since contemplation is valuable in itself. It follows that happiness is some form of contemplation.[42]

And this more complete formulation of that ideal which the old philosophers of nature had sought to carry out in their life, which Socrates had already begun to explicate from the conceptual point of view and about which Plato had previously theorized. But in Aristotle there is more consideration of the contact of the contemplative life with the life of God, which is lacking in Plato because he lacked, as we have seen, the concept of God as *Absolute Mind* and the *Knowing of Knowing*. So the Platonic precept according to which man must as much as possible "assimilate himself to God"

acquired a more precise meaning; to be assimilated to God *means to contemplate the truth just as God contemplates it*, or as the *Eudemian Ethics* explicates, *to contemplate God himself, who is the supreme intellectual being*:

> One must, then, here as elsewhere, live with reference to the ruling principle and with reference to the formed habit and the activity of the ruling principle, as the slave must live with reference to that of the master, and each of us by the rule proper to him. But since man is by nature composed of a ruling and a subject part, each of us should live according to the governing element within himself–(but this is equivocal, for medical science governs in one sense, health in another, the former existing for the latter). And so it is with the theoretic principle; for God is not an imperative ruler, but is the end with a view to which wisdom issues its commands...since God needs nothing. What choice, then, or possession of the natural goods (whether bodily goods, wealth, friends, or other things) will produce the contemplation of God, that choice or possession is best; this is the noblest standard, but any that through deficiency or excess hinders one from the contemplation and service of God is bad; this a man possesses in his soul, and this is the best standard for the soul, to perceive the irrational part of the soul, as such, as little as possible.[43]

7. Friendship and happiness

Aristotle had dedicated two books of the *Nichomachean Ethics* to the treatment of friendship. The thing is explained by different basic reasons. In the first place, friendship is for Aristotle structurally bound to virtue and happiness, hence to the central problems of ethics.[44] In the second place, the problem of friendship, as we have seen, was basically debated by Socrates and especially by Plato and acquired a notable philosophical consistency. In the third place, the structure of Greek society gave a prominence to friendship decisively superior to that given to it in the modern societies, therefore also from this standpoint it is well explained the close attention that the Stagirite dedicated to it.

There are three things that man loves and for which reason he makes friends: *utility, pleasure,* and the *good.* Depending on which one a man seeks, in another man what is the useful, the pleasurable, or the good, different kinds of friendship arise. Therefore, if three values are what he seeks, three must be also the forms of friendship:

> There are accordingly three kinds of friendship, corresponding in number to the three lovable qualities; since a reciprocal affection, known to either party, can be based on each of the three, and when men love each other,

they wish each other well in respect of the quality which is the ground of their friendship. Thus friends whose affection is based on utility do not love each other in themselves, but insofar as some benefit accrues to them from each other. And similarly with those whose friendship is based on pleasure; for instance, we enjoy the society of witty people not because of what they are in themselves, but because they are agreeable to us. Hence in friendship based on utility or on pleasure men love their friend for their own good or their own pleasure, and not as being the person loved, but as useful or agreeable. And therefore these friendships are based on an accident, since the friend is not loved for being what he is, but as affording some benefit or pleasure as the case may be. Consequently friendships of this kind are easily broken off, in the event of the parties themselves changing, for if no longer pleasant or useful to each other, they cease to love each other.[45]

The perfect form of friendship is that between the good, and those who resemble each other in virtue. For their friends wish each alike the other's good in respect of their goodness, and they are good in themselves; but it is those who wish the good of their friends for their friends' sake who are friends in the fullest sense, since they love each other for themselves and not accidentally. Hence the friendship of these lasts as long as they continue to be good; and virtue is a stable quality.[46]

Therefore, the first two forms of friendship are the least valid, yet, in a certain respect they are forms of extrinsic and illusory friendship, since, to use modern terminology, with them one man loves another man not *for what he is* but only *for what he has*; the friend, in large part, is a means to some advantages (wealth, pleasure) that he offers us. The authentic form of friendship is only the third, because with it alone man loves another man *for that which he is*; viz., for the intrinsic goodness of the man.

Just as for being, the reason why Aristotle defines friendship as a virtue is clear, the true form of virtue is the bond that the virtuous man forms with another virtuous man qua virtue itself. And virtue is, as we have seen, that for which and in which man attains fully his own nature and his value as man, and the true form of friendship is precisely the bond of man with man according to the very worth of man. Thus Aristotle can rightly appeal to the same principle to solve the problem that is called (as we will see) the problem of the basic moral choices: "It seems that virtue and the virtuous are the measure in each thing."[47]

Some interpreters of Aristotle believed they have found in the doctrine of friendship a corrective of that egoism or, if you wish, of that egocentrism that in the final analysis is the basic characteristic of the ethical system of the Stagirite. In reality it is not so, in fact he clearly affirms that even in friendship according to virtue the friend seeks in the friend his own good. Friendship as a *gratuitous gift* of itself to the other is a conception totally alien to Aristotle; also in its highest grade friendship is understood as a relationship of giving and having that although purely at a spiritual level must in some way be balanced: "In loving a friend men love what is good for themselves; for the good man in becoming a friend becomes a good to his friend. Each, then, both loves what is good for himself, and makes an equal return in goodwill and in pleasantness; for friendship is said to be equality, and both of these are found most in the friendship of the good." [48]

Aristotle still does not hesitate to affirm expressly that friendship arises toward others "from a sense of friendship toward oneself " [49] and that "everyone wishes well toward himself."[50] But, since there exists in us a worse part and a better part, there are, consequently two different ways of loving oneself. There is the deleterious way of loving the lower part of oneself and wanting for oneself as much wealth and pleasure as possible; and there is, on the contrary, the higher way of loving the most noble part of oneself and the goods relative to this part. Normally one is called an egoist who loves the inferior part of himself and who wants to have the most wealth and pleasures possible; but Aristotle observes that an "egoist" is also one who loves the superior part of himself and wants the most spiritual goods possible. The difference is in the fact that the first is an egoist in the deleterious sense and hence in a negative sense, the second is instead an egoist or self-concerned in the highest sense and hence positive. Here is a fundamental text in this regard:

> That is those who give themselves the preference in regard to objects of this sort [wealth and material goods] that most people usually call lovers of self is plain; for if a man were always anxious that he himself, above all things, should act justly, temperately, or in accordance with any other of the excellences, and in general were always to try to secure for himself the honorable course, no one will call such a man a lover of self or blame him. *But such a man would seem more than the other a lover of self*; at all events he assigns to himself the things that are noblest and best, and gratifies the most authoritative element in himself and in all things obeys this; and just as a city or any other systematic whole is most properly identified with the most authoritative element in it, so is a man; and therefore *the man who loves this and gratifies it is most of all a lover of self*. Besides, a man is said to have or not to have self-control according as his intellect has or has not the control, on the assumption that this is the man himself; and the things men have done from reason are thought most properly their own acts and voluntary acts. That this is the man himself, then, or is so more than anything else, is plain, and also that the good man loves most this part of him. Whence it follows that *he is most truly a lover of self, of another type than that which is a matter of reproach*, and as different from that as living according to reason is from living as passion dictates, and desiring what is noble from desiring what seems advantageous.[51]

In this context it is understandable in what meaning Aristotle considers friendship as necessary to happiness: it goes back to the number of these same superior goods, in the possession of which depends true happiness. In addition, if it is true that the good man tends more to do the good than to receive it, it is also true that precisely for this reason he has need of persons to whom to do good actions. Finally, man is a structurally *political being*, viz., made by living in society with others (of which we will speak in a more detailed way in the exposition of Aristotle's political views) and this same nature has need of others, precisely to enjoy goods, for a man absolutely isolated could not be said to enjoy goods.

Here is a text in which in an paradigmatic manner Aristotle expresses these concepts:

> It is also disputed whether the happy man will need friends or not. It is said that those who are blessed and self-sufficient have no need of friends; for they have the things that are good, and therefore being self-sufficient they need nothing further while a friend, being another self, furnishes what a man cannot provide by his own effort; whence the saying 'when fortune is kind, what need of friends?' But it seems strange, when one assigns all good things to the happy man, not to assign friends, who are thought the greatest of external goods. And if it is more characteristic of a friend to do well by another than to be well done by, and to confer benefits is characteristic of the good man and of excellence, and it is nobler to do well by friends than by strangers, the good man will need people to do well by. This is why the question is asked whether we need friends more in prosperity or in adversity, on the assumption that not only does a man in adversity need people to confer benefits on him, but also those who are prospering need people to do well by. Surely it is strange, too, to make the blessed man a solitary; for no one would choose to possess all good things on condition of being alone, since man is a political creature and one whose nature is to live with others. Therefore even the happy man lives with others; for he has the things that are by nature good. And plainly it is better to spend his days with friends and good men than with strangers or any chance person. *Therefore the happy man needs friends.*[52]

8. Pleasure and happiness

Previously within the ambit of the Socratic schools and within the very Platonic Academy as we have already stated, there was access to lively discussions on pleasures and its relationship with happiness and from these there emerged contrary conclusions. Aristotle discussed basically these conclusions and assumed a position quite original in comparison with them and, in a certain sense, his position had a capacity to mediate the opposed requirements.

For Aristotle pleasure is not a change (a refilling, a completion, an integration, or reintegration), or in general a movement, since it is an *activity* that in every moment is complete: "Seeing seems to be at any moment complete, for it does not lack anything which coming into being later will complete its form; and pleasure; also seems to be of this nature. For it is a whole, and at no time can one find a pleasure whose form will be completed if the pleasure lasts longer."[53]

But, more properly still, for Aristotle pleasure accompanies every activity (be it sensible, pragmatic, or theoretical activity) *and brings it to perfection*: "Pleasure completes the activity not as the inherent state does, but as an end which supervenes as the bloom of youth does on those in the flower of their age. So long, then, as both the intelligible or sensible object and the discriminating or contemplative power are as they should be...."[54]

It is clear therefore what is the novelty of the Aristotelian conception in this regard. When we act or know, whether sensibly or intellectually, we are brought into act, viz., actualized, our potentialities are determined and our *activities* achieve (actuate) their goal relative to their object, which is their own. Precisely because our activities are potentially the object to be realized, they constitute something objectively positive, pleasure accompanies them as *the subjective resonance of that objective, positive thing*. The same life in general, which is precisely an activity and a realization of a positive, is always accompanied by a pleasure.

The aspiration to pleasure, therefore, for Aristotle is wholly natural because it naturally accompanies living and all activities that belong to living precisely as a condition of *"perfection"* or *excellence of these activities*, in the sense which has been analyzed.

Every activity, therefore, has its pleasure; hence every pleasure, in its genera, is precisely a true pleasure. However, as there are *seemly activities* that are good and *unseemly activities* that are bad just so are there *seemly pleasures* that are good and *unseemly pleasures* that are bad. To qualify pleasures, viz., to determine a discriminating criteria and hence to arrange them in order of priority, Aristotle has recourse once again to virtue and the virtuous man:

> The same thing happens in other cases. But in all such matters that which appears to the good man is thought to be really so. If this is correct, as it seems to be, and excellence and the good man as such are the measure of each thing, those also will be pleasures which appear so to him, and those things pleasant which he enjoys. If the things he finds tiresome seem pleasant to someone, that is nothing surprising; for men may be ruined or spoilt in many ways; but the things are not pleasant, but only pleasant to these people and to people in this condition.[55]

But to the good man pleasures *appear* good or evil for some basic precise reasons. In fact, an ontological criteria exists for discriminating between higher pleasures and lower pleasures. The former are those bound to theoretical-contemplative activities of man, the latter are instead those bound to the vegetative and sentient life of man. And in any case, since happiness is bound as we have seen to the theoretical-contemplative activities, they must be held as truly precious only pleasures that are connected to this activity.

9. The psychology of the moral act

Socrates, as we observed in the appropriate place, reduced virtue to *science* and *knowledge* and rejected the notion that man could will or do evil *voluntarily*. Plato had in large part shared this conception; and though in this respect he had specified the irrational forces in the human soul, viz., the concupiscible soul and the irascible soul as capacities opposed to the rational soul. He always believed that human virtue consists in the rule of reason and in the subjugation of those powers to the power of reason itself; so for him as well virtue is, in the ultimate analysis, reason.

Aristotle attempted to overcome this intellectualistic interpretation of moral deeds. Solid realist that he was, he was astute enough to see that virtue is *a knowledge of the good* as well as the *actualization and carrying out, and doing of it, so to speak, the substance of the appropriate actions*; and he tried to determine more closely what were the nature of the complex psychic processes that the moral act presupposed.

In the first place, he clarified what is understood by "involuntary actions" and "voluntary actions." Involuntary are those actions carried out by coercion or through ignorance of the circumstances; voluntary, consequently, are those actions "in which the principle resides in he who acts, if he knows the particular circumstances in which the action unfolds."[56]

But if, up to this point, all appears logical, suddenly the perspective changes, since Aristotle includes among voluntary actions those said to be from impetuosity, from anger, and from desire; and hence he calls voluntary those actions of children and even those of other animals (insofar as they have their origin in them and hence depend on them). It is clear hence that "voluntariety" in this sense, is simply *spontaneous* actions, which have their origin in the subjects that produce them and do not coincide with those that we moderns call by the same name.

The Stagirite continued in his analysis showing that human acts, besides being "voluntary" in the sense clarified, are determined by a "choice" (proaéresiw) and sharpened as thus it would seem to be "something essentially connected with virtue and more than actions able to judge character."[57] In fact choice cannot be exercised by children and animals but only by man who reasons and reflects. And it is precisely that type of reasoning and reflection that concerns the things and actions that depend on us and that are within the realm of the realizables. This type of reasoning and reflection is called by Aristotle *deliberation*. The difference between *deliberation* and *choice* lies in this. Deliberation is concerned with the nature and quality of various actions and the variety of means that must be used to achieve certain goals; it is concerned; that is, with a whole series of things to be realized to reach a goal, or to decide that a more proximate and immediate goal is so ordered. Choice acts with respect to the final goal, rejecting those that are not realizable and, choosing to do those that are. Therefore Aristotle writes: "The object of deliberation and that of choice are the same, except for the fact that which is chosen it has already been determined. In fact an object of choice is that which has already been judged by deliberation. Each man ceases to inquire how he shall act when he has carried back to himself the principle of the action and he has carried back to that part of himself which commands, for it is that which decides."[58]

Here many scholars want to introduce that which we called *will*, insofar as choice is appetite or deliberate desire and hence is not only desire or appetite or only reason. Unfortunately, as soon as we try to improve the Aristotelian position, our effort is shown to be extremely ambiguous and tenuous. First of all, the Stagirite expressly denies that *choice* can be identified with *will* (βούλησις) because *will concerns only goals*, whereas *choice* (just as deliberation) *concerns the means*. Consequently if it is true that choice is that which makes us the source of our actions, viz., responsible, *it is not however that which makes us good*, since such can be only the goals that we propose to ourselves and choice (just as deliberation) concerns only the means. So the primary principle on which our morality depends is rather in the *choice of the ends*.

What is the nature of this choice of the ends? Either (a) an infallible tendency toward the good, to what is truly good, or (b) a tendency to that which *appears* to be good. (a) In the first case, it is evident that choice is not right unless it is voluntary, otherwise, as Socrates said, it will be a form of ignorance, an error, or a mistake. (b) In the second case, it would be necessary to conclude that "what is wished for is not wished for by nature, but according to what each man thinks; and because to one it may appear one thing and to another it might be different, what is wished would be simulatenously contrary."[59] It would mean that no one could be called good or bad or, what is the same thing, that all things would be good precisely because everything done would *appear good*, no matter what its actual condition.

From the dilemma Aristotle believed he could exit in the following way:

> Perhaps we should say that what is wished for in the true and unqualified sense is the good, but that what appears good to each person is wished for by him; and accordingly that the good man wishes for what is truly wished for, the bad man for anything as it may happen just as in the case of our bodies, a man of sound constitution find really healthy food best for his health, but some other diet may be healthy for one who is delicate; and so with things bitter and sweet, hot, heavy, etc. For the good man judges everything correctly; what things truly are, that they seem to him to be, in every area. For special things are noble and pleasant corresponding to each type of character, and perhaps what chiefly distinguishes the good man is that he sees the truth in each kind, being himself as it were the standard and the measure of the noble and the pleasant. It appears to be pleasure that

misleads the mass of mankind; for it seems to them to be a good, though it is not, so they choose what is pleasant as good and shun pain as evil.[60]

But if this is so we move in a circle (a circle wholly analogous to that marked with respect to the relationship between ethical virtue and prudence): to become and to be good one must will good ends, but these are only known if one is good. The truth is that Aristotle understood quite well that we are responsible for our actions, our own moral habits, for the same way in which things appear to us morally, but he was not able to say *because* it is thus and what is the root in us of all this. *He did not know; that is, how to correctly determine the true nature of the will and free choice*; and thus is explained how, although criticizing Socrates, he falls back into the Socratic positions by affirming, for example, that the incontinent errs because at the moment in which he commits the incontinent action he does not have complete knowledge and by affirming that knowledge is determining with respect to moral action.[61] And it is also explained how Aristotle arrived even at saying that once becoming vice ridden one can no longer not be such, even if it were possible in a first moment not to become that way.[62]

However it is legitate to acknowledge that although not truly successful Aristotle did better than all of his predecessors previously had, in affirming that there is something in us on which being good and evil depends, which is not merely irrational desire nor even pure reason; but this "something" eluded him and he did not succeed in specifying it. Moreover, we must objectively recognize that in this respect no Greek succeeded and that Western man will understand the nature of the will and free choice only through Christianity.[63]

II. POLITICS

1. The concept of the State

We have seen earlier that, according to the Stagirite, although the individual good of the individual man and the good of the State are of the same nature (the reason in both cases is virtue), the good of the State is more important, more noble, more complete, and more divine. The reason for this is to be sought in the nature of man, who shows with clarity that he does not have the capacity to live in isolation and needs, precisely in order to be himself, to have relationships with his similars in every moment of his existence.

In the first place, nature has divided men into masculine and feminine who unify to form the first community, viz., the family for procreation and for the satisfaction of the elementary needs (in the nuclear family for Aristotle there is present the slave who as we will see is such by nature). But since families are not sufficient each to itself, villages arise, as a more ample community understood to guarantee in a systematic manner the satisfaction of the needs of life.

But if the family and the village are not sufficient for the satisfaction of the needs of *life in general*, they are not sufficient again to guarantee the condition of the *complete life*; that is, the moral life. This form of life, which can well be called the *spiritual life*, can be guaranteed only by laws, by magistrates, and in general by the complex of organizations of a State. It is in the State that the individual through the laws and political institutions can arise above his egoism and live not according to what is subjectively good but according to what is truly and objectively good. Thus the State, *which is last chronologically*, is instead *first ontologically*, because it represents the whole of which the family and the village are the parts; and from the ontological standpoint the whole precedes the parts, because the whole and only the whole gives meaning to the parts. Just as only the State gives meaning to the other communities and only it is self-sufficient.[1]

Here is a quite famous passage in that the Stagirite develops this concept:

> When several villages are united in a single complete community, large enough to be nearly or quite self-sufficing, the state comes into existence, originating in the bare needs of life, and continuing in existence for the sake of a *good life*. And therefore, if the earlier forms of society are natural, so is the state, for it is the end of them, and the nature of a thing is its end. For what each thing is when fully developed, we call its nature, whether we are speaking of a man, a horse, or a family. Besides, the final cause and end of thing is the best, and to be self-sufficing is the end and the best. Hence it is evident that the state is a creation of nature, and that man is by nature a political animal. And he who by nature and not by mere accident is without a state, is either a bad man or above humanity; he is like the '*tribeless, lawless, hearthless one*,' whom Homer denounces–the natural outcast is forthwith a

lover of war; he may be compared to an isolated piece at draughts. Now, that man is more of a political animal than bees or any other gregarious animals is evident. Nature, as we often say, makes nothing in vain, and man is the only animal who has the gift of speech. And whereas mere voice is but an indication of pleasure and pain, and is therefore found in other animals (for their nature attains to the perception of pleasure and pain and the intimation of them to one another, and no further), the power of speech is intended to set forth the expedient and the inexpedient, and therefore likewise the just and the unjust. And it is a characteristic of man that he alone has any sense of good and evil, of just and unjust, and the like, and the association of living beings who have this sense makes a family and a state. Further the state is by nature clearly prior to the family and to the individual, since the whole is of necessity prior to the part; for example, if the whole body be destroyed, there will be no foot or hand, except homonymously, as we might speak of a stone hand; for when destroyed the hand will be no better than that. But things are defined by their function and power; and we ought not say that they are the same when they no longer have their proper quality, but only that they are homonymous. The proof that the state is a creation of nature and prior to the individual is that the individual, when isolated, is not self-sufficing; and therefore he is like a part in relation to the whole. But he who is unable to live in society, or who has need because he is sufficient for himself, must be either a beast or a God: he is no part of a state.[2]

This is perhaps the most radical defense of the State made in antiquity against the attempts of some currents of Sophism to reduce the polis to a simple fruit of artificial convention and against the extremist denials of the Cynics. Evidently Aristotle, in his vindication of the natural character of the State, goes too far; but it is not necessary to remind the reader once again what strength the Greek political, social, and cultural conditions possessed. The Hellenes, as scholars have long since known, did not have a Church or anything corresponding to it and were inevitably brought to recognize a single type of society that would have a metabiological and spiritual aim and to identify this with the State and with the polis. It is true that with more accuracy, as has been stated, Aristotle would have need to define man as "a social animal," instead as "a political animal"; but it is likewise true that to do this, he would have had to be able to distinguish society from the State and from this distinction he was so far off, that, as we will say better further on, was not even in the condition to understand any another correct form of the State than the City-State, the polis of an Hellenic type, so rooted in the Greek sensibilities that it was his way of conceiving the State and public affairs!

2. The administration of the family

The family that is the original nucleus of which the City-State is composed is constituted by four elements; (*a*) of the relationship of husband and wife, (*b*) of the relationship of father and sons, (*c*) of the relationship of father and servants, (*d*) of the art of procuring things that serve and in particular the riches (the so-called *crematistica*). Aristotle lingers particularly over the third and fourth elements.

Since the administration of the family must acquire determinate qualities and to do this demands adequate instruments, both animate and inanimate, then the workers and slaves"Aristotle thought"are indispensable. The worker is "like an instrument which precedes and conditions the other instruments" and serves for the production of determinate objects and useful goods. Instead the slave does not serve in the production of anything but rather in general "is a worker who serves that which concerns action," "an instrument who serves the doing of things,"[3] that is, in the conduct of life.

But what kind of foundation can be admitted for an institution like that of slavery, viz., an institution that established that a man can be "a living possession" of another man? We have seen that on the part of some Sophists and some minor Socratics challenged or at least cracked the conviction of the soundness of slavery. Aristotle, instead, defended it on the basis of the "natural character" of slavery.

Actually, the metaphysical principles of his system, correctly applied would have brought him to conclusions exactly contrary to this; but here the philosopher allows such a point because conditioned by prejudices and convictions of his time, by bending in a most artificial way his own principles to make them correspond with his convictions. He began from the presupposition that the soul and the mind *by nature* command the body and appetite just as these men in which the soul and mind predominate must have command over those in whom they do not predominate.

And first since he was then convinced that in the masculine the soul and reason predominates more than in the feminine, so he concludes that "the masculine is *by nature* better, the feminine worse, the one called to command, the other to obey."[4]

And for a stronger reason, *by nature* they must be held worse and hence capable only of obedience, and hence slaves, all those men who had the nature endowed with robust bodies but weak minds. Here are the precise words of our philosopher:

> Where then there is such a difference as that between soul and body, or between men and animals (as in the case of those whose business is to use their body, and can do nothing better), the lower sort are *by nature slaves*, and it is better for them as for all inferiors that they should be under the rule of a master. For he who can be, and therefore is, another's, and he who participates in reason enough to apprehend, but to have, is a slave by nature. Whereas the lower animals cannot even apprehend reason; they obey their passions. And indeed the use made of slaves and of tame animals is not very different; for both with their bodies minister to the needs of life.[5]

Here the evident disproportion between the premises and the conclusion is immediately evident besides a good dose of error in the premises themselves. The note that differences man from animal is the reason, and this is the essential and determinate difference; now, the fact that some men have more or less reason cannot change the essence or nature; nature of man is such as long as there is reason, much or little (the quantity does not intrude on the quality in this case). Without reckoning, then, that the difference of intelligence that Aristotle pretends to uncover between man and man is a far from being of the character of that which in the passage read comes to be affirmed.

Naturally, even with the hardening of the principles and the data, Aristotle overworked somewhat their agreement with his reasonings and with the historical realities by which he was conditioned. In fact, slaves were provided, often enough, by the conquests of war (they were hence prisoners). But a war can be *unjust*, the prisoners can be of *high rank*, and in the case of wars of Greeks against Greeks, can be a *Greek* equal in every way "by nature" to those who have made them prisoners. In all these cases slavery is not justifiable "by nature." So? The solution of Aristotle is the following; *by nature* the "barbarian" is inferior and therefore he says with Euripides: "that the Greeks command over barbarians is natural."[6]

But anyone can clearly see that the cure is worse than the disease, again in a sense more damaging to the position of the philosopher, who, to preserve the equality of the Greeks, embraces a typically Hellenic prejudice according to which the Greek is by nature superior to the barbarian, which was a prejudice of an absolutely ethnic character, and as such, fundamentally irrational.

With respect to the *crematistica*,[7] Aristotle distinguishes three kinds of procurement of goods and wealth: (*a*) a natural and immediate mode located through the activity of hunting, sheep-breeding, and agriculture; (*b*) an intermediate mode; that is, mediate, consisting of the exchange of goods with equivalent goods (barter); and (*c*) a nonnatural mode consisting of commerce through money, which was used by all the clever to increase without limit their wealth. Now this third form of *crematistica* is condemned by Aristotle *because there is no limit to the amount of wealth*; and so, who devotes himself to it loses the sense and the ultimate goal of a healthy economy, which is that of satisfying *real needs* and not accumulation of wealth, and he ends changing what is a simple means into that which is an end. Aristotle says wisely:

> Hence some persons are led to believe that getting wealth is the object of household management [the continual accumulation of wealth] and whole idea of their lives is that they ought either to increase their money without limit, or at any rate not to lose it. The origin of this disposition in men is that they are intent upon living only, and not upon living well; and, as their desires

are unlimited, they also desire that the means of gratifying them should be without limit.[8]

A healthy economy tries instead to gain, in the first two ways, so much to satisfy natural needs, *which have a limit fixed by nature*. It is logical, therefore, that he would condemned usury, and hence any form of investment of money intended to produce more money.[9] And although with respect to these positions there is presupposed a socioeconomic situation different than our own, not for this is it less true the basic requirements that they make worthy. When money becomes an end instead of a means, it overturns the meaning of life. Life is used to produce money instead of making money to support life.

3. The citizen

From the analysis of the family Aristotle (after severely criticizing Platonic communitarianism)[10] goes on to consider the State, without deepening the problems relative to villages (which, as we have seen, was the second of the elements constitutive of it). And yet, he presents the second question from a different angle. Because the State is made up of citizens, it is a question of establishing the *nature of the citizen*.

To be a citizen in a City-State, it is not sufficient to live within the territory or enjoy the right of bringing a legal action and not even would it be sufficient to be a descendent of citizens. To be a citizen it is necessary "to participate in the tribunals and the magistracy," it is necessary; that is, *to take part in the administration of justice and to be part of the assembly that legislates and governs the City-State.*[11]

This definition more than ever reflects the peculiar aspect of the Greek City-State, where the citizen is felt to be such only if he participated *directly* in the government of public affairs, in all its aspects (making laws, applying them, administering justice). Consequently, no colonial, no member of a conquered city could be a "citizen" in this sense. But even the workers could not be true citizens, even if they were freed men (that is, even if they were not metics, or strangers, or slaves), because those would not have at their disposition the *time*, which was necessary for the exercise of these functions that to the eyes of Aristotle are essential. And just as the "citizens" are very limited in number, whereas all the other men of the City-State end by being, in some way, means that serve for the satisfaction of the needs of the first. The workers are different from the slaves because although these serve the needs of only one person, they serve the public needs, but for this they did not cease at all to be means.[12]

And so it happens that while Aristotle affirmed that "they are not to be considered citizens all those without whom the City-State would not exist,"[13] history has shown the contrary to be true; but it has demonstrated it only by going through a series of revolutions, and and still have difficulty in translating into reality this truth, that simply, on a theoretical level, has been definitively acquired.

4. The State and its possible forms

The State, the nature of which and whose finality we have seen established, can be attained according to different forms, viz., according to different *constitutions*. Aristotle writes: "A constitution is the structure which gives order to the state by establishing the arrangement of all the duties and especially those of the ruling authority."[14] Now it is clear that since this sovereign authority can be realized in different forms, there will be as many types of constitutions as there are these forms. And the sovereign power can be exercised (*a*) by one man alone, (*b*) by a few men, (*c*) or by a majority of men. But that is not sufficient. Each of these three forms of government can be exercised in a good way and in a bad way, precisely: "The true forms of government, therefore, are those in which the one, or the few, or the many, govern with a view to the *common interest*; but governments which rule with a view to the *private interest*, whether of the one, or of the few, or of the many, are perversions."[15]

There are thus three forms of correct constitutions; *monarchy, aristocracy,* and *constitutional,* to which corresponds likewise forms of degenerate constitutions; *tyranny, oligarchy,* and *democracy.* Here are Aristotle's precise words:

> Of forms of government in which one *rules*, we call that which regards the common interest, kingship; that in which more than one rules, but not many, rule, *aristocracy*; and it is so called, either because the rulers are the best men, or because they have at heart the best interests of the state and of the citizens. But when the many administer the state for the common interest, the government is called by the generic name–a *constitution.*...Of the earlier mentioned forms, the perversions are as follows–of *kingship, tyranny; of aristocracy, oligarchy; of constitutional government,* democracy. For tyranny is a kind of monarchy which has in view the interest of the monarch only; oligarchy has in view the interest of the wealthy; democracy, of the needy: none of them the common good of all.[16]

(The modern reader must consider, for a sound orientation, that the Stagirite intends with the name *democracy* a government that obscures the good for everyone, aiming at the favoring of the interests of the poorest *in an undue way*, and hence gives to the term a negative acceptance that we will render rather with the term *demagoguery*; in fact, Aristotle specifies the notion that the error into which democracy falls is that of maintaining that because all are equal in liberty, all can be and ought to be equal also in everything else.)

What is the best of these three constitutions? The response of Aristotle is polyvalent; chiefly, he stated that all three form of government, when they are right, are *natural* and hence good, indeed because the good of the State consists in aiming at the common good.

It is therefore evident that if in a City-State there exists a man who is excellent in all things, monarchical power should be given to him, and if there exists a group of individual men truly excellent in virtue, they would be able to form an aristocratic government or oligarchy. Here are Aristotle's explicit words:

> If, however, there be some one person, or more than one, although not enough to make up the full complement of a state, whose excellence is so pre-eminent that the excellence or the political capacity of all the rest admit of no comparison with his or theirs, he or they can be no longer regarded as part of a state; for justice will not be done to the superior, if he is reckoned only as the equal of those who are so far inferior to him in excellence and in political capacity. Such a man may truly be deemed a God among men. Hence we see that legislation is necessarily concerned only with those who are equal in birth and in capacity; and that for men of pre-eminent excellence there is no law - they are themselves a law.[17]

Therefore *monarchy* would be, in the abstract, the better form of government, in the situation where there was an exceptional man in a City-State; whereas *aristocracy* would be so in the case in which there were a group of exceptional men. But since such conditions normally are not confirmed, Aristotle, with his strongly realistic sense, indicates the *constitutional* as the form of government most appropriate for the Greek City-State of his time, in which there did not exist one or few exceptional men, but many men who, although they did not excel in political virtue, were still capable of turning to command and being commanders according to the law. The *constitutional* state is practically speaking a *middle way* between oligarchy and democracy, or if you wish, a democracy tempered with oligarchy. In fact, he who governs is a multitude (as in a democracy) and not a minority (as in oligarchy), but it is not a question of poor multitude (different from democracy) but of a well-off multitude insofar as a need to serve in the army and also that excels in warlike abilities. (As we see, the *constitution* adapts the values and destroys the defects of the two degenerate forms and hence in the general schema traced by the Stagirite it is in a somewhat anomalous position anomalous, because it is found on a different level both with respect to the first two complete constitutions, and with respect to the three that are incomplete).

The *constitutional* state, therefore, is the constitution that esteems the middle class that as "middle" offers the best guarantee of stability. Here are the explicit statements of Aristotle:

> But a city ought to be composed, as far as possible, of equals and similars; and these are generally the middle classes. Wherefore the city which is composed of middle-class citizens is necessarily best constituted in respect

of the elements of which we say the fabric of the state naturally consists. And this is the class of citizens which is most secure in a state, for they do not, like the poor, covet other man's goods; nor do others covet theirs, as the poor covet the goods of the rich; and as they neither plot against others, nor are themselves plotted against, they pass through life safely. Wisely then did Phocylides pray–"Many things are best in the mean; I desire to be of a middle condition in my city." Thus it is manifest that the best political community is formed by *citizens of the middle class, and that those states are likely to be well administered in which the middle class is large, and stronger if possible than both the other classes, or at any rate than either singly.*[18]

Also in politics as in ethics, therefore, the concept of the "middle" plays a fundamental role.

5. The ideal State

Of the analyses that Aristotle offers in Books Four, Five and the Six of the *Politics* (dedicated to the examination of the various kinds and species of constitutions, the various forms of revolution, the causes that determine them and the ways with which it is possible to prevent them), in this place it is not possible to speak, given their particularized and even technical character. The Stagirite offers in them the proof of an extraordinary historical consciousness, a truly exceptional and subtle knowledge and a wisdom in understanding political facts and events.

Of greater interest, in what concerns the properly philosophical problematic are instead the last two books dedicated to illustrating the *Ideal State*. And since as we have seen, the conception of the State for Aristotle is fundamentally moral, it is no surprise if he focuses his argument more on its moral and educational problems than on the technical aspects of the institutions and the administration of justice.

It has been seen in ethics that the good is of three different kinds: external goods, corporeal goods, and spiritual goods of the soul. And it has also been seen in what sense the first two are considered as simply means for the realization of the third. And *this holds*–Aristotle says–*both for the individual and for the State.* Also the State must seek the first two types of goods in limited ways and exclusively in function of spiritual goods, because only in them does happiness consist. Here is an very important passage in this regard:

> For, whereas external goods have a limit, like any other instrument, and all things useful are useful for a purpose, and where there is too much of them they must either do harm, or at any rate be of no use, to their possessors, every good of the soul, the greater it is, is also of greater use, if the epithet useful as well as noble is appropriate to such subjects. No proof is required to show that the best state of one thing in relation to another corresponds in degree of excellence to the interval between the natures of which we say that these very states are states: so that, *if the soul is more noble than our*

possessions or our bodies, both absolutely and in relation to us, it must be admitted that the best of either has a similar ratio to the other. Again, it is for the sake of the soul that goods external and goods of the body are desirable at all, and all wise men ought to choose them for the sake of the soul, and not the soul for the sake of them. Let us acknowledge then that *each one has just so much of happiness as he has of excellence and wisdom, and of excellent and wise action.* The Gods are a witness to us of this truth, *for they are happy and blessed, not by reason of any external good, but in themselves and by reason of their own nature.* And herein of necessity lies the difference between good fortune and happiness; for external goods come of themselves, and chance is the author of them, but no one is just or temperate by or through chance. In like manner, and by a similar train of argument, *the happy state may be shown to be that which is best and which acts rightly; and it cannot act rightly without doing right actions, and neither individual or state can do right actions without excellence and wisdom. Thus the courage, justice, and wisdom of a state have the same form and nature as the qualities which give individuals who possess them the name of just, wise or temperate.*[19]

Here are the ideal conditions that must be located in the happy State.

(*a*) With respect to population, which is the first condition of political activity, it must not be too small or too large, but justly measured. In fact a City-State with too few citizens would not be able to be self-sufficient, while the City-State must be sufficient to itself. Instead, that which has too many citizens will be difficult to govern. No one could be a general of a too numerous troop of citizens. No one could be herald in a City-State with too many citizens unless he had a stentorian voice. The citizens could not know each other and hence could not distribute with knowledge the various duties. In sum, Aristotle wanted a City-State that was *to measure man.*[20]

(*b*) Also the territory must be presented in an analogous way. It must be big enough to provide that which is necessary to life, without producing superfluities. It must offer analgous features. It must be difficult to attack and easily defensible, in a favorable position with respect to the hinterlands and with respect to the sea.[21]

(*c*) The ideal qualities of the citizen are–according to Aristotle–exactly those that the Greeks possessed; these are like a *middle way* and like a synthesis of the qualities of the northern peoples and the eastern peoples:

> Those who live in a cold climate and in Europe are full of spirit, but wanting in intelligence and skill; and therefore they retain comparative freedom, but have no political organization, and are incapable of ruling over others. Whereas the natives of Asia are intelligent and inventive, but they are wanting in spirit, and therefore they are always in a state of subjection and slavery. But the Hellenic peoples, which is situated between them, is likewise intermediate in character, being high-spirited and also intelligent. Hence it continues free, and is best-governed of any nation, and, if it could be formed into one state, would be able to rule the world.[22]

It is useless to say that in this judgment the Stagirite is the victim of the same presuppositions that had allowed him to think that the "barbarians" could be slaves "by nature."

(*d*) Aristotle examined hence what are the essential functions of the City-State and what is their ideal distribution.[23] To be sustained in existence a City-State must have (1) farmers who provide the bread, (2) artisans who provide the tools and the manufactured goods, (3) the soldiers who defend it against rebels and enemies, (4) merchants who produce wealth, (5) men who establish what is useful to the community and what are the mutual duties of the citizens, (6) the priests who are concerned with worship.

Consequently, the good City-State will prevent the excrcise of all these functions by all the citizens. First, in the ideal City-State forms of private lives will not be practiced, like those who are peasants or who are merchants or laborers; they are models of the mindless life and live contrary to virtue and in general impede the exercise of virtue, because they do not have sufficient time or liberty. The peasants are therefore slaves and as well as the laborers and merchants who do not have a part in "citizenship." The true citizen is occupied therefore with war, government, and worship. Of themselves, insofar as these functions demand different virtues (the warrior must have power, the judge and legislator prudence), it would need to distribute them to different persons; but this would be difficult to accept in the case of soldiers, who having military power also want political power. The solution that Aristotle proposes is the following. The same persons exercise these offices in different ways: "Nature prescribes that the young have strength and the old have wisdom. Such a distribution of duties will be expedient and also just, and is founded upon a principle of conformity to merit."[24]

Then the citizen will be *first* warriors, *then* counselors, *finally* priests. All those will be affluent, since peasants and workers and merchants foresee that which is necessary for material necessities, they would have all the necessary time to exercise their virtue and to a full attainment of the happy life. And thus "living well" and happiness will be conceded only to the "citizens" of the ideal City-State; all the other men who live in it will be reduced to simple "necessary conditions" and condemned to a marginal human life. We find ourselves faced with the usual historical-social conditioning that so heavily limited Aristotelian thought on this issue and its location in a dimension very alien to us, since, in substance, the philosopher says that it happens that many human beings live a marginal human life or an incomplete human life so that other human beings may live a full or complete human life and that all this is "natural."

(*e*) But there is still an essential point. Happiness of the City-State depends on virtue, but virtue lives in each citizen and therefore the City-State can become and be happy in the measure in which each citizen becomes and is virtuous. How does each man become virtuous and good? In the first place, he must have a certain *natural disposition*, then on this the *attitudes* and *habits* must act, hence *reasoning* and *argument*.[25] Now the education acts precisely on the attitudes and reasoning, and is therefore a factor of enormous importance in the State.

The citizens must be educated in a fundamentally equal way, so that they are capable, in turn, of being obedient and commanding, given that, in turn, they must precisely obey (when they are young) and then command (once they become mature men).[26] But in particular, since the virtue of the good *citizen* and the good *man* is identical, *the education must be substantially to have the aim of forming good men*; that is, it must be able *to realize the ideal established in ethics*; that is, the body living in function of the soul, the lower parts of the soul in function of the higher, and in particular so that the ideal of pure contemplation is realized. The philosopher expressly writes:

> And there must be a corresponding division of actions; the actions of the naturally better part are to be preferred by those who have it in their power to attain to two out of the three or to all, for that is always to everyone the most desirable which is the highest attainable by him. The whole of life is further divided into two parts, business and leisure, war and peace, and of actions some aim at what is necessary and useful, and some at what is honorable. And the preference given to one or the other class of actions *must necessarily be like the preference given to one or the other part of the soul and its actions over the other*; there must be war for the sake of peace, business for the sake of leisure, things useful and necessary for the sake of things honorable. All these points the statesman should keep in view when he frames his laws; he should consider the parts of the soul and their functions, and above all the better and the end; he should also remember the adversities of human lives and actions for men must be able to engage in business and go to war, but leisure and peace are better; they must do what is necessary and indeed what is useful, but what is honorable [that is, *to contemplate*] is better.[27]

The State is not a private citizen, it must impart education that naturally begins with the body, that develops further to reason, will proceed with the education of the impulses, the instincts, and the appetites, and finally will terminate with the education of the rational soul. The traditional Greek physical-musical education assumed in the Aristotelian State and the *Politics* ends with the description of it.

It is hardly necessary to point out that all the lower classes are excluded from education; a technical-professional education for Aristotle is meaningless, because he would educate not only for advantage of *man* but for the advantage of *things* that serve man whereas the true education is an education to be truly and fully a man. These are wonderful requirements, and it has much to recommend it to men of today, except the pretense that so that some can become and be completely human, others must be remain rivetted to the destiny of remaining only a marginal human beings.

Also in politics, in conclusion, the *metaempirical conception of the soul and of the values of the soul are the framework within which the whole argument of Aristotle develops.* Also here Aristotle is very close to Plato, which is not commonly acknowledged; there are certain aberrant aspects of the Platonic republic that the Stagirite criticizes and rejects, but not the basic ideal that it expresses.

FOURTH SECTION

THE FOUNDATION OF LOGIC, RHETORIC, AND POETRY

οἱ ἄνθρωποι πρὸς τὸ ἀληθὲς πεφύκασιν ἱκανῶς καὶ τὰ πλείω τυγχάνουσι τῆς ἀληθείας.

Men are sufficiently endowed for the truth and they achieve the truth for the most part.

Aristotle, *Rhetoric*, A 1.1355a15-17

I. THE FOUNDATION OF LOGIC

1. The concept of logic or "analytics"

Logic does not have a place in the scheme on which the Stagirite divides and systematizes the sciences, and this is not an accident. It is not considered, in fact, either a production of something (thus a productive science) or a moral action (thus a practical science) or even as having a determined content distinct from that of metaphysics or physics or mathematics (thus a theoretical science).

Logic considers instead *the necessary forms of demonstrative argument, in general, which claim to be probative.* Logic shows, hence, thought as a process when there is reasoning: its structure, its elements, the possibility, type, and mode of demonstration, and when it may be used.

Naturally, it is possible to say that logic is a science itself, in the sense that its content is given precisely by the operations of reason; that is, by that *ens tamquam verum (being as true, logical being)* that the Stagirite has distinguished.[1] However, this is only in part outlined in the affirmations of Aristotle, who often avoided the word *logic*, almost incidentally called logic a *science*,[2] and considered it rather a preliminary study; that is, a general propaedeutic to all the sciences. Therefore, the term *organon*, which means "instrument," introduced by Alexander of Aphrodisias to designate logic in its totality (and successively utilized also as a title for the totality of all the Aristotelian works concerning logic), well defines the concept and the goal of Aristotelian logic, which claims to furnish precisely the mental instruments necessary for confronting any kind of inquiry whatever.[3]

It is, however, again to be observed that the term *logic* is not used by Aristotle to designate what we today mean by the term. The term arises in the time of Cicero (and perhaps it is of Stoic origin), but its use is consolidated probably only with Alexander.[4] The Stagirite called logic instead with the term *analytics*, and *Analytics* is the name of the fundamental works of the *Organon.*[5]

"Analytics" (from the Greek ἀνάλυσις, which means resolution) explains the method with which we, by beginning from a given conclusion, *resolve it* precisely into the elements from which it was derived; that is, into the premises from which it arises and hence that ground it and justify it. The analytics is essentially the doctrine of the syllogism, and in effect, it constitutes the fundamental nucleus, the axis around which turns all the other aspects of Aristotelian logic. Moreover, the Stagirite was completely aware of being the discoverer of the syllogism, so much is it true that with total clarity, at the end of the *Sophistic Refutations,* he says that although with respect to rhetorical discourse there were many ancient treatises, on the syllogism there existed absolutely none at all.[6] This is equivalent to saying that since logic (in the Aristotelian sense) is wholly focussed on the syllogism, it is precisely this discovery of the syllogism made possible for the Stagirite the systematization and, hence, the explanation of the whole logical problematic and therefore it is the foundation of logic.

2. The general design of the logical works and the development of Aristotelian logic

To better orient ourselves in the exposition of the issues of logic, it is opportune to outline, through the widest designations, the general design that emerges from the logical writings that have come down to us. They were certainly not composed in the order into which posterity has systematized them in the *Organon*;[7] thus, we have to read them in precisely this systematic order. At the center, as we said, stands the *Analytics* (which Aristotle perhaps considered a single work),[8] which was soon distinguished into the *Prior Analytics* and the *Posterior Analytics*. The former treats the structure of the syllogism in general, its different figures and its different modes, by considering in a formal manner; that is, by prescinding from their truth value and studying them only in terms of consistency or the formal coherence of their reasoning. (In fact, a syllogism may be formally correct or valid that begins from specified premises and deduces the consequences imposed by the given premises; but if the premises are not true, the syllogism, although formally correct, terminates in a conclusion that is not true.) In the *Posterior Analytics*, instead, Aristotle is concerned with the syllogism, which in addition to being formally correct must likewise be true; that is, with the *scientific (demonstrative) syllogism* that is the true and proper demonstration:

> By demonstration–writes Aristotle–I mean the scientific syllogism; I call scientific that syllogism on the basis of which, by the fact of possessing it, we possess science. If then science is as we have posited it, it is necessary for demonstrative science in particular to depend on things which are true and primitive and immediate and more familiar than and prior to and explanatory of the conclusions. For in this way the principles will also be appropriate to what is being proved. The syllogism indeed also exists without these conditions, while demonstration cannot exist without them, since it would not produce science.[9]

Consequently, the *Posterior Analytics* is likewise concerned with the premises, how they are known, and the problems connected to definitions.

In the *Topics*, Aristotle treats instead the *dialectical syllogism*; that is, that syllogism which begins from premises simply based on *opinion* or on the elements that seem to be wholly acceptable or acceptable for the most part, and which hence offer the type of purely *probable* arguments.

Finally in the *Sophistic Refutations*, which in reality may be the final book of the *Topics*,[10] the philosopher is concerned with sophistic arguments.

Since syllogisms are made up of judgments or propositions and these in their turn are made up of concepts and terms, Aristotle must consequently turn to the former and then the latter. He does so in the *Categories* and in the *De Interpretatione*, where there is an analysis in an approximate way of the simplest elements of the proposition; that is, simple notions and primary terms and the judgment and proposition. Therefore, the location of these treatises at the beginning of the *Organon*, almost like a preliminary to the *Analytics* and to the *Topics* would seem to the systematizer of the *Organon* wholly natural. Such a connection undoubtedly exists, but is much more tenuous than was believed to be the case in the past. In particular, it is known that the doctrines of the concept and the proposition, which are presented in the treatises of classical logic and in many parts of the textbook tradition, are for the most part the result of the later reelaboration (especially medieval) of some elements taken from Aristotle.

Finally we must note, not to avoid the historical meaning of the Aristotelian logic, that it arises from a reflection on the procedures that the preceding philosophers had put into practice, principally (as is obvious) beginning from the Sophists, and chiefly taking into account the Socratic procedure, especially as it was extended and probed by Plato. Certainly the mathematical method also had an influence, as revealed by the terminology itself, used to point out many of the logical structures. But mathematics was only *one* component; other sciences exist that could have suggested his discoveries to Aristotle. Aristotelian logic has, therefore, a determinable philosophical origin, it marks the moment in which the philosophical logos, until then completely matured through the structuring of all its problems in the manner which we have seen, becomes capable of stating the problem about its own status and has a precise way of proceeding; and thus, after having learned to reason, the logos succeeds in establishing what the nature of reason is itself, viz., what it is to reason, how much, and on what is it possible to reason. It is a discovery that would be sufficient to give to Aristotle one of the primary places in the history of Western thought.

3. Categories, terms, definitions

The treatise on the *Categories* contains, as we have said, something in some way corresponding to the study of the most simple elements of logic. If we take propositions as "man runs" or "man conquers" and we look for the nexus, viz., if we consider the subject in separation from the predicate, we obtain a word "without connection," viz., separated from any connection with the proposition, e.g., "man," "conquers," "runs" (that is, uncombined terms combined are the source of the proposition). Now, Aristotle says: "Of the things that are said without any combination, each refers to either *substance* or *quantity* or *quality* or *relation* or *where* or *when* or *being-in-position* or *having* or *doing* or *being-affected*."[11] As can be seen, they are the *categories*, which we already recognize from the *Metaphysics*. Here listed as ten in number (perhaps in Pythagorean homage to the perfect number ten), but we know that in reality the number is more exactly eight, because "being in a position" (or "position") and "having" are assumable into other categories.

Consequently if, as we have seen, from the metaphysical standpoint, the categories represent the fundamental meanings of being, it is clear that, *from the logical standpoint*, they must be (as a consequence) *the highest genera within which any term of a proposition is able to be located*. And therefore the passage just read is quite clear, if we separate out the parts of a proposition, each and every term derives its meaning in the ultimate analysis, from one of the categories. Therefore the categories just as they go back to the ultimate meanings of being, also go back to the ultimate meanings to which the terms of a proposition are reducible. Let us take the proposition "Socrates runs" and separate it out; we obtain "Socrates," which goes back to the category of substance, and "runs," which is located in the category of "action." So if I say "Socrates is now in the Lyceum" and break up the proposition, "in the Lyceum" will be reducible to the category of "where," and "now" will be reducible to the category of "when," and so on.

"*Category*" was translated by Boethius with "predicate"; but the translation expresses only in part the meaning of the Greek term and is not wholly adequate; in fact it opens the origin of the term to numerous difficulties, in great part eliminable by maintaining the original meaning. Actually the first category functions always as subject and only improperly as a predicate, as when I say: "Socrates is a man" (that is, "Socrates is a substance"); the others function as predicates (or, you wish, the highest figures of all the possible predicates, the highest genera are solely predicates). And naturally, since the first category constitutes the being on which the being of the others is supported, the first category will be the subject and the other categories could not be except in this subject; hence they alone are capable of being true and proper predicates.

When we fix on the isolated terms of the proposition and take each by itself, we do not have either truth or falsity. Aristotle says: "These things we have listed, taken one by one, in and of themselves, do not constitute an affirmation, which is generated instead by their mutual connection; and indeed each affirmation, as it seems, is true or false, while of the things said without any connection none is true or false, for example, 'man,' 'white,' 'runs,' 'wins.'"[12] What exactly does this mean, that truth (or falsity) is never said of the terms of the proposition *taken singlely*, but *only because they combine in the judgment*, and in the proposition that expresses that combination.

Naturally, since the categories are not simply the terms that result from the breaking apart of the proposition, but the genera to which they are reducible or under which they fall, then the categories themselves are something prior and not further reducible. At the maximum level of universality it can be said that they are "being," but being is not a genus (as we have seen) and hence not definable, precisely because there does not exist anything more general to which we can have recourse to define them.

We have just touched on the problem of the definition, which Aristotle did not consider in the *Categories* but rather in the *Posterior Analytics* and in his other works. However, since the definition concerns terms and concepts it is well to speak of it at this point, as, moreover, the exposition by means of the questions aroused demands.

If it is said that the categories are indefinables because they are the most general, it is because they are the highest genera or predicates. The individuals are indefinable, for different reasons; that is, because they are singulars (καθ' ἕκαστον), and they are the antipodes of the categories, it is possible only to have a perception of them; that is, a purely experiential grasp. But between the categories and the singulars is a whole gamut of notions and concepts, which go from the more universal to the less universal, and some that normally constitute the terms of the judgments and propositions we formulate (the name indicating the individual can be used only as a subject). All these terms, which are between the universality of the categories and the singularity of individuals, we know precisely through their definition (ὁρισμός).

What is the nature of the definition? It not so much means to explain a word but rather to determine what is the object to which the word refers. Therefore the definition that Aristotle gives of the definition is adequately explained as "the locution which expresses the essence [τὸ τί ἦν εἶναι]" or "the locution which expresses the nature [φύσις] of the thing," or "the locution which expresses the substance [οὐσία] of the thing."[13] And to define anything we need the "genus" and the "difference," says Aristotle, or, as has been expressed in the classical formula of Aristotelian thought, the "proximate genus" and the "specific difference."[14] If we wish to know what "man" means we must, by means of an analysis, specify the "proximate genus" in which he is located, which is not that of "living thing" (plants are also living things) but "animal" (animals have besides a vegetative life, also a sentient life), and then we must analyze the "differences" that determine the genus animal, until we find the "ultimate difference" distinctive of man, which is "rationality." Man is, therefore, "*a rational* (specific difference) *animal* (proximate genus)." The essence of things is given by the ultimate or specific difference that characterizes the genus.[15]

Naturally, what holds for the definition of each notion as such holds for the categories; a definition will be sound or not sound but never *true* or *false*, because truth and falsity always imply a combination or separation of notions *and this happens only in the judgment and in the proposition* of which we will now speak.

4. Propositions (*De Interpretatione*)

When we combine two terms (a name and a verb) and we affirm or deny something of something else, viz., as being true or false, then we have a judgment. The judgment is, therefore, an act by which we affirm or deny something of something and the logical expression of the judgment is the enunciation or the *proposition*. Aristotle, actually, does not have a precise terminology in this respect; what we call the *judgment* he indicates rather by the term κατάφασις (*affirmation*) and ἀπόφασις (*negation*); that is, with terms indicating the operations of which the judgment consists; and that which we call the *proposition* he indicates by the term πρότασις. Judgment and proposition constitute the most elementary form of knowledge, that form which makes knowledge directly a nexus between a predicate and a subject. Truth and falsity has its origin in judgment; that is, in the affirmation or negation. Truth is present because what is conjoined in the judgment is conjoined in reality (or because what is separated in the judgment is separated in reality); the false judgment is present instead because what is conjoined in the judgment is not conjoined in reality (or because what is separated in the judgment is not separated in reality). The enunciation or proposition that expresses the judgment, therefore, always expresses affirmations and negations, and it is either true or false.[16] (Note that not just any sentence is a proposition of interest to logic: all sentences that express prayers, invocations, exclamations, and similars are outside of logic and are the concern of rhetoric and poetic discourse; only *apophantic* or declarative discourse enters into the sphere of interest of logic).[17]

The first distinction that must be made among judgments is that between *affirmative judgments* and *negative judgments*, given precisely that to judge is *to affirm or to deny something of something*. (And since in regard to each affirmation and negation there is no middle ground, then, necessarily, either one or the other is true.)[18]

With respect to what in the future will be called the *quantity of terms*; that is, the extension of terms (the greater or lesser universality of the subject), judgments are divided into *universal*, if they are concerned with a universal (for example, "all men are white" or "all men are not white"), and *individual or singular*, if they are concerned with an individual (for example, "Socrates is white" or "Socrates is not white"). In addition, a judgment can concern a universal but not be universal, as in the case of the judgment "a man is white" (or "some men are white" and the corresponding negations); this judgment is said to be a *singular*. (In the *Analytics*, Aristotle will speak, instead, of *indefinite* judgments.) Of universal contradictory propositions and those that are singulars, one but not both is always true or false; instead with the singular contradictory propositions both can be true (e.g., "some man is white," "some man is not white"), which are traditionally called *subcontraries*.[19]

The *De Interpretatione*, finally, considers the *mode* by which something is affirmed or denied of something else, and hence the *modality* of the proposition. We not only join a predicate with a subject and separate them, saying it is or it is not, sometimes, we specify also *in what way a subject* and a predicate are joined or separated; one way is to say "such a subject is such," another is to say "such a subject *must be* such," and other way again is to say "such a subject *can be* such." (We present a particularly illustrative example: someone says "God *exists*," another says, "God *must exist*," and another says "God *can exist*.") Aristotle reduces these propositions implying necessity and possibility to the *assertoric* (declarative) form; and as we have for the necessary proposition "A *is necessarily* that which B is" and for possibility "A *is possibly* that which B is." The negations of these propositions will be "A *is not necessarily* that which B is," and "A *is not possibly* that which B is." He then develops a complex series of considerations about modal propositions.[20] Instead, he can not be said to have noticed the further distinctions of the *hypothetical* judgment and the *disjunctive* judgment.

5. Syllogism

When we affirm or deny something of something else; that is, when we judge and construct propositions, we are not yet reasoning. No one, obviously, reasons by formulating a series of judgments or merely listing a series of propositions evidencing no connection in any way among themselves.

We reason, instead, when we pass from judgment to judgment, from proposition to proposition *that have a relevant connection between them* and that, in a certain sense, are the cause of the assertion of the other proposition, one is called the antecedent and the other is the consequent. There is no reasoning where no connection is asserted. Consequently, the *syllogism* is precisely a complete reasoning; that is, a reasoning process in which the conclusion to which it comes is effectively the consequence that arises, of necessity, from the antecedent.

In general, in a deductive reasoning process; that is, in a syllogism, there must be three propositions, of which two function as antecedents and are hence said to be the *premises*, the third is the consequent; that is, the conclusion that arises from the premises. In the syllogism there are always three terms, of which the one functions as mediator (the middle term) that unites the other two, as we will see.

Let us take a classic example of the syllogism:

(1) If all *sentient things* are *animals.*
(2) And all *men* are *sentient things.*
(3) Then all *men* are *animals.*

It is clear that *all men are animals* is a consequence that necessarily arises from having established that *all sentient things are animals* and that all men are *sentient things.* Where "sentient things" is the term [middle] that warrants the conclusion.

It is in this way that the famous definition given by Aristotle is to be understood:

> Syllogism is a discourse (that is, a reasoning process) in which, something having been stated (that is, the premises) something else necessarily follows from it, solely by reason of their being posited. And with the expression "solely by reason of their being posited" I mean that it follows because of them, and further with the expression "it follows because of them" I mean that no further term is required to have it follow by necessity.[21]

An Italian scholar has given a fine commentary on this passage, "The syllogism is hence to be characterized by the necessity of the consequent [the conclusion] flowing from the antecedent [the premises], by the sole fact that it is laid down. In that sense *the premises are a cause not of the truth or falsity, or in general of the content,* of the consequent [conclusion] considered in itself, but of the process; it is so true that, laying down the antecedent [premises], the consequent [conclusion] cannot not follow from it. The syllogistic premises, therefore, have the value of *hypotheses* and must hence be preceded by the conjunction *if.*[22] In the syllogism, because of the *consistency* generated by the logical form of the reasoning, the truth value must be an extraneous issue, but reference will be made to it, in another persepctive.

Now we will turn to the example of the syllogism that we previously constructed. The first proposition is called the *major premise,* the second the *minor premise,* the third the *conclusion.* The two terms that are united in the conclusion are called the first (which is the subject of the conclusion, "men") the *minor term,* the second (which is the predicate of the conclusion, "animals") the *major term.* And since these terms are combined together through another term, which we have said functions as a hinge, is said to be the *middle term* ("mortal things"); that is, a term that operates as a mediator between the two extremes (the major and the minor terms)."[23]

But Aristotle did not only establish the nature of the syllogism, he produced a series of complex distinctions of the different possible "figures" of the syllogism and the various valid "modes" of each figure.

The different figures (σχήματα) of the syllogism are determined by the various positions that the middle term can occupy with respect to the extremes. Since the middle can be (a) the subject in the major premise and predicate in the minor, or (*b*) the predicate both in the major premise and in the minor, or again (*c*) subject in both premises, *there are three possible figures of the syllogism.* The example we gave earlier is of the first figure, which is, according to Aristotle, the most perfect figure because it is the most natural insofar as it manifests the process of mediation in the clearest way possible.

But since propositions that function as premises can vary in "quantity," viz., they can be either *universal* or *singular*, and in "quality," viz., they can be either *affirmative* or *negative*, multiple combinations are possible for each of the three figures. Aristotle, with a detailed analysis, establishes the nature and number of these possible combinations. These are the "modes" of the syllogism. The conclusions of the Stagirite are the following: there are four valid modes of the first figure, four of the second, and six of the third.

This is not the place to take up the issue of further distinctions between the perfect and the imperfect syllogism, the ways to reduce the second figures to the first, the modes of reduction of the syllogism of the other figures to that of the first, or the rules regarding the conversion of propositions to produce these transformations. Nor is it the place to probe the problem of the nature of *modal* syllogisms that the Stagirite tackled; that is, the problems related to the syllogisms that take into account the *modality* of propositions that operate from a premise (that is, according to whether they concern *simple existence* or imply the modality of *necessity* or *possibility*) with all their possible combinations. This is the most uneven and deeply criticized part of the Aristotelian syllogistic. Finally, because Aristotle did not recognize hypothetical or disjunctive propositions, he did not give us a doctrine of the hypothetical or disjunctive syllogism.[24]

6. Scientific syllogism or demonstration

The syllogism as such, therefore, shows the nature of reasoning itself; that is, what is the structure of inference, and as such it is seen, *as prescinding from the truth value of the premises* (and hence of the conclusion). Instead the "scientific" or "demonstrative" syllogism (or the apodeictic syllogism) differs from the syllogism in general precisely *because it concerns, besides the formal correctness of the inference, likewise the truth value of the premises* (and the consequence as well). Mignucci is correct in his assessment:

> The syllogistic procedure precisely of science is called demonstration; it is a particular type of syllogism, that is different from the syllogism not obviously through the *form*, otherwise it could not be said to be in truth a syllogism, but for the *content* of the premises taken up. In the demonstration, in fact, the premises must be always true, while that is not necessary in the syllogism as such, since in this latter case it is of interest only to determine if a certain consequence follows or does not follow from premises which are laid down, simply on the basis that they have been laid down independently of the truth value which they can have. In the demonstration instead, it being the

procedure which leads to science of the consequent, to know; that is, if the
consequent is true as such or not true, it must be assumed an antecedent
as true, given that from the true, the true necessarily follows.[25]

Hence science, besides the *consistency* of the formal procedure, implies
the *truth* of the content of the premises.

But let us read a passage of the *Posterior Analytics* on this basic point,
already partly discussed:

We think that we have demonstrated knowledge of anything...when we
think we know the causes in virtue of which the thing is what it is and that it
could not be otherwise. "Consequently it is impossible that of which there
is science in the proper sense be different from what we said. Now, if there
is another way of having science we will speak about it in what follows [an
allusion to immediate knowledge by which we grasp first principles, as we
will see below]; for the moment we say that to have science *is to know
through demonstrated conclusions*. By demonstration I mean scientific
syllogism; I mean by scientific syllogism that syllogism on the basis of which,
by the fact of possessing it, we have science. If then to have science is what
we have stated [that is, to know the cause], it is necessary that scientific
demonstration proceed through premises which are true, primary, immediate, better known than, prior to and causes of the conclusions. In such a way
that the principles will be also appropriate to what is being demonstrated.
The syllogism exists in fact without these conditions, *while demonstration
cannot exist without them, since it would not produce science.*[26]

The passage reveals, in an ideal manner, the nature of the Aristotelian
notion of science. It is, fundamentally, a discursive process that aims to
determine the *why* or the *cause* and, of the four causes that are well known,
chiefly the *formal cause* or *essence*. This fundamental cause, by expressing
the essence or nature of the thing, represents precisely the "middle" in
virtue of which we establish the necessary connection of certain properties
with a given subject. Therefore, the meaning of the famous formula that
the Stagirite states in the *Metaphysics* is grasped: "As *in syllogisms*, so in
the processes of generation, the principle of all is *substance*; in fact *syllogisms are dependent on the essence*, and on it acts of generation also
depend."[27]

Therefore the substance (either the *essence, form, or eidos*), just as it is the
center of the metaphysics and the physics, is the center also of the theory of
demonstrated knowledge; that is, of the whole Aristotelian system. Whereas,
the Aristotelian syllogism, in general, implies a rather high degree of for-
malism, the scientific syllogism; that is, the scientific demonstration, *is almost
wholly connected to the metaphysical conception of substance/ousía*, and the
Aristotelian science means an inquiry into substance and all that it implies.
This viewpoint is rather far removed from that assumed by the exact sciences
of the modern period.

In addition, the passage, that we have read, reveals a second fundamental point, viz., what attributes belong to the premises of the scientific or demonstrative syllogism. In the first place, they ought to be *true*, for reasons that we have fully discussed; then they ought to be *primary*; that is, in no need of further demonstration, and *better known and prior*; that is, intelligible of themselves and clear and more universal than the conclusions, and the cause of the conclusions, since they ought to contain the reason or cause.

And thus we achieve a very delicate point in the Aristotelian doctrine of science or demonstrated knowledge. Since the question must inevitably arise *how do we come to know the premises*? It is certainly not through further syllogisms, since in that case it would begin a process to infinity. Hence it must be in another way. What is this way?

7.   Immediate knowledge

The syllogism is necessarily a *deductive process*, insofar as it draws from universal truths less universal and true singulars. But how are the universal truths that operate as deductive premises grasped in the first place? Aristotle's answers are complex: they are grasped by a combination of *epagoge (induction)* and *intuition (mind)* that are, in a certain respect, contrary to the syllogistic process, but that in any case the syllogism itself presupposes.

Induction (ἐπαγωγή) is the "process" by which the universal is grasped from singulars. Notwithstanding what Aristotle says in the *Analytics*,[28] where he attempts to make us see that induction itself can be syllogistically treated, not only does it not succeed, but this attempt remains wholly isolated and he recognizes instead, generally, that *epagoge* is not a reasoning process. Instead, it is a "being lead" from the singulars to the vision of the universal or to a kind of immediate grasp or *intuition* so that in general we might call it immediate knowledge, or, if you wish, through this "process" in which the "middle" (the universal) is given in a certain sense by experience of the individuals or singulars. [In essence *epagoge* is the necessary condition in the "process" of seeing the universal, but it is not sufficient until we bring into play the presence of *mind (nous)*. Then *epagoge and nous* are the necessary and sufficient conditions for the grasp of the universal by the soul. For a further explanation beyond the epistemic recourse must be had to the *De Anima* where, of course, the explanation becomes entangled in a thicket of the enigmatic relations between the separate mind and soul.][29]

Intuition is, instead, the grasp of first principles. Hence also Aristotle admits the intuitive mind. Let us read the locus classicus for this doctrine in the last chapter of the *Posterior Analytics*:

> Since of the intellectual settled dispositions [ἕξαις] by which we grasp truth some are always true, while others admit the false, as opinion and calculation, while mediate knowledge and *immediate knowledge* are always true,

and since there are no other kinds of knowledge which are *more exact than scientific knowledge except immediate knowledge*, and on the other hand the principles of demonstration are more well known, and because all scientific demonstration is constituted argumentatively, there cannot be scientific demonstration of principles, and since there can be *nothing more true than scientific demonstration except immediate knowledge*, immediate knowledge must have for its object the principles. What results from the inquiry not only to what is made of these considerations, but also from the fact that principles of demonstration are not demonstrated; consequently the principle of scientific demonstration is not scientific demonstration. If then we do not have any other kind of true knowledge in addition to scientific knowledge, *immediate knowledge will be the principle of demonstrated conclusions*. Immediate knowledge then can be considered the principle of principles, while demonstrated conclusions in their entirety are in the same relation with the totality of things which immediate knowledge is in with respect to its objects.[30]

This passage, as can be seen, gives a reason for the basic requirement of Platonism: cognitive discourse presupposes at its base a nondiscursive knowledge, the possibility of knowing mediately necessarily presupposes an immediate knowledge.

8. The principles of demonstration

Hence, the premises and principles of demonstration are grasped either through *induction* (*epagoge*) or through *intuition* (*nous*). In this respect note that each of the sciences will assume chiefly its own premises and principles, viz., premises and principles which are peculiar to it and only to it.

In the first place, they will assume the existence of their specific area, or better (in terms belonging to logic) the existence of their *subject* about which all their determination is concerned and which Aristotle called the *subject-genus*. Arithmetic, for example, will assume the existence of unity and number, geometry the existence of spatial magnitude, and so on; and each science will specify its subject by means of *definition*.

In the second place, each science will proceed to define the meaning of a series of terms which belong to it (arithmetic, for example, will define the equal, unequal, etc.; geometry will define the measurable and the incommensurable etc.), but it will *not* assume their *existence*, since *it will demonstrate it*, by proving precisely that they are *characteristics* which belong to their subject-matter.

In the third place, to do this, the sciences must make use of certain "axioms," viz., true proposition which are intuitively true, and these are the principles *through whose power demonstrations are produced*. Here is an example of an axiom: "things equal to the same things are equal to each other."

Therefore Aristotle concludes:

Every demonstrative science has three elements, (1) *that which it posits*, the subject genus whose essential attributes it examines; (2) *the so-called axioms*, which are primary premises of its demonstrations; (3) the *attributes*, the meaning of which it assumes (trans. G. R. G. Mure, McKeon ed. p. 124).[31]

Among the axioms there are some which are "common" to more than one science (like the one cited earlier, others which ground all sciences without exception, like the principle of contradiction (two contradictory predicates cannot be asserted and denied of the same subject, at the same time, and in the same respect), the and the excluded middle, which are strictly connected to the principle of contradiction (it is not possible that there be a middle between two contradictories). There are the famous transcendental principles; that is, applicable to every form of reasoning as such (because applicable for every entity as such), per se nota and hence primary, which Aristotle expressly and fully discusses in the famous Fourth Book of the *Metaphysics*. They are the unconditioned conditions of every demonstration (and are obviously indemonstrables, because every form of demonstration structurally presupposes them).[32] The principle of identity, implicit in the doctrine of Aristotle, is not explicitly taken up for consideration.

9. Dialectical syllogism, eristic syllogism, and fallacies

We have seen that the theory of the *syllogism in general* concerns the formal validity of inference; instead, the theory of the *scientific or demonstrative syllogism* concerns the truth content of the premises. The scientific syllogism exists only when the premises are true and have the characteristics just examined. *When the premises are simply probable; that is, grounded on opinion, then there would be a dialectical syllogism*, which Aristotle discusses in the *Topics*. The goal of this treatise is thoroughly explained by Aristotle as follows:

Our treatise proposes to find a line of inquiry whereby we shall be able to reason *from reputable opinions* about any subject presented to us, and also shall ourselves, when putting forward an argument, avoid saying anything contrary to it. First, then, we must say what syllogism is, and what its varieties are, to grasp *dialectical syllogism*; for this is the object of our search in the treatise before us. Now a syllogism is an argument in which, certain things being laid down, something other than these necessarily comes about through them. It is a demonstration, when the premises from which the syllogism starts are true and primitive, or are such that our knowledge of them has originally come through premises which are primitive and true; and *it is a dialectical syllogism, if it reasons from reputable opinions*. Things are true and primitive which are convincing on the strength not of anything else but of themselves; for in regard to the first principles of science it is improper to ask any further for the why and wherefore of them; each of the first principles should command belief in and by itself. On the other hand, *those opinions are reputable which are accepted by everyone or by the majority or by the wise"viz., by all, or by the majority, or by the most notable and reputable of them.*[33]

The dialectical syllogism, according to Aristotle, serves the purposes of disputation and in particular when it is used to dispute with ordinary people or with learned persons, to single out what are the starting points and how much of their conclusions are acceptable or not acceptable, but not however starting from a point which is not acceptable to them, but from their own point of view. Through this technique we learn hence to dispute with others, by furnishing us with the means to reach agreement with others. In addition, it serves science not only for arguing correctly the pro and the contra of various questions, but in uncovering the primary principles, which, as we know, although syllogistically indemonstrable, can be grasped only inductively and intuitively. However, both induction and the justification of an intuition suppose a discussion structured through the opinions of the people or of the learned:

> It has a further use in relation to the principles used in the several sciences. For it is impossible to discuss them at all from the principles proper to the particular science in hand, *seeing that the principles are primitive in relation to everything else: it is through reputable opinions about them that these have to be discussed*, and this task belongs properly, or most appropriately, to dialectic; for dialectic is the process of criticism wherein lies the path to the principles of all inquiries.[34]

As we can see, in Aristotle, "dialectic" takes on a meaning much different than in Plato (or, if you like, he maintained a weaker and less specific meaning than Plato gave to it, given that, for him, dialectic was especially the science of the relations between the Ideas). But the *Topics* did not probe this second point, and it is limited chiefly to the former and consequently transgressed the limits far into rhetoric.[35]

The term *topoi* (τόποι) means the "places" and indicates metaphorically the ideal outlines to which we return and hence from which the arguments proceed like *sedes et quasi domicilia argumentorum* [the seats and almost-homes of arguments], as Cicero states.[36]

The *Topics* are described thus as "the 'pigeon-holes' from which dialectical reasoning receives its arguments," as Ross correctly states and that thus correctly evaluates this Aristotelian work, which is certainly far from being the least stimulating among the works which make up the *Organon*:

> The last discussion belongs to a bygone mode of thought; it is one of the last efforts of that movement of the Greek spirit towards a general culture, that attempt to discuss all manner of subjects without studying their appropriate first principles, which we know as the sophistic movement. What distin-

guishes Aristotle [from what he says in the *Topics*] from the sophists, at any rate as they are depicted both by him and by Plato, is that his motive is to aid his hearers and reader not to win either gain or glory by a false appearance of wisdom, but discuss questions as sensibly as they can be discussed without special knowledge. But he has himself shown a better way, the way of science; it is his own *Analytics* that have made his *Topics* out of date.[37]

Finally, a syllogism, besides being grounded on premises that are opinions, can be derived from premises that *seem* to be grounded on opinion (but which in reality are not), and then the *eristic* syllogism is produced. The case is also given in which certain syllogisms are *such only in appearance and that seem to conclude, but that in reality conclude only because of some error*, and we have then a *fallacy or paralogism*, viz., *erroneous reasoning.* Consequently, the *Sophistic Refutations* (which is also thought to be the Ninth Book of the *Topics*)[38] study precisely *sophistic refutations* (the term ἔλεγχος means refutation) of sophisms. (As we have seen in the first volume, the Sophists were most frequently identified with the worse part of the group; that is, with the Eristics, who did not aim at anything other than a refutation of the interlocutor by captious arguments.) The correct refutation is a syllogism whose conclusion contradicts the conclusion of the opponent; the refutation of the Sophists, instead (and in general their arguments), were such as to *seem* correct, but in reality they were supported by a series of tricks to deceive the unsuspecting and ignorant. The *Sophistic Refutations* studies all the sources of these possible deceptions with a remarkable perspicuousness, and it examines the more characteristic fallacies from which they are produced.

10. Logic and reality

It is said, rather too frequently by many scholars, that the Aristotelian logic is in some ways distant from reality; logic concerns, in fact, the *universal* whereas reality is instead *individual and singular* in substances, the universal is not reality, reality is not capable of being grasped through logic. If this is so, reality escapes wholly from the logical hammer. Actually it is not so; in fact, such an interpretation supposes that the Aristotelian *primary substance* is the experiential individual, which is not true, as we well know. The singular individual is a *synolon* of matter and form. And if in a sense substance is the *synolon, in a stronger sense* (in a properly ontological and metaphysical and hence primary sense) *substance or ousía is the form or the essence that determines the matter.*[39] The synolon is a τόδε τι; that is, *a determined something*, but the form is also a τόδε τι, viz., *an intelligibly determined being.* Insofar as it is grasped by thought, it becomes *universal* [what is grasped is by being grasped universalized], in the sense that from the ontological structure that determines a thing the form is grasped now as a capacity to refer to many things and hence a capacity to be predicated of many objects (of all those having that structure). The ontological form thus becomes the logical species.

Further mental operations, by analyzing the form, discover the structural possibilities of comprehending them in genera; which represent wider universals and which are as a logical matter or intelligible matter of which the form is the specification, and the genera embrace more and more universality up to the categories (the highest genera or universals). Beyond the categories, thought discovers again a universality that is not dependent on the logical process of being genera, or an analogical relationship; such are *being and unity*. But such operations of thought do not have merely nominal value, because they are grounded on the same structure of the real that is an *eidetic* structure, as we have seen in metaphysics in a detailed way.[40]

As is well known, Kant maintained that Aristotelian logic (which he understood as a purely formal logic) is wholly complete. After the discovery of symbolic logic no one can repeat this judgment, given that the application of symbols, especially, the null class, has enormously enlarged the logical calculus and modified many things. In addition, it is very difficult to affirm that the syllogism is the proper form of all mediation and all inference, as Aristotle instead believed. But whatever objections have been stated and can be mounted against Aristotelian logic and no matter what truth can be derived from the requirements derived from the *New Organon* of Bacon to the *System of Logic* of John Stuart Mill, let alone the requirements involved in Kantian transcendental logic to the Hegelian logic of Reason (the logic of the infinite), or, finally in the logical requirements of the methodology of modern sciences, it is generally certain that Western logic in its totality has its roots in the *Organon* of Aristotle, who, therefore, as we said remains a milestone in the history of Western thought.

II. RHETORIC

1. The Platonic origin of Aristotelian rhetoric

The inquiry into rhetoric has a prior history to Aristotle's consideration of it, beginning from Gorgias (who for the first time attempted a definition and a theoretical exploitation of it) up to Plato (who after having resolutely condemned it, as we saw, tried a partially successful recovery of it). Since, it was precisely on a rhetorical theme that as we know Aristotle began as a writer, composing, and publishing the *Gryllus* (which quickly evaluated the charge on the part of Plato of holding lectures on such a matter in the ambit of the Academy). In the *Gryllus* Aristotle takes a position against Isocrates and the Isocratean rhetoric. He defended the philosophical ideal of the Platonic paideia and seems to accept the perspective that Plato himself had embraced concerning rhetoric, especially in the *Phaedrus*.[1]

Even in the treatise *On Rhetoric* the Stagirite maintains the same basic conception. Rhetoric, if it is to be an authentic rhetoric, cannot be separated from truth and justice and it cannot be based on the emotions or sentiment. The rhetorician must know the things about which he would convince others, just as he must know the soul of the hearers in which he must generate persuasion. In sum, the true art of rhetoric must support the theoretical and moral values and on them, within appropriate limits, it must base itself.

Sometimes scholars have been aware of the fact (and this, in our judgment, is not only a particular confirmation of the general interpretation that we have presented about Aristotle) that the Aristotelian rhetoric "can be considered as a proposal to realize the ideal espoused by Plato in the *Phaedrus*" [2] and in effect, from the beginning to the end of his treatise, the Stagirite has shown a firm conviction that rhetoric is not able and ought not to exist except to serve the values of truth, of justice, and the good. He writes, in fact, expressly: "Rhetoric is useful because things that are true and things that are just have a natural tendency to prevail over their opposites, so that if the decisions of judges are not what they ought to be, the defeat must be due to the speakers themselves, and they must be blamed accordingly."[3] But we will see, in particular, the nature and qualities that are the peculiar characteristics and specific goals of rhetoric.

2. The definition of rhetoric and its relations with dialectic, ethics, and politics

Aristotle, as Plato, was firmly convinced that rhetoric had the task of *teaching* and *inculcating* truth neither about ethico-political values in general nor about particular truths or values. This is, in fact, a task that belongs properly to philosophy, on the one hand, and to the special sciences and arts, on the other. The scope of rhetoric, instead, is that of "persuasion" or, more exactly, that of *discovering the means and ways to persuade in general someone on any subject matter*. The Stagirite writes:

> Rhetoric may be defined as the faculty of observing in any given case the available means of persuasion. This is not a function of any other art. Every other art can instruct or persuade about its own particular subject-matter; for instance, medicine about what is healthy and unhealthy, geometry about the properties of magnitudes, arithmetic about numbers, and the same is true of the other arts and sciences. But rhetoric we look upon as the power of observing the means of persuasion on almost any subject presented to us.[4]

Rhetoric is therefore a sort of methodology of persuasion, an art of analyzing and defining techniques by which a man tries to convince other men, and this specifies its basic structure. Therefore, looked at from its *formal aspect*, rhetoric presents analogies with logic, which studies the structures of thought and reasoning, and in particular it presents analogies with that part of logic Aristotle called *dialectic*. In fact, as we saw, dialectic studies the structure of thought and reasoning that moves not from scientifically based elements, but from elements *based on opinion*, viz., from those elements that appear *acceptable to all or to most men*. Analogously, rhetoric studies those procedures by which men advise, accuse, defend, praise (these, in fact, are all the specific activities involved in persuasion) in general, not however by beginning from scientific knowledge, but from probable opinions.

Rhetoric, therefore, if from the standpoint of form has its control in dialectic, *from the standpoint of content* has it, instead, in ethics and in politics. In fact, if it is true that it, of itself, concerns the structure of persuasion in general, it is also true that men exercise their powers of persuasion especially before a tribunal (to accuse or defend), in the assembly (to counsel and to urge the adoption of the results of determined deliberations) and in general, to praise or blame (about good and evil, about virtue and vice); consequently all that which, as is evident, has to do with doing both in ethics and in politics.

In conclusion, we will say that rhetoric is the analogical correlate or equipollent of dialectic, *if its theoretical foundation is considered*, viz., in its formal procedure; it is, instead, strictly connected with ethics and with politics (and partially with psychology), *if its sphere of application is considered.* Therefore Aristotle can correctly conclude with what follows: "Rhetoric is like an offshoot of dialectic and of ethical studies, which it is appropriate to call politics." [5]

3. The different arguments of persuasion

The distinction between the *formal* aspect and the *content* aspect of rhetoric besides being important for the comprehension of the relationships of rhetoric with dialectic, on the one hand, and with the ethico-political sciences, on the other, is fundamental to understanding the whole Aristotelian treatment of rhetoric, especially the ease with which he passes from one to the other, let alone the various interlacings of methodological considerations with precisely ethico-political as well as psychological considerations.

Referring to the formal aspect of rhetoric, Aristotle distinguishes chiefly, the persuasive arguments that are *technical* from those that are *nontechnical.* The nontechnical arguments (the texts of laws, testimonies, conventions, declarations under torture, and oaths) are already the starting points and we do not find them (we can use them, without need of discovering them).[6] Instead the technical arguments are those specifically belonging to the rhetorician and are of three kinds, in accordance with which (*a*) the orator aims at establishing his credibility, (*b*) the second aims at disposing the soul of the hearer so that he will be convinced through the play of his emotions, (*c*) the third focusses on the intrinsic validity and effectiveness of the arguments themselves. Here is how Aristotle explains this distinction:

> Of the modes of persuasion furnished by the spoken word there are three kinds. The first kind depends on the personal character of the speaker; the second on putting the audience into a certain frame of mind; the third on the proof, or apparent proof, provided by the words of the speech itself. Persuasion is achieved by the speaker's personal character when the speech is so spoken as to make us think him credible. We believe good men more fully and more readily than others; this is true generally whatever the question is, and absolutely true where exact certainty is impossible and opinions are divided. This kind of persuasion, like the others, should be achieved by what the speaker says, not by what people think of this character before he begins to speak. It is not true, as some writers assume in their treatises on rhetoric, that the personal goodness revealed by the speaker contributes nothing to his power of persuasion; on the contrary, his character may almost be called the most effective means of persuasion he possesses. Secondly, persuasion may come through the hearers, when the speech stirs their emotions. Our judgments when we are pleased and friendly are not the same as when we are pained and hostile. It is towards producing these effects, as we maintain, that present-day writers on rhetoric direct the whole of their efforts. This subject shall be treated in detail when we come to speak of the emotions. Thirdly, persuasion is effected through the speech itself when we have proved a truth or an apparent truth by means of the persuasive arguments suitable to the case in question.[7]

Consequently, the works of rhetoricians have scarcely paid attention to the first point and have even obscured the last one, concentrating all their attention on the second, viz., on the manipulation of the emotions. Aristotle instead develops his work in all three directions, emphasizing the third as that which is the most valid.

About the first point, viz., about the character of the orator, the Stagirite points out that to be credible and persuasive, an orator must be or appear to be furnished with three endowments: wisdom, honesty, and benevolence. In fact, speakers make mistakes, in speaking of something and advising on it, either through an absence of wisdom, or because, although knowing what would be appropriate advice, they do not advise it because of dishonesty, or, finally, because, although they know what advice to give or although honest, they are not benevolent toward those with whom they speak. The means by which one can be endowed with such attributes are drawn from the ethical works to which Aristotle refers.[8]

The second point instead is probed by means of a phenomenological analysis, quite rich and vivacious, of the emotions and of the passions that commonly are found in auditors. According to the state of the soul in which the hearers are found, he judges in a different way the same things and therefore an awareness of the psychology of the passions (that awareness; that is, of the human soul that already in the *Phaedrus* Plato had posited as one of the fundamentals of true rhetoric)[9] is indispensable for the orator. This part of the *Rhetoric* reveals a knowledge of human beings that is truly astonishing because it goes not only into the analyses of individual passions but into the description of the different psychic characteristics of the different ages of human life (youth, maturity, and old age) and even to the different dispositions of soul bound to the different characters, which lead to men of different goods of fortune (viz., in the determination of the different psychology of the wealthy man, of the noble man, and of the powerful man).[10]

The third point instead concerns the employment of logical arguments. As we have already said, Aristotle considered this the most important and the most novel. It is also the most technical, and it is what brings back rhetoric to be joined with dialectic, as we now will see.

4. The enthymeme, the example, and the premises of the rhetorical syllogism

As we have already seen, rhetoric does not *teach*, since this is the task of science and most men are not in a condition to follow a scientific reasoning processes. The arguments that rhetoric furnishes must therefore move not from the original premises from which scientific demonstrations spring, but from those that are admitted as *commonly agreed to*, from which dialectic also moves. In addition rhetoric will not descend in its demonstrations through many different steps, through which the common hearer would be lost, but from premises from which conclusions can be rapidly drawn, precisely avoiding logical mediation, for the reasons given. This type of reasoning or rhetorical syllogism is called the *enthymeme*. The enthymeme is therefore a syllogism that moves from probable premises (a form of common opinion and not from first principles), and it is concise and not developed in various steps. In addition, the rhetorical enthymeme makes use of "examples," which do not imply logical mediation of any kind, but make immediately evident what it wants to prove. Just as the rhetorical enthymeme corresponds to the syllogism, so does the *rhetorical example* correspond to *logical induction*, insofar as it corresponds to a completely analogous function. Here are some significant passages with which these notions are explained:

> It is clear, then, that the technical study of rhetoric is concerned with the modes of persuasion. Now persuasion is a sort of demonstration (since we are most fully persuaded when we consider a thing to have been demonstrated); the orator's demonstration is an enthymeme, [and this is, in general, the most effective of the modes of persuasion]; the enthymeme is a sort of syllogism (the consideration of syllogisms of all kinds, without distinction, is the business of dialectic, either of dialectic as a whole or of one of its branches): clearly, then, he who is best able to see how and from what elements a syllogism is produced will also be best skilled in the enthymeme, when he has further learnt what its subject-matter is and in what respects it differs from the syllogisms of logic. For the true and approximately true are approached by the same faculty; it may also be noted that men have sufficient natural instinct for what is true, and usually do arrive at the truth. Hence the man who makes a good guess at truth is likely to make a good guess at what is reputable.[11]
>
> With regard to the persuasion achieved by proof or apparent proof; just as in dialectic there is induction on the one hand and deduction or apparent deduction on the other, so it is in rhetoric. The example is an induction, the enthymeme is a deduction, and the apparent enthymeme is an apparent deduction; for I call a rhetorical deduction an enthymeme, and a rhetorical induction an example. *Everyone who effects persuasion through proof does in fact use either enthymemes or examples*: there is no other way. And since everyone who proves anything at all is bound to use either deductions or inductions (and this is clear to us from the *Analytics*),[12] it must follow that each of the latter is the same as one of the former. The differences between example and enthymeme is made plain by the passages in the *Topics* where induction and deduction have already been discussed.[13] When we base the proof of a proposition on a number of similar cases, this is induction in dialectic, example in rhetoric; when it is shown that, certain propositions being true, a further and quite distinct proposition must also be true in consequence, whether universally or for the most part this is called deduction in dialectic, enthymeme in rhetoric.[14]
>
> It is possible to form deductions and draw conclusions from the results of previous deductions; or, on the other hand, from premises which have not been thus proved, and at the same time are not reputable and so call for proof. Reasonings of the former kind will necessarily be hard to follow owing to their length, for we assume an audience of untrained thinkers; those of the latter kind will fail to be persuasive, because they are based on premises that are not generally admitted or reputable. The enthymeme and the example must, then, deal with what is for the part capable of being other-

wise, the example being an induction, and the enthymeme a deduction. The enythmeme must consist of few propositions, fewer often than those which make up a primary deduction. For if any of these propositions is a familiar fact, there is no need even to mention it; the hearer adds it himself....[15]

5. The three kinds of rhetoric

If from the considerations concerning the form of rhetorical discourse we pass to the considerations concerning its content, then it is necessary to distinguish *three different kinds of rhetoric*. Rhetorical discourse, in fact, can be addressed to either (*a*) political assemblies *by members of the assemblies* to inspire them to judge in specific deliberations, (*b*) to tribunals *by judges* to inspire them to judge in appropriate ways, or (*c*) *to ordinary spectators* and auditors to celebrate determined events or acts. Thus there are the following three kinds of rhetoric; the *deliberative* (political), the *judicial* (forensic), and the *epideictic* (celebratory).

The aim of deliberative rhetoric is to establish the *usefulness* or the harmfulness of a proposed course of *future action* (in any political assembly there is deliberation on the things that concern the future and in general anyone who counsels for or against a course of action can be referring only to the future). The aim of forensic rhetoric is, instead, *to defend or to accuse*, in reference to *past acts* and circumstances (to demonstrate that such acts or circumstances happened or did not happen contrary to what has been established by law). Finally, it is appropriate for epideictic or celebratory rhetoric *to eulogize or diseulogize* and for the most part through *present facts* or events (to recommend those who are worthy of praise or blame).[16]

This distinction of the three kinds of rhetoric, besides the three different kinds of hearers to which they are addressed (the member of the assembly, the judge of the tribunal, and the common auditor), besides the different acts it explains (counseling for and against, defending and accusing, praising and blaming), and besides the different times presupposed (future, past, and present), implies a very precise differences in goals pursued by each type. It is easy to see that (as some scholars do not neglect to point out),[17] the true basis for the diversity of the kinds of rhetoric is their axiological character: deliberative rhetoric has as its goal the value of the *useful,* forensic rhetoric has as its goal the value of *justice*, and celebratory rhetoric has as its goal the value of the *beautiful-good man* [the *kalagathos*]. Also from this standpoint, therefore, the precise metaphysical roots of Aristotelian rhetoric and its finely shaded Platonic requirements are undeniable. Indeed here is a much more eloquent text on the issue in question:

> Rhetoric has three distinct ends in view, one for each of its three kinds. The deliberative orator aims at establishing the *expediency* or the *harmfulness* of a proposed course of action; if he urges its acceptance, he does so on the ground that it will do *good*; if he urges its rejection, he does so on the ground

that it will do *harm*; and all other points, such as whether the proposal is *just* or *unjust*, *honorable* or *dishonorable*, he brings in as subsidiary and relative to this main consideration. The parties in a law-case aim at establishing the justice or injustice of some action, and they too bring in all other points as subsidiary and relative to this one. Those who praise or attack a man aim at proving him worthy of *honor* or the *reverse*, and they too treat all other considerations with reference to this one.[18]

Naturally each of the three kinds of rhetoric has its own appropriate form of argument, which moves from equally unique premises. Aristotle is concerned to explain them in a detailed way with full references to ethics and politics, thus trying to give the most exhaustive possible outline of what must be known by either the political orator, or the judicial orator, or the orator who intends to deliver celebratory discourses, to be able to achieve adequately the aim that each proposed and to achieve complete persuasiveness.[19]

6. The *topoi* of rhetoric

We return now to the *formal aspect* of rhetoric and to its logical structure to bring the discussion to a close. We have seen that rhetoric is substantially learned with dialectic, insofar as its reasonings move from probable premises (from dialectic rhetoric it differs only because it tends to *persuade* and must bring the auditor to a judgment, precisely by means of persuasion). We have seen, in addition, that the example and the enthymeme are the inductive processes and deductive processes that belong to rhetoric. Aristotle further explains that the example can be taken from facts that truly occurred or may be invented; in this last case it constitutes a parable (as for example those in Socratic discourses) or a fable (as for example those in Aesop).[20] Maxims or aphorisms, so precious to the Greeks (remember the importance of the aphorisms attributed to the Seven Sages),[21] is just a premise or a conclusion of an enthymeme or even an enthymeme itself, according to the way in which it is formulated (if it includes in the maxim the reason why it is affirmed it is a true and proper enthymeme).[22]

The enthymeme, like the syllogism, in addition can be either a demonstration or a refutation; the demonstrative enthymeme is that which concludes from premises on which the speaker and the listener agree, that which refutes it is the one that draws a discordant conclusion from that of the adversary.[23]

It is possible to indicate some general sources from which the enthymeme formally considered, viz., prescinding from its specific content, is derived (or from which it has arisen); the so-called *topoi* or general "places" from which they can be drawn (or to which they can be systematically be conducted). The Stagirite states that there are four fundamental rhetorical *topoi*: (*a*) the *topos* of the *possible* and the *impossible*, (*b*) the *topos* of the *future*, (*c*) the *topos* of the *past*, (d) the *topos* of *magnitude*. Here is the Aristotelian text that discusses these *topoi.*

All orators are bound to use the topos of the *possible* and the *impossible;* and to try to show that a thing *has happened*, or *will happen* in the future. Again, the topos of size is common to all oratory; all of us have to argue that things are bigger or smaller than they seem, whether we are making deliberative speeches, speeches of eulogy or attack, or prosecuting or defending in the law-courts....Of the earlier mentioned commonplaces, that concerned with amplification is...most appropriate to epideictic speeches; that concerned with the past, to forensic speeches, where the required decision is always about the past; that concerned with possibility and the future, to deliberative speeches.[24]

Let us illustrate in what sense the possible-impossible are *topoi* or a source of enthymemes. If it is possible that it exists or that it is a thing contrary to another thing that exists, it must be possible and likewise its contrary; for example, if it is possible that a man can be cured, it must likewise be possible that he was sick. If it is possible for a thing to be very difficult, it is possible for a thing to be very easy. If a most excellent thing or action is possible, it is also possible for the same thing or action to be normal in quality.

And here are some examples of things that enter again into the "topos about the past"; if what is normally less likely to occur instead occurred, it can also happen that what is normally more likely to occur occurs; if something occurs that is normally posterior to another thing, that previous thing must already have occurred (if a thing has been forgotten, it must have been known at a previous time).

The *"topos* about the future" is explained by similar examples: if there is a thing that is normally posterior to another thing, it is probable that it will also possess what will follow from this other thing (if it is very cloudy, it probably will rain); if there is a thing that is a goal for another, it is probable that it will also accomplish this other (if someone erects a foundation of a house, they will probably build the house).

Finally to reach his goal, the orator usually *inflates and deflates* the importance of facts and actions that have a relationship with the useful, the just, the seemly, according to the cases and kinds of oratory.[25]

After this general *topos*, Aristotle followed with a particular topos of the true enthymeme and the apparent enthymeme (just as, in the dialectical area, he treated all the deceptions on which the apparent syllogism is based). It is an extremely technical section, but worth the reader's attention and interest.[26]

7.   Conclusions about rhetoric

The last book of the *Rhetoric* treats specific problems of style and composition and hence it takes up problems that although very interesting are part of literary criticism and linguistics more than they are part of philosophy. Let us, instead, give a brief evaluation of rhetoric.

After the great past that rhetoric knew in antiquity, it was condemned to a slow decline in modern times. What are the reasons for this decline? Here is the judgment of two noted English Aristotelian scholars. Ross writes, "If the Rhetoric has now less life in it than most of Aristotle's works, it is probably because speakers are nowadays (and rightly) inclined to rely on natural talent and experience rather than on instruction, and because hearers, though as easily swayed by rhetoric as ever, are rather ashamed of the fact and not much interested in knowing how the trick is done.[27] D. J. Allan instead writes,

> Rhetoric, for such a long time an important part in the education of the gentleman, has almost disappeared today from our school curricula. It is difficult to say if it has disappeared also from modern life or whether it has only been transformed into a too specialized discipline. We think it is a more concrete task of the literary critic to codify the rules of good writing on any manner of subject (what corresponds to Book III of the *Rhetoric* of Aristotle). There is only instead a general ability which associates the lawyer with university teaching, the businessman with preaching; and part of the task of ancient rhetoric would be simply publicity and propaganda, arts, which we fear, they flee from that direct and cynical appeal to the emotions which Aristotle rejected in the introduction to his *Rhetoric*.[28]

The two judgments make a good deal of sense, especially, that of Allan, who specifies correctly the nature of the true modern successors of rhetoric, viz., publicity=advertising and propaganda. However it seems to us that if prescinding from the sociocultural aspect as well as the ethico-political, which have little in common with these modern aspects, and that is, from the elements that we have called *content* and if the aspect that we have called the *formal* is considered, then the element of validity of the Aristotelian rhetoric is still preserved. In fact, the basic problem of Aristotelian rhetoric is this: what are the mechanisms, viz., the logical structures that support the forms of *discourse* (the messages) *that aim to persuade.* And if it is true that today's publicity=advertising and propaganda aim to persuade, the Aristotelian requirement, which is unchanged in its meaning, is no less true, if applied to these modern types of rhetoric. But we will speak further, on this issue. Not only has the meaning of the Aristotelian requirements remained unchanged if applied to these new forms of persuasion, but, it better reflects the response and reaches analogous conclusion to those Aristotle achieved. He who wishes to persuade making use of modern means of persuasion tries again to create for himself in the first place *credibility* (which corresponds to the analogous characteristic of credibility of the ancient orators, of which the Stagirite speaks). In addition both propaganda and publicity=advertising try *to play on the feelings of the public to give them certain dispositions*; and the enormous audio-visual apparatus of which they avail themselves is only a massive instrument of pressure intended to produce in the public the *desired dispositions*.

Finally, the most typical logical vehicle of which propaganda and advertising=publicity make use, viz., the *slogan*, it is easy to see, corresponds to the ancient aphorism and it is either a premise or a conclusion of an enthymeme, if not simply an enthymeme. The fact, then, that today rhetoric focusses precisely on human emotions, human passions, and a series of means linked to human irrationality that Aristotle abhorred, but that he knew very well to be very useful for convincing, means only that the techniques of persuasion are today become divorced from morality, whereas Aristotle intended to firmly bind them to moral values.

III. POETICS

1. The notion of the productive sciences

We have seen that the third kind of science is the "poietic sciences" or the "productive sciences." These sciences, as indicated by their name, teach us how to do and produce things, objects, instruments, according to rules and precise knowledge.

As is obvious we are speaking about the various arts or, as we said again with the Greek term, of *technai*. The Greeks, however, in formulating the notion of art, focussed more than us today on the *cognitive aspect* that it implies, emphasizing in a special manner the contraposition between art and experience; experience implies, in fact, a chiefly mechanical repetition and does not go beyond the knowledge of the *that*; that is, of the *de facto* given, whereas art goes beyond the pure datum and touches on knowledge of the *why* or comes close to it, and as such it constitutes a form of knowledge. Therefore, it is clear why the arts are included in the general outline of knowledge, and why they are arranged hierarchically on the third or last level, insofar as they are knowledges, it is true, but knowledges that do not have their goals within the subject who knows. Thus it is not a knowledge that accrues to the benefit of the agent or producer (as is practical knowledge), since it is done *for the benefit of the object produced.*

The poietic sciences, in their entirety, are not of interest, except indirectly, to the philosophical inquiry. The "seemly arts" are an exception, because they are distinguished from all the others, both in their structure, and in their goals. Aristotle says: "Some things that nature does not make, art makes; instead others *imitate them.*"[1]

There are arts that fulfill and organize nature in some way and have, therefore, as goals the mere pragmatically useful, whereas the arts that instead imitate nature itself, by reproducing or recreating some aspects, with pliable material, with colors, sounds, or words, have goals that *are not identical with the goal of mere pragmatic utility.* They are the so-called seemly arts, which Aristotle analyzes in the *Poetics.* Actually, the Stagirite limits himself to the treatment of poetry, and, within poetry, only tragedy and he subordinates it to epic poetry (in one part of the work, since lost, he also treats comedy; however, some things he says are of value for all the seemly arts in general, or at least to be extended also to the other seemly arts).

The treatment of the poetic art, if it is to follow the schema of the sciences of which we have spoken at the beginning, must follow the treatment of the practical sciences; but since, as we have noted, poetry has special characteristics and in the *Poetics* Aristotle imposed a type of discourse analogous to that imposed in the *Rhetoric,* it is more reasonable to speak of it in this section.

The question posed by the Stagirite is this. What is the nature of poetic discourse and what is its purpose? There are two notions on which we must concentrate our attention to understand the response given by our philosopher to the question: (*a*) the notion of *mimesis* and (*b*) that of *catharsis*.

2. Poetic *mimesis*

We shall begin by discussing the notion of *mimesis*. Plato had forcefully reproached art precisely because it is a *mimesis*; that is, an imitation of phenomenal things that (as we know) are in their turn imitations of eternal models of the Ideas. Thus art is a copy of a copy, an appearance of an appearance, which diminishes its veracity to an evanescent point.

Aristotle clearly opposes this mode of conceiving art and interpreted artistic *mimesis* according to a different perspective. He conceived of it as an activity that far from passively reproducing the appearance of things, almost recreates the things according to a new dimension. Let us read a key passage in this regard:

> From what we have said it will be seen that *the poet's function is to describe, not the thing that has happened, but a kind of thing that might happen, i.e. what is possible as being probable or necessary.* The distinction between historian and poet is not in the one writing prose and the other verse–you might put the work of Herodotus into verse, and it would still be a species of history; it consists really in this, *that the one–describes the thing that has been, and the other a kind of thing that might be.* Hence poetry is something *more philosophical and of graver import than history, since its statements are of the nature rather of universals, whereas those of history are singulars.* By a universal statement I mean one as to what such or such a kind of man will probably or necessarily say or do–which is the aim of poetry, though *it affixes proper names to the characters*; by a singular statement, one as to what, say, Alcibiades did or had done to him.[2]

The passage is illuminating in many respects.

(*a*) In the first place, Aristotle understands well that poetry is not poetry because it uses verse; it could dispense with using verse and equally be poetry. The poet has to be the poet of a story instead of verses, because he is a poet only in virtue of his mimetic or creative power, and he creates or imitates actions not verses.[3] And, in general, it can be well said that the means used by art are not that which makes it is true that the art is indeed art.

(*b*) In the second place, Aristotle specifies likewise correctly that poetry (and art in general) does not depend even on its object, or better *on the truth content of its object*. It is not the *historical truth* of the persons, of facts, and of the circumstances that he represents that gives value to art. Art can also narrate something that actually happened, but it becomes art only if to these things is added a certain *quid* (*what*) that is lacking in purely historical narrative (remember that the Stagirite understands historical narrative chiefly as a chronical, as the description of persons and facts only chronologically connected). If the *History* of Herodotus were to be put into verse, it would still not be poetry; however, things that actually happened and are narrated by Herodotus would become poetry. How? Aristotle replies: "And if he should come to take a subject from actual history, he is none the less a poet for that; *since some historic occurrences may very well be in the probable and possible order of things; and it is in that aspect of them that he is their poet.*"[4]

(*c*) It is clear, in the third place, that poetry has a superiority over history, for the *different way* in which it treats facts. Actually, whereas history is bound entirely to the singular, and considers it precisely *insofar as it is singular*, poetry, when it touches on facts that touch on history, *transfigures* them, so to speak, in virtue of its mode of treating them, seeing them "under the aspect of possibility and of probability," and thus making them give rise to a wider significance, and in a certain sense *universalizes* this object. Aristotle used precisely the technical term *universal* (τὰ καθόλου).[5] But what kind of "universal" can this be in poetry, what kind of universal is it that (as we have read in the passage from which we began) does not disdain the use of proper names?

(*d*) Evidently, this has nothing to do with the *logical universals*, the type treated in theoretical philosophy and, in particular, logic. In fact, whether poetry does not reproduce experiential truth, it in no way deals with ideal types, "abstract" truths, or more precisely logical truths. Poetry not only can and must release itself from reality and present facts and persons not as they are but as *they could be or ought to be*, but, Aristotle expressly says, *it can also introduce the irrational and the impossible and can thus speak falsehoods and make appropriate use of paralogisms* (that is, of fallacious reasonings). And it can do this by the agreement that makes the impossible and irrational *probable*.[6] The Stagirite is led to say: "The impossible probable is to be preferred to the unbelievable possible."[7]

"With regard to the requirements of poetry, a credible impossibility is always to be preferred to an unbelievable possibility."[8]

Naturally, things being so, poetry could well represent the Gods in fallacious ways, the way the common people represent them, and like a belief of the common people are made part of life.

(*e*) The universality of the representational function of poetry arises from its power to reproduce events "according to the law of probability and necessity"; that is, from its capacity to recreate events in a manner such that they are joined into a completely unitary whole, almost as in an organism in which all the parts have their meaning within the functioning of the whole of which they are a part. Valgimigli has grasped better than anyone these points in a passage that we want to quote, because it is so illuminating:

History has an extrinsic and chronological coherence, poetry an intrinsic and spiritual one. What history narrates is the bare fact arranged in its place within a chronological series; but a series or chronological arrangement can be simply juxtaposition, and not necessarily co-ordinated and dependent. What poetry represents is wholly sharp and strict in its consequential nature and coherence and concentration of parts which nothing can move or destroy without entering a void whence disgrace and ruin may be found together. Because one thing which happens *in consequence* of another–poetry is different than that which happens after–history. Hence we can no longer say that the object of *mimesis* is a datum of reality. If it is so, it does not hold as such, but only insofar as it is conceived in its being and its becoming, according to the law of verisimilitude and necessity. The law of unity, coherence, cohesion, concentration, whence all the elements which compose myth; that is, the *mimesis* of action, they adhere to each other, they are both necessary, they compenetrate each other in a fluid mutuality and they aim at agreement toward a single goal which is concretized in an attitude toward life, in an active and present power, as a living and complete organism. And this is the fundamental law that firmly maintains the whole Aristotelian *Poetics*, which interprets it from beginning to end in every proposition, which illuminates every obscurity, which abolishes contradictions, which insinuates into the more subtle particulars of poetical technique, and which again today, it is well to secure its escort to any one who attempts the mystery of poetry and art.[9]

Consequently, says Valgimigli with terminology taken from Benedetto Croce, the universal in the arts is "the *concrete universal,* but in the greatest of its concretization."[10] It could be also said the "imaginative universal," by using more modules from G. B. Vico. But it is obvious that this terminology carries us decisively beyond Aristotle. Notwithstanding that, it is clear, from the considerations developed earlier, that in the famous passage from which we began, the Stagirite has intuited this, although somewhat vaguely and confusedly. Poetry is more philosophical than history, but it is not philosophy. The universal found in poetry is not the logical universal and hence, it is something unique, having its own value, although not having the value of true history or the value of true logic. The Platonic position is therefore clearly surpassed.

3. The beautiful

Modern aesthetics has habituated us to consider the problems of art in such a way that it seems difficult to us to define art without previously defining the *beautiful* and thus it succeeds in making us think that it is next to impossible to solve these problems. In reality, we have already seen that this notion was not at all clear in antiquity. Plato, as we know, joined the beautiful with the erotic more than with art; and Aristotle who joined it with art, did not define it except in a passing way in the *Poetics.* And here is the definition he gave:

To be beautiful, a living creature, and every whole made up of parts, must not only present a certain *order* in its arrangement of parts, but also be of a certain definite magnitude. Seemliness is a matter of size and order, and therefore impossible either in a very minute creature, since our perception becomes indistinct as it approaches instantaneity; or in a creature of vast size–one, say, 1,000 miles long–as in that case, instead of the object being seen all at once, the unity and wholeness of it is lost to the beholder....[11]

The same notion is expressed in the *Metaphysics,* where the beautiful is connected to mathematics:

Now since the good and the beautiful are different (for the former always implies conduct as its subject, while the beautiful is found also in motionless things), those who assert that the mathematical sciences say nothing of the beautiful or the good are in error. For these sciences state and prove a very great deal about them; for if they do not expressly mention them, but prove attributes which are their results or their formulas, it is not true to say that they tell us nothing about them. The chief forms of the beautiful are *order* and *symmetry* and *definiteness*, that the mathematical sciences demonstrate in a special degree.[12]

The beautiful, then, for Aristotle, implies order, symmetry of parts, quantitative determination; in a word we can say *proportion*.

It is understandable now how by applying these canons to tragedy, Aristotle wants it neither too long or too short, but capable of being grasped with the mind as in a glance from beginning to end. And the same thing certainly would hold, for him, for every work of art.[13]

Aristotle's way of conceiving the beautiful brings to mind the clear Hellenic injunction of "nothing in excess" and the "measure" and in particular the clear notion of Pythagorean thought that in the "limit" located perfection and completion.

4. *Catharsis*

We have said that Aristotle is fundamentally concerned with tragedy and that in relation to tragedy he develops his theory of art. Here we cannot enter into the details of the discussion; but one point should be emphasized, although presented in regard to his theory of art in close connection with the definition of tragedy, it also holds for the arts in general. The Stagirite writes: "A tragedy, then, is the imitation of an action that is serious and also, as having magnitude, complete in itself; in language with pleasurable accessories, each brought in separately in the parts of the work; in a dramatic, not narrative form; with incidents arousing pity and fear, *wherewith to accomplish its catharsis of such emotions.*"[14]

The original used the expression *catharsis of the passions* (κάθαρσις τῶν παθημάτων), which is somewhat ambiguous, and it has been consequently the object of differing interpretations. Some maintain that Aristotle speaks of the *purification of the passions* in a moral sense, almost of their "sublimation" achieved by means of the elimination of what is harmful in them. Others, instead, understand the *"catharsis* of the passions" in the sense of the *temporary removal or elimination of the passions*, in an almost physiological sense, hence in the sense of a venting and hence *liberation from the passions.*[15]

Aristotle must have explained more basically the sense of *catharsis*, in the second book of the *Poetics*, which unfortunately is lost. However there are two passages in the *Politics* that give hints and that we would like to quote, given the importance of the issue. In the first passage we read: "Besides the flute is not an instrument which expresses moral qualities, but arouses unbridled emotions of a kind useful only on those occasions in which the purpose was to produce a *catharsis* rather then an increase in knowledge."[16] In a second, fuller, and more circumscribed passage there are further specifications:

> We accept the division of melodies proposed by certain philosophers into melodies of character, melodies of action, and passionate or inspiring melodies, each having, as they say, a mode corresponding to it. But we maintain further that music should be studied, not for the sake of one, but of many benefits; that is to say, with a view to education, or *catharsis*...music may also serve for intellectual enjoyment, for relaxation and for recreation after exertion. It is clear, therefore, that all the modes must be employed by us, but not all of them in the same manner. In education the modes most expressive of character are to be preferred, but in listening to the performances of others we may admit the modes of action and passion also. For feelings such as pity and fear, or, again, enthusiasm, exist very strongly in some souls, and have more or less influence over all. Some persons fall into a religious frenzy, and we see them restored as a result of the sacred melodies–when they have used the melodies that excite the soul to mystic frenzy–as though *they had found healing and purification*. Those who are influenced by pity or fear, and every emotional nature, must have like experience, and others in so far as each is susceptible to such emotions, and all are in a manner *purged and their souls lightened and delighted. The melodies that purge the passions likewise give an innocent pleasure to mankind.*[17]

From these passages it is clear that poetic *catharsis* is certainly not a *purification of a moral nature* (since it is expressly distinguished from it), but it is likewise not reducible to a *purely physiological event*. It is probable or in any case possible that, although with uncertainty and waverings, that Aristotle saw in that pleasing liberation which the work of art produced something analogous to what we today call *aesthetic pleasure*. Plato had condemned art–among other things–also because it let loose the emotions and passions, freeing them from the rational element that should control them. Aristotle exactly overturned the Platonic interpretation: art does not charge, but is a discharge of emotion, and that type of emotion which is achieved, not only is not harmful but is restorative of health.

CONCLUSIONS ABOUT ARISTOTELIAN PHILOSOPHY

εἰ μὲν φιλοσοφητέον φιλοσοφητέον καὶ
εἰ μὴ φιλοσοφητέον φιλοσοφητέον·
πάντως ἄρα φιλοσοφητέον. εἰ μὲν γὰρ
ἔστι, πάντως ὀφείομεν φιλοσοφεῖν
οὔσης αὐτῆς· εἰ δὲ μὴ ἔστι, καὶ οὕτως
ὀφείομεν ζητεῖν οὐκ ἔστι φιλοσοφία,
ζητοῦντες δὲ φιλοσοφοῦμεν, ἐπειδὴ τὸ
ζητεῖν αἰτία τῆς φιλοσοφίας ἐστίν.

If one must philosophize, one must
philosophize, and if one does not
philosophize, one must equally
philosophize; in any case therefore one
must philosophize; if, then, philosophy
exists, we must maintain in all ways to
philosophize, given that it does exist; if
instead it does not exist, even in this case
we must inquire how philosophy does
not exist; but, by inquiring, we
philosophize, since to inquire is the
cause of philosophy.

Aristotle, *Protrepticus*, Frag. 2

I. THE DESTINY OF ARISTOTELIAN PHILOSOPHY

Aristotelian speculation has had an influence of a historical and also a superhistorical nature that has not perhaps been equaled in the whole sweep of the total cultural experience of the West. If immediately after his death Aristotle was silenced and was not understood within the very walls of the Peripatos (just as, moreover, Plato himself ends in being no longer understood within the confines of the Academy), revived, already at the end of the ancient period, in the sphere of Greek thought itself, with the entrance on the stage of history of the Greek commentators who in their search for secure support looked to him; from Alexander of Aphrodisias (200 CE) to the array of various Neoplatonic commentators. Already in the sixth century Boethius introduced to the West the logic by translating the *Organon* (of which the culture absorbed, in a first moment, chiefly the *Categories* and the *De Interpretatione*) while in the twelfth century, the whole interest of the Western world was fundamentally centered on Aristotelian logic. But already at the beginning of the ninth century the Arabs (from the middle East to Spain) received fundamentally all Aristotelian thought, commenting, and reinterpreting it in a basic way. And in great part through the influence of the Arabs the interest in the thought of the Stagirite flowed again into the West, and in the thirteenth and fourteenth centuries we see, by the Scholastics, to the most magnificent reflourishing that Aristotelianism had known. In this period Aristotle lost, therefore, almost all his historical configuration of a man from a particular period of time and became instead a symbol of the "Philosopher" par excellence. He became "the master of those who know," almost an emblem of all that reason can say with its own power, outside of faith.

And after the Scholastic flowering he is then reinterpreted in a new way, which lasted from the fifteenth century to the end of the seventeenth century (chiefly in the University of Padua), and which in the attempt to return to the genuine Aristotle; that is, to the Aristotle without the embellishments in which he had been covered by the Scholastics, in reality, ends by identifying Aristotle with the naturalistic anti-Platonic dimension, as we have seen. In the nineteenth century, there followed the flourishing of philological studies and the great edition of all the works of our philosopher under the editorship of Bekker, Aristotle enters again if only partially, into the ongoing philosophical culture; both Phenomenology and Heidegger draw from Brentano, whose masterpiece *Being and Time* starts exactly from the book of Brentano, *The Multiple Meanings of Being According to Aristotle*. Aristotle is then considered as a point of reference by all the currents of Neoscholasticism. About the rebirth of studies of an historical-philological nature promoted by the new method of Jaeger developed in the course of the nineteenth century, we have already said what happened in the introductory section.

Consequently, precisely because of the spiritual leadership very often exercised by Aristotelian thought and by the figure of Aristotle, there arises, an indiscriminate love that achieves true and proper contortions of acts of worship (one of the last Aristotelians at the beginning of the modern age refused to look in the telescope simply because did not want to attribute any error to Aristotle). Likewise there was truly absurd aversion and disrespect for Aristotle that was likewise indiscriminate and irrationally hostile and visceral, not only in the area of theoretical studies but even in that of histories of philosophy. Consequently it does not happen frequently that one meets a correct and measured evaluation of the totality of the thought of the Stagirite.

Let us record, by way of example, one of the most captious and partisan judgments given by the best French historian of ancient philosophy of the late modern period, in this way the reader can have some adequate idea of what we are speaking about. L. Robin writes:

> It would, perhaps, be a fair description of Aristotle to say that he was too much and too little a philosopher. He was a skilful and tricky dialectician, but was neither deep nor original. The invention which is most clearly his consists in well-coined formulas, verbal distinctions which are easy to handle. He set up a machine whose works, once set in motion, give the illusion of penetrating reflection and real knowledge. The misfortune is that he used this machine to attack both Democritos and Plato. So he for a long time turned science away from paths in which it might fairly soon have made decisive progress. On the other hand...he was a might encyclopaedist and a master-teacher. He possessed all the knowledge of his day, and was able to systematize it with great art in lectures and treatises. The amount and variety of his works and his undeniable gifts of elaboration and presentation, although they are not the same thing as the very spirit of inquiry in science and philosophy, are, apart from special historical circumstances, what have earned his philosophy and name their incomparable authority.[1]

Naturally, Robin himself finishes *in point of fact* by denying his own assessment, such as it is, in the carrying out of his work, for he was forced to dedicate to Aristotle more space than to any other thinker, in particular more space than he allots to Plato, and what he says in presenting Aristotle in detail subverts his final judgment. But we wanted to read this assessment simply as a model, viz., to show the acrimony and enmity, to the point of irrationality that conditions the judgment of historians who ought to be beyond "such mischief."

II. THE ACHIEVEMENTS AND APORIAS OF ARISTOTELIAN PHILOSOPHY

Those who have followed us to this point will be capable of evaluating the destiny of Aristotelianism for reasons other than those of its simple "historical circumstances," or worse, "its encyclopedism," or still worse, "its well-turned definitions."

In the first place, they will remember the achievements of his metaphysics. The reform of the Platonic notion of the Ideas and together with it the probing of the fundamental results of the Second Voyage carried Aristotle to the great discovery of the immobile Movent; that is to say, to the discovery of the Absolute, the supreme *intelligible realities*, the supreme *Mind* or *Intelligence* (the *self-thinking thought*, the *self-thinking intelligence*). And it is to this discovery that the whole of the West, in different ways will be drawn. Medieval theologians made use of it in their reinterpretations of the notion of God about which the Scriptures speak. Hegel does not hesitate to consider this speculative idea "the best and most free" and to see in it the primary historical intuition of the Absolute as self-thinking thought. The aporias that resulted from this discovery are likewise notable; his absolute transcendent, without any communication with the world and human beings, must make its connection to the world very difficult to comprehend (and the structuring itself of the world as well) and to men with it. The world exists eternally, and eternally tends toward the primary Principle, but it is not because He *wishes* or *projects* this, but only because, being the supreme Good, as such He can only attract; but if this is so, He attracts in a necessary manner and almost mechanistically (like a magnet attracts). Without numbering, then, the theological aporias that arise from Aristotle having admitted other Minds (although lower) in addition to and under the primary one. From all these difficulties only the understanding of creation would be able to offer a way out; but it is a doctrine unknown to the whole of the Greeks. In any case, having grasped the Absolute as spirit (mind) and as knowing, as an immaterial entity, and cognizant is the greatest achievement of ancient metaphysics. In addition to the principal discovery we must emphasize, although only in passing, the importance of the speculative predicaments especially of a metaphysical significance, *being, category, substance, accident, matter, form, act, and potency* and all those linked to them, about which arguments have been focused for many centuries (also when, as in the age of rationalism and of empiricism, it will be attempted to give to them completely novel meanings).

In what concerns the Aristotelian physics (cosmology included), the argument does not change. We know that the physics of the Stagirite is, in reality, *a metaphysics of the sensible* and as such must be evaluated; it develops a different argument with respect to that which Galileo will open as the great phase of modern science; and when historians reproach Aristotelian physics for having precisely impeded science up to Galileo, they forget also what this metaphysics of nature had contributed to the improvement of that *logos* which will create the true science of nature.

Also in psychology the Aristotelian achievements are important. Once again such achievements have little to do with the modern empirical science that carries the same name, because the psychology of the Stagirite has a strongly metaphysical base and is not precisely capable of being substituted for it, since it proceeds according to different principles. The explanation of knowledge as a progressive dematerialization of form, which begins in the senses and terminates in the intellect-mind is probably the greatest contribution of the Stagirite in this area. The aporias implicated in the Platonic doctrine of *anamnesis* is overcome with a shrewd use of the notions of potency and act, as we have seen. But a further aporia reappeared on a higher level; in us there is *Nous*, an immaterial "entity" that acts by "making" actual the highest kind of knowledge (which are then the highest form of dematerialization). This *Nous* is something that "comes from the outside" and is immortal; it is the "divine in us." But how it comes from the outside into us, what its origin and its destiny is, Aristotle does not say. And all the successive interpretations are simply beside the point, because Aristotle cannot structurally say it; either he must have recourse to the eschatological myth of Plato, grasped by him in his youthful exoteric writings but then left completely to fall into obscurity, or from the beginning he would have had to make an appeal to an understanding of a doctrine similar to creation.

The acquisitions of the *Ethics* were also important and had a very great influence, in all periods of history. In the moral thought of Aristotle there is more of the Platonic than is generally acknowledged. The notion at the base of the Aristotelian ethics is fundamentally that which is Socratic-Platonic, according to which the essence of man is given by his soul and hence the true values are the values of the soul, with respect to which the other goods assume only an instrumental meaning. Instead, the Aristotelian ethics lacks the religious and eschatological dimension that is precisely Platonic, and it is this lack (together with an attentive phenomenology of a realistic character that Aristotle probes fully) that makes Aristotelian ethics appear more different than Plato's although it is not so in reality. The Socratic-Platonic "care of the soul" is the basic notion; virtue is only the virtue of the soul, just as happiness is only the happiness of the soul. From the distinction of the parts of the soul is deduced the principal distinction of the virtues and in the higher part of the soul is located the highest virtue. It is in any case fundamental that Aristotle demonstrated that also by prescinding from Platonic religious reasons, that type of ethics is supported likewise on a purely philosophical base. Aristotle attempted, in addition, to push beyond Socrates and Plato, by explaining the psychology of the moral act, reevaluating those volitional elements that Plato introduced in the soul beginning from the *Republic*, but that then he did not basically exploit. But this time, the success is relative: Aristotle understood that *liberty* is determinative in our moral actions; but then, he did not succeed in determining the nature of will and free choice, and free choice repeatedly slips away in the very requirements in which he attempts to affirm it. Also he, like Plato, places in knowledge (or to use his language, in the *intellectual virtues*) the highest part of the *areté* of human beings and in the contemplation of the truth posits what makes man fully and completely himself. Aporias remain in the Aristotelian ethics, such as the determination of the true source of moral action: ethical virtue, on the one hand, suppose for their realization the intellectual virtue of prudence (*phrónesis*), but practical wisdom can exist only where there is ethical virtue (and vice versa). In addition, to become good it is necessary to will good ends, but the true good ends are only recognized by those who are already good; so, from the beginning it revolves in a circle. Another is the rational choice in which scholars chiefly encounter will and liberty, in truth for Aristotle is only the *choice of the means* and not of the ends (which are willed prior to *the choice of the means*). Also Aristotelian ethics is in large measure overly optimistic about the power of reason (intellectualism): the key that characterizes a complete man (just as it characterizes God) is reason and knowledge not will.

Even more accentuated are the aporias of politics (which "remember" is an integral part of ethics). In addition to a splendid intuition (like the definition of man as necessarily a political animal and a series of propositions arising from this) we find the theorizing about *slavery* and about *ethnic superiority*. Aristotle did not see beyond the polis and continued to believe that the polis is a politically the most perfect institution. His pupil Alexander the Great went on to Hellenize the barbarians and opened new ways to history, but the Stagirite could understand nothing of all of this. The barbarians were, for him, *by nature* inferior beings, and hence, they could not be made the equals to Greek man, nor could they be Hellenized, nor could they be the true active subjects of a political organism different from the polis. We saw fully how, actually, these aporias do not derive so much from his philosophical principles, as from the historical-cultural contingencies according to which he was conditioned. But this is much more interesting because it shows how in the adequate comprehension of man and his destiny there is not only the speculative component that comes into play. Applied to human beings, the purely philosophical principles demonstrate a susceptibility to a large amount of manipulation and plasticity. In particular, Aristotle could not give a true meaning to human beings, because he could not put them into relation with God. Because his God is not a creator, He is not interested in human beings and He is a stranger both to the destiny of individuals and to the destiny of peoples. Human beings will always exist and they will exist for always (since neither the world nor the living species have an origin), but their value lays in concrete individuals, as carriers and transmitters of their *eidos*, viz., of the rationality that they incarnate and in the measure in which they enflesh it. Still the individual man, *from the aspect of his individuality*, ends by being rather insignificant. Only the revolution of Christianity will know how to reevaluate man precisely *as an individual* and will know how to explain the true root of goodness and evil, viz., moral responsibility. And only the "notion" of the "sons of God" offers the means for definitively eliminating the distinctions of man-woman, freeman-slave, Greek-barbarian and all the others connected to them and will know how to understand in what consists the true equality of each one and of all human beings.

Of the significance and importance of Aristotelian logic we have already spoken at length; it would be difficult to support and demonstrate that the new logics of the modern age could have existed if Aristotle had never written the *Organon*. But that does not mean, as is evident, that henceforth the syllogism would be, as Aristotle claimed, the form of every and any correct argument and also the structure of every mediation and inference. Moreover, in the various branches of philosophical knowledge Aristotle himself largely gave value to other procedures, not only to those that are deductive. And we have also seen that induction and Platonic intuition itself point out, in Aristotle, the declared limits of syllogistic deduction. But Aristotelian logic remains, in any case, as the stock from which successive logics are the outgrowths.

Finally, about the relationship of Aristotle with Plato we have said all that is necessary in the beginning section. Here, in conclusion, we wish only to add this: the making immanent of the Ideas and their "transformation" into essences (viz., into the intelligible structure of the sensible, as we have seen, has been carried not only to the negation of the existence of supersensible substances as *minds or intelligences* (instead of being intelligibles), but opens into a further aporia;—what relationship exists between these immanent intelligible essences and the human mind and the transcendent mind? Do the immanent intelligibles depend or not depend on the transcendent intelligence? If they depend, in what way do they depend on it? He ought to have made of the intelligible essences the thoughts themselves of the creative intelligence and to consider them as exemplary causes, exploiting that intuition only vaguely glimpsed in Plato in the doctrine of the Demiurge, but quickly compromised in the context of Platonic thought itself, given that the Demiurge is only an inferior God, conditioned by the world of the Ideas. Also from these aporias there is only the exit provided by the understanding of creation.

To conclude the exposition and interpretation of the thought of Aristotle, which is certainly the most complete expression and almost the synthesis of classical philosophy, which is the form of philosophy speculatively and metaphysically most developed, we wish, by bringing the discourse in a circle with respect to what we said in the Preface, to refocus on one point. In defending philosophy against its enemies, Aristotle wrote in the *Protrepticus*, "Whether we ought to philosophize, or whether we ought not to philosophize, we need to philosophize; but between philosophizing and not philosophizing there is no choice, because in any case it is to philosophize." This means that if we ought to philosophize, we certainly philosophize; if we ought not philosophize, then we need to philosophize to demonstrate that we ought not; but this is in any case to philosophize. We hence cannot possibly desist from philosophizing. Consequently, when Aristotle expresses these sacrosanct truths, he was far from suspecting that precisely his philosophy would be in large part determinative in the history of the content of human philosophizing; there are precisely more Aristotelian notions, principles, and categories to be often invoked pro and contra to philosophize, but with the result that the dilemma just mentioned *a priori* is shown to be inevitable.

Man nowadays must not believe that, after Marx and Freud, he has definitively abandoned the classical discussion of philosophy, of which the Aristotelian is the most typical form. However, he will take refuge rigorously in the strict confines of the empirical sciences if not limiting himself exclusively to adversarial politics or he will consign to it his entire existential anxiety and then he will attempt to assert something of a metaregional and metaempirical nature. When he does so, he will find himself back again in that inexorable dilemma mentioned earlier, and more and more–whether he knows it or not–he will find himself reasoning again according to categories, which by direct filiation or by a dialectic and mediated transformation and contraposition, are derived from Aristotle and classical philosophy, and which in him has found its most complete expression. Consequently, not only is it folly to renounce philosophizing, but since we must inevitably philosophize, it is likewise folly to believe that it can be limited to the present, since the present is not intelligible without the past from which it is born and in addition it is never truly attained or it is only attained in an illusory way; because the actual is already the moment that has fled, but what is it that resists beyond the moment; and, within limits, the truly actual is only the eternal.

NOTES

FIRST PART—FIRST SECTION

CHAPTER ONE

(THE MEDIATION BETWEEN THE WRITTEN AND THE ORAL)

1. Plato was born in Athens in 427 BCE. His correct name was Aristocles (the name of his grandfather), and Plato was a nickname. *Diogenes Laertius*, 3.4 writes: "He learnt gymnastics under Ariston, the Argive wrestler. And from him he received the name of Plato on account of his robust build, in place of his original name that was Aristocles, after his grandfather, as Alexander informs us in his *Successions of Philosophers*. But others affirm that he got the name Plato from the breadth of his style, or from the breadth of his forehead, as suggested by Neanthes." (Remember that in Greek πλάτος means *capaciousness, abundance, range* and the nickname Plato is derived from this word). Plato's father numbered among his ancestors King Codrus; on his mother's side, Solon. It is not a surprise that when he came of age Plato would aspire to enter politics: his birth, intelligence, and personal attitudes all combined to move him in that direction. This is the biographical datum, in fact, that deeply affected his thought.

Aristotle (*Metaphysics*, A 6) writes that Plato was initially a follower of the Heraclitean Cratylus, and then of Socrates (Plato met Socrates when he was twenty years old). It is clear, hence, that Plato was associated with Socrates, at first, for the same reasons that the other young men associated with Socrates; namely, not simply to become philosophers but rather to better prepare themselves for a political career. But events were to lead Plato in another direction.

Plato's first involvement in political activity must have taken place in 404–403, when the aristocrats seized power and his two cousins, *Charmides*, and Critias, were involved with the oligarchy. But it undoubtedly must have been a bitter and disappointing experience because of the violent and factious methods that Plato saw used by those in whom he had placed his confidence.

But his disgust for the political methods practiced in Athens must have reached a highpoint in 399, when Socrates was condemned to death. The democrats (who had then seized power) were responsible for the condemnation of Socrates. And so Plato became convinced that for the time being it was better to distance himself from militant politics.

After 399 Plato was in Megara with other Socratics, guests of Euclid (probably to avoid possible persecutions that could have come down on them as members of the Socratic circle). But Plato did not remain very long in Megara.

Diogenes Laertius, tells us: "Next he proceeded to Cyrene on a visit to Theodorus the mathematician, thence to Italy to see the Pythagorean philosophers Philolaus and Eurytus, and thence to Egypt to see those who interpreted the will of the Gods....Plato also intended to make the acquaintance of the Magians, but was prevented by the wars in Asia." (3.6,7). There is no confirmation of these voyages to Cyrene and Egypt in the *Seventh Letter*, although we know with certitude of his voyage to Italy in 388 BC. when he was forty years of age and in succeeding years.

He was certainly moved by a desire to get to know about Pythagorean communities (he met in fact Archytas as we know from the *Seventh Letter*, 388C). During this voyage Plato was invited to Syracuse in Sicily by the tyrant Dionysius I. Plato certainly hoped to inculcate in this tyrant the ideal of the philosopher-king (that he had already proposed in the *Gorgias*, a work that very probably preceded the voyage). Plato in Syracuse got into conflict with the tyrant and with the court (simply by maintaining the principles espoused in the *Gorgias*,); and, instead developed a strong bond of friendship with Dion, a relative of the tyrant, in whom Plato thought he had found someone with the potential to become a philosopher-king. Dionysius at this point was so infuriated with Plato says, *Diogenes Laertius*, (3.19)—that he prevailed on a Spartan ambassador to sell him off as a slave in Aegina (but perhaps, more simply, he was limited to sending him off to Aegina, which was at war with Athens, where Plato would be treated as a slave). Fortunately he was rescued by Anniceris of Cyrene who found him in Aegina *(Diogenes Laertius*, 3.20).

On his return to Athens he founded the Academy (in a gymnasium situated in a park dedicated to the hero Accademus, whence the name Academy) and the *Meno*, was probably the first pronouncement of his new School. The Academy was successful very quickly and attracted young men as well as well-known scholars in great numbers.

In 367 Plato returned to Sicily a second time. Dionysius I was dead and had been succeeded by his son Dionysius II who, Dion reported, was better disposed than the father with respect to Plato aims. But Dionysius II turned out to have the same qualities as his father. Only because he was embroiled in a war did Dionysius II allow Plato to return to Athens.

In 361 Plato went to Sicily a third time. After he had returned to Athens,—Dion had taken refuge there,—he was persuaded by Dion to accept a new and urgent invitation from Dionysius II (for the purpose of finishing his philosophical preparation), hoping that, in this way, Dionysius would complete his education. But it was a grave error to believe in the change of sentiments of Dionysius. Plato certainly would have lost a great deal except for the intervention of Archytas and the Tarantineans who served him. (Dion returned, in 357, seized power in Syracuse, but not for long. He was killed in 353.)

In 360 Plato returned to Athens and took up the direction of the Academy until his death, which occurred in 347 BCE.

The writings of Plato have come down to us intact. The arrangement that was given to them (a task that was completed by the grammarian Thrasyllus, but begun already prior to him) is based on the content of the writings themselves. The thirty-six works have been subdivided into the following nine tetralogies:

I: *Euthyphro, Apology of Socrates, Crito, Phaedo*;
II: *Cratylus, Theaetetus, Sophist, Statesman*;
III: *Parmenides, Philebus, Symposium, Phaedrus*;
IV: *Alcibiades I, Alcibiades I,I, Hipparchus, Amatores*;
V: *Theages, Charmides, Laches, Lysis*;
VI: *Euthydemus, Protagoras, Gorgias, Meno*;
VII: *Hippias minor, Hippias major, Ion, Menexenus*;
VIII: *Clitophon, Republic, Timaeus, Critias*
IX: *Minos, Laws, Epinomis, Letters*.

Remember that the pagination of the various dialogues to which all scholars refer is that of the fifteenth century edition of Stephanus; it is placed in the margins in all modern editions and translations.

To avoid burdening the text, in the course of our exposition we generally will cite only works explicitly used as evidence, while we will provide a rich and detailed bibliography in volume V, *s.v.*; we ask the reader's indulgence.

2. *Symposium*, 219A; *Republic* VIII, 519B.

3. *Phaedo*, 99C–D.

4. *Phaedrus*, 278D.

5. The necessity for introducing a new criterion and a new model to read and understand Plato (partially begun by Robin, Heinrich Gomperz and especially by J. Stenzel) has been presented in a systematic way for the first time by the School of Tübingen, in a particular way in the following works: H. Krämer, *Arete bei Platon und Aristoteles. Zum Wesen und zur Geschichte der platonischen Ontologie* (Heidelberg, 1959 (Amsterdam, 1967²); K. Gaiser, *Platons Ungeschriebene Lehre. Studien zur systematischen und geschichtlichen. Begrundung der Wissenschaften in der Platonischen Schule. With the addition of Testimonia Platonica. Quellentexte zur Schule und mündlichen Lehre Platons*, (Stuttgart, 1963, 1968²); H. Krämer, *Platone e i fondamenti della metafisica. Saggio sulla teoria dei principi e sulle dottrine non scritte di Platone con una raccolta dei documenti fondamentali in edizione bilingue e bibliografia. Introduzione e traduzione di G. Reale*, (Milan, 1982, 1989³), this work was composed appropriately for the Center for Metaphysical Research of the Catholic University directly at my invitation [the volume has been published by State University of New York Press with the title *Plato and the Foundations of Metaphysics*, (Albany, 1990)]; K. Gaiser, *Platone come scrittore filosofico. Saggio sull'ermeneutica dei dialoghi platonici* (Naples, 1984), a work published only in Italian. To these works add T. A. Szlezák, *Platon und die Schriftlichkeit der Philosophie. Interpretationen zu den frühen und mittleren Dialogen* (Berlin, 1985); Introduzione e traduzione di G. Reale (Milan, 1989²); G. Reale, *Per una nuova interpretazione di Platone. Rilettura della metafisica dei grandi dialoghi alle luce delle "Dottrine non scritte,"* (Milan, 1990⁷, the first edition is from 1984), but published in a provisional and partial rough draft. The work of L. Robin, to which we made reference earlier, is the famous *La Théorie Platonicienne des Idées et des Nombres d'après Aristote* (Paris, 1908, Hildesheim, 1963); of J. Stenzel see especially *Zahl und Gestalt bei Platon und Aristoteles* (Leipzig-Berlin, 1924, Darmstadt, 1959³); the brief article from Heinrich Gomperz is very interesting (but with a far-reaching perspective): "Platons philosophisches System," in *Proceedings of the Seventh International Congress of Philosophy* (London, 1931), pp. 426–431 (published in an English translation in Gomperz, *Philosophical Studies* [Boston, 1953], pp. 119–24). Very interesting from our perspective is J. N. Findlay, *Plato. The Written and Unwritten Doctrines* (London, 1974). A full bibliography on the issue may be found in Krämer, *Plato*, pp. 418ff.

Among the scholars who have in different ways contributed to the articulation of the model of the traditional interpretation, three deserve particular mention: D. Ross, *Plato's Theory of Ideas* (Oxford, 1951, 1953²); P. Merlan, *From Platonism* to *Neoplatonism* (The Hague, 1953, 1968³; republished in 1975) and, by the same author, numerous articles now collected in *Kleine philosophische Schriften*, (Hildesheim-New York, 1976); C. J. DeVogel, numerous articles now collected in *Philosophia. Part I: Studies in Greek Philsophy* (Van Gorcum:Assen, 1970), pp. 153–292. Rereading these works carefully in the light of the new paradigm produces interesting results.

The final works on Plato by H. G. Gadamer deserve particular mention: "Platons ungeschriebene Dialektik," in *Idee und Zahl. Studien zur platonischen Philosophie* (Heidelberg, 1968), pp. 121–47, reedited many times.

Let us mention, finally, that the numbering of the *Testimonia Platonica* that we use is that of the now classic work of Gaiser; along with this we will also cite the collection in Krämer that can be found in *Plato*, pp. 358ff. that side by side with the Greek text can be found our Italian translation [the American edition does not have the Greek text but does have the testimonies among the appendices].

6. Of F. Schleiermacher see especially the *Einleitung* to the impressive series of translation of the works of Plato (1804ff.), which today can be found republished in K. Gaiser (editor), *Zehn Beiträge zum Platonverständnis* (Hildesheim, 1969), pp. 1–32. For the understanding of this *Einleitung* the pages of Krämer, *Plato*, pp. 33–149 and Reale, *Plato*, pp. 71–87 and passim are fundamental. Let us remember that the thesis of Schleiermacher is a true hermeneutic model *only* in the measure in which it proposes and defends in a systematic manner the *self-sufficiency of the Platonic writings*; all the rest involves, instead, the complex articulation of this model, which in the modern period has had a great amount of complex variation, although always keeping secure the thesis of the autonomy of the writings. Keep in mind again that many criticisms made (in the course of 1800s and in the first half of the 1900s) about Schleiermacher do not concern his basic thesis, because of its complex articulations. For the demonstration of this view consult our *Plato*, passim.

7. F. Nietzsche, *Gesammelte Werke. Viertes Band: Vorträge, Schriften und Vorlesungen* 1871–1876 (Musarion Ausgabe, München), p. 370. Nietzsche criticizes another thesis of Scheiermacher, but it is the criticism of this position that demonstrates his extraordinary and farsighted understanding of the basic problem.

8. *Phaedrus*, 274B–278E. For an interpretation and detailed commentary, see Krämer, *Plato*, 36ff.; Szlezák, *Platon*, 7–48; Reale, *Plato*, 89–106, cfr. also Gaiser, *Platone come scrittore*, 77–101.

9. *Phaedrus*, 275C–D.

10. *Phaedrus*, 278B–E.

11. *Phaedrus*, 278C.

12. *Seventh Letter*, 340B–345C. cf. Krämer, *Plato*, 44ff.; 105–113; Szlezák, *Platon*, 386–405; Reale, *Plato*, 105–121.

13. *Seventh Letter*, 341C–E.

14. *Seventh Letter*, 344C–D.

15. These very significant expressions are found in the *Seventh Letter*, on the following pages: 341A–B; 344B–D.

16. *Seventh Letter*, 344D–E.

17. Aristotle, *Physics*, Δ2. 209b 11–17 (Gaiser, *Test. Plat.*, 54A = Krämer, 4).

18. Simplicius, *In Arist.* Phys., 151, 6–9 Diels (Gaiser, *Test. Plat.*, 8 = Krämer, 2).

19. Simplicius, *In Arist. Phys.*, 453, 22–30 Diels (Gaiser, *Test. Plat.*, 23B = Krämer, 3).

20. Aristoxenos, *Harm. elem.*, II, 39–40 Da Rios (Gaiser, *Test. Plat.*, 7 = Krämer, 1).

21. *Seventh Letter*, 340B–D; 341C–E; 344D.

22. *Seventh Letter*, 345B.

23. Reale, *Plato*, passim.

24. In the modern age W. Lennemann, *System der platonischen Philosophie* (Leipzig 1792–1795) especially has spread this conception and after him Hegel in the citation given earlier [p. 27 Italian text].

25. G.W.F. Hegel, "Vorlesungen über die Geschichte der Philosophie," in *Sämtliche Werke...herausgegeben von H. Glockner, Vierte Auflage der Jubiläumsausgabe*, (Stuttgart-Bad Cannstatt, 1965), vol. 18, pp. 179ff.

26. K. Gaiser, "La teoria dei Principi in Platone," *Elenchos* 1 (1980):45–75; the passage cited is on p. 48.

27. Cfr. *Republic*, VI–VIII, passim; *Laws*, XII, 960Bff.

28. For the bibliography connected to this issue see volume V, *s.v.*

29. On the significance of this term and on its use in the dialogues, see Szlezák, *Platon*, 376–385.

30. These allusions are very numerous. Some of the most important are collected by Krämer, *Plato*, Appendix II, pp. 358ff. (see the references of the Platonic writings to the "unwritten doctlrines,") with Greek text and my translation on facing pages [American edition without Greek text, Appendix 2, pp. 199-202 (nn.1-11)]. Cfr. also Reale, *Plato*, passim.

31. Krämer, *Plato*, 148.

32. Gaiser, *Platone come scrittore*, 46.

33. Szlezák, *Platon*, 66; cfr. also 328ff.

34. This is exactly the path opened by the School of Tübingen that we have adopted in our *Plato*, passim.

CHAPTER TWO

(THE IMPORTANT PROBLEMS THAT HAVE BESET

THE INTERPRETATION OF PLATO)

1. G. W. Leibniz, *Die philosophischen Schriften*, C. J. Gerhardt edition, Vol. III (Berlin, 1887; 1978^2), p. 637.

2. See, for an idea of how the problem of the "system" is generally misunderstood, E. N. Tigerstedt, *Interpreting Plato* (Uppsala, 1977).

3. Krämer, *Platon*, 177f.

4. Gaiser, *La teoria*, 48f.

5. J. W. Goethe, "Plato, als Mitgenosse einer christlichen Offenbarung," in *Goethes Werke*, XXXII (in the collection "Deutsche National-Litteratur. Historisch-kritische Ausgabe" 113.Bd), p. 140.

6. Cf. volume I, 239–252.

7. K. Jaspers, *Die grossen Philosophen* (München, 1957), 267ff.

8. T. Gomperz, *Griechische Denker* (Leipzig, 1896–1897).

9. K. F. Hermann, *Geschichte und System der platonischen Philosophie* (Heidelberg, 1839).

10. In addition to the work of Hermann cited in the prior note, the works of L. Campbell has been decisive and especially the remarkable work of W. Lutoslawski, *The Origin and Growth of Plato's Logic* (London, 1905[2]; 1897[1]). The most recent work on this issue is H. Thesleff, *Studies in Platonic Chronology* (Helsinki, 1982).

11. Hegel, *Vorlesungen über die Geschichte der Philosophie*, cit., 188ff.

12. Cf. W. Hirsch, *Platons' Weg zum Mythos* (Berlin, 1971).

13. See the bibliography in volume V, *s.v.*

14. *Phaedo*, 67B–C; 68A; 114C.

15. *Gorgias*, 527A–B.

16. *Phaedo*, 114D.

17. Cf. *Timaeus*, 29B–C. See Reale, *Plato*, 519–521.

18. *Timaeus*, 29C–D.

19. Gaiser, *Platone come scrittore*, 44. On this attribute of myth consult *Phaedo*, 114D (check the text presented earlier [p. 51 Italian edition]); *Laws*, X, 903B.

20. Cf. *Phaedrus*, 276E.

SECOND SECTION—CHAPTER ONE

(THE SECOND VOYAGE)

1. Cf. *Phaedo*, 96A–102A. For a detailed analysis check our *Plato*, pp. 147–177, where we present the fullest and most detailed analysis so far that has been done of this passage.

2. W. Goodrich, "On *Phaedo*, 96A–102A and on the δεύτερος πλοῦς 99D," *Classical Review* 17 (1903): 381–484 and 18 (1904): 5–11.

3. *Phaedo*, 99B–D.

4. Eustachius, *In Odyss.*, p. 1453. This quite beautiful image of the second voyage (δεύτερος πλοῦς), which, in the metaphorical sense in which Plato used it, we have taken up as the chief key for the interpretation of Plato's thought, as well as *before* and *after* Plato, with the general approval of many scholars. In general it has been

correctly understood with the sole exception (up till now) of A. A. Long, who writes: "R. thinks that Plato's *deuteros plous* is 'second' and superior to the method of the phisikoi, exemplified by Anaxagoras; but that cannot be right (cf. W. J. Goodrich, *Classical Review* 17 [1903], 383). Nor does it, as such, consist in the 'scoperta del soprasensibile e delle Idee'...but in ὑποθέμενος ἑκάστοτε λόγον ὃν ἂν κρίνω ἐρρωμενέστατον εἶναι (*Phd.* 100A)" (The *Classical Review* 3 [1982]: 40). But Long is incorrect because the very phrase which he cites states what I say: in fact the "hypotheses" of which this text speaks *are exactly those which introduce the Ideas*, and hence the metasensible, as for the rest, the whole of the *Phaedo*, confirms it and the text that we recorded demonstrate in so clear manner as to exclude any reasonable doubt. Consult the analysis presented in our *Plato*, pp. 147–167 (check also our previous translation with commentary of the *Phaedo*, [Brescia:Editrice La Scuola, 1970; 1986[10]], passim).

5. *Phaedo*, 99D–100A.

6. *Phaedo*, 100A–101D.

7. *Phaedo*, 101D–E.

8. *Phaedo*, 101E–102A.

9. *Phaedo*, 107A–B.

10. *Parmenides*, 134E–135B.

11. *Seventh Letter*, 341C.

12. *Timaeus*, 28C.

13. *Philebus*, 28D–29A.

14. We remind the reader that our work *Plato*, passim., must be read for a detailed documentation of all that we have stated.

CHAPTER TWO

(THE PLATONIC THEORY OF THE IDEAS)

1. On the doctrine of the Ideas, its origins and its philosophical meaning, the scholarly literature is very considerable. See our volume V, *s.v.*

2. On this thesis the volume of V. E. Alfieri, *Atomos Idea. L'origine del concetto dell'atomo nel pensiero greco* (Florence, 1953; Galatina, 1979[2]), p. 54 [60[2]]).

3. G. Calogero, *Storia della logica antica* (Bari:Laterza, 1967), p. 269.

4. Diels-Kranz, 59B4 (see also *Reale*, I:111ff.).

5. P. Friedländer, *Platon*, Vol. I (Berlin, 1964[3]), p. 13.

6. Cf. *Symposium*, 219A; *Republic* VII, 519B.

7. Reale, *Plato*, pp. 169–221.

8. *Phaedo*, 65C–66A.

9. *Statesman*, 286A (cf. also *Phaedo*, 85E; *Philebus*, 64B; *Sophist*, 246B, 247D; *Epinomis*, 981B).

10. Diels-Kranz, 13B3; cf. *Reale*, I:46.

11. Diels-Kranz, 30B9; cf. *Reale*, I:98.

12. The fundamental work on this thesis is still H. Gomperz, "ΑΣΩΜΑΤΟΣ," *Hermes* 67 (1932):155–167.

13. Let us remember especially the expression τὸ παντελῶς ὄν (cf. *Republic* V, 477A; *Sophist*, 248E), τὸ ὄν ὄντως and οὐσία ὄντως οὖσα (*Phaedrus*, 247C–E). But Plato quite frequently used many other analogies.

14. *Phaedo*, 78D–79A.

15. *Phaedo*, 75C–D.

16. Cf. earlier, pp. 60f.

17. Cf. *Republic* V, 478E–479D.

18. Cf. *Phaedo*, 66C; *Republic*, VI, 485A–B; VII, 521C–D; cf. also, VI, 509Dff.; VII, 514Aff.

19. Aristotle, *Metaphysics*, A 6.987A–B; M 4.1078b–1079a.

20. Here, like *Protagoras*, he posited *man as "measure" of all things* (cf. *Reale*, I:230ff.).

21. *Cratylus*, 439B–440A.

22. *Cratylus*, 385E–386E.

23. *Republic*, V, 475E–476A.

24. *Republic*, V, 479A.

25. *Republic*, VI, 484B.

26. *Republic*, VII, 537C.

27. Aristotle, *Metaphysics*, A9, 990b13; Alexander of Aphrodisias, *In Arist. Metaph.* 80, 9ff. Hayduck (= Aristotle, *De ideis*, frag. 3 Ross). For a detailed analysis of this argument, see E. Berti, *La filosofia del primo Aristotele* (Padua, 1962), pp. 208ff.; W. Leszl, *Il "De Ideis" di Aristotele e la teoria platonica delle Idee* (Florence, 1975), 141ff.

28. An excellent list of the expressions with which Plato indicated the immanence of the Ideas and with that he indicated the transcendence has been furnished by D. Ross, *Plato's Theory of Ideas*, cit., pp. 228ff., and has been reported by us in *Plato*, 199ff., note 61.

29. *Timaeus*, 51B–52A.

30. We will see that this form of *dualism* has a precise "bipolar" structure; cf. earlier, pp. 69ff.

31. *Phaedrus*, 247C–E; cf. *Republic*, VI, 509D (see Reale, *Plato*, pp. 204f.).

32. Cf. *Phaedo*, 100C–D; cf. also 74D.

33. Cf. *Euthyphro*, 6D–E, and our edition with introduction and commentary to this dialogue (Brescia, 1984⁶).

34. *Timaeus*, 68D.

Notes / 401

CHAPTER THREE
(THE UNWRITTEN DOCTRINES AND METAPHYSICS)

1. *Phaedo*, 101E; *Republic*, VI, 510B; 511B.

2. Cf. *Reale* I:208ff.

3. Cf. Aristotle, *Metaphysics*, M 4.1078b–1079a.

4. *Seventh Letter*, 344D.

5. Aristotle, *Metaphysics*, A 6.987b18–21 (Gaiser, *Test. Plat.* 22A = Krämer, 9).

6. Theophrastus, *Metaphysics*, 6b11–16 (Gaiser, *Test. Plat.*, 30 = Krämer, 8).

7. Sextus Empiricus, *Adv. math.*, x, 258 and 262 (Gaiser, *Test. Plat.*, 32 = Krämer, 12).

8. Heraclitus, we recall, said this: "from all things the *one* and from the *one* all things." (Diels-Kranz, 22B11), a fragment that we chose as the epigraph of the treatment of Presocratic philosophy from its origins (cf. *Reale*, I:33) and the many times we appeal to the One.

9. Cf. Krämer, *Plato*, pp. 155f. and the testimony on page 156, note 6.

10. Proclus, *In Plat. Parm.*, pp. 38ff. Klibansky-Labowsky, parts of which have only come down to us in the translation of William of Moerbeke (Gaiser, *Test. Plat.*, 50).

11. *Republic* VI, 509B.

12. Simplicius, *In Arist. Phys.*, p. 248, 13–16 Diels (Gaiser, *Test. Plat.*, 31 = Krämer, 13).

13. See P. Philippson, *Untersuchungen über den griechischen Mythos*, (Zürich, 1944).

14. Ibid., pp. 65f. [Italian edition].

15. Aristotle, *Metaphysics*, G 1.1004b27–1005a2.

16. Especially by Sextus Empiricus, *Adv. math.*, X, 263ff. (Gaiser, *Test. Plat.*, 32 = Krämer, 12); Simplicius, *In Arist. Phys.*, pp. 247, 30f. Diels (Gaiser, *Test. Plat.*, 31 = Krämer, 13); various passages in *Divisiones Aristoteleae* (Gaiser, *Test. Plat.*, 43 and 44 = Krämer, 27–31).

17. The first scholar to correctly explain and reevaluate this doctrine was P. Wilpert, *Zwei aristotelische Frühschriften über die Ideelehre* (Regensberg, 1949). See also; Krämer, *Arete*, pp. 282–379; 438ff.; Krämer, *Plato*, pp. 159f.; Gaiser, *Platons*, pp. 24f;73–88;177f.;Gaiser,"Quellenkritische Probleme der indirekten Platonüberlieferung," in *Idee und Zahl. Studien zur platonischen Philosophie* (Heidelberg 1968), pp. 31–84 and especially pp. 63ff.; Reale, *Plato*, pp. 261ff.

18. Cf. Aristotle, *Metaphysics*, M 7, 1078b7–12; cf. what we said in *Plato*, pp. 244f.

19. O.Töplitz, "Das Verhältniss von Mathematik und Ideelehre bei Plato," in *Quellen und Studien zur Geschichte der Mathematik, Astronomie und Physik*, 1 (1929/31), pp. 3–33, now in the collection with different studies edited by O. Becker, *Zur Geschichte der griechischen Mathematik* (Darmstadt, 1965), pp. 45–75. This thesis

was accepted and spread by J. Stenzel, P. Wilpert, and consequently by Gaiser and Krämer.

20. Cf. Aristotle, *Metaphysics*, M 8.1084a12–b2; Λ 8.1073a18–22 (Gaiser, *Test. Plat.*, 61 and 62).

21. Friedländer, *Platon*, p. 13.

22. On these issues consult the excellent pages of W. Tatarkiewicz, *History of Aesthetics*, vol. I: *Ancient Aesthetics* (The Hague-Paris-Warszawa, 1970), passim.

23. Aristotle, *Metaphysics*, A 6.987b14–18 (Gaiser, *Test. Plat.*, 22A = Krämer 9). Consult also volume V, *s.v.*

24. This is the famous fragment of *Parmenides*, Diels-Kranz 28B3.

25. Gaiser, *Platons*, p. 89.

26. Gaiser, *Platons*, p. 299.

CHAPTER FOUR

(THE METAPHYSICS OF THE IDEAS)

1. Cf. earlier, p. 16.

2. Gaiser, *Platone come scrittore*, p. 89; the fragment cited is by Heraclitus, Diels-Kranz, 22B93.

3. *Republic*, VI, 504A–505B.

4. *Republic*, VI, 506D–507A.

5. *Republic*, VI, 507A–509C.

6. *Republic*, VII, 508B–509C.

7. Consult the outline of these questions we have traced in *Plato*, pp. 312ff. (with the respective analytic solutions).

8. Plotinus, *Enneads*, 5.5.6.

9. For a clarification consult H. Krämer, "Uber den Zusammenhang von Prinzipienlehre und Dialektik bei Platon. Zur Definition des Dialektikers Politeia 534 B/C," *Philologus* 110 (1966):35–70 (now in the volume edited by J. Wippern, *Das Problem der Ungeschriebenen Lehre Platons. Beiträge zur Verständnis der platonischen Prinzipienlehre* [Darmstadt, 1972], pp. 394–448);H. Krämer,"ΕΠΕΚΕΙΝΑ ΤΗΣ ΟΥΣΙΑΣ. Zu Platon Politeia 509B," *Archiv für Geschichte der Philosophie* 51 (1969):1–30; Krämer, *Plato*, 184–98; Szlezák, *Platon*, 271–326; Reale, *Plato*, 293–333.

10. Consult the range of the interpretations that we traced in *Plato*, 335ff.

11. *Parmenides*, 126A–128E.

12. *Parmenides*, 128E–135C.

13. *Parmenides*, 135C–166C.

14. Plotinus, *Enneads*, 6.1–3.

15. A. E. Taylor, *Plato* (London, 1949[6]), 389.

16. *Sophist*, 241D–242A.

17. *Sophist*, 258A–259B.

18. *Sophist*, 242C.

19. Consult *Sophist*, 242D–245D.

20. For a detailed analysis consult Reale, *Plato*, 359–79.

21. Just as Porphyry had done as Simplicius writes: *In Arist. Phys.*, 453, 30ff. Diels (Gaiser, *Test. Plat.*, 23B = Krämer, 11).

22. J. Stenzel, *Studien zur Entwicklung der platonischen Dialektik von Sokrates zu Aristoteles* (Darmstadt, 1961[2]; 1917[1]).

23. *Philebus*, 16Cff.

24. *Philebus*, 18A–B.

25. *Philebus*, 28C–31A.

26. *Philebus*, 64Aff.

27. M. Pohlenz, *Der hellinische Mensch* (Göttingen, 1947), p. 422 [Italian edition].

28. *Republic*, VI, 504A–506B.

29. Diels-Kranz, 22B93.

30. Consult Reale, *Plato*, pp. 405–21 and 471–507, where we present a most detailed analysis of these issues.

CHAPTER FIVE

(THE DOCTRINE OF THE DEMIURGE AND COSMOLOGY)

1. Aristotle, *Metaphysics*, Δ11.1019a1–4.

2. On these questions see Krämer, *Plato*, pp. 164 and 176ff., Reale, *Plato*, 427ff.

3. Cf. *Reale*, I:88ff.

4. *Republic* V, 477Aff.

5. The riddle goes like this: there is *a man* who is *not a man* (= eunuch), who drags *a rock* which is *not a rock* (= pumice), to a *bird* which is *not a bird* (= bat), on a *plant* which is *not a plant* (= a reed). The appeal of this riddle suggests in a splendid manner the fundamental ambiguity of the μεταξύ, of the sensible that is *both being and non-being* and is *not either (pure) being or non-being.*

6. *Republic* V, 478E–479D. It is appropriate to point out that *nonbeing*, of which Plato speaks in this passage, would seem to be *nothing* (nonbeing in the absolute sense). However the text and context allow us to believe that Plato meant rather, the opposite material principle (the sensible Dyad), that, as we know, become assimilated to nonbeing, since, for our philosopher, being is a "mixture," which depends on the determination and delimitation of the *indeterminate* and *unlimited* (and such is instead the Dyad of the great-and-small that is in fact the unlimited). Note in

addition, the elusive hints (which we have pointed out in the italic print) to the *One* (which is explicated in the Ideas) in opposition to phenomenal-sensible things *doubles*, and *greats* and *smalls* (allusions to the Dyad of the great-and-small in which they partake); pay attention also to the initial statement that sensible intermediate being "partakes of both," that is, "in being and nonbeing"; but it is clear that the "participation" in nonbeing is possible only if it is something (indeed the indeterminate and the unlimited). In conclusion, this passage is very clear, if these specific meanings are given to "being" and to "nonbeing," that Plato in his metaphysics gave to them and that is reflected in a perfect way in his protologic.

7. On this issue find a full treatment in Reale, *Plato*, 425–622, to which we will refer many times.

8. Consult the rich bibliography published in the last ten years on the *Timaeus* (which has been for a long time the most read and most influential dialogue of Plato) found in H. Cherniss, "Plato (1950–1957)," *Lustrum* 4 (1959): 208–277; L. Brisson, "Platon 1958–1975," *Lustrum* 20 (1977): 286f.; L. Brisson, "Platon 1975–1980," *Lustrum* 25(1983): 295ff. (with the related reference). The most extended treatment of the metaphysical grounding of the dialogues is found in Reale, *Plato*, 509–622; again, 509ff. where other important bibliographical information can be found.

9. *Timaeus*, 27E–28B.

10. *Timaeus*, 28B–29A.

11. *Timaeus*, 29A–B.

12. Cf. earlier note 6.

13. *Timaeus*, 50C.

14. Cf. *Timaeus*, 50C, 51A, 52C.

15. *Timaeus*, 51E–52B. Note that Plato, here, specifies that which in the passage read earlier from the *Republic* was pointed out with ignorance; that is, no cognition of nonbeing (which corresponds to the material Principle here treated). In fact, it (*a*) is not cognizable with the senses; (*b*) is graspable only with a spurious reason; that is, "bastard reason" (λογισμῷ τινι νόθῳ); (*c*) it is believed to be evil. Actually, what is known (whether sensibly or rationally) is determinate, whereas the material Principle is indeterminate, which is cognizable only through a "bastard reasoning."

16. *Timaeus*, 52B.

17. *Timaeus*, 52C; cf. Reale, *Plato*, 543ff.

18. *Timaeus*, 50B–C; cf. Reale, *Plato*, 536–543.

19. *Timaeus*, 30A.

20. *Timaeus*, 52D–53B; cf. Reale, *Plato*, 546ff.

21. *Timaeus*, 47E–48B; cf. Reale, *Plato*, 531–535.

22. Cf. Aristotle, *Physics*, Δ 2.209b11–17 (Gaiser, *Test. Plat.*, 54A = Krämer, 4); Aristotle, *Metaphysics*, A6.987b1ff.; 988a10ff. (Gaiser, *Test. Plat.*, 22A = Krämer 9); Theophrastus, *Metaphysics*, 6a23–b5 (Gaiser, *Test. Plat.*, 30 = Krämer, 8);

Simplicius, *In Arist. Phys.*, 248, 5–15 Diels (Gaiser, *Test. Plat.*, 31 = Krämer, 13; Simplicius, *In Arist. Phys.*, pp. 430, 34–431, 16 Diels (Gaiser, *Test. Plat.*, 55B); cf. Reale, *Plato*, 549–559.

23 Cf. Aristotle, *Metaphysics*, Z 10.1036a9–12;Z 11.1037a5–13;H 6.1045a33–35;K 1,1059b14–21 and our commentary to the *Metaphysics*, in these places. See especially H. Happ, *Hyle. Studien zum aristotischen Materie-Begriff* (Berlin–New York, 1971), 581–615.

24. Cf. *Theaetetus*, 176A–B. The most famous testimony of the "unwritten doctrine," in which Plato connects the Dyad of the great-and-small with the "cause of evil" (τοῦ κακῶς αἰτία) is from Aristotle, *Metaphysics*, A 6.988a14 (Gaiser, *Test. Plat.*, 22A = Krämer, 9).

25. *Timaeus*, 29E–30A.

26. *Timaeus*, 53A–B, 56C, 68D–69B.

27. *Timaeus*, 30B–31A; cf. Reale, *Plato*, 572ff.

28. *Timaeus*, 31B–32C; cf. Reale, *Plato*, 575ff.

29. *Timaeus*, 32C–33B; cf. Reale, *Plato*, 578ff.

30. *Timaeus*, 33B–34A; cf. Reale, *Plato*, 579ff.

31. Cf. the paragraph that follows and notes 36–38.

32. Cf. the paragraph that follows and notes 39–40.

33. Cf. the paragraph that follows and notes 41–44.

34. *Timaeus*, 47E–48A, says that everything around this world is born exactly from the mixture of necessity and intelligence: μεμειγμένη γὰρ οὖν ἡ τοῦδετοῦκόσμου γένεσις ἐξ ἀνάγκης τε καὶ νοῦσυστάσεως ἐγεννήθη.

35. Aristotle, *Metaphysics*, A 6.987b14–18 (Gaiser, *Test. Plat.*, 22A = Krämer, 9).

36. Cf. *Timaeus*, 37D–39D.

37. *Timaeus*, 37D 3–7.

38. *Timaeus*, 38B6–8: note the strong expressions: xrÉnow...μετ᾿ οὐρανοῦ γέγονεν and, in addition: κατὰ τὸ παράδειγμα.

39. *Timaeus*, 53A–B.

40. Cf. earlier note 34. For a clarification of this issue consult Reale, *Plato*, 563–71.

41. Cf. *Timaeus*, 34B–35B; see Reale, *Plato*, 585–98, with further information that we gave there.

42. *Timaeus*, 34A–36D.

43. The expression coined by the Rennaissance *anima copula mundi* could be attached in a perfect way to the Platonic conception.

44. Cf. *Timaeus*, 40A–B; 41D–42B.

45. For completeness, let us remember that the creationism of the Demiurge is also explicated in the comparison of the Ideas to *artifacts*; that is, of the Ideas of artificial objects, as Plato states in Book X of the *Republic*. Therefore the Demiurge

presupposes the existence of the general Ideas and those of natural things (those to which he refers and that inspire him, as models, in the construction of the cosmos), but "he creates" (in the Hellenic sense) all those things that inspired men, as models, in the production of all the objects of their arts. For a clarification of the issues and for an interpretation and commentary of the related texts consult Reale, *Plato*, 439–53.

46. *Timaeus*, 37A; 29A.

47. Cf. Reale, *Plato*, pp. 463–70; 605ff.

48. Cf. *Timaeus*, 29E, 41B.

49. *Timaeus*, 68D.

50. See the argument that the Demiurge has with the created gods, in the *Timaeus*, 41A–D. His "power," which he invites these gods to share, is that of making the one-into-many. Already in the *Gorgias*, 507E–508B Plato states that heaven, earth, gods, and men "are held together by *order*, by wisdom and by rectitude," and that indeed this makes of the world a "cosmos" and not something disordered and unruly." In this sense the indirect tradition summarized the Demiurgic activity, saying that the Platonic God "always geometricizes" (Plutarch, *Quaest. conviv.* VIII 2). And indeed this is the nature of the *unity-in-multiplicity*. (Remember the passage of the *Timaeus*, 41A–D, earlier, p. 240 and the passage of the *Gorgias*, 507E–508B, earlier, pp.179-80).

CHAPTER SIX

(EPISTEMOLOGY AND DIALECTIC)

1. For a detailed analysis of the dialogue see our edition (Brescia:La Scuola, 1986[11]).

2. *Meno*, 80D.

3. *Meno*, 81C–D (cf. our comments, pp. 39ff.).

4. *Meno*, 82B–86C (cf. the comments and clarification of this point in our edition, pp. 45–60).

5. *Meno*, 85D–86B.

6. Cf. *Phaedo*, 73Cff.

7. Consult on this argument the clarifications of J. Moreau, *Le sens du platonisme* (Paris, 1976), 115ff.

8. *Phaedo*, 74D–75D.

9. On the importance of Platonic *anamnesis* one can profitably read the pages of M.F. Sciacca, inspired by the objective *a priori* in the Rosminian sense, in *Platone* (Milan, 1967), I:38ff.

10. *Phaedrus*, 249B–C.

11. *Phaedrus*, 249E–250A.

12. *Timaeus*, 41D–E.

13. As P. Natorp claims *Platos Ideelehre* (Leipzig, 1903) [and the current of thought inspired by Kantianism, about which the reader can find enough information and a discussion in A. Levi, *Sulle interpretazioni immanentische della filosofia di Platone* (Turin, n.d. [but published in 1920)].

14. For the reader who wants to clarify the issue of *anamnesis* in all its aspects, we point out the voluminous work of C. E. Huber, *Anamnesis bei Plato,* (München, 1964). For recent studies see volume V, *s.v.*

15. *Republic*, V, 476E–477B.

16. Cf. *Meno*, 97Aff.

17. Consult what is said in paragraphs 4 and 5 passim.

18. Cf. *Republic*, VI, 509Cff.

19. *Republic*, VII, 533C–D.

20. *Republic*, VII, 534B–D.

21. *Timaeus*, 68D.

22. *Phaedrus*, 265C–266B.

23. *Sophist*, 253C–D.

24. *Philebus*, 15D.

25. *Philebus*, 16C–17A.

26. Cf. Reale, *Plato*, passim.

CHAPTER SEVEN

(THE CONCEPTION OF ART AND RHETORIC)

1. *Ion*, passim; *Meno*, 99Dff.; *Phaedrus*, 244Aff. and especially, 245Aff.

2. *Phaedrus*, 245A.

3. *Republic* X, 598B.

4. *Republic* X, 602A–B.

5. *Republic* X, 603A–B.

6. Cf. *Republic* II and X.

7. An analysis of the Idea of Beauty considered in itself and for itself has been done by Plato in the *Hippias major*,; but the dialogue has been one of those that has been the most neglected, because it was considered inauthentic. See, for the contrary view, our student's work M. T. Liminta, *Il problema della bellezza. Autenticità e significato dell'Ippia maggiore di Platone* (Milan:Celuc, 1974), in which—among other things—he explains in detail the reasons why Plato rejected a purely autonomous aesthetic of the beautiful (and also of art).

8. *Republic*, III, 387B.

9. In *Reale*, I:149–90 the section on the *Sophist*, passim.

10. Cf. the first part of the *Gorgias*, with our comments, pp. 17–46.

11. Cf. *Gorgias*, 463Bff.

12. *Phaedrus*, 260D–E.

13. Cf. *Phaedrus*, 263Bff.

14. Cf. *Phaedrus*, 270Bff.

THIRD SECTION—CHAPTER ONE

(THE MYSTICAL-RELIGIOUS-ASCETIC)

1. Here is a summarizing and eloquent passage of a Neoplatonist, which states clearly the final Greeks interest in the thought of Plato. "I maintain...that on the one hand, the philosophy of Plato and his principle was uncovered through the good will of the highest Gods...that this philosophy after having received its perfection and then returning as it were to itself and becoming invisible to many who professed to philosophize, and who desire to engage in the investigation of true being, it again advanced into the light. But, on the other hand, I think that the secret doctrine especially about the divine mysteries (which is purely established on a sacred foundation and which perpetually exists with the Gods themselves), became thence apparent to such as are capable of enjoying it for a time, through one man [Plato] whom I should not err in calling the primary guide and interpreter of the most holy mysteries into which souls separated from earthly places are initiated, and of those entire and stable visions, which those participate who genuinely embrace...a happy and blessed life. But this philosophy shone forth at first from him so augustly and secretly as if from sacred temples and as if it were from a secure and stable innermost secret precinct of the most holy inaccessible place" (Proclus, *The Platonic Theology*, cap. 1).

2. Especially in the *Phaedo*, but then also in his succeeding writings.

3. Cf. *Gorgias*, 48Cff.

4. Cf. *Gorgias*, 492Df.

5. Cf. *Gorgias*, 492Eff.

6. Cf. *Phaedo*, 70Aff.

7. Cf. *Gorgias*, and *Phaedo*, passim.

CHAPTER TWO

(THE IMMORTALITY OF THE SOUL)

1. There are three proofs in the *Phaedo*, as H. Bonitz has soundly demonstrated in "Die imphädon enthaltenen Beweise für die Unsterblichkeit der menschlechen Seele," first published in *Hermes* and now in *Platonische Studien*, last edition (Hildesheim, 1968), 293–323 (scholars who speak of four or more proofs in the *Phaedo*, ignore Bonitz's documentation).

2. It can be found in a brief exposition in our edition of the *Phaedo*, xxxviiiff.

3. See our comments to the *Phaedo*, 85–92.

4. *Phaedo*, 79A–80B.

5. *Phaedo*, 102B–107B.

6. *Republic*, 610E–611A.

7. *Phaedrus*, 245C–246A.

8. Cf. earlier, pp. 113ff.; also p. 240.

9. Cf. *Gorgias*, 523A; 527A.

10. Cf. the following paragraph.

11. *Gorgias*, 523D–524A.

12. *Gospel of John*, 5:22.

13. *Gorgias*, 525B–C.

14. *Phaedo*, 113D–114C.

15. *Phaedo*, 114D–155A.

16. *Phaedo*, 81C–82C.

17. See earlier, pp. 113ff. and 240.

18. *Timaeus*, 42B–D.

19. *Republic*, X, 618A.

20. *Republic*, X, 617D–E.

21. *Republic*, X, 619B.

22. *Republic*, X, 619D–E.

23. Cf. earlier, note 15.

24. *Republic*, X, 621B–D.

25. Cf. *Phaedrus*, 246A–249D.

26. *Phaedrus*, 248C.

27. *Phaedrus*, 248E–249B.

28. Cf. earlier, pp. 113ff.

29. Cf. earlier, p. 151 and note 18 above.

CHAPTER THREE

(THE NEW MORAL ASCETIC)

1. Cf. earlier, pp. 57ff.

2. *Gorgias*, 492E.

3. *Phaedo*, 66B–67B.

4. *Theaetetus*, 176A–B.

5. *Laws*, IV, 716C.

6. Cf. *Reale*, I:208ff.

7. *Laws*, V, 726A–729A; cf. also V, 743E.

8. *Phaedo*, 83B–E.

9. *Republic*, IX, 585D–E.

10. *Republic*, IX, 586D–E.

11. We have spoken about Eudoxus, *Reale*, III:63–4.

12. *Philebus*, 67B.

13. *Philebus*, 66E–67A.

14. *Laws*, V, 732D–733D.

15. *Laws*, V, 734C–E.

16. *Phaedo*, 69A–D.

17. Cf. *Laws*, V, 731C: "you need to know first of all that the unjust man *is not so voluntarily*"; *Laws*, IX, 860 D–E: "the doer of a wrong, you will grant, is a bad man, and a bad man is *what he is against his will*. But it is mere nonsense to talk of the voluntary doing of an *involuntary* act. Ergo, he who declares the doing of a wrong involuntarily must regard the doer of it as acting contrary to his own will, and I in particular am bound at this moment to accept the position."; *Timaeus*, 86E: "For *no man is voluntarily bad*, but the bad become bad by reason of al ill disposition of the body and bad education...things which are hateful to every man and *happen to him against his will*."

CHAPTER FOUR

(THE MYSTICISM OF PHILIA AND EROS)

1. For an accurate interpretation of the *Lysis*, we suggest the work of our student M. Lualdi, *Il problema della philia e il Liside platonico* (Milan:Celuc, 1974).

2. *Lysis*, 219C–D.

3. On the issue of love see, for clarifications, G. Kreuger, *Einsicht und Leidenschaft* (Frankfurt, 1939;1963³); G. Calogero, *Il Simposio di Platone* (Bari, 1946²); L. Robin, *La théorie platonicienne de l'amour* (Paris, 1968³); as well as Stenzel, *Platone educatore*, pp. 142ff.; and Jaeger, *Paideia*, II, pp. 299ff. Cf. further bibliography in volume V, *s.v.*

4. *Symposium*, 202E–203A.

5. *Symposium*, 203C–E.

6. *Symposium*, 206E.

7. *Symposium*, 210A–212A.

8. *Phaedrus*, 250D–E.

9. *Phaedrus*, 251A–B.

CHAPTER FIVE

(PLATO A PROPHET?)

1. Cf. Platone, *Dialoghi*, trans. F. Acri (Milan, 3d ed.), p. 5.

2. *Gorgias*, 527B–D; cf. also, what we pointed out earlier, pp. 147ff.

3. Plato, *Republic*, II, 361E–362A. The Greek text, to be exact, has the term ἀνασκινδυλευθήσεται, which means "will be impaled." However the translation of Acri (and of other scholars) "will be crucified" is plausible. In fact, during Plato's time, the Greeks did not practice real "crucifixion," but "impalement," *which is precisely the kind of punishment from which "crucifixion" is derived*. On the other hand, the Jews themselves would introduce "crucifixion" in place of "impalement" through the influence of the Romans.

4. Acri, *Platone, Dialoghi*, 9.

CHAPTER SIX

(THE ETHICAL-RELIGIOUS COMPONENT)

1. See *Republic*, X, 611B–C (cf. also IX, 589C–D, 590C–D).

2. *Phaedrus*, 246Aff.

3. Cf. *Phaedrus*, 246A–B.

4. L. Robin, *La théorie platonicienne de l'amour* (Paris, 1968[3]), pp. 134f.

5. Ibid., 135.

6. In our judgment, the argument would be fully clarified. In fact the precisions that Plato made about the pair of horses representing the human soul, by pointing that one is beautiful and good, like the parents from which it is derived, the other is the opposite like the parents from which it comes, becomes much clearer, if it is connected with what Plato stated in the *Timaeus*, where he speaks of *Identity* and *Difference* as two of the three component elements of the rational soul, which are precisely derived from indivisible Identity and divisible Identity and from indivisible Difference and divisible Difference. This discourse, hence, would reflect a full development; but in this place we have thought it appropriate to limit ourselves to the basic outline of the problem.

7. *Gorgias*, 503D–504D.

8. *Gorgias*, 507C–508A. See also what we said in this respect, in our Introduction and in our comments to the *Gorgias*, (Editrice La Scuola, 1985[7]), pp. LIff. and 173, by integrating with what we now say and in particular with the important analysis of Krämer in the place indicated in the notes that follow.

9. On this issue the examination made by H. Krämer in *Arete*, pp. 57–83 is fundamental.

10. Cf. earlier, pp. 157ff.

11. Cf. *Republic*, VI, 500Bff.; we presented the passage, earlier, pp. 202ff.

12. Cf. Reale, *Plato*, 620ff.

13. Cf. *Symposium*, 203Bff.

14. Cf. *Symposium*, 189C–193D. We will make a detailed treatment of this problematic in another place.

15. Cf. *Phaedrus*, 250Cff.

FOURTH SECTION—CHAPTER ONE

(THE POLITICAL COMPONENT)

1. On the *Letters* of Plato we suggest two volumes to the reader: one already a classic, G. Pasquali, *Le lettere di Platone* (Florence, 1938; 1967²), and one recent one, M. Isnardi Parente, *Filosofia e politica nelle lettere di Platone* (Naples, 1970). For a detailed analysis of the *Seventh Letter*, consult L. Edelstein, *Plato's Seventh Letter*, (Leiden, 1966), cf. bibliography in volume V, *s.v.*

2. V. von Wilamowitz-Moellendorff, *Platon* (Berlin, 1959⁵; 1918¹).

3. Jaeger, *Paideia*, II:129–647.

4. Remember especially K. Hildebrandt, *Platon* (Berlin, 1933). The volumes that have come from England and America do not report this interpretation, instead they persistently argue against Plato, considering him an enemy of democracy, e.g., K. R. Popper, *The Open Society and Its Enemies* (London, 1945) republished many times and A. H. S. Crossman, *Plato Today* (New York, 1937) against these positions consult R. B. Levinson, *In Defense of Plato* (Cambridge [Mass.], 1953).

5. *Seventh Letter*, 324B–C.

6. *Seventh Letter*, 325C–326B.

7. For a clarification of this interpretation of the *Gorgias*, see our edition and in particular the Introduction, xi–lviii.

8. *Gorgias*, 521D.

9. Plato tells about it, in detail, in his *Seventh Letter*; cf. earlier the biographical note 1, pp. 393ff.

10. Cf. *Gorgias*, passim.

11. We will see that Plato designs his ideal State, in the *Republic*, even as a magnification of the soul.

12. Cf. *Phaedo*, 66C; *Republic*, IV, 421E–422A.

CHAPTER TWO

(THE *REPUBLIC* OR THE IDEAL STATE)

1. A. E. Taylor, *Plato*, pp. 412ff.

2. Ibid., 413f.

3. Ibid., p. 414.

4. Jaeger, *Paideia*, II, passim.

5. Cf. In particular the works of Popper and Crossman cited in note 4 of the preceding chapter.

6. The work of Popper is now published in Italian.

7. Cf. especially the work of Levinson, *In Defense of Plato*, and the various articles of different authors collected and published by R. Bambrough, *Plato, Popper and Politics*, (Cambridge-New York, 1967).

8. Cf. in *Reale* I:195–256; that is, the whole section dedicated to Socrates.

9. Cf. earlier, pp. 211-2ff.

10. See *Reale* I:183ff.

11. *Republic*, II, 368C–369B.

12. Cf. *Republic*, II, 369B.

13. Cf. *Republic*, II, 369Cff.

14. Cf. *Republic*, II, 373Cff.

15. Cf. *Republic*, II, 375Aff.

16. Cf. *Republic*, II, 376Dff. and III, passim.

17. Cf. *Republic*, II, 377B; III, 398A.

18. Cf. *Republic*, III, 398Cff.

19. Cf. *Republic*, III, 403Cff.

20. Cf. *Republic*, III, 403D.

21. Cf. *Republic*, III, 410Bff.

22. Cf. *Republic*, III, 412Bff.

23. Cf. *Republic*, III, 415A–D; IV, 423C–D.

24. Cf. *Republic*, IV, 419Aff.

25. Cf. *Republic*, IV, 423Cff.

26. Cf. *Republic*, IV, 428Bff.

27. Cf. *Republic*, IV, 429Aff.

28. Cf. *Republic*, IV, 430Dff.

29. Cf. *Republic*, IV, 432Bff.

30. *Republic*, IV, 435E.

31. *Republic*, IV, 436B.

32. *Republic*, IV, 441D–442D.

33. Cf. *Republic*, IV, 444D.

34. Cf. *Republic*, V, 449Cff.

35. *Republic*, V, 455D–456A.

36. Cf. *Republic*, V, 457A.

37. Cf. *Republic*, V, 457C–D.

38. Cf. *Republic*, V, 458Eff.

39. Cf. *Republic*, V, 460Bff.

40. Cf. *Republic*, V, 461D.

41. *Republic*, V, 462A–E.

42. Taylor, *Plato*, 277.

43. Jaeger, *Paideia*, II:243.

44. As we saw earlier (pp. 213–14), Plato reaches intuitively, to some assertions that, if consciously clarified, would have brought him to the discovery of the individual and his values; but he used these assertions in opposite directions.

45. *Republic*, V, 473C–D.

46. *Republic*, VI, 499B–D.

47. *Republic*, VI, 500B–501C.

48. Cf. *Republic*, VI, 505A; VII, 540A–B (we present this passage on page 204).

49. Cf. *Republic*, VI and VII, passim.

50. Jaeger, *Paideia*, II:518.

51. Cf. *Republic*, VI, 504Dff.

52. Cf. *Republic*, IV, 435D; VI, 503E–504E. The meaning of this *long way* has been explained by Jaeger, *Paideia*, II:483ff.

53. Cf. *Republic*, VI, 525Dff.

54. *Republic*, VII, 536D–537A.

55. *Republic*, VII, 537C.

56. Ibid.

57. *Republic*, VI, 486A.

58. *Republic*, VIII, 537D.

59. Cf. *Republic*, VII, 539E.

60. *Republic*, VII, 540A–B.

61. *Republic*, VII, 540C.

62. Cf. *Republic*, VII, 520E–521B.

63. *Republic*, VIII, 544D–E.

64. Cf. *Republic*, VIII, 545Dff.

65. Cf. *Republic*, VIII, 550Cff.

66. Cf. *Republic*, VIII, 555Bff.

67. *Republic*, VIII, 560B.

68. Cf. *Republic*, VIII, 560Cff.

69. *Republic*, VIII, 562A–564A.

70. *Republic*, VIII, 569B–C.

71. Here is a passage that illustrates their point, where Plato touches a series of themes, which, although on a purely intuitive level, anticipates some principles of psychoanalysis: "In the matter of our desires I do not think we sufficiently distinguished their nature and number. And so long as this is lacking our inquiry will lack clearness.—Well, said he, will our consideration of them not still be opportune?—By all means. And observe what it is about them that I wish to consider. It is this. Of our unnecessary pleasures and appetites *there are some lawless ones, I think, which probably are to be found in us all, but which, when controlled by the laws and the better desires in alliance with reason,* can in some men be altogether got rid of, or so nearly so that only a few weak ones remain, while in others the remnant is stronger and more numerous. What desires do you mean? he said.—*Those, said I, that are awakened in sleep when the rest of the soul, the rational, gentle and dominant part, slumbers,* but the beastly and savage part, replete with food and wine, gambols and, repelling sleep, endeavors to sally forth and satisfy its own instincts. You are aware that in such case there is nothing it will not venture to undertake as being released from sense of shame and all reason. It does not shrink from attempting to lie with a mother in fancy or with anyone else, man, god, or brute. It is ready for any foul deed of blook; it abstains from no food and, in a word, falls short of no extreme of folly and shamelessness.—Most true, he said.—But when, I suppose, a man's condition is healthy and sober, and he goes to sleep after arousing his rational part and entertaining it with fair words and thoughts, and attaining to clear self-consciousness, while he has neither starved nor indulged to repletion his appetitive part, so that it may be lulled to sleep and not disturb the better part by its pleasure or pain, but may suffer that in isolated purity to examine and reach out toward and apprehend some of the things unknown to it, past, present, or future, and when he has in like manner tamed his passionate part, and does not after a quarrel fall asleep with anger still awake within him, but if he has thus quieted the two elements in his soul and quickened the third, in which reason resides, and so goes to his rest, you are aware that in such case he is most likely to apprehend truth, and the visions of his dreams are least likely to be lawless.—I certainly think so, he said.—This description has carried us too far, but the point that we have to notice is this, that in fact *there exists in every one of us, even in some reputed most respectable, a terrible, fierce, and lawless brood of desires, which it seems are revealed in our sleep*" (*Republic*, IX, 571A–572B).

72. *Republic*, IX, 573C.

73. *Republic*, IX, 576A.

74. Cf. *Republic*, IX, 589D; 590D–E.

75. Cf. *Republic*, X, 608Cff.

76. Cf. *Republic*, X, 618Cff.

77. *Republic*, IX, 591C–592B.

78. Jaeger, *Paideia*, II:355.
79. Jaeger, *Paideia*, II:356.
80. Ibid.

CHAPTER THREE
(THE MAN OF THE STATE, THE WRITTEN LAWS, AND THE CONSTITUTION)

1. *Statesman*, 301D.
2. *Statesman*, 301C–E.
3. Cf. *Statesman*, 300Cff.
4. *Statesman*, 302E–303B.
5. *Statesman*, 283D.
6. *Statesman*, 283E.
7. *Statesman*, 284B–E.
8. Cf. *Statesman*, 305D.
9. Cf. *Statesman*, 304Aff.
10. Cf. *Statesman*, 306Aff.
11. *Statesman*, 311B–C.

CHAPTER FOUR
(THE "SECOND STATE" OF THE *LAWS*)

1. Taylor, *Plato*, pp. 464ff.
2. *Laws*, IX, 875C–D.
3. *Laws*, V, 739B–E.
4. *Laws*, V, 739A; 739E.
5. *Laws*, V, 739B.
6. *Laws*, III, 693D–E.
7. Cf. *Laws*, III, 698A–B.
8. *Laws*, VI, 757A–D.
9. *Laws*, IV, 716C.

CHAPTER FIVE
(THE POLITICAL COMPONENT AND THE PROTOLOGIC)

1. *Republic*, VII, 517C.

2. *Republic*, VII, 540A–B.

3. On this issue and its connection with the *"Unwritten Doctrines,"* see Aristotle, *Eudemian Ethics*, A 8.1218a15–28. (Krämer, 25); Iamblichus, *Protrepticus*, cap. 6, pp. 37, 26ff. Pistelli = Aristotle, *Protrepticus*, frag. 5 Ross (Gaiser, *Test. Plat.*, 34 = Krämer, 26).

4. *Republic*, IV, 422E–423B. At the beginning of the decisive part of this passage, it speaks of "very many City-States and not a City-State" and it adds "something said playfully." This point is most understood. In fact the Greek τὸ τῶν παιζόντων is interpreted "as comes to play of the πόλεις," a kind of play the various weights of which would be called πόλεις. Instead, the exact sense is "something said playfully." And the play would be this: οὐ πόλις ἀλλὰ πόλεις, or πολεῖς, understood as an epic accusative plural of πολύς. Fraccaroli (Platone, *La Reppublica* (Florence 1932, p. 171, note 1), who reported this interpretation, rejected it for these reasons: "This second interpretation however is less probable, because there is no way that an application of this proverb can be made." Instead, in the parameters of the interpretation that we support, it takes on a perfect import, focussed exactly on the thematic of the *one* and the *many*, and expresses with perfect playful allusions the ultimate protological truth.

5. *Republic*, V, 462A–B.

6. *Republic*, IV, 443D–444A.

7. Krämer, *Arete*, 83–118 (cf. also pp. 118–145).

8. Aristotle, *Politicus*, frag. 2 Ross; cf. Reale, *Plato*, 379–85.

9. *Laws*, IV, 716C.

10. The passage of the *Timaeus* presented by us many times is in 68D; the passage of the *Laws*, is X, 903E–904A, about which Gaiser has given excellent explanations in *Platone come scrittore*, pp. 146ff. To understand the passage well, it is necessary to read and meditate on the whole section from 902D–904D.

FIFTH SECTION—CHAPTER ONE
(THE MYTH OF THE CAVE)

1. *Republic*, VII, 514Aff. On the influence of this myth on ancient and modern authors and the remarkable reelaborations that have been done to it, see K. Gaiser, *Il paragone della caverna Variazioni da Platone ad oggi* (Naples:Bibliopolis, 1985).

2. *Republic*, VII, 514A–517A.

3. Krämer, *Plato*, p. 194; cf. also Gaiser, *Il paragone*, p. 16.

4. *Republic*, VII, 515C.

5. *Republic*, VII, 518Dff.

6. Jaeger, *Paideia* II:295f., note 77 (pp. 417–418).

CHAPTER TWO

(SUMMITS OF PLATONISM)

1. *Republic*, VI, 511B.

2. W. Jaeger, *Studien zur Entstehungsgeschichte der Metaphysik des Aristoteles* (Berlin, 1912), p. 141.

3. *Phaedo*, 79A.

4. Cf. Jaeger, *Paideia*, II:492ff.

5. *Timaeus*, 41A–D.

6. Cf. *Timaeus*, 37A; cf. also 29A.

7. On this argument see Reale, *Plato*, pp. 425–622.

8. Cf. *Symposium*, 205B; *Sophist*, 219B, 265B, 266B.

9. *Sophist*, 266B.

10 Cf. Reale, *Plato*, passim.

11. *Theaetetus*, 176B.

12. *Republic*, X, 613B.

ARISTOTLE

FIRST SECTION—CHAPTER ONE

(A CRITICAL PREMISE)

1. Aristotle (as we know from Apollodorus Chronicus, quoted in DL 5.9; LCL 1:453) was born in the first year of the ninety-ninth Olympiad; that is, in 384/383 BCE, at Stagira, in Macedonia. The citizens already had been colonized by Ionions for a long time, and they spoke an Ionion dialect. The father of Aristotle, whose name was Nicomachus, was a valued physician and was in the service of King Amyntas III of Macedonia (the father of Philip of Macedonia). It is hence presumed, at least for a certain period of time, that the young Aristotle lived with his family at Pella, which was the site of the royal palace of the Amyntas and at which the court also lived. If up to this point Nicomachus had taught his son the medical art we do not know, given that he died when Aristotle was still very young. We know, with certainty that in his eighteenth year; that is, in 366/365, Aristotle came to Athens, embarking on the completion of his intellectual formation, and he entered almost immediately into the Platonic Academy. It was certainly at the school of Plato that Aristotle matured and consolidated his own philosophical avocation in a decisive way, so much so that he remained in the Academy for twenty years; that is, until Plato died. We do not know with any accuracy the precise role of Aristotle within the ambit of the Platonic school. Certainly he gave lectures on rhetoric, but beyond these his contributions must have been fundamental in the numerous discussions about the whole sweep of the subjects with which the Academy was concerned (and the discussions engaged not only with Plato and other Academics, but all the best-known persons of different backgrounds who were guest at the Academy, starting from the famous scientist Eudoxus, who probably, in the first years in which Aristotle was present at the Academy, was the most influential presence, because Plato during that period was in Sicily). It is certain that, in the period of twenty years that passed during his stay at the Academy, being the decisive years in the life of a man, Aristotle acquired the Platonic principles in their substance and defended them in his writings; and together he subjected them to a penetrating criticism, attempting to move them in new directions. (It is certainly not happenstance by which a very young Aristotle is understood as a character in the Platonic *Parmenides*, a dialogue, as we know, as an answer already to certain criticisms of the theory of Ideas. In fact some of the criticism about the theory of Ideas we read in the Aristotelian *Metaphysics*, go back to analogous criticisms that can be read in the *Parmenides*,). On the death of Plato (347), when by now he had arrived at the "mezzo del cammin di nostra vita" ("the midpoint of our life's journey") [Dante, *La Divina Commedia*], Aristotle decided not to remain in Athens at the Academy because of the direction that the school had taken under Speusippus (who led the currents further from that which was the convictions matured by him), and therefore he departed from Athens and went to Asia Minor.

This will begin a new and most important phase in the life of Aristotle. In the company of a famous companion from the Academy, Xenocrates, he took up residence first at Assos (which is on the coast of the Troads) where he founded a school together with the Platonists Erastus and Coriscus who were originally from the city of Skepsis; and they became advisers to Hermias, a competent statesman, ruler of Atarneus and Assos. At Assos Aristotle stayed for three years. He then went on to Mytilene on the island of Lesbos, probably at the urging of Theophrastus (who was much later to become the successor of Aristotle himself), who was born in a place on the island itself. Both the phase of the teaching at Assos and the phase at Mytilene are fundamental. It is probable that the Stagirite taught courses at Assos on the more properly philosophical disciplines and that at Mytilene he instead concentrated on research into the natural sciences by beginning and consolidating his important collaboration with Theophrastus, which was to have such a large part in the destiny of the Peripatos.

A new period in the life of Aristotle began in 343/342 BCE Philip of Macedon called him to the court, and he took on the education of Philip's son Alexander; that is, of someone who was to revolutionize Greek history, at the time thirteen years of age. Let us remember that previously the father of Aristotle had ties to the Macedonian court and that hence Philip could also have known of the young Aristotle himself; in any case, certainly Hermias, who had linked his political activity to that of Macedonians, had spoken to the ruler about Aristotle in glowing terms. Unfortunately we know very little of the relationship established by these two exceptional persons (the first one of the greatest philosophers and the other one of the greatest political figures of all times) that destiny had bound together. It is certain that, if Aristotle could share the idea of unifying Greek City-States under the Macedonian hegemony, he did not understand in any case the idea of the Hellenizing of the barbarians and the equalization of them with the Greeks. The political genius of his student, in this area, opened historical perspectives more novel and audacious than the political categories would permit him to grasp, given that his categories were essentially conservative and, in a certain respect, reactionary. Aristotle remained at the Macedonian court until Alexander achieved sole political power; that is, until about 336 (but it is also possible that after 340 he returned to Stagira, because of Alexander actively pursuing his military and political ambitions).

Finally, in 335/334 BCE, Aristotle returned to Athens and rented some buildings near a small temple dedicated to Apollo Lyceus, whence came the name of "Lyceum" given to the school. Because Aristotle imparted his teaching by walking in a garden annexed to the buildings, the school was called also a *Peripatos* (from the Greek word *peripatos* = a walkway, an ambulatory), and his followers were thus said to be *Peripatetics*. The Peripatos was opposed thus to the Academy, and for a certain period of time, it eclipsed it entirely. These were the most productive years for Aristotle; the years that would see the great systematization of the philosophical and scientific works that have been preserved for us.

In 323 BCE, Alexander died. In Athens there was a strong anti-Macedonian reaction, in which Aristotle became embroiled, being guilty by assocation, as the teacher of the great conqueror (formally he was charged with impiety for having written a poem in honor of Hermias that was the kind written for a God). To avoid his enemies, he went back to Chalcis, where he had inherited property from his mother, leaving Theophrastus in charge of the Peripatos. He died in 322 BCE, after a few months of exile. The writings of Aristotle, as is known, are divided into two large groups: the *exoteric* (which are composed mostly in dialogue form and were destined to be read by the public at large), and the *esoteric* or *acroamatic* (which instead are the result of and based upon the teaching of Aristotle and were not meant for publication, but only to be heard by his students and hence they were the exclusive heritage of the school).

The first group of writings have been completely lost and of them there exists only their titles and some fragments. Perhaps the first of the exoteric works was the *Gryllus* or *On Rhetoric*, (in which Aristotle defended the Platonic position against Isocrates), and the final work was the *Protreptic* or *On Philosophy*. The other works from his youth worth mentioning are *On the Ideas*, the *Eudemus*, or *On Soul*. The efforts of modern scholars have been focussed particularly on these works and so a certain number of fragments have been recovered. Other works of the first literary period are empty titles for us simply. The most complete, accurate, informed, and balanced reconstruction of these works has been given by E. Berti, *La filosofia del prima Aristotele* (Padua, 1962); the reader will find references and discussion of all the literature concerning the argument. (Cf. also M. Untersteiner, *Aristotele, Della Filosofia* [Rome, 1963], as well as *Aristotle and Plato in the Mid-Fourth Century, Symposium*, Aristotelicum, ed. Düring, I. and Owen, G. E. L., Oxford, 1957 [Göteborg, 1960]). Among the list of these works, in our judgment, should be included also the *Treatise on the Cosmos for Alexander*, which Aristotle probably wrote at the Macedonian court (for teaching his illustrious student) with the same elegant style and method used in the works destined for the public at large (consult G. Reale, *Aristotele, Trattato sul cosmo* [Naples, 1974]). On the contrary, the great works derived from Aristotle's teaching have come down to us. These works are concerned with the whole gamut of the philosophical problematic and some of the branches of the natural sciences. Let us first consider the works that are more properly philosophical. The *Corpus aristotelicum*, in its actual arrangement, begins with the *Organon*, the title bestowed upon it in late antiquity and that encompasses all the logical treatises together. They are *Categories, De Interpretatione, Prior Analytics, Posterior Analytics, Topics, Sophist*,ical Refutations. Following them are the works of natural philosophy; that is, the *Physics, De Caelo, De Generatione et Corruptione, Meteorologica*,. Connected to these works are the works on psychology, which include *De anima*, and a group of shorter treatises known since medieval times under the title of *Parva Naturalia*. The most famous work is, of course, the fourteen books that constitute what came to be called the *Metaphysics*,. Then come the treatises on moral and political philosophy, *Nicomachean Ethics, Eudemian Ethics, Magna Moralia*, and the *Politics*,. Finally there are the *Rhetoric*, and *Poetics*,. (Among the works concerned with the natural sciences are the imposing *History of Animals, The Parts of Animals, The Movement of Animals, The Generation of Animals*; these are works that fit into the history of science more than into the history of philosophical problems.) With respect to the list or catalogues of all the titles of the Aristotelian works handed down in the ancient catalogues and the various problems connected to them we refer the reader to the superb work of P. Moraux, *Les listes anciennes des ouvrages d'Aristote* (Louvain, 1951).

The totality of the Aristotelian writings was left by Theophrastus as an inheritance to Neleus, son of the Coriscus, to whom Aristotle was bound in deep friendship during the period at Assos. The descendents of Neleus hid these writings in a cellar of the house where they stayed until a bibliophile named Apellicon (who was a soldier in the pay of the Mithridates) acquired them. From the hands of Apellicon they passed to those of Sulla, who during the first Mithridatic war confiscated them and brought them to Rome, where the work of transcription begun by Apellicon was continued. Finally Andronicus of Rhodes about the middle of the first century before the common era prepared and succeeded in publishing an adequate edition of the Aristotelian works. Andronicus was the tenth successor of Aristotle in the Peripatos (consult Strabo 13.1.54 [608–609] and Plutarch, *Sylla* 26.1–2 [468A–B]).

And from then on first through the efforts of the great Greek commentators, then through Arabic philosophy, to the medievals and into the Renaissance these works for a long time were the most frequently read, meditated on, commented on, and reinterpreted among all those that have survived from antiquity.

The citations of the works of Aristotle are based on the classical edition of I. Bekker, *Aristotelis Opera* (Berlin, 1831; reprinted by O. Gigon, Berlin, 1960), the Greek capital letter indicates the number of the book (the ancients divided their works into books), the Arabic number that immediately follows indicates the chapter, whereas the succeeding numbers indicate the page; the letters "a" and "b" indicate the columns, respectively, the right-hand or left-hand column on the page (Bekker's edition has two columns per page); finally the numbers after the letters indicate the lines within the columns used by Bekker.

2. DL 5.1; LCL 1:445.

3. W. Jaeger, *Aristotele. Grundlegung einer Geschichte seiner Entwicklung* (Berlin, 1923), translated by Richard Robinson, *Aristotle: Fundamentals of the History of his Development* (Oxford, 1934; 1948).

4. We say this bearing in mind the scholars who have not fallen into the extreme and paradoxical position, as for example, Zürcher did in his work *Aristoteles' Werk und Geist* (Paderborn, 1952), we have given ample attention to this work in our article "J. Zürcher e un tentativo di rivoluzione nel campo degli contemporanei" in the Supplement to the *Rivista di filosofia neoscolastica, Aristotele nella critica e negli studi contemporanei* 48 (Milan, 1956) 108–143; consult G. Reale, *The Concept of First Philosophy and the Unity of the Metaphysics*, of Aristotle, (Albany, 1980) 483, trans. J. R. Catan. Zürcher claims that 80 percent of the Aristotelian works that we read were rewritten by Theophrastus!

5. See in this regard especially the volume of Berti cited earlier especially note 1.

6. For a brief characterization of the principal writings see G. Reale, *Introduzione a Aristotele* (Bari, 1974) 12ff. In English consult the compressed but complete account of J. Owens, *A History of Ancient Western Philosophy* (Englewood Cliffs, N.J., 1960), 285–94 especially notes 6–22. See also Reale, *Aristotele, Trattato sul cosmo*. For an examination of the same issue see also the by now classic work of E. Bignone, *L'Aristotele perduto e la formazione filosofica di Epicuro*, 2 vols. (Florence, 1936; 1973).

7. Consult P. Aubenque, *Le problème de l'être chez Aristote* (Paris, 1962) 9ff.

8. For the adequate defense of what we have asserted we advise the reader to consult our volume, G. Reale, *The Concept of First Philosophy and the Unity of the Metaphysics*, of Aristotle (Albany, 1980), trans. J. R. Catan, hereinafter *The Concept of First Philosophy*.

CHAPTER TWO

(THE BASIC POINTS OF CONTACT BETWEEN

PLATO AND ARISTOTLE)

1. Cf. Jaeger, *Studien zur Entstehungsgeschichte der Metaphysik des Aristoteles*, 141; cf. earlier, p. 238.

2. *Metaphysics*, L 7.1072b13ff.: ſk toiayÈthw a›ra aÂrxh„w h›rthtai Ã oyÂranÜw kaá hÀ fyÈsiw.

3. Cf. Reale, Plato, pp. 509–622.

4. Plato conceived the inquiry into natural phenomena and hence the science of physics as structurally bound to mythical narration [a likely story] (because it was connected to becoming), as we have already explained; therefore, he judged these inquiries to not be serious, even if very important. Cf. ibid., 519–523.

5. Consult G. Reale, *Aristotele, La Metafisica, traduzione, introduzione e commento* 2 Vols. Naples, 1968 (1978²); see especially A 6 and A 9 and the commentary volume I:174–182; 189–212, as well as Books M and N passim and all of Book Z (we have also published an *edito minor*, from Rusconi, Milan 1978: 1984², but without the commentary, for that it is necessary to use the large edition that we published with Loffredo). hereinafter referred to as *Metafisica*.

6. *Nicomachean Ethics*, A 1,1094a3 τάγαθόν, οὗ πάντ ἐφίεται. Cf. also *Metaphysics*, Λ 7.1072b1ff.

7. Cf. Reale, *Plato*, 252–255.

8. Cf. ibid., 534ff.

9. See our commentary on the *Metafisica*, passim, and especially that to Books Z H Θ.

10. *Diogenes Laertius*, 5.1. Cf. earlier, p. 247, the epigraph that we used to characterize the first section, by connecting this statement of Diogenes with the truly emblematic statement of Aristotle: "If there were nothing eternal, there would not be any becoming" (*Metaphysics*, B 4.999b5ff.).

CHAPTER THREE

(THE BASIC DIFFERENCES

BETWEEN PLATO AND ARISTOTLE)

1. Proclus, *In Tim.* 338c–d; Aristotle, *Eudemus*, frag. 4 Ross p. 17. The translation of the fragments of the esoterica was taken from David Ross, *The Works of Aristotle*, Vol. XII *Select Fragments* (Oxford, 1952) which can also be found in the convenient translation by J. Barnes and Gavin Lawrence in J. Barnes, *The Complete Works of Aristotle. The Revised Oxford Translation* (Princeton, 1984) 2 vols.

2. Proclus, *In Plato. Remp.* 2.349.13–26 Kroll; Aristotle, *Eudemus*, frag. 5 Ross pp. 17–18.

3. Augustine, *Contra Julian Pelag.*, 4.15.78; Aristotle, *Protrepticus,* frag. 10b Ross p. 42.

4. It is significant that works like the *Physics*, *De Caelo*, *On Generation and Corruption*, and *The Movement of Animals* give primacy to the immobile Movent as a reason for the various natural phenomena of which they give an account.

SECOND SECTION—CHAPTER ONE
(METAPHYSICS)

1. Consult *Metaphysics*, E.1 passim.

2. Consult Reale, *Metafisica*, 1:3ff and the biographical references listed there. We have sometimes used Ross's translation, which is included in J. Barnes, *The Complete Works of Aristotle*, vol. 2, 1552–1728, for ease of reference hereinafter cited as J. Barnes, *Aristotle* by volume and page. Any departures from the Ross translation will be noted.

3. Cf. especially *Metaphysics*, Books A, α, B.

4. Cf. especially *Metaphysics*, Books Γ, as well as Books E 2–4; K 3.

5. Cf. especially *Metaphysics*, Books Z, H, and Θ, passim.

6. Cf. especially *Metaphysics*, Books E 1, and all of Λ.

7. For the explicit documentation of these points and for those views we stated throughout this section consult Reale, *The Concept of First Philosophy*, passim.

8. Aristotle *Metaphysics*, E 1.1026a27–29 and K 7.1064b9–14.

9. Even if it was not of Aristotelian coinage, the term is, however, in a completely Aristotelian spirit. In *Metaphysics*, Γ 3.1005a33ff Aristotle specifies those who are concerned with such knowledge as "one kind of thinker who is even *beyond the natural philosopher*" (τοῦ φυσικοῦ τις ἀνωτέρω), insofar as the physicist is concerned with nature, which only constitutes one of the genera of being (whereas above this there exists another genera of being). See also *Metaphysics*, A 8 passim (where the Naturalists are criticized, precisely because they admit only one genera of being); E 1 and Λ passim.

10. Cf. *Metaphysics*, E 1.1026a18–23 "Consequently there are three theoretical philosophies: physics, mathematics and theology [= metaphysics]. It is certain, in fact, that if the divine exists, it is a reality of this kind. And it is certain, also, that the highest science must have as its object the highest kind of reality. And while the theoretical sciences are superior to the other sciences, this is, in its turn, superior to the other theoretical sciences"; A 2.983a4–10, "It [metaphysics], in fact, among all the sciences is the most divine and worthy of honor. But a science can be divine only in these two senses: either because it is the science that God possesses in the highest degree, or, also, because it has as its object divine things. Now only wisdom [= metaphysics] possesses both of these characteristics; in fact, it is a common conviction of all that God is a cause and principle, and also that God, either exclusively or in the highest degree, has this kind of knowledge."

11. Aristotle, *Metaphysics*, A 2, passim, also for the notions that follow.

12. Aristotle, *Metaphysics*, A 2.983a10ff.

13. Aristotle, *Metaphysics*, A 3–10.

14. Reale, *The Concept of First Philosophy*, 31ff.

15. Aristotle, *Metaphysics*, Λ 4–5 and 6–8.

16. Cf. Aristotle, *Physics*, A 2–3. (We refer, for an examination of these problems, to our work "L'impossibilità di intendere univocamente l'essere e la tavola dei significati di esso secondo Aristotele," *Rivista di filosofia neoscolastica* 56 (1964): 286–326. In English, consult J. Owens, *The Doctrine of Being in the Aristotelian Metaphysics*, (Toronto, 1978 revised edition) 107–135, hereinafter *DoBAM*.

17. Consult Aristotle, *Metaphysics*, N 2, passim.

18. Consult Aristotle, *Metaphysics*, Γ 2.1003a33–b6.

19. Consult Aristotle, *Metaphysics*, Γ 2.1003b5–10.

20. Consult G. Reale in the article cited in note 16 earlier and our commentary to Γ, E, and K of the *Metafisica*,.

21. For an examination of the problems, see J. Ownes, *DoBAM*.

22. Consult Aristotle *Metaphysics*, Δ 7, E 2–4 and further citations that we gave in our work cited in note 16 earlier and our Introduction to the *Metafisica*, pp. 30ff. We remember that the first of the Aristotelian lists of the meanings of being was made by F. Brentano, in a now classic work, *Von der mannigfachen Bedeutung des Seienden nach Aristoteles* (Freiburg im Bresgau, 1862; Darmstadt, 1960). English translation, *On the Several Senses of Being in Aristotle*, trans. Rolf George (Berkeley, 1975).

23. Consult Aristotle, *Metaphysics*, E 2.1026b21.

24. There are eight in the list of the *Metaphysics*, and the *Physics*, ten in the list in the *Categories*, and the *Topics*, (but the ninth category is reducible to the fourth and the tenth to the seventh; see the list).

25. Consult Aristotle, *Metaphysics*, Z 4.1030a21–23.

26. Consult Aristotle, *Metaphysics*, Z 4.1030a32–b3.

27. Consult Aristotle, *Metaphysics*, Z 4.1029a21.

28. Consult the massive documentation adduced by Brentano in *The Several Senses of Being*, trans. Rolf George and passim.

29. For arguments on this problem during the previous century consult the following works now classic, F. A. Trendelenburg, *Geschichte der Kategoreinlehre* (Berlin, 1846), 196–380; H. Bonitz, "Ueber die Kategorien des Aristoteles," *Sitzungsberichte der Kaiserlichen Akad. d. Wissensch. Philos.–hist. Klasse*, Bd. 10, Heft 5 (Vienna, 1853), 591–645; O. Apelt, "Die Kategorienlehre des Aristoteles," *Beiträge zur Geschichte der griech. Philos.* (Leipzig, 1891), 101–216; and the volume of Brentano's already cited many times. Trendelenburg maintains that Aristotle deduced the categories from grammar. Apelt speaks rather of a logical deduction. Bonitz and Brentano proposed instead an ontological deduction. There is a full discussion of these issues in our article: "Filo conduttore grammaticale e filo conduttore ontologico nella deduzione delle categorie aristoteliche," *Rivista di filosofia neoscolastica*, XLIX (1957): 423–457 (there is a consistent misspelling in the text of Trendelenburg's name [Trendelemburg]).

30. Cf. especially *Metaphysics*, Book Θ, passim. For a detailed analysis of the doctrine see our article, "La dottrina aristotelica della potenza dell'atto e dell'entelechia

nella Metafisica," in *Studi di filosofia e di storia della filosofia in onore di Francesco Olgiati* (Milan, 1962), pp. 145–207.

31. On these two final meanings of being consult, *Metaphysics*, E 2–4 and our commentary, vol. I, 506–16.

32. *Metaphysics*, Z 1.1028b2–7.

33. Concerning what we said here in short, the reader can consult what we said more fully documented in the Introduction to our commentary on the *Metaphysics*, pp. 45ff. (Cf. also G. Reale, "La polivocità della concezione aristotelica della sostanza," *Scritti in onore di Carlo Giacon*, [Padua, 1972], 17–40) and especially in the commentary to Books Z and H, passim.

34. *Metaphysics*, Z 2, passim.

35. *Metaphysics*, Z 3.1029a33ff. For Aristotle the primary intelligible is *per natura [by nature]* that which is ontologically primary; *for us* the sensible is primary and the ontological is secondary, because that through which we know are the sensibles and the senses, and we achieve the intelligible only through and *after* the sensible.

36. Cf. also *Metaphysics*, Z 2, passim; Z 11.1037a10–17; Z 16.1040b34–1041a3; Z 17.1041a6–9.

37. Cf. also *Metaphysics*, Z 4–12 and H 2–3 with our commentary, vol. I, 572–621 and vol. II, 19–30.

38. *Metaphysics*, Z H, passim.

39. Cf. the detailed references that we gave in the Introduction to our commentary on the *Metaphysics*, vol. I, 51ff., as well as the comentary to Book Z, passim.

40. *Metaphysics*, Z 17.1041b28.

41. Zeller, *DPG*, II:344ff.

42. Cf. *Metaphysics*, Z 7–9 (and our commentary, vol. I, 589–606).

43. Cf. *Metaphysics*, Z 13–16 (and our commentary, vol. I, 621–634).

44. *Metaphysics*, Z 17.1041b5–9.

45. *Metaphysics*, Z 17.1041b11–28; cf. also H 2.1043b10ff.

46. *Metaphysics*, Z 12, passim.

47. Cf. *Metaphysics*, Z 3.1029a3–7: "We call *matter* for example the bronze, *form* the structure and the formal shape, *synolon* that which results from these; that is, the statue. Consequently if the form is *a prior and greater being* (πρότερον καὶ μᾶλλον ὄν) with respect to the matter, for the same reason it is also prior to the composite."

48. Cf. earlier note 30.

49. Cf. *Metaphysics*, H 2.

50. Cf. *Metaphysics*, Λ 6–8.

51. Cf. *Metaphysics*, Θ 8, passim. This axiom of the *priority of act over potency* is very important, and, as we will see, it constitutes one of the principles on which the metaempirical inference to the immobile Movent was made to pivot. Here is the

passage of the *Metaphysics*, (Θ 8.1050a4ff.) in which the ontological *priority* of act over potency is explained "But act is also *prior in substance*. Firstly, because the things that are posterior in the order of generation, are primary in the order of *form* and *substance*: for example the adult is prior to the infant and the man is prior to the seed: the one, in fact, possesses the actuated form, the other, instead, does not. In the second place, it is prior because all those things which come into being proceed toward a principle; that is, toward the *goal* (or *end*): in fact, the goal constitutes a principle and becoming takes place in function of the end. And the *end is the act*, and thanks to it the potency is acquired: in fact, animals do not see because they possess sight, but they have sight to see....In addition, matter is in potency because *it can achieve the form*; and when, then, it is in act, then it is in possession of its form....But act is also prior to potency according to substance in another sense: in fact, eternal beings are prior to the corruptible ones in substance, and nothing which is in potency is eternal."

52. Cf. for example, *Metaphysics*, K 9; consult earlier pp. 201-3.

53. Cf. *Metaphysics*, H 6, passim.

54. Cf. *Metaphysics*, Λ 6–9.

55. Cf. *Metaphysics*, Λ 6–7.

56. Cf. *Metaphysics*, Λ 7.1072b3.

57. Just as, for example, F. Brentano, "Ueber den Creationismus des Aristoteles," *Sitzungsberichte der Akademie der Wissensch. in Wein. Philos.-hist. Klasse*, Bd. 101, 1882, 95–126; idem., *Aristoteles und seine Weltanschauung* (Leipzig, 1911; Darmstadt, 1967), and again idem., *Psychologie des Aristoteles* (Mainz, 1867; Darmstadt, 1967), 234–250 [English translation: *The Psychology of Aristotle*, trans. Rolf George (Berkeley, 1977) (the appendix entitled "Von dem Wirken, insbesondere dem schöpferischen Wirken des Aristotelischen Gottes," ["Of the Activity, Especially the Creative Activity, of Aristotle's God," pp. 162–80].

58. D. Ross, *Aristotle* (London, 1923).

59. Cf. *Metaphysics*, Λ 6, passim.

60. Cf. *Metaphysics*, Λ 7.1072b13–18 and 24–30.

61. Cf. *Metaphysics*, Λ 7.1072b18–24.

62. Cf. *Metaphysics*, Λ 9.1072b34–35.

63. Cf. *Metaphysics*, Λ 7.1072a5–13.

64. Cf. *Metaphysics*, Λ 8, passim.

65. Homer, *Iliad*, II, v. 204.

66. Cf. *Metaphysics*, Λ 8.1073b1–3: "That the movents are substances, then, and that one of these is first and another second according to the same order (κατὰ τὴν αὐτὴν τάξιν) as the movements of the stars, is evident."

67. Cf. *Metaphysics*, Λ 9.1074b21–27.

68. Cf. *Metaphysics*, Λ 9.1074b28–35.

69. In other words, God is *only* loved and not *also, a lover*; He is the one loved [object], *not the one who loves* [*subject*]. For Aristotle, just as for Plato, it is inconceivable that God (the Absolute) would love anything (anything other than Himself), since love is a tendency to possess something that one lacks, and God lacks nothing. (The notion of love as a gratuitous gift is entirely unknown to the Greeks). In addition God cannot love, because it is pure intelligence (Mind), and according to Aristotle, pure intelligence *cannot be acted upon* and therefore cannot love (cf. the passage of the *De anima*, which we recorded earlier on pp. 311-2ff.)

70. For a clarification of all these problems concerning the Aristotelian metaphysics, the reader will find all the necessary information in the ample bibliography presented in J. Owens, *DoBAM*, 425–446, and in the select bibliography that can be found in the third edition and translation of our volume, *The Concept of First Philosophy and the Unity of the Metaphysics of Aristotle*, 424–97 (Appendix C), and in the general bibliography found in vol. II of our commentary on the *Metaphysics*, of Aristotle, 449–502.

CHAPTER TWO
(PHYSICS)

1. Cf. *Metaphysics*, E 1.1025a28ff.

2. See the position that Aristotle takes up in relation to the Presocratic philosophy of *physis* in *Metaphysics*, A 8, passim.

3. On the Aristotelian concept of nature see especially the second book of the *Physics*, of which Hamelin has given a good commentary: *Aristote, Physique II, Traduction et commentaire* (Paris, 1932²). On the issue see also the clear pages of A. Mansion, *Introduction à la Physique Aristotélicienne* (Louvain-Paris, 1945²), 92ff. and passim.

4. Cf. *Physics*, Books E Z H Θ; but also the books that precede, that are concerned in large measure with movement or the concepts strictly connected to it.

5. Cf. *Physics*, Γ 1.201a10–11 and *Metaphysics*, K 9.1065b33:"ἡ τοῦ δυνατοῦ ᾖ δυνατὸν ἐντελέχεια κίνησίς ἐστιν."

6. Cf. *Physics*, Γ 1–2. The doctrine is repeated verbatim from the *Physics*, in the *Metaphysics*, K 9.1066b5ff: "Being either is only in act or it is in potency, or it is, both, in act and in potency: and this is verified both for substance, and for quality, and for the remaining categories. Movement does not exist outside these things: in fact, movement always takes place according to the categories of being, but there is nothing common to all and so it does not enter into a single category. Each of these categories, in all things, exists in two different ways..., so that there must be as many kinds of movement as there are categories of being."

7. Cf. *Physics*, E 1–2.

8. Cf. *Physics*, A 5ff.;cf. also E 1–2.

9. Cf. *Physics*, B, in particular Chapters 7–8; see in this regard Mansion, *Introduction à la Physique Aristotélicienne*, 251–281.

10. *Physics*, B 4–6, on that consult Mansion, ibid., 292–314.

11. *Physics*, Δ, passim.

12. *Physics*, Δ 1.208b6–8

13. *Physics*, Δ 1.208b19–21.

14. *Physics*, Δ 2.209a31–b2.

15. *Physics*, Δ 4.210b34–211a1.

16. *Physics*, Δ 4.212a6.

17. *Physics*, Δ 4.212a14–21.

18. *Physics*, Δ 5.212b16–22.

19. *Physics*, Δ 7.213b30–33. Here is how Aristotle explains the origin of this conviction: "the void is thought to be a place with nothing in it. The reason for this is that people take what exists to be body, and hold that while every body is in place, void is place in which there is no body, so that where there is no body, there must be void."

20. J. M. Dubois, *Le temps et l'instant selon Aristote* (Paris, 1967), has dedicated an exhaustive analysis to the doctrine of time.

21. *Physics*, Δ 10.217b32–218a8.

22. *Physics*, Δ 11.218b21–23.

23. *Physics*, Δ 11.219a22–25.

24. *Physics*, Δ 11.219b1–2: "τοῦτο γὰρ ἐστιν ὁ χρόνος, ἀριθμὸς κινήσεως κατὰ τὸ πρότερον καὶ ὕστερον."

25. *Physics*, Δ 11.219a26–30.

26. *Physics*, Δ 14.209a21–26.

27. For the clarification of these problems consult the volume of Dubois, *Le temps et l'instant selon Aristote*, pp. 259ff.

28. *Physics*, Γ 4–8.

29. *Physics*, Γ 6.207a7–15.

30. *Metaphysics*, Θ 8.1050b20–27.

31. Cf. *De Caelo*, A 3.270b16ff. In this passage, after having said the aither "is not subject to increase of diminution, unaging or to the other affections," Aristotle explains, "The common name [aither], too, which has been handed down from our distant ancestors even to our own day, seems to show that they conceived of it in the fashion which we have been expressing....And so implying that the primary body is something else beyond earth, fire, air, and water, they gave the highest place a name of it own, aither [αἰθήρ], derived from the fact that it 'runs always' [ἀεὶ θεῖν] for an eternity of time." Consult also *Meteorologica*, A 3.339b16ff.

32. Note that if such a denomination is absent in the esoterica, it was already present in the exoterica; in addition it is found already in the *Epinomis*, (a dialogue

attributed to Plato), 981C. On the question, see Reale, *Aristotele, Trattato sul cosmo*, pp. 102ff.

33. *Metaphysics*, B 4.999b5ff.; cf. *Physics*, Θ, passim.

34. A new (even if in many respects arguable) interpretation of Aristotelian physics has recently been published by W. Wieland, *Die aristotelische Physik* (Göttingen, 1962). We mention it as a stimulating antithesis to our own interpretation.

CHAPTER THREE

(PSYCHOLOGY)

1. For the bibliography on this work, we suggest F. A. Trendelenburg, *Aristotelis De anima, libri tres* (Berlin, 1872) this commentary remains fundamental; it was republished at Graz in 1957); G. Rodier, *Aristote, Traité de l'âme* (Paris, 1947); D. Ross, *Aristotle, De anima*, (Oxford, 1961); G. Movia, *Aristotele, L'anima* (Naples, 1979).

2. These treatises are available in the *Loeb Classical Library Series*, rev. ed. 1957 (reprinted in 1964 translated by W. S. Hett).

3. *De anima*, B 1.412a19–22.

4. *De anima*, B 1.412a27–28.

5. *De anima*, B 1.412b4–6.

6. *De anima*, B 1.413a4–7.

7. *De anima*, B 2.413b24–29.

8. *Metaphysics*, Λ 3.1070a24–26.

9. *De anima*, B 3.414a29–31.

10. *De anima*, B 3.414b20–415a12.

11. Ross, *Aristotle*, p. 198.

12. *De anima*, B 4.416b20–23.

13. *De anima*, B 4.415a26–b7.

14. *De anima*, B 5.417a17–20.

15. *De anima*, B 5.418a3–6.

16. Ross, *Aristotle*, p. 202; cf. *De anima*, B 5.417b6ff.

17. *De anima*, B 12.424a17–24 (for a clarification of this point consult Trendelenburg, *Aristoteles, De anima*, pp. 337ff.

18. *De anima*, Γ 1.425a14–20.

19. *De anima*, Γ 3.428b18–25.

20. *De anima*, B 3.414a32–b6.

21. *De anima*, Γ 10.433a21.

22. *De anima*, Γ 10.433a25–26.

23. *De anima,* Γ 4.429a10–b10.

24. *De anima,* Γ 5.430a10–23.

25. *De gener. animalium,*B 3.736b27–28.

26. *De anima,* Γ 5.430a13.

27. *De anima,* A 4.408b18–29.

CHAPTER FOUR

(MATHEMATICS)

1. *Metaphysics,* M 2, passim.

2. *Metaphysics,* 3.1078a25ff.

3. *Metaphysics,* 3.1077b31ff.

4. Concerning the criticism that Aristotle makes about the Academics, see especially Books M and N of the *Metaphysics,* passim.

THIRD SECTION—CHAPTER ONE

(ETHICS)

1. Cf. for example *Nicomachean Ethics,* A 3 at the beginning.

2. *Nicomachean Ethics,* K 10.1181b15.

3. *Nicomachean Ethics,* A 2.1094b7–10.

4. *Nicomachean Ethics,* A 2.1094a28–b2.

5. Ross, *Aristotle,* p. 280.

6. *Nicomachean Ethics,* A 1.1094a1–3.

7. *Nicomachean Ethics,* A 2.1094a18–22.

8. *Nicomachean Ethics,* A 4.1095a17–20.

9. *Nicomachean Ethics,* A 5.1095b19.

10. *Nicomachean Ethics,* A 5.1095b24–26.

11. *Nicomachean Ethics,* A 5.1096a5–7.

12. *Nicomachean Ethics,* A 5.1096b32–35.

13. *Nicomachean Ethics,* A 7.1097b22–1098a20.

14. *Nicomachean Ethics,* I 4.1166a16–17.

15. *Nicomachean Ethics,* I 8.1169a2–3.

16. *Nicomachean Ethics,* K 7.1178a2–3.

17. *Nicomachean Ethics,* A 8.1098b12–15.

18. *Nicomachean Ethics,* A 8.1099a31–b7.

19. *Nicomachean Ethics,* A 10.1101a7–8.

20. Cf. more on p. 237 earlier.

21. *Nicomachean Ethics*, A 13.1102bB2–3.

22. *Nicomachean Ethics*, A 13.1102b23–31.

23. *Nicomachean Ethics*, B 1.1103a33–b2.

24. *Nicomachean Ethics*, B 6.1106a26–b7.

25. *Nicomachean Ethics*, B 6.1106b18–28.

26. *Nicomachean Ethics*, B 6.1107a6–8.

27. *Eudemian Ethics*,B 3.

28. *Nicomachean Ethics*, Book E, passim.

29. *Nicomachean Ethics*, E 1.1129b27–30.

30. *Nicomachean Ethics*, E 5.1133b32–1134a1.

31. Cf. *Nicomachean Ethics*, D 3ff.

32. Cf. *Nicomachean Ethics*, Z 1.

33. *Nicomachean Ethics*, Z 5.1140b4–6.

34. *Nicomachean Ethics*, Z 12.1144a6–9.

35. *Nicomachean Ethics*, Z 13.1144b31–33.

36. *Nicomachean Ethics*, B 6.1006b36–1007a2.

37. Cf. *Nicomachean Ethics*, Z 13.

38. Cf. *Nicomachean Ethics*, Z 12.

39. Zeller-Mondolfo, *La filosofia dei Greci nel suo sviluppo storico*, Parte II, Vol. 6 ed. A. Plebe, p. 72.

40. *Nicomachean Ethics*, Z 7.1141a34–b2.

41. *Nicomachean Ethics*, K 7.1177b19–1178a2.

42. *Nicomachean Ethics*, K 8.1178b21–32.

43. *Eudemian Ethics*,Θ 3.1249b6–23.

44. *Nicomachean Ethics*, Books Θ and I.

45. *Nicomachean Ethics*, Θ 3.1156a6–21.

46. *Nicomachean Ethics*, Θ 3.1156b7–12.

47. *Nicomachean Ethics*, I 4.1166a12–13.

48. *Nicomachean Ethics*, Θ 5.1157b33–1158a1.

49. *Nicomachean Ethics*, I 4.1166a2–11.

50. *Nicomachean Ethics*, Θ 7.1159a12.

51. *Nicomachean Ethics*, I 8.1168b23–1169a6.

52. *Nicomachean Ethics*, I 9.1169b3–22.

53. *Nicomachean Ethics*, K 4.1174a14–19.

54. *Nicomachean Ethics*, K 4.1174b31–1175a1.

55. *Nicomachean Ethics*, K 5.1076a15–22.

56. *Nicomachean Ethics*, Γ 1.1111a22–24.

57. *Nicomachean Ethics*, Γ 2.1111bff.

58. *Nicomachean Ethics*, Γ 3.1113a2–7 (we depart from Plebe's interpretation of the term προαίρεσις, which in our view is not appropriately rendered by *proponimento* [purpose, resolution, intention], but is better rendered with *scelta* [choice], which is a much clearer term.

59. *Nicomachean Ethics*, Γ 4.1113a20–21.

60. *Nicomachean Ethics*, Γ 4.1113a23–b2.

61. *Nicomachean Ethics*, H 1ff.

62. *Nicomachean Ethics*, Γ 5.

63. For a profound meditation on the Aristotelian ethics, we suggest *Aristote, L'éthique à Nicomaque, Introduction, traduction et commentaire*, by R. A. Gauthier and J. Y. Jolif (Louvain-Paris, 1970^2) 2 vols. of two books each. In this work a general bibliography may be found and especially one concerning the various questions about Aristotelian ethics.

CHAPTER TWO

(POLITICS)

1. *Politics*, A 1.

2. *Politics*, A 2.1252b27–1253a29.

3. For all these expressions consult *Politics*, A 4, passim.

4. *Politics*, A 5.1254b13–14.

5. *Politics*, A 5.1254b16–26.

6. Euripides, *Iphigenia in Aulis*, v. 1400; cf. *Politics*, A 2.1252b8.

7. Cf. *Politics*, A 8ff.

8. *Politics*, A 9.1257b38–1258a2.

9. Cf. *Politics*, A 10.

10. Cf. *Politics*, Book B.

11. *Politics*, Γ 1.

12. *Politics*, Γ 5.

13. *Politics*, Γ 5.1278a3.

14. *Politics*, Γ 6.1278b8–10.

15. *Politics*, Γ 7.1279a28–31.

16. *Politics*, Γ 7.1279a32–b10.

17. *Politics*, Γ 13.1284a3–14.

18. *Politics*, Δ 11.1295b25–38.

19. *Politics*, H 1.1323b7–36.

20. *Politics*, H 4.

21. *Politics*, H 5–6.

22. *Politics*, H 7.1327b23–33.

23. Cf. *Politics*, H 8ff.

24. *Politics*, H 9.1329a14–17.

25. Cf. *Politics*, H 13.

26. *Politics*, H 14.

27. *Politics*, H 14.1333a26–b3.

FOURTH SECTION—CHAPTER ONE
(THE FOUNDATION OF LOGIC)

1. Cf. *Metaphysics*, E 2–4.

2. Cf. *Rhetoric*, A 4.1359b10 where it speaks of an "analytic science" (and *analytics* as we will immediately see, for Aristotle, is *logic*).

3. Cf. T. Waitz, *Aristotelis Organon*, 2 Vols. (Lipsiaw, 1844–1846; republished Aalen, 1965), Vol. II, 293ff.

4. Cf. Ross, *Aristotle*, p. 29.

5. Aristotle cited these writings in addition under the title *Analytics* as well as with the phrase *Writings on the Syllogism*; cf. M. Mignucci, *Aristotele, Gli Analitici Primi* (Naples, 1969), p. 40 and note 2.

6. *Sophist*,ic Refutations 34.183b34f.; 184a8ff.

7. See the state of the question in Mignucci, *Aristotele, Gli Analitici Primi*, pp. 19ff. Cf., in addition, V. Sainati, *Storia dell'Organon aristotelico* (Florence, 1968).

8. Waitz, *Organon*, I:366f.

9. *Post. Anal.*, A 2.71b17–25.

10. As the final book of the *Topics*, (Iota) Waitz considers it throughout the other books in his edition of the *Organon*; cf. the justification he gives in vol. II, 528f. Cf. also the information given by Mignucci, *Aristotele, Analitici Primi*, 19, note 2.

11. *Categories*, 4.1b25–27.

12. *Categories*, 4.214–10.

13. See the various places in that these definitions can be understood in Waitz, *Aristoteles Organon*, II:398.

14. Cf. the passages in Waitz, *Aristoteles Organon*, II:399.

15. See in particular *Metaphysics*, Z 12.

16. *De Interpretatione*, chapters 1 and 9.

17. *De Interpretatione*, 4.17a1–7.

18. *De Interpretatione*, 5–6

19. *De Interpretatione*, 7.

20. *De Interpretatione*, 9ff.

21. *Prior Analytics*, A 1.24b18–22.

22. M. Mignucci, *La teoria aristotelica della scienza* (Florence, 1965), 151.

23. Cf. *Prior Analytics*, A 4.

24. On all the questions here only hinted at, the reader can find the necessary explanations and the necessary clarifications in the Introduction and the commentary of the Mignucci volume cited many times earlier.

25. M. Mignucci, *La teoria aristotelica della scienza*, 110f.

26. *Post. Anal.*, A 2.71b9–25.

27. *Metaphysics*, Z 9.1034a30–32.

28. *Prior Analytics*, B 23.

29. See the passages cited by Bonitz, *Index Aristotelicus*, 264a.

30. *Post. Anal.*, B 19.100b5–17.

31. *Post. Anal.*, A 10.76b11–16.

32. See the *Metaphysics*, Γ 3–8 and our commentary vol. I:329–357.

33. *Topics*, A 1.100a18–b23.

34. *Topics*, A 2.101a36–b4.

35. For a detailed exposition of the Aristotelian "dialectic," cf. C. A. Viano, *La logica di Aristotele* (Turin, 1955), Chapter 4, passim.

36. Cicero, *De Oratore* 2.39.162 (cf. Aristotle, *Topics*, H, at the end).

37. Ross, *Aristotle*, 86ff.

38. See earlier note 10.

39. In *Metaphysics*, Z 7.1032b1ff. Aristotle says that without middle terms: "we call 'form' (*eidos*) the essence of each thing and the *primary substance*."

40. We suggest going to our commentary on Book Z of the *Metaphysics*, for all the requisite clarifications; Book Z is truly essential for understanding the entire thought of Aristotle. The logic (just as all the other parts of Aristotelian thought) cannot be understood except on the basis of the doctrine of substance-form just as it has been determined in that book.

CHAPTER TWO
(RHETORIC)

1. For a reconstruction of the *Gyrllus* see Berti, *La filosofia del primo Aristotele*, pp. 159ff.

2. Gomperz, *GP*, IV:617.

3. *Rhetoric*, A 1.1355a20–23.

4. *Rhetoric*, A 2.1355b26–34.

5. *Rhetoric*, A 2.1356a25–27.

6. *Rhetoric*, A 2.1355b35ff.; A 15.1375a22ff.

7. *Rhetoric*, A 2.1356a1–20.

8. *Rhetoric*, B 4.1378a5ff.

9. Plato, *Phaedrus*, 270Aff.

10. *Rhetoric*, B 2–17.

11. *Rhetoric*, A 1.1355a3–18.

12. Cf. *Prior Analytics*, B 23 and *Post. Anal.*, A 1.

13. Cf. *Topics*, A 1.100a25ff.; A 12.105a13ff.

14. *Rhetoric*, A 2.1356a35–b17.

15. *Rhetoric*, A 2.1375a7–18.

16. Cf. *Rhetoric*, A 3.1358a36ff.

17. See, for example, O. Kraus, *Neue Studien zur aristotelischen Rhetorik* (Halle, 1907).

18. *Rhetoric*, A 3.1358b20–29.

19. *Rhetoric*, A 4–14.

20. *Rhetoric*, B 20.

21. See *Reale*, I:142ff.

22. *Rhetoric*, B 21.

23. Cf. *Rhetoric*, B 22.1396b23ff.

24. *Rhetoric*, B 18.1391b27–1392a7.

25. Cf. *Rhetoric*, B 19.

26. Cf. *Rhetoric*, B 23–26. On the issue, consult A. Russo, *La filosofia della retorica in Aristotele* (Naples, 1962), 111ff.

27. Ross, *Aristotle*, 412.

28. D. J. Allan, *The Philosophy of Aristotle* (Oxford, 1970).

CHAPTER THREE
(POETICS)

1. *Physics*, B 8.199a15–17.

2. *Poetics*, 9.1451a36–b11.

3. *Poetics*, 9.1451b27ff.

4. *Poetics*, 9.1451b29–33.

5. *Poetics*, 9.1451b7.

6. Cf. *Poetics*, 24.1460a13ff.

7. *Poetics*, 24.1460a26ff.

8. *Poetics*, 25.1461b11ff.

9. M. Valgimigli, *Aristotele, Poetica* (Bari, 1968[7]), pp. 13f.

10. Ibid., 28.

11. *Poetics*, 7.1450b34–1451a4.

12. *Metaphysics*, M 3.1078a31–b2.

13. Cf. *Poetics*, 7.

14. *Poetics*, 6.1449b24–28.

15. Among the many articles on the argument we suggest the article by W. J. Verdenius, "Κάθαρσις τῶν παθημάτων," in *Autour d'Aristote* (Louvain, 1955), 367–73

16. *Politics*, Θ 6.1341a21–24.

17. *Politics*, Θ 7.1341b32–1342a16.

FIFTH SECTION—CHAPTER ONE

(CONCLUSIONS)

1. Robin, *Greek Thought and the Origins of the Scientific Spirit* (New York/Russell & Russell, 1928[1]; reissued 1967), trans. M. R. Dobie, p.308